COMPETING PHILOSOPHIES IN AMERICAN POLITICAL ECONOMICS

Selected Readings with Essays and Editorial Commentaries

JOHN E. ELLIOTT
University of Southern California

and

JOHN COWNIE
Federal City College

Goodyear Publishing Company, Inc.
Pacific Palisades, California

Library of Congress Cataloging in Publication Data

Elliott, John E comp.
Competing philosophies in American political economics.

1. Economics—History—United States—Addresses, essays, lectures. 2. Economics—History—Addresses, essays, lectures. I. Cownie, John, joint comp. II. Title. II. Title.
HB119.A2E48 330'.0973 74-11828
ISBN 0-87620-182-6

COMPETING PHILOSOPHIES IN AMERICAN POLITICAL ECONOMICS

Pacific Palisades, California 90272

Y-1826-0

Current printing (last digit):

10 9 8 7 6 5 4 3 2 1

Printed in the United States of America

To Rosie
and
To Cathie and Henry

CONTENTS

PREFACE xiii

INTRODUCTION 1

1 CLASSICAL LIBERALISM, CONSERVATISM, AND ECONOMIC INDIVIDUALISM 4

CLASSICAL LIBERALISM 4

1.1 The Foundations 7
Adam Smith

1.2 Extensions and Reformulations 13
John S. Mill

1.3 The Classical Theory of Economic Policy 20
Warren J. Samuels

A NOTE ON MODERN LIBERALISM AND MODERN CONSERVATISM 22

1.4 Liberal and Conservative: Turn and Turnabout 23
Max E. Fletcher

1.5 Free Enterprise and Democracy 29
Overton H. Taylor

CONSERVATISM 36

1.6 Classical Conservatism 37
Clinton Rossiter

CONSERVATIVE ECONOMIC INDIVIDUALISM 42

1.7 Laissez-Faire Conservatism 44
Clinton Rossiter

2 RADICAL CRITIQUES OF CAPITALISM: MARXISM AND SOCIALISM 51

MARX'S THEORY OF CAPITALISM 51

2.1 The Communist Manifesto 55
Karl Marx and Friedrich Engels

2.2 Marx's Theory of Capitalist Development 63
Karl Marx

2.3 Capitalism, Communism, and Alienation 71
Karl Marx

2.4 Anarchism, Marxism, and Liberalism 79
Marshall S. Shatz

SOCIALISM AND THE ROLE OF THE STATE IN THE ECONOMIC REFORM OF CAPITALISM 86

2.5 Marx's Theory of the State 88
Paul M. Sweezy

2.6 Evolutionary Socialism 92
Edward Bernstein

2.7 Fabian and Guild Socialism 101
Walter S. Buckingham, Jr.

AMERICAN RADICALISM: THORSTEIN VEBLEN 106

2.8 The Engineers and the Price System 107
Thorstein Veblen

3 KEYNES AND THE POST-KEYNESIAN SYNTHESIS 115

KEYNES AND THE POST-KEYNESIAN SYNTHESIS 115

3.1 Post-Post-Keynes: The Shattered Synthesis 116
Daniel R. Fusfeld

3.2 Keynes and the Post-Keynesian Synthesis 118
John M. Keynes

HOW KEYNES "CAME TO AMERICA" 122

3.3 Alvin H. Hansen: The American Keynes 124
Robert Lekachman

3.4 Functional Finance 128
Abba P. Lerner

3.5 Deficits and Fiscal Policy 131
James Buchanan

3.6 How Keynes Came to America 136
John K. Galbraith

KEYNESIAN ECONOMICS AND OTHER PHILOSOPHIES OF CAPITALISM 141

3.7 Must Conservatives Repudiate Keynes? 141
Ernest van den Haag and Henry Hazlitt

3.8 Keynes: A Neo-Marxist Perspective 147
Paul M. Sweezy

3.9 Keynes and the Socialists 151
G.D.H. Cole

THE LIBERAL STRAND OF THE KEYNESIAN SYNTHESIS 157

3.10 Keynesian Economics and Social Reform Liberalism 158
Donald S. Watson

3.11 Keynes and the Classical Liberal Tradition 162
Paul Streeten

3.12 The Public-Policy Ideas and Political Tendencies of Keynesian Economists 170
Overton H. Taylor

3.13 Challenge to Affluence 174
Gunnar Myrdal

3.14 What's Wrong with American Economics? 182
Leon H. Keyserling

THE CONSERVATIVE STRAND OF THE POST-KEYNESIAN SYNTEHSIS 188

3.15 Rules for Fiscal Policy 190
James Buchanan

3.16 Power without Property 197
Adolf A. Berle

3.17 Conservative Economic Policy 200
Henry C. Wallich

3.18 Liberal Versus Conservative Strands of Neo-Keynesianism 206
Robert Lekachman

3.19 The New Economics: Handmaiden of Inspired Truth 208
Richard B. Du Boff and Edward S. Herman

THE SHATTERED SYNTHESIS 214

3.20 Post-Post-Keynes: The Shattered Synthesis 215
Daniel R. Fusfeld

4 JOSEPH SCHUMPETER AND THE THEORY OF CAPITALIST TRANSFORMATION 220

SCHUMPETER'S ANSWER TO MARX AND KEYNES 220

4.1 Summary of Schumpeter's Theory of the Business Cycle 222
Rendigs Fels

4.2 Schumpeter's Answer to Marx and Keynes: Inequality and Instability 227
Joseph A. Schumpeter

SCHUMPETER'S ANSWER TO KEYNES AND HANSEN 232

4.3 Schumpeter's Answer to Keynes and Hansen: Secular Stagnation 232
Joseph A. Schumpeter

SCHUMPETER, CONSERVATISM, AND LIBERALISM 237

4.4 Creative Destruction and Monopoly 238
Joseph A. Schumpeter

CAN CAPITALISM SURVIVE? 243

4.5 Can Capitalism Survive? 244
Joseph A. Schumpeter

4.6 Joseph A. Schumpeter: Critical Evaluation 252
Allen M. Sievers

SCHUMPETER, CONTEMPORARY ECONOMIC THOUGHT, AND PUBLIC POLICY 258

5 JOHN KENNETH GALBRAITH: POWER, AFFLUENCE, AND THE NEW INDUSTRIAL STATE 260

COUNTERVAILING POWER 260

5.1 Countervailing Power: Exposition 262
John K. Galbraith

5.2 Countervailing Power: Critique 268
Walter A. Adams

THE PROBLEMS OF AFFLUENCE 273

5.3 Problems of Affluence 274
John K. Galbraith

5.4 Private Versus Public: Could Kenneth Galbraith Be Wrong? 279
Henry C. Wallich

CORPORATE POWER, TECHNOLOGY, AND POLICY 285

5.5 The New Industrial State 286
John K. Galbraith

5.6 The Close of the Galbraithian System 293
Scott Gordon

ECONOMICS AND THE PUBLIC PURPOSE 297

5.7 Economics and the Public Purpose 297
John K. Galbraith

5.8 Utopian Reformism 305
Paul M. Sweezy

6 RADICAL REFORM FROM THE RIGHT: THE INDIVIDUALIST CONSERVATISM OF THE NEO-LIBERALS 311

6.1 Neo Liberalism 312
Donald S. Watson

THE ROAD TO SERFDOM 316

6.2 The Road to Serfdom: Exposition 318
Friedrich A. Hayek

6.3 The Road to Serfdom: Critique 329
Henry C. Wallich

THE NEO-LIBERAL CASE FOR COMPETITIVE MARKETS 331

6.4 The Competitive Market and Optimal Allocative Efficiency 332
Carl F. Christ

6.5 Capitalism and Freedom 338
Milton Friedman

6.6 A Note on Friedman's Freedom 342
C. B. Macpherson

MODIFIED LAISSEZ-FAIRE: THE ECONOMIC ROLE OF GOVERNMENT 347

6.7 The Economic Role of Government 348
Friedrich A. Hayek

6.8 The Great Society: A Libertarian Critique 351
Murray N. Rothbard

NEO-LIBERALISM AND MAJOR ECONOMIC ISSUES 355

Monetary and Fiscal Policy 355

6.9 A Monetary and Fiscal Framework for Economic Stability 356
Milton Friedman

Monopoly and Big Business 362

6.10 Critique of Big Business 364
George Stigler

Inequality and the Distribution of Income 368

6.11 Inequality and Income Distribution 369
Henry C. Wallich

Critique of Economic Growth 375

6.12 Critique of Economic Growth 376
E. J. Mishan

RADICAL CRITIQUE OF AMERICAN CAPITALISM: CONVERGENCE OF EXTREMES 380

6.13 Dissent in Economics: The Convergence of Extremes 381
Mancur Olson and Christopher K. Clague

7 RADICAL REFORM FROM THE LEFT: NEO-MARXISM, THE NEW LEFT, AND DEMOCRATIC SOCIALISM 387

NEO-MARXISM 387

7.1 Monopoly Capitalism 389
Paul A. Baran and Paul M. Sweezy

7.2 Critique of Monopoly Capital 401
Robert Heilbroner

7.3 Workers Under Neo-Capitalism 404
Ernest Mandel

7.4 Capitalist Expansion, Ideology, and Imperialism 412
Arthur MacEwan

THE NEW LEFT AND THE NEW RADICALISM 419

7.5 The Challenge of Radical Political Economics 421
Raymond S. Franklin and William K. Tabb

7.6 Neocapitalism and the New Left 430
Greg Calvert and Carol Neiman

7.7 The Political Economy of the New Left: An Outsider's View 438
Assar Lindbeck

7.8 Economics of the New Left 446
Stephen Hymer and Frank Roosevelt

DEMOCRATIC SOCIALISM AND ECONOMIC REFORM 452

7.9 Why Socialism in America 453
Michael Harrington

7.10 Equality and Social Justice 460
C. A. R. Crosland

7.11 Small is Beautiful: Critique of Industrialized Capitalism and Socialism 466
E. F. Schumacher

7.12 The Democratic Welfare Community 476
Gunnar Myrdal

PREFACE

The market for college textbooks typically exemplifies the properties associated with ''monopolistic competition'': a large number of sellers, each attempting to differentiate its product in the buyers' minds. The role of a Preface is often then to distinguish a text (hopefully favorably) from an embarrassing surfeit of competitors. Because entry into textbook competition is relatively easy, and because success breeds imitation, the task of differentiation can be formidable. Occasionally, however, a text or anthology breaks new ground—or at least cultivates it in a substantially different way. Here, the task of a Preface is different, namely, to explain the greater-than-usual differentiation and to indicate where and how the book may be used.

To the best of our knowledge, this book is unique in its scope and depth of examination of the major competing philosophies in American political economics. The Introducion that follows identifies the major dimensions and issues that comprise the concept ''economic philosophies,'' and describes briefly the book's organization. Not surprisingly, the focus (chapter 3) is on the ''post-Keynesian synthesis'' in economic thought and policy—the persuasive and highly influential interpretation of economic life, with a prescription for its social control—provided by the English economist John Maynard Keynes and his successors. Other chapters provide perspective by discussing such pre-Keynesian philosophies as classical liberalism and Marxism (chapters 1-2) or by comparing competing views in the post-Keynesian era (chapters 4-7).

Reading selections have been edited and abridged to provide the greatest possible exposure to thinkers and points of view, and the selections are supplemented and linked by short essays and editorial commentaries. A glance at the Table of Contents shows the range and quality of the *dramatis personae* represented in the readings themselves. Smith, Mill, Marx, Keynes, Schumpeter, Galbraith, Friedman: these and others who best illustrate particular economic philosophies, or who have made a significant impact on economic thought, are represented in exposition and as critics of one another.

Although the book may be used in a variety of courses, in manuscript form it has been tested in three: comparative economic systems, history of economic thought, and principles of economics. In the comparative systems course, it bolsters and supplements the analysis of classical and contemporary capitalism. In the history of economic thought, it provides broader perspective on economic philosophies and thereby supplements readings on the more technical dimensions of economic analysis. In principles of economics, it introduces students to major historical figures and prominent contemporary contributors in the discipline, and provides effective illustrations of controversy.

We would like to thank those who have helped us in this project, with the traditional exoneration from responsibility for our mistakes. Professor Daniel Fusfeld of the University of Michigan read the entire manuscript and made numerous helpful suggestions. Professor Joyce Pickersgill of California State University at Fullerton gave a useful critique of an early version of the manuscript. Our students at the University of Southern California and the Federal City College have given yeoman service by reading and student testing several prepublication editions. Alfred W. Goodyear and Steve Lock of Goodyear Publishing Company have given wise counsel at various stages in the manuscript's development. Colette Conboy, Jane Hellesoe-Henon, Janice Sadler, Tom Moule, and others at Goodyear have helped guide the manuscript through preparation and production. Perhaps most important, we would like to thank the many "economic philosophers" whose writings have been reprinted and evaluated here and whose perceptive studies provide insight and perspective on the major economic issues in American public life.

John E. Elliott

John Cownie

INTRODUCTION

This is a book on competing philosophies in contemporary American "political economics." It is concerned with public economic policy, the role of government in economic life, and the impact of government policy and economic reform on individual freedoms and economic order. It endeavors to give a broad perspective to debates among economists and controversies over political economics by focusing on ideas and philosophies concerning the economic order. Controversy and debate on issues of public concern include (1) technical economic analysis—questions of the logical structure of economic theories and historical-statistical studies of economics in practice. It includes also (2) different visions of the past history and future prospects of the economic system; (3) value judgments concerning competing goals of public policy (for example, stability, growth, justice); and (4) judgments concerning noneconomic variables and institutions (for example, the functioning of government, the relations of social classes).

This combination of economic analysis, historical vision, value judgments about social goals, and assessment of the relations of the economy to social and political institutions is roughly what we mean by "economic philosophy"; and it is economic philosophy in this broad sense—more precisely, the economic philosophies of economists—with which we are concerned in this book. Emphasis is placed on those prominent systems of thought most pertinent to understanding and evaluating economic controversy and dissent in American society in the 1970s.

The immediate starting point for a critical examination and comparison of contemporary economic philosophies is the "post-Keynesian synthesis." If Adam Smith (*Wealth of Nations,* 1776) may be taken as the founding father figure of economics as a field of study and archetype in the classical liberal philosophy of economic individualism, John Maynard Keynes (*The General Theory of Employment, Interest and Money,* 1936) may be described as the intellectual father of that system of thought that has dominated thinking about the economy and economic policy in the industrialized, mixed capitalist economies in Western Europe and the United States for approximately the last quarter of a century.

In a sense, the post-Keynesian synthesis is an extension of classical-neoclassical economics and classical liberalism, with a nod in the direction of Marx and the socialists (although Keynes himself was clearly a rebellious student of the former and personally disdainful of the latter). For this reason, historical perspective is invaluable; the first two chapters of this book examine and compare the economic philosophies of classical liberalism, conservatism, Marxism, and socialism. These pre-Keynesian ideas about the economic order not only provide historical and intellectual background to Keynes and the post-Keynesian synthesis; they continue as well to influence significantly the major philosophies of dissent from the post-Keynesian synthesis.

Like the classical and neoclassical economists before him, Keynes accepted private ownership of property and espoused competitive markets as a means to coordinate economic life and control private economic power. And like the classical liberals of the late-eighteenth–early-nineteenth centuries, he felt that the state could be limited to the provision of a general framework within which the market system and private enterprise could do their work. Like Marx, however, Keynes perceived laissez-faire capitalism to be inherently unstable and subject to periodic crises, breakdowns, depressions, and unemployment. But whereas Marx perceived capitalism's economic problems to be systemic, rooted in the institutions of private ownership, and incapable of resolution save through a radical transformation to the new and different system of socialism, Keynes and the post-Keynesians believed that capitalism could be reformed—that its tendency toward depressions could be eliminated through an appropriate blend of central controls and private initiative, and that "modified" capitalism could then resolve other economic problems efficaciously.

The post-Keynesian synthesis, anticipated by Keynes in the mid-thirties and actually popularized, extended, and applied in the postwar years by a number of his followers and successors, brought together the Keynesian analysis of monetary and fiscal management and the neoclassical theory of market processes and a pricing system operative within an institutional framework of private ownership. In the synthesis, Keynesian-type policies and institutions were to regulate aggregate levels of demand, output, income, employment, prices, and the overall rate of economic growth, while the microeconomic institutions and processes of the market place and private enterprise were to determine the allocation of resources and distribution of income.

The post-Keynesian synthesis also stimulated a convergence or at least a modus vivendi between liberal and conservative views of the economic order. By focusing on stable prosperity and growth, the liberal wing of the post-Keynesian synthesis acceded to a truce on questions of conflict between rich and poor, business and labor, and the more and less powerful in society. Focusing upon the contributions of large-scale corporations and corporate managers to economic growth and stability, the conservative wing acceded to a new, positive role for government management in the economy and the abandonment of such pre-Keynesian values and verities as small government and annually balanced budgets.

But the post-Keynesian synthesis has not been without its critics. Some, like Joseph Schumpeter and, later, John Kenneth Galbraith stood apart from it and criticized one or another of its tenets. Others, notably neoliberals or individualist-conservatives such as Friedrich Hayek, Milton Friedman, and

James Buchanan, drawing partly on the classical-liberal philosophy, have provided neoconservative dissent from the Right. In the 1960s and 1970s, still others, notably contemporary Marxists and socialists, also have drawn upon earlier strains of thought (for example, classical Marxism and socialism) in constructing their radical critiques of the post-Keynesian synthesis. Partly in response to issues raised by the critics, partly in response to developments in society and the economy at large, the post-Keynesian synthesis began to crack by the late 60s, with more open debate between its liberal and conservative wings.

Essentially, the method used in succeeding chapters is comparison and contrast. We concentrate on a relatively small number of representative figures who best illustrate particular viewpoints or who have had a large impact on the course of economic thought or policy: Smith, Mill, Marx, Keynes, Hansen, Schumpeter, Galbraith, Hayek, Friedman, Baran, and Sweezy. The leading representatives speak for themselves, both in exposition and as critics of one another. Critical analyses by other scholars are included primarily to further explain the thinking of these representatives. The readings are supplemented by short essays and commentary, designed to link the readings together and to place them in context.

1 CLASSICAL LIBERALISM, CONSERVATISM, AND ECONOMIC INDIVIDUALISM

Why study classical liberalism and conservatism in a book about contemporary economic philosophies? The answer is straightforward. Classical liberalism emerged as a radical philosophy in the eighteenth century. In the modified form of laissez-faire conservatism, it became the pervasive conservative philosophy of the nineteenth century, and continued its preeminence well into the twentieth. Because all contemporary economic philosophies are largely either adaptations of or hostile reactions to classical liberalism, knowledge of classical liberalism and its variants is indispensable to a clear understanding of competing views of contemporary American capitalism.

In this chapter, we will first examine the leading tenets of classical liberalism, with special reference to the thinking of Adam Smith and John Stuart Mill, late-eighteenth- and mid-nineteenth-century architects of classical economic theory and classical liberalism. Later in the chapter, we will describe briefly the contrasting philosophy of classical conservatism and the transformation of classical liberalism to laissez-faire conservatism.

CLASSICAL LIBERALISM

The economic theory of classical liberalism focused on division of labor and thereby specialization among workers, consequent market exchange of mass-produced goods, and the functioning of the competitive market. Seeking their own self-interest, Adam Smith argued, individuals are led, as if by an "invisible hand," to "serve an end which was no part of their intentions." The "hand" in the metaphor is competition, perceived as large numbers of sellers and buyers of any particular product, with mobility of resources and freedom to enter into competition in any particular area of the economy. The hand is "invisible" because it is unconscious and impersonal. Under competitive conditions, consumers, producers, workers, and other economic units are too small relative to the market as a whole to significantly influence its workings, and they therefore must adapt as best they can to impersonal forces beyond their control. The competitive market economy has no central plan or planner to guide, regulate, and control economic life. Yet, through the interaction of demands and supplies in markets for goods and resources, economic life is coordinated, regulated, and controlled. Resources are allocated, more or less efficiently, to produce what the market demands; output is distributed among the various agents (workers, landlords, capitalists) who produce it. These socially beneficial results are the ends that are no part of any individual's intention.

The policy corollary to this economic theory is that the proper functions of government are sharply limited. In brief, government should maintain a framework within which individuals can energetically pursue their own self-interest, controlled by the competitive marketplace. Its proper activities include maintaining national defense and internal law and order, protecting competition by preventing unfair business practices, enforcing lawful contracts, and promoting exchange by such means as providing a stable monetary system and maintaining convenient avenues of transportation. In addition, most of the classical liberals expected government to provide a minimum of support to those who were unable to work and could look to no one else for help.

It is worth emphasizing, however, that in supporting the concept of a limited state, classical liberals were not doctrinaire advocates of laissez-faire. Extensive analysis of the writings of Adam Smith, the archetype of classical liberal economists, shows that his works were grounded too much in common sense to permit any single generalization to characterize his views concerning the proper activities of government. Thus, Smith recognized that if the state were to provide a framework within which all citizens may pursue a measure of self-interest, it may well be required to place some restrictions on the efforts of some individuals to exert economic power over others. It is true that Smith felt there was a strong presumption against governmental regulations beyond those needed to preserve domestic peace and justice. However, this presumption was largely the result of his observations of the attempts at regulation by the governments of his time. Outside of "peace and justice" operations, Smith saw the economic activities of such governments as consisting chiefly in the perpetuation of mercantilistic practices, legal monopolies, and settlement and apprenticeship laws. Smith had specific and pragmatic objections to such activities, and he could not place much confidence in the economic judgment of such governments. Where Smith observed more enlightened governments pursuing what he regarded as sensible economic policies, he was willing to condone somewhat more latitude in the range of their concerns.

Adam Smith (and the classical liberals generally) realized that the "laws of the market" did not operate to produce perfect harmony within society; yet Smith did espouse the idea that the market could be counted upon to produce a broad pattern of appropriate economic relationships. The "invisible hand" of the market did not eliminate all economic problems, and still less did it guarantee social justice; but it did guide men toward the rational patterns of exchange necessary in the classical liberals' notion of a rational and well-ordered economy. Thus classical liberals saw the economic role of government as arising primarily from the facts that in some areas the laws of the market could not operate and that in other areas individuals could deliberately obstruct the workings of the market for personal gain. In effect, classical liberals proposed not laissez-faire, but a functional division of labor between an important but limited public sector, providing a sociopolitical framework of essentially nonmarketable goods and services, and a private sector, functioning within that framework to coordinate individual economic decisions through market exchange.

The mid-nineteenth century restatement of classical liberalism by John Stuart Mill develops even more clearly this pragmatic blend of market processes and government policies. Indeed, Mill may be regarded as a transition figure between the classical liberalism of the late eighteenth–early nineteenth century and the democratic social reform liberalism of the late nineteenth–early twentieth century.

On the one hand, Mill had a deep and abiding faith in the efficacy of competition and market processes. The major alternative to competition, he felt, was not cooperation, but monopoly; and the failure to understand the benefits of competition was his major criticism of mid-nineteenth-century socialists. On the other hand, he clearly recognized a strategic role for government, not only in providing important nonmarketable goods and a framework for private enterprise, but in serving, through the social process of democracy, as agent of the workers and the poor in the reform of the economic system.

Mill's most frequently cited principle concerning these matters was a distinction between the "laws" of production (which "partake of the character of physical truth") and those of distribution (which are "a matter of human institution solely"). Strictly speaking, this distinction is too sharply drawn. As Marx, among others, quickly pointed out, production and distribution are interdependent, and there are therefore limits on the extent to which a modified capitalist system may tinker with the redistribution of income and/or property. Loosely formulated, however, Mill's distinction reflects the homey wisdom that the institutional structure of society (for example, the distribution of land ownership in England, which had its roots in the Norman conquest, feudal privilege, and inheritance) is scarcely governed by the immutable "natural laws" of the market, but may well be open to reform.

The selections immediately following consider the classical liberal view of the appropriate economic roles of market processes and government. Selection 1.1 is the classic statement on the subject by Smith. Note especially Smith's third function of government. A major portion of debate among contemporary economic philosophies is concerned with determining precisely what these "works and institutions" (the "agenda" of government, as Keynes called it) are to be and what their proper magnitude (the size of government relative to the private sector) is. Selection 1.2 is Mill's mid-nineteenth-century restatement of "laissez-faire and its exceptions." As Warren Samuels observes in selection 1.3, the exceptions are so important and numerous that a guiding principle is needed to give perspective. Samuels' proposal, drawing upon the work of contemporary British neoliberal Lionel Robbins, is the concept of "market-plus-framework."

1.1 The Foundations

Adam Smith

OF THE NATURAL AND MARKET PRICE OF COMMODITIES

. . . When the price of any commodity is neither more nor less than what is sufficient to pay the rent of the land, the wages of the labor, and the profits of the stock employed in raising, preparing, and bringing it to market, according to their natural rates, the commodity is then sold for what may be called its natural price.

The actual price at which any commodity is commonly sold is called its market price. It may either be above, or below, or exactly the same with its natural price.

The market price of every particular commodity is regulated by the proportion between the quantity which is actually brought to the market and the demand of those who are willing to pay the natural price of the commodity, or the whole value of the rent, labor, and profit which must be paid in order to bring it thither. Such people may be called the effectual demanders, and their demand the effectual demand, since it may be sufficient to effectuate the bringing of the commodity to market. It is different from the absolute demand. A very poor man may be said in some sense to have a demand for a coach and six; he might like to have it; but his demand is not an effectual demand, as the commodity can never be brought to market in order to satisfy it.

When the quantity of any commodity which is brought to market falls short of the effectual demand, all those who are willing to pay the whole value of the rent, wages, and profit which must be paid in order to bring it thither cannot be supplied with the quantity which they want. Rather than want it altogether, some of them will be willing to give more. A competition will immediately begin among them, and the market price will rise more or less above the natural price, according as either the greatness of the deficiency or the wealth and wanton luxury of the competitors happen to animate more or less the eagerness of the competition. Among competitors of equal wealth and luxury the same deficiency will generally occasion a more or less eager competition, according as the acquisition of the commodity happens to be of more or less importance to them. Hence the exorbitant price of the necessaries of life during the blockade of a town or in a famine.

When the quantity brought to market exceeds the effectual demand, it cannot be all sold to those who are willing to pay the whole value of the rent, wages, and profit which must be paid in order to bring it thither. Some part must be sold to those who are willing to pay less, and the low price which they

Excerpted from Adam Smith, *An Inquiry Into the Nature and Causes of the Wealth of Nations*, (New York: Random House, 1938), pp. 24–27, 29–31, 34–38, 40, 42–43.

give for it must reduce the price of the whole. The market price will sink more or less below the natural price, according as the greatness of the excess increases more or less the competition of the sellers, or according as it happens to be more or less important to them to get immediately rid of the commodity. The same excess in the importation of perishables will occasion a much greater competition than in that of durable commodities; in the importation of oranges, for example, than in that of old iron.

When the quantity brought to market is just sufficient to supply the effectual demand and no more, the market price naturally comes to be either exactly, or as nearly as can be judged of, the same with the natural price. The whole quantity upon hand can be disposed of for this price and cannot be disposed of for more. The competition of the different dealers obliges them all to accept of this price but does not oblige them to accept of less.

The quantity of every commodity brought to market naturally suits itself to the effectual demand. It is the interest of all those who employ their land, labor, or stock, in bringing any commodity to market, that the quantity never should exceed the effectual demand; and it is the interest of all other people that it never should fall short of that demand.

If at any time it exceeds the effectual demand, some of the component parts of its price must be paid below their natural rate. If it is rent, the interest of the landlords will immediately prompt them to withdraw a part of their land; and if it is wages or profit, the interest of the laborers in the one case, and of their employers in the other, will prompt them to withdraw a part of their labor or stock from this employment. The quantity brought to market will soon be no more than sufficient to supply the effectual demand. All the different parts of its price will rise to their natural rate, and the whole price to its natural price.

If, on the contrary, the quantity brought to market should at any time fall short of the effectual demand, some of the component parts of its price must rise above their natural rate. If it is rent, the interest of all other landlords will naturally prompt them to prepare more land for the raising of this commodity; if it is wages or profit, the interest of all other laborers and dealers will soon prompt them to employ more labor and stock in preparing and bringing it to market. The quantity brought thither will soon be sufficient to supply the effectual demand. All the different parts of its price will soon sink to their natural rate, and the whole price to its natural price.

The natural price, therefore, is, as it were, the central price, to which the prices of all commodities are continually gravitating. Different accidents may sometimes keep them suspended a good deal above it, and sometimes force them down even somewhat below it. But whatever may be the obstacles which hinder them from settling in this center of repose and continuance, they are constantly tending toward it.

The whole quantity of industry annually employed in order to bring any commodity to market naturally suits itself in this manner to the effectual demand. It naturally aims at bringing always that precise quantity thither which may be sufficient to supply, and no more than supply, that demand.

But though the market price of every particular commodity is in this manner continually gravitating, if one may say so, toward the natural price, yet sometimes particular accidents, sometimes natural causes, and sometimes particular regulations of police, may, in many commodities, keep up the market price, for a long time together, a good deal above the natural price.

When by an increase in the effectual demand, the market price of some particular commodity happens to rise a good deal above the natural price, those who employ their stocks in supplying that market are generally careful to conceal this change. If it was commonly known, their great profit would tempt so many new rivals to employ their stocks in the same way that, the effectual demand being fully supplied, the market price would soon be reduced to the natural price and perhaps for some time even below it. If the market is at a great distance from the residence of those who supply it, they may sometimes be able to keep the secret for several years together and may so long enjoy their extraordinary profits without any new rivals. Secrets of this kind, however, it must be acknowledged, can seldom be long kept; and the extraordinary profits can last very little longer than they are kept.

* * *

A monopoly granted either to an individual or to a trading company has the same effect as a secret in trade or manufactures. The monopolists, by keeping the market constantly understocked, by never fully supplying the effectual demand, sell their commodities much above the natural price and raise their emoluments, whether they consist in wages or profit, greatly above their natural rate.

The price of monopoly is upon every occasion the highest which can be got. The natural price, or the price of free competition, on the contrary, is the lowest which can be taken, not upon every occasion indeed, but for any considerable time together. The one is upon every occasion the highest which can be squeezed out of the buyers, or which, it is supposed, they will consent to give; the other is the lowest which the sellers can commonly afford to take and at the same time continue their business.

The market price of any particular commodity, though it may continue long above, can seldom continue long below, its natural price. Whatever part of it was paid below the natural rate, the persons whose interest it affected would immediately feel the loss and would immediately withdraw either so much land, or so much labor, or so much stock, from being employed about it that the quantity brought to market would soon be no more than sufficient to supply the effectual demand. Its market price, therefore, would soon rise to the natural price. This at least would be the case where there was perfect liberty.

OF SYSTEMS OF POLITICAL ECONOMY

The general industry of the society never can exceed what the capital of the society can employ. As the number of workmen that can be kept in employment by any particular person must bear a certain proportion to his capital, so the number of those that can be continually employed by all the members of a great society must bear a certain proportion to the whole capital of that society and never can exceed that proportion. No regulation of commerce can increase the quantity of industry in any society beyond what its capital can maintain. It can only divert a part of it into a direction into which it might not otherwise have gone; and it is by no means certain that this artificial direction is likely to be more advantageous to the society than that into which it would have gone of its own accord.

Every individual is continually exerting himself to find out the most advantageous employment for whatever capital he can command. It is his own advantage, indeed, and not that of society, which he has in view. But the study of his own advantage naturally or, rather, necessarily leads him to prefer that employment which is most advantageous to the society.

First, every individual endeavors to employ his capital as near home as he can and consequently as much as he can in the support of domestic industry, provided always that he can thereby obtain the ordinary or not a great deal less than the ordinary profits of stock. . . .

Secondly, every individual who employs his capital in the support of domestic industry necessarily endeavors so to direct that industry that its produce may be to the greatest possible value.

The produce of industry is what it adds to the subject or materials upon which it is employed. In proportion as the value of this produce is great or small, so will likewise be the profits of the employer. But it is only for the sake of profit that any man employs a capital in the support of industry; and he will always, therefore, endeavor to employ it in the support of that industry of which the produce is likely to be of the greatest value, or to exchange for the greatest quantity either of money or of other goods.

But the annual revenue for every society is always precisely equal to the exchangeable value of the whole annual produce of its industry, or rather is precisely the same thing with that exchangeable value. As every individual, therefore, endeavors as much as he can both to employ his capital in the support of domestic industry, and so to direct that industry that its produce may be of the greatest value, every individual necessarily labors to render the annual revenue of the society as great as he can. He generally, indeed, neither intends to promote the public interest nor knows how much he is promoting it. By preferring the support of domestic to that of foreign industry, he intends only his own security; and by directing that industry in such a manner as its produce may be of the greatest value, he intends only his own gain, and he is in this, as in many other cases, led by an invisible hand to promote an end which was no part of his intention. Nor is it always the worse for the society that it was no part of it. By pursuing his own interest, he frequently promotes that of the society more effectually than when he really intends to promote it. I have never known much good done by those who affected to trade for the public good. It is an affectation, indeed, not very common among merchants, and very few words need be employed in dissuading them from it.

What is the species of domestic industry which his capital can employ, and of which the produce is likely to be of the greatest value, every individual, it is evident, can, in his local situation, judge much better than any statesman or lawgiver can do for him. The statesman, who should attempt to direct private people in what manner they ought to employ their capitals, would not only load himself with a most unnecessary attention but assume an authority which could safely be trusted not only to no single person but to no council or senate whatever, and which would nowhere be so dangerous as in the hands of a man who had folly and presumption enough to fancy himself fit to exercise it.

To give the monopoly of the home market to the produce of domestic industry, in any particular art of manufacture, is in some measure to direct private people in what manner they ought to employ their capitals and must, in almost all cases, be either a useless or a hurtful regulation. If the produce of domestic can be brought there as cheap as that of foreign industry, the regulation is evidently useless. If it cannot, it must generally be hurtful. It is the maxim of every prudent master of a family never to attempt to make at home what it will cost him more to make than to buy. The tailor does not attempt to make his own shoes but buys them of the shoemaker. The shoemaker does not attempt to make his own clothes but employs a tailor. The farmer attempts to make neither the one nor the other but employs those different artificers. All of them find it for their interest to employ their whole industry in a way in which they have some advantage over their neighbors and to purchase with a part of its produce, or what is the same thing, with the price of a part of it, whatever else they have occasion for.

What is prudence in the conduct of every private family can scarce be folly in that of a great kingdom. If a foreign country can supply us with a commodity cheaper than we ourselves can make it, better buy it of them with some part of the produce of our own industry, employed in a way in which we have some advantage. The general industry of the country, being always in proportion to the capital which employs it, will not thereby be diminished, no more than that of the above-mentioned artificers, but only left to find out the way in which it can be employed with the greatest advantage. It is certainly not employed to the greatest advantage when it is thus directed toward an object which it can buy cheaper than it can make. The value of its annual produce is certainly more or less diminished when it is thus turned away from producing commodities evidently of more value than the commodity which it is directed to produce. According to the supposition, that commodity could be purchased from foreign countries cheaper than it can be made at home. It could, therefore, have been purchased with a part only of the commodities or, what is the same thing, with a part only of the price of the commodities, which the industry employed by equal capital would have produced at home, had it been left to follow its natural course. The industry of the country, therefore, is thus turned away from a more, to a less, advantageous employment, and the exchangeable value of its annual produce, instead of being increased, according to the intention of the lawgiver, must necessarily be diminished by every such regulation. . . .

All systems either of preference or of restraint, therefore, being thus completely taken away, the obvious and simple system of natural liberty establishes itself of its own accord. Every man, as long as he does not violate the laws of justice, is left perfectly free to pursue his own interest his own way and to bring both his industry and capital into competition with those of any other man or order of men. The sovereign is completely discharged from a duty, in the attempting to perform which he must always be exposed to innumerable delusions, and for the proper performance of which no human wisdom or knowledge could ever be sufficient—the duty of superintending the industry of private people and of directing it toward the employments most suitable to the interest of the society. According to the system of natural liberty, the sovereign has only three duties to attend to; three duties of great importance, indeed, but plain and intelligible to common understandings: first, the duty of protecting the society from the violence and invasion of other independent societies; secondly, the duty of protecting, as far as possible, every member of the society from the injustice or oppression of every other member of it, or the duty of establishing an exact administration of justice; and, thirdly, the duty of erecting and maintaining certain public works and certain public institutions which it can never be for the interest of any individual, or small number of individuals, to erect and maintain, because the profit could never repay the expense to any individual or small number of individuals, though it may frequently do much more than repay it to a great society. . . .

The interest of the dealers in any particular branch of trade or manufactures, is always in some respects different from, and even opposite to, that of the public. To widen the market and to narrow the competition is always the interest of the dealers. To widen the market may frequently be agreeable enough to the interest of the public; but to narrow the competition must always be against it and can serve only to enable the dealers, by raising their profits above what they naturally would be, to levy, for their own benefit, an absurd tax upon the rest of their fellow-citizens. The proposal of any new law or regulation of commerce which comes from this order ought always to be listened to with great precaution and ought never to be adopted till after having been long and carefully examined, not only with the most scrupulous, but with the most suspicious attention. It comes from an order of men whose interest is never exactly the same with that of the public, who have generally an interest to deceive and even to oppress the public, and who accordingly have, upon many occasions, both deceived and oppressed it. . . .

People of the same trade seldom meet together, even for merriment and diversion, but the conversation ends in a conspiracy against the public or in some contrivance to raise prices. It is impossible indeed to prevent such meetings, by any law which either could be executed, or would be consistent with liberty and justice. But though the law cannot hinder people of the same trade from sometimes assembling together, it ought to do nothing to facilitate such assemblies, much less to render them necessary.

Consumption is the sole end and purpose of all production, and the interest of the producer ought to be attended to only so far as it may be necessary for promoting that of the consumer. The maxim is so perfectly self-evident that it would be absurd to attempt to prove it. But in the mercantile system, the interest of the consumer is almost constantly sacrificed to that of the producer;

and it seems to consider production, and not consumption, as the ultimate end and object of all industry and commerce. . . .

It cannot be very difficult to determine who have been the contrivers of this whole mercantile system; not the consumers, we may believe, whose interest has been entirely neglected; but the producers, whose interest has been so carefully attended to; and among this latter class our merchants and manufacturers have been by far the principal architects. In the mercantile regulations, which have been taken notice of in this chapter, the interest of our manufacturers has been most peculiarly attended to; and the interest, not so much of the consumers, as that of some other sets of producers, has been sacrificed to it.

1.2 Extensions and Reformulations

John S. Mill

1. We must set out by distinguishing between two kinds of intervention by the government, which, though they may relate to the same subject, differ widely in their nature and effects, and require, for their justification, motives of a very different degree of urgency. The intervention may extend to controlling the free agency of individuals. Government may interdict all persons from doing certain things; or from doing them without its authorization; or may prescribe to them certain things to be done, or a certain manner of doing things which it is left optional with them to do or to abstain from. This is the *authoritative* interference of government. There is another kind of intervention which is not authoritative: when a government, instead of issuing a command and enforcing it by penalties, adopts the course so seldom resorted to by governments, and of which such important use might be made, that of giving advice, and promulgating information; or when, leaving individuals free to use their own means of pursuing any object of general interest, the government, not meddling with them, but not trusting the object solely to their care, establishes, side by side with their arrangements, an agency of its own for a like purpose. Thus, it is one thing to provide schools or colleges, and another to require that no person shall act as an instructor of youth without a government licence. There might be a national bank, or a government manufactory, without any monopoly against private banks and manufactories. There might be a post-office, without penalties against the conveyance of letters by other means. . . .

2. It is evident, that the authoritative form of government intervention has a much more limited sphere of legitimate action than the other. It requires a much stronger necessity to justify it in any case; while there are large depart-

Excerpted from John Stuart Mill, *Principles of Political Economy, with Some of their Applications to Social Philosophy* (London: Longmans Green, 1926), pp. 942–78.

ments of human life from which it must be unreservedly and imperiously excluded. Whatever theory we adopt respecting the foundation of the social union, and under whatever political institutions we live, there is a circle around every individual human being which no government, be it that of one, of a few, or of the many, ought to be permitted to overstep: there is a part of the life of every person who has come to years of discretion, within which the individuality of that person ought to reign uncontrolled either by any other individual or by the public collectively. That there is, or ought to be, some space in human existence thus entrenched around, and sacred from authoritative intrusion, no one who professes the smallest regard to human freedom or dignity will call in question: the point to be determined is, where the limit should be placed; how large a province of human life this reserved territory should include. I apprehend that it ought to include all that part which concerns only the life, whether inward or outward, of the individual, and does not affect the interests of others, or affects them only through the moral influence of example. With respect to the domain of the inward consciousness, the thoughts and feelings, and as much of external conduct as is personal only, involving no consequences, none at least of a painful or injurious kind, to other people; I hold that it is allowable in all, and in the more thoughtful and cultivated often a duty, to assert and promulgate, with all the force they are capable of, their opinion of what is good or bad, admirable or contemptible, but not to compel others to conform to that opinion; whether the force used is that of extra-legal coercion, or exerts itself by means of the law.

Even in those portions of conduct which do affect the interest of others, the onus of making out a case always lies on the defenders of legal prohibitions. It is not a merely constructive or presumptive injury to others which will justify the interference of law with individual freedom. To be prevented from doing what one is inclined to, or from acting according to one's own judgment of what is desirable, is not only always irksome, but always tends, *pro tanto,* to starve the development of some portion of the bodily or mental faculties, either sensitive or active; and unless the conscience of the individual goes freely with the legal restraint, it partakes, either in a great or in a small degree, of the degradation of slavery. Scarcely any degree of utility, short of absolute necessity, will justify prohibitory regulation, unless it can also be made to recommend itself to the general conscience; unless persons of ordinary good intentions either believe already, or can be induced to believe, that the thing prohibited is a thing which they ought not to wish to do.

It is otherwise with governmental interferences which do not restrain individual free agency. When a government provides means for fulfilling a certain end, leaving individuals free to avail themselves of different means if in their opinion preferable, there is no infringement of liberty, no irksome or degrading restraint. One of the principal objections to government interference is then absent.

3. A second general objection to government agency is that every increase of the functions devolving on the government is an increase of its power, both

in the form of authority, and still more, in the indirect form of influence. Many, in latter times, have been prone to think that limitation of the powers of the government is only essential when the government itself is badly constituted; when it does not represent the people, but is the organ of a class, or coalition of classes: and that a government of sufficiently popular constitution might be trusted with any amount of power over the nation, since its power would be only that of the nation over itself. This might be true, if the nation, in such cases, did not practically mean a mere majority of the nation, and if minorities were only capable of oppressing, but not of being oppressed. Experience, however, proves that the depositaries of power who are mere delegates of the people, that is of a majority, are quite as ready (when they think they can count on popular support) as any organs of oligarchy to assume arbitrary power, and encroach unduly on the liberty of private life. Hence it is no less important in a democratic than in any other government, that all tendency on the part of public authorities to stretch their interference, and assume a power of any sort which can easily be dispensed with, should be regarded with unremitting jealousy. Perhaps this is even more important in a democracy than in any other form of political society; because, where public opinion is sovereign, an individual who is oppressed by the sovereign does not, as in most other states of things, find a rival power to which he can appeal for relief, or, at all events, for sympathy.

4. A third general objection to government agency rests on the principle of the division of labour. Every additional function undertaken by the government is a fresh occupation imposed upon a body already overcharged with duties. A natural consequence is that most things are ill done; much not done at all, because the government is not able to do it without delays which are fatal to its purpose; that the more troublesome, and less showy, of the functions undertaken, are postponed or neglected, and an excuse is always ready for the neglect; while the heads of the administration have their minds so fully taken up with official details, in however perfunctory a manner superintended, that they have no time or thought to spare for the great interests of the state, and the preparation of enlarged measures of social improvement.

But these inconveniences, though real and serious, result much more from the bad organization of governments, than from the extent and variety of the duties undertaken by them. Government is not a name for some one functionary, or definite number of functionaries: there may be almost any amount of division of labour within the administrative body itself.

5. But though a better organization of governments would greatly diminish the force of the objection to the mere multiplication of their duties, it would still remain true that in all the more advanced communities the great majority of things are worse done by the intervention of government, than the individuals most interested in the matter would do them, or cause them to be done, if left to themselves. The grounds of this truth are expressed with tolerable exactness in the popular dictum, that people understand their own business

and their own interests better, and care for them more, than the government does, or can be expected to do. This maxim holds true throughout the greatest part of the business of life, and wherever it is true we ought to condemn every kind of government intervention that conflicts with it.

It must be remembered, besides, that even if a government were superior in intelligence and knowledge to any single individual in the nation, it must be inferior to all the individuals of the nation taken together.

6. I have reserved for the last place one of the strongest of the reasons against the extension of government agency. Even if the government could comprehend within itself, in each department, all the most eminent intellectual capacity and active talent of the nation, it would not be the less desirable that the conduct of a large portion of the affairs of the society should be left in the hands of the persons immediately interested in them. The business of life is an essential part of the practical education of a people; without which, book and school instruction, though most necessary and salutary, does not suffice to qualilfy them for conduct, and for the adaptation of means to ends. Instruction is only one of the desiderata of mental improvement; another, almost as indispensable, is a vigorous exercise of the active energies; labour, contrivance, judgment, self-control: and the natural stimulus to these is the difficulties of life.

A people among whom there is no habit of spontaneous action for a collective interest—who look habitually to their government to command or prompt them in all matters of joint concern—who expect to have everything done for them, except what can be made an affair of mere habit and routine—have their faculties only half developed; their education is defective in one of its most important branches.

7. The preceding are the principal reasons, of a general character, in favour of restricting to the narrowest compass the intervention of a public authority in the business of the community: and few will dispute the more than sufficiency of these reasons, to throw, in every instance, the burthen of making out a strong case, not on those who resist, but on those who recommend, government interference. *Laissez-faire,* in short, should be the practice: every departure from it, unless required by some great good, is a certain evil.

8. Now, the proposition that the consumer is a competent judge of the commodity, can be admitted only with numerous abatements and exceptions. He is generally the best judge (though even this is not true universally) of the material objects produced for his use. These are destined to supply some physical want, or gratify some taste or inclination, respecting which wants or inclinations there is no appeal from the person who feels them; or they are the means and appliances of some occupation, for the use of the persons engaged in it, who may be presumed to be judges of the things required in their own habitual employment. But there are other things, of the worth of which the demand of

the market is by no means a test; things of which the utility does not consist in ministering to inclinations, nor in serving the daily uses of life, and the want of which is least felt where the need is greatest. This is peculiarly true of those things which are chiefly useful as tending to raise the character of human beings. The uncultivated cannot be competent judges of cultivation.

Education, therefore, is one of those things which it is admissible in principle that a government should provide for the people. The case is one to which the reasons of the non-interference principle do not necessarily or universally extend.

With regard to elementary education, the exception to ordinary rules may, I conceive, justifiably be carried still further. There are certain primary elements and means of knowledge, which it is in the highest degree desirable that all human beings born into the community should acquire during childhood. If their parents, or those on whom they depend, have the power of obtaining for them this instruction, and fail to do it, they commit a double breach of duty, towards the children themselves, and towards the members of the community generally, who are all liable to suffer seriously from the consequences of ignorance and want of education in their fellow-citizens. It is therefore an allowable exercise of the powers of government to impose on parents the legal obligation of giving elementary instruction to children. This, however, cannot fairly be done, without taking measures to insure that such instruction shall be always accessible to them, either gratuitously or at a trifling expense.

9. Let us now consider another class of cases, where there is no person in the situation of a consumer, and where the interest and judgment to be relied on are those of the agent himself; as in the conduct of any business in which he is exclusively interested, or in entering into any contract or engagement by which he himself is to be bound.

Among those members of the community whose freedom of contract ought to be controlled by the legislature for their own protection, on account (it is said) of their dependent position, it is frequently proposed to include women: and in the existing Factory Acts their labour, in common with that of young persons, has been placed under peculiar restrictions. But the classing together, for this and other purposes, of women and children, appears to me both indefensible in the principle and mischievous in practice. Children below a certain age *cannot* judge or act for themselves; up to a considerably greater age they are inevitably more or less disqualified for doing so; but women are as capable as men of appreciating and managing their own concerns, and the only hindrance to their doing so arises from the injustice of their present social position.

10. A second exception to the doctrine that individuals are the best judges of their own interest, is when an individual attempts to decide irrevocably now what will be best for his interest at some future and distant time. The presumption in favour of individual judgment is only legitimate, where the judgment is grounded on actual, and especially on present, personal experience; not where it is formed antecedently to experience, and not suffered to be reversed even after experience

has condemned it. These considerations are eminently applicable to marriage, the most important of all cases of engagement for life.

11. The third exception which I shall notice, to the doctrine that government cannot mangage the affairs of individuals as well as the individuals themselves, has reference to the great class of cases in which the individuals can only manage the concern by delegated agency, and in which the so-called private management is, in point of fact, hardly better entitled to be called management by the persons interested than administration by a public officer. Whatever, if left to spontaneous agency, can only be done by joint-stock associations, will often be as well, and sometimes better done, as far as the actual work is concerned, by the state. Government management is, indeed, proverbially jobbing, careless, and ineffective, but so likewise has generally been joint-stock management. The directors of a joint-stock company, it is true, are always shareholders; but also the members of a government are invariably taxpayers; and in the case of directors, no more than in that of governments, is their proportional share of the benefits of good management equal to the interest they may possibly have in mismanagement, even without reckoning the interest of their ease. It may be objected, that the shareholders, in their collective character, exercise a certain control over the directors, and have almost always full power to remove them from office. Practically, however, the difficulty of exercising this power is found to be so great, that it is hardly ever exercised except in cases of such flagrantly unskillful, or, at least, unsuccessful management, as would generally produce the ejection from office of managers appointed by the government.

12. To a fourth case of exception I must request particular attention, it being one to which, as it appears to me, the attention of political economists has not yet been sufficiently drawn. There are matters in which the interference of law is required, not to overrule the judgment of individuals respecting their own interest, but to give effect to that judgment: they being unable to give effect to it except by concert, which concert again cannot be effectual unless it receives validity and sanction from the law. For illustration, I may advert to laws diminishing the hours of labour.

13. Fifthly; the argument against government interference, grounded on the maxim that individuals are the best judges of their own interest, cannot apply to the very large class of cases, in which those acts of individuals with which the government claims to interfere, are not done by those individuals for their own interest, but for the interest of other people. This includes, among other things, the important and much agitated subject of public charity. Though individuals should, in general, be left to do for themselves whatever it can reasonably be expected that they should be capable of doing, yet when they are at any rate not to be left to themselves, but to be helped by other people, the question arises whether it is better that they should receive this help exclusively from individuals, and therefore uncertainly and casually, or by systematic arrangements, in which society acts through its organ, the state.

This brings us to the subject of Poor Laws.

Apart from any metaphysical considerations respecting the foundation of morals or of the social union, it will be admitted to be right that human beings should help one another; and the more so, in proportion to the urgency of the need: and none needs help so urgently as one who is starving. The claim to help, therefore, created by destitution, is one of the strongest which can exist, and there is prima facie the amplest reason for making the relief of so extreme an exigency as certain to those who require it as by any arrangements of society it can be made.

In so far as the subject admits of any general doctrine or maxim, it would appear to be this—that if assistance is given in such a manner that the condition of the person helped is as desirable as that of the person who succeeds in doing the same thing without help, the assistance, if capable of being previously calculated on, is mischievous: but if, while available to everybody, it leaves to every one a strong motive to do without it if he can, it is then for the most part beneficial.

14. Another class of cases which fall within the same general principle as the case of public charity, are those in which the acts done by individuals, though intended solely for their own benefit, involve consequences extending indefinitely beyond them, to interests of the nation or of posterity, for which society in its collective capacity is alone able, and alone bound, to provide. One of these cases is that of Colonization.

15. The same principle which points out colonization, and the relief of the indigent, as cases to which the principal objection to government interference does not apply, extends also to a variety of cases, in which important public services are to be performed, while yet there is no individual specially interested in performing them, nor would any adequate remuneration naturally or spontaneously attend their performance. Take for instance a voyage of geographical or scientific exploration. The information sought may be of great public value, yet no individual would derive any benefit from it which would repay the expense of fitting out the expedition; and there is no mode of intercepting the benefit on its way to those who profit by it, in order to levy a toll for the remuneration of its authors. Again, it is a proper office of government to build and maintain lighthouses, establish buoys, etc., for the security of navigation: for since it is impossible that the ships at sea which are benefited by a lighthouse should be made to pay a toll on the occasion of its use, no one would build lighthouses from motives of personal interest, unless indemnified and rewarded from a compulsory levy made by the state.

16. The preceding heads comprise, to the best of my judgment, the whole of the exceptions to the practical maxim, that the business of society can be best performed by private and voluntary agency. It is, however, necessary to add, that the intervention of government cannot always practically stop short at the limit which defines the cases intrinsically suitable for it. In the particular circumstances of a given age or nation, there is scarcely anything really important to the general interest, which it may not be desirable, or even necessary, that the government should take upon itself, not because private individuals cannot effectually perform it, but because they will not.

1.3 The Classical Theory of Economic Policy

Warren J. Samuels

The Market-Plus-Framework Interpretation

THE PROBLEM

The genius of the classical economists was to propose a system of socioeconomic organization and proceed to analyze, however imperfectly, the operation of such a system. At the heart of this was a theory of economic policy, one vital to the understanding and analysis of contemporary Western society.

But the discussion by, no less than the subsequent interpretation of, the classical economists concerning their theory of economic policy focused and has continued to focus on certain facets with the consequence that other facets, as well as the system as a whole, have remained unobtrusive, unspecified, and misunderstood. Analysis of the classicists' writings discloses a much more sophisticated and complete classical theory of economic policy than has been hitherto generally appreciated.

Certainly, there must be a place for the value system represented by the *doctrine* of laissez faire. There can hardly be any question that the classical economists were advocates of the market system, with a connotation of the minimization of government activity, reliance upon market forces to resolve the basic economic problems (resource allocation, income distribution, and the like), and private property and free private enterprise with private participation as buyers and sellers, consumers and investors, i.e., as private economic actors. It is, after all, just such ideas that the doctrinal slogan of laissez faire signifies. But any thorough statement of the classical theory of economic policy must go beyond doctrine into the practical realities of the way in which the classical economists dealt with the fundamental problems involved in any theory of economic policy and must specify as completely as possible the basic components to which the classical system reduces.

The context of relevance is rather the market-plus-framework interpretation of the classical theory of economic policy, which is taken as the most meaningful analysis of the classical policy system yet formulated.

In his *Theory of Economic Policy,* Lord Robbins attempted specifically to absolve the classicists from the false criticisms of having a narrow class bias, a belief in *Harmonielehre,* and an extreme laissez-faire stand on policy. Affirmatively, Lord Robbins' interpretation of the classical theory of economic policy emphasized (a) economic liberalism, or "the system of economic freedom";

(b) the createdness of whatever mutuality of interest or order exists, and a correlative reformist orientation; and (c) the importance of the framework within which private activity is undertaken, the provision of which is one of the functions ascribed to government. The general view, then, adopted by Lord Robbins is that of the "market-plus-framework" approach.

His thematic emphasis is upon the fact, operation, and significance of the framework within which individual or private economic activity and market forces operate and are constrained. According to Lord Robbins, "The invisible hand which guides men to promote ends which were no part of their intention, is not the hand of some god or some natural agency independent of human effort; it is the hand of the lawgiver, the hand which withdraws from the sphere of the pursuit of self-interest those possibilities which do not harmonize with the public good." The classical economists, he argues, ". . . never conceived the system of economic freedom as arising *in vacuo* or functioning in a system of law and order so simple and so minimal as to be capable of being written down on a limited table of stone (or a revolutionary handbill) and restricted to the functions of the night watchman. Nothing less than the whole complex of the Benthamite codes—Civil, Penal and Constitutional was an adequate framework for their system." This framework Lord Robbins sees as involving ". . . the provision of a set of rules which so limited and guided individual initiative, that the residue of free action undirected from the centre could be conceived to harmonize with the general objects of public interest." The framework, then, is of the greatest importance: "Indeed," writes Lord Robbins, "in any logical scheme, we must regard the provision of such a framework as *prior* to the recommendation of economic freedom," and "it is to betray a total absence of acquaintance with the literature to suppose that the prior necessity of the framework would ever have been called in question." To Lord Robbins, the classicists "regarded the appropriate legal framework and the system of economic freedom as two aspects of one and the same social process."

The notion of a sharp separation between the political and the economic spheres, so far as the classical economists were concerned, is then, according to Lord Robbins, erroneous. If by the economic sphere is meant private economic activity, then it is composed of free action, yes, but of a "residue of free action" remaining after the withdrawal "from the sphere of the pursuit of self-interest those possibilities" which are determined through the legal process to be against the social interest. The legal process is not exogenous or superimposed; rather, it is a part of a larger process, inclusive also of private economic activity, through which the adjustment and reconciliation of interests takes place.

The whole logic of classical economics and theory of economic policy was based rather on the *createdness* of any harmonious order, upon the necessity to create such harmony as could be achieved by developing an appropriate and effective institutional system or framework. Both society and market were seen as artifacts, and as artifacts that were evolving. Despite occasional ex-cathedra allegations about an automatic harmony and notwithstanding a preoccupation with the facts and problems of economic adjustment, the classical economists did not take the institutional system for granted. To the classicists' discussions of the magnificent workings of the automatic market place, there must be juxtaposed their theory of social control, the institutions of which were to channel individual interests into amenable lines and thereby *create* harmony. Lord Robbins' framework may be considered as a system of social control to create that harmony, or alternately, to create the conditions of order: "If [the classical economists] assumed anywhere a harmony, it was never a harmony arising in a vacuum but always very definitely within a framework of law." Within the constraints of the market-plus-framework interpretations specified by Lord Robbins, the transformation or conversion of private interest into social interest was accomplished not only through the medium of the competitive market place but also through the legal process, which become "two aspects of one and the same social process," namely, the total economic decision-making process.

THE APPROACH

The market-plus-framework interpretation of the classical theory of economic policy, particularly as elucidated by Lord Robbins, has the great virtue of specifying more completely what the classical theory of policy was all about than had been indicated by the ambiguous but doctrinally useful laissez-faire or laissez-faire-plus-exceptions views. It has replaced a caricature with a more complete analysis. The most significant particular contributions *in re* the classical policy system include: (a) calling attention to the importance of the institutional organization of society and economy as a mode additional to market forces or private participation for the resolution of the basic economic problems; (b) establishing the createdness of order and of the resolution of the problems of freedom and control, and continuity and change, thereby directing attention to a more accurate understanding of the complexities of establishing mutuality of interests and to the role of the system of social control; and (c) suggesting the subtleties involved in reconciling freedom and order. The market-plus-framework interpretation indicates that the classical economists were more sophisticated than the doctrinally oriented approaches would allow.

A NOTE ON MODERN LIBERALISM AND MODERN CONSERVATISM

The term "liberal" when applied to a present-day political economist denotes something considerably different from the classical liberalism described above. Modern American Liberalism will be treated in later chapters, but a brief remark is in order here. The early American liberalism of Thomas Jefferson hinged upon two postulates about the relationship between politics and economics. First, a truly democratic order was to be best realized in a nation composed largely of small farms, augmented by the necessary number of small businesses; in other words, democracy required an economy built upon a very large number of small and independent units of production. Second, the chief threat to the realization of such a system came from the advocates of big business, and these advocates, such as Alexander Hamilton, were known to favor governmental intervention to help the "infant industries" of America in getting established. Thus, the rhetoric of Jeffersonian democracy coupled together the cause of the small farmer and businessman with antagonism toward governmental intervention in the workings of the economy.

However appropriate in Jefferson's day, there was strong evidence a century later that the linkage was no longer sensible. In fact, it seemed apparent to many that the rights of individuals in the economic sphere could be protected only if the government would take firm steps to limit the influence of the large-scale economic power blocs that had arisen. This latter school of thought, which has come to support a variety of governmental economic activities, encompasses what will be called here "modern social reform liberalism," or simply "liberalism." The school of thought that has continued to maintain that the chief threat to democratic capitalism is unwarranted governmental intervention in the economy will be called "modern conservatism," or simply "conservatism." (There is one exception. Friedrich Hayek, Milton Friedman, and other contemporary economists who could be described as "conservative," in the sense that the term is defined here, insist upon designating themselves as "liberal," to emphasize their close intellectual bond with classical liberalism. To avoid confusion, we will refer to this group of economists as neoliberals–individualist-conservatives.)

The historical reversal of the policy positions of liberal and conservative thinkers is described by Max Fletcher in selection 1.4. In selection 1.5, Overton H. Taylor distinguishes between classical and contemporary liberalism, and relates each to the development of political democracy.

1.4 Liberal and Conservative: Turn and Turnabout

Max E. Fletcher

The economic conservative prefers not to be called a conservative; he is really, he insists, a nineteenth-century liberal. What is not so generally recognized is that the economic liberal—while happy with the label—exhibits the most important distinguishing attribute of the nineteenth-century conservative: a lack of faith in the concept of an automatic, self-regulating economy. The twentieth

Excerpted from Max E. Fletcher, "Liberal and Conservative: Turn and Turnabout," ***Journal of Economic Issues*****, September 1968, pp. 312–22. Reprinted by permission of the publisher and the author.**

century has thus witnessed two complete ideological turnabouts. The conservative has been busily engaged in dressing himself in the shucked-off garments of the liberal; the liberal, having stripped himself of his earlier garb, now finds himself wearing the abandoned trappings of the conservative.

Economic liberalism, as it developed during the nineteenth century, was identified primarily by adherence to a joint belief in the concepts of a self-regulating market economy and laissez faire. The two parts of this program, although tied in a bundle by the liberal, are really separate, but not necessarily independent, concepts. The belief in a self-regulating market economy leads logically to the espousal of a governmental hands-off-business policy, but the reverse need not be true. In fact, a general sentiment favoring laissez faire developed long before the self-regulating market economy was recognized as a possibility. The development of capitalistic techniques and the stimulus of expanding trade, coupled with the ineffectiveness of central governments, enabled businessmen in one industry after another to break loose from restrictions and assert what they regarded as their rights of industrial liberty—even in the age that we continue to label the mercantilist era.

This was relaxation in practice, however, not in principle. When abandonment of restraints brought social upheaval, governments stepped back into the picture to control the process of change. Enclosure acts, for example, allowed for the overthrow of antiquated land tenure rules, but the Tudors and early Stuarts maintained a sufficient balance between "habitation" and "improvement" that the enclosure movement was decelerated. At the same time another series of legislative enactments (Statute of Artificers, Poor Laws, Act of Settlement) attempted to cushion the impact of economic change by restricting the process and providing relief for the "victims" of such change.

Generalization of the principle of laissez faire came only toward the end of the eighteenth century. Until that time the necessity of state intervention was justified on the basis of an assumed conflict between individual self-interests and social welfare. Although particular groups of businessmen might persuade the state authorities that the interests of society would not be jeopardized were they freed from central control, the ultimate authority of the state in the economic arena was never seriously challenged. Government intervention might be invoked at any time to bring about an artificial identification of social and private interests by imposing limitations on individual liberties.

A general policy of laissez faire, a general hostility to the very idea of state regulation, could not be seriously proposed until it could be established that there was a natural harmony of interests private and social, which would be achieved if only the state would refrain from economic meddling. This was the key contribution of the Physiocrats and Adam Smith, in Adam Smith's version, as set forth in *The Wealth of Nations*.

Guided by his belief in this natural harmony of economic interest —developed in the writings of the Physiocrats and Adam Smith, but rounded into a system by the later "classical" economists, especially Ricardo, J. B. Say, and John Stuart Mill—the liberal during the nineteenth century successfully swept away, over the determined opposition of the conservative, one after another of the governmental roadblocks standing in the way of achievement of such natural harmony. Corn laws, poor laws, guild restrictions, navigation acts, anti-incorporation laws, most restraints on banking—all fell before the mighty thrusts of the liberal. By the beginning of the 1860s all the major countries had adopted free or relatively free markets as their chief economic instrument: free markets for men, for money, for land, and for goods and services. Both in England and abroad, the economic sphere had been "liberated" from the inhibiting, enervating hand of the mercantilist state and placed under the guidance of market forces.

If it is a fact that the adoption of the self-regulating market system was urged by the nineteenth-century liberal, it is equally true that the nineteenth-century conservative conceived his task to be the opposition to the wholesale adoption of such a system, and once the system was adopted, to fight for its modification. The conservative of an earlier day was thus consistently "interventionist," as is his latter-day counterpart, today's liberal. The economic liberal sought to "liberate" economic activities from the governmental controls imposed in all prior societies; the conservative sought to "conserve" the principle that the state should have the unquestioned right to intervene in "private" economic affairs in order to set right things that were amiss.

Almost from the beginning of the nineteenth century to the end, the power of the conservative was used to mitigate the workings of the market system. In England the role of the conservative was so apparent that the era was called the period of "Tory social reform." The reform work begun by the Earl of Shaftesbury in securing the passage of the early factory acts and the Ten-Hours Bill was continued by Disraeli, both as novelist and as Tory prime minister. In these movements the position was taken that a laissez-faire policy did not fulfill the requirements of national well-being; that the general welfare accordingly had to be sought through conscious regulation instead of trusting to the operation of unfettered economic forces. By the end of the century even the British industrialist was coming round to his point of view. In Germany, the first social legislation was put through by the arch-conservative Bismark and his Prussian backers, on the basis of the belief that the government was the proper authority to care for the workingman, not the market. And in the United States, where the laissez-faire philosophy was officially sanctified by the constitution and federal laws, the most significant breaches of the laissez-faire attitude —provision of central banking, federal aid to business, and protective tariffs—were promoted by the more conservative political parties.

By the close of the nineteenth century a curious paradox had developed. The doctrines of laissez faire and an automatic, self-regulating market system had been canonized and had been accepted as a new religion. But the prophets of this new religion found it increasingly difficult to put down their doubts concerning the truthfulness of their own dogma. This can clearly be seen in England, the early home of economic liberalism. There the Liberal party, which had proudly carried the banner of laissez faire and control by the market in an earlier period, had become converted by the end of the century to moderate state capitalism. Between 1905 and 1914 the party secured the adoption of a legislative reform program that sidestepped the unrestricted market forces in several areas: workmen's compensation, old-age pensions, sickness, invalidity, and unemployment insurance, and reform of the landholding system. World War I vastly increased the restraints on the operations of the market. The English liberal had thus turned full-about. The market was dethroned, the government waited to be crowned.

In the United States the turnabout of the liberal was just as complete as in England, but the process of change was both more complex and more long-drawn-out. Toward the end of the nineteenth century there were increasing doubts about the tenability of [liberal] assumptions. Laws were deemed necessary to prevent [people] from buying adulterated foods or from working in plants where the machinery was improperly safeguarded. And in a society of unequals, the strong and clever, in the absence of government controls, proved only too likely to exploit the weak and the ignorant.

Further, the natural or automatic working of the law of supply and demand dictated a degree of competition that was not readily forthcoming. In an age of pools, trusts, and mergers, government regulation seemed to be necessary to ensure a fair price, since producers had found that their self-interest often impelled combination to cushion the impact of competition.

Even the wave of regulatory legislation which was passed around the turn of the century, however, while it led to some qualifications of the self-regulating market economy concept, was not sufficient to destroy faith in the idea itself. Substantially free markets did, after all, still work—and work effectively, at least through the 1920s. The denouement—or, better, the coup de grâce—was reserved for the Great Depression of the 1930s and the Keynesian Revolution.

John Maynard Keynes provided, in his *General Theory of Employment, Interest and Money,* an intellectually respectable alternative to the thesis that a market-directed economy would inevitably make the adjustments necessary to maximize production and employment. According to Keynes, such an economy could reach a position of stable equilibrium at *any* level of output. This being the case, the only means of getting a market economy off dead-center if it were stuck at an under-full-employment level of output was government intervention—government tinkering with the money markets, tax levels or the rate of acquisition of government goods and services, such as public works. The Keynesian program swept the field. It could shortly be said by economists, with much truth, that "we're all Keynesians," that is, interventionists. They had come to believe that the identification of private and social interests rested on the benevolence and competence of the government authority.[1]

[1]Samuel H. Beer has recently pointed out that the same *volte-face* has taken place in the political as in the economic sphere: "The modern liberal, as a champion of strong and active central government in the service of nation-wide purposes, becomes the heir of Hamilton, while the modern conservative, as the opponent of centralization and friend of states rights and localism, represents the Jeffersonian tradition." "Liberalism and the National Idea," *The Public Interest,* No. 5, Fall 1966, p. 72.

The prospects for a return to the self-regulating market economy in the postwar period appeared anything but bright. The few persons still dedicated to the principle of a market-directed economy, to a belief in economic individualism and laissez faire, seemed to be living in a world gone by. The hopelessness of their position is graphically illustrated in the writings of University of Chicago economist Henry Simons. For liberty to survive, according to Simons, a wholesale reordering of institutions and "rules of the game" was necessary: elimination of private monopoly in all its forms (which meant breaking up General Motors, Ford, Chrysler, General Electric, Westinghouse, U.S. Steel, and so forth, as well as the labor unions), abolition of fractional-reserve deposit banking, drastic changes in the whole tax system, elimination of the tariff system, and limitations upon advertising and selling activities. In other words, to achieve liberty, such a comprehensive remodeling of economic society was necessary that only a leviathan state could do the job! Sales of this nostrum were not very brisk. And somewhat similar proposals of Hayek and von Mises also sparked little interest.

With the fortunes of economic conservatism at such a low ebb such a short time ago, how can the present respectability of the belief in economic individualism and a market-oriented economy be explained? The answer lies partly in the realm of ideas, partly in the area of work-a-day experience. As for the ideas, they are in important part those of the late Harvard economist Joseph A. Schumpeter and the economists at the University of Chicago.

Joseph Schumpeter's chief contribution in this area was his *Capitalism, Socialism, and Democracy*. Here was a program with sales appeal, for it called for no major overhaul of the economy. In fact prudence demanded just the reverse. Letting government remove its crippling restrictions from business and capitalism would again function satisfactorily, as it did in an earlier age when left alone. There would be depressions, it is true, but depressions are the price of progress. Besides, recovery would come about much more rapidly in the absence of government intervention. The recuperative powers of the economy were great; patent medicines, such as the New Deal, only interfered with the self-healing process. As for the argument of the earlier liberal economists that a market economy could only work properly in the absence of concentrated economic power, Schumpeter asked only that proponents of such views look about them. In what industries would they find the greatest efficiency, the most rapid rate of economic advance? Not in those industries most closely approaching the nineteenth-century ideal of atomistic competition, such as farming and bituminous coal mining. Technical change came only where it could be afforded, where firms had the resources that innovation called for and the market power to protect such innovations until they had a chance to pay off. "Bigness" was therefore not a vice of modern-day capitalism, but a virtue. Other writers, such as Peter Drucker, A. A. Berle, the editors of *Fortune,* and David Lilienthal, have embroidered on this theme with the discovery that the modern corporation has developed a sense of social responsibility, and therefore needs little centralized control or direction.

The Chicago School, building on the work of Frank Knight and Henry Simons, has had significant success in getting across the message that there is an intimate relationship between economic freedom and political freedom. Milton Friedman, in particular, has persistently called for a re-examination of the respective roles of governments and markets in our society and the enlargement of individual freedom through greater reliance on competitive markets. His role as economic advisor to Barry Goldwater in the 1964 presidential campaign is consistent with this set of beliefs. So successful has Friedman been in converting students and professional colleagues to his point of view that it is the rare university today whose economics department does not house at least one ardent supporter of the Friedman position.

At the same time, much of the glamor associated with centralism has begun to rub off. If the uncontrolled market could make mistakes, so could the planners—only bigger ones.

It would be tidier if it could be maintained that today's economic conservative believes not only in a self-regulating market economy but in the same "model" of self-regulating economy as did the nineteenth-century economic liberal. Such clearly is not the case. The belief in the harmony of private and social interests, in the absence of erratic, unpredictable government intervention, is common to both. But some of the institutional arrangements venerated in the nineteenth century are no longer defended. The gold standard, for example, with its provisions for automatic changes in the money supply and price level, is dead. But it is believed that its successor, the Federal Reserve system, can only avoid being a destabilizing force in the economy if it is placed on automatic pilot and given a fixed course to follow. Many conservatives are also willing to dispense with the companion to the gold standard, the annually-balanced budget, provided that the budget is unbalanced by the natural workings of the economy, a boom automatically providing a budgetary surplus and thereby reducing inflationary pressures, a recession automatically bringing about a deficit and thereby 'braking" the recession. There is thus a somewhat enlarged role for government to play, but by and large government does not act, it reacts.

A general lack of faith in the self-regulating market principle prompts the modern liberal to take the view that the government must act, not simply react. If there is private affluence and public poverty, then government must restrict the sovereignty of the consumer, must channel more spending into public uses. "Automatic stabilizers" are good as far as they go, but they do not go far enough. If economic instability becomes acute, only discretionary government policies can right the balance. If market power is concentrated then, unless "countervailing" power develops spontaneously, it is the responsibility of government either to break up the original power or to promote the development of countervailing power. In this view, then, the present-day liberal envisions an economy with the government as full partner. Along with the economic conservative of a century ago, he finds it necessary for the state to intervene to bring about an enforced identification of private and social interests.

The terms "economic liberal" and "economic conservative" may best be defined in terms of acceptance or rejection of a market-directed economy. Thus the individuals of the nineteenth century who sought to "conserve" the principle that the final authority in economic affairs was the government by that token deserved the name of conservative, while those persons who attempted successfully to "liberate" economic activities from the purview of government in favor of control of economic affairs by markets were truly liberals. Today the conservative is the one who attempts to "conserve" this latter outlook, while the liberal promotes the "liberation" of the economic sphere from full market control, favoring a more active role for government.

This suggests that the two positions, in practice, are not so bipolar. Few conservatives favor absolute control by the market, and few liberals are in sympathy with an unlimited amount of government control of the economy. The comparison might best be visualized in terms of a continuum, with an economic system featuring uncontrolled markets at one extreme, an economic system typified by all-out government planning and control at the other, and with various mixtures of market control and government control in between. Those persons with conservative leanings find their places toward the free-market end of this spectrum. Liberals range themselves along the government planning and control end. "Moderate" conservatives and "moderate" liberals—both of whom wish to retain the market-oriented economy, but recognize the need for a certain amount of government intervention—bunch closely together in the middle.

1.5 Free Enterprise and Democracy

Overton H. Taylor

HISTORY OF THE WORD "LIBERAL"

As is indicated by the word "liberal" itself, and demonstrated by the entire history of "liberalism," we liberals—apart from extremists who misuse and are not entitled to the name—are friends of liberty and loyal heirs of the main American tradition, aiming at the nearest feasible approach to a society of (in the main) voluntarily co-operating, free individuals. But by an accident in the history of American political terminology, the word "liberal" has come into general use here only in the quite recent period, which has been marked by some new enlargements of the sphere of activity of the people's government. And in this period the expansion of our government—while occurring chiefly under the pressure of prevailing conditions and the resulting insistent needs and demands of the popular majority—has been brought about through a movement

From Overton H. Taylor, "Free Enterprise and Democracy," in *Saving American Capitalism*, edited by Seymour E. Harris (New York: Knopf, 1950), pp. 331–40. Reprinted by permission of the editor.

led precisely by those (the liberals) most anxious to see the full blessings of liberty extended to *all* Americans. Not the group's liberal purpose, however, but merely its support (in seeming conflict with that purpose) of new governmental economic controls has been most clearly evident to the public. Thus it has come about that, ignoring both the literal and the older historic meaning of the word, our national usage means by "liberals" persons advocating a degree and kind of humanitarian "big government"; a thing which the conservative opposition can all too easily represent as, and which if misdirected can degenerate into, a general, dangerous curtailment of traditional and still desirable private liberties.

BIRTH OF THE LIBERAL CREED

The old gospel of entirely or very "free enterprise" and very limited government is today identified in our politics with conservatism, and even in that quarter is not much more than a wistful memory. But in the epoch of its birth—the late eighteenth and early nineteenth centuries, the epoch of the American and French Revolutions and England's first steps toward democracy—the same gospel (with a subtle difference) was a vital part of the *liberal* creed. Along with the ideal and theory of political democracy, it was then the first philosophy of the liberal-democratic movement to emancipate the common people from oppression by the privileged few. For in that age, this movement was directed against the regimes established in the preceding epoch—regimes of despotic monarchy, oligarchy (actual rule, under the reigning monarchs, by small groups of aristocratic landowners and rich merchants), and "mercantilism," the economic policy of those governments. The character of mercantilism, above all, is the key to the original, liberal meaning of the gospel of free enterprise. Mercantilism was a system of governmental promotion and friendly control of high "capitalist" enterprise and wide control of economic affairs for the benefit of the ruling, privileged, rich minorities and to bolster up the military power of each great imperial nation-state, and not for the sake of improving the economic welfare of the common people. In short, the liberal movement in its earliest phase was a revolt against the alliance of "big government" and what was then "big business."

LIBERALISM VERSUS MERCANTILISM

It was in opposition to mercantilism that the first liberal economists—Adam Smith and others—developed the ideal and theory of an economic system of universal free enterprise, free competition, and free trade. Governments were to function only as "impartial umpires." Central in mercantilist policy were lavish grants of legal monopolies to associations of established, wealthy businessmen, and a mass of restrictive regulations of the normal, gain-seeking activities of "little" businessmen and of farmers, working men, and the people as consumers. And so, by opposition, it became the central idea of the liberal economists that a regime of minimal government and maximal economic freedom for all individuals would subject the former monopolies and all businesses to competitive pressures beneficial to the public; distribute opportunities impartially to all the people, and elicit from all the people their best productive efforts and contributions to the common welfare; and in general, harmonize the self-interest of each individual with the collective interest of mankind. With its strong individualism, that economic-liberal philosophy combined, inseparably, a no less strong internationalism. All individuals everywhere were to have large, equal, and sacred freedoms to pursue their interests anywhere, across as well as within the national frontiers; and the national governments were to be made to stop "interfering" in the economic world in those ways which had favored the already rich and oppressed the common people, as well as served the spirit of aggressive nationalism, to the detriment of international trade, prosperity, and peace.

ECONOMIC LIBERALISM AND POLITICAL DEMOCRACY

Now that ideal and theory of the free world economy attained a fairly full development and some influence a few decades before the ideal and theory of political democracy—the other half of the complete philosophy of nineteenth-century liberalism—became of equal, practical importance. In other words, the main body of the liberal reformers first tried for a while only to make the old, pre-democratic kind of government as little harmful as possible by curtailing its powers and sphere of activity, before they went on to the further effort to replace it with a new kind of government, so organized as to be responsive and responsible to all the people. But then in the second, more complete, phase of the liberal movement, most leading advocates of fully democratic, popular government long remained also advocates of minimal government and the economic system of free, unregulated, individual enterprise, competition, and trade. The utmost freedom for all individuals at all consistent with their common welfare was still the first concern. Fear of "big government" as likely to be oppressive misgovernment, perverted to the ends of a rich, powerful, and selfish few, was still the dominant fear. Generations of experience of the old type of government had produced in the people a deep distrust of government in general, which could die out only with the gradual, full development of, and new generations of experience under, political democracy. Political democracy at first was usually thought of, not as enabling the popular majority to control and use a widely active, strong government to attain their ends by positive action, but rather as enabling the people to protect themselves from too much government, by using the vote as a veto on ambitious governmental plans.

Moreover, the theory of the ideal "free market" economy still impressed most democratic leaders as a "democratic" conception in its own sphere and the logical counterpart of political democracy. Free competition of all enterprises for the patronage of the people would oblige them to serve all the people as amply, well, and cheaply as possible, just as political "free competition" of parties, candidates, ideas, and programs for the votes of the people would force *them* into line with prevailing popular desires. Thus, through the early decades of the nineteenth century, free enterprise and democracy were as a rule supported together in pro-popular, progressive, liberal, and democratic quarters, and opposed together in well-to-do and conservative quarters. For example, in this country then it was the Jeffersonian and, later, the Jacksonian Democrats who preached free enterprise and limited government along with full political democracy. The Hamiltonian Federalists and, later, the Whigs—representatives of the northern, larger business interests and forerunners of the present-day Republican Party—were not supporters either of free enterprise or of full democracy. Instead, those early parties of the "well born," well-to-do, and conservative families in our land still more or less openly favored a regime of oligarchy or rule, in effect, by themselves; a strong and active federal government, responsive mainly to their interests and ideas; and an economic policy on the part of that government akin to the traditions of European mercantilism.

THE ENGLISH EXPERIENCE

Not only here but in every country of what was to be the democratic-capitalist world, conversion of business leaders to the creed of free enterprise and democracy was a more or less late development. But this development occurred earliest—in the early-to-middle decades of the nineteenth century—and most completely, in England, the first country to go through the Industrial Revolution or enter the industrial machine age. For the rise of the new industrialism, in England then and later elsewhere, transferred the controlling voice in the business community to a new set of men with new attitudes. In the place of the former class of "merchant princes," whose hopes of large profits lay in monopolistic and/or state-aided control of markets, there arose the new class of manufacturing capitalists, whose hopes lay at first in a wholly free competition of ever improving methods of production. Having as their best route to profits free exertion of their own individual enterprise and ingenuity, the new industrialists in general tended to be more independent, "rugged individualists," asking the state only to give them a wide, free, unobstructed field for their endeavors. Moreover, in the special case of the early British industrialists, their whole situation—never fully, in all aspects, repeated elsewhere—gave them inducements to become especially complete supporters of democracy and humane reforms as well as of free enterprise, and of free trade abroad as well as free enterprise at home. As it bears on other points yet to come in my narrative and argument, let me now spell out this last point briefly.

In Britain's old-world social hierarchy of a century and more ago, not her businessmen but her landowning aristocrats and "gentlemen" were and had been the ruling class. No matter how rich they were the businessmen in general ranked only as members of the middle class, and had much tendency to be, in feeling, a part of the common people. And this now became more significantly true than it had been earlier; the earlier "merchant princes" had been accepted into the governing-class circles and could feel identified with the old, traditional, social and political system of the country. But the new industrialists in most cases rose from humbler social origins and long retained "democratic" feelings. And those feelings were often accentuated by the tendency of their social superiors—the aristocrats and "gentlemen"—to dislike their "pushing" ways and so to snub them. Again, being the chief "backers" of and first gainers from the technological progress in industry which was transforming society, the industrialists tended to aspire to be leaders of social progress in general —leading supporters of new, progressive ideas in all fields, including politics. Also, industrialism required a mass market, enlargement of the market for all commodities to include all the people, or progressive elevation of mass living standards. This requirement aligned the interests of the businessmen with democratic progress. They could well support political democracy, for it enlarged their own political influence as well as that of the working people, and as yet any fears that the latter would use the new political system against them were lulled by the fact that the gospel of free enterprise was still a part of the democratic creed. In the higher, nonbusiness circles of the aristocracy and gentry, or patrician landlords, there was in that half-century just after the French Revolution much reactionary fear of democracy, of the new cult of liberty or individualism, and of all progressivism. There was a vigorous growth of a new conservative or Tory philosophy of authoritarian, "paternal" government over all the people and the economy by the ancient, limited, hereditary ruling class. But in the main the British industrial capitalists opposed that reaction and joined the liberal, democratic, progressive movement. And finally, the resulting political alignment of labor and capital together against the "Tory Landlords" became crystallized around the special issue of the corn laws, or agricultural protectionism, versus the complete freedom of foreign trade which the British industrialists, in their special situation in that epoch, desired as in both their own and the national interest. They saw free trade as the way to cheapen food and thus lower money wages without injuring labor, and as a means of facilitating expansion of industrial exports in exchange for imported food and raw material.

SELF-INTEREST AND THE COMMON WELFARE

Such were the backgrounds of the first and fullest adoption, by any national business community, of the entire philosophy of the now old, obsolescent, early, special form of "liberalism" which included the gospel of very free enterprise and very limited government. Nor did its adoption by business at once transform the old liberalism into the new conservatism it has since become; that transformation was to be another, still later, development, and is yet to be explained here. The mid-nineteenth-century British liberal businessmen had, I think—in a measure not often excelled by normal, not saintly, human beings—the true liberal, generous, humane, idealistic, democratic, and progressive spirit. At the same time it is true, as I have indicated, that a shrewd perception of where their own interests lay in the special circumstances they confronted in their time and country had very much to do with making them adherents of the liberal outlook. They should not on that account be singled out for special censure. The tendency to be much influenced by self-interest in arriving at political opinions—which even so are usually honest and sometimes valid beliefs as to what public policies are morally right and best for the welfare of the entire community—is a tendency not at all peculiar to businessmen or to any class, in any epoch or society. It is an all but universal human weakness. . . . The point is, there was a time, especially in England, when conditions were such that a genuine liberalism, in the form then current, harmonized with the interests and so had the support of business, together with the common people.

THE AMERICAN EXPERIENCE

There was never at any time in this country, however, or indeed elsewhere outside of England, any complete parallel to that situation in mid-nineteenth-century England. American business, for example, never as a whole accepted the old economic-liberal views on the question of the tariff, or on that of the trusts—free trade abroad, or free competition at home. Conditions here, during and after our industrial revolution, which came later by a few decades than England's, did not so generally align the interests of our industrialists with those policies. We have had, in great numbers, our own ruggedly individualistic captains of industry; but by and large our business leaders in the past have sought and won much active, governmental help—interference for their benefit in the economy—and governmental tolerance of their own collusive endeavors to build up monopolies and to handicap their competitors. Since we never had a European-model aristocracy, the top layer of the American business community has always constituted our topmost social class, wielding from the outset a very great influence over all American life. Through all generations and changes in our country, and despite steady growth of the reality and vigor of our political democracy, this group has continued to seek to retain its early control over government, and insure a mixed set of policies: protection of the business freedoms desired by big interests, and active furtherance of their designs entailing restrictions of the free enterprise of other people. Until very recently, American progressivism had to concentrate its efforts mainly on the task of ending business control and misuse of government, or in other words perfecting our real, political democracy. And despite some appearances to the contrary at times, I think it is true that until very recently American individualism—the ideal of great freedom for all individuals and very limited government—remained more a popular than a business ideal. Precisely that fact is what now gives our business defenders of free enterprise, the opponents of present-day liberal, democratic, governmental controls over business, an unfair advantage in political debate.

EXPANSION OF DEMOCRACY AND THE RIFT WITH BUSINESS

Meanwhile, there began long ago in the democratic-capitalist world as a whole and even in mid-nineteenth-century England, a rift in the early harmony —which was never complete even there—of business, democracy, and free enterprise. Democracy began to go beyond removal of the pre-democratic governmental controls over individual enterprise which had suited the "big business" of an earlier day, and impose new and different controls of its own on the new industrialists. For while the Industrial Revolution and its consequence, the new industrial capitalism, brought great benefits to all the people, they also brought new evils into being; and as governments became more democratic and responsive to popular needs, they were obliged even while professing the free-enterprise creed in general, to begin to take on new functions and evolve new organs in the effort to alleviate the new evils. Thus, for example, the English Factory Acts came into being in the very heyday of the country's devotion to extreme individualistic liberalism. And a steady, gradual expansion of government and social legislation of many kinds followed, there and elsewhere, right on down to the present.

Also, in the meantime, in a minority quarter far to the left of and unconnected with that main trend but adding still more to the distress of business, socialist movements got under way. The grain of truth in their gospel was and is the fact that under industrial capitalism a measure of conflict does exist between the interests of the class of owners (and their agents, managers), and those of the class of wage-earning workers. The two "classes" have a common interest in high production, but a clash of interests over the division of the proceeds. The old economic-liberal theory of the potential, perfect harmony of all interests in the ideal free-market economy evaded recognition of the fact of "classes" and the partial conflict of their interests. On the other hand the socialist view falsely depicts that conflict as an absolute one, denies the actual bond of common interests between the "masses" and the "capitalists," and holds that democracy must in the end become incompatible with and abolish private capitalism. The socialist body of doctrine is, I believe, in definite error, and a threat to all individual liberties including those most vital to the working people. But its spread has been stimulated by the labor-capital conflict, the slowness of democracy in developing controls over business for the general welfare, and the resistance of business to the moderate controls and reforms which alone can preserve a viable union of the democratic, liberal state and the business economy.

CONSERVATIVE REDEFINITION OF FREE ENTERPRISE, AND TODAY'S LIBERALISM

Now it was in the reaction of business and its friends against the menace of socialism and the expanding activities of democratic governments, that, in the late nineteenth and early twentieth centuries, the old, originally liberal, economic ideal and theory of the free-enterprise economy became, by a subtle change, the gospel of conservatism. The reorientation involved little apparent change in economic theory. The neo-classical economists and the pro-business popularizers of their teachings appeared to be only further elaborating and refining the scheme of thought of Adam Smith and his immediate successors, the old classical economists. But what had been the vision of a group of liberal reformers, of a possible, ideal economy, now became an unreal, alleged account of the mode of operation of a later, actual system which was *not* a realization of the original ideal. And above all, the utopia now confused with reality, now was defended or exalted in contrast not with the original alternatives —despotism, oligarchy, mercantilism, all business monopolies, and the remains of feudalism—but with the new, advancing, and dreaded alternatives—mild democratic control over capitalism and, as the frightful specter seen as looming beyond that, socialism.

Finally, when the old economic-liberal theory had thus been refitted to the uses of, and taken over by, conservatism, liberal thought began its new, recent and current, still confused gropings toward a new vision, of a really possible and sound "middle way" between the extremes of entirely free enterprise, and socialism. Thus far, this latest development has attained great importance only in this country. In Europe, socialism has become the creed of the discontented "many" and their sympathetic leaders; the main conservative forces there have turned back to ancient anti-democratic, authoritarian ideas; and the term "liberalism" there still means as a rule the old creed of extreme individualism, now supported only by tiny, ineffective groups of essentially conservative although anti-authoritarian intellectuals. But the current new or latter-day American liberalism, despite its meausre of conflict with that older creed, is the true continuation of the old, authentic, liberal movement, in the new conditions of today.

CONSERVATISM

At the time of its emergence and early development, classical liberalism was a liberal, even radical, philosophy of economic reform. By contrast, classical conservatism, as represented by such figures as Edmund Burke (1729–97) and contemporary American political philosopher Russell Kirk (*The Conservative Mind,* 1953), is characterized by a strong preference for gradual change that sustains intact the best in the aristocratic heritage of the past.

Unlike classical liberalism, which was intimately linked with classical (and later neoclassical) economic theory, classical conservatism is a social philosophy with implications for the economic order, but little economic theory of its own. Our interest in classical conservatism here stems largely from its impact, along with that of classical liberalism, upon *laissez-faire conservatism,* the dominant economic philosophy in the United States from the Civil War to the Great Depression of the 1930s. Laissez-faire conservatism might be described with simplification as a popularized amalgam of classical liberalism and classical conservatism.

Though by no means diametrically opposed to the main tenets of classical liberalism, classical conservatives such as Burke drew subtle but important distinctions in three main dimensions of their thought:

(1) *The nature of man:* While recognizing the existence of different economic functions and social classes (for example, workers, landlords,

capitalists), classical liberalism, with its focus on rational pursuit of self-interest and atomistic competition, contained an important equalitarian strain —restricted, to be sure, to equality of *opportunity* rather than of economic position, but there, nonetheless. Classical conservatism, by contrast, perceived of men as members of social groups and emphasized inequalities in talents and capacities for leadership.

(2) *Market processes and the private sector:* Classical conservatism gives qualified support to market processes, but more for their contributions to freedom, social pluralism, the balance of social power, and the preservation of private property than to competitive economic efficiency. A strong private sector of the economy is espoused more for its contributions to self-reliance and protection against potential governmental tyranny than for its role in promoting prosperity and meeting consumer demands.

(3) *Economic role of government:* Like classical liberalism, classical conservatism advocates a limited government, but limited in size rather than in economic function. In the conservative view, government's role in economic life should be restricted more because of the potential corrupting effect of the concentration of economic power than because efficiency dictates an appropriate functional division between private and public sectors of the economy. On the other hand, if necessary to maintain order, stability, and security, a conservative state might well take on functions beyond those of a classical liberal state (for example, comprehensive social security programs), or even intervene in market processes.

In selection 1.6, Clinton Rossiter describes the leading dimensions of classical conservatism.

1.6 Classical Conservatism

Clinton Rossiter

The Conservative holds rather strong opinions about man's nature, his capacity for self-government, his relations with other men, the kind of life he should lead, and the rights he may properly claim. On these opinions, which taken together represent a stiff questioning of the bright promises of Liberalism, rests the whole Conservative tradition.

Man, says the Conservative . . . is a fabulous composite of some good and much evil, a blend of several ennobling excellencies and several more degrading imperfections . . . As no man is perfect, so no man is perfectible. If educated properly, placed in a favorable environment, and held in restraint by tradition and authority, he may display innate qualities of rationality, sociabil-

Excerpted from Clinton Rossiter, *Conservatism in America* (New York: Random House, 1962), pp. 21–24, 27–28, 31–32, 34–35, 37–38, 40–41. Reprinted by permission of the publisher and Mrs. Clinton Rossiter.

ity, industry, and decency. Never, no matter how he is educated or situated or restrained, will he throw off completely his other innate qualities of irrationality, selfishness, laziness, depravity, corruptibility, and cruelty. Man's nature is essentially immutable, and the immutable strain is one of deep-seated wickedness. . . .

The Conservatism that celebrates Burke holds out obstinately against two popular beliefs about human relations in modern society: individualism and equality. Putting off a discussion of individualism for a few pages, let us hear what the Conservative has to say about the explosive question of equality.

Each man is equal to every other man in only one meaningful sense: he is a man, a physical and spiritual entity, and is thus entitled by God and nature to be treated as end rather than means. From the basic fact of moral equality come several secondary equalities that the modern Conservative recognizes, more eloquently in public than in private: equality of opportunity, the right of each individual to exploit his own talents up to their natural limits; equality before the law, the right to justice on the same terms as other men; and political equality, which takes the form—and a rather distressing form it often seems—of universal suffrage. Beyond this the conservative is unwilling to go. Recognizing the infinite variety among men in talent, taste, appearance, intelligence, and virtue, he is candid enough to assert that this variety extends vertically as well as horizontally. Men are grossly unequal—and, what is more, can never be made equal—in most qualities of mind, body, and spirit.

The good society of Conservatism rests solidly on this great truth. The social order is organized in such a way as to take advantage of ineradicable natural distinctions among men. It exhibits a class structure in which there are several quite distinct levels, most men find their level early and stay in it without rancor, and equality of opportunity keeps the way at least partially open to ascent and decline. At the same time, the social order aims to temper those distinctions that are not natural. While it recognizes the inevitability and indeed the necessity of orders and classes, it insists that all privileges, ranks, and other visible signs of inequality be as natural and functional as possible. The Conservative, of course—and this point is of decisive importance—is much more inclined than other men to consider artificial distinctions as natural. Equity rather than equality is the mark of his society; the reconciliation rather than the abolition of classes is his constant aim. When he is forced to choose between liberty and equality, he throws his support unhesitatingly to liberty. Indeed, the preference for liberty over equality lies at the root of the Conservative tradition, and men who subscribe to this tradition never tire of warning against the "rage for equality." Some of the Conservative's best thoughts are directed to society and the social process. The key points of his social theory appear to be these:

Society is a living organism with roots deep in the past. The true community, the Conservative likes to say, is a tree, not a machine. It rose to its present strength and glory through centuries of growth, and men must forbear to think of it as a mechanical contrivance that can be dismantled and reassembled in one generation. Not fiat but prescription, not the open hand of experiment but the hidden hand of custom, is the chief creative force in the social process.

Society is cellular. It is not an agglomeration of lonely individuals, but a grand union of functional groups. Man is a social animal whose best interests are served by co-operating with other men. Indeed, he has no real meaning except as contributing member of his family, church, local community, and, at certain stages of historical development, occupational association. The group is important not only because it gives life, work, comfort, and spiritual support to the individual, but because it joins with thousands of other groups to form the one really stubborn roadblock against the march of the all-powerful state. The Conservative is careful not to ride the cellular analogy too hard, for he is aware that it can lead to a social theory in which man loses all dignity and personality.

In addition to intrinsic groups like the family and church, a healthy society will display a balanced combination of "institutions": constitution, common law, monarchy or presidency, legislature, courts, civil service, armed services and subdivisions, colleges, schools, forms of property, corporations, trade unions, guilds, fraternal orders, and dozens of other instrumentalities and understandings that mold the lives of men.

Society is structured. The Conservative, as we have learned already, recognizes the existence of classes and orders as a positive good. . . .

Society is a unity. In the healthy community all these groups and institutions and classes fit together into a harmonious whole, and attempts to reshape one part of society must inevitably disturb other parts. The Conservative, though something of a pluralist, never loses sight of the ultimate unity into which all the parts of society must finally merge.

Society cannot be static. Change is the rule of life, for societies as for men. A community cannot stand still; it must develop or decay. And the Conservative must not be afraid to abandon patently outworn institutions and ideals. . . . In recognizing, however grudgingly, this great social truth, the Conservative shows himself to be neither a reactionary nor a standpatter. Yet he is just as emphatically not a liberal or radical, and he therefore sets severe conditions upon social change, especially if it is to be worked by active reform. Change, he insists, must never be taken for its own sake; must have preservation, if possible even restoration, as its central object; must be severely limited in scope and purpose; must be a response to an undoubted social need—for example, the renovation or elimination of an institution that is plainly obsolete; must be worked out by slow and careful stages; must be brought off under Conservative auspices, or with Conservatives intervening at the decisive moment. . . .

Unity, harmony, authority, security, continuity—these are the key elements of social stability. In longing for a society in which peace and order reign, the Conservative comes closest to the utopianism that he ridicules in others. . . . The Conservative's ideas about government display an unusual degree of symmetry, and he is rarely stumped by practical questions about its nature, structure, and purpose. . . .

Man, he insists, is a political as well as social animal; government is necessary to his existence as man. . . . Government, like the family out of which it arose, is nature's unforced answer to timeless human needs. Natural in origin, it is also natural in development. Like society, it is a tree rather than a machine. Laws and institutions are the result of centuries of imperceptible growth, not the work of one generation of constitution-makers. . . .

Society must be stable. Although men can never hope to see their community completely stable, they can create an endurable condition of peace and order. . . .

Government is a positive, if not entirely unmixed, blessing. . . . Government serves genuine purposes that cannot be fulfilled by any other means. Any time-honored instrument that is so essential to man's liberty and security cannot be considered inherently evil.

Government, in the Conservative view, is something like fire. Under control, it is the most useful of servants; out of control, it is a ravaging tyrant. The danger of its getting out of control is no argument against its extended and generous use. Held within proper limits, government answers in all these purposes:

It defends the community against external assault.

It is the symbol of unity, the focus of that patriotic fervor which turns a lumpy mass of men and groups into a living unity.

It establishes and administers an equitable system of justice, which alone makes it possible for men to live and do business with one another.

It protects men against the violence they can do one another. By the judicious use of force, it ensures "domestic tranquillity."

It secures the rights of men, including the right of property, against the assaults of license, anarchy, and jealousy.

It adjusts conflicts among groups and regulates their activities, thus acting as the major equilibrating force in the balance of social forces.

It promotes public and private morality, without which freedom cannot long exist. In league with church and family, it strives to separate men's virtues from their vices and to keep the latter under tight rein. It does all this by encouraging or at least protecting organized religion, by supporting the means of education, by enacting laws against vice, and by offering a high example of justice and rectitude. It aids men in their pursuit of happiness, chiefly by removing obstacles in the path of individual development.

Finally, government acts as a humanitarian agency in cases of clear necessity. It relieves human suffering by acts of care and charity, and in more developed communities it may guarantee each citizen the minimum material requirements of a decent existence. In discharging this function, government operates under three clear restrictions. First it can achieve only limited success as a welfare agency. . . . Many of man's ills, especially those that are spiritual in nature, are not curable by legislation. Second, it must do its good works of charity and philanthropy at the lowest and most personal levels. Third, there is, as Peter Viereck insists, a "line of diminishing returns for humanitarianism. Beyond it, the increase in security is less than the loss in liberty." The humanitarian function of government will always remain secondary to its great duties to ensure tranquillity, establish justice, secure rights and property, and raise the level of morality. . . .

The Conservative neither fears nor worships the political state. He hopes that these functions will be discharged justly, virtuously, and with a minimum of compulsion or interference with the lives of men. He can get as angry as any old-fashioned Liberal at the inefficiencies and petty tyrannies of bureaucracy. Yet he attaches too much importance to political authority and activity ever to fall prey, even when his party is out of power, to the simple doctrine that the best government is the least and the least government the best. One mark of the best government, to be sure, is that it employs the least force; but the reduction of force, which Ortega considered the essence of civilization, is a problem of reforming men, not of limiting the size or scope of government.

Man's place in society, especially his relations to government, presents a continuing problem on which the Conservative refuses to take a doctrinaire stand. In general, he tries to strike a workable compromise between the needs of the community and the rights of the individual, both of which he champions eloquently whenever they are ignored or despised.

The Conservative refuses to make the easy, he would say demagogic, distinction between "human rights" and "property rights." Property, in his view, is a human right, as important to man's existence and improvement as any other right. . . .

Property makes it possible for a man to develop in mind and spirit. Tools, house, land, clothes, books, heirlooms—how can anyone deny that these are as essential as the air to man's growth to maturity and wisdom?

Property makes it possible for a man to be free. Independence and privacy can never be enjoyed by one who must rely on other persons or agencies—especially government—for food, shelter, and material comforts. Property gives him a place on which to stand and make free choices; it grants him a sphere in which he may ignore the state.

Property is the most important single technique for the diffusion of economic power.

Property is essential to the existence of the family, the natural unit of society.

Property provides the main incentive for productive work. Human nature being what it is and always will be, the desire to acquire and hold property is essential to progress.

Finally, property is a powerful conservative agent, giving added support and substance to that temperament which helps to stabilize society.

The Conservative defense of private property is most certainly not a defense of its abuse, neglect, or existence in grotesque forms and exaggerated concentrations. Nor is it primarily a defense of industrial capitalism or large-scale private enterprise.

It should be plain that the Conservative, contrary to popular belief, is not an extreme individualist. He may be willing to concede numerous arguments of the unqualified individualists, for neither his own respect for the dignity of the individual nor his dislike of the busy-body state is surpassed by that of any man. Yet he cannot agree to the full implications of individualism, which is based, so he thinks, on an incorrect appraisal of man, society, history, and government. In his own way, the full-blooded individualist is as much a perfectionist as the socialist, and with perfectionism the Conservative can have no truck.

In particular, the Conservative refuses to go all the way with economic individualism. His distrust of unfettered man, his devotion to groups, his sense of the complexity of the social process, his recognition of the real services that government can perform—all these sentiments make it impossible for him to subscribe whole-heartedly to the dogmas and shibboleths of economic individualism: laissez-faire, the negative state, enlightened self-interest, the law of supply and demand, the profit motive. While the Conservative may occasionally have kind words for each of these notions, especially when he hears them derided by collectivists and blueprinters, he is careful to qualify his support by stating other, more important social truths. For example, while he does not for a moment deny the prominence of the profit motive, he insists that it be recognized for the selfish thing it is and be kept within reasonable, socially imposed limits.

At the same time that he expresses doubts about unqualified laissez-faire, the Conservative expresses horror over unqualified socialism. If pressed for a precise solution to the problem of government and the economy, if asked to draw a fine line between their respective spheres, he answers that precise solutions and fine lines are cruel and dangerous delusions. Between collectivism and laissez-faire there are many possible points of temporary adjustment. The stable, just, and productive economy is a mixture of individual enterprise, group co-operation, and government regulation according to the traditions and needs of each people. Beyond this the undoctrinaire Conservative refuses to pursue the issue, except to preach again from his favorite text: in regulating the economy in the public interest government cannot by right treat men unjustly and cannot by nature solve all or even a majority of their problems.

CONSERVATIVE ECONOMIC INDIVIDUALISM

There is no doubt that sharp disagreements about the proper scope of governmental activity existed among the framers of the United States Constitution. Alexander Hamilton and other Federalists saw a proper role for government in the protection and encouragement of the new nation's manufacturing industries, and in general they favored the cause of a relatively strong central government. Thomas Jefferson and the Republicans idealized the concept of a nation of small and independent farmers and, at least in principle, were opposed to any very active central government. Jefferson's thinking, however, remained well within the fairly moderate spirit of classical liberalism as it has been described above. It is not possible to say with certainty how and why conservative, laissez-faire individualism came to displace classical liberalism as the dominant social philosophy in the United States. What is certain is that in late-nineteenth-century America, that aspect of classical liberalism which emphasized the "natural order" of social phenomena had survived and developed, while that aspect which dictated a pragmatic approach to the determination of governmental functions had largely vanished.

Herbert Spencer, writing in England in the middle years of the nineteenth century, espoused laissez-faire in its most doctrinaire form. He held the sole legitimate function of government to be protection of citizens from external aggression and internal violence; a state that attempts to do more than this automatically becomes oppressive. Any regulation of commerce is decried as meddling with the processes of nature, and accordingly is roundly condemned. Spencer started from the same premises as did his predecessors and contemporaries in the classical liberal school, but he was exceptional in allowing no compassion or sympathy for the unfortunate to disturb the cold logic with which these premises were pursued. He saw in social relationships just another instance of the competition for survival that the biologist Charles Darwin had suggested extended to all living species. The natural order would function best if the unfit were allowed to perish in competition, just as the fit were allowed to enjoy the fruits of their success. Social Darwinism, with its vehement denunciation of any attempts at social welfare legislation, enjoyed considerable influence for a time in England and was later popularized in the United States, where its leading exponent was William Graham Sumner.

Sumner also invoked the "authority" of Darwin's biological theories to justify a doctrine of minimum government activity and maximum freedom of individual economic enterprise. His writings were especially important in America because they provided for his time (the late nineteenth and early twentieth centuries) a continuing rationalization for laissez-faire in a period when it was becoming increasingly incompatible with some of the other ideals of American democracy. In particular, the laissez-faire strand in the thought of Jeffersonians had been intertwined with strong feelings that individuals should have a feasible opportunity to make themselves economically independent by working energetically on small farms or in other small-scale enterprises. In Sumner's day, the hard realities of a growing industrial society were shrinking these opportunities and suppressing the equalitarian and humanitarian facets of the democratic creed. Men of Sumner's persuasion kept alive the ideal of economic individualism at a time when this ideal was extracting an ever-higher cost in terms of other democratic values.

Differences, as well as similarities, between the laissez-faire conservative and classical liberal variants of economic individualism should be noted. Laissez-faire conservatism inherited from classical liberalism the psychological assumption of self-interest and the economic vision of socially beneficial market processes. But differences traceable to the influence of classical conservatism are also significant. Classical liberalism emphasized competition as an impersonal and automatic social process, individual freedom to compete, and limited government. Conservative individualism emphasized property rights of enterprises, even clearly monopolistic ones, and insisted upon small, laissez-faire, but probusiness government. In short, while classical liberalism in England had been "a liberalizing social philosophy of economic reform, laissez-faire conservatism in the United States became increasingly a defense of the *status quo,* an identification of the 'American way of life' with an aristocracy of wealth, and a monistic dominance of business interests.''[1]

Conservative economic individualism or laissez-faire conservatism, as thus described, ''rose to prominence between 1865 and 1885, to ascendency between 1885 and 1920, to domination and virtual identification with the 'American way' in the 1920s.''[2] It provided the rhetoric, and together with classical liberalism and classical-neoclassical economic theory the substance, for the conservative defense of the status quo against both New Deal reforms and the Keynesian revolution in economic thought and policy. And it ''has continued to play a rear-guard function of reaction against the extension of liberal social reform in the years since 1945.''[3] Although since the 1930s the concept of economic individualism has not had sufficient influence to thwart efforts at social reform,[4] it nevertheless remains an important force in shaping the thinking of many Americans, and it retains in its more sophisticated forms the backing of the conservative element among contemporary American economists.

The main tenets of laissez-faire conservatism are described by Clinton Rossiter in selection 1.7.

1.7 Laissez-Faire Conservatism

Clinton Rossiter

Laissez-faire conservatism . . . rose to prominence between 1865 and 1885, to ascendancy between 1885 and 1920, to domination—to virtual identification with ''the American Way''—in the 1920's. . . .

It is not easy to state the principles of laissez-faire conservatism. The prophets of the rising faith seemed often to preach in a babble of tongues. Few of them claimed to be political or social theorists; practically none could take the long or deep view of man and his place in the community. Even William Graham Sumner of Yale, the most brilliant and consistent of this group and a scholar of the first magnitude, was quite unspeculative in his political thinking. . . .

[1] John E. Elliott, *Comparative Economic Systems* (Englewood Cliffs, N.J.: Prentice-Hall, 1973), p. 105.

[2] Clinton Rossiter, *Conservatism in America* (N.Y.: Random House, 1962), p. 131.

[3] Elliott, *Comparative Economic Systems,* p. 103.

[4] Contemporary radical critics dissent from this view. Especially since World War II, they argue, an alliance of the large corporations, government, and the military, endorsed by conservatives and accepted by pragmatic liberals, has prevented any truly major social reform. See the various readings in chapter 7.

Excerpted from Clinton Rossiter, *Conservatism in America* (New York: Random House, 1962), pp. 21–24, 27–28, 31–32, 34–35, 37–38, 40–41. Reprinted by permission of the publisher and Mrs. Clinton Rossiter.

Despite this apparent confusion, the American Right seems to have been guided between the Civil War and the Great Depression by a set of common principles. . . . The spokesmen of laissez-faire conservatism wasted few thoughts on man. They ignored almost completely his nature and needs as social, religious, or political animal. The only man who seems to have counted in their thinking was *homo economicus*.

Their opinion of this man was a confusing blend of harshness and hopefulness. The key trait of his immutable nature was a deep current of selfishness that rose to the surface most frequently in the form of intense acquisitiveness. Man's most important earthly need—and right and duty—was to satisfy his acquisitive instincts. . . .

This selfish individual, who would neither sow nor reap unless prodded by material discomfort and beckoned by material gain, was in the world by and for himself. No one owed him a living; he owed no one support. If he was rich, powerful, and happy, he could thank his own talents; if he was poor, frustrated, and miserable, he could blame his own faults. He must, in any case, take the consequences of his behavior. . . .

Laissez-faire conservatives seized joyfully on the bright principle of equality, but their interpretation of it was so twisted that they may certainly be classed as anti-equalitarians. Here, at least, their assumptions and even their public statements remained basically conservative. The only real equality, so it appears in their writings, was equality of economic liberty. . . . Men were equal in the right to acquire and hold property, in the right to be free of government interference in their business, and, most important, in the *lack* of any right to the assistance of government in pursuing their acquisitive ends. "All grants of exclusive privileges"—whether to the highest-placed industrialist or the lowest-placed laborer—were "against common right, and void." In addition, most preachers of the new gospel acknowledged in passing that men were equal before the law and at the polls. But the significant equality was equality of opportunity—"equality in self-reliance."

None of these men ever asserted the fact of a rough equality in talents and virtues or the desirability of equality in status and property. Quite the contrary, many of them echoed Adams in insisting on the harsh reality of natural inequalities among men, and Calhoun in asserting that the competition resulting from these inequalities was the great spur to progress. . . .

The twin doctrines of equality of opportunity and inequality of ability led the laissez-faire conservative inexorably to a belief in natural aristocracy, which, however, he rarely peddled under so honest a label. Underlying this belief was a characteristically American concept of class: classes were a fact of life, and hard-headed men would shape their thinking to the existence of a social order. Yet the order was made up of classes, not castes; the way up and the way down were open to all.

The men at the top of this order formed the most natural and socially valuable of all aristocracies: the aristocracy of personal achievement. The best of such men, the "captains of industry," were those who had risen from the bottom, from "that sternest but most efficient of all schools—poverty." . . .

The capstone of this theory of aristocracy was the so-called "Gospel of Wealth." The natural aristocrat, elevated above his fellow men by his superior energy and ability, had not only the right but the duty to lead them wisely and well. He was bound, in addition, to live an exemplary private life as a model for the young men who would succeed him and old men who would not. Finally, if he was one of the chosen few who had been favored with excessive wealth, he was to use this wealth wisely; he was obliged to act as "the steward of great riches." No one preached the Gospel of Wealth more fervently than Andrew Carnegie, who considered "the man of wealth . . . the mere agent and trustee for his poorer brethren, bringing to their service his superior wisdom, experience, and ability to administer, doing for them better than they would or could do for themselves. . . .

The rights of man were another area of political speculation in which laissez-faire conservatives thought only those thoughts that served their immediate purposes. . . . Like all Americans, they loved "liberty, charming liberty," but it was liberty defined largely in economic terms.

A few tough-minded men like Sumner scoffed at the notion of natural rights, insisting that liberty was something that had been earned in struggle and recognized in law. Most leaders of this school, however, declaimed in ornate language about "the holy rights of free men." Two rights in particular claimed their devotion. The first, the right of property, was elevated to a position of unchallenged primacy. It was the essence of liberty, the definition of right, in Sumner's words, "the condition of civilization." While the right to property was being raised over all other rights, the concept of property was expanded far beyond the ownership of personal possessions. The United States Steel Corporation was "private property," and government had no more authority to interfere in its operation than to take away half the acreage of every farmer in the country. As to the income tax, that was mere "theft."

The second right to which laissez-faire conservatives devoted special attention was freedom of contract, the right of a man freely—without support or interference from government—to buy and sell property or labor. Sure that the welfare of society depended upon free competition among "equal" individuals, the [Supreme] Court defended the precious rights of laborers to get work by promising not to join unions, of scrubwomen and elevator operators to make the best bargain they could with employers, and of underpaid bakers to work just as long as they wanted.

The laissez-faire justices must not be written off as blatant hypocrites. They were bitterly anti-labor, no doubt of that; yet they were so hypnotized by the dogma of individualism and the fiction of equality of bargaining power that combinations of workers and protective laws appeared to them as direct threats to liberty and progress.

In their thinking about the nature and purpose of government, laissez-faire conservatives abandoned the principles of Federalism and adopted those of Jeffersonian democracy. The progressive agrarians of 1800 had had reason to fear government. In their experience it had been an oppressive tool of the rich, a means for perpetuating privilege and legalizing inequality. As a result, their leading thinkers expressed suspicion of political power in the most general language. The conservative industrialists of 1880 had reason to fear it, too. They had learned, also by experience, that government based on a broad suffrage could be a tool of the masses as well as of the classes. Faced by the new progressivism of the new agrarians, they seized upon the noble phrases in which the generalized suspicion of government had first been expressed and went forth to battle against regulation of rates and schedules, income taxes, anti-trust legislation, and all other attempts to "legislate equality."

Laissez-faire conservatives looked on government as something inherently inefficient, because anything it could do the private enterprise of acquisitive men could do "twice as cheap and ten times as fast"; inadequate, because there were severe natural limitations to collective as opposed to individual action; unintelligent, because it inevitably attracted men unwilling or unable to make good in the real business of life; arbitrary, because political power had a peculiarly corrupting effect; and undemocratic, because it seemed always bent on interfering with liberty, property, and equality of opportunity. The idea that government could do anyone much good was considered ridiculous and heretical. The idea that it could do a great deal of harm was considered the beginning of political wisdom.

Few laissez-faire conservatives were as consistent as Sumner, who blasted away at protective tariffs and minimum-wage laws with magnificent impartiality. Some argued, often sincerely, that tariffs, land grants, subsidies, bounties, favorable patent laws, hard-currency laws, and other aids to business enterprise were aids to the whole community or simply "the rules of the game," not special privileges or tinkerings with the natural laws of a free economy. Others were sufficiently shocked by the growth of monopoly, inequality, and gross dishonesty to recommend that government take action to restore competition or to protect workers and consumers. Most spokesmen for the business community, however, continued to hammer away at government as the one genuine threat to human liberty. In their mistrust of authority, contempt for "politicians," glorification of the individual, and adherence to the concept of "the policeman state," they came very near to a theory of philosophical anarchy. . . . Government was not merely dangerous; in the good society it was irrelevant.

* * *

. . . They were intensely conservative about inherited institutions and arrangements like family, church, school, property, and the class system, and they apparently assumed that their adventures in finance and industrial expansion would leave the good old ways untouched. All these institutions were asked to serve in the noble cause of economic liberty.

The authentic laissez-faire conservative, like the authentic Revolutionary of 1776, believed devoutly in the existence of a higher law that dictated individual conduct, controlled the workings of society, set limits to government, and promised prosperity to men and progress to nations. His version of higher law was narrow and twisted, yet he was convinced that he, too, had somehow got hold of absolute truth. This conviction lent an air of sanctity and finality to laissez-faire conservatism that accounts for much of the passion with which its spokesmen assaulted advocates of reform. Men who tampered with the established order were not only fools for ignoring the advice of leaders of enterprise, but idiots for challenging eternal verities. "God and Nature have ordained the chances and conditions of life on earth once and for all," Sumner wrote. "The case cannot be opened. We cannot get a revision of the laws of human life."

This new version of the law of nature pointed to inevitable progress. While there were some doubters, notably Sumner, among the more solid of its oracles, most laissez-faire conservatives professed to believe with Carnegie in the "certain and steady progress of the race." Although the doctrine of inevitable progress strayed far from the Conservative tradition, it had a thoroughly conservative purpose and in fact served nobly as a defense of the established order. Since the order was itself the promise of progress, all reforms could be branded as reactionary meddling.

Laissez-faire conservatism, whether as articulate philosophy or mere bundle of prejudices, gained virtually complete domination over the minds of Americans who were or hoped to be solid and respectable. Champions of the new faith, most of whom needed no encouragement from men of industrial wealth, were active in every corner of American life. The articles of this faith were taught in schools and colleges, preached from thousands of pulpits, made the basis of official policy, and advanced as the moral of countless speeches, poems, tracts, and novels. While many conservative Americans deplored the excesses and injustices of industrial capitalism, they deplored them in the language of Carnegie and Sumner. There was little room for alternative political and social philosophies. Laissez-faire conservatism, as packaged for general consumption, seemed to express the realities and fill the needs of the new America. Like all working philosophies, it was the product of a small, self-conscious minority, yet it trickled down through the social order to infect and inspire several generations of American conservatives.

We have looked into laissez-faire conservatism with unusual care because knowledge of its history and principles is the key to an understanding, not only of the mind of the modern Right, but of the development of the whole American political tradition. . . .

In defiance or ignorance of the spirit of nineteenth-century Conservatism, but true to its practical and opportunistic character, the Right made a peace of convenience and profit with the two mighty forces of the age: democracy and industrialism. Instead of fighting a rear-guard action against the advance of democracy, it recognized that popular government was here to stay and set out to control such government to its own ends. Instead of resisting the rise of industrialism, it acted as the chief agent and became the chief beneficiary of technological change. In short, instead of practising a dogged conservatism and reaping the usual harvest of unpopularity, it made a most unconservative bid for the admiration of its own age and the plaudits of posterity. It did all this in casual confidence that neither democracy nor industrial expansion would shake old values and corrupt old institutions.

Not only did laissez-faire conservatives accept the hopeful teachings of Liberal democracy; they saw themselves as the legitimate trustees of this great tradition. They did this by identifying capitalism with democracy, by convincing themselves that the economic liberty of John D. Rockefeller was the same thing, only better, as the all-embracing liberty of Thomas Jefferson. This was not, of course, an altogether miraculous feat. The democratic dogma had always incorporated two quite different biases—one toward political liberty, the other toward property—and every man had a right to read it his own way. The laissez-faire conservatives, it might be argued, were the true heirs of Locke.

What made it possible for laissez-faire conservatism to stage this unintentional ideological coup was the shift in the style and concern of political thought from ethics to economics. The intellectual climate of the age was profoundly materialistic. Politics, religion, education, culture, social affairs—all seemed dwarfed by the tremendous events taking place in the arena of economic enterprise. The political thinking of the giants who strode about this arena and of the many people who applauded them was inevitably warped toward economic considerations. In the pages of their tracts, liberty is property, man is an economic unit, the aristocracy is the handful of men who have survived in the struggle. Progress is equated with growth, the free man with the successful entrepreneur, life with earning a living. Thomas Jefferson with Herbert Spencer, and equality before God and the law with "equality of opportunity"—that is, with outrageous inequalities in status and possession. . . .

Laissez-faire conservatism was no monopoly of Carnegie and Rockefeller; it was an outlook on life that had a broad appeal. Its extreme apostles, to be sure, were elitists with a vengeance, but most men who held it were neither rich nor powerful nor, for that matter, self-conscious. . . .

Finally, despite its patronage of change and premature acceptance of democracy, laissez-faire conservatism was at bottom a conservative political faith. It is a mistake, I think, to treat it simply as an aberration of nineteenth-century Liberalism. I would consider it equally an aberration of Conservatism, a philosophy preservative in purpose and traditionalist in principle. The men who shared this philosophy were fundamentally conservative, for they opposed all change except industrial expansion, feared reform as a threat to the established order, and presumed to have inherited a system based on political and social truth. Many articles of their faith were essentials of the Conservative tradition: the inevitability of stratification, persistence of natural inequalities, necessity of aristocracy, importance of religion and morality; sanctity of property, unwisdom of majority rule, urgency of constitutionalism, and folly of all attempts at social and economic leveling. To be sure, laissez-faire conservatives defined several of these concepts in their own way, but the twists they gave to aristocracy and property were nothing compared to the havoc they wreaked upon democracy and equality. Where they clearly strayed from Conservatism was in their glorification of rugged individualism and consequent disregard for the community, their choice of struggle over harmony and contract over status as the bases of sound human relations, their fatuous optimism and confidence in progress (from which a substantial minority dissented), and their unabashed, all-pervading materialism. They were the first Right in Western history to turn violently against government, the only Right to push individualism so far as to assert that a man could never be helped, only harmed, by the assistance of the community. . . . This creed was neither Conservatism in the tradition of Burke (or even Adams) nor Liberalism in the tradition of Mill (or even Jefferson). It was, in a word, laissez-faire conservatism.

2 RADICAL CRITIQUES OF CAPITALISM: MARXISM AND SOCIALISM

It is convenient for the purpose of analysis to separate capitalism's critics into radicals and reformers. Reformers, whether liberal or conservative, are defined as those who see specific defects in the capitalist system, but who nonetheless argue that with suitable modifications capitalism can (and probably should) be preserved. Radicals, by contrast, are defined here as those who believe the inadequacies and "evils" of capitalism to be the result of the nature of the system itself. Changes in capitalism, even if relatively significant, cannot remove the basic contradictions that radicals see as necessary parts of the system. Radical critiques therefore prescribe or predict that capitalism must or will be replaced by a fundamentally different economic order if a just and humane society is to be achieved.

In practice, distinctions between reform and radical thought can become blurred. As noted below, non-Marxian socialists have frequently voiced radical criticisms while at the same time advocating measures for the reform of the capitalist system and, on occasion, making common cause with liberal reformers. The major part of this chapter, however, deals with analyses that only can be considered radical. Marx's theory of capitalism is discussed in the first part of the chapter. Post-Marxian socialism, and its relation to democratic reform, is examined in the second part. The chapter closes with a brief discussion of an American radical, Thorstein Veblen.

MARX'S THEORY OF CAPITALISM

Marxism is a broad term used here to designate the social philosophy and social science of Karl Marx and his followers. Marx wrote in the middle and later years of the nineteenth century, chiefly in England, and to a great extent his work reflects the conditions of the time and place in which he wrote. Although he developed a theory of history within which the period of capitalism was for any society but one stage, the majority of Marx's own writing concerned itself with the processes by which a society passed into, through, and out of the stage of capitalism.

In Marx's view, three circumstances largely govern the ways in which goods are produced and distributed in capitalist society. First, production is generally organized by individuals for market exchange. Second, ownership of the means of production (natural resources and capital goods) is monopolized by a small minority of the population ("capitalists"). The third characteristic, derivable from the first two, is that the vast majority of the population ("workers") must work for the minority in order to gain access to the economic necessities of life. The only thing that a worker is capable of furnishing for sale (or exchange) is his own "labor power." He must sell his labor power to a capitalist, who in normal circumstances will pay him only a subsistence wage. The capitalist combines labor power with means of production to produce economic goods that have a certain market value. The difference between this value and the legitimate costs of producing the goods—the wages that must be paid the workers, depreciation, and the cost of raw materials—is "surplus value"; it goes to capitalists in the form of profits, rent, and interest. The capitalist occupies a key organizing position in this economic system, and both his own psychological drives and the competition to which he is subject impel him to pursue his occupation with great vigor. He acquires surplus value by any avenue of business open to him; some of it of course is used for his own necessities and pleasures, but a great deal of it is invested in additional capital, which further broadens the range of his operations. Thus, Marx identifies capitalism as a highly dynamic system that has been responsible for tremendous advances in technique and increases in production.

Granting capitalism its due does not prevent Marx from forecasting its ultimate demise, however. Within the logic of the capitalist economic system, Marx finds a series of "contradictions," and these contradictions imply the eventual downfall of the system itself. The American neo-Marxist Paul Sweezy identifies the four most important of the contradictions as follows. First, when capitalists attempt to increase surplus value by implementing technological change, they create unemployment, which in turn holds down wages and restricts the power of workers to consume the output of the capitalists' businesses. Second, as more and more capital accumulates, the rate of profit begins to fall; when capitalists respond by interrupting the processes of production and accumulation, economic crises and depressions result. Third, as a capitalist country grows wealthier, it devotes an ever greater share of its resources to increasing its productive powers; because the ability of the workers to purchase consumption goods increases less rapidly or decreases, and because the willingness of capitalists to consume is limited, eventually the means of production are left to lie idle and stagnation replaces economic expansion. Fourth, technological change, capital accumulation, and recurrent crises combine to virtually guarantee the growth of the scale of production and the ever-increasing concentration of capital under the control of trusts and monopolies. By increasing the market power of capitalists, monopoly increases class conflicts. By reinforcing capitalism's contradictions, it tends to increase the length and severity of capitalism's crises and depressions.

In their attempt to combat these contradictions, capitalists use the political power of the state, over which they have final control. Workers may be either repressed or granted minor concessions, as particular situations seem to indicate. But states become even more important in the attempts of national groups of capitalists to maintain and to improve their own positions at the expense of all other countries. In their zeal to preserve their own small segment of the world economy, the capitalists of a given nation generally desire to exploit all other nations, capitalist and noncapitalist alike. There are certain short-run advantages in concentrating on the latter, for they are less likely to fight back, and wars can be both destructive and dangerous to capitalists. In the long run, however, empire building also can lead to war, for the interests of the various imperialist powers are bound to come into conflict with each other.

Marx is not specific about just which of mature capitalism's specific problems is most likely to trigger its final downfall, but he need not be. If his prognoses are correct, if workers are to become more misearble, business cycles more severe, capital more concentrated, imperialism and wars the accepted form of conducting international affairs, then the final destruction of capitalism is assured even if the exact form is not specified. The most important aspect of this destruction would be the ascendance of the industrial proletariat, the working class, to the dominant position in the new society. A new economic structure would emerge, embodying techniques and relations of production and distribution appropriate to the circumstances of an advanced industrialized society, and upon this structure a new superstructure would develop.

Although Marx analyzed capitalism in economic terms, he defined it sociologically—in terms of the dominance of the property-owning capitalist class. Thus, by what Joseph Schumpeter has called a "brilliant stroke of analytic strategy," Marx linked the movement of the working class to social power within the process of industrialization to the establishment of a socialist society and the assumption of ownership and control of industrial capital by a worker state.

It hardly need be said that capitalism has not yet satisfied all of the predictions that Marx made for it. On the other hand, it is undeniable that the Marxian analysis has yielded insights into the workings of the capitalist system, and continues to do so through its impact on contemporary American Marxists (see chapter 7). By extending Marxian theory as well as analyzing its areas of predictive success and failure, these followers of Marx provide a radical critique of contemporary American-style capitalism.

The following selections examine several of the major dimensions of Marx's theory of capitalist development and the relations of Marxian economics to non-Marxian economic theory. In selection 2.1, Marx and Engels present basic ideas on historical change, class struggles between workers and capitalists, and the prospective demise of capitalism. Note what Joseph Schumpeter called Marx's "hymn of praise" to capitalism's industrializing proclivities.

Selection 2.2, taken from Marx's major work on economic theory, *Capital* (1867), presents his mature analysis of the process of capital accumulation and its effects: industrialization, concentration and centralization of capital, and periodic redundancy and unemployment of workers as labor-saving inventions substitute capital for labor.

Marx's critical analysis and evaluation of capitalism was characterized by a fundamental dualism. On the one hand, he recognized and lauded capitalism's proclivities toward capital accumulation, technological progress, and industrialization. On the other hand, he identified "contradictions" and conflicts in the capitalist order that would eventually bring its downfall. Henry K. Grossman stresses the confluence, in Marx's vision of capitalism's demise, of the "objective" tendencies of capitalist development and decay and the "subjective" trends in the class struggle.[1] The objective tendencies, by themselves, would yield a prediction of economic breakdown, a failure, as Joseph Schumpeter phrases it (see chapter 4), of the "capitalist engine." These tendencies, in conjunction with his historical vision of the dynamics of social and economic change, explain Marx's disdain for the coup d'état or premature political revolution. Many decades, and perhaps centuries, are required for capitalism to accumulate capital and promote industrialization and modern technologies, and for capitalism's inherent contradictions to emerge, heighten, and finally overwhelm its dynamic progressive properties. On the other hand, the radical transformation of the capitalist economic order to a new and different economic system will not occur automatically. Capitalism must be "overthrown." The agent for revolutionary change is the industrial working class. Goaded by decades of exploitation and class conflict, the victims of these "subjective" trends will seize social power and control over the means of production by an act of political revolution. They will succeed, however, only when the time is ripe and "objective" preconditions have been laid.

In recent years, "humanist socialists" have turned increasingly to the "young Marx," especially the Marx of the *Economic and Philosophical Manuscripts* of 1844. In these writings, Marx indicted the capitalist industrialization process for its tendencies toward "alienation" or "estrangement" of man —from the products he produces, from the processes of work and production, from nature and human nature, and from his fellow man. By contrast, ideal socialism or communism may be characterized as an unalienated society in which men and women, in cooperative association, would be free to develop their human potentials. Excerpts from Marx's views on the relationships among alienation, capitalism, and communism are presented in selection 2.3.

Students of Marx have often noted similarities between Marxism and anarchism and the role of anarchist elements both in Marx's theory of capitalism (for example, his critique of the dehumanizing effects of machinery and the division of labor under conditions of private property) and his vision of socialism (for example, the "withering away of the state" and the "conscious regulation" of the division of labor). Anarchism, in turn, as a social and economic philosophy, has familial connections with both liberalism and socialism. In selection 2.4, Marshall Shatz identifies the leading properties of classical, nineteenth century anarchism and some of its relationships to other

[1] Henry K. Grossman, "The Evolutionist Revolt Against Classical Economics," *Journal of Political Economy*, October, December 1943.

economic philosophies. In modified form, the spirit of anarchism lives on in some of the writings of contemporary neoliberalism (selection 6.8), the New Left (selection 7.6), and democratic socialism (selection 7.11).

2.1 The Communist Manifesto

Karl Marx and Friedrich Engels

BOURGEOIS AND PROLETARIANS

The history of all hitherto existing society is the history of class struggles.

Freeman and slave, patrician and plebian, lord and serf, guild-master and journeyman, in a word, oppressor and oppressed, stood in constant opposition to one another, carried on an uninterrupted, now hidden, now open fight, a fight that each time ended, either in a revolutionary reconstitution of society at large, or in the common ruin of the contending classes.

In the earlier epochs of history, we find almost everywhere a complicated arrangement of society into various orders, a manifold gradation of social rank. In ancient Rome we have patricians, knights, plebians, slaves; in the Middle Ages, feudal lords, vassals, guild-masters, journeymen, apprentices, serfs; in almost all of these classes, again, subordinate gradations.

The modern bourgeois society that has sprouted from the ruins of feudal society, has not done away with class antagonisms. It has but established new classes, new conditions of oppression, new forms of struggle in place of the old ones.

Our epoch, the epoch of the bourgeoisie, possesses, however, this distinctive feature: It has simplified the class antagonisms. Society as a whole is more and more splitting up into two great hostile camps, into two great classes directly facing each other—bourgeoisie and proletariat.

From the serfs of the Middle Ages sprang the chartered burghers of the earliest towns. From these burgesses the first elements of the bourgeoisie were developed.

The discovery of America, the rounding of the Cape, opened up fresh ground for the rising bourgeoisie. The East-Indian and Chinese markets, the colonization of America, trade with the colonies, the increase in the means of exchange and in commodities generally, gave to commerce, to navigation, to industry, an impulse never before known, and thereby, to the revolutionary element in the tottering feudal society, a rapid development.

The feudal system of industry, in which industrial production was

From Karl Marx and Friedrich Engels, *Manifesto of the Communist Party*, edited and annotated by Friedrich Engels (New York: International Publishers, 1932), pp. 9–21. Reprinted by permission of the publisher.

monopolized by closed guilds, now no longer sufficed for the growing wants of the new markets. The manufacturing system took its place. The guild-masters were pushed aside by the manufacturing middle class; division of labor between the different corporate guilds vanished in the face of division of labor in each single workshop.

Meantime the markets kept ever growing, the demand ever rising. Even manufacture no longer sufficed. Thereupon, steam and machinery revolutionized industrial production. The place of manufacture was taken by the giant, modern industry, the place of the industrial middle class, by industrial millionaires—the leaders of whole industrial armies, the modern bourgeois.

Modern industry has established the world market, for which the discovery of America paved the way. This market has given an immense development to commerce, to navigation, to communication by land. This development has, in its turn, reacted on the extension of industry; and in proportion as industry, commerce, navigation, railways extended, in the same proportion the bourgeoisie developed, increased its capital, and pushed into the background every class handed down from the Middle Ages.

We see, therefore, how the modern bourgeoisie is itself the product of a long course of development, of a series of revolutions in the modes of production and of exchange.

Each step in the development of the bourgeoisie was accompanied by a corresponding political advance of that class. An oppressed class under the sway of the feudal nobility, it became an armed and self-governing association in the medieval commune; here independent urban republic (as in Italy and Germany), there taxable "third estate" of the monarchy (as in France); afterwards, in the period of manufacture proper, serving either the semi-feudal or the absolute monarchy as a counterpoise against the nobility, and, in fact, corner-stone of the great monarchies in general—the bourgeoisie has at last, since the establishment of modern industry and of the world market, conquered for itself, in the modern representative state, exclusive political sway. The executive of the modern state is but a committee for managing the common affairs of the whole bourgeoisie.

The bourgeoisie has played a most revolutionary role in history.

The bourgeoisie, wherever it has got the upper hand, has put an end to all feudal, patriarchal, idyllic relations. It has pitilessly torn asunder the motley feudal ties that bound man to his "natural superiors," and has left no other bond between man and man than naked self-interest, than callous "cash payment." It has resolved personal worth into exchange value, and in place of the numberless indefeasible chartered freedoms, has set up that single, unconscionable freedom—Free Trade.

It has been the first to show what man's activity can bring about. It has accomplished wonders far surpassing Egyptian pyramids, Roman aqueducts, and Gothic cathedrals; it has conducted expeditions that put in the shade all former migrations of nations and crusades.

The bourgeoisie cannot exist without constantly revolutionizing the instruments of production, and thereby the relations of production, and with them the whole relations of society. Conservation of the old modes of production in unaltered form, was, on the contrary, the first condition of existence for all earlier industrial classes. Constant revolutionizing of production, uninterrupted disturbance of all social conditions, everlasting uncertainty and agitation distinguish the bourgeois epoch from all earlier ones.

The need of a constantly expanding market for its products chases the bourgeoisie over the whole surface of the globe. It must nestle everywhere, settle everywhere, establish connections everywhere.

The bourgeoisie has through its exploitation of the world market given a cosmopolitan character to production and consumption in every country. To the great chagrin of reactionaries, it has drawn from under the feet of industry the national ground on which it stood. All old-established national industries have been destroyed or are daily being destroyed. They are dislodged by new industries, whose introduction becomes a life and death question for all civilized nations, by industries that no longer work up indigenous raw material, but raw material drawn from the remotest zones; industries whose products are consumed, not only at home, but in every quarter of the globe. In place of the old wants, satisfied by the production of the country, we find new wants, requiring for their satisfaction the products of distant lands and climes. In place of the old local and national seclusion and self-sufficiency, we have intercourse in every direction, universal inter-dependence of nations.

The bourgeoisie, by the rapid improvement of all instruments of production, by the immensely facilitated means of communication, draws all nations, even the most barbarian, into civilization. The cheap prices of its commodities are the heavy artillery with which it batters down all Chinese walls, with which it forces the barbarians' intensely obstinate hatred of foreigners to capitulate. It compels all nations, on pain of extinction, to adopt the bourgeois mode of production; it compels them to introduce what it calls civilization into their midst, i.e., to become bourgeois themselves. In a word, it creates a world after its own image.

The bourgeoisie has subjected the country to the rule of the towns. It has created enormous cities, has greatly increased the urban population as compared with the rural, and has thus rescued a considerable part of the population from the idiocy of rural life.

More and more the bourgeoisie keeps doing away with the scattered state of the population, of the means of production, and of property. It has agglomerated population, centralized means of production, and has concentrated property in a few hands. The necessary consequence of this was political centralization. Independent, or but loosely connected provinces, with separate interests, laws, governments and systems of taxation, became lumped together into one nation, with one government, one code of laws, one national class interest, one frontier and one customs tariff.

The bourgeoisie, during its rule of scarce one hundred years, has created more massive and more colossal productive forces than have all preceding generations together. Subjection of nature's forces to man, machinery, application of chemistry to industry and agriculture, steam-navigation, railways, electric telegraphs, clearing of whole continents for cultivation, canalization of rivers, whole populations conjured out of the ground—what earlier century had even a presentiment that such productive forces slumbered in the lap of social labor?

We see then that the means of production and of exchange, which served as the foundation for the growth of the bourgeoisie, were generated in feudal society. At a certain stage in the development of these means of production and of exchange, the conditions under which feudal society produced and exchanged, the feudal organization of agriculture and manufacturing industry, in a word, the feudal relations of property became no longer compatible with the already developed productive forces; they became so many fetters. They had to be burst asunder; they were burst asunder.

Into their place stepped free competition, accompanied by a social and political constitution adapted to it, and by the economic and political sway of the bourgeois class.

A similar movement is going on before our own eyes. Modern bourgeois society with its relations of production, of exchange and of property, a society that has conjured up such gigantic means of production and of exchange, is like the sorcerer who is no longer able to control the powers of the nether world whom he has called up by his spells. For many a decade past the history of industry and commerce is but the history of the revolt of modern productive forces against modern conditions of production, against the property relations that are the conditions for the existence of the bourgeoisie and of its rule. It is enough to mention the commercial crises that by their periodical return put the existence of the entire bourgeois society on trial, each time more threateningly. In these crises a great part not only of the existing products, but also of the previously created productive forces, are periodically destroyed. In these crises there breaks out an epidemic that, in all earlier epochs, would have seemed an absurdity—the epidemic of over-production. Society suddenly finds itself put back into a state of momentary barbarism; it appears as if a famine, a universal war of devastation had cut off the supply of every means of subsistence; industry and commerce seem to be destroyed. And why? Because there is too much civilization, too much means of subsistence, too much industry, too much commerce. The productive forces at the disposal of society no longer tend to further the development of the conditions of bourgeois property; on the contrary, they have become too powerful for these conditions, by which they are fettered, and no sooner do they overcome these fetters than they bring disorder into the whole of bourgeois society, endanger the existence of bourgeois property. The conditions of bourgeois society are too narrow to comprise the wealth created by them. And how does the bourgeoisie get over these crises? On the one hand by enforced destruction of a mass of productive forces; on the other, by the conquest of new markets, and by the more thorough exploitation of the old ones. That is to say, by paving the way for more extensive and more destructive crises, and by diminishing the means whereby crises are prevented.

The weapons with which the bourgeoisie felled feudalism to the ground are now turned against the bourgeoisie itself.

But not only has the bourgeoisie forged the weapons that bring death to itself; it has also called into existence the men who are to wield those weapons—the modern working class—the proletarians.

In proportion as the bourgeoisie, i.e., capital, is developed, in the same proportion is the proletariat, the modern working class, developed—a class of laborers, who live only so long as they find work, and who find work only so long as their labor increases capital. These laborers, who must sell themselves piecemeal, are a commodity, like every other article of commerce, and are consequently exposed to all the vicissitudes of competition, to all the fluctuations of the market.

Owing to the extensive use of machinery and to division of labor, the work of the proletarians has lost all individual character, and, consequently, all charm for the workman. He becomes an appendage of the machine, and it is only the most simple, most monotonous, and most easily acquired knack, that is required of him. Hence, the cost of production of a workman is restricted, almost entirely, to the means of subsistence that he requires for his maintenance, and for the propagation of his race. But the price of a commodity, and therefore also of labor, is equal to its cost of production. In proportion, therefore, as the repulsiveness of the work increases, the wage decreases. Nay more, in proportion as the use of machinery and division of labor increases, in the same proportion the burden of toil also increases, whether by prolongation of the working hours, by increase of the work exacted in a given time, or by increased speed of the machinery, etc.

Modern industry has converted the little workshop of the patriarchal master into the great factory of the industrial capitalist. Masses of laborers, crowded into the factory, are organized like soldiers. As privates of the industrial army they are placed under the command of a perfect hierarchy of officers and sergeants. Not only are they slaves of the bourgeois class, and of the bourgeois state; they are daily and hourly enslaved by the machine, by the over-looker, and, above all, by the individual bourgeois manufacturer himself. The more openly this despotism proclaims gain to be its end and aim, the more petty, the more hateful and the more embittering it is.

The less the skill and exertion of strength implied in manual labor, in other words, the more modern industry develops, the more is the labor of men superseded by that of women. Differences of age and sex have no longer any distinctive social validity for the working class. All are instruments of labor, more or less expensive to use, according to their age and sex.

No sooner has the laborer received his wages in cash, for the moment escaping exploitation by the manufacturer, than he is set upon by the other portions of the bourgeoisie, the landlord, the shopkeeper, the pawnbroker, etc.

The lower strata of the middle class—the small tradespeople, shopkeepers, and retired tradesmen generally, the handicraftsmen and peasants—all these sink gradually into the proletariat, partly because their diminutive capital does not suffice for the scale on which modern industry is carried on, and is swamped in the competition with the large capitalists, partly because their specialized skill is rendered worthless by new methods of production. Thus the proletariat is recruited from all classes of the population.

The proletariat goes through various stages of development. With its birth begins its struggle with the bourgeoisie. At first the contest is carried on by individual laborers, then by the work people of a factory, then by the operatives of one trade, in one locality, against the individual bourgeois who directly exploits them. They direct their attacks not against the bourgeois conditions of production, but against the instruments of production themselves; they destroy imported wares that compete with their labor, they smash machinery to pieces, they set factories ablaze, they seek to restore by force the vanished status of the workman of the Middle Ages.

At this stage the laborers still form an incoherent mass scattered over the whole country, and broken up by their mutual competition. If anywhere they unite to form more compact bodies, this is not yet the consequence of their own active union, but of the union of the bourgeoisie, which class, in order to attain its own political ends, is compelled to set the whole proletariat in motion, and is moreover still able to do so for a time. At this stage, therefore, the proletarians do not fight their enemies, but the enemies of their enemies, the remnants of absolute monarchy, the landowners, the non-industrial bourgeois, the petty bourgeoisie. Thus the whole historical movement is concentrated in the hands of the bourgeoisie; every victory so obtained is a victory for the bourgeoisie.

But with the development of industry the proletariat not only increases in number; it becomes concentrated in greater masses, its strength grows, and it feels that strength more. The various interests and conditions of life within the ranks of the proletariat are more and more equalized, in proportion as machinery obliterates all distinctions of labor and nearly everywhere reduces wages to the same low level. The growing competition among the bourgeois, and the resulting commercial crises, make the wages of the workers ever more fluctuating. The unceasing improvement of machinery, ever more rapidly developing, makes their livelihood more and more precarious; the collisions between individual workmen and individual bourgeois take more and more the character of collisions between two classes. Thereupon the workers begin to form combinations (trade unions) against the bourgeoisie; they club together in order to keep up the rate of wages; they found permanent associations in order to make provision beforehand for these occasional revolts. Here and there the contest breaks out into riots.

Now and then the workers are victorious, but only for a time. The real fruit of their battles lies, not in the immediate result, but in the ever expanding union of the workers. This union is furthered by the improved means of communication which are created by modern industry, and which place the workers of different localities in contact with one another. It was just this contact that was needed to centralize the numerous local struggles, all of the same character, into one national struggle between classes.

This organization of the proletarians into a class, and consequently into a political party, is continually being upset again by the competition between the workers themselves. But it ever rises up again, stronger, firmer, mightier. It compels legislative recognition of particular interests of the workers, by taking advantage of the divisions among the bourgeoisie itself. Thus the ten-hour bill in England was carried.

Altogether, collisions between the classes of the old society further the course of development of the proletariat in many ways. The bourgeoisie finds itself involved in a constant battle. At first with the aristocracy; later on, with those portions of the bourgeoisie itself whose interests have become antagonistic to the progress of industry; at all times with the bourgeoisie of foreign countries. In all these battles it sees itself compelled to appeal to the proletariat, to ask for its help, and thus, to drag it into the political arena. The bourgeoisie itself, therefore, supplies the proletariat with its own elements of political and general education, in other words, it furnishes the proletariat with weapons for fighting the bourgeoisie.

Further, as we have already seen, entire sections of the ruling classes are, by the advance of industry, precipitated into the proletariat, or are at least threatened in their conditions of existence. These also supply the proletariat with fresh elements of enlightenment and progress.

Finally, in times when the class struggle nears the decisive hour, the process of dissolution going on within the ruling class, in fact within the whole range of old society, assumes such a violent, glaring character, that a small section of the ruling class cuts itself adrift, and joins the revolutionary class, the class that holds the future in its hands. Just as, therefore, at an earlier period, a section of the nobility went over to the bourgeoisie, so now a portion of the bourgeoisie goes over to the proletariat, and in particular, a portion of the bourgeois ideologists, who have raised themselves to the level of comprehending theoretically the historical movement as a whole.

Of all the classes that stand face to face with the bourgeoisie today, the proletariat alone is a really revolutionary class. The other classes decay and finally disappear in the face of modern industry; the proletariat is its special and essential product.

The lower middle class, the small manufacturer, the shopkeeper, the artisan, the peasant, all these fight against the bourgeoisie, to save from extinction their existence as fractions of the middle class. They are therefore not revolutionary, but conservative. Nay more, they are reactionary, for they try to roll back the wheel of history. If by chance they are revolutionary, they are so only in view of their impending transfer into the proletariat; they thus defend not their present, but their future interests; they desert their own standpoint to adopt that of the proletariat.

The "dangerous class," the social scum (*Lumpenproletariat*), that passively rotting mass thrown off by the lowest layers of old society, may, here and there, be swept into the movement by a proletarian revolution; its conditions of life, however, prepare it far more for the part of a bribed tool of reactionary intrigue.

The social conditions of the old society no longer exist for the proletariat. The proletarian is without property; his relation to his wife and children has no longer anything in common with bourgeois family relations; modern industrial labor, modern subjection to capital, the same in England as in France, in America as in Germany, has stripped him of every trace of national character. Law, morality, religion, are to him so many bourgeois prejudices, behind which lurk in ambush just as many bourgeois interests.

All the preceding classes that got the upper hand, sought to fortify their already acquired status by subjecting society at large to their conditions of appropriation. The proletarians cannot become masters of the productive forces of society, except by abolishing their own previous mode of appropriation, and thereby also every other previous mode of appropriation. They have nothing of their own to secure and to fortify; their mission is to destroy all previous securities for, and insurances of, individual property.

All previous historical movements were movements of minorities, or in the interest of minorities. The proletarian movement is the self-conscious, independent movement of the immense majority, in the interest of the immense majority.

In depicting the most general phases of the development of the proletariat, we traced the more or less veiled civil war, raging within existing society, up to the point where that war breaks out into open revolution, and where the violent overthrow of the bourgeoisie lays the foundation for the sway of the proletariat.

Hitherto, every form of society has been based, as we have already seen, on the antagonism of oppressing and oppressed classes. But in order to oppress a class, certain conditions must be assured to it under which it can, at least, continue its slavish existence. The serf, in the period of serfdom, raised himself to membership in the commune, just as the petty bourgeois, under the yoke of feudal absolutism, managed to develop into a bourgeois. The modern laborer, on the contrary, instead of rising with the progress of industry, sinks deeper and deeper below the conditions of existence of his own class. He becomes a pauper, and pauperism develops more rapidly than population and wealth. And here it becomes evident, that the bourgeoisie is unfit any longer to be the ruling class in society, and to impose its conditions of existence upon society as an over-riding law. It is unfit to rule because it is incompetent to assure an existence to its slave within his slavery, because it cannot help letting him sink into such a state, that it has to feed him, instead of being fed by him. Society can no longer live under this bourgeoisie, in other words, its existence is no longer compatible with society.

The essential condition for the existence and sway of the bourgeois class, is the formation and augmentation of capital; the condition for capital is wage-labor. Wage-labor rests exclusively on competition between the laborers. The advance of industry, whose involuntary promoter is the bourgeoisie, replaces the isolation of the laborers, due to competition, by their revolutionary combination, due to association. The development of modern industry, therefore, cuts from under its feet the very foundation on which the bourgeoisie produces and appropriates products. What the bourgeoisie therefore produces, above all, are its own grave-diggers. Its fall and the victory of the proletariat are equally inevitable.

2.2 Marx's Theory of Capitalist Development

Karl Marx

The General Law of Capitalist Accumulation

1—THE INCREASED DEMAND FOR LABOUR-POWER THAT ACCOMPANIES ACCUMULATION, THE COMPOSITION OF CAPITAL REMAINING THE SAME

In this chapter we consider the influence of the growth of capital on the lot of the labouring class. The most important factor in this inquiry, is the composition of capital and the changes it undergoes in the course of the process of accumulation.

The composition of capital is determined by the proportion in which it is divided into constant capital or value of the means of production, and variable capital or value of labour-power, the sum total of wages.

Growth of capital involves growth of its variable constituent or of the part invested in labour-power. A part of the surplus-value turned into additional capital must always be retransformed into variable capital, or additional labour-fund. If we suppose that, all other circumstances remaining the same, the composition of capital also remains constant (*i.e.,* that a definite mass of means of production constantly needs the same mass of labour-power to set in motion), then the demand for labour and the subsistence-fund of the labourers clearly increase in the same proportion as the capital, and the more rapidly, the more rapidly the capital increases. Since under special stimulus to enrichment, such as the opening of new markets, or of new spheres for the outlay of capital in consequence of newly developed social wants, etc., the scale of accumulation may be suddenly extended, merely by a change in the division of the surplus-value or surplus-product into capital and revenue, the requirements of accumulating capital may exceed the increase of labour-power or of the number of labourers; the demand for labourers may exceed the supply, and, therefore, wages may rise. This must, indeed, ultimately be the case if the conditions supposed above continue. For since in each year more labourers are employed than in its predecessor, sooner or later a point must be reached, at which the requirements of accumulation begin to surpass the customary supply of labour, and, therefore, a rise of wages takes place. The more or less favourable circumstances in which the wage-working class supports and multiplies itself, in no way alter the fundamental character of capitalist production. As simple reproduction constantly reproduces the capital-relation itself, *i.e.,* the relation of capitalists on the one hand, and wage-workers on the other, so reproduction on

---

Excerpted from Karl Marx, *Capital,* volume I (New York: Random House, 1900).

a progressive scale, *i.e.,* accumulation, reproduces the capital relation on a progressive scale, more capitalists or larger capitalists at this pole, more wage-workers at that. The reproduction of a mass of labour-power, which must incessantly re-incorporate itself with capital for that capital's self-expansion; which cannot get free from capital, and whose enslavement to capital is only concealed by the variety of individual capitalists to whom it sells itself, this reproduction of labour-power forms, in fact, an essential of the reproduction of capital itself. Accumulation of capital is, therefore, increase of the proletariat.

But just as little as better clothing, food, and treatment do away with the exploitation of the slave, so little do they set aside that of the wage-worker. A rise in the price of labour, as a consequence of accumulation of capital, only means, in fact, that the length and weight of the golden chain the wage-worker has already forged for himself, allow of a relaxation of the tension of it. In the controversies on this subject the chief fact has generally been overlooked, viz., the *differentia specifica* of capitalistic production. Labour-power is only sale-able so far as it preserves the means of production in their capacity of capital, reproduces its own value as capital, and yields in unpaid labour a source of additional capital. The conditions of its sale, whether more or less favourable to the labourer, include therefore the necessity of its constant re-selling, and the constantly extended reproduction of all wealth in the shape of capital. Wages, by their very nature, always imply the performance of a certain quantity of unpaid labour on the part of the labourer. Altogether, irrespective of the case of a rise of wages with a falling price of labour, etc., such an increase only means at best a quantitative diminution of the unpaid labour that the worker has to supply. This diminution can never reach the point at which it would threaten the system itself. Apart from violent conflicts as to the rate of wages (and Adam Smith has already shown that in such a conflict, taken on the whole, the master is always master), a rise in the price of labour resulting from accumulation of capital implies the following alternative:

Either the price of labour keeps on rising, because its rise does not interfere with the progress of accumulation. Or, on the other hand, accumulation slackens in consequence of the rise in the price of labour, because the stimulus of gain is blunted. The rate of accumulation lessens; but with its lessening, the primary cause of that lessening vanishes, *i.e.,* the disproportion between capital and exploitable labour-power. The mechanism of the process of capitalist production removes the very obstacles that it temporarily creates. The price of labour falls again to a level corresponding with the needs of the self-expansion of capital, whether the level be below, the same as, or above the one which was normal before the rise of wages took place. Thus, when the industrial cycle is in the phase of crisis, a general fall in the price of commodities is expressed as a rise in the value of money, and, in the phase of prosperity, a general rise in the price of commodities, as a fall in the value of money.

The law of capitalistic accumulation, metamorphosed by economists into a pretended law of nature, in reality merely states that the very nature of accumulation excludes every diminution in the degree of exploitation of labour, and every rise in the price of labour, which could seriously imperil the continual reproduction, on an ever enlarging scale, of the capitalistic relation.

2—RELATIVE DIMINUTION OF THE VARIABLE PART OF CAPITAL SIMULTANEOUSLY WITH THE PROGRESS OF ACCUMULATION AND OF THE CONCENTRATION THAT ACCOMPANIES IT

Once given the general basis of the capitalistic system, then, in the course of accumulation, a point is reached at which the development of the productivity of social labour becomes the most powerful lever of accumulation.

Apart from natural conditions, such as fertility of the soil, etc., and from the skill of independent and isolated producers (shown rather qualitatively in the goodness than quantitatively in the mass of their products), the degree of productivity of labour, in a given society, is expressed in the relative extent of the means of production that one labourer, during a given time, with the same tension of labour-power, turns into products. The mass of the means of production which he thus transforms, increases with the productiveness of his labour. The growing extent of the means of production, as compared with the labour-power incorporated with them, is an expression of the growing productiveness of labour. The increase of the latter appears, therefore, in the diminution of the mass of labour in proportion to the mass of means of production moved by it, or in the diminution of the subjective factor of the labour process as compared with the objective factor.

But, if the progress of accumulation lessens the relative magnitude of the variable part of capital, it by no means, in doing this, excludes the possibility of a rise in its absolute magnitude.

The development of the productiveness of social labour presupposes co-operation on a large scale. It is only upon this supposition that division and combination of labour can be organised, and the means of production economised by concentration on a vast scale; instruments of labour which, from their very nature, are only fit for use in common, such as a system of machinery, can be called into being; huge natural forces can be pressed into the service of production; and the transformation can be effected of the process of production into a technological application of science. Co-operation on a large scale can realise itself only in the increase of individual capitals, only in proportion as the means of social production and the means of subsistence are transformed into the private property of capitalists. The basis of the production of commodities can admit of production on a large scale in the capitalistic form alone. But all methods for raising the social productive power of labour that are developed on this basis, are at the same times methods for the increased production of surplus-value or surplus-product, which in its turn is the formative element of accumulation. They are, therefore, at the same time methods of the production of capital by capital, or methods of its accelerated accumulation. The continual re-transformation of surplus-value into capital now appears in the shape of the increasing magnitude of the capital that enters into the process of production. This in turn is the basis of an extended scale of production, of the methods for raising the productive power of labour that accompany it, and of accelerated production of surplus-value. If, therefore, a certain degree of accumulation of capital appears as a condition of the specifically capitalist mode of production, the latter causes conversely an accelerated accumulation of capital. With the accumulation of capital, therefore, the specifically capitalistic mode of production developes, and with the capitalist mode of production the accumulation of capital. Both these economic factors bring about, in the compound ratio of the impulses they reciprocally give one another, that change in the technical composition of capital by which the variable constituent becomes always smaller and smaller as compared with the constant.

Every accumulation becomes the means of new accumulation. With the increasing mass of wealth which functions as capital, accumulation increases the concentration of that wealth in the hands of individual capitalists, and thereby widens the basis of production on a large scale and of the specific methods of capitalist production. The growth of social capital is effected by the growth of many individual capitals. All other circumstances remaining the same, individual capitals, and with them the concentration of the means of production, increases in such proportion as they form aliquot parts of the total social capital. At the same time portions of the original capitals disengage themselves and function as new independent capitals. Besides other causes, the division of property, within capitalist families, plays a great part in this. With the accumulation of capital, therefore, the number of capitalists grows to a greater or less extent. Two points characterise this kind of concentration which grows directly out of, or rather is identical with, accumulation. First: The increasing concentration of the social means of production in the hands of individual capitalists is, other things remaining equal, limited by the degree of increase of social wealth. Second: The part of social capital domiciled in each particular sphere of production is divided among many capitalists who face one another as independent commodity-producers competing with each other. Accumulation and the concentration accompanying it are, therefore, not only scattered over many points, but the increase of each functioning capital is thwarted by the formation of new and the subdivision of old capitals. Accumulation, therefore, presents itself on the one hand as increasing concentration of the means of production, and of the command over labour; on the other, as repulsion of many individual capitals one from another.

This splitting-up of the total social capital into many individual capitals or the repulsion of its fractions one from another, is counteracted by their attraction. This last does not mean that simple concentration of the means of production and of the command over labour, which is identical with accumulation. It is concentration of capitals already formed, destruction of their individual independence, expropriation of capitalist by capitalist, transformation of many small into few large capitals. This is centralisation proper, as distinct from accumulation and concentration.

The laws of this centralisation of capitals, or of the attraction of capital by capital, cannot be developed here. A brief hint at a few facts must suffice. The battle of competition is fought by cheapening of commodites. The cheapness of commodities depends, *ceteris paribus,* on the productiveness of labour, and this again on the scale of production. Therefore, the larger capitals beat the smaller. It will further be remembered that, with the development of the capitalist mode of production, there is an increase in the minimum amount of individual capital necessary to carry on a business under its normal conditions. The smaller capitals, therefore, crowd into spheres of production which Modern Industry has only sporadically or incompletely got hold of. Here competition rages in direct proportion to the number, and in inverse proportion to the magnitudes, of the antagonistic capitals. It always ends in the ruin of many small capitalists, whose capitals partly pass into the hand of their conquerors, partly vanish. Apart from this, with capitalist production an altogether new force comes into play—the credit system.

In its beginnings, the credit system sneaks in as a modest helper of accumulation and draws by invisible threads the money resources scattered all over the surface of society into the hands of individual or associated capitalists. But soon it becomes a new and formidable weapon in the competitive struggle, and finally it transforms itself into an immense social mechanism for the centralisation of capitals.

Competition and credit, the two most powerful levers of centralization, develop in proportion as capitalist production and accumulation do. However, the progress of centralisation is by no means dependent upon the positive growth of the volume of social capital. Centralisation may take place by a mere change in the distribution of already existing capitals. Centralisation in a certain line of industry would have reached its extreme limit, if all the individual capitals invested in it would have been amalgamated into one single capital.

This limit would not be reached in any particular society until the entire social capital would be united, either in the hands of one single capitalist, or in those of one single corporation.

Centralisation supplements the work of accumulation, by enabling the industrial capitalists to expand the scale of their operations. The economic result remains the same, whether this consummation is brought about by accumulation or centralisation.

It is evident, however, that accumulation is a very slow process as compared with centralisation, which needs but to alter the quantitative grouping of the integral parts of social capital. The world would still be without railroads, if it had been obliged to wait until accumulation should have enabled a few individual capitals to undertake the construction of a railroad. Centralisation, on the other hand, accomplished this by a turn of the hand through stock companies. Centralisation, by thus accelerating and intensifying the effects of accumulation, extends and hastens at the same time the revolutions in the technical composition of capital, which increase its constant part at the expense of its variable part and thereby reduce the relative demand for labor.

The masses of capital amalgamated over night by centralisation reproduce and augment themselves like the others, only faster, and thus become new and powerful levers of social accumulation. Hence, if the progress of social accumulation is mentioned nowadays, it comprizes as a matter of course the effects of centralisation. The additional capitals formed in the course of normal accumulation serve mainly as vehicles for the exploitation of new inventions and discoveries, or of industrial improvements in general. However, the old capital likewise arrives in due time at the moment when it must renew its head and limbs, when it casts off its old skin and is likewise born again in its perfected industrial form, in which a smaller quantity of labor suffices to set in motion a larger quantity of machinery and raw materials. The absolute decrease of the demand for labor necessarily following therefrom will naturally be so much greater, the more these capitals going through the process of rejuvenation have become accumulated in masses by means of the movement of centralisation.

On the one hand, therefore, the additional capital formed in the course of accumulation attracts fewer and fewer labourers in proportion to its magnitude. On the other hand, the old capital periodically reproduced with change of composition, repels more and more of the labourers formerly employed by it.

3—PROGRESSIVE PRODUCTION OF A RELATIVE SURPLUS-POPULATION OR INDUSTRIAL RESERVE ARMY

The accumulation of capital, though originally appearing as its quantitative extension only, is effected, as we have seen, under a progressive qualitative change in its composition, under a constant increase of its constant, at the expense of its variable constituent.

The specifically capitalist mode of production, the development of the productive power of labour corresponding to it, and the change thence resulting in the organic composition of capital, do not merely keep pace with the advance of accumulation, or with the growth of social wealth. They develop at a much quicker rate, because mere accumulation, the absolute increase of the total social capital, is accompanied by the centralisation of the individual capitals of which that total is made up; and because the change in the technological composition of the additional capital goes hand in hand with a similar change in the technological composition of the original capital. With the advance of accumulation, therefore, the proportion of constant to variable capital changes. Since the demand for labour is determined not by the amount of capital as a whole, but by its variable constituent alone, that demand falls progressively with the increase of the total capital, instead of, as previously assumed, rising in proportion to it. It falls relatively to the magnitude of the total capital, and at an accelerated rate, as this magnitude increases. With the growth of the total capital, its variable constituent or the labour incorporated in it, also does increase, but in a constantly diminishing proportion. It is capitalistic accumulation itself that constantly produces, and produces in the direct ratio of its own energy and extent, a relatively redundant population of labourers, *i.e.,* a population of greater extent than suffices for the average needs of the self-expansion of capital, and therefore a surplus-population.

In all spheres, the increase of the variable part of capital, and therefore of the number of labourers employed by it, is always connected with violent fluctuations and transitory production of surplus-population, whether this takes the more striking form of the repulsion of labourers already employed, or the less evident but not less real form of the more difficult absorption of the additional labouring population through the usual channels. With the magnitude of social capital already functioning, and the degree of its increase, with the extension of the scale of production, and the mass of the labourers set in motion, with the development of the productiveness of their labour, with the greater breadth and fullness of all sources of wealth, there is also an extension of the scale on which greater attraction of labourers by capital is accompanied by their greater repulsion; the rapidity of the change in the organic composition of capital, and in its technical form increases, and an increasing number of spheres of production becomes involved in this change, now simultaneously, now alternately. The labouring population therefore produces, along with the accumulation of capital produced by it, the means by which itself is made relatively superfluous, is turned into a relative surplus population; and it does this to an always increasing extent. This is a law of population peculiar to the capitalist mode of production.

But if a surplus labouring population is a necessary product of accumulation or of the development of wealth on a capitalist basis, this surplus population becomes, conversely, the lever of capitalistic accumulation, nay, a condition of existence of the capitalist mode of production. It forms a disposable industrial reserve army, that belongs to capital quite as absolutely as if the latter had bred it at its own cost. Independently of the limits of the actual increase of population, it creates, for the changing needs of the self-expansion of capital, a mass of human material always ready for exploitation. With accumulation, and the development of the productiveness of labour that accompanies it, the power of sudden expansion of capital grows also; it grows because the technical conditions of the process of production themselves—machinery, means of transport, etc.—now admit of the rapidest transformation of masses of surplus product into additional means of production. The mass of social wealth, overflowing with the advance of accumulation, and transformable into additional capital, thrusts itself frantically into old branches of production, whose market suddenly expands, or into newly formed branches, such as railways, etc., the need for which grows out of the development of the old ones. In all such cases, there must be the possibility of throwing great masses of men suddenly on the decisive points without injury to the scale of production in other spheres. Overpopulation supplies these masses. The course characteristic of modern industry, viz., a decennial cycle (interrupted by smaller oscillations), of periods of average activity, production at high pressure, crisis and stagnation, depends on the constant formation, the greater or less absorption, and the re-formation of the industrial reserve army of surplus population. In their turn, the varying phases of the industrial cycle recruit the surplus population, and become one of the most energetic agents of its reproduction. The expansion by fits and starts of the scale of production is the preliminary to its equally sudden contraction; the latter again evokes the former, but the former is impossible without disposable human material, without an increase in the number of labourers independently of the absolute growth of the population. This increase is effected by the simple process that constantly "sets free" a part of the labourers; by methods which lessen the number of labourers employed in proportion to the increased production. The whole form of the movement of modern industry depends, therefore, upon the constant transformation of a part of the labouring population into unemployed or half-employed hands.

Taking them as a whole, the general movements of wages are exclusively regulated by the expansion and contraction of the industrial reserve army, and these again correspond to the periodic changes of the industrial cycle. They are, therefore, not determined by the variations of the absolute number of the working population, but by the varying proportions in which the working class is divided into active and reserve army, by the increase of diminution in the relative amount of the surplus-population, by the extent to which it is now absorbed, now set free.

The industrial reserve army, during the periods of stagnation and average prosperity, weighs down the active labour-army; during the periods of over-production and paroxysm, it holds its pretensions in check. Relative surplus population is therefore the pivot upon which the law of demand and supply of labour works. It confines the field of action of this law within the limits absolutely convenient to the activity of exploitation and to the domination of capital.

4—THE GENERAL LAW OF CAPITALISTIC ACCUMULATION

The greater the social wealth, the functioning capital, the extent and energy of its growth, and, therefore, also the absolute mass of the proletariat and the productiveness of its labour, the greater is the industrial reserve-army. The same causes which develop the expansive power of capital, developes also the labour-power at its disposal. The relative mass of the industrial reserve-army increases therefore with the potential energy of wealth. But the greater this reserve-army in proportion to the active labour-army, the greater is the mass of a consolidated surplus-population, whose misery is in inverse ratio to its torment of labour. The more extensive, finally, the lazurus-layers of the working-class, and the industrial reserve-army, the greater is official pauperism. *This is the absolute general law of capitalist accumulation.*

Within the capitalist system all methods for raising the social productiveness of labour are brought about at the cost of the individual labourer; all means for the development of production transform themselves into means of domination over, and exploitation of, the producers; they mutilate the labourer into a fragment of a man, degrade him to the level of an appendage of a machine, destroy every remnant of charm in his work and turn it into a hated toil; they estrange from him the intellectual potentialities of the labour-process in the same proportion as science is incorporated in it as an independant power; they distort the conditions under which he works, subject him during the labour-process to despotism the more hateful for its meanness; they transform his life-time into working-time, and drag his wife and child beneath the wheels of the Juggernaut of capital. But all methods for the production of surplus value are at the same time methods of accumulation; and every extension of accumulation becomes again a means for the development of those methods. It follows therefore that in proportion as capital accumulates, the lot of the labourer, be his payment high or low, must grow worse. The law, finally, that always equilibrates the relative surplus-population, or industrial reserve army, to the extent and energy of accumulation, this law rivets the labourer to capital more firmly than the wedges of Vulcan did Prometheus to the rock. It establishes an accumulation of misery, corresponding with accumulation of capital. Accumulation of wealth at one pole is, therefore, at the same time accumulation of misery, agony of toil, slavery, ignorance, brutality, mental degradation, at the opposite pole, *i.e.*, on the side of the class that produces its own product in the form of capital.

2.3 Capitalism, Communism, and Alienation

Karl Marx

Alienated Labour

We have begun from the presuppositions of political economy. We have accepted its terminology and its laws.

Political economy begins with the fact of private property; it does not explain it. It conceives the *material* process of private property, as this occurs in reality, in general and abstract formulas which then serve it as laws. It does not *comprehend* these laws; that is, it does not show how they arise out of the nature of private property. Political economy provides no explanation of the basis for the distinction of labour from capital, of capital from land. When, for example, the relation of wages to profits is defined, this is explained in terms of the interests of capitalists; in other words, what should be explained is assumed. Similarly, competition is referred to at every point and is explained in terms of external conditions. Political economy tells us nothing about the extent to which these external and apparently accidental conditions are simply the experssion of a necessary development. Exchange itself seems an accidental fact. The only motive forces which political economy recognizes are *avarice* and the *war between the avaricious, competition*.

Thus we have now to grasp the real connexion between this whole system of alienation—private property, acquisitiveness, the separation of labour, capital and land, exchange and competition, value and the devaluation of man, monopoly and competition—and the system of *money*.

Let us not begin our explanation, as does the economist, from a legendary primordial condition.

We shall begin from a *contemporary* economic fact. The worker becomes poorer the more wealth he produces and the more his production increases in

From *Karl Marx: Early Writings*, translated and edited by T. B. Bottomore, pp. 120–33, 152–60, 162, 167–71, 176–78, 187.

power and extent. The worker becomes an ever cheaper commodity the more goods he creates. The *devaluation* of the human world increases in direct relation with the *increase in value* of the world of things. Labour does not only create goods; it also produces itself and the worker as a *commodity,* and indeed in the same proportion as it produces goods.

This fact simply implies that the object produced by labour, its product, now stands opposed to it as an *alien being,* as a *power independent* of the producer. The product of labour is labour which has been embodied in an object and turned into a physical thing; this product is an *objectification* of labour. The performance of work is at the same time its objectification. The performance of work appears in the sphere of political economy as a *vitiation* of the worker, objectification as a *loss* and as *servitude to the object,* and appropriation as *alienation*.

All these consequences follow from the fact that the worker is related to the *product of his labour* as to an *alien* object. For it is clear on this presupposition that the more the worker expends himself in work the more powerful becomes the world of objects which he creates in face of himself, the poorer he becomes in his inner life, and the less he belongs to himself. What is embodied in the product of his labour is no longer his own. The greater this product is, therefore, the more he is diminished. The *alienation* of the worker in his product means not only that his labour becomes an object, assumes an *external* existence, but that it exists independently, *outside himself,* and alien to him, and that it stands opposed to him as an autonomous power. The life which he has given to the object sets itself against him as an alien and hostile force.

Political economy conceals the alienation in the nature of labour in so far as it does not examine the direct relationship between the worker (work) and production. Labour certainly produces marvels for the rich but it produces privation for the worker. It produces palaces, but hovels for the worker. It produces beauty, but deformity for the worker. It replaces labour by machinery, but it casts some of the workers back into a barbarous kind of work and turns the others into machines. It produces intelligence, but also stupidity and cretinism for the workers.

So far we have considered the alienation of the worker only from one aspect; namely, *his relationship with the products of his labour*. However, alienation appears not merely in the result but also in the *process* of *production,* within *productive activity* itself. How could the worker stand in an alien relationship to the product of his activity if he did not alienate himself in the act of production itself? The product is indeed only the *résumé* of activity, of production. Consequently, if the product of labour is alienation, production itself must be active alienation—the alienation of activity and the activity of alienation. The alienation of the object of labour merely summarizes the alienation in the work activity itself.

What constitutes the alienation of labour? First, that the work is *external* to the worker, that it is not part of his nature; and that, consequently, he does not fulfil himself in his work but denies himself, has a feeling of misery rather than well-being, does not develop freely his mental and physical energies but is physically exhausted and mentally debased. The worker, therefore, feels himself at home only during his leisure time, whereas at work he feels homeless. His work is not voluntary but imposed, *forced labour*. It is not the satisfaction of a need, but only a *means* for satisfying other needs. Its alien character is clearly shown by the fact that as soon as there is no physical or other compulsion it is avoided like the plague. External labour, labour in which man alienates himself, is a labour of self-sacrifice, of mortification. Finally, the external character of work for the worker is shown by the fact that it is not his own work but work for someone else, that in work he does not belong to himself but to another person.

We have now considered the act of alienation of practical human activity, labour, from two aspects: (1) the relationship of the worker to the *product of labour* as an alien object which dominates him. This relationship is at the same time the relationship to the sensuous external world, to natural objects, as an alien and hostile world; (2) the relationship of labour to the *act of production* within *labour*. This is the relationship of the worker to his own activity as something alien and not belonging to him, activity as suffering (passivity), strength as powerlessness, creation as emasculation, the *personal* physical and mental energy of the worker, his personal life (for what is life but activity?), as an activity which is directed against himself, independent of him and not belonging to him. This is *self-alienation* as against the above-mentioned alienation of the *thing*.

We have now to infer a third characteristic of *alienated labour* from the two we have considered.

Since alienated labour: (1) alienates nature from man; and (2) alienates man from himself, from his own active function, his life activity; so it alienates him from the species. It makes *species-life* into a means of individual life. In the first place it alienates species-life and individual life, and secondly, it turns the latter, as an abstraction, into the purpose of the former, also in its abstract and alienated form.

For labour, *life activity, productive life,* now appear to man only as *means* for the satisfaction of a need, the need to maintain his physical existence. Productive life is, however, species-life. It is life creating life. In the type of life activity resides the whole character of a species, its species-character; and free, conscious activity is the species-character of human beings. Life itself appears only as a *means of life*.

Conscious life activity distinguishes man from the life activity of animals. Only for this reason is he a species-being. Or rather, he is only a self-conscious being, i.e. his own life is an object for him, because he is a species-being. Only for this reason is his activity free activity. Alienated labour reverses the relationship, in that man because he is a self-conscious being makes his life activity, his *being,* only a means for his *existence*.

Just as alienated labour transforms free and self-directed activity into a means, so it transforms the species-life of man into a means of physical existence.

Consciousness, which man has from his species, is transformed through alienation so that species-life becomes only a means for him. (3) Thus alienated labour turns the *species-life of man,* and also nature as his mental species-property, into an *alien* being and into a *means* for his *individual existence*. It alienates from man his own body, external nature, his mental life and his *human* life. (4) A direct consequence of the alienation of man from the product of his labour, from his life activity and from his species-life, is that *man* is *alienated* from other *men*. When man confronts himself he also confronts *other* men. What is true of man's relationship to his work, to the product of his work and to himself, is also true of his relationship to other men, to their labour and to the objects of their labour.

In general, the statement that man is alienated from his species-life means that each man is alienated from others, and that each of the others is likewise alienated from human life.

Let us now examine further how this concept of alienated labour must express and reveal itself in reality. If the product of labour is alien to me and confronts me as an alien power, to whom does it belong? If my own activity does not belong to me but is an alien, forced activity, to whom does it belong? To a being *other* than myself. And who is this being?

The *alien* being to whom labour and the product of labour belong, to whose service labour is devoted, and to whose enjoyment the product of labour goes, can only be *man* himself. If the product of labour does not belong to the worker, but confronts him as an alien power, this can only be because it belongs to *a man other than the worker*. If his activity is a torment to him it must be a source of *enjoyment* and pleasure to another. Not the gods, nor nature, but only man himself can be this alien power over men.

Consider the earlier statement that the relation of man to himself is first *realized, objectified,* through his relation to other men. If he is related to the product of his labour, his objectified labour, as to an *alien,* hostile, powerful and independent object, he is related in such a way that another alien, hostile, powerful and independent man is the lord of this object. If he is related to his own activity as to unfree activity, then he is related to it as activity in the service, and under the domination, coercion and yoke, of another man.

Thus, through alienated labour the worker creates the relation of another man, who does not work and is outside the work process, to this labour. The relation of the worker to work also produces the relation of the capitalist (or whatever one likes to call the lord of labour) to work. *Private property* is, therefore, the product, the necessary result, of *alienated labour,* of the external relation of the worker to nature and to himself.

Private property is thus derived from the analysis of the concept of *alienated labour;* that is, alienated man, alienated labour, alienated life, and estranged man.

We have, of course, derived the concept of *alienated labour (alienated life)* from political economy, from an analysis of the *movement of private property*. But the analysis of this concept shows that although private property appears to be the basis and cause of alienated labour, it is rather a consequence of the latter, just as the gods are *fundamentally* not the cause but the product of confusions of human reason. At a later stage, however, there is a reciprocal influence.

Only in the final stage of the development of private property is its secret revealed, namely, that it is on one hand the *product* of alienated labour, and on the other hand the *means* by which labour is alienated, *the realization of this alienation*.

This elucidation throws light upon several unresolved controversies—

> *1. In the wage system labour appears not as an end in itself but as the servant of wages.*
>
> *An enforced* increase in wages *would be nothing more than a* better remuneration of slaves, *and would not restore, either to the worker or to the work, their human significance and worth.*
>
> *Even* equality of incomes *would only change the relation of the present-day worker to his work into a relation of all men to work. Society would then be conceived as an abstract capitalist.*
>
> *2. From the relation of alienated labour to private property it also follows that the emancipation of society from private property, from servitude, takes the political form of the* emancipation of the workers; *not in the sense that only the latter's emancipation is involved, but because this emancipation includes the emancipation of humanity as a whole. For all human servitude is involved in the relation of the worker to production, and all the types of servitude are only modifications or consequences of this relation.*

Private Property and Communism

Communism is the positive expression of the abolition of private property, and in the first place of universal private property. In taking this relation in its *universal aspect* communism is, in its first form, only the generalization and fulfillment of the relation. The domination of material property looms so large that it aims to destroy everything which is incapable of being possessed by everyone as private property. It wishes to eliminate talent, etc. by *force*. Immediate physical possession seems to it the unique goal of life and existence. The role of *worker* is not abolished, but is extended to all men. The relation of private property remains the relation of the community to the world of things. This communism, which negates the *personality* of man in every sphere, is only the logical expression of private property, which is this negation. Universal *envy* setting itself up as a power is only a camouflaged form of cupidity which re-establishes itself and satisfies itself in a different way. The thoughts of every individual private property are *at least* directed against any *wealthier* private property, in the form of envy and the desire to reduce everything to a common level; so that this envy and levelling in fact constitute the essence of competition. Crude communism is only the culmination of such envy and levelling-down on the basis of a *preconceived* minimum. How little this abolition of private property represents a genuine appropriation is shown by the abstract negation of the whole world of culture and civilization, and the regression to the *unnatural* simplicity of the poor and wantless individual who has not only not surpassed private property but has not yet even attained to it.

The community is only a community of *work* and of *equality of wages* paid out by the communal capital, by the *community* as universal capitalist. The two sides of the relation are raised to a *supposed* universality; *labour* as a condition in which everyone is placed, and *capital* as the acknowledged universality and power of the community.

1. The first positive annulment of private property, crude communism, is, therefore, only a *phenomenal form* of the infamy of private property representing itself as positive community.

2. Communism *(a)* still political in nature, democratic or despotic; *(b)* with the abolition of the state, yet still incomplete and influenced by private property, that is, by the alienation of man. In both forms communism is already aware of being the reintegration of man, his return to himself, the supersession of man's self-alienation. But since it has not yet grasped the positive nature of private property, or the *human* nature of needs, it is still captured and contaminated by private property. It has well understood the concept, but not the essence.

3. *Communism* is the *positive* abolition of *private property,* of *human self-alienation,* and thus the real *appropriation* of *human* nature through and for man. It is, therefore, the return of man himself as a *social,* i.e. really human, being, a complete and conscious return which assimilates all the wealth of previous development. Communism as a fully developed naturalism is humanism and as a fully developed humanism is naturalism. It is the *definitive* resolution of the antagonism between man and nature, and between man and man. It is the true solution of the conflict between existence and essence, between objectification and self-affirmation, between freedom and necessity, between individual and species. It is the solution of the riddle of history and knows itself to be this solution.

Thus the whole historical development, both the *real* genesis of communism (the birth of its empirical existence) and its thinking consciousness, is its comprehended and conscious process of becoming; whereas the other, still undeveloped, communism seeks in certain historical forms opposed to private property a *historical* justification founded upon what already exists, and to this end tears out of their context isolated elements of this development and asserts them as proofs of its historical pedigree. In doing so, it makes clear that by far the greater part of this development contradicts its own assertions, and that if it has ever existed its past existence refutes its pretension to *essential being*.

It is easy to understand the necessity which leads the whole revolutionary movement to find its empirical, as well as its theoretical, basis in the development of *private property,* and more precisely of the economic system.

The positive supersession of *private property,* as the appropriation of *human* life, is, therefore, the positive supersession of all alienation, and the return of man from religion, the family, the state, etc. to his *human,* i.e. social life.

4. Just as *private property* is only the sensuous expression of the fact that man is at the same time an *objective* fact for himself and becomes an alien and non-human object for himself; just as his manifestation of life is also his alienation of life and his self-realization a loss of reality, the emergence of an *alien* reality; so the positive supersession of private property, i.e. the *sensuous* appropriation of the human essence and of human life, of objective man and of human *creations,* by and for man, should not be taken only in the sense of *immediate,* exclusive *enjoyment,* or only in the sense of *possession* or *having.* Man appropriates his manifold being in an all-inclusive way, and thus as a whole man.

Private property has made us so stupid and partial that an object is only *ours* when we have it, when it exists for us as capital or when it is directly eaten, drunk, worn, inhabited, etc., in short, *utilized* in some way. But private property itself only conceives these various forms of possession as *means of life,* and the life for which they serve as means is the *life* of *private property*—labour and creation of capital.

The supersession of private property is, therefore, the complete *emancipation* of all the human qualities and senses.

Just as society at its beginnings finds, through the development of *private property* with its wealth and poverty (both intellectual and material), the materials necessary for this *cultural development,* so the fully constituted society produces man in all the plenitude of his being, the wealthy man endowed with all the senses, as an enduring reality. The resolution of *theoretical* contradictions is possible *only* through practical means, only through the *practical* energy of man. Their resolution is not by any means, therefore, only a problem of knowledge, but is a *real* problem of life which philosophy was unable to solve precisely because it saw there a purely theoretical problem.

Socialism begins from the *theoretical* and *practical sense perception* of man and nature as essential beings. It is positive human *self-consciousness,* no longer a self-consciousness attained through the negation of religion; just as the *real life* of man is positive and no longer attained through the negation of private property, through *communism.* Communism is the phase of negation of the negation and is, consequently, for the next stage of historical development, a real and necessary factor in the emancipation and rehabilitation of man. Communism is the necessary form and the dynamic principle of the immediate future, but communism is not itself the goal of human development—the form of human society.

Needs, Production, and Division of Labour

We have seen the importance which must be attributed, in a socialist perspective, to the *wealth* of human needs, and consequently also to a *new mode of production* and to a new *object* of production. A new manifestation of *human* powers and a new enrichment of the human being. Within the system of private property it has the opposite meaning. Every man speculates upon creating a *new* need in another in order to force him to a new sacrifice, to place him in a new dependence, and to entice him into a new kind of pleasure and thereby into economic ruin. Everyone tries to establish over others an alien power in order to find there the satisfaction of his own egoistic need. With the increasing mass of objects, therefore, the realm of alien entities to which man is subjected also increases. Every new product is a new *potentiality* of mutual deceit and robbery. Man becomes increasingly poor as a man; he has increasing need of *money* in order to take possession of the hostile being. The power of his *money* diminishes directly with the growth of the quantity of production, i.e. his need increases with the increasing *power* of money. The expansion of production and of needs becomes an *ingenious* and always *calculating* subservience to inhuman, depraved, unnatural and *imaginary* appetites. Private property does not know how to change crude need into *human* need; its *idealism* is *fantasy, caprice* and *fancy*. No eunuch flatters his tyrant more shamefully or seeks by more infamous means to stimulate his jaded appetite, in order to gain some favour, than does the eunuch of industry, the entrepreneur, in order to acquire a few silver coins or to charm the gold from the purse of his dearly beloved neighbour. The entrepreneur accedes to the most depraved fancies of his neighbour, plays the role of pander between him and his needs, awakens unhealthy appetites in him, and watches for every weakness so that later on he may claim the remuneration for this labour of love.

In order to supersede the *idea* of private property communist *ideas* are sufficient, but *genuine* communist activity is necessary in order to supersede *real* private property. History will produce it, and the development which we already recognize in thought as self-transcending will in reality involve a severe and protracted process.

Alienation is apparent not only in the fact that *my* means of life belong to *someone else,* that *my* desires are the unattainable possession of *someone else,* but that everything is *something different* from itself, that my activity is *something else,* and finally (and this is also the case for the capitalist) that *an inhuman power* rules over everything.

The consideration of *division of labour* and *exchange* is of the greatest interest, since they are the *perceptible, alienated* expression of human *activity* and *capacities* as the activity and capacities *proper to a species.*

To state that *private property* is the basis of the *division of labour* and *exchange* is simply to assert that *labour* is the essence of private property; an assertion which the economist cannot prove and which we wish to prove for him. It is precisely in the fact that the *division of labour* and *exchange* are manifestations of private property that we find the proof, first that *human* life needed *private property* for its realization, and secondly, that it now requires the supersession of private property.

2.4 Anarchism, Marxism, and Liberalism

Marshall S. Shatz

Anarchism, of all the major currents of modern social and political thought, has probably been subject to the grossest misunderstandings of its nature and objectives. Anarchism can trace its intellectual lineage back more than a century and a half, and political movements inspired by it have been appearing in most of the countries of the Western world for about a hundred years. Yet today it is still necessary to ask, just what *is* anarchism?

First of all, it is necessary to point out that anarchism is a positive social doctrine embodying a critique of human society as it exists and a vision of a better form of social order. Although the words "anarchism" and "anarchy" are often confused and are sometimes used interchangeably even in anarchist literature, there is a vital difference between them. The word "anarchy" is generally associated with a state of chaos, confusion, disorder. Some anarchists, to be sure, regarded such a condition as a necessary or even desirable means of achieving their ends. But even the most revolution-minded anarchist regarded "anarchy" only as a stepping-stone to "anarchism," a transitional phase in which the old would be destroyed so that the new might emerge.

By the same token, anarchism is not synonymous with terrorism (or, as it is sometimes, and misleadingly, termed, "nihilism"). Of all the misconceptions of anarchism, the one that dies hardest is the belief that anarchism is inseparable from assassination, bomb-throwing, and dynamiting. The meaning of anarchism is not exhausted by the acts of violence carried out at certain periods by some of its adherents.

To identify still more specifically the philosophical sphere to which anarchism belongs, it should be stressed that anarchism is an antipolitical, and not merely apolitical doctrine. It regards political authority, and its modern embodiment the state, as the root of all evil, and the extirpation of that evil as its cardinal task. The political realm is the starting point of anarchism, and its objective is a political one, even if it calls for the abolition of politics altogether and the replacement of the state by new forms of human association.

Anarchism's foremost rivals and objects of criticism have always been liberalism, on the one hand, and socialism, or more specifically, Marxism, on the other. Anarchism not only occupies itself with the same range of issues as these two systems, but it shares many of their premises and aspirations. At one

---

end of the anarchist spectrum it is sometimes difficult to tell the anarchist individualist from the liberal, while at the other the anarchist communist becomes almost indistinguishable from the socialist. It has been observed that anarchism employs a liberal critique of socialism and a socialist critique of liberalism. Nonetheless, in doing so anarchism retains its separate identity, and in actuality liberalism and Marxism prove to have more in common with each other than either does with anarchism.

Most anarchists share with liberals their high valuation of individualism. Such disparate contributors to the anarchist tradition as Max Stirner and Josiah Warren proclaimed the sovereignty of the individual, and even those anarchists who advocated some form of communism generally justified it as the social arrangement that would prove most conducive to the full flowering of the individual. Liberalism's traditional hostility to encroachment by the state on individual freedom finds an echo in anarchism's abhorrence of state authority. There is a point at which the anarchist and the liberal defender of civil rights seem to be speaking the same language, as they criticize the intrusion of the state into the private life of the individual and denounce bureaucratic despotism. The anarchists, however, go considerably further in their criticism, for they wish not merely to restrict the authority of the state but to abolish it altogether. Liberalism regards constitutional government and the rule of law as essential instruments for safeguarding the freedom of the individual in society. Anarchism regards both the very principle of government, however democratic its forms, and the notion that law is a necessary framework for the life of society, as instruments solely of tyranny.

In economic matters, anarchism denies the sanctity of private property and the free marketplace, institutions that liberalism, even in its modern welfare-state form, has traditionally upheld. From William Godwin onward, anarchists have criticized the exploitative character of capitalism in much the same terms as the socialists. Even those anarchists who did not favor the complete abolition of private property agreed that an individual's economic rewards should be limited to the proceeds of his own labor, and accordingly they advocated restrictions on the accumulation and utilization of property that would be unacceptable to most liberals. With the advent of Marxism, the majority of anarchists accepted the main outlines of its critique of capitalism and its objective of abolishing private ownership of the means of production. At least until the expulsion of Bakunin and his followers from the First International in 1872, Marxism and anarchism were but two branches of the international socialist movement, and even thereafter they proceeded in many respects along parallel lines.

Throughout their history, however, the anarchists have repudiated the authoritarian element in socialism, an element which, in their estimation, had first appeared in the utopian projects of the early socialists and then been enshrined in Marxism. They suspected that socialism harbored a conception of society as something greater than the sum of its parts, as a collective entity with claims of its own which might override the claims of the individuals composing it. To the anarchists this seemed to represent little improvement over the submission to authority demanded by the state. Their suspicions appeared confirmed by the program of the Marxists, who insisted that the capitalist state must first be seized and put to use before it could be abolished forever, that it would without fail gradually wither away but could not merely be annihilated on the day of the revolution. Marxism and anarchism, therefore, though united in their antipathy to the existing order and their devotion to the cause of the laboring class, remained distinct and mutually hostile movements. In a sense too socialist for the liberals and too liberal for the socialists, the anarchists found capitalism and Marxism equally distasteful—a distaste reciprocated in full measure by their opponents, who vied with each other in denouncing the "forces of anarchy."

The specific economic doctrines and political programs of anarchism, however, are themselves reflections of a more fundamental anarchist vision of things. It is this underlying vision even more than the quarrel over state authority that explains the truly passionate animosity toward Marxism that runs as a leitmotiv through so much of anarchist history, from Bakunin to the anarchist elements in the New Left today, from the Russian Revolution to the Spanish Civil War. To the anarchists, Marxism has always represented not just a misguided and potentially dangerous set of tactics for achieving the downfall of an order they both ostensibly rejected, but a fundamentally different perception of the world and of man's purpose in it. If the anarchists have devoted nearly as much energy to denouncing Marxism as they have to denouncing the "bourgeois" system, it is because they have regarded the Marxists as potential heirs of the system rather than its sworn enemies.

The most basic and far-reaching antagonisms between anarchism and Marxism stem from their different conceptions of the relationship between man and nature. In Marxism, nature is something that man must master; he asserts himself over it, exploits it, and harnesses it to his own purposes. There is an inherent opposition between man and nature that is expressed in man's quest to gain control over the forces of nature through his labor, to turn them to productive economic purposes, and to create the man-made world in which his own nature will realize itself. The modern industrial system, for all the evils it perpetrates and the sufferings it inflicts in its capitalist form, carries out this task with stunning efficiency. Thus the *Communist Manifesto,* while condemning the capitalist system, is filled with admiration for the productive forces it has created. In the country where it first became an official ideology, Marxism itself has been the instrument for creating those "colossal productive forces." One of Marxism's primary functions in the Soviet Union has been to provide ideological sanction for an unparalleled drive to transform a backward agrarian society into a modern industrial one, the ultimate result of which is to be the advent of communism.

If it is man's purpose to master nature and subject it to his will, he must consciously control and channel his own energies into productive endeavor. Labor, the purposeful application of human forces to the environment, becomes the central, even the defining characteristic of mankind; and it was in terms of improvements in the organization of human labor that Marx interpreted man's entire history. At the very least, such an outlook places a premium on self-discipline, organization, rationalism, and all the other personal and social qualities that enable men to make the concerted and persistent effort creation of a man-made environment requires.

Such, in the briefest terms, is the Marxist conception of the road man must take to the ultimate attainment of freedom and self-realization. In this respect the spirit of Marxism is very similar to the spirit of liberalism, which also envisages the improvement of mankind in terms of material progress through the development of science and technology. Both differ radically from anarchism, which is animated by quite another spirit. Anarchism views the relationship between man and nature essentially as one of harmony, not as one of opposition. Human society is not a collective enterprise for the mastery of nature but an organic outgrowth of nature, and the ills of society stem from efforts to impose artificial constraints on its free, spontaneous development. This sentiment manifests itself in anarchist thought and practice in a variety of ways. It is expressed, for instance, in the recurrent anarchist image of human life as an unpatterned flow of free creativity, just as spontaneous and unplanned, but also as intrinsically harmonious, as nature itself.

"Spontaneity" is one of the key words of anarchism. Seeking to restore man to nature rather than conquer it, anarchism celebrates the free play of human impulses. It wishes to release the natural forces of the personality rather than control them the better to direct them into economically productive areas. For this reason, while Marx dismissed the "idiocy of rural life," the anarchists traditionally felt a strong affinity for the peasantry. It seemed to them that the peasants lived in exemplary harmony with their physical and social environment; their labor was meaningful in that it directly satisfied their material needs, and their communities and personal relationships were formed naturally, in response to the demands of life. It was precisely the "elemental" quality of their existence that the anarchists, in contrast to Trotsky, found so attractive.

To say that anarchism "rejected" modern industry and technology is too simple a judgment. The anarchists did view productive labor differently from the Marxists, however, and their attitude toward its modern industrial form was consequently qualified and ambiguous. Work, to most anarchists, is an activity meant to fulfill the basic material needs of the individual and, in addition, to satisfy his spiritual need for self-expression. Anarchism views work in terms of the spontaneous creativity of the individual artist rather than in terms of the collective and planned creativity of man reshaping his environment. To borrow a distinction drawn by the Dutch historian Johan Huizinga the anarchist sees man less as *Homo faber,* man the maker, than as *Homo ludens,* man the player. The function of his labor is not to remake the world around him but to manifest the creative forces of his personality.

With this as its central aspiration, anarchism sees no need for large and complex forms of social or economic organization. It is in the small community, with its numerous voluntary associations of like-minded individuals, that a man can best satisfy both his material and his spiritual needs. Anarchism condemns the state not merely because it deems it exploitative and coercive, but because it considers it an artificial and unnatural framework for the life of society. A communal organization welling up from below, in direct response to the true needs of its members, represents the proper social arena for their activities. The state, with its powerful administrative and economic bureaucracies, imposes its authority from above, without the direct sanction of the individual or his immediate community. Regardless of its form, it inevitably develops objectives of its own, and without fail it will seek to harness the energies of the society it rules and turn them to the pursuit of purposes alien to it.

From this perspective the "unhistorical" character of the anarchist outlook becomes more intelligible. Marxism, with its theory of historical materialism, and liberalism, with a concept of progress that is less determinate but also linked to economic development, perceive the world in strictly historical terms. Both embody a sense of development through time, of a gradual unfolding of human capacity as history proceeds. This sense of historical time is either absent or weakly developed in the views of the anarchists. The anarchist does not feel that the defects of human society stem from underdevelopment, from incomplete mastery of the forces of the environment, and lack of fulfillment of human potential, which material progress can be expected to remedy in the course of time. If man's better impulses do not now manifest themselves fully, it is because they are being repressed and thwarted by external conditions. Remove those conditions, allow men to act in accordance with their true nature, and they will spontaneously create a harmonious form of social organization.

With anarchism's underlying character in mind, it should not be too difficult to understand why liberalism and Marxism have had so much greater success in the modern world. The relationship they perceive between man and nature is a productive and dynamic one, and it has enabled them to serve as highly effective ideologies of industrialization. Much of the remarkable industrial expansion of Western Europe and North America in the nineteenth century owed its vigor to the liberal ideology and the social, political, and economic institutions it created. And twentieth-century Soviet Marxism, with its endless exhortations to increase production, develop industry and technology, and thereby lay the foundations for communism, has exhibited some of the basic assumptions and aspirations of nineteenth-century capitalism; it has thus been able to serve as a substitute for the entrepreneurial spirit that was too weakly developed in most of Eastern Europe to assume the task of industrialization itself. The anarchists, on the other hand, have always been more skeptical about modern industrial civilization, not only rejecting the hardships it visited on the workers and the sheer ugliness it produced, as did Marxism, but questioning its ultimate purpose. It is very difficult to imagine an anarchist sitting down to write such a work as *Das Kapital,* with its minute—and enthralled—investigation of the intricacies of the capitalist economic system. An anarchist would simply not be sufficiently interested in the details of economic production or deem them of sufficient importance to devote himself to such an enterprise.

This does not mean that historical anarchism was inherently anti-industrial, or that all anarchists merely wished to turn the clock back to a world of simple peasants and independent craftsmen (though some, of course, such as

Tolstoy, would have liked nothing better). Peter Kropotkin, for instance, appreciated many aspects of modern technology and tried to integrate them into his vision of the anarchist society; anarcho-syndicalism tried to adapt anarchist principles to the modern factory system and trade-union organization; and the anarchist movements that sprang up among the Jewish garment workers of London and New York were entirely urban-oriented. But it is true that anarchism called into question the very essence of industrial-technological civilization: the seemingly compulsive urge to maximize economic production, and the mammoth scale of the institutions which that urge generated. Such a civilization, the anarchist believed, uproots the individual from his natural environment, isolates him from his fellows, and thwarts his self-development and self-enjoyment. The latter can be achieved only in the small, voluntary community where the individual can engage in meaningful personal relationships and truly creative labor. To be sure, these are the ultimate objectives of Marxism, too. But the Marxist utopia, the classless society in which the state has withered away—really an anarchist utopia, as has often been pointed out—can dawn only at the end of the long historical process of economic development, and not before; it is relegated to a future which, in the history of Marxism, has tended to grow ever more remote. The anarchist insists on releasing the spontaneous impulses of the human personality right now, rather than damming them up for the present in order to generate a better future. As a result, even those anarchists who acknowledged the benefits of modern industry proposed courses of action that would probably have proved incompatible with it. Even if they accepted the factory and the railroad, they rejected the pattern of political and economic organization that had made them possible, planning to restructure the industrial order as a vast network of autonomous producers' associations, each managing its own segment of the industrial system and entering into voluntary agreements with others. During the great industrial expansion of the nineteenth and twentieth centuries, therefore, anarchism appeared to be running counter to the prevailing forces of history, making a heroic but futile effort, if not actually to turn back the clock, then at least to stop its further progress.

If the character of anarchism as we have described it helps to explain its failure in the past, however, it also helps to explain its remarkable revival in recent years, a revival, one senses, that has astonished even the remnants of the anarchist movement. Although nothing like the anarchist movement of the past has been resurrected, the anarchist tradition has been rediscovered, the literature of anarchism is being read once again, and an assortment of social thinkers and political groups are claiming to have found inspiration in anarchist ideas. The renewal of interest in anarchism today can be traced to the growing awareness of the price that has been paid for the immense productivity and material abundance of modern industrial technology: industrial man has become separated from living nature as he has surrounded himself with more and more of his own products—and more and more of his own wastes; he has grown estranged from his neighbors and increasingly subject to the authority of remote, impersonal bureaucracies, both public and private; and he has felt his personal significance diminish as he has come to be regarded primarily as a producer and consumer of goods rather than as an individual whose true purpose is self-expression and self-growth. Many of the values against which the achievements of industrial society are increasingly being measured and found wanting are values that have long been harbored and defended by the anarchist tradition, and the growing consciousness of those values in the contemporary mind has been accompanied by a rediscovery of anarchism.

It might well be argued that anarchism is in fact a luxury which the post-industrial world is only now beginning to be able to afford. The material abundance provided by modern technology, in conjunction with the vastly increased leisure available, has at last created conditions in which serious attention can be paid to the preservation and enjoyment of the natural environment, to a more balanced and multifaceted kind of personal growth, and to a more intensive cultivation of communal relationships. In the nineteenth and early twentieth centuries, when strong concentrations of political and economic power, hierarchical forms of organization, and the self-discipline of the work ethic were required to forge the modern industrial system, anarchism seemed an anachronism, a nostalgic longing for a freer and simpler age. In the contemporary context, however, the traditional doctrines of anarchism take on new meaning, as modern society begins to shift its emphasis from the task of generating material wealth to the task of utilizing it to enrich social and personal life.

To point out the relevance of anarchism today is hardly to advocate uncritical acceptance of it; on the contrary, awareness of its defects becomes all the more important as its attractiveness increases. Some of the questions raised by anarchism's critics in the past have never been adequately answered and must still be asked today. Anarchism has yet to prove itself a viable approach to economic organization. Even if anarchism does seem more applicable to a post-industrial society of abundance and leisure than to a society in the process of industrializing, the problem still remains of maintaining in some way the economic productivity that has generated such abundance and leisure. To individuals surfeited and bored with the products and services of modern technology, a more simple and unencumbered way of life may have considerable appeal—especially when their communal experiments form mere enclaves in the larger society and can still fall back upon those products and services when necessary. Subsequent generations might find it more difficult to appreciate the simple life or to devote themselves to self-cultivation if most of their energies must be taken up by a struggle for subsistence. As in the past, anarchism as a social philosophy faces the delicate task of finding a practical adjustment to modern conditions rather than turning its back upon them.

These reservations suggest that anarchism as an all-embracing ideology, as a total alternative to the existing structure of society, is as fraught with contradictions today as it was in the past (though of course Marxism and liberalism have hardly proved themselves free of contradictions of their own). But anarchism does have the capacity to offer a timely and provocative challenge to prevailing values and institutions which, many people feel, are now beginning to yield diminishing returns. Contemporary anarchist currents appear to be drawing upon the most fruitful and creative facets of the anarchist tradition, approaching it as a relatively untapped source of inspiration rather than as a program or blueprint. If anarchism has a living role to play in social and political thought today, it is as an instrument of constructive criticism, a refreshing antidote to some of the self-inflicted poisons of life in the urban-industrial society. By no means does it have all of the answers to the problems of modern man and his society. But the questions it asks, though they trace their origins all the way back to the eighteenth century, seem remarkably fresh and inspiriting today.

SOCIALISM AND THE ROLE OF THE STATE IN THE ECONOMIC REFORM OF CAPITALISM

At this point, a reader familiar with the theory and practice of the Keynesian revolution (see chapter 3) may be tempted to interject: "But wait a minute. Suppose that old-style, laissez-faire capitalism *is* characterized by conflicts between workers and capitalists, and *is* accompanied by depressions. Cannot, indeed does not, the modern democratic state regulate and control the business cycle, thereby reducing capitalism's main "contradiction," and redistribute income from rich to poor, thereby ameliorating its central conflict? And does not democratic economic reform thus constitute a partnership between public and private sectors of the economy that will give capitalism a new lease on life and, albeit in modified form, prevent or indefinitely postpone its demise?"

The answers given to these questions by the various post-Marxian radical critics of capitalism differ significantly, and are an important component in the intellectual background to current debates over the appropriate role of government in economic life.

Marx's position, and that of orthodox Marxists generally, is that genuine economic reform through governmental action is unattainable in a capitalist society. First, capitalism's contradictions and conflicts are deeply rooted in its underlying institutions, notably, concentrated private ownership of the means of production by the capitalist class. Therefore, only a truly radical transformation to a new and different economic system characterized by worker-social ownership and control of the means of production is sufficient to resolve capitalism's problems. Second, the state, even the modern representative democratic state, cannot serve as an agent for genuine economic reform because it is controlled not by citizens in general but essentially by capitalist industrialists. In the Marxian view, economic power begets political power. The state, in effect, is the political arm of the bourgeoisie, the instrument whereby the dominant, property-owning class sustains its control over the economic system. Of course, capitalists may permit government to make minor concessions or modifications (for example, old age insurance), to reduce the revolutionary fervor of the workers. And the broader social interests of capitalists in the long-run continuity of the capitalist system may stimulate certain reforms (for example, factory legislation, maximum working hours). But *genuine* economic reform requires the elimination of the *source* of capitalist exploitation and crises, namely private ownership of the means of production, and the establishment of socialism. The capitalist class, in control of both the economy and the state, would certainly not accede to its eviction from power, or to the use of "its" state as eviction agent for the proletariat. These ideas on the Marxian theory of the state are summarized by Paul Sweezy in selection 2.5.

In the latter nineteenth and early twentieth centuries, a major debate raged both within and without the Marxian socialist movement on the questions of the relations between democracy and socialism, and on the possible use of the democratic state as a vehicle for the economic reform of capitalism and the eventual establishment of a socialist economy. The German social democrat Edward Bernstein, in *Evolutionary Socialism* (1899) and other works, led Marxist "revisionists" in restating and modifying both Marx's economic theories and his view of the role of the democratic state. The concentration and centralization of capital, Bernstein argued, would facilitate the transition, through democratic political means, to a socialist economy. Capitalism was certainly characterized by depressions and exploitation of labor. However, because of industrialization and economic growth, capitalism's economic crises were becoming more tolerable and its conflicts less, not more, intense. Therefore, the purely economic case for capitalism's impending demise was losing its force. On the other hand, Bernstein contended, Marx had overemphasized the influence of the capitalist class on the state and underestimated its capacity for democratic reforms, especially if reforms are made in a peaceful and gradual way and embody a consensus of different groups—workers, labor unions, cooperatives, and small bourgeoisie. Selection 2.6 summarizes Bernstein's revisionist interpretation of Marxism, with special reference to the practicality of democratic economic reform.

The Marxist revisionists constituted a connecting link between Marxian and non-Marxian socialism. In the early decades of the twentieth century, non-Marxian socialists in both Europe and the United States continued to combine radical criticism of old-style, laissez-faire capitalism with a vision of a more just and humane socialist organization of the economy. Democratic socialists, especially in Great Britain (notably R. H. Tawney and G. B. Shaw, the Webbs, and others associated with the Fabian Society) and in the United States (Eugene Debs and Norman Thomas), espoused democracy, both as the organizing principle of a socialist economy and as the principal means of moving from capitalism to socialism.

It is at this point that democratic socialist and liberal democratic reform of capitalism fuse and lines of demarcation become blurred. Moderate non-Marxian socialists have traditionally espoused the democratic reform of capitalism as the means of eventually establishing (however gradually) a socialist economy, whereas liberal reformers propose democratic reforms as a means of improving and sustaining a modified form of capitalism. But both display a deep faith in the democratic process as the vehicle for reform, control, and organization of economic life. Hence, the specific reforms of the two groups often coalesce. Comparison of the views of such liberal social reform contributors to the post-Keynesian synthesis as Gunnar Myrdal or Alvin Hansen (chapter 3), the ideas of John Kenneth Galbraith on "social imbalance" (chapter 5), and the writing of such contemporary "democratic collectivists" as Michael Harrington (chapter 7) illustrates the continued influence of democratic socialist thought and the close affinity between moderate socialists and liberal democratic reformers.

As the process of economic reform proceeded in the twentieth century, democratic socialists increasingly turned their attention to the questions of the transition from capitalism to socialism and the appropriate organization of a socialist economy. In Great Britain, two main strands of the socialist movement emerged: one, associated with R. H. Tawney, G.D.H. Cole, and others, focused upon worker control of industry and, in today's terminology, direct or "participatory" democracy. These "guild socialists," as they came to be called, sharply criticized bureaucracy, centralization, and autocracy in both large-scale private corporations and the political state, and they advocated a democratic and decentralized reconstruction of the economic order around "guilds" of workers.

The second main strand of democratic socialism, associated especially with the Fabian Society, focused on the worker as a citizen, indirect or representative democracy, and the role of the democratic state as an agent for economic reform, social control, and centralized management and planning of economic life.

In selection 2.7, Walter Buckingham compares and contrasts these two main strands of democratic socialist thought. As we shall see in chapter 7, this distinction between centralized and decentralized forms of democratic socialism roughly parallels and anticipates the division in contemporary radical-but-democratic socialist dissent in the United States between the ideas of the New Left and the more traditional critique of democratic collectivists.

2.5 Marx's Theory of the State

Paul M. Sweezy

THE PRIMARY FUNCTION OF THE STATE

There is a tendency on the part of modern liberal theorists to interpret the state as an institution established in the interests of society as a whole for the purpose of mediating and reconciling the antagonisms to which social existence inevitably gives rise. This is a theory which avoids the pitfalls of political metaphysics and which serves to integrate in a tolerably satisfactory fashion a

Excerpted from Paul M. Sweezy, *The Theory of Capitalist Development* (New York: Monthly Review Press, 1942), pp. 240–51. Reprinted by permission of the publisher.

considerable body of observed fact. It contains, however, one basic shortcoming, the recognition of which leads to a theory essentially Marxian in its orientation. A critique of what may be called the class-mediation conception of the state is, therefore, perhaps the best way of introducing the Marxian theory.

The class-mediation theory assumes, usually implicitly, that the underlying class structure, or what comes to the same thing, the system of property relations is an immutable datum, in this respect like the order of nature itself. It then proceeds to ask what arrangements the various classes will make to get along with each other, and finds that an institution for mediating their conflicting interests is the logical and necessary answer. To this institution powers for maintaining order and settling quarrels are granted. In the real world what is called the state is identified as the counterpart of this theoretical construction.

The weakness of this theory is not difficult to discover. It lies in the assumption of an immutable and, so to speak, self-maintaining class structure of society. The superficiality of this assumption is indicated by the most cursory study of history. The fact is that many forms of property relations with their concomitant class structures have come and gone in the past, and there is no reason to assume that they will not continue to do so in the future. The class structure of society is no part of the natural order of things; it is the product of past social development, and it will change in the course of future social development.

Once this is recognized it becomes clear that the liberal theory goes wrong in the manner in which it initially poses the problem. We cannot ask: Given a certain class structure, how will the various classes, with their divergent and often conflicting interests, manage to get along together? We must ask: How did a particular class structure come into being and by what means is its continued existence guaranteed? As soon as an attempt is made to answer this question, it appears that the state has a function in society which is prior to and more fundamental than any which present-day liberals attribute to it.

A given set of property relations serves to define and demarcate the class structure of society. From any set of property relations one class or classes (the owners) reap material advantages; other classes (the owned and the non-owners) suffer material disadvantages. A special institution capable and willing to use force to whatever degree is required is an essential to the maintenance of such a set of property relations. Investigation shows that the state possesses this characteristic to the fullest degree, and that no other institution is or can be allowed to compete with it in this respect. This is usually expressed by saying that the state, and the state alone, exercises sovereignty over all those subject to its jurisdiction. It is, therefore, not difficulty to identify the state as the guarantor of a given set of property relations.

The state is the product of a long and arduous struggle in which the class which occupies what is for the time the key positions in the process of production gets the upper hand over its rivals and fashions a state which will enforce that set of property relations which is in its own interest. In other words any particular state is the child of the class or classes in society which benefit from the particular set of property relations which it is the state's obligation to enforce. A moment's reflection will carry the conviction that it could hardly be otherwise. As soon as we have dropped the historically untenable assumption that the class structure of society is in some way natural or self-enforcing, it is clear that any other outcome would lack the prerequisites of stability. If the disadvantaged classes were in possession of state power, they would attempt to use it to establish a social order more favorable to their own interests, while a sharing of state power among the various classes would merely shift the locale of conflict to the state itself.

That such conflicts within the state, corresponding to fundamental class struggles outside, have taken place in certain transitional historical periods is not denied. During those long periods, however, when a certain social order enjoys a relatively continuous and stable existence, the state power must be monopolized by the class or classes which are the chief beneficiaries.

As against the class-mediation theory of the state, we have here the underlying idea of what has been called the class-domination theory. The former takes the existence of a certain class structure for granted and sees in the state an institution for reconciling the conflicting interests of the various classes; the latter, on the other hand, recognizes that classes are the product of historical development and sees in the state an instrument in the hands of the ruling classes for enforcing and guaranteeing the stability of the class structure itself.

It is important to realize that, so far as capitalist society is concerned, 'class domination' and 'the protection of private property' are virtually synonymous expressions. Hence when we say with Engels that the highest purpose of the state is the protection of private property, we are also saying that the state is an instrument of class domination. This is doubtless insufficiently realized by critics of the Marxian theory who tend to see in the notion of class domination something darker and more sinister than 'mere' protection of private property. In other words they tend to look upon class domination as something reprehensible and the protection of private property as something meritorious. Consequently, it does not occur to them to identify the two ideas. Frequently, no doubt, this is because they have in mind not capitalist property, but rather private property as it would be in a simple commodity-producing society where each producers owns and works with his own means of production. Under such conditions there are no classes at all and hence no class domination. Under capitalist relations, however, property has an altogether different significance, and its protection is easily shown to be identical with the preservation of class dominance. Capitalist private property does not consist in things—things exist independently of their ownership—but in a social relation between people. Property confers upon its owners freedom from labor and the disposal over the labor of others, and this is the essence of all social domination whatever form it may assume.

The recognition that the defense of private property is the first duty of the state is the decisive factor in determining the attitude of genuine Marxist socialism towards the state. 'The theory of the Communists,' Marx and Engels wrote in the *Communist Manifesto,* 'can be summed up in the single sentence:

Abolition of private property.' Since the state is first and foremost the protector of private property, it follows that the realization of this end cannot be achieved without a head-on collision between the forces of socialism and the state power.

THE STATE AS AN ECONOMIC INSTRUMENT

The state has always been a very significant factor in the functioning of the economy within the framework of the system of property relations which it guarantees.

First, state power is invoked to solve problems which are posed by the economic development of the particular form of society under consideration, in this case capitalism. In the earlier period a shortage of labor power, in the later period over-exploitation of the laboring population were the subjects of state action. In each case the solution of the problem required state intervention. Many familiar examples of a similar character readily come to mind.

Second, we should naturally expect that the state power under capitalism would be used first and foremost in the interests of the capitalist class since the state is dedicated to the preservation of the structure of capitalism and must therefore be staffed by those who fully accept the postulates and objectives of this form of society. This is unquestionably true, but it is not inconsistent to say that state action may run counter to the immediate economic interests of some or even all of the capitalists provided only that the overriding aim of preserving the system intact is promoted. The legal limitation of the working day is a classic example of state action of this sort. The intensity of class antagonism engendered by over-exploitation of the labor force was such that it became imperative for the capitalist class to make concessions even at the cost of immediate economic advantages. For the sake of preserving domestic peace and tranquility, blunting the edge of class antagonisms, and ultimately avoiding the dangers of violent revolution, the capitalist class is always prepared to make concessions through the medium of state action. It may, of course, happen that the occasion for the concessions is an actual materialization of the threat of revolution. In this case their purpose is to restore peace and order so that production and accumulation can once again go forward uninterruptedly.

Let us summarize the principles underlying the use of the state as an economic instrument within the framework of capitalism. In the 1st place, the state comes into action in the economic sphere in order to solve problems which are posed by the development of capitalism. In the 2nd place, where the interests of the capitalist class are concerned, there is a strong predisposition to use the state power freely. And, finally, the state may be used to make concessions to the working class provided that the consequences of not doing so are sufficiently dangerous to the stability and functioning of the system as a whole.

It should be noted that none of these conclusions lends support to the revisionist view that socialism can be achieved through a series of piecemeal reforms. On the contrary, they grow out of and supplement the basic principle that the state exists in the first instance for the protection of capitalist property relations. Reforms may modify the functioning of capitalism but never threaten its foundation.

THE QUESTION OF THE FORM OF GOVERNMENT

Democracy does not alter the basic significance of the state in relation to the economy. The existence of democracy is, of course, a matter of prime importance particularly to the working class. Only under a democratic form of government can the working class organize freely and effectively for the achievement of its ends, whether they happen to be socialist or merely reformist in character. It is for this reason that one of the first demands of the labor movement in all non-democratic countries has always been the establishment of democratic forms of government. Moreover, for the ruling class democracy has always constituted a potential threat to the stability of its position and has consequently been granted grudgingly, with limitations, and usually only under severe pressure.

Democracy brings the conflicts of capitalist society into the open in the political sphere; it restricts the freedom of the capitalists to use the state in their own interests; it reinforces the working class in demanding concessions; finally, it even increases the possibility that the working class will present demands which threaten the system itself and so must be rejected by the capitalists and their state functionaries regardless of the consequences. These are all matters of the greatest importance in determining the actual course of capitalist evolution; but they do not contradict the principles set forth in the preceding section. There is, in other words, nothing in the nature of democracy to make us change our view of the fundamental functions and limits of state action in capitalist society.

2.6 Evolutionary Socialism

Edward Bernstein

The Economics of Revisionism

THE DISTRIBUTION OF WEALTH IN THE MODERN COMMUNITY

The capitalist, according to the theory of Marx, must produce surplus value in order to obtain a profit, but he can only draw surplus value from living labour. In order to secure the market against his competitors he must strive after a

Excerpted from Edward Bernstein, *Evolutionary Socialism,* (New York: B. W. Huebsch, 1909, Schocken Books, 1961). Reprinted by permission of Schocken Books.

cheapening of production and this he attains, where the lowering of wages is resisted, only by means of an increase of the productivity of labour; that is by the perfecting of machinery and the economising of human labour. But in reducing human labour he places so much labour producing surplus value out of its function, and so kills the goose that lays the golden egg. The consequence is a gradually accomplished lowering of the profit rate, which through counteracting circumstances, is certainly temporarily hindered, but is always starting again. This produces another intrinsic contradiction in the capitalist mode of production. Profit rate is the inducement to the productive application of capital; if it falls below a certain point, the motive for productive undertakings is weakened—especially as far as concerns the new amounts of capital which enter the market as off-shoots of the accumulated masses of capital. Capital shows itself as a barrier to capitalist production. The continued development of production is interrupted. Whilst on the one hand every active particle of capital tries to secure and increase its rate of profit by means of a feverish strain of production, congestion in the expansion of production already sets in on the other. This is only the counterpart of the transactions leading to relative over-production, which produces a crisis in the market of use values. Over-production of commodities is at the same time manifesting itself as over-production of capital. Here as there, crises bring about a temporary arrangement. Enormous depreciation and destruction of capital take place, and under the influence of stagnation a portion of the working class must submit to a reduction of wages below the average, as an increased reserve army of superabundant hands stands at the disposal of capital in the labour market.

Thus after a time the conditions of a profitable investment of capital are re-established and the dance can go on anew but with the intrinsic contradiction already mentioned on an increased scale. Greater centralisation of capital, greater concentration of enterprises, increased rate of exploitation.

Now, is all that right?

Yes and no. It is true above all as a tendency. The forces painted are there and work in the given direction. And the proceedings are also taken from reality. The fall of the profit rate is a fact, the advent of over-production and crises is a fact, periodic diminution of capital is a fact, the concentration and centralisation of industrial capital is a fact, the increase of the rate of surplus value is a fact. So far we are, in principle, agreed in the statement. When the statement does not agree with reality it is not because something false is said, but because what is said is incomplete. Factors which influence the contradictions described by limiting them, are in Marx either quite ignored, or are, although discussed at some place, abandoned later on when the established facts are summed up and confronted, so that the social result of the conflicts appears much stronger and more abrupt than it is in reality.

The number of shareholders and the average amount of their holding of shares has been of rapid growth.

This division of national wealth, for which word in the great majority of cases one may substitute national surplus value, is shown again in the figures of the statistics of incomes.

It is quite wrong to assume that the present development of society shows a relative or indeed absolute diminution of the number of the members of the possessing classes. Their number increases both relatively and absolutely. If the activity and the prospects of social democracy were dependent on the decrease of the "wealthy," then it might indeed lie down to sleep. But the contrary is the case. The prospects of socialism depend not on the decrease but on the increase of social wealth.

Socialism, or the social movement of modern times, has already survived many a superstition, it will also survive this, that its future depends on the concentration of wealth or, if one will put it thus, on the absorption of surplus value by a diminishing group of capitalist mammoths.

Whether the social surplus produce is accumulated in the shape of monopoly by 10,000 persons or is shared up in graduated amounts among half-a-million of men makes no difference in principle to the nine or ten million heads of families who are worsted by this transaction. Their struggle for a more just distribution or for an organisation which would include a more just distribution is not on that account less justifiable and necessary. On the contrary, it might cost less surplus labour to keep a few thousand privileged persons in sumptuousness than half-a-million or more in wealth.

If society were constituted or had developed in the manner the socialist theory has hitherto assumed, then certainly the economic collapse would be only a question of a short span of time. Far from society being simplified as to its divisions compared with earlier times, it has been graduated and differentiated both in respect of incomes and of business activities.

If the working class waits till "Capital" has put the middle classes out of the world it might really have a long nap.

THE CLASSES OF ESTABLISHMENTS IN THE PRODUCTION AND DISTRIBUTION OF SOCIAL WEALTH

If the continual improvement of technical methods and centralisation of businesses in an increasing number of branches of industry is a fact whose significance scarcely any crazy reactionaries can hide from themselves, it is a no less well-established fact that in a whole series of branches of industry small and medium-sized undertakings appear quite capable of existing beside the large industries. In industry there is no development according to a pattern that applies equally to one and all branches. Businesses carried on throughout according to routine, continue as small and medium-sized undertakings, whilst branches of technical trades which were thought to be secured for small businesses are absorbed for ever one fine day by a large organisation.

A whole series of circumstances allows the continuance and renewal of small and medium enterprises. They can be divided into three groups.

First, a great number of trades or branches of trades are nearly equally adapted for small and medium undertakings as for large enterprises, and the advantages which the latter have over the former are not so important that they can outweigh the peculiar advantages of the smaller home industries. This is, as everyone knows, the case, amongst others, with different branches of wood, leather, and metal work. Or, a division of labour is found where the large industry carries out one-half and three-quarters of the manufacture and when the finishing processes are done by smaller enterprises.

Secondly, when the product must be made accessible to the consumer, small establishments are, in many cases, favourable to its manufacture, as is shown most clearly in bakeries.

Last, but not least, the large industry itself gives life to smaller and medium trades partly by production on a large scale producing a corresponding cheapening of materials of work (auxiliary materials, half-manufactured goods), partly by the liberating of capital, on the one hand, and the "setting free" of workers on the other. In great and small amounts new capital is always entering the market seeking utilisation, and the demand on the market for new goods increases steadily with the wealth of the community.

In spite of the continued changes in the grouping of industries and the internal organisation of the establishments, we have this picture on the whole to-day: that the large industry does not continuously absorb the smaller and medium industries, but that it is growing up beside them. Only the very small enterprises decline relatively and absolutely. But as regards the small and medium industries they do increase.

If the collapse of modern society depends on the disappearance of the middle ranks between the apex and the base of the social pyramid, if it is dependent upon the absorption of these middle classes by the extremes above and below them, then its realisation is no nearer in England, France, and Germany to-day than at any earlier time in the nineteenth century.

But a building can appear outwardly unchanged and substantial and yet be decayed if the stones themselves or important layers of stones have become rotten. The soundness of a business house stands the test of critical periods; it remains, therefore, for us to investigate what is the course of the economic crises which are peculiar to the modern order of production, and what consequences and reactions are to be expected in the near future from them.

THE CRISES AND POSSIBILITIES OF ADJUSTMENT IN MODERN ECONOMY

Signs of an economic world-wide crash of unheard-of violence have not been established, nor can one describe the improvement of trade in the intervals between the crises as particularly short-lived. Much more does a third question arise which after all is partly contained already in the second—namely: (1) whether the enormous extension of the world market, in conjunction with the extraordinary shortening of time necessary for the transmission of news and for the transport trade, has so increased the possibilities of adjustment of disturbances; and (2) whether the enormously increased wealth of the European states, in conjunction with the elasticity of the modern credit system and the rise of industrial Kartels, has so limited the reacting force of local or individual disturbances that, at least for some time, general commercial crises similar to the earlier ones are to be regarded as improbable.

Over-production is to a certain extent unavoidable. But over-production in single industries does not mean general crises. If it leads to such an one, either the industries concerned must be of such importance as consumers of the manufactures of other industries, as that their stagnation also stops these industries, or indeed they must take from them, through the medium of the money market—that is, through the paralysis of general credit—the means of carrying on production. But it is evident that there is always a lessening probability of this latter result. The richer a country is, the more developed its credit organisation—which is not to be confused with a more widely spread habit to produce with borrowed capital. For here the possibilities of adjustment multiply in an increasing measure.

There remains then only so much, that the capacity for production in modern society is much greater than the actual demand for products determined by the buying capacity; that millions live insufficiently housed, insufficiently clad, and insufficiently nourished, in spite of abundant means at hand for sufficient housing, nourishment, and clothing; that out of this incongruity, overproduction appears again and again in different branches of production, so that either actually certain articles are produced in greater amounts than can be used—for example, more yarn than the present weaving mills can work—or that certain articles are produced not indeed in a greater quantity than can be used, but in a greater quantity than can be bought; that in consequence of this, great irregularity occurs in the employment of the workers, which makes their situation extremely insecure, weighs them down in unworthy dependence, brings forth over-work here and want of work there; and that of the means employed to-day to counteract the most visible part of this evil, the Kartels represent monopolist unions—on the one side against the workers, and on the other against the great public—which have a tendency to carry on warfare over the heads of these and at their cost with the same kind of monopolist unions in other industries or other lands, or, by international or inter-industrial agreements, arbitrarily to adapt production and prices to their need of profit. The capitalistic means of defence against crises virtually bear within themselves the possibilities of a new and more hopeless serfdom for the working classes, as well as of privileges of production which revive in acute form the old guild privileges. It appears to me to be much more important at present, from the standpoint of the workers, to keep before our eyes the possibilities of Kartels and trusts than to prophesy their "impotence." It is for the working class a subordinate question whether these combinations will be able, in the course of time, to attain their first-mentioned object—the warding off of crises. But it becomes a question full of importance as soon as expectations of any kind as regards the movement for the emancipation of the working classes are made dependent upon the question of the general crisis. For then the belief that Kartels are of no effect against crises may be the cause of very disastrous neglect.

The problem of crises cannot be solved by a few well-preserved catchwords. We can only investigate what elements of modern economy work in favour of crises and what work against them. It is impossible to pre-judge a priori the ultimate relation of these forces to one another, or their development. Unless unforeseen external events bring about a general crisis—and as we have said that can happen any day—there is no urgent reason for concluding that such a crisis will come to pass for purely economic reasons. Local and partial depressions are unavoidable; general stagnation is not unavoidable with the present organisation and extension of the world market, and particularly with the great extension of the production of articles of food.

The Tasks and Possibilities of Social Democracy

THE POLITICAL AND ECONOMIC PRELIMINARY CONDITIONS OF SOCIALISM

What are the preliminary conditions of the realisation of socialism? Historical materialism sees them first in the modern development of production. With the spread of the capitalistic large enterprises in industry and agriculture there is assumed to be a lasting and steadily-increasing material cause for the impetus to a socialistic transformation of society. In these undertakings production is already socially organised, only the management is individualistic and the profit is appropriated by individuals, not on the ground of their labour, but of their share of capital. The active worker is separated from the possession of his instruments of production, he is in the dependent condition of a wage-earner, from which he does not escape as long as he lives, and the pressure of it is rendered sharper by the uncertainty which is joined with this dependence both on the employer and on the fluctuations in the state of trade. Like production itself, the conditions of existence for the producers press towards the socialisation and the co-operative organisation of production and exchange. As soon as this development is sufficiently advanced the realisation of socialism becomes an imperative necessity for the further development of the community. To carry it out is the task of the proletariat organised as a class party which for this purpose must take possession of the political government.

According to that, we have as the first condition of the general realisation of socialism a definite degree of capitalist development, and as the second the exercise of political sovereignty by the class party of the workers, *i.e.*, social democracy. The dictatorship of the proletariat is, according to Marx, the form of the exercise of this power in the transition period.

But what is the modern proletariat?

If one counts in it all persons without property, all those who have no income from property or from a privileged position, then they certainly form the absolute majority of the population of advanced countries. But this "proletariat" would be a mixture of extraordinarily different elements, of classes which have great differences.

The modern wage-earners are not of the homogeneous mass, devoid in an equal degree of property, family, etc., as the *Communist Manifesto* foresees; that it is just in the most advanced of the manufacturing industries that a whole hierarchy of differentiated workmen are to be found between whose groups only a moderate feeling of solidarity exists.

But even if we assume that this differentiation does not exist in the industrial working classes or that it exercises no effect on the mode of thinking of the workmen concerned, yet the industrial workers are everywhere the minority of the population. In Germany, together with industrial home-workers, some 7,000,000 out of 19,000,000 people earning incomes are industrial wage-earners. We have besides the technical civil service, the shop employees, the agricultural labourers.

Meanwhile, the desire of the industrial working classes for socialistic production is for the most part more a matter of assumption than of certainty.

DEMOCRACY AND SOCIALISM

The trade unions concern themselves with the profit rate in production as the co-operative stores concern themselves with the profit rate on the sale of goods. The fight of the workmen organised in trade unions for the improvement of their standard of life is from the standpoint of the capitalist a fight between wage rate and profit rate.

The trade unions are the democratic element in industry. Their tendency is to destroy the absolutism of capital, and to procure for the worker a direct influence in the management of an industry. [But there are] limits to which the function of a trade union can extend in a democracy, and beyond which it has no place in a democratic community. Independently of whether the state, the community, or capitalists are employers, the trade union as an organisation of all persons occupied in certain trades can only further simultaneously the interests of its members and the general good as long as it is content to remain a partner. Beyond that it would run into danger of degenerating into a close corporation with all the worst qualities of a monopoly. It is the same as with the co-operative society. The trade union, as mistress of a whole branch of production, the ideal of various older socialists, would really be only a monopolist productive association, and as soon as it relied on its monopoly or worked upon it, it would be antagonistic to socialism and democracy, let its inner constitution be what it may. Why it is contrary to socialism needs no further explanation. Associations against the community are as little socialism as is the oligarchic government of the state. But why should such a trade union not be in keeping with the principles of a democracy?

This question necessitates another. What is the principle of democracy?

The answer to this appears very simple. At first one would think it settled by the definition "government by the people." But even a little consideration tells us that by that only quite a superficial, purely formal definition is given, whilst nearly all who use the word democracy to-day understand by it more than a mere form of government. We shall come much nearer to the definition if we express ourselves negatively, and define democracy as an absence of class government, as the indication of a social condition where a political privilege belongs to no one class as opposed to the whole community.

Democracy is in principle the suppression of class government, though it is not yet the actual suppression of classes. In a democracy the parties, and the classes standing behind them, soon learn to know the limits of their power, and to undertake each time only as much as they can reasonably hope to carry through under the existing circumstances. Even if they make their demands rather higher than they seriously mean in order to give way in the unavoidable compromise—and democracy is the high school of compromise—they must still be moderate. The right to vote in a democracy makes its members virtually partners in the community, and this virtual partnership must in the end lead to real partnership. With a working class undeveloped in numbers and culture the general right to vote may long appear as the right to choose "the butcher"; with the growing number and knowledge of the workers it is changed, however, into the implement by which to transform the representatives of the people from masters into real servants of the people.

Universal suffrage in Germany could serve Bismarck temporarily as a tool, but finally it compelled Bismarck to serve it as a tool. In 1878 it could bring Bismarck into a position to forge the weapon of socialistic law, but through it this weapon became blunt and broken, until by the help of it Bismarck was thoroughly beaten.

Is there any sense in maintaining the phrase of the "dictatorship of the proletariat" at a time when in all possible places representatives of social democracy have placed themselves practically in the arena of Parliamentary work, have declared for the proportional representation of the people, and for direct legislation—all of which is inconsistent with a dictatorship.

The phrase is to-day so antiquated that it is only to be reconciled with reality by stripping the word dictatorship of its actual meaning and attaching to it some kind of weakened interpretation. The whole practical activity of social democracy is directed towards creating circumstances and conditions which shall render possible and secure a transition (free from convulsive outbursts) of the modern social order into a higher one.

Social democracy does not wish to break up society and make all its members proletarians together; it labours rather incessantly at raising the worker from the social position of a proletarian to that of a citizen, and thus to make citizenship universal. It does not want to set up a proletarian society instead of a civic society, but a socialist order of society instead of a capitalist one.

Finally, it is to be recommended that some moderation should be kept in the declaration of war against "liberalism." It is true that the great liberal movement of modern times arose for the advantage of the capitalist bourgeoisie first of all, and the parties which assumed the names of liberals were, or became in due course, simple guardians of capitalism. Naturally, only opposition can reign between these parties and social democracy. But with respect to liberalism as a great historical movement, socialism is its legitimate heir, not only in chronological sequence, but also in its spiritual qualities, as is shown moreover in every question of principle in which social democracy has had to take up an attitude.

The aim of all socialist measures, even of those which appear outwardly as coercive measures, is the development and the securing of a free personality. Their more exact examination always shows that the coercion included will raise the sum total of liberty in society, and will give more freedom over a more extended area than it takes away. The legal day of a maximum number of hours' work, for example, is actually a fixing of a minimum of freedom, a prohibition to sell freedom longer than for a certain number of hours daily, and, in principle, therefore, stands on the same ground as the prohibition agreed to by all liberals against selling oneself into personal slavery. It is thus no accident that the first country where a maximum hours' day was carried out was Switzerland, the most democratically progressive country in Europe, and democracy is only the political form of liberalism.

There is actually no really liberal thought which does not also belong to the elements of the ideas of socialism. Even the principle of economic personal responsibility which belongs apparently so entirely to the Manchester School cannot, in my judgment, be denied in theory by socialism nor be made inoperative under any conceivable circumstances.

Liberalism had historically the task of breaking the chains which the fettered economy and the corresponding organisations of law of the middle ages had imposed on the further development of society. That it at first strictly maintained the form of bourgeois liberalism did not stop it from actually expressing a very much wider-reaching general principle of society whose completion will be socialism.

Socialism will create no new bondage of any kind whatever. The individual is to be free, not in the metaphysical sense, as the anarchists dreamed—*i.e.,* free from all duties towards the community—but free from every economic compulsion in his action and choice of a calling. Such freedom is only possible for all by means of organisation. In this sense one might call socialism "organising liberalism," for when one examines more closely the organisations that socialism wants and how it wants them, he will find that what distinguishes them above all from the feudalistic organisations, outwardly like them, is just their liberalism, their democratic constitution, their accessibility.

If democracy is not to excel centralised absolutism in the breeding of bureaucracies, it must be built up on an elaborately organised self-government with a corresponding economic, personal responsibility of all the units of administration as well as of the adult citizens of the state. Nothing is more injurious to its healthy development than enforced uniformity and a too abundant amount of protectionism or subventionism.

To create the organisations described—or, so far as they are already begun, to develop them further—is the indispensable preliminary to what we call socialism of production. Without them the so-called social appropriation of the means of production would only result presumably in reckless devastation of productive forces, insane experimentalising and aimless violence, and the political sovereignty of the working class would, in fact, only be carried out in the form of a dictatorial, revolutionary, central power, supported by the terrorist dictatorship of revolutionary clubs.

It is not my intention to unfold pictures of the future. I am not concerned with what will happen in the more distant future, but with what can and ought to happen in the present, for the present and the nearest future. And so the conclusion of this exposition is the very banal statement that the conquest of the democracy, the formation of political and social organs of the democracy, is the indispensable preliminary condition to the realisation of socialism.

2.7 Fabian and Guild Socialism

Walter S. Buckingham, Jr.

From the earliest times socialist thought has contained two contradictory doctrines regarding the management of public industries. One is the syndicalist principle of workers' control; the other is the principle adopted by the Fabian Society of centralized, expert control in behalf of the entire community. In the years following the formation of the Fabian Society, the conflict between these two doctrines was never resolved and both continued to develop concurrently.

To the Fabians, the state was potentially good and could be used as an instrument for abolishing "unearned" incomes, meaning rents, interest, and certain types of profit. The government could also be used for owning and managing industries, for promoting justice, and for mitigating the existing extremes in economic well-being.

To the Fabians, Parliament represented the will of the majority. It was, therefore, democratic and should be retained, not overthrown. Parliament had simply never before represented the working people. But if enough workers' representatives could be elected, then Parliament would obviously express the workers' wishes. Thus the task to be done was political and educational but not revolutionary.

Another outstanding characteristic of the Fabians was their profound respect for experts. Possibly because the Fabians were for the most part middle- and upper-class intellectuals rather than representatives of the working class they did not hesitate to recommend that economic and other problems be attacked by committees of trained or experienced specialists rather than by delegates or workers. Basically, Sidney and Beatrice Webb (who, more than anyone else, molded Fabian political theory) were planners. Their orderly minds were more revolted by inefficiency than by the loss of personal or political freedom.

The early Fabians made a distinct contribution to socialist economic theory. Rejecting the Marxist theory of distribution, the Fabians, particularly Sidney Webb and Bernard Shaw, preferred to pursue the classical economics of Adam Smith, Stanley Jevons, and John Stuart Mill to a socialist conclusion.

Wealth, declared the Fabians, was social. This was a necessary conclusion because modern industrial organization made it impossible to distinguish the

---

Excerpted from Walter S. Buckingham, Jr., *Theoretical Economic Systems*, pp. 296–311.

contribution made to the final product by each factor of production or each individual person.

The Fabians agreed with Ricardo that rent is a differential payment which accrues to the owners of any land that is more productive than the poorest land in cultivation.

According to the Fabians, this was sufficient in itself to justify nationalization of land and the abolishing of landlords.

This same analysis of land rent can be applied to capital and other resources and factors of production. An admired and respected contemporary of the early Fabians, Alfred Marshall of Cambridge, had introduced the concept of the quasi-rent, meaning the excess income which some resources receive over that amount which they would yield at equilibrium in pure competition. The Fabians went beyond Marshall to argue that all kinds of capital, and even skills and ability, are rewarded by the same differential payments which, like Ricardo's land rent, are based on the price of the product at the "margin of cultivation."

The Fabians proposed to tax away these bonuses where they could be found but to permit, for incentive purposes, income differentials based on productivity. Fabian distribution theory would collect surplus for society as a whole. The state, which owned the wealth, would use the surplus, or rent, to provide social services such as education, medical care, and insurance or else to provide certain basic goods free of charge.

The early Fabians were also concerned with the problem of economic power and its effect on the distribution of income and wealth.

Private property was condemned because it led to private monopoly which held prices unreasonably high, restricted production, caused great extremes in economic well-being, and led to recurring and perhaps permanent unemployment. The state was always envisaged as preventing these unhappy consequences by playing an ever larger role along the lines of (1) regulation of industry, (2) municipal ownership and administration of industry, and (3) taxation of rent and interest.

The Fabians' penetrating analyses of private power always led to restriction or abolition of private property and a corresponding expansion of the role of the government. Unfortunately the Fabians' rather naïve faith in democratic institutions blinded them to the fact that government ownership and regulation does not abolish power but merely transfers it to the state. In a mature, democratic society, power may be safer in the government than in private hands, but it certainly continues to exist and to pose serious problems of control or dispersal.

The Fabians did not reject the Marxian doctrine of the inevitability of socialism, but they supplemented it with a belief in gradualism. Socialism could be "helped along." They promoted all kinds of progressive legislation such as inheritance taxes, social security, income taxes, labor legislation, and the like on the theory that a step toward democracy must be a step toward socialism and vice versa.

As soon as it was organized, the Fabian Society recognized a trend toward municipal ownership of utilities which existed in the 1880's. Until this time, direct municipal operation of industrial enterprises and even local services had been very limited.

During the 1870's, however, several English cities discovered that there were numerous advantages to be gained through municipal ownership of gas and water companies.

Quickly seeing the possibilities of promoting public ownership on this basis, the Fabians began such a vigorous campaign to extend municipal industries that for many years they were referred to as "gas and water socialists." In addition to ordinary utilities, municipal ownership and operation was advocated for such diverse undertakings as pawnshops, hospitals, steamboats, bakeries, and fire insurance underwriting. The general socialist feeling at the turn of the century was that public ownership of enterprise in a socialist state would be predominantly municipal in form.

The early Fabian theory of the transition to socialism involved the transfer of private industry to public ownership through bankruptcy, forced sale to municipal governments, or threat of municipal competition. Increased labor union organization and political agitation by labor and socialist groups would lead to increased political awareness and activity by working people. This, together with the gradual extension of the franchise to propertyless classes and women would lead to a demand for economic security and social guarantees provided by the state. These measures would be expensive and could only be financed through higher taxes on income, property, and inheritance. These taxes would not only be necessary but would be demanded by the working class in order to ameliorate the existing extremes in income. Thus rent, interest, and profits would be confiscated by the state. This transfer of unearned income would not occur in a lump sum but gradually by installments.

This process would be cumulative. As the public sector of the economy grew, the private sector would find it harder to compete. Wages would be higher in the public sector (due to governmental policy), and private firms would consequently have to raise wages in order to get labor. This would bring further downward pressure on profit margins, which were already squeezed by taxation, and would lead to a demand on the landlords for lower rents. The city, which was taxing rental income, would experience a decrease in revenue as rents fell and would then raise the tax rate. The landlord class, squeezed from both sides, would gradually disappear. The business capitalists would be disappearing at the same time through the process of municipalization.

The faith in parliamentary methods and the perhaps exaggerated belief in the benevolent state held by most of the early Fabians was not shared by all socialists at that time. A different or special kind of socialism, based in part on syndicalism, arose and became known as guild socialism or guildism. The leading economists who were exponents of guildism, such as J. A. Hobson, R. H. Tawney, and G. D. H. Cole, looked toward quite a different form of industrial organization than most of the Fabians envisaged. While the Fabians relied on the worker as a citizen who could create and maintain a democratic state, the guild socialists tended to rely on the worker as an economic producer who would offest state power. However, some of the strongest exponents of guildism were also Fabians themselves, and all were deeply influenced by the environment of British politics; so guildism resembled the reasonable, nonrevolutionary Fabian reformism more than the revolutionary anarchy of continental syndicalism.

Relatively mild as it appeared, however, guildism contained two germinal ideas which closely resembled continental syndicalism. One of these was a conviction that workers' interests could be properly represented in Parliament only by workers' delegates themselves. The second was a conviction that *direct* control over production by the workers, in addition to public ownership, was a necessary requisite of a democratic socialist state.

The first conviction was formulated by G. D. H. Cole, who developed a pluralistic basis for the socialist state. To Cole, the individual was a consumer, a producer, and a citizen as well as a worker; since he belonged to several interest groups, he could hardly be properly represented by one geographically elected delegate. To Cole, true democratic representation had to be functional. Man could only realize expression of his highest aspirations if he took part in both political and industrial management functions himself. Several representatives, one for each of his several interests, would be necessary, and this would involve a reorganization of both Parliament and the electoral system on a functional basis.

The other belief, that of direct workers' control over production, was based on a traditional conception, which had been expressed by Robert Owen and John Stuart Mill, of the worker as a self-governing craftsman. To the guildists, socialism could not satisfy the desires of workers by merely transferring property titles to the state. This would only substitute bureaucrats for capitalists, and workers would still have no control over their working conditions. There could be no such thing as harmonious labor-management relations in either private or public enterprise. The mere existence of any kind of management made labor-management strife inevitable. Labor would have to assume positive control over the operation of the industrial enterprise and eliminate management as a function separate from labor.

Guild socialism was thus highly idealistic. Its challenge to orthodox socialism was based on the idea that power and responsibility should be widely dispersed among working people, not centralized in a state bureaucracy. Freedom had to be based on free organization at every level of economic life in order to be real.

Ownership was to be vested in the state, but administration was to be on a federation principle of workers controlling through their guilds. These firms and industries would then be operated "as a trust" for the public.

Thus economic control by labor was to be secured independently of political control of the government although there was hope for eventual control of political institutions as well. The movement for control and eventual ownership by the workers would be more rapid in such industries as the building trades where the smaller amount of capital involved would strengthen labor's bargaining position.

Guild socialism thus advocated a different kind of "socialization." In industries such as building construction, expropriation would be unnecessary since workers could force private enterprise out of business by bargaining pressure or competition. For industries such as coal mining, guildists demanded nationalization by the state just like other socialists. Ownership was to be vested in the state, but control and administration were to be by the workers through their guilds.

To quote Cole:

> *The real aim . . . must be not merely the expropriation of the capitalist, but the supercession of his economic functions and his replacement by the workers in every sphere of his economic and social power. For it is by this capture and assumption of social and economic functions that the workers will alone make possible an equitable distribution of the national income and a reasonable reorganization of Society as a whole.*

In the economy envisaged by the guild socialists, each producing firm would be owned and managed by a guild of workers. Industries would be organized into guilds representative of the firms, and, finally, all would be organized into a national producers' guild. Even the professions and civil services like health and education would be similarly organized. Individuals in their consumer interests would be organized into a system of guilds not unlike the existing consumer cooperatives although producers' and workers' interests were assumed to be more important and would have preferences over consumers' interests.

Replacing the market system as a means of allocating materials would be bargaining between guilds. The traditional functions of government would be performed by local, regional, and national "communes" which would represent the people in their various capacities, members being elected by producers, consumers, civil service guilds, and the like. For example, the guild which distributes a commodity would base its selling price on the price it paid to the manufacturing guild plus its own costs of distribution. It would submit this price to the cooperative society representing the consumers. If the price were not accepted or if the two could not agree on a price, the question would go to the local, regional, or national commune (depending on the type of market involved) which would act as arbitrator. If it were decided, for social reasons, to sell a particular commodity at either more or less than its cost of production, then the commune again would determine the allocation of the resulting surplus or loss.

Guildism was charged with emotion; yet it had to include a strong faith in human abilities to assume that striking workmen could take over and operate a complicated business. Some guildists argued that the state should continue to exist as an organ of democratic action for the nation. Others envisaged the state's replacement by a sort of federal structure representing functional organizations of producers, consumers, civic interests, and cultural interests.

AMERICAN RADICALISM: THORSTEIN VEBLEN

Neither Marxism nor socialism has played as direct a role in American politics or political economics as in European. In part, this is probably explained by special circumstances and characteristics of the American experience: relatively greater upward economic mobility and lesser inequality; abundant natural resources; a greater ratio of land to labor; the "safety valve" of a large and open frontier; the existence of a large internal market unfettered by barriers to trade and exchange; the relative absence of a feudal past or a rigid class structure. In part, it probably reflects the relative failure of American Marxists and socialists to adapt their European heritage of radical criticism to American conditions.[2]

The ranks of the political economists in the United States, however, have included homegrown radicals—less sweeping in their indictment of capitalism and less intense in their identification of a class struggle between workers and capitalists than was Marx, and less committed to traditional socialist measures such as nationalization of enterprise, but at least equally sharp in their diagnoses of social and economic ills and equally willing to contemplate or propose reforms in the institutional structure of the economic system.

The heyday of laissez-faire conservatism and Social Darwinism in the latter decades of the nineteenth century was not without dissenting voices, but the reform movement in the United States reached a peak in the "progressive era" of roughly two decades just before World War I. It was during this era—which witnessed the passage of the Interstate Commerce Commission Act of 1887 (regulating railroads); the Sherman (1890), Clayton (1914), and Federal Trade Commission (1914) Acts (to control monopoly); and the Pure Food and Drug Act (1906)—that one dimension of the classical liberal creed (laissez-faire) was progressively abandoned for the sake of another (effective competition). And it was during this era also that the concept of pluralist democracy—partly through private action (for example, early efforts at collective bargaining) and partly through proposals and programs for more effective government regulation of the economy in the interests of farmers, workers, consumers, and small businessmen—seriously challenged the assumption of corporate monism so prominent in laissez-faire conservatism. In short, it was an era in which liberalism shifted from the essentially conservative function of defense of the existing social order to regain, in a broader setting, the critical and reformist spirit of the classical liberalism of the late eighteenth–early nineteenth centuries.

It is interesting that mainstream economists, typically, were not deeply involved in the dissent and critique of the progressive era. During these years, American economists, in the orthodox, neoclassical tradition, generally focused upon improvements in the tools of economic analysis, notably refinements in the theory of competitive markets and the allocation of resources.

[2] See, for example, Daniel Bell, *Marxian Socialism in the United States*. Princeton, N.J.: Princeton University Press, 1967.

Probably the most prominent and certainly the most eccentric and iconoclastic economist in the dissenting tradition during this period was Thorstein Veblen, born in the Midwest, of Norwegian stock. Throughout his colorful career, beginning with *The Theory of the Leisure Class* (1899), Veblen developed a vision of capitalist development trenchant in its criticism and sweeping in its scope, and an alternative to both economic orthodoxy and Marxism-socialism.

The major theme in Veblen's various works, as in Marx's analysis, was conflict. Even more than Marx, Veblen identified technological change as the underlying cause of the evolutionary change in economic institutions, and perceived attitudes and theories as parts of a surrounding superstructure that tends to lag behind the changing pace of technological and economic developments. But in contrast to Marx, Veblen did not perceive the dominant conflict in modern industrial society to be that between workers and capitalists. In Veblen's interpretation, workers tend to be a bit awed by, and in any event to emulate, those with greater wealth and higher incomes. And the economic functions and positions of Marx's capitalist industrialists are divided in Veblen's analysis between two opposing groups: first, the "captains of finance," together with "absentee owners" and financial executives (for example, accountants and salesmen), whose major concerns are maximizing profit through control of markets and various forms of financial manipulation; and second, the "engineers," for example, production experts and technological specialists, whose primary concern is production and whose values are efficiency and workmanship.

Conflict between these two groups, as described in selection 2.8, could eventually result in a revolutionary takeover of the industrial system by the technicians *if* they recognize their potential power, based on their indispensability. (Another Veblenian alternative: a mésalliance between the captains of finance, the state, and the military in defense of the "vested interests"—a sort of fascistic military-industrial complex.) Characteristically, Veblen stopped short of definitive predictions, contenting himself with critique, satire, and identification of radical alternatives—unsettling to conventional patterns of thought as well as to the existing power structure.

2.8 The Engineers and the Price System

Thorstein Veblen

The Captains of Finance and the Engineers

In more than one respect the industrial system of today is notably different from anything that has gone before. It is eminently a system, self-balanced and com-

Excerpted from *The Engineers and the Price System*.

prehensive; and it is a system of interlocking mechanical processes, rather than of skillful manipulation. It is mechanical rather than manual. It is an organization of mechanical powers and material resources, rather than of skilled craftsmen and tools; although the skilled workmen and tools are also an indispensable part of its comprehensive mechanism. It is of an impersonal nature, after the fashion of the material sciences, on which it constantly draws. It runs to "quantity production" of specialized and standardized goods and services. For all these reasons it lends itself to systematic control under the direction of industrial experts, skilled technologists, who may be called "production engineers," for want of a better term.

This industrial system runs on as an inclusive organization of many and diverse interlocking mechanical processes, interdependent and balanced among themselves in such a way that the due working of any part of it is conditioned on the due working of all the rest. Therefore it will work at its best only on condition that these industrial experts, production engineers, will work together on a common understanding; and more particularly on condition that they must not work at cross purposes. These technological specialists whose constant supervision is indispensable to the due working of the industrial system constitute the general staff of industry, whose work it is to control the strategy of production at large and to keep an oversight of the tactics of production in detail.

It is essential that that corps of technological specialists who by training, insight, and interest make up the general staff of industry must have a free hand in the disposal of available resources, in materials, equipment, and man power, regardless of any national pretensions or any vested interests. Any degree of obstruction, diversion, or withholding of any of the available industrial forces, with a view to the special gain of any nation or any investor, unavoidably brings on a dislocation of the system; which involves a disproportionate lowering of its working efficiency and therefore a disproportionate loss to the whole, and therefore a net loss to all its parts.

And all the while the statesmen are at work to divert and obstruct the working forces of this industrial system, here and there, for the special advantage of one nation and another at the cost of the rest; and the captains of finance are working, at cross purposes and in collusion, to divert whatever they can to the special gain of one vested interest and another, at any cost to the rest. So it happens that the industrial system is deliberately handicapped with dissension, misdirection, and unemployment of material resources, equipment, and man power, at every turn where the statesmen or the captains of finance can touch its mechanism; and all the civilized peoples are suffering privation together because their general staff of industrial experts are in this way required to take orders and submit to sabotage at the hands of the statesmen and the vested interests. Politics and investment are still allowed to decide matters of industrial policy which should plainly be left to the discretion of the general staff of production engineers driven by no commercial bias.

In effect, the progressive advance of this industrial system towards an all-inclusive mechanical balance of interlocking processes appears to be approaching a critical pass, beyond which it will no longer be practicable to leave its control in the hands of business men working at cross purposes for private gain, or to entrust its continued administration to others than suitably trained technological experts, production engineers without a commercial interest. What these men may then do with it all is not so plain; the best they can do may not be good enough; but the negative proposition is becoming sufficiently plain, that this mechanical state of the industrial arts will not long tolerate the continued control of production by the vested interests under the current businesslike rule of incapacity by advisement.

From an early point in development there set in a progressive differentiation, such as to divide those who designed and administered the industrial processes from those others who designed and managed the commercial transactions and took care of the financial end. So there also set in a corresponding division of powers between the business management and the technological experts. It became the work of the technologist to determine, on technological grounds, what could be done in the way of productive industry, and to contrive ways and means of doing it; but the business management always continued to decide, on commercial grounds, how much work should be done and what kind and quality of goods and services should be produced; and the decision of the business management has always continued to be final, and has always set the limit beyond which production must not go.

With the continued growth of specialization the experts have necessarily had more and more to say in the affairs of industry; but always their findings as to what work is to be done and what ways and means are to be employed in production have had to wait on the findings of the business managers as to what will be expedient for the purpose of commercial gain.

The result has been, uniformly and as a matter of course, that the production of goods and services has advisedly been stopped short of productive capacity, by curtailment of output and by derangement of the productive system. There are two main reasons for this, and both have operated together throughout the machine era to stop industrial production increasingly short of productive capacity. (a) The commercial need of maintaining a profitable price has led to an increasingly imperative curtailment of the output, as fast as the advance of the industrial arts has enhanced the productive capacity. And (b) the continued advance of the mechanical technology has called for an ever-increasing volume and diversity of special knowledge, and so has left the businesslike captains of finance continually farther in arrears, so that they have been less and less capable of comprehending what is required in the ordinary way of industrial equipment and personnel.

Hitherto these men who so make up the general staff of the industrial system have not drawn together into anything like a self-directing working force; nor have they been vested with anything more than an occasional, haphazard, and tentative control of some disjointed sector of the industrial equipment, with no direct or decisive relation to that personnel of productive industry that may be called the officers of the line and the rank and file. It is still the unbroken privilege of the financial management and its financial agents to "hire and fire." The final disposition of all the industrial forces still remains in the hands of the business men, who still continue to dispose of these forces for other than industrial ends. And all the while it is an open secret that with a reasonably free hand the production experts would today readily increase the ordinary output of industry by several fold,—variously estimated at some 300 per cent to 1200 per cent of the current output. And what stands in the way of so increasing the ordinary output of goods and services is business as usual.

Right lately these technologists have begun to become uneasily "class-conscious" and to reflect that they together constitute the indispensable General Staff of the industrial system. Their class consciousness has taken the immediate form of a growing sense of waste and confusion in the management of industry by the financial agents of the absentee owners. They are beginning to take stock of that all-pervading mismanagement of industry that is inseparable from its control for commercial ends. All of which brings home a realization of their own shame and of damage to the common good. So the engineers are beginning to draw together and ask themselves, "What about it?"

It would be hazardous to surmise how, how soon, on what provocation, and with what effect the guild of engineers are due to realize that they constitute a guild, and that the material fortunes of the civilized peoples already lie loose in their hands. But it is already sufficiently plain that the industrial conditions and the drift of conviction among the engineers are drawing together to some such end.

They are becoming class-conscious, and they are no longer driven by a commercial interest, in any such degree as will make them a vested interest in that commercial sense in which the syndicated owners and the federated workmen are vested interests. They are, at the same time, numerically and by habitual outlook, no such heterogeneous and unwieldy body as the federated workmen, whose numbers and scattering interest has left all their endeavors substantially nugatory. In short, the engineers are in a position to make the next move.

By comparison with the population at large, including the financial powers and the kept classes, the technological specialists which come in question here are a very inconsiderable number; yet this small number is indispensable to the continued working of the productive industries. And there is the patent fact that such a thing as a general strike of the technological specialists in industry need involve no more than a minute fraction of one per cent of the population; yet it would swiftly bring a collapse of the old order and sweep the timeworn fabric of finance and absentee sabotage into the discard for good and all. The industrial dictatorship of the captain of finance is now held on sufferance of the engineers and is liable at any time to be discontinued at their discretion, as a matter of convenience.

On The Danger of a Revolutionary Overturn

It has been argued, and it seems not unreasonable to believe, that the established order of business enterprise, vested rights, and commercialized nationalism, is due presently to go under in a muddle of shame and confusion, because it is no longer a practicable system of industrial management under the conditions created by the later state of the industrial arts. Twentieth-century technology has outgrown the eighteenth-century system of vested rights. The experience of the past few years teaches that the usual management of industry by business methods has become highly inefficient and wasteful, and the indications are many and obvious that any businesslike control of production and distribution is bound to run more and more consistently at cross purposes with the community's livelihood, the farther the industrial arts advance and the wider the industrial system extends. So that it is perhaps not reasonably to be questioned that Vested Interests in business are riding for a fall. But the end is not yet; although it is to be admitted, regretfully perhaps, that with every further advance in technological knowledge and practice and with every further increase in the volume and complexity of the industrial system, any businesslike control is bound to grow still more incompetent, irrelevant, and impertinent.

The established order of business rests on absentee ownership and is managed with an eye single to the largest obtainable net return in terms of price. The underlying population is dependent on the working of this industrial system for its livelihood; and their material interest therefore centers in the output and distribution of consumable goods, not in an increasing volume of earnings for the absentee owners. Hence there is a division of interest between the business community, who do business for the absentee owners, and the underlying population, who work for a living; and in the nature of the case this division of interest between the absentee owners and the underlying population is growing wider and more evident from day to day; which engenders a certain division of sentiment and a degree of mutual distrust. With it all the underlying population are still in a sufficiently deferential frame of mind toward their absentee owners, and are quite conscientiously delicate about any abatement of the free income which their owners come in for, according to the rules of the game as it is played.

The business concerns which so have the management of industry on this plan of absentee ownership are capitalized on their business capacity, not on their industrial capacity; that is to say, they are capitalized on their capacity to produce earnings, not on their capacity to produce goods. Their capitalization has, in effect, been calculated and fixed on the highest ordinary rate of earnings previously obtained; and on pain of insolvency their businesslike managers are now required to meet fixed income-charges on this capitalization. Therefore, as a proposition of safe and sane business management, prices have to be maintained or advanced.

From this businesslike requirement of meeting these fixed overhead charges on the capitalization there result certain customary lines of waste and obstruction, which are unavoidable so long as industry is managed by businesslike methods and for businesslike ends. These ordinary lines of waste and obstruction are necessarily (and blamelessly) included in the businesslike conduct of production. They may for convenience be classed under four heads: (a) Unemployment of material resources, equipment and manpower, in whole or in part, deliberately or through ignorance; (b) Salesmanship (includes, e.g., needless multiplication of merchants and shops, wholesale and retail, newspaper advertising and bill-boards, sales-exhibits, sales-agents, fancy packages and labels, adulteration, multiplication of brands and proprietary articles); (c) Production (and sales-cost) of superfluities and spurious goods; (d) Systematic dislocation, sabotage and duplication, due in part to businesslike strategy, in part to businesslike ignorance of industrial requirements (includes, e.g., such things as cross-freights, monopolization of resources, withholding of facilities and information from business rivals whom it is thought wise to hinder or defeat). There is, of course, no blame, and no sense of blame or shame attaching to all this everyday waste and confusion that goes to make up the workday total of businesslike management. All of it is a legitimate and necessary part of the established order of business enterprise, within the law and within the ethics of the trade.

Salesmanship is the most conspicuous, and perhaps the gravest, of these wasteful and industrially futile practices that are involved in the businesslike conduct of industry; it bulks large both in its immediate cost and in its meretricious consequences.

It is doubtless within the mark to say that, at an average, one-half the price paid for goods and services by consumers is to be set down to the account of salesmanship—that is, to sales-cost and to the net gains of salesmanship. But in many notable lines of merchandise the sales-cost will ordinarily foot up to some ten or twenty times the production-cost proper, and to not less than one hundred times the necessary cost of distribution.

It is reasonable to believe that this state of things, which has been coming on gradually for some time past, will in time come to be understood and appreciated by the underlying population, at least in some degree. And it is likewise reasonable to believe that so soon as the underlying population come to realize that all this wasteful traffic of salesmanship is using up their productive forces, with nothing better to show for it than an increased cost of living, they will be driven to make some move to abate the nuisance. And just so far as this state of things is now beginning to be understood, its logical outcome is a growing distrust of the business men and all their works and words. But the underlying population is still very credulous about anything that is said or done in the name of Business, and there need be no apprehension of a mutinous outbreak, just yet.

Closely related to the wasteful practices of salesmanship as commonly understood, if it should not rather be counted in as an extension of salesmanship, is that persistent unemployment of men, equipment, and material resources, by which the output of goods and services is kept down to the "requirements of the market," with a view to maintaining prices at a "reasonably profitable level." Such unemployment, deliberate and habitual, is one of the ordinary expedients employed in the businesslike management of industry.

All this is well known to the Guardians of the Vested Interests, and their knowledge of it is, quite reasonably, a source of uneasiness to them. But they see no help for it; and indeed there is no help for it within the framework of "business as usual," since it is the essence of business as usual. So also, the

Guardians are aware that this businesslike sabotage on productive industry is a fruitful source of discontent and distrust among the underlying population who suffer the inconvenience of it all; and they are beset with the abiding fear that the underlying population may shortly be provoked into disallowing those Vested Interests for whose benefit this deliberate and habitual sabotage on production is carried on.

If the country's productive industry were competently organized as a systematic whole, and were then managed by competent technicians with an eye single to maximum production of goods and services; instead of, as now, being manhandled by ignorant business men with an eye single to maximum profits; the resulting output of goods and services would doubtless exceed the current output by several hundred per cent. But then, none of all that is necessary to save the established order of things. All that is required is a decent modicum of efficiency, very far short of the theoretical maximum production.

There is, of course, the chance, and it is by no means a remote chance, that the rapidly increasing volume and complexity of the industrial system may presently bring the country's industry into such a ticklish state of unstable equilibrium that even a reasonable modicum of willful derangement can no longer be tolerated, even for the most urgent and most legitimate reasons of businesslike strategy and vested rights. In time, such an outcome is presumably due to be looked for. There is, indeed, no lack of evidence that the advanced industrial countries are approaching such a state of things, America among the rest.

How soon the limit of tolerance for willful derangement is due to be reached, would be a hazardous topic of speculation.

Those gifted, trained, and experienced technicians who now are in possession of the requisite technological information and experience are the first and instantly indispensable factor in the everyday work of carrying on the country's productive industry. They now constitute the General Staff of the industrial system.

Therefore any question of a revolutionary overturn, in America or in any other of the advanced industrial countries, resolves itself in practical fact into a question of what the guild of technicians will do. In effect it is a question whether the discretion and responsibility in the management of the country's industry shall pass from the financiers, who speak for the Vested Interests, to the technicians, who speak for the industrial system as a going concern. There is no third party qualified to make a colorable bid, or able to make good its pretensions if it should make a bid.

The chances of anything like a Soviet in America, therefore, are the chances of a Soviet of technicians. And, to the due comfort of the Guardians of the Vested Interests and the good citizens who make up their background, it can be shown that anything like a Soviet of Technicians is at the most a remote contingency in America.

The vested rights of absentee ownership are still embedded in the sentiments of the underlying population; and the assertion is still quite safe that anything like a Soviet of Technicians is not a present menace to the Vested Interests in America.

By settled habit the technicians, the engineers and industrial experts, are a harmless and docile sort, well fed on the whole, and somewhat placidly content with the "full dinner-pail" which the lieutenants of the Vested Interests habitually allow them. It is true, they constitute the indispensable General Staff of that industrial system which feeds the Vested Interests; but hitherto at least, they have had nothing to say in the planning and direction of this industrial system, except as employees in the pay of the financiers.

The technicians are a "safe and sane" lot, on the whole; and they are pretty well commercialized, particularly the older generation, who speak with authority and conviction, and to whom the younger generation of engineers defer, on the whole, with such a degree of filial piety as should go far to reassure all good citizens. And herein lies the present security of the Vested Interests; for the whole-hearted co-operation of the technicians would be as indispensable to any effectual movement of overturn as their unwavering service in the employ of the Vested Interests is indispensable to the maintenance of the established order.

3 KEYNES AND THE POST-KEYNESIAN SYNTHESIS

KEYNES AND THE POST-KEYNESIAN SYNTHESIS

For more than a quarter of a century, thinking about economic issues and policies in the United States has been dominated by a blend of the macroeconomic analysis of the late English economist John Maynard Keynes and his followers and the microeconomic analysis found in the central tradition of economic thought from Adam Smith through English neoclassical economist Alfred Marshall and his followers. This blend may be appropriately described as either a "grand neo-classical synthesis," as suggested by Paul Samuelson,[1] or as a "post-Keynesian synthesis," as suggested by Daniel Fusfeld.

Keynes himself anticipated the "post-Keynesian synthesis" in his seminal work, *The General Theory of Employment, Interest and Money,* published (in 1936) during the depression of the thirties. Steeped in the traditions of academic orthodoxy as a student of the great British neoclassicist Alfred Marshall, Keynes essentially accepted the neoclassical analysis of how the competitive price system in a market capitalist economy allocates resources under full employment conditions. "If," he emphasized, "nations can learn to provide themselves with full employment by their domestic policy," then a framework will have been created "which allows the classical medicine to do its work" and in which "the wisdom of Adam Smith" can be implemented.[2]

While essentially accepting neoclassical microeconomics, Keynes sharply dissented from orthodox views concerning macroeconomics, notably the idea that through reliance upon flexible prices in labor, goods, and money markets, the economy normally tends toward stable equilibrium at full employment. The core of Keynes' critique of laissez-faire capitalism (and here he agreed with Marx) was that left to its own devices, a competitive market capitalist economy does not automatically function so as to sustain full-employment utilization of resources. Indeed, Keynes argued, unemployment and depression is the usual rule, full employment and prosperity the special case. From this critique, Keynes derived a provocative and influential policy conclusion. Governments,

[1] Paul A. Samuelson, *Economics,* 7th ed. (N.Y.: McGraw-Hill, 1967), p. 351.

[2] John M. Keynes, "The Balance of Payments of the United States," *Economic Journal,* June 1946, p. 186.

through control over spending, taxing, and the money supply, should guide the macroeconomic affairs of industrialized capitalist economies toward full employment.

In short, macroeconomic policies were perceived by Keynes as complementary to private enterprise and market price systems, their function being to provide a monetary and fiscal framework within which the market economy can allocate resources and distribute income efficaciously. Indeed, if we grant, with Keynes, the view that market capitalism is not automatically self-regulating at full employment, and if we grant also that contemporary societies will not tolerate depression and unemployment, the real alternative to Keynesian-style capitalism is not laissez-faire but a more radical reconstruction of the economic order (for example, socialism, fascism, communism). Keynesian monetary and fiscal policies then can be regarded as an effort to sustain and "save" a moderately reformed capitalism.

In selection 3.1, Fusfeld describes cogently the major dimensions of the post-Keynesian synthesis. Selection 3.2 shows clearly the deep extent to which the roots of the synthesis may be found in the writings of Keynes.

3.1 Post-Post-Keynes: The Shattered Synthesis

Daniel R. Fusfeld

Events of the past five years have shattered a synthesis of economic theory and policy that has dominated thinking about economic issues in the United States for a quarter of a century. This synthesis, referred to by many economists as "post-Keynesian," was based on the national-scale macroeconomics of John Maynard Keynes together with the revived, closeup microeconomics of Alfred Marshall and his followers. The systems of these two great economists were unified in a framework of theory and policy, the principal professional exponent of which has been Paul Samuelson of MIT. The theoretical elements were taught to two generations of college students in Samuelson's great introductory economics text, titled simply and conclusively *Economics,* and by its many imitators. The policy principles were developed through a series of national administrations and expressed in the annual reports of the President's Council of Economic Advisers.

And for years it all seemed to be working. The synthesis appeared to provide an efficient analytical framework for understanding and running modern, industrial economies. Policies derived from Keynesian theory seemed capable of sustaining high levels of employment and high rates of economic growth. Marshallian neoclassical economics seemed to explain adequately enough how resources were allocated and incomes distributed in a private, market-oriented economy. In crude terms, producers were seen as responding to consumer demand to turn out the products and services that maximize consumer welfare. Rewards were proportionate to an individual's contribution to production. Economic growth was ensured by the savings and enterprise of a success-oriented private-enterprise economy.

Much of the system rested on the assumption that competition would prevail and concentrated economic power could not control markets for its own benefit. To ensure competition and prevent monopolies from building up, the post-Keynesian synthesis required strong antitrust legislation, and where "natural" monopolies existed, such as in utilities or railroads, vigorous regulation by government agencies was prescribed. But such government intervention in the economic system, it was felt, could be limited. In fact, a number of studies in the 1950s seemed to show that the extent of monopoly was not increasing and that competitive pressures tended to erode monopolistic positions.

The primary role of government was to ensure full employment and growth by the proper mix of spending, taxation, and monetary policy. Although economic problems of a variety of sorts were found, they could largely be resolved as long as full employment and growth were sustained. Even poverty might be ended by a growing economy, for it would bring higher material standards of living and spread them to the poor. The rich might get richer, but the poor would get richer too. The paradigm sketched by the post-Keynesian synthesis was of a benign social order that would move mankind toward a better and more stable future.

Economic growth played a crucial role in the post-Keynesian synthesis, which postulated a smooth expansion of output through increases in productivity financed by savings. Imbalances and discontinuities in the inner workings of the economic machinery are foreclosed by substitution of one factor of production for another; for example, relatively abundant machinery would fill in for labor when manpower became scarce. Short-run imbalances may occur, according to this theory, but they will be overcome in the long run by the flexibility of the private-enterprise economy and its ability to adjust to changing circumstances.

The underlying political implications of this theory of economic growth should be obvious. The theory was developed at a time when planning was being used in the Soviet Union to achieve high rates of economic growth. Indeed, during the early and mid-1960s, when U.S. growth speeded up and Soviet growth slowed down, the U.S. growth rate at its *peak* reached only as high as the Soviet growth rate at its *trough*. Planning was also being used in many underdeveloped countries that were moving toward a variety of socialist types of development programs. Yet the leading Western economists were saying that the traditional forces of the free market in a private-enterprise economy would generate the optimal growth path.

Furthermore, they said, economic growth could provide the resources for a series of domestic reforms and improvements: ending poverty, expanding opportunity, solving urban problems, building houses and highways, even shooting at the moon, although that was mostly a Cold War enterprise. All this could be done, mind you, without rocking the boat by redistributing income or breaking up the great industrial and financial centers of power. The structure of wealth and power would remain untouched.

Economic growth could also provide the resources for aid to the Third World. Aid programs would help keep those nations on our side in the Cold War. Aid would help them take off into sustained economic growth, making their economies more like ours, eventually allowing the aid programs themselves to taper off and end—according to the scenario sketched by W. W. Rostow in his *Stages of Economic Growth,* which was appropriately subtitled "An Anti-Communist Manifesto."

Finally, the post-Keynesian synthesis played a part in the ideological foundations of American foreign policy. Containment of communism and the strategy of the Cold War were based on the belief that communism contained the seeds of its own downfall. Tensions and conflicts within the Soviet Union and the Communist bloc were expected to weaken and perhaps destroy communism as a threat to the free world and its predominantly capitalistic economy. Meanwhile, private enterprise in the managed Western economies would move strongly ahead toward continually higher living standards, economic strength, and material resources. Containment would prevent war, while economic growth would lead the West to superiority and victory.

3.2 Keynes and the Post-Keynesian Synthesis

John M. Keynes

Concluding Notes on the Social Philosophy towards which the General Theory Might Lead

The outstanding faults of the economic society in which we live are its failure to provide for full employment and its arbitrary and inequitable distribution of wealth and incomes.

Up to the point where full employment prevails, the growth of capital depends not at all on a low propensity to consume but is, on the contrary, held back by it; and only in conditions of full employment is a low propensity to consume conducive to the growth of capital. Moreover, experience suggests that in existing conditions saving by institutions and through sinking funds is

Excerpted from *The General Theory of Employment, Interest, and Money* by John Maynard Keynes. Reprinted by permission of Harcourt Brace Jovanovich, Inc., The Royal Economic Society, and Macmillan, London and Basingstoke.

more than adequate, and that measures for the redistribution of incomes in a way likely to raise the propensity to consume may prove positively favourable to the growth of capital.

Thus our argument leads towards the conclusion that in contemporary conditions the growth of wealth, so far from being dependent on the abstinence of the rich, as is commonly supposed, is more likely to be impeded by it. One of the chief social justifications of great inequality of wealth is, therefore, removed. I am not saying that there are no other reasons, unaffected by our theory, capable of justifying some measure of inequality in some circumstances. But it does dispose of the most important of the reasons why hitherto we have thought it prudent to move carefully.

For my own part, I believe that there is social and psychological justification for significant inequalities of incomes and wealth, but not for such large disparities as exist to-day. There are valuable human activities which require the motive of money-making and the environment of private wealth-ownership for their full fruition. Moreover, dangerous human proclivities can be canalised into comparatively harmless channels by the existence of opportunities for money-making and private wealth, which, if they cannot be satisfied in this way, may find their outlet in cruelty, the reckless pursuit of personal power and authority, and other forms of self-aggrandisement. It is better that a man should tyrannise over his bank balance than over his fellow-citizens; and whilst the former is sometimes denounced as being but a means to the latter, sometimes at least it is an alternative. But it is not necessary for the stimulation of these activities and the satisfaction of these proclivities that the game should be played for such high stakes as at present. Much lower stakes will serve the purpose equally well, as soon as the players are accustomed to them.

There is, however, a second, much more fundamental inference from our argument which has a bearing on the future of inequalities of wealth; namely, our theory of the rate of interest. The justification for a moderately high rate of interest has been found hitherto in the necessity of providing a sufficient inducement to save. But we have shown that the extent of effective saving is necessarily determined by the scale of investment and that the scale of investment is promoted by a *low* rate of interest, provided that we do not attempt to stimulate it in this way beyond the point which corresponds to full employment. Thus it is to our best advantage to reduce the rate of interest to that point relatively to the schedule of the marginal efficiency of capital at which there is full employment.

There can be no doubt that this criterion will lead to a much lower rate of interest than has ruled hitherto; and, so far as one can guess at the schedules of the marginal efficiency of capital corresponding to increasing amounts of capital, the rate of interest is likely to fall steadily, if it should be practicable to maintain conditions of more or less continuous full employment—unless, indeed, there is an excessive change in the aggregate propensity to consume (including the State).

I feel sure that the demand for capital is strictly limited in the sense that it would not be difficult to increase the stock of capital up to a point where its marginal efficiency had fallen to a very low figure. This would not mean that the use of capital instruments would cost almost nothing, but only that the return from them would have to cover little more than their exhaustion by wastage and obsolescence together with some margin to cover risk and the exercise of skill and judgment. In short, the aggregate return from durable goods in the course of their life would, as in the case of short-lived goods, just cover their labour-costs of production *plus* an allowance for risk and the costs of skill and supervision.

Now, though this state of affairs would be quite compatible with some measure of individualism, yet it would mean the euthanasia of the rentier, and, consequently, the euthanasia of the cumulative oppressive power of the capitalist to exploit the scarcity-value of capital. Interest to-day rewards no genuine sacrifice, any more than does the rent of land. The owner of capital can obtain interest because capital is scarce, just as the owner of land can obtain rent because land is scarce. But whilst there may be intrinsic reasons for the scarcity of land, there are no intrinsic reasons for the scarcity of capital.

I see, therefore, the rentier aspect of capitalism as a transitional phase which will disappear when it has done its work. And with the disappearance of its rentier aspect much else in it besides will suffer a sea-change. It will be, moreover, a great advantage of the order of events which I am advocating, that the euthanasia of the rentier, of the functionless investor, will be nothing sudden, merely a gradual but prolonged continuance of what we have seen recently in Great Britain, and will need no revolution.

In some respects the foregoing theory is moderately conservative in its implications. For whilst it indicates the vital importance of establishing certain central controls in matters which are now left in the main to individual initiative, there are wide fields of activity which are unaffected. The State will have to exercise a guiding influence on the propensity to consume partly through its scheme of taxation, partly by fixing the rate of interest, and partly, perhaps, in other ways. Furthermore, it seems unlikely that the influence of banking policy on the rate of interest will be sufficient by itself to determine an optimum rate of investment. I conceive, therefore, that a somewhat comprehensive socialisation of investment will prove the only means of securing an approximation to full employment; though this need not exclude all manner of compromises and of devices by which public authority will co-operate with private initiative. But beyond this no obvious case is made out for a system of State Socialism which would embrace most of the economic life of the community. It is not the ownership of the instruments of production which it is important for the State to assume. If the State is able to determine the aggregate amount of resources devoted to augmenting the instruments and the basic rate of reward to those who own them, it will have accomplished all that is necessary. Moreover, the necessary measures of socialisation can be introduced gradually and without a break in the general traditions of society.

Our criticism of the accepted classical theory of economics has consisted not so much in finding logical flaws in its analysis as in pointing out that its tacit assumptions are seldom or never satisfied, with the result that it cannot solve the economic problems of the actual world. But if our central controls succeed in establishing an aggregate volume of output corresponding to full employment as nearly as is practicable, the classical theory comes into its own again from this point onwards. If we suppose the volume of output to be given, i.e. to be determined by forces outside the classical scheme of thought, then there is no objection to be raised against the classical analysis of the manner in which private self-interest will determine what in particular is produced, in what proportions the factors of production will be combined to produce it, and how the value of the final product will be distributed between them. Again, if we have dealt otherwise with the problem of thrift, there is no objection to be raised against the modern classical theory as to the degree of consilience between private and public advantage in conditions of perfect and imperfect competition respectively. Thus, apart from the necessity of central controls to bring about an adjustment between the propensity to consume and the inducement to invest, there is no more reason to socialise economic life than there was before.

To put the point concretely, I see no reason to suppose that the existing system seriously misemploys the factors of production which are in use. There are, of course, errors of foresight, but these would not be avoided by centralising decisions. When 9,000,000 men are employed out of 10,000,000 willing and able to work, there is no evidence that the labour of these 9,000,000 men is misdirected. The complaint against the present system is not that these 9,000,000 men ought to be employed on different tasks, but that tasks should be available for the remaining 1,000,000 men. It is in determining the volume, not the direction, of actual employment that the existing system has broken down.

Thus I agree that the result of filling in the gaps in the classical theory is to indicate the nature of the environment which the free play of economic forces requires if it is to realise the full potentialities of production. The central controls necessary to ensure full employment will, of course, involve a large extension of the traditional functions of government. Furthermore, the modern classical theory has itself called attention to various conditions in which the free play of economic forces may need to be curbed or guided. But there will still remain a wide field for the exercise of private initiative and responsibility. Within this field the traditional advantages of individualism will still hold good.

Let us stop for a moment to remind ourselves what these advantages are. They are partly advantages of efficiency—the advantages of decentralisation and of the play of self-interest. The advantage to efficiency of the decentralisation of decisions and of individual responsibility is even greater, perhaps, than the nineteenth century supposed; and the reaction against the appeal to self-interest may have gone too far. But, above all, individualism, if it can be purged of its defects and its abuses, is the best safeguard of personal liberty in the sense that, compared with any other system, it greatly widens the field for the exercise of personal choice. It is also the best safeguard of the variety of life, which emerges precisely from this extended field of personal choice, and the loss of which is the greatest of all the losses of the homogeneous or totalitarian state. For this variety preserves the traditions which embody the most secure and successful choices of former generations; it colours the present with the diversification of its fancy; and, being the handmaid of experiment as well as of tradition and of fancy, it is the most powerful instrument to better the future.

Whilst, therefore, the enlargement of the functions of government, involved in the task of adjusting to one another the propensity to consume and the inducement to invest, would seem to a nineteenth-century publicist or to a contemporary American financier to be a terrific encroachment on individualism, I defend it, on the contrary, both as the only practicable means of avoiding the destruction of existing economic forms in their entirety and as the condition of the successful functioning of individual initiative.

The authoritarian state systems of to-day seem to solve the problem of unemployment at the expense of efficiency and of freedom. It is certain that the world will not much longer tolerate the unemployment which, apart from brief intervals of excitement, is associated—and, in my opinion, inevitably associated—with present-day capitalistic individualism. But it may be possible by a right analysis of the problem to cure the disease whilst preserving efficiency and freedom.

HOW KEYNES "CAME TO AMERICA"

Although Keynes anticipated the post-Keynesian synthesis, the "post-" is appropriate for two major reasons. First, Keynes addressed his most famous and highly influential work, *The General Theory of Employment, Interest, and Money,* to his fellow economists. Even some of them found it "in many places incoherent, ambiguous, and obscure. Keynes enjoyed the privileges of a pathfinder, leaving it to others to tidy up after him."[3] The explanation, popularization, and extension of Keynes' work have occupied the attention of many first-rate economists, including Alvin Hansen, Abba Lerner, and Paul Samuelson. Second, the *General Theory* was primarily a theoretical work rather than a guide to policy. The translation of Keynesian economics into recommendations for public policy and the implementation of those recommendations in the creation of "guided" or "managed" capitalist systems occupied a succeeding generation of economists and policy makers in the United States and other industrialized capitalist economies.

The following four selections discuss these dimensions of post-Keynesian economics more fully. In selection 3.3, Lekachman describes the major economic ideas of Alvin Hansen, often called the "American Keynes." Hansen's role in translating, clarifying, extending, and applying the Keynesian message was enormous. But he was also an important contributor in his own

[3] Allen M. Sievers, *Revolution, Evolution and Economic Order* (Englewood Cliffs, N.J.: Prentice-Hall, 1962), p. 12.

right to the analysis of prosperity and depression, and was especially known for his Americanized version of the theory of secular or long-run "stagnation." First presented in 1938, it is summarized here by Lekachman.

In selection 3.4, Abba Lerner states from his Keynesian perspective the basic principles of macroeconomic policy. Lerner's exposition underscores three key points. First, Lerner suggests, there is nothing sacrosanct or "sound" about an annually balanced governmental budget. The appropriate goal is a balanced economy, at full-employment utilization of its resources. To this end, the means of monetary and fiscal management should be functionally applied. Second, although Keynesian economics is especially relevant to issues of depression and unemployment, the analysis and policy recommendations can be and were turned into reverse gear by Keynesians for the purposes of analyzing and controlling inflation. Third, Keynes, in the *General Theory,* made three recommendations for curbing depression and promoting full employment: (1) an expansion in the money supply (to decrease interest rates and stimulate private investment); (2) an increase in government expenditures (to supplement private investment); and, (3) measures that would lower interest rates and reduce taxes (to increase the propensity to consume and thereby expand consumption). Although capable of being subsumed under (3), the creation of budget deficits by tax cuts (as, for example, in 1964) was not specifically mentioned. Clearly, Keynes' expectation was that the major thrust of an antidepressionary government program would be government expenditures, especially "government investment" in public works projects. Lerner shows that the basic logic of Keynesian policy involves adjustments in overall tax levels as well as government expenditures and other policy instruments.

Selection 3.5, by James Buchanan, illustrates two major points: first, that budget deficits (and surpluses) play a strategic role in Keynesian-type fiscal policy; and second, that the basic theory of aggregate demand and its policy implications for the promotion of economic stability are not restricted to a particular school of economic theory or social philosophy. Rather they are widely shared throughout the economics profession and are consistent with different views on the agenda of government in contemporary society. (Buchanan is a prominent "neo-liberal" or "individualist-conservative" who, like Hayek, Friedman, and others, advocates a limited role for government in economic life. See chapter 6.)

It should be understood that the major application of Keynesian economics to public policy did *not* occur under the auspices of the New Deal. Although the Roosevelt administration came to embrace a mild Keynesianism by the late 1930s, Keynes and most Keynesians believed the deficits of the New Deal years were too little (never appreciably more than 3 percent of the GNP), too late, and too inconsistently and cautiously applied. The real demonstration that large-scale deficits could galvanize a depressed economy and catapult it to full-employment prosperity came during World War II. The application of Keynesian-type policy in a major way occurred in the postwar period. And the explicit conversion of presidential leadership in the United States to Keynesian views awaited the Kennedy-Johnson (and Nixon-Ford) administrations. In selection 3.6, Galbraith describes how Keynes "came to America" and how the principles of macroeconomic policy came to be applied by both Republican and Democratic administrations.

3.3 Alvin H. Hansen: The American Keynes

Robert Lekachman

The leader of American Keynesianism was Harvard's Alvin H. Hansen. . . . Hansen became the most influential expositor of Keynesian doctrine both to fellow professionals and to a wider public, the inventor of an American version of Keynes's prediction of capitalism's long-run future, and inevitably the target of the ill-informed and the prejudiced in and out of public life.

Hansen's own career is an example of the power of the Keynesian analysis. . . . In his early writings [he held] a cautious, even conservative estimate of the potentialities of public intervention. There was little evidence in these works of sympathy with Keynes's activist preferences.

But as a result of his own reconsiderations and discussions with colleagues and students, Hansen rapidly shifted his ground. His 1938 collection of essays, *Full Recovery or Stagnation,* contained an old and a new Hansen. . . . A concluding group of essays devoted to the 1937 recession, the concept of pump-priming, and the doctrine of secular stagnation clearly represented an endorsement of a larger role of government in general and of Keynesian public finance policy in particular.

Once begun, the evolution of Hansen's opinions continued undeviatingly. His 1941 *Fiscal Policy and Business Cycles* completed his shift toward Keynesian attitudes and Keynesian analysis. In Hansen's formulation Keynes became both more concrete and more comprehensible, for it was the strength of *Fiscal Policy and Business Cycles* that its author gave the flesh of American statistics to the bones of abstract theory. . . .

The advantages especially in the United States of Hansen's careful, detailed approach appeared particularly in the handling of the consumption function. Keynes's treatment had been a priori, abstract, and unadorned by example. In contrast, Hansen, who had come to value highly the income-consumption relation, first looked at the consumption function from a cyclical standpoint and illustrated his argument with some genuine statistics of family income. Then he applied a long-run secular analysis to the data, computing lines of relationship between recorded income and consumption data. He rounded out his case for the concept with a statistical appendix prepared by Paul Samuelson which dealt closely with the major data on incomes and expen-

Excerpted from Robert Lekachman, *The Age of Keynes* (New York: Random House, 1966). Reprinted by permission of the publisher.

ditures collected by Simon Kuznets, the pioneer investigator of the national income magnitudes.

Hansen was equally persuasive in his exposition on public spending and taxing. His long chapter on Keynesian fiscal policy, "Pump-Priming and Compensatory Fiscal Policy," centered upon the distinction between the two concepts of deficit finance.

As Hansen defined pump-priming, it "carries with it the implication that a certain volume of public spending . . . will have the effect of setting the economy going on the way toward full utilization of resources on its own power without further aid from government." Within the Roosevelt administration, there were some optimists who were convinced that a short period of government deficit would rapidly stimulate business confidence, increase private investment, and eliminate the need for further deficits.

Compensatory spending implied a less euphoric outlook, "merely that public expenditures may be used to compensate for the decline in private investment." By this time Hansen was convinced that the prime reason for economic depression was inadequate private investment. Compensatory expenditure simply supplemented private investment. As businessmen raised their investment expenditures of their own accord, compensatory spending could decline. It was a short step from the identification of this role for government to the notion of a federal budget balanced not each year but over the entire business cycle. As the economy contracted, compensatory spending would generate deficits. The deficits, according to the value of the multiplier, would raise the national income by amounts larger than themselves. Symmetrically, during expansion, surpluses would accrue as the usual consequence of rising tax receipts and constant or declining public expenditures. In a typical business cycle, the algebraic sum of the deficits and the surpluses would total zero.

The power of compensatory spending depended upon the size of the multiplier. What was a sensible value in the United States? Hansen accepted the estimate of the Columbia economist John Maurice Clark that the leakages[1] were on the order of one-third. Thus, it followed that $1 billion of new investment or $1 billion of additional public spending, financed by debt or created credit, would produce an increase in consumer spending initially of $667 million, then of two-thirds of $667 million, and so on in a diminishing progression. Including the initial $1 billion added to national income, the total effect of the government's action or of a private increase in investment would equal $3 billion. The multiplier, 3, was as always the reciprocal of the leakages. With great care and the aid of a series of vivid charts, Hansen made this multiplier process as concrete and plausible as it had been abstract and confusing in Keynes's version.

Hansen completed his exposition with a piece of synthesis. Borrowing from his brilliant student Paul Samuelson's investigations, Hansen demon-

[1] Leakage is the portion of income which is saved, devoted to the payment of debts and taxes, or expended on imported goods. Keynes's guess at a higher percentage of leakage for England was associated with the much greater importance of imported goods in England than in the United States.

strated that the older principle of acceleration[2] could be combined with the multiplier to generate a model of cyclical fluctuation.

What Hansen had written was a teachable version of Keynesian economics, applied in some statistical detail to the American economy. If he had done no more, his leading position among American Keynesians would have been secure. In fact he enunciated the only truly original American extension of Keynesian economics until at least the 1950s. This was the notion of secular stagnation, a sufficiently plausible and persistent vision of the American situation as to deserve a section of its own.

In 1938 Alvin Hansen was president of the American Economic Association. . . . Few presidential addresses can have been more influential than the speech which Alvin Hansen delivered in Detroit on December 28, 1938. Entitled "Economic Progress and Declining Population," it amounted to the bold statement that not even compensatory spending, much less pump-priming, could lift the American economy to satisfactory levels of economic activity.

Why was this so? As the answer went, "We are passing, so to speak, over a divide which separates the great era of growth and expansion of the nineteenth century from an era which no man, unwilling to embark on pure conjecture, can as yet characterize with clarity or precision." How had the American economy so altered as to pass from growth in the nineteenth century to somnolence in the twentieth? Hansen's answer was composed of three elements. Most important was the rate of population growth. Second, American dynamism in the nineteenth century had been stimulated also by the opening of successive continental frontiers and the exploitation of the natural resources of the West. And there was a third major source of economic energy: new inventions and their application. These were the three pillars of investment, and investment, earlier as later, was the source of rapid growth and satisfactory employment.

A mature economy was that of a nation no longer spurred by high investment. Such was the condition of the American economy. Consider first the overriding role of population change. From the *Wealth of Nations* onward, economists had recognized the importance of a rapid increase in population as a stimulus to high investment. As Hansen reminded his audience, Adam Smith had demonstrated that growing populations facilitated a finer division of labor and higher per capita productivity. More than that, larger populations facilitated the extension of the market for finished goods. . . .

Even if nothing else of economic significance occurs, a rapidly expanding population will demand more capital [because of higher output]. But it is plain that a rapidly expanding population will call not only for more goods than will a stationary population but also for a drastically different assortment of goods. A growing population implies rapid family formation, which in turn causes a buoyant demand for new housing and household furnishings. A stationary

[2] The acceleration principle is symmetrical to the multiplier. It assumes that there is a definable relation between increases in consumption and increases in investment.

population requires only replacement of that portion of the housing stock which becomes unusable. Moreover, since it contains a higher proportion of the elderly, the demand for personal services—medical, domestic, even custodial—increases. Housing involves large capital expenditure; personal service does not. Hence any shift from a rapidly increasing population to a slowly increasing or stationary population must imply a declining ratio of capital to output as a whole. . . .

To say the least, any substantial decline in the rate of population growth must have . . . seriously adverse effects upon investment incentives.

In fact, the population rate of growth had slowed. In a central passage, Hansen summarized the American experience:

> *In the decade of the nineteen-twenties the population of the United States increased by 16,000,000—an absolute growth equal to that of the prewar decade and in excess of any other decade in our history. In the current decade we are adding only half this number to our population, and the best forecasts indicate a decline to a third in the decade which we are about to enter. . . .*

What accounted for the remainder of the nineteenth-century growth in capital investment were Hansen's second and third influences, the exploitation of new frontiers and resources and the stimulus of technical invention. The atmosphere of the twentieth century was less propitious to these varieties of investment as well. As far as frontiers were concerned, "These outlets for new investment are rapidly being closed." This was not only a matter of the completion of settlement in the American West; it was the result also of the narrowing of opportunities for foreign investment. Foreign investment had served France and England during the nineteenth century as a substitute for an open land frontier. But, said Hansen ominously, "No one is likely to challenge the statement that foreign investment will in the next fifty years play an incomparably smaller role than was the case in the nineteenth century."

If population growth was slowing to a halt, if frontiers were closing, and if foreign investment was shrinking, what was left as a last hope was a "world in which we must fall back upon a more rapid advance of technology than in the past if we are to find private investment opportunities adequate to maintain full employment." Under the circumstances everything possible must be done to encourage the emergence of new industries. In the past spectacular novelties like railroads, electricity, and automobiles had created massive investment booms. In the future we would be compelled to rely still more heavily upon the important innovation.

Nevertheless, the outlook was scarcely brighter here than elsewhere, for a whole array of "institutional developments" restricted initiative and damped opportunity. Among the impediments to investment in new industries and processes were "the growing power of trade unions and trade associations, the development of monopolistic competition, of rivalry for the market through expensive persuasion and advertising, instead of through price competition." Price competition compelled even reluctant businessmen to acquire cost-cutting new techniques even if the price was the scrapping of old equipment which was still physically usable. The price of delay was speedy elimination by rivals of superior alertness. But where monopoly, oligopoly, or monopolistic competition characterized the market, patents might be suppressed, old equipment used until it wore out, and investment and innovation alike held to a minimum.

Thus, at the end of his exploration, Hansen concluded that "The main problem of our times, and particularly in the United States, is the problem of full employment." It was an era marked by weak business recoveries and protracted depressions: "This is the essence of secular stagnation—sick recoveries which die in their infancy and depressions which feed on themselves and leave a hard and seemingly immovable core of unemployment."

A grim . . . problem.

3.4 Functional Finance

Abba P. Lerner

The essential idea of Functional Finance is very simple. It is that the financial activities of the government should be judged not by any traditional canons of fiscal propriety but by considering the effects of each act and deciding whether these effects are desired or not.

The effects that government should consider are primarily the effects on the public, in whose interest the government is supposed to be acting. The effects on the government are always relatively unimportant.

The effects can be considered in their most simple and literal sense. For example, two effects of any tax payment are that the taxpayer has less money and that the government has more money. The first of these effects is important, so that the tax should be imposed if there is a good reason for wanting the taxpayer to have less money. The effect on the government, namely, that the government will have more money is not important because the government can always get more money quite easily without impoverishing any taxpayer. If the government needs more money for any purpose it can simply create some money, either directly by printing it or indirectly by borrowing it from the banks.

From this it follows that taxes should never be imposed simply because the government needs money. Economic transactions, like purchases or sales of

From Abba P. Lerner, "An Integrated Full Employment Policy," *International Postwar Problems* (New York: American Labor Conference on International Affairs, January 1946), pp. 69–73. Reprinted by permission of the author.

goods, should be taxed only when it is thought desirable to discourage these transactions. Individuals should be taxed only to the extent that it is desired to make the taxpayer poorer. The government should borrow money only if it desires to replace cash in the hands of the public by government IOU's (and should lend money or repay debt if it wishes to bring about the opposite effect). The government should sell goods if it is desirable that the public should have goods instead of cash, and should buy goods if it is desirable that the public should have more cash instead of the goods. For these are the effects of the government action and it is the distinguishing mark of reasonable behavior that action is governed only by a consideration of its effects. Functional Finance is nothing but the systematic application of this principle of rationality to governmental financial activities.

Every governmental financial activity can be reduced to one or more of six basic elements. The six elements form three pairs, one of each pair being the reverse of its partner. The three pairs of elementary financial instruments are:

1. Buying and Selling
2. Subsidizing and Taxing (i.e., giving money to people and taking money from people)
3. Lending and Borrowing

These six elements include everything that the government can do in the economic field. Everything else can be considered as a combination of two or more of the elements. Requisitioning, for example, is equivalent to *Buying* the goods from an individual and then taking the money away from him by *Taxation*.

All this is related to the problem of full employment because the level of employment depends on the rate at which money is being spent on all goods and services together. The greater the total rate of spending, that is, the greater the amount of money spent on all goods and services every day of every week, both by the public and by the government, the greater will be the number of men and women that employers will find it profitable to employ. If the total rate of spending is low, employers will not be able to sell at a profit the output of all the people who want to work, and we will have unemployment. The degree of unemployment will depend on the degree to which the total rate of spending is below that level which would make it profitable to employ all who want to work.

A total rate of spending *above* this ideal level would mean that the public is trying to buy more goods than it is possible to produce even when everybody has a job. When everybody who wants to work is already working, such a great demand for goods cannot increase employment further. It can only raise prices and start an inflation.

Since inflation and unemployment should be prevented if possible, and since these scourges result from too high or too low a total rate of spending, it is impossible to avoid the conclusion that one of the most important duties of the government is to direct its financial policies toward keeping the total rate of spending from going too high or too low.

The three pairs of instruments fit so well into such a conception of the financial duties of the government that it is easy to identify Functional Finance with a policy for keeping the total rate of spending in the economy at the right level for preventing inflations and unemployment.

Buying goods and services directly increases the total rate of spending and is appropriate when the rate of spending is deficient. *Selling* goods (that have been acquired by the government in the past) naturally has the opposite effect, absorbing excessive spending, and is appropriate when the rate of spending is too high. (Government buying includes the undertaking of public works, the acquisition of products for storage, as has been done with cotton and wheat, and the purchase by the government of the products of industry for purposes such as war.)

Subsidies increase the total rate of spending by encouraging the transactions which are subsidized or simply by increasing the amount of money that the receivers of the subsidy can spend. Taxes work in the opposite direction by discouraging the transactions subject to the tax or simply by diminishing the amount of money that the taxpayers have left to spend. Subsidies may in fact be considered as negative taxes.

Lending by government has the effect of making it easier for borrowers to obtain loans which they could then spend either on consumption or more probably on investment in new construction. (Although government lending is rare, the repayment of government debt has exactly the same effects and must be included in government lending.) *Borrowing* by the government has the opposite effects, making it harder for borrowers to obtain loans by diminishing the expenditure out of such loans and so lowering the total rate of spending.[1]

Thus the six fiscal instruments provide the government with six ways of dealing with an excessive total rate of spending and six ways of dealing with a deficiency in the total rate of spending. If spending is excessive the government can cut down on its *Buying* or its *Subsidies* or its *Lending* (an increase in debt repayment counting as an increase in lending), or it can step up its *Selling* or its *Taxes* or its *Borrowing*. In other words it can cut down on the first item in one of the three pairs of elementary governmental financial instruments or step up the second item in one of them. If the total rate of spending is deficient the whole business is simply reversed. The government can then step up the first item in one of the three pairs of instruments or it can cut down on the second element in one of them.

[1]If the government borrows from banks holding excess reserves, this effect will not come about. The excess reserves would permit the banks to lend to the government without reducing their loans to other borrowers. The same is true if the government borrows from individuals who have an excess of cash which they would otherwise have kept idle. In all such cases the effects are just as if the government had created new money—bank money or cash money as the case may be.

Sometimes it is said that borrowing from the banks is inflationary (meaning that it tends to increase the total rate of spending). This is not correct. Government borrowing from the banks can never make it easier for others to borrow.

3.5 Deficits and Fiscal Policy

James Buchanan

The Economics of Unbalanced Budgets: Deficit Financing

As a general rule, unbalanced budgets will exert more effects on the macroeconomic variables than will balanced budgets.

Budgets may be unbalanced in two directions. Government expenditures may exceed tax revenues or tax revenues may exceed government expenditures. We shall try to ascertain the economic effects of *deficit financing,* the term that is commonly used to refer to the first sort of budget unbalance.

WAYS OF CREATING A DEFICIT

A budget deficit is defined as an excess of expenditures over receipts during a specified accounting period, normally a fiscal year. There are several ways in which a deficit may be created.

First of all, expenditures may be increased while tax revenues remain stable. Secondly, expenditures may remain unchanged while taxes are reduced.

Expenditure Increase

Let us assume that the rate of taxation remains stable, that is to say, the receipts of the government from the private sector are not changed. A deficit is to be created by an increase in the rate of public or governmental outlay. Quite clearly, the effects of this operation will depend on the type or form of the expenditure. We shall first assume that the government increases its rate of purchasing real goods and services from the domestic private economy. For example, the expenditure increment may take the form of expanded outlay on components for the space exploration program.

The effects may best be analyzed in terms of the investment or income multiplier analysis. Assuming, for the moment, that all secondary or indirect repercussions of the government's action may be neglected, the expanded purchases will increase total spending (public and private) for goods and services. The net impact must be expansionary. If unemployed resources exist, and if these resources are of the sort that may be absorbed by generalized

Excerpted with permission from James Buchanan, *The Public Finances,* rev. ed. Homewood, Ill.: Richard D. Irwin, Inc., pp. 89–108.

increases in aggregate demand, then an increase in national real income will take place. If the resources that are unemployed are not capable of being absorbed readily in expanding industries, and if serious institutional rigidities in the structure of wages and prices are present, the increase in demand may generate price-level increases, even in the face of some observed resource unemployment. If, before the deficit creation, all resources capable of being effectively employed are currently employed in the economy, the result of the expansionary force will be primarily that of increasing the general level of prices, that is, inflation. In this case, little if any increase in real, as opposed to money, national income will take place. Regardless of the initial situation, however, the effects of deficit financing are to increase national *money* income.

To what extent will national money income rise? Here we may rely more directly on the analysis of the investment multiplier. If the additional expenditure is financed in such a way that purchasing power in the private sector is not reduced, the full multiplier effects will be exerted. National money income will rise by the full amount of the deficit during the initial spending period. As this additional income remains in the circular flow through successive income periods, the total addition to national money income will be some multiple of the initial increment to spending represented by the deficit. If this increment takes the form of a once-and-for-all single period deficit, national money income for any single period will never increase more than the increase in spending. But if the spending increase takes the more normal form of an increase in the *rate* of purchase, that is, if deficits are continued in being over a sequence of income periods, national money income will tend to increase from its previous level by the appropriately calculated multiple of the continuing deficit. The value of this multiplier depends . . . on the marginal propensity to save.

Reduction in Taxes

Taxation withdraws purchasing power from the private sector of the economy. A reduction in taxation, with the rate of public spending remaining unchanged, restores purchasing power to private hands. The initial effect is to increase private income receipts. In this first stage, the deficit so created does nothing to increase directly either public or private spending. The difference in effect at this first stage distinguishes the tax reduction and the expenditure increase methods of deficit creation.

As private incomes are increased by tax reduction, individuals and families will be encouraged to increase rates of private spending on goods and services. This is the second stage of the income-spending process. If the entire amount of the tax-induced income increase should be spent, the effects would be identical with that of the public expenditure increase, save for the one-stage lag in time. But private families will not normally spend the full amount of an increase in income. Some share of the income increment will be saved. Therefore, somewhat less than the full amount of the deficit will return directly to the circular flow, and only that share that does so return will set off multiplier effects on national money income. A tax reduction will tend, therefore, to be less expansionary in effect than an equivalent increase in public spending, provided that the secondary effects of the two operations are similar. If tax reduction should, by reducing high marginal rates on personal incomes, provide some incentive for investment outlay, the larger multiplier effects of an expenditure-created deficit might be more than offset.

FINANCING A BUDGET DEFICIT

A budget deficit, regardless of the method by which it is created, must be financed. The effects of the whole operation may be influenced more by the means of financing than by the means of creating the deficit. A deficit implies a rate of public outlay in excess of tax receipts. This must be made up by funds—purchasing power—and this must be secured from some source other than current taxes. There are two basic ways of securing such funds: borrowing or creating money. As the following discussion will indicate, these two ways have not been carefully distinguished.

Borrowing from the "Public"

If a governmental unit decides to finance a deficit by borrowing from the "public," that is, from individuals and nonfinancial institutions, it will offer government securities in exchange for current purchasing power, currency or deposit claims. This operation will withdraw current purchasing power from the private economy, purchasing power that might otherwise have been used to purchase private securities or consumer goods and services. Only if the funds should be drawn from private hoards, from wholly idle balances, would there be no reduction in private spending. To the extent that the financing side does withdraw purchasing power from the private sector, government borrowing from the "public" resembles taxation in its macroeconomic effect. Financing a deficit in this manner must be contractionary, in and of itself. The public expenditure of the funds will fully return the withdrawn monetary resources to the spending-income flow, but the net effect on the size of this flow is not likely to be great except in those cases, which seem relatively rare, where a good share of the borrowed funds come out of private hoards. Some expansionary effect from the combined operation may be predicted, but in many instances this effect will be small and may, under some conditions, be negligible.

This analysis clearly indicates that deficits should be financed by borrowing from the "public" only when it seems desirable to limit sharply the expansionary effects. This financing method is, therefore, appropriate when deficits are created for other than "fiscal policy" purposes, for example, during war periods when the political pressures are such that adequate taxation cannot be achieved. If the very purpose of creating a deficit is to generate expansion in the income-spending flow, it seems the height of folly to dampen this expansion by financing the deficit in a contractionary way.

Borrowing from Commercial Banks

The full expansionary effects of budget deficits take place only when the funds are secured in such a manner that private purchasing power is not significantly reduced. When commercial banks have excess reserves and utilize these to purchase government securities, this is more or less the case. The government's borrowing of these otherwise idle funds allows them to be activated and to flow (via the public spending process) into the income-spending stream. An important secondary effect of this operation is that exerted on the supply of money in the system. The utilization of these otherwise excess and idle commercial bank reserves to finance deficits will allow for an expansion of the total stock of currency and bank deposits to some multiple of the initial amount "borrowed" by the government. Since, however, banks possess excess reserves prior to the borrowing operation, there is no assurance that these deposit multiplier effects will be influential in encouraging further expansions in national money income. Nevertheless, the secondary effects on the money supply, if these are allowed to take place by the monetary authorities, can provide a source of elasticity in the money-credit system and can facilitate the working out of the multiplier effects of the deficit. The financing of the deficit through borrowing from commercial banks that possess excess reserves takes on main characteristics of the second method of securing funds, namely, money creation. Only in some rather limited definitional sense can this operation be called "borrowing."

If, however, the government attempts to sell securities to commercial banks when reserves are not in excess, the borrowing operation takes on characteristics of borrowing from the "public," as previously discussed. The operation is necessarily restrictive since banks must, in this case, use funds in purchasing the securities that they would otherwise have used in purchasing private earning assets. The demand for private "bonds" is reduced; prices are pushed down, and interest rates are driven up. The expansionary effects of the public spending side of the deficit are, to a considerable extent, offset by the reduction in private investment caused by the tightening up of funds available for private securities.

"Borrowing" from the Federal Reserve Banks

The "sale" of government securities to the Federal Reserve banks in order to finance a budget deficit should not be included under the rubric "borrowing" at all, and the continued confusing usage tends to muddle popular discussion. This form of financing is the modern institutional equivalent of the second method of securing funds that was mentioned, *money creation*. To call this operation "borrowing" tends to confuse the useful distinction that should be made between genuine borrowing, through which purchasing power is actually transferred *to* government and *away* from other uses in exchange for an interest return, and money creation, which involves a net addition to the total of purchasing power. As the preceding section indicated, the sale of government securities to the commercial banks can represent a genuine borrowing operation if funds are withdrawn from alternative bank investments. No differential addition to the total money supply need take place. On the other hand, if excess reserves are present, the sale of securities to commercial banks also generates net money creation.

The sale of government debt instruments to the Federal Reserve banks, coupled with the expenditure of these funds in the purchase of public goods and services, not only adds to the spending flow of the economy without offsetting effects on the financing side; the combined operation also increases the stock of money in the system, generating possible multiplier effects of quite another sort.

In the twentieth century, Western governments are not likely to resort to the more crude method of deliberate currency creation when the same results may be accomplished by "borrowing" from central banks. Insofar as the public is fully cognizant of the fact that "borrowing" from central banks is really money creation, the method of financing a deficit is legitimate. It becomes the most appropriate method when the maximum expansionary effects of the deficit are desired, for example, at the bottom of a deep depression. The method of financing is wholly inappropriate when the deficits are created for reasons other than those of economic stabilization.

CONCLUSIONS

We have distinguished between the creation of deficits and financing them. Deficits created by expenditure expansion were shown to be more expansionary than like deficits created by tax reduction under restricted conditions.

The financing of a deficit can be as important as the means of creating it in determining its effect. The maximum expansionary effects are achieved through a sale of securities to Federal Reserve banks. Not only does this method of financing leave private purchasing power undisturbed; it also causes a net addition to the total money stock, an addition which can be a multiple of the initial size of the deficit. This addition to the money stock can, itself, generate further expansionary effects on money income.

Where excess reserves are present, the securing of funds from commercial banks has a similar effect. Either of these methods is essentially equivalent to money creation.

If, on the other hand, it should prove desirable to finance the deficit in the least expansionary manner, the funds should be secured through the sale of government securities to the "public." Securities sold should be exchanged for current purchasing power which will be withdrawn from the spending stream.

3.6 How Keynes Came to America

John K. Galbraith

The most influential book on economic and social policy so far in this century, *The General Theory of Employment Interest and Money* by John Maynard Keynes, was published in 1936 in both Britain and the United States.

By common, if not yet quite universal, agreement, the Keynesian revolution was one of the great modern accomplishments in social design. Yet those responsible have had no honors and some opprobrium. For a long while, to be known as an active Keynesian was to invite the wrath of those who equate social advance with subversion. Those concerned developed a habit of reticence. As a further consequence, the history of the revolution is, perhaps, the worst told story of our era.

It is time that we knew better this part of our history and those who made it, and this is a little of the story.

Before the publication of *The General Theory,* Keynes had urged his ideas directly on President Roosevelt, most notably in a famous letter to the *New York Times* on December 31, 1933: "I lay overwhelming emphasis on the increase of national purchasing power resulting from government expenditure which is financed by loans." And he visited FDR in the summer of 1934 to press his case, although the session was no great success; each, during the meeting, developed some doubts about the general good sense of the other.

In the meantime, two key Washington officials, Marriner Eccles, the exceptionally able Utah banker who was to become head of the Federal Reserve Board, and Lauchlin Currie, a recent Harvard instructor who was its assistant director of research and later an economic aide to Roosevelt (and later still a prominent victim of McCarthyite persecution), had on their own account reached conclusions similar to those of Keynes as to the proper course of fiscal policy. When *The General Theory* arrived, they took it as confirmation of the course they had previously been urging.

Paralleling the work of Keynes in the thirties and rivaling it in importance, though not in fame, was that of Simon Kuznets and a group of young economists and statisticians at the University of Pennsylvania, the National Bureau of Economic Research and the United States Department of Commerce. They developed from earlier beginnings the now familiar concepts of National Income and Gross National Product and their components, and made estimates

---

of their amount. Included among the components of National Income and Gross National Product were the saving, investment, aggregate of disposable income and the other magnitudes of which Keynes was talking. As a result, those who were translating Keynes's ideas into action could now know not only what needed to be done but how much. And many who would never have been persuaded by the Keynesian abstractions were compelled to belief by the concrete figures from Kuznets and his inventive colleagues.

However, the trumpet—if the metaphor is permissible for this particular book—that was sounded in Cambridge, England, was heard most clearly in Cambridge, Massachusetts. Harvard was the principal avenue by which Keynes's ideas passed to the United States.

In the late thirties, Harvard had a large community of young economists, most of them held there by the shortage of jobs that Keynes sought to cure. They had the normal confidence of their years in their ability to remake the world and, unlike less fortunate generations, the opportunity. They also had occupational indication of the need. Massive unemployment persisted year after year. It was degrading to have to continue telling the young that this was merely a temporary departure from the full employment norm, and that one need only obtain the needed wage reductions.

Paul Samuelson, who subsequently taught economics to an entire generation and who almost from the outset was the acknowledged leader of the younger Keynesian community, has compared the excitement of the young economists, on the arrival of Keynes's book, to that of Keats on first looking into Chapman's Homer. Some will wonder if economists are capable of such refined emotion, but the effect was certainly great. Here was a remedy for the despair that could be seen just beyond the Yard. It did not overthrow the system but saved it. To the nonrevolutionary, it seemed too good to be true. To the occasional revolutionary, it was. The old economics was still taught by day. But in the evening and almost every evening from 1936 on, almost everyone in the Harvard community discussed Keynes.

This might, conceivably, have remained a rather academic discussion. As with the Bible and Marx, obscurity stimulated abstract debate. But in 1938, the practical instincts that economists sometimes suppress with success were catalyzed by the arrival in Cambridge from Minnesota of Alvin H. Hansen. He was then about fifty, an effective teacher and a popular colleague. But, most of all, he was a man for whom economic ideas had no standing apart from their use.

Most economists of established reputation had not taken to Keynes. Faced with the choice between changing one's mind and proving that there is no need to do so, almost everyone gets busy on the proof. So it was then. Hansen had an established reputation, and he did change his mind. Though he had been an effective critic of some central propositions in Keynes's *Treatise on Money,* an immediately preceding work, and was initially rather cool to *The General Theory,* he soon became strongly persuaded of Keynes's importance.

He proceeded to expound the ideas in books, articles and lectures and to apply them to the American scene. He persuaded his students and younger colleagues that they should not only understand the ideas but win understanding in others and then go on to get action. Without ever seeking to do so or being quite aware of the fact, he became the leader of a crusade. In the late thirties Hansen's seminar in the new Graduate School of Public Administration was regularly visited by the Washington policy-makers. Often the students overflowed into the hall.

The officials took Hansen's ideas, and perhaps even more his sense of conviction, back to Washington. In time there was also a strong migration of his younger colleagues and students to the capital. Among numerous others were Richard Gilbert, later a principal architect of Pakistan's economic development, who was a confidant of Harry Hopkins; Richard Musgrave, later at Princeton and other universities, and now once again back at Harvard, who applied Keynes's and Hansen's ideas to the tax system; Alan Sweezy, now of the California Institute of Technology, who went to the Federal Reserve and the WPA; George Jaszi, who went to the Department of Commerce; G. Griffith Johnson, who served at the Treasury, the National Security Resources Board and the White House; and Walter Salant, now of the Brookings Institution, who served influentially in several Federal agencies. Keynes wrote admiringly of this group of young Washington disciples.

The discussions that had begun in Cambridge continued through the war years in Washington where most of the earlier participants were now serving. One of the leaders, a close friend of Hansen's but not otherwise connected with the Harvard group, was the late Gerhard Colm of the Bureau of the Budget. Colm, a German refugee, had made the transition from a position of influence in Germany to one of major responsibility in the United States government in a matter of some five years. He played a major role in reducing the Keynesian proposals to workable estimates of costs and quantities. Keynesian policies became central to what was called postwar planning and designs for preventing the re-emergence of massive unemployment.

Meanwhile, others were concerning themselves with a wider audience. Seymour Harris, another of Hansen's colleagues and an early convert to Keynes, became the most prolific exponent of the ideas in the course of becoming one of the most prolific scholars of modern times. He published half a dozen books on Keynes and outlined the ideas in hundreds of letters, speeches, memoranda, Congressional appearances and articles. Professor Samuelson, mentioned above, put the Keynesian ideas into what became (and remains) the most influential textbook on economics since the last great exposition of the classical system by Alfred Marshall. Lloyd Metzler at the University of Chicago applied the Keynesian system to international trade. Lloyd G. Reynolds gathered a talented group of younger economists at Yale and made that university a major center of discussion of the new ideas.

Meanwhile, with the help of the academic Keynesians, a few businessmen were becoming interested. Two New England industrialists, Henry S. Dennison of the Dennison Manufacturing Company in Framingham, Massachusetts, and Ralph Flanders of the Jones and Lamson Machine Company of Springfield, Vermont (and later United States Senator from Vermont), hired members of the Harvard group to tutor them in the ideas. Before the war they had endorsed them in a book, in which Lincoln Filene of Boston and Morris E. Leeds of Philadelphia had joined, called *Toward Full Employment.* It was only slightly more readable and even less read than Keynes. In the later war years, the Committee for Economic Development, led in these matters by Flanders and Beardsley Ruml, and again with the help of the academic Keynesians, began evangelizing the business community.

In Washington during the war years, the National Planning Association had been a center for academic discussion of the Keynesian ideas. At the end of the war Hans Christian Sonne, the imaginative and liberal New York banker, began underwriting both the NPA and the Keynesian ideas. With the CED in which Sonne was also influential, the NPA became another important instrument for explaining the policy to the larger public. (In the autumn of 1949, in an exercise combining imagination with rare diplomacy, Sonne gathered a dozen economists of strongly varying views at Princeton and persuaded them all to sign a specific endorsement of Keynesian fiscal policies. The agreement was later reported to the Congress in well-publicized hearings by Arthur Smithies of Harvard and Simeon Leland of Northwestern University.)

In 1946, ten years after the publication of *The General Theory,* the Employment Act of that year gave the Keynesian system the qualified but still quite explicit support of law. It recognized, as Keynes had urged, that unemployment and insufficient output would respond to positive policies. Not much was said about the specific policies but the responsibility of the Federal Government to act in some fashion was clearly affirmed. The Council of Economic Advisers became, in turn, a platform for expounding the Keynesian view of the economy and it was brought promptly into use. Thus in only a decade had the revolution spread.

Those who nurture thoughts of conspiracy and clandestine plots will be saddened to know that this was a revolution without organization. All who participated felt a deep sense of personal responsibility for the ideas; there was a varying but deep urge to persuade.

Something more, however, was suspected. And there was some effort at counterrevolution. Nobody could say that he preferred massive unemployment to Keynes. And even men of conservative mood, when they understood what was involved, opted for the policy—some asking only that it be called by some other name. The Committee for Economic Development, coached by Ruml on semantics, never advocated deficits. Rather, it spoke well of a budget that was balanced only under conditions of high employment. Those who objected to Keynes were also invariably handicapped by the fact that they hadn't (and couldn't) read the book. It was like attacking the original Kama Sutra for pornography without being able to read Sanskrit.

President Eisenhower's first Chairman of the Council of Economic Advisers was Arthur F. Burns of Columbia University and the National Bureau of Economic Research (and later adviser and Chairman of the Federal Reserve Board under Richard Nixon). Mr. Burns had credentials as a critic of Keynes. A man who has always associated respectability with mild obsolescence, his introduction to the 1946 annual report of the National Bureau was called "Economic Research and the Keynesian Thinking of Our Time." He made his own critical interpretation of the Keynesian underemployment equilibrium and concluded, perhaps a trifle heavily, that "the imposing schemes for governmental action that are being bottomed on Keynes's equilibrium theory must be viewed with skepticism." Alvin Hansen replied rather sharply.

But if Burns regarded Keynes with skepticism, he viewed recessions (including ones for which he might be held responsible) with antipathy. In his 1955 report as Chairman of the Council of Economic Advisers, he said, "Budget policies can help promote the objective of maximum production by wisely allocating resources *first between private and public uses;* second, among various government programs." (My italics.) Keynes, reading these words carefully—government action to decide as between private and public spending—would have strongly applauded. And, indeed, a spokesman for the National Association of Manufacturers told the Joint Economic Committee that they pointed "directly toward the planned and eventually the socialized economy."

After the departure of Burns, the Eisenhower Administration incurred a deficit of $9.4 billion in the national income accounts in the course of overcoming the recession of 1958. This was by far the largest deficit ever incurred by an American government in peacetime; it exceeded the total peace-time expenditure by FDR in any year up to 1940. No administration had ever given the economy such a massive dose of Keynesian medicine. With a Republican administration, guided by men like Mr. Randall and Mr. Weeks, following such policies, the academic Keynesians at Harvard and elsewhere were no longer vulnerable.

Presidents Kennedy and Johnson continued what is now commonplace policy. Advised by Walter Heller, a remarkably skillful exponent of Keynes's ideas, they added the new device of the deliberate tax reduction to sustain aggregate demand. And they abandoned, at long last, the double talk by which advocates of Keynesian policies combined advocacy of measures to promote full employment and economic growth with promises of a promptly balanced budget. "We have recognized as self-defeating the effort to balance our budget too quickly in an economy operating well below its potential," President Johnson said in his 1965 report.

Now, as noted, Keynesian policies are the new orthodoxy. Economists are everywhere to be seen enjoying their new and pleasantly uncontroversial role.

The purpose of this essay is to pay respect to those who pioneered the Keynesian revolution in America. We should take pride in the men who brought it about. It is hardly fitting that they should have been celebrated only by the reactionaries. The debt to the courage and intelligence of Alvin Hansen is especially great. Next only to Keynes, his is the credit for saving what even conservatives still call capitalism.

KEYNESIAN ECONOMICS AND OTHER PHILOSOPHIES OF CAPITALISM

The umbrella of the post-Keynesian synthesis, even at its height, did not encompass all the various economic philosophies of capitalism. In selection 3.7, Ernest van den Haag and Henry Hazlett debate the question of the appropriate response of conservatives to Keynesian analysis and policy. Haag suggests qualified acceptance; Hazlitt, like many laissez-faire conservatives and conservative business groups,[4] opts for unqualified rejection.

Paul Sweezy (selection 3.8) provides a contemporary neo-Marxist critique of Keynesian economics. While praising Keynes himself, and recognizing the tremendous advances in theoretical and statistical technique made by Keynesian economists, Sweezy criticizes the societal and class-bound character of Keynesian thinking and its lack of historical and political perspective.

The late G.D.H. Cole, prominent British democratic socialist, assesses (in selection 3.9) the implications of Keynesian economics for the socialist movement. Although he finds much to praise in Keynes' critique of laissez-faire capitalism, Cole questions the full applicability of a full-employment policy within the framework of private enterprise and a strictly macroeconomic policy.

3.7 Must Conservatives Repudiate Keynes?

Ernest van den Haag and Henry Hazlitt

No, says Ernest van den Haag

Conservatives often object to the economics of Lord Keynes with more heat than light. They feel that his economic doctrines are outright socialism, or will lead to it, or, at least, to a vast extension of government control and power over

[4] See, for example, National Association of Manufacturers, *The American Individual Enterprise System* (N.Y.: McGraw-Hill, 1947).

From Ernest van den Haag and Henry Hazlitt, "Must Conservatives Repudiate Keynes?" *National Review*, 4 June 1960. Reprinted by permission of the publisher.

the economy. Conservatives also fear that Keynesianism brings fiscal and ultimately political irresponsibility through deficit financing, inflation, and the handing out of political bribes by a government which can obtain the necessary money through increasing the national debt. Now, I am opposed to all these evils. Yet I favor the basic Keynesian theory. In my opinion, it does not lead to any of these evils but helps to avoid them.

The association of Keynes' economics with political leftism—in this country with the New Deal—is an historical accident which helps to explain their reputation among conservatives, but does not justify it. The theory itself is politically neutral and applicable in both capitalist and socialist societies without changing the institutions of either. Thus I see no need to oppose it from a conservative viewpoint, though Communists must and do oppose it because Keynes' theory shows clearly that depression and inflation can be cured within the capitalist system—whereas the Communist dogma requires capitalism to suffer and die from depression.

DEPRESSION AND INFLATION

Economic depression is a major and drawn-out reduction of aggregate sales, production, prices, employment and income—a massive non-utilization of resources, the owners of which would like to have them utilized to earn income. Depression occurs when total expenditure on goods and services by consumers, business and government is insufficient to purchase total output at current prices. The lost sales, with or without lower prices, cause lower production, employment and income. There are many possible reasons for the insufficiency of total expenditure which is the basic characteristic of depression. They vary, moreover, from depression to depression, although in most cases the portion of their income consumers fail to spend—their intended savings—exceeds the amount businessmen raise and invest successfully. If business adds less money to total expenditure, via investment, than consumers subtract, via saving, total expenditure is reduced and thus total income. For income is but expenditure viewed from the recipients' side. Some goods are not transformed into income but frozen into inventories, while people who would like to cannot afford to buy them because of lack of income. The inventories devalue with falling prices. And this leads to still less demand, lower prices, less production and ultimately less income. Once set in motion, the process becomes cumulative and to some extent self-propelling. For instance, when prices fall or sales lack, some businesses cannot go on producing for they are losing money. Business and consumers postpone purchases in hope or fear of further price reductions; inventories accumulate without being replenished, and new investment declines—things get worse before they get better.

No improvement is likely until expenditure stops falling. This may happen only when intended savings no longer exceed investment expenditure—when income is very low, that is, after a long period in which fewer people work than want to, and work less, produce less and get less income than they want, and even the reduced output is hard to sell—though people's needs are less satisfied than ever. Keynes may have been wrong in believing that a depression could go on indefinitely, that an equilibrium (a situation that has no endogenous tendency to change) may be reached at a very low level of income, employment and production. But even if this is not the case, the process of decline can be long drawn out, with baneful effects.

Even if it were true that unemployment could be reduced by reducing the price of labor (wage rates)—and there is much doubt on the feasibility and usefulness of such a measure—the process would be lengthy. The expectation of reduced wage rates would reduce hiring, production and sales, as do all other expected price reductions in depression. One might as well recommend death as a remedy for illness. Moreover, wage rates could be reduced indefinitely without reducing unemployment if marginal value productivity falls with them, as may be the case if prices fall—just as, in inflation, wage rates can be increased indefinitely if prices are. Both processes are undesirable. It seems fortunate that the wage rate decrease is unfeasible as well.

Before we look for safer and more effective remedies, it will be instructive to glance at inflation, which in many ways is the reverse of depression. In depression, total expenditure is insufficient to buy total output at current prices when resources are fully utilized. Hence, output is reduced or insufficient to utilize productive resources to the extent desired by their owners. In inflation, total expenditure exceeds the amount needed to buy the total output available at current prices. Hence, in inflation, prices are bid up and rise as output at first is increased. But if all resources are already utilized, higher prices cannot be matched by higher production.

Undesirable effects on income distribution and the general pattern of economic activity are associated with both inflation and depression—though they differ. Depression involves hypoactivity, inflation hyperactivity, often in the wrong direction. Inflation, like depression, distorts production patterns, but depression leads to prompt decreases of production, while inflation does not —at least not at first. Depression favors creditors, inflation debtors. The cumulative effect of depression, however, tends to damage everybody. And the cumulative effect of inflation, too, tends to weaken the fabric of the economy although the damage is not quite so obvious to most. One reason is that depression means less money income for almost everyone, whereas inflation means more money income for almost everyone—and people do not discover immediately or give proper weight to the discovery that the dollars they receive are worth less than before.

Depression is, by and large, the converse of inflation: spending less than the amount needed to purchase current (not to speak of maximum) output at current prices. If the remedy against inflation is to decrease spending, the remedy against depression is to increase it.

The means available are the same as those available to control inflation. Since the evil is opposite, they must be used in the opposite direction. Business expenditure can be facilitated by decreasing interest rates; government spending can be increased directly, for instance, by increasing pensions; the expenditures of business and consumers can be increased by reducing taxes while keeping government expenditures stable.

Before discussing the Keynesian approach further, let me stress that it is meant to counter and cure major swings of business activity and prices. Minor fluctuations occur all the time and are best countered by the adjustments of Federal Reserve policy which have always been undertaken since the beginning of central banking. A person's changes from buoyant to more pensive moods do not call for the measures suitable for manic-depressive cycles; or, to change metaphors, a competent physician does not prescribe penicillin for a cold, though he may use it should the cold become pneumonia.

Many people feel that the attempt to remedy depression may land us in inflation. By this logic we should never irrigate land for it may lead to inundation; nor should we drain swamps for it may lead to aridity. And if we should not try to remedy depression for fear of inflation, we should not try to remedy inflation either for it may lead to depression. This is obviously absurd. In the attempt to keep spending at the correct level—no more and no less than needed to purchase total output when all or nearly all resources are being used, at current prices—we may sometimes have to reduce spending; at other times we may have to increase it. There is no reason to believe that we cannot increase or decrease spending by the right amount. After all, we will notice changes in employment, production, prices, etc. and accordingly reduce or augment the increase or decrease of expenditure.

MORE GOVERNMENT CONTROLS?

Does increasing the rate of expenditure of the economy—and thus demand, production and income—involve an extension of government controls? Far from it. The means by which the level of total spending is influenced have been used since the beginnings of the free enterprise system. The government has always spent money, created money and taxed. Interest rates have always helped control spending. In the past, these instruments of economic policy have not always been used so as to bring about the desired long-run effects. Undue weight was given, say to the effect of interest rates on government financing which is surely less important than the effect on the economy as a whole—on business financing, for instance. Similarly, taxation, in addition to being a way of giving money to the government, has the important effect of decreasing the income available to the taxed; which in inflation is desirable and in depression is not. These effects occur regardless of whether we are conscious of them. But by realizing the foreseeable effects of our action, we may act so as to bring about the desired and avoid the undesired effects. This, too, is hardly a novelty. Indeed, in inflation the government has always resorted to the instruments which Lord Keynes proposes should be used for analogous though opposite purposes in depression. Conservatives have usually applauded the anti-inflationary use of these instruments. Why do they oppose their anti-depressive use?

Surely not because they like depression, though perhaps they are more aware of the danger of inflation. Yet the political dangers of depression can hardly be overestimated. Without the depression of the 1930s, there would have been neither a Roosevelt nor a Hitler. Probably no Second World War —not to speak of the present threat of a third one. Depression impairs loyalty to both democracy and capitalism as much, if not more, than inflation.

Surely the objection that the proposed remedies against depression constitute socialism is absurd. They do not involve nationalization; or any form of government economic activity or control, not now pursued (such as taxing or spending or regulating the issuance of money) and, on the contrary, by lightening the tax burden, they stimulate private enterprise. Contrary to what is believed by some, public works—genuine or boondoggles—are not required to remedy depression.

What is needed in depression is additional spending, additional purchases to sell what we are capable of producing and willing to consume. The government can spend directly by purchasing goods and services. But this is neither necessary nor particularly helpful. Additional private spending is much more to the point. This can be brought about by the government taking less income away from prospective spenders—business and consumers—through reduced taxation, and even by giving them money (for example, higher pensions). There is no need for an increase in government activity—public works or services.

Subsidies to particular economic groups such as farmers should be avoided, for in addition to increasing spending, they make the group more attractive than it would otherwise be, and thus unnecessarily distort the patterns of production. If subsidies are given, they should be received by non-economic groupings, such as veterans, the old, or the young—groups that cannot be joined for the sake of the subsidy. For similar reasons, subsidies should always be in money, never in kind; nor should we ever undertake public works for the sake of employment. Public works should be undertaken when needed—not to employ people. For people can be employed by increasing the rate of private spending; and they then are led to produce what consumers want, rather than unwanted post office frescoes.

Some fear that the Keynesian anti-depression prescription will be followed because of its obvious appeal, but not the less attractive anti-inflation prescription. Hence, we might be in permanent wild inflation. The evidence —Germany, France, England, the United States, Italy—gives little support to that fear. Moreover, if people want to pursue an inflationary policy, nothing can stop them. But people's inclination to do so will be strengthened by depressive phenomena and weakened if we avoid or promptly remedy these—which can be done without inflation.

One final point: the remedy against depression that I'm advocating —increasing expenditure enough to permit the sale of the goods that would be produced if resources are utilized to the extent desired by their owners—is not basically different from what occurs when depression is cured spontaneously.

(Only the spontaneous cure may keep us waiting for years.) When depression is relieved spontaneously, expenditure increases because someone spends more—for example, businessmen increase investment—and thus more is purchased and produced. The money in either case is created by the banking system, which under normal circumstances creates 90 per cent of all money spent through the act of lending, for example, "monetizing debt." Whether the government initiates the process or private business makes little difference. In either case it is "automatic." And in either case, if too much money is created, inflation occurs. Hence, to be consistent, those who oppose increases of expenditure through newly created money as inflationary would have to oppose any transition from depression to prosperity. Such a transition always involves a slight rise in prices which is necessary to stimulate production. But it need not amount to inflation—to a rise in the price level not needed for or correlated to a rise in production.

Yes, repeats Henry Hazlitt

According to Keynesian theory, economic depressions occur because of an "insufficiency of total expenditure." It would seem to follow that the remedy for the depression is for the government to increase the supply of money, to create more "purchasing power," in order to raise total expenditures to a level that restores "full employment."

But the Keynesian analysis begins at an arbitrary and unanalyzed starting point. Why has expenditure suddenly become insufficient? There may be any number of reasons. There may have been a sudden collapse of commodity prices or demand (as in 1920 and 1929) without any corresponding reduction in wage-rates. In that case people will not buy the same volume of goods at the same level of prices as before. But manufacturers cannot reduce prices because of their high labor costs. The result is unemployment. The remedy would be a sufficient reduction in wage-rates to make possible resumption of full production and sales at the now lower level of prices and of (monetary) demand. This would not, of course, mean any reduction in real wages. But the unions, the Keynesians and the politicians insist that such a money reduction in wage rates is unthinkable, and their insistence itself makes it "unfeasible." As wages cannot then be adjusted downward to the new level of prices, prices must be adjusted upward again to wages. This is achieved by increasing the money supply, either directly or indirectly, through cheap money policies, increased government spending and deliberate deficits.

In brief, the Keynesian remedy for unemployment, no matter how caused, is always more inflation. This is not merely the conclusion of a "gloomy economic moralist." Jacob Viner correctly predicted in 1936 that "In a world organized in accordance with Keynes' specifications there would be a constant race between the printing press and the business agents of the trade unions."

In Mr. Van Den Haag's version, original Keynesianism is somewhat diluted. He does not believe in socialism, and therefore presumably repudiates (though not explicitly) Keynes' proposal to socialize investment. As against

Keynes, also, he does not believe in public works "for the sake of employment." But his own remedies are politically even more dangerous. In times of depression, he is for starting subsidies and pensions, not to farmers, but to "non-economic groupings, such as veterans, the old, or the young." That just about covers everybody. As experience has shown, it creates a vested interest of such immense political power that no one later dares to suggest any reduction (let alone termination) of the pensions. They become permanent; they are increased almost automatically in every election year; and in subsequent depressions any new pensions must be piled on top of the existing ones.

Mr. Van Den Haag tries to reassure us by pointing out that after an inflation has worked great havoc, as in Germany, France and Italy, or when it has reached alarming dimensions, as in England, it can sometimes be stopped. It can—by a clear-sighted and courageous *repudiation* of the Keynesian remedies, as happened dramatically in 1957, when the Bank of England raised its discount rate to 7 per cent.

3.8 Keynes: A Neo-Marxist Perspective

Paul M. Sweezy

Keynes' Achievements I

The true nature of Keynes' achievement was to reform neo-classical economics, to bring it back into contact with the real world from which it had wandered farther and farther since the break with the classical tradition in the nineteenth century; and it was precisely because he was one of them and not an outsider that Keynes could exercise such a profound influence on his colleagues. The very same reasons, however, account for the fact that, as we shall see below, Keynes could never transcend the limitations of the neo-classical approach which conceives of economic life in abstraction from its historical setting and hence is inherently incapable of providing a scientific guide to social action.

. . . . The opportunity to which Keynes responded was essentially a crisis in traditional economics, a crisis which was both accentuated and laid bare by the Great Depression. He was able to demonstrate that his fellow economists, by their unthinking acceptance of Say's Law, were in effect asserting the impossibility of what was actually happening. From this starting point he was able to go on to a penetrating analysis of the capitalist economy which shows that depression and unemployment far from being impossible, are the norms to which that economy tends, and which explode once and for all the myth of a harmony between private and public interests which was the cornerstone of

Excerpted from Paul M. Sweezy, "What Has Keynes Contributed to the Analysis of Capitalism?" *Science and Society*, October 1946. Reprinted by permission of the publisher.

nineteenth century liberalism. But Keynes stopped here in his critique of existing society. Our troubles, he believed, are due to a failure of intelligence and not to the breakdown of a social system; "the problem of want and poverty and the economic struggle between classes and nations," he wrote in 1931, "is nothing but a frightful muddle, a transitory and unnecessary muddle."

That Keynes held this view was, of course, no accident. He could reject Say's Law and the economic conclusions based on it because he thought they were largely responsible for the muddle; but it never occurred to him to question, still less to try to escape from, the broader philosophical and social tradition in which he was reared. The major unspoken premise of that tradition is that capitalism is the only possible form of civilized society. Hence Keynes, exactly like the economists he criticized, never viewed the system as a whole; never studied the economy in its historical setting; never appreciated the interconnectedness of economic phenomena on the one hand and technological, political, and cultural phenomena on the other. Moreover, he was apparently quite ignorant of the fact that there was a serious body of economic thought, as closely related to the classical school as the doctrines on which he himself was brought up, which attempted to do these things. In Keynes' eyes, Marx inhabited a theoretical underworld . . . and there is no evidence that he ever thought of any of Marx's followers as anything but propagandists and agitators.

. . . . I raise the issue only in order to show that the school of thought to which Keynes belongs is rather isolated and one-sided, that some of his most important discoveries were taken for granted by socialist economists at least a generation before Keynes began to write, and that many of the most vital problems of the capitalist system are completely ignored in *The General Theory*. Marx rejected Say's Law from the outset; already before 1900 his followers were carrying on a spirited debate among themselves not only on the subject of periodic crises but also on the question whether capitalism could be expected to run into a period of permanent or chronic depression. Keynes ignores technological change and technological unemployment, problems which figure as an integral part of the Marxian theoretical structure. Keynes treats unemployment as a symptom of a technical fault in the capitalist mechanism, while Marx regards it as the indispensable means by which capitalists maintain their control over the labor market. Keynes completely ignores the problems of monopoly, its distorting effect on the distribution of income and the utilization of resources, the huge parasitic apparatus of distribution and advertising which it foists upon the economy. A socialist can only blink his eyes in astonishment when he reads that there is "no reason to suppose that the existing system seriously misemploys the factors of production which are in use. . . . When 9,000,000 men are employed out of 10,000,000 willing and able to work, there is no evidence that the labor of these 9,000,000 men is misdirected." Many other examples of the insularity and comparative narrowness of the Keynesian approach could be cited. But perhaps most striking of all is Keynes's habit of treating the state as a *deus ex machina* to be invoked whenever his human actors, behaving according to the rules of the capitalist game, get themselves into a dilemma from which there is apparently no escape. Naturally, this Olympian interventionist resolves everything in a manner satisfactory to the author and presumably to the audience. The only trouble is—as every Marxist knows—that the state is not a god but one of the actors who has a part to play just like all the other actors.

Nothing that has been said should be taken as belittling the importance of Keynes' work.

But while it is right to recognize the great importance of Keynes, it is no less essential to recognize his shortcomings. They are for the most part the shortcomings of bourgeois thought in general: the unwillingness to view the economy as an integral part of a social whole; the inability to see the present as history, to understand that the disasters and catastrophies amidst which we live are not simply a "frightful muddle" but are the direct and inevitable product of a social system which has exhausted its creative powers, but whose beneficiaries are determined to hang on regardless of the cost.

Keynes' Achievements II

Apart from minor matters of formulation and emphasis, I am prepared to stand by what I wrote a decade and a half ago about Keynes and Keynesian economics. In particular, I still believe that his greatest achievements were freeing economics from the tyranny of Say's Law and exploding the myth of capitalism as a self-adjusting system which reconciles private and public interests.

In this connection, however, I would like to amend what I wrote earlier, not because the amendment is of any particular importance in itself but because it provides a logical introduction to the remarks which constitute the substance of what follows.

Starting from the rejection of Say's Law, I wrote, Keynes "was able to go on to a penetrating analysis of the capitalist economy which shows that depression and unemployment, far from being impossible, are the norms to which the economy tends." This now seems to me to be a misleading statement of the case. Keynes in fact did not "show" anything of the kind, at least not in the sense of furnishing a logical, consistent, and convincing set of reasons why it should be so. He *believed* that the inducement to invest was, so to speak, naturally weak and that the structure of the system was such that a weak inducement to invest would result in depression and unemployment. His analysis was focused on this structure, and he gave reasons (essentially downward rigidity of wage and interest rates) why it could not generate full employment in the absence of a strong inducement to invest. But he had very little indeed to say about why the inducement to invest should be chronically weak, and this, after all, lies at the heart of the matter.

It is not hard to infer from remarks scattered here and there throughout the *General Theory* that Keynes believed that at any given time the demand for capital is narrowly limited and hence that the maintenance of a strong inducement to invest depends almost entirely on what are often called exogenous factors. Perhaps the most explicit statement of this thesis occurs on page 307:

Excerpted from Robert Lekachman, ed., *Keynes General Theory: Report of the Decades* (New York: St. Martin's Press, 1900). Reprinted by permission of the publisher.

> *During the nineteenth century, the growth of population and of invention, the opening up of new lands, the state of confidence and the frequency of war over the average of (say) each decade seem to have been sufficient, taken in conjunction with the propensity to consume, to establish a schedule of the marginal efficiency of capital which allowed a reasonably satisfactory average level of employment to be compatible with a rate of interest high enough to be psychologically acceptable to wealth-owners.*

So much for the nineteenth century. What of the twentieth? On the following page, we read: "To-day and presumably for the future the schedule of the marginal efficiency of capital is, for a variety of reasons, much lower than it was in the nineteenth century." One might expect to find this followed by a discussion of the "variety of reasons," but if so one would be disappointed. Keynes turns immediately to the downward stickiness of the rate of interest and forgets all about the flagging marginal efficiency of capital. Nor does a careful reading of the rest of the *General Theory,* or of his other writings either for that matter, yield any but casual and often peripheral remarks bearing on the subject.

About all one can say, then, is that Keynes seems to have been of the opinion that "the growth of population and of invention, the opening up of new lands, the state of confidence and the frequency of war," taken all together, had lost much of their efficacy as stimulants to the demand for capital. This is not much of a theory, and it is even less impressive when one looks, in even the most superficial way, at the historical record. On a world scale, population growth has speeded up rather than the reverse, and in an economic sense there has been no lack of underdeveloped lands. Nor can one very well complain about a shortage of wars during the twentieth century. That leaves the state of confidence, which is obviously a reflection rather than a cause of the underlying situation. The truth would seem to be that the "vision" of capitalism as a system always in imminent danger of falling into a state of stagnation—a vision which permeates, and in a sense even dominates, the *General Theory*—is based more on intuition and generalizing from British experience of the 1920's and early 1930's than on any serious analysis of the factors affecting the inducement to invest.

Among Keynes' followers, only Hansen undertook to develop a *theory* of the tendency to stagnation. This theory turns out, however, to be little more than an elaboration, in terms of U.S. experience, of Keynes' casual remark quoted above. . . .

Thus neither Keynes nor his followers really provided an explanation of the stagnation of the 1930's. Their whole analysis was directed to showing that *if* the inducement to invest is weak, the capitalist system, left to itself, will stagnate. But they had nothing very enlightening to say about *why* it should be (or remain) weaker than it had been in the past.

. . . . The *General Theory* shows absolutely no trace of "monopolistic thinking," and its tremendous impact and prestige doubtless served as an additional bulwark of the traditional assumption of universal competition. My own opinion now, many years later, is that it was the stubborn commitment to this assumption—the refusal to contemplate, let alone work out the implications of, the possibility that monopoly (or oligopoly) had become the norm—which accounts for the failure of Keynesians and non-Keynesians alike to make any progress in developing a satisfactory theory of what happened during the 1930's.

Keynes not only did nothing to overcome this profoundly anti-historical character of received economic theory; on the contrary, his example and prestige did much to strengthen it. It is therefore really no cause for surprise that Keynes' followers were incapable of transcending his strictly limited vision of capitalist reality. Nor, considering the usual relation between master and epigone, can we say that it is a cause of surprise that in vital respects they took a long step back from the position occupied by Keynes. He was deeply convinced that capitalism is *not* a system of economic harmonics and that its gravest failing was precisely its chronic tendency to depression and stagnation. His followers, with one or two honorable exceptions, cheerfully abandoned this disturbing and at the same time challenging view and gave themselves over to comforting speculations about full-employment equilibria, warranted growth rates, and similar fancies.

Now that stagnation is once again with us, at least in the most advanced and monopolistic of the capitalist countries, now that its abeyance during the forties and early fifties can be clearly seen to have been the result of war, the aftermath of war, and preparation for war—now that these things are being driven home by practical experience to even the dullest observer of the current economic scene, the stage would seem to be set for bourgeois economics to attempt a new step forward. . . . It may not be out of place to suggest that before this could happen, bourgeois economics would first have to recover the ground lost since Keynes—to recapture his vision of capitalism, not as the best of all possible worlds but as a system of profound contradictions and deeply rooted self-destructive tendencies.

3.9 Keynes and the Socialists

G.D.H. Cole

THE SOCIALISTS AND THE KEYNESIANS

Keynes constructed a new kind of Economics of which the principal lesson was that it was the State's business to maintain a condition of full employment, instead of trusting to the working of "economic laws" to bring such a condi-

From G.D.H. Cole, *Socialist Economics* (London: Victor Gollancz, 1950). Reprinted by permission of David Higham Associates, Ltd.

tion about. It was the State's business, Keynes argued, to ensure that there should be enough demand in the market to clear all that could be produced at prices adequate to cover costs, including normal profits. This should be accepted as a definite responsibility of the Government—of course, with the addition that there should not be too much demand either, only just enough to hold things steady *and progressive,* in a condition of dynamic equilibrium deliberately brought about by wise economic planning, not naturally happening when nothing was done to induce it.

Once this idea was accepted, there were plenty of ways of acting on it. Public capital expenditure to fill in the gap left by inadequate private investment, or alternately subsidies to business men designed to induce them to take up capital more freely, or, on a different tack, increased consuming power engendered by tax remissions or, alternatively, by actual subsidies to consumption. Monetary inflation Keynes did not urge; but he did agree that the banking system ought to stand ready to create enough credit to finance the requirements of full employment. He wanted monetary policy to become the servant of productive development, not an independent and capricious power whose dictates industry had to obey. He treated the rate of interest, not as a sacred thing to which production had to accommodate itself, but as an instrument that could be regulated by public action to help bring about a lightening of the dead hand of unearned income. Therewith, he played ducks and drakes with the time-honoured notion that an annually balanced budget—or indeed a balanced budget at all—was a *sine qua non* of economic rationality. A budget deficit, that is, the State paying out more than it received in taxes—might be the very best way to maintain employment and production in face of a threatened recession in demand. Keynes knocked down the shibboleths of economic orthodoxy, row upon row, with a consummate skill that even his bitterest opponents had to admire. Within a few years he transformed traditional economics from a jeremiad into a practical programme for making the capitalist system work.

No: that is not quite fair. Keynes had no devotion to the capitalist system as such. Indeed, the entire dispute about Capitalism and Socialism seemed to him to be mainly beside the point. His remedies would serve to render workable either Capitalism or Socialism, or indeed any other system that was compatible with the State's acceptance of the responsibility for ensuring full employment. He made this sound easy—if only the manipulators of public economic policy could be persuaded to behave in a reasonably intelligent fashion.

This new Keynesian Economics deeply affected the thought of Socialists as well as of "progressives" of all sorts who were not Socialists. Keynes made the planning of employment seem so much more important than anything else, at a time when the thoughts of both politicians and economists had become fixed perforce on the disease of unemployment in both its long-term and its cyclical forms. Hitherto, most Socialists had contended that the disease of unemployment was incurable except by socialisation—that is, by the State taking over industry and employing every available person, and at the same time so distributing purchasing power as to ensure that there would be a demand for all that socialised industry could produce. But now it appeared, if Keynes were right, that full employment could be maintained without socialisation, merely by manipulating the correct levers at the centre, in the money and investment markets. There might be a case for socialising this or that industry on other grounds—to prevent monopolistic restriction, or to improve productive efficiency by rationalisation—but not in order to cure unemployment; for that could be done by other, and much less disturbing, methods.

The only economists who were not deeply affected by this revolution in traditional economic thought were the Marxists, who, having a complete and distinct economic theory of their own that had diverged from orthodox theory a century ago and thereafter gone its own way, regarded Keynesism as merely the latest dodge to save Capitalism from itself by invoking the State as its ally. Nothing, the Marxists continued to assert, could save Capitalism from recurrent crises, all leading up to the final crisis in the course of which it would be submerged in world revolution. Some Marxists, indeed, went so far as to admit that Keynes' nostrums might prove potent enough to stave off capitalist crisis for some time. Professor Varga, the leading theoretician of the Soviet Union, came near to saying this, and was made to eat his words—though he spat some of them out again in the process.

The Socialist economists who were not full-blooded Marxists were in a different case; for most of them had no belief in the inevitability of "Capitalism's Final Crisis." They had been for a long time past calling on the Government to ease unemployment by "public works policy"—that is, by providing useful jobs for workers for whom profit-seeking Capitalism appeared to have no use. They had been contending on this issue with the orthodox economists who argued either that the effect of State action to provide work would be an equivalent diminution in private investment or that, even if extra jobs could be provided, the result would be to throw the economic system out of balance and to lead on to an inflationary crisis. Keynes' new doctrines came as a powerful reinforcement of what they had been saying, and as a great relief to their minds, because they were now able to argue for State action with the grain of traditional economic theory, and not against it as heretics and pariahs foolish enough to be taken in by economic "quacks." Above all, the socialist economists in academic jobs, who had to spend their days teaching students the things that were needed for passing examinations, were immensely reassured, and set to work happily to teach the new Keynesian economics, with a sense that a bridge between the classical tradition and Socialism had been successfully built.

Indeed, it is hardly too much to say that most of the non-Marxist socialist economists swallowed Keynes whole, and became his most fervent disciples. As one who did not, I, in my capacity as a teacher, passed from one discomfort to another. The things I had been arguing, largely on a basis laid by J. A. Hobson, at the risk of spoiling my pupils' examination chances, suddenly became part of the new orthodoxy; and I found myself trying to brake the enthusiasm of students who expected far too much from them. For I continued to believe that, great as was the advance made by Keynes in the techniques of economic manipulation, his conclusions were partly vitiated by his habit of reasoning in terms of global demand and supply, or at any rate of "capital goods" and "consumers' goods" as global divisions of the total product of industry, instead of breaking up the productive system into much smaller and more differentiated groups of real persons and things.

Thus, when Keynes spoke of maintaining total "investment" at an adequate level, I began at once to think of the actual forms of this investment—machines of different sorts, specialised buildings, ships, new minesinkings, farm equipment, and so on. And when Keynes spoke of "full employment" I began at once to think of actual men and women, living in particular places and possessing both particular skills, dexterities and aptitudes, and also family attachments and wills to work more or less hard or efficiently. I do not mean that I found other economists ignoring these real factors; but I did find an undue readiness to believe that they were secondary to the main thing—which was to manipulate global demand for investment and consumption goods by making the right budgetary adjustments and accommodating to these the flows of credit out of the banking system, the rates of interest on borrowed money, and the "public works policy" of the State—which last thus appeared not as a prime mover, but rather as one among a number of budgetary devices for keeping economic activity at a high level. I was sceptical about all this, not as doubting its correctness and usefulness up to a point, but as holding that it left many too many of the real factors in the situation out of account.

For, can the State really, by following the Keynesian prescription, maintain full employment without setting inflationary tendencies to work, unless it is in a position to control, broadly, what is to be produced and when, and what is to be charged for it, and also the broad distribution of purchasing power, as well as its global amount? I do not think it can. I am not suggesting that, in order to achieve *and maintain* full employment without inflation, it is necessary for the State to take charge of the entire economy, to fix all prices, or to regulate the whole distribution of incomes among individuals. But I do believe that, in order to achieve the desired result, the State must be in a position to direct investment into particular branches of production, to control the location of industry in order to bring balanced employment to the workers rather than expect them to migrate in large masses in search of work, and to regulate the course of prices and incomes in such a way as to secure a tolerable correspondence between the flow of consumers' goods and services and the demand for them, and at the same time to keep costs at such a level as to enable exporting industries to hold a satisfactory place in the world market.

But I go further than this. Although it would be theoretically possible for the State to exercise all these powers by "controls," without taking any considerable executive functions into its own hands, I cannot conceive of such an arrangement working in practice, except very ill. Control without executive responsibility or financial accountability for the results of the orders given is an instrument that has its uses, and is indeed indispensable if we are to avoid both an excessive concentration of authority and an undue absence of it; but it is an instrument that has grave disadvantages—not least the irritation it is bound to cause among those who have to carry out the orders and to bear the brunt of what ensues.

Take the case of investment. The State can, no doubt, in theory, channel private investment into the forms of development it thinks best; but in practice, if it relies on "controls," it has to do this mainly by forbidding types of investment which it thinks less desirable, or actually disapproves. Even if the effect is not that of reducing the total volume of investment—as it may well be—it is unlikely to be very satisfactory in securing the right balance among the permitted types of investment. In order to achieve this, the State must itself become an investor, and therewith an owner of capital assets: not necessarily the sole owner, but investor and owner on a considerable scale, not only in a limited group of "public service" industries, but over a wide field, covering potentially every major type of capital development. This is apart from the fact—certainly no less important—that "controls" may be quite ineffective in securing a correct total volume of investment at periods when a stimulus, rather than a deterrent, is called for.

Take again the closely related problem of industrial location. The State, if it tries to secure a right distribution and a right local balance of employment openings merely by control, will be in precisely the same difficulty. In this case it can do something—and is actually doing something—by the development of Industrial Trading Estates and New Towns; but that reinforces my point, for such action involves direct public investment, even if plenty of room is left for private capital to operate within the framework of direct public provision.

Or take price regulation. Here, if anywhere, one would expect the control mechanism to be able to work without direct assumption of responsibility by the State. It is, however, notoriously difficult to fix the right prices except for a narrow range of highly standardised goods, most of which are either crude or semi-manufactured foodstuffs or materials. Control can be most easily extended beyond this field by promoting the production of certain "utility" lines of standard qualities and specifications; but this method cannot be extended very far without beginning to impinge on justifiable variety of output, and therewith on consumers' choice. Beyond these limits the State cannot easily tell what prices are fair unless it is itself engaged in production and in a position to check the private producers' costs by its own experience, either in publicly owned factories or in establishments in which it has at any rate a part interest in ownership and administration.

Finally, take the case of incomes—for the moment not wages but those paid for managerial, professional, and administrative work. If most industries are privately owned and public employment is confined to a narrow group, there will be a strong tendency for private industry to set the standards of payment for such jobs, and for public employments to have to fall in with the capitalist practice. We have seen this occurring already in the case of the new public boards and corporations.

This matters, not only because it is an essential part of socialist policy to reduce differences of earned, as well as of unearned, income, but also because the example of high earnings in the upper ranges of employment naturally sets up, in any society that is moving towards Socialism, a strong pressure all down the scale for higher incomes, beyond what can be afforded without putting inflationary forces in motion. The spectacle of high top salaries leads to demands for high salaries lower down, and also to demands for high wages, not as a reward for high productivity, but as a claim to higher status and a nearer approach to equality.

It is sometimes argued that this need not happen if a very progressive system of taxation on the higher incomes reduces the real inequality of spending power within reasonable bounds. But this view is psychologically incorrect. Rightly or wrongly, men measure relative status in terms of income before, and not after, direct taxation. It is, moreover, an extraordinary and in the long run indefensible process to begin by distributing much more in earned incomes than the recipients are to be allowed to keep, and then to redress undue inequalities by taking back a higher and higher proportion as the income rises. This is a good enough way of dealing with unearned incomes: its extension to earned incomes is a logical absurdity, save as a purely transitional method.

In effect, then, I am arguing that the Keynesian apparatus for maintaining economic equilibrium at a high level will not work in practice unless the State, through some publicly responsible agency—or rather through many such agencies—owns and conducts a large part of the apparatus of production. This does not mean that it is necessary to nationalise everything—heaven forbid! It does mean that the "public sector" of industry must be large enough to set the tone for the rest, leaving private industry to operate within a framework of public enterprise, rather than the other way around. This "public sector" can be itself highly diversified. It can include, besides nationally owned and unified industries and services, state-owned and partly state-owned enterprises in industries still left largely under other forms of ownership. It can include Co-operative Societies, both of consumers and of producers. It can include locally and regionally organised, as well as nationally unified services. It can also have many diverse forms of internal administration, from the Post Office type and the National Board type to various experiments in "workers' control" and industrial democracy. Public enterprise does not and should not mean uniformity: nor should it mean the elimination of competition except where national unification is clearly necessary on grounds of economic efficiency.

The upshot of the argument is that the Keynesian revolution in economic thought is to be welcomed and accepted by Socialists up to a point, but cannot be taken as a substitute for Socialism, or for a socialist economic theory which goes a long way beyond it. Keynesism is after all, in the last analysis, a very elaborate mechanism for *offsetting* rather than curing certain glaring deficiencies in the working of capitalist society. Keynes did not say that he could do away with the inherent instability of Capitalism, with its tendency to engender alternating booms and slumps, with its speculative aberrations, and with its marked preference for monopolistic restriction. He claimed only that he knew how to prevent these tendencies from doing nearly as much harm as they had done in the past. He did not meet even the purely economic case of the

Socialists against the capitalist system—much less their whole case, with its large moral and psychological elements.

Accordingly, though Keynesian economics is a great advance on the *laissez-faire*-based economics that preceded it, this advance in no way makes less necessary the formulation of the quite distinct economic theory appropriate to a socialist society. Socialist economists can build on Keynes to a quite considerable extent; and to a still greater extent they can use Keynes as a stick for beating more reactionary economists over the head. But Keynes was no Socialist; he had no deep-seated faith in democracy to drive him on to formulate an economic theory that would meet the needs of a society committed to working out the implications of the democratic attitude in every aspect of social life, including the economic.

THE LIBERAL STRAND OF THE KEYNESIAN SYNTHESIS

Is Keynesian economics "radical," "liberal," or "conservative," or none of these? Do Keynesian policy prescriptions really serve to "save" American capitalism or to transform it? The relationships between the post-Keynesian synthesis and various strands of contemporary thinking about issues of public economic policy are subtle and complex, and have been modified in the course of time. At the outset, Keynesian analysis and policy prescriptions were widely regarded as liberal and reformist in character, by both the economics profession and the general public. In neoclassical orthodoxy, the economy is presumed to automatically tend toward full employment. *From this perspective,* the deliberate use of monetary and fiscal policies to promote full employment, price stability, and economic growth, and the expansion of the public debt through purposeful creation of federal government deficits, seemed definitely liberal and reformist. This characterization of Keynesian economics was heightened by its association in popular discussion with the depression and the reforms of the New Deal, by Keynes' cautious critique of inequality in the distribution of income, and by the obviously liberal, reformist proclivities of many Keynesian economists (for example, Hansen).

The liberal dimensions of the Keynesian analysis and its relationship to left-of-center, social reform liberalism are described in the next five selections. In selection 3.10, Donald Watson contrasts reform liberalism and conservatism as contemporary economic philosophies, placing Keynes and Keynesian-type policies squarely under the former heading. In selection 3.11, Paul Streeten puts Keynes' analysis and recommendations in a broader perspective by identifying some of their implicit value premises, and comparing these premises with the tradition of classical liberalism and classical economic theory. In selection 3.12, Overton Taylor distinguishes between the relatively conservative character of some of Keynes' ideas and the left-of-center uses to which Keynesian-style policies may be put. In selection 3.13, Gunnar Myrdal, prominent advocate of liberal democratic social reform, presents a "challenge to affluence." He links the problem of unemployment in an otherwise affluent economy to poverty, inequality, and racial discrimination. In selection 3.14, Leon Keyserling, chairman of the Council of Economic Advisers during the Truman administration and perennial liberal gadfly, criticizes the timidity, skewed priorities, and neglect of allocative and distributive issues in the expansionary monetary and fiscal policies of the 1960s.

3.10 Keynesian Economics and Social Reform Liberalism

Donald S. Watson

REFORM LIBERALISM

What are the characteristics of reform liberalism at the present time? Reform liberalism stands for the general-welfare state, for the positive and active intervention of government in economic affairs. This economic philosophy, or more broadly, this attitude of mind has been known under many other names—New Deal, Fair Deal, Square Deal, progressivism, social planning, the welfare state, social control, the positive state, regulated capitalism, the new freedom, the general-welfare state, reformism, and, of course, unmodified and unqualified "liberalism."

Fundamental Criticism of the Market

Reform liberalism occupies a position between laissez faire and socialism. But the position is not necessarily midway between them, and it should be added that there has been no obvious tendency for the position of reform liberalism to drift closer to one of the extremes. In its beginnings late in the nineteenth century, reform liberalism repudiated the doctrines that uncritically praised the market as a social institution. Reform liberals have continued to be skeptical, where they are not overtly hostile, of the market as a coordinating mechanism. Innumerable statements expressing disbelief in the social efficacy of the market could be garnered from the writings of reform liberals. The criticisms have ranged from almost the total denial of any usefulness of the market—such ut-

Excerpted from Donald S. Watson, *Economic Policy: Business and Government* (Boston: Houghton Mifflin, 1960), pp. 64–71. Reprinted by permission of the publisher.

terances being common in the 1930's—to analytically qualified appraisals of a proper role for the market. Reform liberals want economic activity to lead to the realization of humanitarian values, to the freedom and dignity of man to social justice.

The fundamental criticism of the market proceeds from the high positions that equality and humanitarianism occupy in the ethics of reform liberalism. The popular slogans of "social justice" and of "human rights before property rights" amount to denunciation of the unequal distribution of incomes that arises in a market economy. Inequality itself is strongly criticized, but more than that, the criticism has gone on to point to discrepancies between market results and social needs. This can be done in two general ways. One is to measure the family income required for a minimum standard of decency, and then to estimate the number of millions of families with incomes below the minimum level. It is then implicit that there is something wrong with an economic system permitting such a result. The other general way of censuring the market is to take particular problems, such as housing, medical care, and diets. For each of these a standard of adequacy can be set up; it is then demonstrated that the low-income groups cannot (or do not) afford the adequate housing (or medical care, or diets) said to be socially needed.

Another side of the reform-liberal criticism of the inequality of incomes is the distinction between property and labor incomes. Emotionally this is again the tension between property rights and human rights; ethically it is a problem of economic justice. The recipients of property incomes are the privileged, the possessors of power, the vested interests. They are the minority favored by the operation of the market. Those who receive labor incomes are the great majority, exposed to the vicissitudes and fluctuations of a market that rewards too many with too low incomes.

Reform liberals have also denounced the market for waste and inefficiency. The excessive destruction of natural resources in the past has been laid at the door of the market. There have been other such specific charges along with the continuing general attack on the wastes of competition. Reform-liberal thought holds firmly to the belief that what remains of the efficiency of the market—some good points are awarded it—has been steadily diminishing over the decades, owing to the continual decline of competition.

To correct or to supplant the market, reform liberalism looks to social control. Considered broadly, social control can be exercised by private interest groups such as labor unions, consumers' cooperatives, farmers' organizations, as well as by government. But of course in most contexts social control means government control. This is more than the turn of a phrase, because reform-liberal thought tends to identify government with society. Consciously or unconsciously, government is seen as both the voice and the power of society, and as the means to accomplish its purposes. In addition, reform liberalism is imbued with the thought that the historical changes in economic, political, and social institutions lead in the direction of even more social control. History does indeed have a meaning to the reform liberal: steady progress through advancing social control. The efficiency of the market is thought to be declining owing to changes in technology that lead to ever greater economies of large-scale production, and owing to the growth and power of business corporations and labor unions. Along with these trends democracy has become more effective, and the techniques of social control have steadily improved.

The Methods of Social Control

Reform liberals tend to be pragmatic, and are proud of it, in their choices or recommendations of methods of economic control. Within the last generation, however, there has been a distinct tendency to prefer large-scale, comprehensive solutions, solutions to which the term planning has often been applied. Planning is visualized as a technique, or a set of techniques, made possible by the advance of knowledge in many fields, and made necessary by the growth of large-scale production, the increasing interdependence of economic life, and the emergence of social problems. Planning can take many forms—the unified development of large river valleys, the coordination of federal and state conservation policies, the coordination of the transportation industries, the improvement of social insurance, and so on. The emphasis on planning in reform-liberal thought in the last generation has also had the consequence of stressing national solutions to economic problems; the federal government possesses more power than all the states taken together, and it is capable of tidy, integrated, and comprehensive solutions.

The Concern for Stability and Security

Because of its direct and sympathetic concern for the low-income groups, with their exposure to unemployment and loss of income, reform liberalism has given much attention to the instabilities of the economy. In prosperous periods, reform liberals have pointed to the plight of groups with very low incomes. By doing so, reform liberals attempt to puncture the smugness and complacency generated by prosperity. The heavy unemployment and the lowered incomes of farmers and wage-earners in periods of depression stimulate strong denunciation of the whole system of private enterprise. Reform liberals imperatively demand government action to raise levels of employment and of income. In short, then, reform liberalism looks upon the business cycle as an unmitigated evil and places an emphasis which can be hardly exaggerated upon the policy of full employment.

Ever since the early 1930's economic stability has been in the forefront of discussion of national economic policy. Though not alone in demanding that the federal government guarantee continuing economic stability, reform liberalism has come to be associated with the goal of full employment and with the advocacy of whatever means should prove necessary to attain this goal. Thus the reform-liberal position was identified in the middle 1930's with deficit spending, in the late 1930's with the slightly more sophisticated compensatory fiscal policy, and in the postwar period with fiscal policy as the means to stability. In the late 1950's many reform-liberal economists were willing to tolerate some degree of price inflation for the sake of full employment.

The names of two economists are linked with the problem of stability and reform-liberal economic policy. One is Lord Keynes, the British economist whose theories are commonly and more or less correctly credited with having provided the analytical basis for the New Deal deficit-spending policies in the middle 1930's. The impact of Keynes' theory upon economics was strong enough to justify the term "revolution"; more than that, a school of Keynesians quickly emerged. Reform liberals seized Keynes' ideas and some of his offhand remarks as fresh and brilliant proof of the inherent weakness of private enterprise and of the necessity of continuous, direct, and strong government action. The leader of the Keynesians became Alvin H. Hansen of Harvard University who developed the stagnation thesis, namely, that the problem of stability and full employment is more than that of counteracting cyclical depressions, because of a permanent deficiency of aggregate demand. The gap, Hansen and others argued, must be made up by large-scale government programs—public works, regional resource development, health facilities, education, urban development, and so on. Thus the maintenance of stability was to mean a great expansion of other government functions.

Besides the business cycle there are of course other causes of losses of incomes—illness, accidents, the infirmities of age, death of the breadwinner, and so on. Social insurance is the provision against losses of income from the insecurities of life in the modern economy. Reform liberalism has been a powerful force behind the drive for a broader system of social insurance.

The Meaning of Reform Liberalism for Contemporary Economic Policy

It would be an exaggeration to attribute the existence of all actual economic policies to the efforts of reform liberals. But if many economic policies can be considered as reforms, certainly the reform liberals can take much of the credit. This clearly holds true for labor legislation, social insurance, public housing, and similar measures. In demanding a continuous extension and improvement of government controls, reform liberals believe that it is all part of the march of democracy, of the advancement of the people, and of inevitable historical progress. It is an essentially optimistic outlook. The optimism of reform liberalism stems in part perhaps from its conception of human nature—seeing more goodness in man and more possibility of happiness through material advances and suitable institutions. Then, too, reform liberalism places much store in the progress of technology; economic institutions and government controls ought to change and keep pace with the applications of science. This idea is familiar through well-worn figures of speech—the laws or economic controls suitable to the horse-and-buggy age are not appropriate to the automobile (or the jet or the nuclear or the electronic) age.

3.11 Keynes and the Classical Liberal Tradition

Paul Streeten

The purpose of this essay is to bring out some of the value premises implicit in Keynes's analysis and recommendations, and to relate these premises to the great classical tradition of British economic thought.

THE HARMONY OF INTERESTS

The doctrine that there is a harmony of interests in society was one of the main inspirations for the formulation of economic laws. Like a leitmotif it runs through the whole of economic theory. It is so deep-rooted that some of the fiercest critics of the harmony theory were themselves its victims. The terminology changed and numerous qualifications and modifications were introduced in the course of time. Nevertheless, the common origin is clearly recognizable.

The economists inherited the doctrine from the philosophers of natural law. For Adam Smith economic laws were the decrees of a benevolent and beneficent natural order which turns man's stupid and selfish interests into the common good. Bentham no longer had Adam Smith's faith in the natural order. For him the ends which the economic system pursues are the ends of men, not of Nature. The market is a mechanism (not an organism) designed by men to serve their will.

It is useful to distinguish between a *crude* and the various versions of a *modified* harmony doctrine. According to the crude harmony doctrine the free play of self-interests automatically promotes the interest of society. There is no need for government regulation. Each, by promoting his own interest, simultaneously promotes the interest of "all" (in some significant sense).

According to the modified harmony doctrine the "interest of society," or the "interest of *all,*" does not automatically coincide with the interests of each of its members, although it is in the interest of all, and in some sense also in the interest of *each,* to promote the social interest. The theory assumes different degrees or layers of self-interest, only one of which leads to harmony. The most commonly discussed obstacle to the realization of this kind of self-interest is ignorance, but there are others. Conflicts can arise if we think we want to follow certain courses which would not really be to our advantage.

Thus the crude version of the harmony doctrine tends to lead to a liberal laissez-faire view of policy, whereas the modified version *may* provide reasons

Excerpted from Paul P. Streeten, "Keynes and the Classical Tradition," in *Post-Keynesian Economics*, edited by Kenneth K. Kurihara (New Brunswick, N.J.: Rutgers University Press, 1954).

for government regulations. Harmony may have to be engineered. But according to both versions there is, actually or potentially, behind the manifold activities of individuals and groups, a coordination of activities towards a purpose. Both imply that there is a subject, a will, a plan and a rational adaptation of means towards an end in society. Society is looked upon as a super-individual or a large family with a unified goal which is simultaneously the (properly defined) goal of each of its members. Hence the teleological implications of such terms as "the economy," "social welfare," "economic organization," "economic function," "equilibrium," "maximum social welfare," "economic laws," etc.

Two difficulties inherent in the utilitarian philosophy have strengthened the need to have recourse to a cruder version of the harmony doctrine with its liberal policy implications, particularly in economics. The first is the impossibility to calculate and compare *in practice* the effects on happiness of a particular measure. It seems both simpler and safer to rely on the spontaneous harmony of egoisms than to perform an impossible calculation. This argument for noninterference from the complete ignorance of the effects of interference can still be found in the most up-to-date controversies.

The second aid to the cruder harmony version is the difficulty of deriving both actual (hedonistically determined) and moral behavior from the all-powerful motives of pleasure and pain. The dangerous logical jump from "we must do what we think will please us" to "we ought to do what pleases others" is greatly eased if identity of interests can be postulated.

INCOME DISTRIBUTION

Keynesian theory strengthened the utilitarian tradition because it resolved one of the great moral dilemmas of the neoutilitarians. Since Bentham it was held that a more egalitarian income distribution would raise general welfare. But inequality, it was thought, is required in order to safeguard sufficient savings. Saving is the source of investment and investment is an essential condition of economic progress and of a rising standard of living of all, including the poor. Equality would defeat its own purpose by reducing the wealth not only of the rich but also of the poor.

Keynes showed that a more equal distribution raises welfare not only on the Benthamite argument that a pound transferred from a rich to a poor man reduces the utility of the former by less than it increases the utility of the latter. It would also in certain conditions speed up investment and economic progress (at any rate in the short run). He thus removed, in his own words, "one of the chief social justifications of great inequality of wealth" and thus, in the words of Schumpeter, he "smashed . . . the last pillar of the bourgeois argument . . . into dust."

This argument has its forerunners among the early critics of liberal-utilitarian economics. Greater equality [they held], would set free vast productive powers, as well as all kinds of other virtues.

These early critics, like Keynes and some modern "Liberal-Socialists" (e.g., Lerner, Meade) had no sympathy for detailed planning. They believed as strongly as the liberals whom they attacked in the virtues of the free market and the pricing system. What distinguished the critics from the orthodox liberals is their conviction that if only some particular institutional arrangement which causes an "artificial disturbance" could be corrected, free exchange could be relied upon to produce a social optimum.

To the demand to reform property and inheritance laws, other critics added monopoly and the concentration of economic power. Veblen thought that if only financiers could be got out of the way the engineers could be relied upon to produce a social optimum. List, in a somewhat different tradition, believed that once manufacturing industry had been developed behind a protective tariff free trade would maximize income. Wicksell and Keynes stressed the possibility that the natural rate may diverge from the market rate of interest and that this may cause trouble. Others have emphasized wage rigidities. The common feature of all these criticisms is that the classical scheme comes into its own as soon as certain institutional "disturbances," which the classics were supposed to have ignored, were removed. The purpose of economic policy is conceived to be the removal of brakes on the free-wheeling economic process, not the provision of active power.

Like ignorance in Bentham's scheme, these obstacles were thought to prevent the achievement of an underlying harmony of interests. But once they are removed, the elegant and anonymous operation of free competition could be relied upon to maximize the common welfare. Thus some of the fiercest critics of liberal doctrine tacitly accepted its fundamental tenet.

It may seem that Keynesian measures of regulating investment as a means of achieving and maintaining full employment represent a break with the liberal-utilitarian tradition for two reasons: first, they appear to violate the *liberal* tradition because they are interferences not only with the *distribution* but also with the *production* sphere. Second, they seem to make the canons of *utilitarianism* redundant, because they appear to promote the interests of all at the expense of none.

INTERFERENCE WITH THE SPHERE OF PRODUCTION

The unqualified laissez-faire dogma was first modified for the sphere of distribution, particularly clearly by J. S. Mill. Adam Smith and Ricardo already had drawn a sharp distinction between production (always to be understood as including exchange) and distribution. Their proof of the liberal doctrine was much more successful in relation to production than to distribution. Adam Smith's well-known theory of the division of labor was a convincing demonstration that specialization and free exchange reduce costs and increase benefits. But this proof was frequently considered to apply also without further discussion to the sphere of income and property distribution.

J. S. Mill, who was influenced by the socialist critics, challenged the principle of *laissez faire* for the sphere of distribution. But production, he still believed, should, on the whole, be left to look after itself. With this qualification the doctrine entered into British welfare economics and is still widely accepted today.

Seen against this background, Keynes appears as a proponent of a different tradition. In some respects his views resemble those of Continental and American critics of liberalism who tried to show that production will not "look after itself." According to Keynes, government action is necessary, not only and not mainly in order to correct undesirable distributional results, but also and largely in order to maintain total effective demand and thus full employment and production.

In this respect Keynes has more in common with conservative advocates of production policies like Friedrich List than with the British classics or socialists. Both List and Keynes held that productive powers would lie stagnant unless released by certain types of state action. Both saw in the state not an agency whose activity is confined to (usually undesirable forms of) consumption and redistribution, but a powerful stimulant to production. But both also believed that, once the productive forces were released, the liberal system would work well.

Yet, from a different point of view, Keynes appears much more closely aligned with the liberals than with the antiliberals. Although List and other advocates of production policy on the one hand, and Keynes on the other, share the belief that the state has to take certain actions in order to create the right environment for private self-interest to work beneficially, there is an important difference. The Protectionists advocate interference with particular branches of production and regulation of the composition of output, whereas Keynes believed that if "we suppose the volume of output to be given, i.e., to be determined by forces outside the classical scheme of thought, then there is no objection to be raised against the classical analysis of the manner in which private self-interest will determine what in particular is produced, in what proportions the factors of production will be combined to produce it, and how the value of the final product will be distributed between them. . . . It is in determining the volume, not the direction, of actual employment that the existing system has broken down."

There were, of course, many Keyneses. The Keynes of the *General Theory* has, in spite of his production policies, greater faith in *laissez faire* than the Keynes of *The End of Laissez-Faire*. We have already noticed that their preoccupation with "artificial disturbances" was the hallmark of those critics who remained steeped in liberal thought in spite of their criticism of the classical arguments. They pilloried such evils as the maldistribution of income (the liberal socialists), monopoly, and financial ill-management (radical liberals, Veblen), etc. Keynes's analysis, faithful to this tradition, brings to light another type of obstacle to what is believed would otherwise be the successful operation of the market. The rigidity of the rate of interest (together, possibly, with the rigidity of wage rates) due to speculation is another distorting element. State interference is necessary tin order to establish, according to the *Treatise,* coincidence of the market rate with the natural rate and, according to the

General Theory, the full-employment rate. At the same time, a series of other "complications" are ignored.

In spite of his unorthodox views on production policy, Keynes, particularly later in life, stood faithfully in the liberal-utilitarian tradition. He was not, of course, a laissez-faire utilitarian. But then neither was Bentham, Mill, Sidgwick or Pigou. One can believe in the greatest happiness principle without believing that the greatest happiness is the automatic result of free market forces. Positive government action is necessary in order to safeguard the great happiness or general welfare. The characteristic *utilitarian* feature and the relic of the harmony doctrine is the belief, which Keynes shared with Bentham and Mill, that the economic welfare of a nation is something that the government can and should discover and promote. The *liberal* feature is the conviction that the promotion of economic welfare requires only a little tampering here and there, and that, for the rest, the automatic play of self-interest is a better driving force than any practical alternative.

Neither the utilitarian nor the liberal component of this conviction is shared, e.g., by some members of the historical school, by the Marxists, or by the Schumpeterians, who reject the notion of a "common well-being" and who look upon government policies as the outcome of the struggle between different interests.

INTEREST HARMONY AND ANTIDEPRESSION POLICIES

If the first objection to looking upon Keynes as a liberal and a utilitarian was that his recommendations *violate liberal* canons, the second is that they do *not require* utilitarian canons. It may appear at first sight that the whole dispute about distribution and its relation to economic welfare, which is at the heart of recent controversies in welfare economics, is irrelevant for the policies with which Keynesian economics is concerned.

In some spheres, interests seem to coincide and there, at any rate, quasi objective recommendations would appear to be possible. Monetary policy is occasionally quoted as an example. Thus it might seem quite safe to say that prosperity and stability are better than depression and fluctuations, and that measures which increase and prolong general prosperity are in the general interest. Professor Frank H. Knight wrote recently: "The business cycle . . . is not a problem of conflict of interests, since practically no one profits from depressions." Many of the quibbles of welfare economics about how to achieve the best allocation of given and already fully, though not optimally, employed resources may appear trivial in comparison with the problem of how to increase the employment of resources, to reduce unemployment of men and promote prosperity.

It may seem that Keynesian measures are designed to promote the "interests of all" in a sense which makes it unnecessary to compare and weight interests, since nobody is harmed. Thus even those who believe that every man's enjoyment is unique and incommensurable with any other man's could still subscribe to Keynesian measures. Surely everyone prefers prosperity to depression and stability to fluctuations, except possibly for a few speculators. If this were true, the utilitarian assumption of the comparability of individual utilities could be dropped. Measures to achieve full employment would not present any of the awkward problems of comparing and weighting which a policy of "tightening up," i.e., of rendering more efficient an already fully employed economy, would have to face. It would seem that we could increase the national cake without reducing anybody's slice.

Yet, this appearance is deceptive for at least three reasons. (1) Some people are bound to lose in any case. (2) Harmony would not prevail even if nobody were to lose pecuniarily. (3) Even if problems of redistribution could be side-stepped in the short run, they might become urgent in any long-run policy to maintain full employment. Moreover, the acceptance of Keynesian policies would, once again, bring allocative and thus distributional problems into the foreground.

In the first place, some people are bound to lose even through antidepression policies. Fixed income receivers will be worse off. It is, of course, true that they could be compensated or, if not, that their losses are negligible in comparison with the gains (which is a value judgment and involves interpersonal comparisons). There is therefore a greater degree of harmony here than in policies designed to restore, say, free trade or competition. Yet, there is hardly ever complete harmony.

Second, and perhaps more important, post-Keynesian experience and controversy suggest that there is neither general agreement on Keynes's analysis nor a general harmony of those interests which are affected by Keynesian measures, quite apart from the disharmony which arises from the reduced incomes of fixed income receivers.

Opposition may arise from misunderstanding. This is possible even in the Benthamite scheme. It could, in principle, be cleared up and harmony be established. But opposition may arise in spite of, or rather because of, a full understanding of the implications of Keynesian measures. Some people oppose them because they do not want full employment, either because they believe it undermines the discipline of workers, or because they fear that, if trade unions are strengthened through full employment, the share of profits will fall; or even if it is not expected to fall, entrepreneurs may fear that their power and status in society would be reduced.

Keynes himself believed more strongly in a harmony of interests in this respect than the later experience of full-employment conditions would warrant. He ascribed the opposition to antidepression policies to the stupidity of bankers and believed that the removal of risks and the increase in profits would commend these policies to entrepreneurs. In fact, their opposition is perfectly rational, both on economic and political grounds. These policies undermine their bargaining power. Decisions which in slump conditions would have been in their power become in conditions of full employment matters of government policy, such as redistribution, the rate of investment and progress.

Many consider full employment an objective which involves a sacrifice, a "price," foregone opportunities. Some of these costs cannot be expressed in money terms (e.g., the anticipated loss of liberty) and are, perhaps, not strictly economic. But the crucial point is that there is no harmony of interests. Even in the short run, a dilemma between unemployment and controls may arise, if inflation is ruled out.

A measure of agreement might perhaps be reached by drawing a distinction between antidepression policies and full-employment policies. Many who would reject the latter might accept the former, though it would be difficult to reach agreement on where the line between the two should be drawn. But there is more wide-spread agreement on the desirability of avoiding very high, long-term unemployment than on the desirability of maintaining full employment.

Even if there were complete national harmony on antidepression policies, conflict will still arise with the interests of other nations and hence with the value systems of those who have international welfare at heart. Changes in the balance of payments and changes in the terms of trade resulting from antidepression policies will have repercussions abroad. Some of these changes may be welcomed by foreigners, but others will require adjustments which they may not be willing to make. The harmony doctrine is even less plausible if we attempt to apply it to the world economy.

The third reason why Keynesian policies do not avoid interest conflicts is this: Keynes's own analysis applies to the short run. It is easier to stimulate investment sufficiently to *attain* full employment, than it is to sustain this level of investment, and thus full employment, over a prolonged period of time. In the short run investment generates income but not consumption output. In the long run, however, investment also yields increased consumption output. If the investment required to generate full-employment *income* is the same as the investment required to yield the *output* which is demanded under continued full employment, full employment will be maintained. But this would be an odd coincidence. It is quite possible that the investment required to generate full-employment income is larger than (a) the investment required to meet effective demand or (b) the investment which can be worked profitably with a given population (or a given rate of population increase). In other words, full-employment investment may fall off, either (a) because there is insufficient consumption demand for the goods which it helps to produce indirectly, or (b) because the labor force required to work in conjunction with the fixed capital equipment is too small. In either case excess capacity will emerge and investment will be reduced. It will be impossible to maintain full employment. In order to avoid case (a) consumption would have to be raised, and in order to avoid both (a) and (b) policies designed to transfer labor from the investment goods industries to the consumption goods trades would have to be carried out. In such a situation a redistribution of income from the wealthier to the poorer might have to play an essential part. Such a redistribution would reduce the investment required to generate income and would help to prevent the generation of excess capacity in relation to either demand or the available labor force. It appears therefore that the distribution of income may play an important part in maintaining full employment over a period of time.

Finally, even if full agreement could be reached on antidepression policies, the wide-spread *knowledge* of Keynesian *analysis,* and the *adoption* of Keynesian *remedies* would bring the problem of interest conflicts into the forefront again, even if one could assume that it lies dormant in a world of undiagnosed and uncured unemployment.

In conditions of large-scale unemployment one group's gain need not spell another's loss. But with the adoption of antidepression policies, and a fortiori with full-employment policies, conflicts become once again acute. Measures which were before socially costless, or had a negative social cost, now involve genuine sacrifices. The question how to weigh gains against losses arises as a result of the adoption of policies which might meet with unanimous approval.

SUMMARY

What then, is Keynes's position in the classical tradition?

1. Keynes's thought is unmistakably in the classical liberal-utilitarian tradition. He can be considered as a harmony theorist in the sense that he looked upon the economic activities of a nation as if they were those of an individual or a family, i.e., as if they had a common purpose which, properly understood, is also the purpose of each individual. The common good, public welfare, maximum output, etc., are for him meaningful concepts and desirable objectives.

2. It may appear that Keynes's recommendations represent a break with the classical tradition for the paradoxical reasons (a) that they involve interference with *production,* not merely with distribution; and (b) that, by apparently promoting the interests of each and all they seem to make the *utilitarian* calculus superfluous. But (a) does not represent a break with the *harmony* tradition and the appearance of (b) is deceptive, for losses of some kinds are bound to occur.

3. Advocates of production policies have often accepted the meaningfulness and desirability of maximizing the common welfare, in particular in the light of consideration 2 (b). Keynes, in particular, advocated the regulation of *aggregates* only. He stood in the *liberal* tradition in the sense that the interferences which he advocated aim at the removal of particular breaks on the free pursuit of the common good.

4. For several reasons, Keynesian measures do not in fact meet with applause from all and each. (a) Some are bound to lose in any case. (b) Nonmaterial considerations may cause opposition even where there is no strictly economic loss. (c) Long-run maintenance of full employment may require redistribution.

5. In a country, or in a world, pledged to full employment not only the classical problems of interest conflicts come into their own again, but new problems of the distribution of economic power and its conscious manipulation arise.

3.12 The Public-Policy Ideas and Political Tendencies of Keynesian Economists

Overton H. Taylor

Keynes was decidedly not in the tradition of "pure economics," but rather in that of "political economy," in the sense that, like all the great "political economists" of the eighteenth and nineteenth centuries, he was interested above all in the quest for wise decisions on national policies. He directed his efforts toward developing a way of discovering, not only how and how well or ill a nation's economy in any period is working, but also what policies on the part of the nation's government are required to cause or enable its economy to work as well as possible. He aspired to be not only, for the social-economic organism, a physiologist but a physician, able not only to diagnose its ailments, but also to prescribe the right remedies for them. And his analysis of the mode of causation of general economic depressions led him directly to his recommendations about the lines on which governments should act to cure, or better, to prevent them. . . . The immediate cause of a depression is an insufficiently large flow of money in the system, as the population's income and outlay for all goods and services, to constitute, at the existing levels of production costs and prices, an adequate demand for a full-employment output; therefore, the policy problem is how best to bring about an appropriate increase of the effective supply and flow of money, or the flow of spending, and people's incomes and respendings, in the whole economy.

Now the pre-Keynesian, classical type of "monetary policy," based on traditional "monetary theory," had sought to accomplish that result in such situations simply by making more central-bank funds available to and through all ordinary banks, as lenders to borrowing and investing business firms, at lowered interest rates. This was expected to induce the business firms to increase their borrowings and investment spendings, with the further result of also increasing the incomes and consumption spendings of the people; and thus to bring about recovery of employment, income, demand, prices, profits, and production. But the ineffectiveness or inadequacy of this policy or "medicine," in a severe depression, was simultaneously demonstrated both by the Keynesian analysis and by actual experience with the depression of the early 1930's. When in general the profit expectations of business for the near or visible future were below zero, and the thirst of the owners of money for "liquidity" made it impossible greatly to increase the supply and lower the cost of borrowable capital funds for business use, the efforts of the central banks to work in this direction proved unavailing. They could and did enable the banks to lend more freely at somewhat lower interest rates, but they could not lower the latter *sufficiently* or make all lenders in the system follow suit and keep up the active flow of money into business or investment uses, or—the real crux—induce the business world substantially to increase its borrowings and investment outlays, by any feasible lowering of the interest costs, when prospective profits on the required investment outlays were nil or negative. The problem was not how to increase the supply or quantity or stock of money—that was no problem—but how to increase *spending,* incomes, and demand for labor and for producers' goods and consumers' goods. And the only way to do this on a sufficient scale was for the government, as by far the largest and freest-to-act spending agency in society, to greatly increase its volume and rate of spending to a point far in excess of its tax revenues, borrow and spend over and beyond the latter the "created" bank money or central-bank funds which business enterprises were not willing to borrow and invest, and thus pour new additional money into active, general circulation, via the incomes and spendings of all of the initial recipients or beneficiaries of the new additional government spendings. As this remedy began to work, and the increases of people's incomes and spendings became increasingly general all through the economy, and demand and production and employment revived, so would the profit prospects and investment spendings of business also then increase, and the upward spiral, replacing the downward spiral into the depression, would be under way. With renewed growth of the people's incomes, the government's tax revenues would also grow, and at the appropriate point it could begin to taper off the enlargement of its spendings, and allow the growth of its tax revenues to overtake them, and repay some of the debt contracted to finance the budgetary deficit, and carry the rest permanently (meeting the interest charges on it) with the aid of the large tax revenues that a continually, increasingly prosperous society could easily afford.

Now in the United States it happened that the early New Deal administration stumbled or groped its way into doing, among other things, much along this line of the later Keynesian recommendations, *before* Keynes wrote and published his *General Theory*—before he *made* the analysis and recommendations discussed in this chapter, at all. The "blind" responses of a bold, energetic, versatile, and determined government to the actual conditions, popular demands, and practical exigencies confronting it led it onto a path which the brilliant "new economics" of Keynes then came along just in time to "rationalize" or confirm as the highest wisdom, after the event. Understandably then, a great number of the able young American professional economists and advanced students of economics, of that time, received the new "Keynesian" gospel with the greatest enthusiasm, and became its lifelong devotees. They had been feeling severely frustrated by the near-non-existence in the pre-Keynesian economics, which they had been brought up on, of any "light" on the pressing practical problem now confronting them, and their country, as to what the latter could and should do to cure or cope with the terrible depression. Many were already in sympathy with the New Deal government's efforts and expedients, in spite of their violation of all the "sound principles of political economy," which they had been taught; and this flirtation with "heresies" opposed to and by everything in their previous professional educations was at best uncomfortable. But now a great economist of unchallengeable competence and eminence endorsed and advocated lavish governmental deficit spending to engender economic recovery, and showed convincingly just why it was needed and how it would work. Naturally, a very large percentage of the members of the then rising generation of American economists quickly became pure, thorough, and ardent Keynesian economists.

Moreover, the prevalent American association of Keynesian economics that the New Deal, which thus grew up and persisted, and the generally reputed "radicalism" of the latter, led also to a prevalent association in American minds—both among economists and among the members of the general public—of Keynesian economics with relatively "radical" or "left-of-center" political views on all or most kinds of public issues; whereas in contrast the other American economists who did not immediately, fully embrace "the new economics" but remained in some ways critical of it and more attached to the older classical tradition of thought in their discipline, were commonly assumed to be in all cases extreme and adamant political "conservatives." These too simple and absolute attachments of political labels to the groups of economists responding somewhat differently to the ideas of Keynes have done no good to the work and thought of the profession as a whole, or to its standing with the public. And it is of some importance here to ask what can be truly said about the real "political philosophies," if any, of these modern types or groups of "political economists."

With regard to Keynes himself, it is on the whole clear to all careful students of his career and writings that his own ideals and aims were relatively conservative, in the sense that he wanted to see preserved, and sought through his own work to help preserve, both "capitalism" and liberal democracy; the economic system made up mainly of largely free, private enterprises and competitive markets; democratic governments serving not the many as against the few but the common welfare and the just freedoms of all as impartially as possible, and enlarging their roles or spheres of authority and activity only to the quite limited extent that he deemed necessary in the interests of the best working, strength, and stability of that economic system; and all the private, individual freedoms for all, of the liberal-democratic and economic-liberal traditions. In advocating that national governments should vary and adjust their programs of taxation, borrowing, and spending in accordance with the changing needs of the national economies, or as required to preserve in the latter at all times the appropriate total flows of money-income and spending and demand for all goods and services, and thus preserve continuous full employment, steady economic growth, and stable price levels; Keynes meant to advocate only this one limited departure from *laissez faire,* or moderate degree and kind of governmental "intervention" in the economic world, *in order to strengthen and preserve* the "free-enterprise system" by curing what always had been its worst defect—proneness to recurrent, devastating depressions, with mass unemployment—and removing the main cause of subversive, radical attacks upon it. This Englishman never supported or flirted with socialism; he disliked the English Labor party as a "class" party, had a very low opinion of the economics and intellectual system of Karl Marx, and was very clearly on the whole an adherent of the individualistic, libertarian tradition of nineteenth-century English liberalism.

At the same time, on topics connected with thrift or saving, interest on loans of money, and traditional canons of "sound" public finance, Keynes frequently uttered radical-sounding remarks and epigrams. His belief that, in economically advanced and prosperous societies, thrifty saving could be and was being overdone, with not beneficial but harmful consequences, made him seem a foe of this central "virtue" in the traditional "capitalist" ethos, and a subversive "radical" in the eyes of all-out conservatives of a certain type. And so of course did his belief—the other side of that same coin—that even the most (by ordinary standards) "wasteful" or "extravagant" spending, both private and public, when or if needed to cure or prevent the far greater economic and human wastes of mass unemployment, should be infinitely preferred to the latter. Then also, his theory that the interest-incomes of those who make "saved" money available for investment in production, are not their deserved and needed rewards and incentives for difficult and virtuous and always socially useful saving, but merely bribes paid to induce them to allow business firms to use or invest the money they would save anyway and simply "hoard" if not paid their interest—this theory of course does seem to have affinities with ancient anticapitalist ideas about all interest as "usury." And in advocating governmental and central-banking policies designed to lower interest rates as far as possible, Keynes in one passage spoke with pleasure of "the euthanasia of the *rentiers*" toward which this could lead. His sympathies lay with the active businessmen or entrepreneurs who got things done, not with the passive capitalists or creditors who merely charge for the use of what they own. And in his *Tract on Monetary Reform,* written long before he produced his *General Theory,* he very significantly expressed the view that the trend, in much of economic history, of gradual inflation or rising price levels and falling real value of the money unit, had the beneficial result of gradually reducing the real burden or retarding drag of old debts and interest charges upon all active business and productive enterprise. It is not surprising that such ideas have helped to cause many more ordinary or typical conservative minds to distrust this "flexible, enlightened," reforming-to-conserve, "conservative" thinker, who in addition had these particular, unorthodox, and eccentric views. But in spite of them, it remains clear that his over-all main purpose was conservative.

The personal outlook of Keynes himself, however, and the possible, long-run institutional results of different, possible, actual developments of Keynesian governmental economic policies, as carried out in practice, may be different matters. Repeated enlargements of the government's budget at times of incipient depression, to enlarge the income-flow in the system and prevent depression, *could* lead gradually into socialism, through growth of the share of the nation's income and wealth taken over, and used in ways determined, by its government. Conservative governments can develop and use the general policy ideas of Keynes on truly conservative lines and with conservative results; but governments or parties-in-power with socialistic or "welfare-state" ideas and purposes can develop and use the same general policy ideas or methods in their own directions also. And the English Labor or Socialist government, of the period 1945 to 1950, did so. What Keynesian economics as such leads to in the sphere of governmental policies is not so much a political direction as a set of ideas or devices which can be used to assist developments in either direction —strengthening and perpetuation of the "system of free enterprise," or gradual change toward socialism—depending on the views and aims, having other sources, of those politically in control.

* * *

3.13 Challenge to Affluence

Gunnar Myrdal

UNEMPLOYMENT

The Need for More Than Expansion

The first inference to be drawn from the present situation in the labour market of the United States is undoubtedly that business should be given a spurt to expand rapidly. All other measures are otherwise hopeless. . . .

There are, however, a number of qualifications to the view that America only needs business expansion in order to cure unemployment.

American unemployment is increasingly a structural one. Every year, indeed every month, that a high level of unemployment is tolerated makes full employment more difficult to attain as a policy goal.

This structural character of unemployment in America means, first, that already at the present low rate of economic growth and at the present high and rising level of unemployment there is a scarcity of educated and skilled labour which shows up in the high figures for overtime among employees belonging to this èlite. A rising trend of business activity would very soon be bottlenecked by a lack of this type of worker, long before the hard core of unemployed —those of an inferior quality—had become absorbed. Expansion simply cannot proceed very far before it meets this physical limitation, which must also have inflationary effects since wages must tend to rise. A balanced employment situation cannot be achieved purely by business expansion.

Excerpted from Gunnar Myrdal, *Challenge to Affluence* (New York: Random House, 1965), pp. 23–24, 26–30, 32–36, 40–43, 50–54, 57–62, 64–69, 92–93. Reprinted by permission of the publisher.

The Need for Education, Training and Retraining

The present situation of large-scale structural unemployment in the United States is caused by the absence of jobs that could easily be done by such workers as are released during the process of technological development, and by a lag in the adjustment of a high percentage of young and older workers —adjustment in point of quality—to the changed labour demand.

From the policy point of view, there are two ways of overcoming the present discrepancy in America between the direction of labour demand, when it is permitted to expand, and the existing quality of the unutilized labour supply. One way is to expand production in fields which will demand labour of the quality that exists or can easily be acquired. The other is to change the quality of the labour supply by education and training. As we shall see, the two types of policy-induced changes are closely interrelated.

We shall first discuss the second way of overcoming the discrepancy between the quality of labour demanded and supplied. As technological developments, and formalized procedures in recruitment, continuously increase the demand for educated and highly trained workers and decrease it for the less well educated and trained, greatly increased facilities for education and training are imperatively demanded. If, moreover, we bear in mind the demographic changes under way, it becomes clear that these facilities must initially be placed at the disposal of young people: given the particularly rapid growth of people in the younger age groups, educational and training facilities must be expanded much more rapidly for these than proportionally to the population increase.

Besides general schooling, America needs very much greater efforts in the field of vocational training.

At the same time there is urgent need for the retraining of older workers, so as to prevent the emergence of a group of second-class citizens who are permanently unemployed or only casually employed. We must bear in mind, however, that only in an expanding economy can there be any real chance of successfully rehabilitating workers who have been laid off or are in the danger zone.

With widespread unemployment and little general expansion, the retrained will have difficulty in finding jobs and will easily be pushed back to their previous status. All efforts will then have been in vain and productive resources will have been wasted.

The Need for Increasing Labour Demand Generally and in Special Sectors

We have stressed that the first and most obvious step in a policy designed to eliminate the waste of large-scale unemployment must be to give the economy as much of a spurt towards expansion as it can safely take, given the relative scarcity of such educated and trained labour as is now available. . . .

In addition to this policy of general economic expansion, efforts are needed to increase labour demand in special sectors of the economy. To a large extent such efforts harmonize well with the need for raising the quality of the labour force discussed in the previous section. Thus to increase facilities for education and training means to provide and employ more teachers, and more teachers of these teachers. The same is true in the field of health and in the social services. The care and protection of human beings, and the improvement of their health, culture, and happiness, is generally less well provided for in America, particularly so far as the lower strata are concerned, than in the most advanced welfare states in Western Europe.

Though technological development will increase the productivity of the labour force engaged in these occupations, there are such huge unsatisfied needs in this sector that an expansion of its labour demand should be a main policy goal.

In such a situation it may almost be looked upon as fortunate that America is in such dire need of rebuilding its cities, clearing its huge slums, and reconstructing its obsolete and inadequate transportation system, particularly in metropolitan districts. . . .

UNEMPLOYMENT AND POVERTY

The Emergence of an "Underclass"

The facts about unemployment and its immediate causes are well known in America.

Less often observed and commented upon is the tendency of the changes under way to trap an "underclass" of unemployed and, gradually, unemployable persons and families of the bottom of a society in which, for the majority of people above that level, the increasingly democratic structure of the educational system creates more and more liberty—real liberty—and equality of opportunity, at least over the course of two generations.

America's image of itself was, and is, that of a free and open society where anyone of sound body and soul, and with the necessary drive, can find work (at least when business is on the upturn) and can climb to the highest and most rewarding positions.

Not that reality ever agreed entirely with it. And over the last few generations a process has been under way which, though in the main opening up more opportunities to more people, has closed some opportunities to some. And now in the end it threatens to split off a true "underclass"—not really an integrated part of the nation at all but a useless and miserable substratum.

The New Threat

. . . There is something threatening in the most recent changes and in the trend for a foreseeable future. The displacement of unskilled and even of much skilled labour has a definiteness that must compel us to stop and think. To take advantage of the expansion of demand for highly educated and trained labour—an expansion that would be even more rapid if the rate of economic growth were higher—the displaced worker must go so far to meet requirements of education and training that he simply cannot think of jumping the gap, no matter how alert and enterprising he may be. He needs to be helped to do it by society or he will not be able to do it at all.

What is happening is similar to the disappearance more than half a century ago of the "self-made man" from the highest positions as a result of the widening of college education and a parallel rise in the demands for formal education and leadership-training in business, as it became increasingly large-scale, organized, and stratified. This process has continued steadily downwards, first to middle positions, and then to ever lower strata in industry and commerce, until now it is beginning to make unskilled and many skilled workers redundant.

This is a new threat. For when the process has proceeded as far as that, without a parallel change by way of educating and training the *whole* labour force to correspond to the new demands, there is no longer a great space underneath for economic advance and social mobility, as there was when the self-made man disappeared at the top. Those not needed are true "outcasts". They have simply become unemployed, and indeed largely unemployable. It is almost as difficult for them to get and hold a good job as it long ago became for a boot-black to end as president of a great corporation. *In society at large there is more equality of opportunity today than there ever was. But for the bottom layer there is less or none.*

Poverty

If poverty be defined [1965] as having to live on an annual income of under $4,000 for multiple-person families and $2,000 for unattached individuals, 38 million Americans, or more than one-fifth of the nation, were poor in 1960. In deprivation (defined as above poverty but short of the requirements for what in America is now considered a modestly comfortable standard of living—from $4,000 to $6,000 for families and from $2,000 to $3,000 for unattached individuals) were more than 39 million people, or again more than one-fifth of the nation. Utter destitution—the situation of people with less than half the poverty income—was the destiny of more than 12½ million Americans, or nearly 7 per cent of the population of the United States.

The proportion of people in these various categories of deprivation, poverty, and destitution has been decreasing since the depression years, first rapidly and then slowly. The slow-down has become particularly marked during the last decade; the number of families living in extreme misery with incomes under $1,000 per year seem actually to have increased a little. Income distribution did follow a tendency towards gradual equalization until the last decade, but then the relative economic stagnation began to reflect itself in a new tendency to increasing economic inequality.

Increased Inequality in the Midst of General Equality

It is perfectly possible for the majority of Americans to live, together with practically everyone they have primary contact with, in a situation of full and even overfull employment, with brisk demand and competition for their labour, while they read in the newspapers that there is large and growing unemployment beneath them. That this can be so is the result of unemployment being to a large extent structural in character.

With increasing distress at the bottom of American society, ever greater social mobility, liberty and equality of opportunity, and a generally rising economic and cultural level, may be perfectly possible in majority America. More and more individuals and families may move further away from the neighbourhood of the dividing line. Social welfare policies have been specially framed, as I said previously, to give greater security for that middle group in the nation. And it might even be possible for some individual from below the poverty line to pass successfully above it—the false corollary being that America is still the free and open society of its cherished image and well established ideals.

But as less and less work is required of the type that people in the urban and rural slums can offer, they will be increasingly isolated and exposed to unemployment, underemployment and plain exploitation. There is an ugly smell rising from the basement of the stately American mansion.

LIBERTY AND EQUALITY—THE CENTRAL ISSUE IN THE ECONOMIC STAGNATION PROBLEM

Eradication of Poverty as an Economic Interest and a Necessity for Economic Progress

The eradication of poverty has now become an economic interest as well as almost a political necessity, if America is to escape from the rut of relative economic stagnation with high and rising unemployment and underemployment. . . .

We revealed the complexity with which a low level of education and training, and, generally, a low quality of labour supply, is interrelated with poverty and all that poverty implies. The conclusion is that, to be successful, a full employment policy must aim at gradually eradicating poverty.

Efforts to educate and train the young, and to re-educate such adults as need it must meet with far greater difficulties, be far less effective and, consequently, even from a financial point of view imply far more waste, the longer these people are poor, live in urban and rural slums, and are afflicted by all the other consequences of poverty. To an extent, but as we know from experience only to an extent, poverty will decrease as economic expansion and fuller employment get under way: but direct measures of a surgical nature are also needed.

The structural character of contemporary unemployment makes it important that there be public investment in the education, training and retraining of workers right from the start. Otherwise scarcity of personnel with high levels of education and training will soon set a ceiling to the rise in production and most probably cause a recession long before anything in the neighbourhood of full employment has been achieved. Since the low quality of part of the labour supply is intertwined with poverty in a vicious circle, vigorous measures must be taken, also from the very start, to reduce poverty itself.

All this implies public expenditure designed initially to improve the lot of the American poor. The reason why such a redistribution policy must be to the general economic interest, and not merely benefit the poor themselves, is, of course, that their unemployment, and their low productivity when they are working, represents the main unutilized or underutilized resource in America. The majority of Americans now living in comfortable circumstances should become better off, not worse off, as a result of such a policy.

The Unmet Needs

Our account of the actual extent of poverty in America proves that the abundance and affluence of American society is highly exaggerated by public opinion. A fifth of the American people is now officially recognized as living in poverty. Of these a very sizable percentage is really destitute. And above the poverty-stricken fifth of the nation there are at least as many with no substantial lot or part in the abundance believed to be so characteristically American. For a large minority the affluent society is nothing but a myth.

The fact is, of course, that there is a very large volume of elementary needs in America crying to be met, and that these, translated into effective demands, could sustain a rapid growth in production for a long time to come.

In view, however, of the technological revolution under way, and of the American capacity to expand production of material goods in almost every field if a higher rate of growth were permitted, a rise in living standards for the underprivileged becomes an almost necessary condition for rapid, long-term advance. Even apart from the urgent need for improving the quality of that part of the labour force that is at present either redundant or underemployed in low productivity occupations, and *if only for the initial purpose of building a more solid foundation in aggregate demand for the expansion of production, large-scale redistributional reforms are urgently called for.*

Redistributional Reforms

Redistributional reforms should be looked upon as no less important from the point of view of laying a stable basis for the achievement of a rapid and steady expansion of the American economy, and for high employment, than from the point of view of social justice.

The reform implying least governmental intervention in the economy is, of course, a reduction of the tax burden in the lower income brackets. The prevalence in the tax system of the United States—including that of the states and the municipalities—of taxes on real property, and of sales taxes of various sorts, imply, as a recent study by the Tax Foundation has revealed, that the tax burden in the lower and middle income strata is decisively regressive. This cannot possibly be in accordance with the nation's ideals for the distribution of the tax burden. A reform is overdue, and would immediately put more purchasing power into the hands of those Americans whose consumption is insufficient.

Nor would urgently needed reforms of the social security system require more than a minimum of governmental intervention in the economy. In this field the United States is still far behind those other countries that share its basic values.

An improvement in the unemployment benefit system (particularly for the underemployed and the casually employed) is no less necessary. It is not only a question of raising the level of unemployment benefits, but also of making them available on a national scale for all who are unemployed (even though they may have some shifting or menial job) or have not been employed long enough to qualify under present rules. The financial burden of an improvement of this form of social security—as of most others—will tend to be heaviest in the beginning, but to taper off as the economy expands and full employment is restored. Unemployment relief will then in fact cease to be much of a problem.

Related to reforms in the field of social security are a number of others that require no direct intervention of a governmental kind in the running of the economy. Thus it is of urgent importance that minimum wage legislation should be made comprehensive, and not remain inapplicable in many occupations in which the setting of a wage floor is particularly important, as for instance in hotels and restaurants, in some retail stores, and in hospitals and laundries. Even after the change in minimum wage legislation two years ago some 16 million workers are still uncovered.

Other Governmental Action

So far we have touched upon redistributive schemes that can be operated mainly on a cash basis or, in any case, without much government intervention in the economy. It should be clear, however, that in addition to those reforms there is a need for policies that involve the government more directly in steering the economy, mostly by providing such enterprises and services as belong properly to the public sector since they could hardly be forthcoming from private business.

We have already dealt with the urgent need for much greater efforts in the fields of education and of the training of the young, particularly among the poorer strata, and of retraining old workers now afflicted by unemployment or employed in low-productivity occupations. The need for radical and comprehensive education, and for an unemployment policy directed to the rehabilitation and reallocation of workers, is necessarily implied.

Much the same is true in respect of health protection and medical care. The training of doctors and nurses must be considerably expanded and speeded up.

In filling these needs much larger resources will have to be allocated to the building of schools and hospitals.

There are many other public investments that are now irrationally neglected. There is, of course, no excuse for a rich country to tolerate huge slums in the big cities and lesser ones in the smaller cities, while allowing a large part of its manpower and of its other productive resources to go to waste. Up to the present public efforts in the way of slum clearance have not only been feeble in the extreme, but have perversely favoured the middle third of the nation and often left the poor in worse slums than before. This has been the reality behind the euphemistic term ''urban renewal''—which in Detroit is popularly referred to as ''Negro removal''.

Closely related to the slum clearance problem is that of making American cities better servants of human life and efficient labour. Huge investments are needed for this purpose: and these are specially urgent, because more than the whole population increase is now swelling the number of city dwellers and, in particular, of those in the big metropolitan districts.

. . . There is a serious and irrational bias against public investment and consumption in America. This results from a combination of high-pressure salesmanship for private consumption with a traditional suspicion against increasing public budgets. It cannot possibly correspond, however, to what people would really prefer if they could as readily follow their impulses to buy the means of collective consumption as to buy private consumers' goods, and if the former were equally well advertised.

The Identity of the Two Goals

All these major reforms are clearly in the interests of social justice, which Americans interpret as liberty and equality of opportunity. At the same time, it is the thesis of this book that a reorientation of American policy in the direction of such reforms is a precondition for establishing an expansion of the economy that is not only rapid at the start but remains steady. *Never in the history of America has there been a greater and more complete identity between the ideals of social justice and the requirements of economic progress.* The latter goal is unattainable unless large-scale policy measures are inaugurated to reach the former.

Negative Inference

If our analysis is correct and the following propositions are accepted:

that unemployment and underemployment in America is increasingly becoming structural;

that a readjustment of the quality of the labour supply to fit the labour demand is therefore a condition for full employment;

that this readjustment requires large-scale policy efforts in the fields of education, training, and retraining;

that such efforts, if they are not to be ineffective or wasted, presuppose in their turn a powerful attempt to eradicate poverty;

that rapid and steady growth of the economy in the present stage of technological development also requires the mobilization of the vast unmet needs among the poor and in the public sector, in order to stabilize aggregate demand on a high and rising level;

that the surplus of manual labour released by technical development in agriculture and manufacturing industry, even if decreased by this increase in aggregate demand, must be reemployed by means of a vast increase in construction work of various sorts, which at the same time necessitates retraining and implies the satisfaction of unmet needs;

then it is also clear that blocking these reforms, or pursuing them on a smaller scale or more slowly than may be required, will result in a failure to realize a sufficiently rapid and at the same time a sufficiently steady growth, and to reach a full employment economy.

A boom, in whatever way induced, will then soon be broken by a new recession, without ever having fully utilized the productive resources and, in particular, the labour force. As a trend, rising unemployment levels will then still prevail.

I have referred to a bigger role for government, but by this I do not mean a bigger bureaucracy. I find American government offices appallingly big in relation to the functions they perform. And many functions should themselves disappear with better planning.

At the same time there is bound to be a bigger role for the government for a number of reasons. The government will have to take increased responsibility for organizing public consumption in the fields of education and health. It will have to redistribute incomes on a considerable scale by its taxation, its social security schemes and its agricultural policies. It will have to invest far more than at present in slum clearance and low-rent housing, and, indeed, in a complete renewal of the cities and their transport systems, as well as in the development of national resources as a whole. More generally, it will have to take the responsibility for a larger part of consumption and investment and, consequently, for a great deal of employment and production. And all this activity will have to be co-ordinated in the light of two converging ideals—that of greater social justice on the one hand, and that of a more rapid and steady expansion of the economy on the other.

3.14 What's Wrong with American Economics?

Leon H. Keyserling

. . . Clearly, the best judgments about national economic policies are not to be discerned in the mist of ratiocination, but in the light of actual experience. For

Excerpted from Leon H. Keyserling, "What's Wrong with American Economics," *Challenge*, May/June 1973. Reprinted by permission of the publisher.

about twenty years to date, there must have been a lot wrong with these policies, in that they have worked poorly most of the time, and not nearly well enough at any time.

THE FIRST REQUIREMENT: OPTIMUM ECONOMIC GROWTH

The first requirement imposed upon our economic system (or any other, for that matter) is to sustain an optimum rate of real economic growth, i.e., that sufficient to assure reasonably full but not excessive use of growing production capabilities. Large idleness means large waste, plus arrant discontent; and no nation can afford that. At least since 1953, our average annual growth performance has fallen lamentably short of the optimum. We have experienced what might be called a "roller-coaster" prosperity, with aborted periods of upturn being followed by periods of stagnation and then recession. This cycle is now on the way to repeating itself for the fifth time within two decades. Moreover, each successive upturn, at its peak, has tended to leave us with more unused manpower and plant than the peak of the previous upturn.

The upturn from 1961 to around the middle of 1970 was claimed by the proponents of "The New Economics" to augur a significant break in the unsatisfactory pattern, through application of superior national policies. There was much prideful talk about the "longest peacetime advance on record" (viewing the Vietnam engagement as minor in an economic sense). But the highly unsatisfactory upturn from 1961 to 1964 was a largely "autonomous" reaction to the preceding recession; there were no new and large injections of stimulative national policy. And even after the massive tax reductions of 1964 (erroneous, for reasons soon to be discussed), there was general agreement by early 1966 that an absolute downturn was in prospect, which was postponed mainly by the vast and unexpected acceleration of spending for the South-Asian war. Even with this, a pronounced slowdown in the rate of real economic growth took effect from 1966 onward, although few identified it or proposed remedial action until the recession began in 1970.

During the period 1953–1972 as a whole, our average annual rate of real economic growth was only 3.5 percent. Meanwhile, conservatively estimated on the basis of the historical record and other relevant analysis, a real growth rate averaging annually in the neighborhood of 4.3 percent was needed during this period to maintain reasonably full resource use. The costs of this long-term retreat from reasonably full resource use have been staggering. During 1953–1972 as a whole, the difference between the actual and the optimum growth rate involved the forfeiture of almost $1.8 *trillion* of total national production, measured in 1970 dollars, and about 45 million man-years of employment opportunity. And if we were to do no better in future—which seems the prospect without a veritable revolution in national economic policies—we would forfeit during 1973–1980 another $1.7 *trillion* of total national production, again measured in 1970 dollars, and 16.5 million man-years of employment opportunity, the very much lower employment loss being due to trends in productivity, patterns of employment, and pay. The employment deficiency is based upon the true level of unemployment, taking into account full-time unemployment as officially measured, the full-time equivalent of part-time unemployment, and the concealed unemployment of those not officially counted as unemployed because shortage of job opportunity dissuades them from "participation" in the civilian labor force.

It has been argued in various quarters that our recent or current national output would be adequate in the future if income distribution were improved and allocations to the public sector were enlarged. Granted the need for these changes, this argument is frivolous. For the changes themselves are much easier to obtain, both economically and politically, when growth is high than when it is low. And although we may use unwisely much of what we produce, we cannot put to wiser use what we do not produce; and our pressing needs, both domestic and international, extend even beyond our optimum growth capabilities in the foreseeable future. Most important, low growth means high unemployment, the evil of evils.

The environmentalists advance the further argument that economic growth brings in its wake a host of ills, including pollution of the air and water. But the additional resources required to build factories and other facilities which do not pollute, and to build automobiles which do not emit noxious fumes, will be unavailable without optimum growth—or they would be available without such growth only at the price of creating an irreconcilable conflict between those who want to abolish pollution and those who want better schools, improved health services, the restoration of our deteriorating urban areas, and the like.

THE SECOND REQUIREMENT: MEETING PRIORITY NEEDS

The failure to deal even tolerably with the great priorities of our domestic needs—too enduring to be fairly attributable to the Vietnam war—is inseparably associated with the unsatisfactory rate of economic growth. At existing tax rates, the $1.8 *trillion* shortfall in economic growth since 1953 has brought about a loss of at least $450 billion in tax revenues at all levels of government. And if the low average growth rate were to persist through 1980, we would forfeit more than another $400 billion in tax revenues, again measured in 1970 dollars.

The amplitude of common knowledge on the subject makes it unnecessary to detail the quantitative and qualitative shortages of facilities and services in our public schools; in available medical care at tolerable costs; in decent housing and urban renewal efforts; in modern transportation systems; in antipollution programs; in treatment of our senior citizens and disabled people; in the care of disadvantaged children; in programs to restore reasonable "parity" of income and public services to farm families and others in rural areas; and in other efforts to liquidate poverty and reduce deprivation (above poverty, but below an acceptable American standard of living).

THE THIRD REQUIREMENT: SOCIAL JUSTICE

A perfect definition of justice is not available, but gross injustice is easy to define, and it is all around us. As late as 1971 (and available data indicate that there has been further maldistribution since then), 42 percent of the total money income flowing to all multiple-person families went to the highest income fifth, and 66 percent to the highest two-fifths, while only 6 percent went to the lowest fifth, and only 18 percent to the lowest two-fifths. Among unattached individuals or single-person families, 50 percent went to the highest fifth, and 74 percent to the highest two-fifths, while only 3 percent went to the lowest fifth, and only 11 percent to the lowest two-fifths. This is iniquitous in terms of social justice, and, for reasons soon to be disclosed, utterly incompatible with a satisfactory growth performance.

MISAPPLICATION OF LORD KEYNES: THE ALLOCATIONS PROBLEM

Several decades ago, Lord Keynes observed that the maldistribution of income was generating too low a level of consumption, relative to the growing ability to produce. He found that an excessive share of total income accruing to those higher up in the income structure, who spend smaller portions of their incomes for immediate consumption than those lower down in the structure, generated more saving for private investment than could enduringly be absorbed. Hence, overcapacity, and massive unemployment of manpower and plant. Keynes therefore proposed that public borrowing be used to tap off the excessive private saving and put it to work through investment in enlarged public goods and services, which he also deemed manifestly desirable per se. But this was not *all* of the thought of the great Englishman. He insisted that this "compensatory" program could not succeed unless many other measures were adopted to improve the distribution of private income.

When the New Economics, from 1961 onward, came to wrestle with the evil of inadequate economic growth, the diagnosis upon which Keynes focused was clearly applicable, although the situation was not nearly as acute as the one he confronted. In each period of upturn during 1953–1964, during the "roller-coaster" performance, the rate of growth in the investment which adds to plant and equipment had far outrun the rate of growth in consumption, which on analytical grounds should include both private consumption and public demand for goods and services. Income maldistribution all along the line, abetted by public policies, contributed to these misallocations of resources and economic activity.

But the New Economics took the position that it made little difference *where* the effort to increase demand was injected into the economy. Ignoring the central concern of most of the great economists about allocation of resources and incomes, the new thinkers forgot that the injection of increased *power* to spend would not *pro tanto* increase *actual* spending or demand, if the injections were grossly misplaced. Thus there was repeated resort to massive tax reductions, especially in 1964, which greatly augmented the availability of funds to those who were already "oversaving" and/or relatively overinvesting. Meanwhile, the composition of the tax reductions did not sufficiently augment the spending power of consumers. Simultaneously, the reckless tax reduction prevented the needed increases in allocations to public demand. In practical results, the New Economics gave the economy a very temporary "shot in the arm," followed by all of the unfortunate developments since 1966, abetted, to be sure, by the mistakes of later public officials who said "We are all Keynesians now."

The prevalent policy of insufficient expansion of the money supply in the long run accompanied by a fantastic increase in interest rates is subject to the same criticism. It was designed ("successfully") to reduce the real economic growth rate far below the optimum rate; and all of the inevitable consequences followed. The policy stimulated what needed restraint and repressed what needed expansion, thus feeding the fat and starving the lean. And the policy has been grossly inflationary, because rising interest costs are pyramided throughout the price structure.

The policy of repressed public spending, in all its aspects, has had precisely the same misallocating effects.

THE CONFUSION BETWEEN MEANS AND ENDS

The neglect of appropriate attention to the three great ends of growth, priorities, and justice (depending basically upon the allocation of resources and incomes) implies necessarily that the specific policies and programs are not properly developed and applied. For policies in such fields as taxation, money, social security, housing, agriculture, income supports and welfare, and the international economy—to mention some of the most important—are merely *means* toward the three great ends, and must fall short if these ends are not constantly defined and reviewed in highly quantitative terms. Practically every policy I define as a "means" affects the distribution of income and resources in one way or another; and how can these policies be satisfactory if we do not bear constantly in mind what allocations we need on economic and social grounds?

A striking example of the failure to move toward this equilibrium or balance is to be found in the recent and current "control" efforts with respect to prices, wages, and profits. For these, too, are merely means toward allocations of resources and incomes in accord with the three great ends. The controls program has been applied and judged as if the *sole* purposes were to restrain the rate of price inflation. But at least equally important is the role of wages in the expansion of consumption toward improved equilibrium and optimum economic growth. Regardless of whether wage trends are now running too high or too low, it is amazing that the role of wages in consumption never surfaces in the public evaluation of the controls. My own belief is that we have suffered under a controls program which, in the name of fighting inflation, is excessively repressive upon growth, priorities, and justice.

THE ERRONEOUS CAMPAIGN AGAINST INFLATION

What I have said above emphasizes the point that a rising, stable, or falling price level is not good or bad per se. It all depends upon the impact of price trends upon the three great ends I have stressed—a matter almost completely disregarded in the prevalent approaches.

In addition, whether price increases are good or bad should be judged in terms of the causes and consequences of the particular type of inflation we are experiencing. To illustrate: Let us assume for a moment that the same amount of price inflation as we have had since 1966 had been generated (a result which I challenge for reasons to be stated) by successful programs to maintain optimum economic growth and minimum unemployment; launch a more effective war against poverty; clear the slums and build the homes our people need; renovate our cities; modernize social security; and bring rural income and living standards up to some tolerable level of parity with those of others. The inflation thus generated would have been a wonderful bargain or tradeoff. In contrast, this same amount of actual inflation, accompanied and aggravated by contrived neglect of these crucial tasks through policies and programs avowedly designed to fight inflation, has been a cruel, stupid, and indefensible inflation.

All empirical evidence since 1953 has made it increasingly plain, contrary to the trade-off theory, that *we have more inflation when idle resources increase, and less inflation when they are reduced.* Although this has been demonstrated many times, a few examples will suffice. During 1958–1966, when the average annual rate of real economic growth was 4.9 percent and unemployment dropped from 6.8 percent to 3.8 percent, the average annual increase in consumer prices was only 1.5 percent. But during 1966–1972, when the average rate of real economic growth was only 3.1 percent and when unemployment rose from 3.8 percent to 5.6 percent, the average annual rate of consumer price inflation was 4.3 percent. The performance record from 12 months before the freeze to date again illustrates clearly that substantial reduction in the rate of inflation commenced well before the freeze as the economy moved from recession to a much higher though inadequate rate of economic growth. Most recently, there have been disturbing signs of an intensification of the inflationary process; and I believe this to be due mainly to the still inadequate economic performance and the vast uncertainties about the near future and about current national economic policies.

The theoretical reasons in support of the overwhelming empirical evidence are clear. During periods of low or negative growth, those who administer their prices attempt to compensate for inadequate volume by lifting their prices faster; reduced productivity gains increase *per unit* cost and lead to price increases; shortages of such public services as medical care and housing, aggravated by repressed public programs, add to inflationary pressures; exorbitant interest rates, undertaken to fight inflation, are inflationary per se. In addition, sharp changes in business expectations prompt price changes, usually upward no matter in which direction the economy is moving. It by now seems axiomatic that, in the long run, a stable and optimum rate of economic growth generates less *net* price inflation than the roller-coaster performance. And even were this more questionable than I deem it to be, the advantages of optimum economic performance immensely outweigh any marginal benefits in the area of prices which anyone might claim (I believe mistakenly) to result from holding the economy back and starving social programs.

THE CONSERVATIVE STRAND OF THE POST-KEYNESIAN SYNTHESIS

In the last quarter century or so, the relation between Keynesian economics and the liberal-conservative debate in the United States has undergone a subtle but dramatic change. One side of the post-Keynesian synthesis has been the acquiescence of conservatives both inside and outside the economics profession to the Keynesian revolution. (Recall selection 3.7 by Ernest van den Haag.) During and after World War II, large-scale corporations and their ideological supporters came to accept the use of monetary and fiscal policies to promote the economic stability necessary to sustain and extend corporate profits. A new variant of economic conservatism arose which became an integral part of the post-Keynesian synthesis rather than a rearguard criticism of it. Managerial capitalism, as this variant of economic conservatism has come to be called, combines support for a modified Keynesian macroeconomic role for government with an elaborate rationale justifying the roles of both large-scale corporations and their "new-style," nonowning manager-executives in the "private" sector.

In a now-classic policy statement in the early postwar years, the Committee for Economic Development promulgated the moderate or modified Keynesianism of "progressive" or "liberal" business groups in the United States.[5] On the one hand, the CED clearly recognized the crucial role of aggregate demand in determining the overall performance of the economy, the possibility of depression or inflation because of insufficient or excessive demand, the limitations of the annually balanced budget rule, and the consequent need for government action to sustain stable prosperity. On the other hand, the CED maintained contact with pre-Keynesian values and verities (for example, economic freedom, economy in government, debt reduction) and proposed primary reliance on automatic stabilizers built into the internal workings of the fiscal system (for example, progressive income tax, unemployment compensation payments), rather than on discretionary policy tools (for example, public works expenditures). In other publications, the CED both reflected and contributed to the spread of the emerging consensus that corporate business and government were complementary and compatible institutions in modern managerial capitalism.

[5] *Taxes and the Budget: A Program for Prosperity in a Free Economy* (New York: Committee for Economic Development, 1947).

The conservative strand of the post-Keynesian synthesis is described in the next three readings. Selection 3.15, by James Buchanan, shows how conservative Keynesianism can make common cause with neo-liberalism (chapter 6). Evaluating rules for fiscal policy, Buchanan commends budgetary balance at high-level employment, criticizes "functional finance" (recall Abba Lerner's discussion in selection 3.4), and comments favorably on the concept of the annually balanced budget.

In selection 3.16, Adolf Berle, former "braintruster" in the Roosevelt administration, and co-author with Gardner Means of the classic *The Modern Corporation and Private Property* (1932), describes the limitations on corporate power in the contemporary American economy. Classically, Berle suggests, "property" implied both an active controlling function (management) and a passive receptive function (beneficial ownership). A separation of these two dimensions of property has taken place in the large-scale corporation, whose managers have become increasingly free from the control of stockholder-owners (as well as from the controls traditionally exerted by the competitive market place). But corporate economic power, though "far reaching" and largely loosened from its traditional checks, is "never absolute"; it is offset by a modern check-and-balance system, including public opinion, oligopolistic rivalry, the need for profits, and governmental intervention.

In *The Cost of Freedom* (1960) and other works (selection 3.17), Henry Wallich, professor of economics at Yale University and a member of Eisenhower's Council of Economic Advisers, has presented the case for "modern" or "progressive conservatism." His views lie somewhere between Keynesian orthodoxy and the individualist conservatism of Friedman, Buchanan, and others (chapter 6). As presidential adviser, he advocated the use of monetary and fiscal policies to promote stable prosperity. Wallich recognizes the role of large-scale organization in both business and government, and the technological and social changes that have brought about concentrations of economic power, but he emphasizes the reality and desirability of sustained decentralization and freedom in economic life.

If one side of the post-Keynesian synthesis was the acquiescence of conservatives to the Keynesian revolution, the other was the taming of the reformist zeal of liberal Keynesians. With the passage of time, Keynesian economics itself became a "new orthodoxy." A new generation of economists accepted with virtual unanimity the participation of government in the promotion of economic recovery and the maintenance of stable full employment. The need for reallocation of resources and redistribution of income in a fully employed economy was largely dropped in the liberals' sacrifice to consensus. Keynesian economics became respectable partly by becoming palatable, and it became palatable partly by becoming more neutral politically and ideologically. Once the basic thrust of Keynesian analysis and policy—the necessity and feasibility of conscious governmental action designed to promote full employment, economic stability, and growth—was accepted, the older contrast between *liberal* Keynesianism and *conservative* pre- or anti-Keynesianism became increasingly obsolete. The more current debate became that between liberal and conservative strands of the post-Keynesian synthesis over such questions as fiscal versus monetary policy, discretionary versus automatic policy instruments, government expenditures versus tax cuts, government employment versus stimulation of the private sector, priority for full employment versus priority for price stability.

An overview of the contrast between liberal and conservative strands of the post-Keynesian synthesis, with particular reference to the debates of the 1960s, is given in selection 3.18 by Lekachman. Walter Heller (chairman of the Council of Economic Advisers during the Kennedy-Johnson administrations and leading advocate of expansionary monetary and fiscal policies) has described this tempering of the liberal reformist zeal of the post-Keynesian synthesis as the "decline of the doctrinaire."[6] By contrast, John K. Galbraith, whose views on American capitalism will be explored more fully in chapter 5, has categorized the political compromise that chose tax cuts rather than expanded government spending and generous employment and antipoverty programs as "reactionary Keynesianism."[7] In selection 3.19, Richard Du Boff and Edward Herman sharply criticize neo-Keynesian orthodoxy from the perspective of the new radicalism of the 1960s and 1970s.

3.15 Rules for Fiscal Policy

James Buchanan

We shall discuss here separate rules for fiscal policy, that is, alternative schemes of budgetary adjustment in response to changes in the values for income, employment and prices.

THE BALANCED BUDGET RULE

Prior to the Great Depression of the 1930's, the only accepted rule for fiscal policy was that the government's budget should not be adjusted in response to changes in the level of economic activity, that the budget should not be used deliberately as a weapon for macroeconomic policy. The budget should be made on the basis of the principle of maintaining balance in the fiscal accounts over the appropriate accounting period, normally accepted as the fiscal year.

Since any strict adherence to the principle or rule of the annually balanced budget means that fiscal policy is not to be employed directly for stabilization

[6] Walter W. Heller, *New Dimensions of Political Economy* (New York: W. W. Norton, 1967).

[7] John K. Galbraith, *Hearings on the January 1965 Economic Report of the President* (Washington, D.C.: U.S. Government Printing Office, 1965).

Excerpted with permission from James Buchanan, *The Public Finances*, rev. ed. Homewood, Ill.: Richard D. Irwin, pp. 119–33.

purposes, the implication of this view is that the primary instrument of macroeconomic policy becomes monetary policy along with reliance on the self-correcting forces within the economy itself. Monetary policy, conceived as a deliberately employed means of influencing the state of the economy, has been long accepted, especially in the form of the manipulation of central bank rates. Nevertheless, the weight given to the self-correcting forces in the economy was also of major importance before the onset of the Great Depression.

The economic theories of Lord Keynes, themselves born in the Great Depression, were of great influence in emphasizing the absence of satisfactory self-correcting mechanisms in the economy under nationally managed currency systems and the necessity for positive governmental action designed to achieve satisfactory levels of income and employment. Until this influence made itself felt, the standard feature of fiscal orthodoxy was that of the annually balanced government budget.

Once it was widely recognized that the federal budget might be purposefully unbalanced to achieve desired levels of income and employment, economists tended to abandon the balanced budget rule on the grounds that it is overly restrictive. It came to be widely accepted that the maintenance of full employment along with stable growth are more important than any strict adherence to an ancient fiscal rule; therefore, if necessary, the government budget should be deliberately unbalanced as required. *Fiscal policy,* as such, was introduced into the discussion.

What is to be said in favor of the rule of the annually balanced budget? In suggesting the rather wholesale abandonment of this rule, many economists seem to have overlooked the important function that the rule does play in the complex process of fiscal decision making. Economists, on the average, seem to have paid perhaps too much attention to the objectives for macroeconomic policy and not sufficient attention to the other equally important aspects of budgetary and fiscal institutions.

The balanced budget rule serves a control function. Taxing and spending decisions are made by legislative bodies. And representative government being as it is, the legislator, regardless of his personal integrity, is constantly under pressure from two opposing forces. Constituents want lower taxes, and they rarely make the connection between taxes and specific public services. At the same time, voters want tax reductions and federal expenditure projects (veterans' hospitals, missile installations, river basin developments, and so on) in their local areas. Unless some central control feature exists to keep these two opposing forces in some rough equality with each other, the limited degree of rationality that is present in legislative decisions will be still further reduced. Only the balanced budget rule tends to provide such a control feature. It was, and continues to be, largely respect for this time-honored fiscal principle (considered to be wholly out of date by many modern analysts) that has kept public spending and tax revenues in rough correspondence with each other over the postwar period.

It is easy to see that abandonment of the faith in the balanced budget rule or principle tends to bias decision making in the direction of deficit financing. Legislators will rarely create surpluses since the tax cutters and the expenditure expanders are the pressure groups, not the tax increasers and the expenditure cutters. Therefore, insofar as post-Keynesian attitudes are allowed to exert influences on legislators, federal budgets will tend to show more unbalance on the deficit side than on the surplus side.

Does this suggest that the principle of the annually balanced budget should necessarily be restored to its former place as the model for fiscal responsibility? It is difficult to give an unqualified answer to this question. We may say that if the job of macroeconomic policy can successfully be carried out by nonfiscal means, the rule for the annually balanced budget will allow "better" decisions concerning the size of the over-all budget to be made. But there are also disadvantages to placing the full job of macroeconomic policy on the alternative to fiscal policy, namely monetary policy. There are no easy solutions here. It seems clear that some adherence to the orthodox rule of budget balance must be maintained but that legislative bodies must be willing to depart from this rule when the economic situation warrants. If the nonfiscal means of combatting either severe recession or inflation are insufficiently powerful to accomplish the task, employment, growth, and price-level stability criteria must generally take precedence over the balanced budget rule. But given vigorous and rational application, these nonfiscal weapons do seem to be of sufficient strength to accomplish the desired goals of macroeconomic policy. On the whole, we conclude that the rule for budget balance should be retained as a guide for responsible fiscal decisions during times of normal economic activity, including minor recessions and inflations. And the departure from this rule solely or even primarily to accelerate rapid economic growth seems to be highly questionable policy. Governments should be willing to abandon this rule only when prolonged and serious depression is present or when inflation is proceeding at a dangerous pace.

BUDGET BALANCE AT HIGH-LEVEL INCOME AND EMPLOYMENT

In the years since World War II a fiscal policy rule has been proposed, and to some extent adopted, which represents a compromise between the principle of the annually balanced budget and the direct utilization of the budget for macroeconomic policy purposes. This proposed rule or principle is that of budget balance at the most desirable level of national money income, with built-in or automatic unbalance during periods of recession or inflation.

At any given time, a certain aggregate national income or GNP is required to generate the highest level of resource employment that is consistent with stability in the purchasing of the monetary unit. As was pointed out previously, the degree of unemployment that this level of income represents will depend on the institutional structure. The first step in applying this fiscal rule is that of estimating the "most desirable" or the effective "full employment" GNP. The yield of the alternative tax structures can then be estimated on the basis of the assumption that national income is, in fact, generated at the desired level. The rule states that decisions made regarding taxes and public spending should always be made *on the assumption that the high-level income is to be maintained, and that balance between the two sides of the account should be present.* For each new item of public spending that is adopted, the Congress should expect to increase the tax rate sufficiently to finance fully the expenditure at the high-level national income. In this way, through the pairing off of expenditure increments with tax increments, it is hoped that the desirable control features of the balanced budget principle may be reatined.

Actually, national income may fall below or lie above the level that is estimated to be the most desirable and upon which the tax-expenditure decisions are presumably made. But this fiscal rule is designed to guarantee the presence of more or less automatic adjustment in the budget when income levels change.

Built-in Stabilizers

The important means through which this is accomplished is built-in flexibility on both the tax and the expenditure sides of the account. If taxes are levied on the basis of income, either personal or corporate, a proportional rate structure will produce less total revenue at lower national incomes than at higher ones. But, insofar as the structure contains progressive elements, the change in tax revenues as income changes will be proportionately greater than the income change itself. Not only does a person pay less tax at an annual income of $10,000 than he does at $20,000 because the base of the tax is reduced; he also shifts to a lower bracket for which a lower rate of tax is applied. Further, this built-in flexibility in revenue yield is reinforced if the tax structure imposes relatively heavier rates on those elements of income that are especially subject to change when national income changes. The important place of the corporation income tax in the federal revenue system is relevant here. Corporate profits is one of the first income sectors to be reduced when the level of total demand falls; similarly, profits tend to move up rapidly when aggregate demand increases. Since the corporation income tax bears primarily on corporate profits, its yield changes much more than proportionately as national income changes. It possesses major advantages as a "built-in stabilizer."

On the expenditure side, many items of public spending are somewhat insensitive to national income changes. As national income falls, government demand for real goods and services does not fall. Therefore, outlay on these real goods and services is reduced only insofar as buying prices are reduced. And, given considerable stickiness in prices against downward shifts in demand, little reduction in government expenditure can be expected. The effects are not symmetrical with respect to national income increases. As national income goes up, government spending for a fixed amount of real goods and services will increase with the increase in purchase prices, but not to the same extent that tax revenues increase. But, aside from government spending for real goods and services which does not vary greatly over the income cycle, some important public expenditures vary inversely with national income. If social security payments and unemployment compensation are determined on the basis of certain predefined rules of eligibility, a decline in the overall level of income and employment will cause these transfer payments to increase. Other budgetary items such as aid to veterans, aid to families with dependent children, aid to agriculture, etc., may also vary inversely with national income. Considerable built-in flexibility may thus be present on the expenditure side of the budget, but experience has shown that this is of considerably less significance than the flexibility on the tax side.

Postwar Experience under the Rule

The proposal for using the federal budget as a macroeconomic policy tool only to the extent that the corrective forces can be made quasi-automatic and independent of day-to-day decisions on taxes and expenditures was strongly advanced in the early 1950's. The Committee for Economic Development, an organization of leading American businessmen, recommended this principle as a guiding rule for budgetary policy. And to a certain extent, in part deliberately, in part accidentally, this rule was followed in practice in the 1950's, although, of course, there was no official statement of its adoption or applicability. The continued high-level rates of taxes over the whole of the period since World War II acted to guarantee a high sensitivity of tax yields to shifts in national income. This, coupled with the relative insensibility of public spending, caused deficits to occur almost automatically during recessions and surpluses to occur during periods of threatened inflation. Supplementary fiscal action was taken, but the major impact of budgetary policy in the 1950's came about because of the built-in flexibility features.

To the extent that Congress indicated a willingness to allow the built-in stabilizers to adjust tax yields and expenditures in a compensating manner during the postwar decades, the rule of the annually balanced budget was no longer the dominant fiscal orthodoxy held by American political leaders.

FUNCTIONAL FINANCE

A rule propounded much earlier in the late 1930's and early 1940's directly as a result of the Keynesian analysis [is] "functional finance." It is based on the idea that the federal budget should be used as the major instrument for achieving macroeconomic objectives and that budgetary changes should be made as often as desired and in whatever magnitude is desired. The allocative function of the budget should be relegated to secondary rank. This rule of "functional finance" is associated in the early post-Keynesian literature with the writings of Professor Abba Lerner.

In the depression condition of the 1930's, the employment objective did seem to overwhelm all others in importance. Early statements of the fiscal policy rule tended to be somewhat extreme and oversimplified. For example, the statement was made that the *only* purpose of taxation was that of preventing inflation. As long as inflation was not threatened, public expenditures were to be financed by the creation of money. Stated in this oversimplified manner, the functional finance rule ignores the basic purpose of the fiscal structure, which is to provide certain collective goods and services. And the decision concerning the appropriate amount of these goods and services is not properly made by limiting budgetary adjustments to the accomplishment of macroeconomic objectives.

Modern statements of this rule are more sophisticated. The rule states simply that the federal budget should be purposefully used at all times with a view toward maintaining desired values for the macroeconomic variables: national income, employment, price levels, rates of growth. The admittedly useful control features inherent in the balanced-budget rule are less important than the achievement of these objectives. No attempt need be made, according to functional finance proponents, to balance the budget in any single accounting period, nor should the principle of budget balance either at high income or at potential GNP be adopted. The criteria for budgetary planning should be direct, not indirect. Budget balance may be the result but it should never be the aim of budgetary planning.

The proponents of this budgetary rule normally place less reliance on monetary policy as an appropriate macroeconomic instrument than do those who favor either of the alternative rules. In the pure Keynesian analysis, monetary policy is quite ineffective in insuring a reversal of a slump or recession due to the floor that is allegedly placed under the interest rate. Once this floor is reached, monetary policy is presumed to become ineffective, since it is only through interest rate reductions that stimulus can come, in this model. Several objections have been raised to this argument, but these will not concern us here. If, however, monetary policy is ineffective, fiscal policy must be allowed a more important role, especially on downswings. The modern advocate of functional finance desires that the budget be deliberately unbalanced at the onset of a downturn. Taxes should be reduced, but, more importantly, public spending should be increased.

On the upturn it has been generally recognized, even by the extreme Keynesians, that monetary policy is relatively more effective. There is no ceiling on the interest rate. Hence functional finance advocates are less emphatic on the need for surplus creation during inflationary booms. They may, however, raise serious objections to the application of monetary policy on the upswing of the cycle. They agree that it can be effective, but they do not like its results. The high interest rates that may be required impinge differentially on the investment sector of the economy. And this is recognized to conflict with accelerating the rate of growth, a conflict that we have already discussed.

When we turn to considerations of practical politics, the functional finance approach may be criticized. It seems clearly to embody a bias toward deficit creation, given the existence of democratic decision-making institutions. Legislative bodies will be highly responsive to the needs of the economy during periods of recession when the signs indicate that both a reduction in taxation and an increase in spending is suggested. On the other hand, neither legislative nor executive bodies seem likely to respond to inflation by tax increases and government curtailment. If the economy should be guided from above by a single decision-making agency, interested only in maximizing the well-being of all the citizens, there seems no doubt but that the functional finance rule would be the most desirable of all those discussed. But this kind of decision-making body does not exist, nor would we want it to exist in a democratic society. Hence we must always examine the rule as it would exist in practice, not how it might work in a wholly ideal decision-making world. In practice, either this rule or the one discussed previously tends to weaken seriously the controls over public spending.

This does not suggest that the ideas that are summarized in the "functional finance" approach to macroeconomic policy have not done much to awaken governments to their responsibility for insuring that national income and high employment, along with price-level stability and steady growth, should be fostered where possible. Certainly, should a severe depression occur, the budget would be deliberately used in the manner that functional finance suggests. All alternative rules that might previously exist would simply be scrapped. Similarly, if runaway inflation should commence, there seems little doubt that surplus creation would be followed, actively or passively. Therefore, in the sense of very wide sweeps in the economy, we may say that we live, in the [1970's], in a regime of "functional finance." The debate is not on this point, however. It concerns the applicability of the budget as an instrument of macroeconomic policy during periods of reasonable "normalcy" in the economy, when slight recessions and slight boomlets appear along a steady but variable growth path. In this setting fiscal policy, generally, is less adaptable, and the question of the appropriate rule to be followed remains, perhaps, an open one.

CONCLUSIONS

In this article alternative rules for fiscal policy have been discussed. The first was that of the annually balanced budget. This rule, which represented the dominant fiscal orthodoxy prior to the 1930's, does possess highly desirable control features which many economists have overlooked. The rule tends to cause more responsible decisions to be made concerning the appropriate amount of government spending. However, during periods of economic recession or boom, the rule, if literally applied, tends to be perverse in its effects on the economy. The budget provides a possibly corrective force in achieving desirable levels for the macroeconomic variables.

The rule of budget balance at high income and employment represented a compromise of sorts between the annually balanced budget principle and functional finance. The rule attempted to combine the control features of budget balance with the stabilization features of functional finance through the employment of the so-called built-in stabilizers, which tend automatically to produce deficits in recession and surpluses in booms. To some extent, this rule was practiced, although not explicitly, during the decade of the 1950's.

This rule of budget balance at high employment must be modified in applicability when the economy grows. The level of income at which balance in the accounts is to be maintained grows through time, and this fact makes necessary a rather continuous adjustment of the tax-spending structure in order to prevent the emergence, or potential emergence, of a "full employment surplus." It is this emendation that the economists of the 1960's have added to the principle of budget balance at high employment, and it was the analysis here, in terms of budget balance at "potential GNP", that provided the background for the major tax cut proposals in 1963.

This rule, which departs still further from the control features inherent in the balanced budget, does not seem widely different from the earlier proposed rule, that of "functional finance." Here the primary purpose of the government fiscal structure is that of achieving the goals of macroeconomic policy. This rule will be followed with respect to wide and major changes in the level of economic activity. For more "normal" periods, characterized by relatively minor fluctuations, the rule would work well only in a regime of an economic tsar. With democratically elected representatives making fiscal choices, the wholesale departure from the rule of budget balance may produce serious bias toward continuous deficit financing and, as a result, secular inflation.

3.16 Power Without Property

Adolf A. Berle

The flowing tide of evolution has downgraded the traditional possessor-owners of individualist enterprise to the legal position of passive claim-holders and to the economic position of *rentiers*. Conversely, their decision-making functions have been aggregated, and have been placed in the administrations of great organizations, namely, corporations. In result, the greatest part of American economic enterprise, formerly individualist, has been regrouped and consolidated into a few hundred non-Statist, collective cooperative institutions.

These clearly have economic advantages, and have produced economic benefits. All this depends on organization; but economic organization, like all organization, depends upon and generates power.

LIMITATION AND CONTROL OF ECONOMIC POWER

Economic power, far-reaching though it can be, is decidedly more limited than the vast and unsolved enigma of power in general. It is never absolute.

Absent combination with other forms, economic power is indeed impressive but not uncontrollable.

The Great Limitation: Pluralism, Including Competition

No organization wielding economic power is disassociated from other organizations likewise wielding economic power (actual or potential competitors, suppliers, large buyers, and so forth), or from other institutions in the community wielding other forms of power—for example, organized labor and the political State. No element of the current American industrial system is removed from contact with and dependence on other parts of that system. The relationship with and interdependence of each organization on other organizations is frequently direct and immediate, limiting its capacity to act. In contemporary United States, the power of any organization, however great and strong, is subject not only to the laws of its being but to the added limitation that failure or refusal by it to function means that some other organization—whether a competing organization or an agency of the State—will emerge, undertaking to produce, employ, supply, or distribute, that is, to provide a tolerable equivalent. The economic power of an American corporation, therefore, is capable of application only within certain limits. At present, the greatest continuous restraint on the use of economic power in the United States is its pluralism: the fact that no single organization has been permitted to grasp more than a limited number of functions, or even, as a rule, to achieve monopoly in any one function. In the main (though not universally) the result at present is an equipoise of strong organizations.

Classically, pluralism in this context means possibility of competition by rival organizations or industries. This, of course, assumes the existence, or possibility of ready creation, of competing units. In the case of a monopoly this assumption may not be valid. Consequently there is a consistent preoccupation of American politics and American law to destroy, or prevent emergence of, monopoly.

In place of the classical "market place conditions," the present American system of "oligopoly" has emerged: two to five powerful corporations dominating each of the most important industries. Competition exists between these units. But it is "imperfect" because the powerful organizations tend to behave in about the same way under any given set of conditions.

The protection in such a system is that each of the few large units can and will with gusto enter the field and the market of any other unit in the industry which handles its affairs badly. While the system of oligopoly does not hold out the old hope of an "optimum" set of market conditions reached through competition, it does erect a substantial limitation on the power of each unit in it. Of no less importance is the fact that it does set up a base permitting a degree of planning (that is, consensus on objectives, methods, and desired results) which affords a measure of stabilization.

The Need for Profits

A second limitation is the obvious need for profits. It is true that the profit motivation has an impact rather different from that assumed by the classical economists. Profits mean one thing to a possessor-owner who is immediately and directly enriched or impoverished. They mean another to corporation managers, executives, and laborers whose compensation is not immediately related to them. But it is still true that a non-Statist economic organization cannot continue to exist and enjoy power (let alone enhance its position) unless it makes profits. Therefore the operation of such organizations must be directed toward reaping profits, and they must move within the general limitations of the profit system.

The "Public Consensus"—The "Corporate Conscience"

This limitation is intangible, imponderable in character, but wholly real. It may be called limitation by "public consensus." This is the existence of a set of ideas, widely held by the community, and often by the organization itself and the men who direct it, that certain uses of power are "wrong," that is, contrary to the established interest and value system of the community. Indulgence of these ideas as limitation on economic power, and regard for them by the managers of the great corporations, is sometimes called—and ridiculed as—the "corporate conscience." The ridicule is pragmatically unjustified. The first sanction enforcing limitations imposed by the public consensus is a lively appreciation of that consensus by corporate managements. This is the reality of the "corporate conscience." Violation leads to loss of prestige, public standing, and popular esteem for the men in the organization itself as loyalty to it is undermined. Deprivation of prestige is one of the very ancient methods by which a society enforces its value systems upon individuals and groups within it. And if loss of prestige does not produce results more acceptable to the community, other and more forceful means of imposing the ideas embodied in the public consensus of community commonly appear.

Political Intervention

Misuse of economic power may provoke a degree of irritation or distress leading to the emergence or energizing of the action of a more powerful counterforce. Periodic interventions of the Government of the United States into specific economic fields have occurred where economic power was thought to have been abused or to have failed to serve the community.

The Granger movement leading to the establishment of the Interstate Commerce Commission in 1887 was such an incident. Continuing abuses of power by railroads at the turn of the century led President Roosevelt in 1903 to cause the Congress to give that Commission (that is, to take from the railroad corporation and give to the Government of the United States) power to fix railroad rates. Other notable instances were assumption of economic power by the Federal government through passage of the Public Utilities Holding Company Act of 1934, and of the Rural Electrification Act of 1935.

However powerless any individual may be to deal with economic organization on the economic plane, he does have, in the American democracy, a solid and respected power in the political field. If enough individuals consider that they are aggrieved, they can energize a political intervention. Our studies may have downgraded the individual as an economic factor. But he is still very much alive, visible, and active as a political factor.

Economic power thus is not only not absolute; it functions in the possibility that competing organizations or quite other forms of power—political (Statist) or organized labor—may intervene. In American society, the ultimate limitation on economic power is the possibility of energizing, in any one of various ways, the political power of the government.

3.17 Conservative Economic Policy

Henry C. Wallich

. . . . Conservatism is an attitude, an approach, more than a specific set of doctrines. Its specific policies must change with the times—anything else would be ossification, not conservatism. And conservatism must flow from convictions, if it is to be more than opportunism and defense of vested interests. What are the economic issues, and what stand does conservatism take on them? . . .

The main features of a conservative attitude are not hard to discern. Conservatism takes an organic view of society, as something that has grown up over time and cannot be arbitrarily changed—very different from a set of building blocks that can be shuffled and reassembled whenever someone invents a new model. Conservatism puts more stock in experience than in abstract reasoning. It is skeptical of broad solutions, preferring to go step by step. . . .

These almost instinctive attitudes shape the specific policies advocated by conservatives, but certainly do not commit them to any unvarying doctrine. This applies with particular force to the economic field. Our economy cannot stand still for long; it must expand or sink into depression. Expansion requires invention and brings social change. Conservatives, if they want to preserve principles, must accept and even promote changes in outward form. They will be selective about change, and try to bring it about with a minimum of distur-

Excerpted from Henry C. Wallich, "Conservative Economic Policy," *The Yale Review*, Autumn 1956.

bance. They will not, if they are wise, resist it. Conservatism is not conservationism.

* * *

What are the economic policies that should flow from a conservative attitude? They must be molded, of course, to meet the challenge of the times. Perhaps the dominant challenge to be encountered by a conservative administration will be to encourage rapid growth of the economy without inflation. . . .

At first blush, ''growth'' as a top policy goal seems to be something of a stranger to the conservative vocabulary, where ''stability'' and ''balance'' are more at home. Isn't such emphasis bound to lead away from truly conservative preoccupations, toward a paroxysm of materialism? Does it make sense to speed up when we are not sure what lies at the end of the road?

On second thought, conservative concerns like these must retreat into the background when confronted with the realities of the situation. The most obtrusive of these realities is Russia. There are still those who seem to think that the best way of countering the growth of the Russian economy is to deny that it is occurring. A more rational approach is to speed up our own expansion. Whatever the future may hold, we dare not let ourselves be overtaken.

Another and more congenial urgency arises from the great many things still to be done in our own country. Education, health, housing, roads, raising of the lowest income brackets, all demand a rapidly growing national income. Growth also serves as a substitute for greater equalization, if all participate in it. The enlargement of the cake softens the argument over the size of the slices.

Granted that growth is urgent, shouldn't a conservative government rely on natural forces to supply it? Isn't rapid growth an outstanding characteristic of a free economy? The answer, like so many in economics, is yes and no. Our economy has turned in a fine performance in raising income and living standards. It has done this primarily, however, because American consumers and businessmen have saved and ploughed back into the economy part of their income. Had they decided to consume more of current output and save less, growth would have been less. The economy would still have done well by us, by making the most efficient use possible of the resources that existed. But the system does not decide by itself what percentage of output is to be ploughed back to create new resources. Precisely because it is a free system, this decision is in the hands of its users. A free economy, therefore, may be operating with high efficiency, and yet have little growth—if little new capital is fed into it. By the same token, an inefficient economy, such as the Russian, may nevertheless advance rapidly if living standards are held down so as to allow a high rate of investment.

A free economy, therefore, does not assure fast growth under all circumstances. What can be done to create circumstances favorable to growth? The first and biggest ingredient of an active growth policy is the obvious one of staying out of depressions. Our success in this endeavor since the war should not blind us to the very real difficulties that we may encounter farther along the road. But accelerated growth is only one of many compelling reasons, of course, why everything must be done to prevent a new disaster, and we have cause to believe that if we avoid speculative excesses, we can also stave off a severe depression.

The second step toward accelerated growth would be to invigorate the body economic—to expand its little grey cells, through more education and research, to quicken its reflexes, by removing rigidities and sharpening incentives. Conservatives will want their government to move circumspectly, however, and to leave private enterprise the elbowroom it needs.

But important as these things are, they are not the core of the question. The core is capital formation. To get the expansion we want, we must invest more. Over the last five years, investment in the American economy has run at a rate of about 15 percent of the gross national product. In a relatively poor country like West Germany, it has been averaging 25 percent, even after reconstruction was largely completed. The result: Germany's gross national product has advanced 7 percent annually, ours, 3 to 4 percent.

How much an economy invests depends partly on incentives—profits, markets, new techniques, competition—and partly on the savings that become available. Incentives and savings are both strongly influenced by the tax system. High personal and corporate rates take some of the zest out of the hunt for profit. They also take some of the wherewithal that large and small businesses and wealthy individuals might otherwise put into such ventures.

This is a conclusion at which one arrives reluctantly, because it seems to open up a conflict between social equity and progress. If we try to even up the income distribution by means of progressive taxation, we reduce savings and curtail investment incentives and so slow down growth. If we want to accelerate growth, we have to accept inequality of income. Yet this conflict is easier to resolve for the conservative than for the liberal, the conservative being more concerned about equality of opportunity than equality of shares. From a dollars-and-cents point of view, it is quite obvious that over a period of years, even those who find themselves at the short end of inequality have more to gain from faster growth than from any conceivable income redistribution. A speed-up in real output of only one extra percent per year will soon lift even the economically weakest into income brackets to which no amount of redistribution could promote them.

The conservative social conscience is put at ease by this observation. Political thinkers have sought to defend differences in income and wealth on grounds of natural law, or property rights, or simply as one of the facts of life. For the economist, economic inequality acquires a functional justification thanks to the growth concept. Its ultimate results benefit even those who at first seem to be losers.

Inequality is losing its sharp edge, moreover, thanks to the reshaping of our living habits by modern technology. Not the least among science's miracles is the way in which it has shrunk the difference between living standards. The basic mechanics of life in the $5,000 and the $25,000 household have become very similar. The $25,000 home contains better models of the same equipment and a few more frills, its owner enjoys a few exclusive luxuries. But as contrasted with 50 years ago, the closing of the gap is startling.

The challenge of rapid growth, which we have been discussing so far, is intimately connected with a second issue that conservative economic policy will have to meet: the problem of inflation. In its early stretches, inflation looks like a primrose path to rapid growth. The proponents of this route argue—not always consistently—two positions. Some of them say that inflation is positively desirable because it bolsters the prospects of business and so encourages investment. Others accept inflation with moderate reluctance, as the inevitable by-product of an expansionary policy. Both share the belief that all the fuel that easy money and big government spending can generate should be pumped under the boilers to keep pressure at a peak. This high-pressure economy, it is argued, will bring every last available resource and unemployed worker into production. By pushing output to its absolute maximum at all times, we shall also get the fastest rate of growth. About the degree of inflation that this procedure would involve its supporters differ, but few deny that we would feel it.

Conservatives cannot accept this forced-draft type of economy. The path of inflation to them looks like a short cut into a blind alley. . . . Deliberate inflation, if not a crime, is at least of very debatable morality, because it involves an attempt to deceive people, and works hardships on those least able to defend themselves: the unorganized, the dependent, the old. Very probably it is also a mistake, like most attempts to fool all the people all of the time. For a few years, quite likely, the inflationary prescription may work. The economy, working under full steam and with the safety valves tied down, would expand more rapidly. But eventually, these forced-draft measures would exact their penalty. The lid may blow off, control of inflation may be lost altogether, the economy may spiral off into chaos. Or if this escape is blocked, we may see incentives dulled by over-full employment and perennial sellers' markets, while rising prices discourage saving and distort investment motivations. The economy then slows down. In the long run, enough friction and imbalance may develop to plunge it into a deep depression. No one, of course, can predict with assurance how soon and how intensely any of these repercussions would make themselves felt. But the prospect is there—an incalculable risk and for that reason all the more distasteful to conservatives.

Among the most likely—and probably earliest—consequences of inflation are economic controls. Price and wage controls, material allocations, foreign trade and currency controls might help stave off the evil day when the final bill for an inflationary boom is presented. But they would not stave it off forever, and they are in themselves alien to the economic and political temper of the American people. Pursued to their bitter end, economic controls would threaten even our political liberties. That risk is too high a price to pay for accelerated growth when there are other ways open to us.

A third challenge to conservative economic policy will be the strengthening of the American enterprise system. This is a challenge of a nature different from those posed by growth and by inflation. It concerns the enduring structure of our economy, rather than the current functioning. It is all the more basic for that reason.

In the conservative view of things, free enterprise is more than a method of producing goods and services. It is a way of life. Free enterprise is a highly efficient economic system, but above all it is the system best suited to a free society.

In the United States, the alternative to free enterprise is not socialism; in contrast to Europe, no one seriously questions private property. The alternative is a more centralized system, in which the government would play a stronger role. We know from the experience of two wars that such a system can be effective in an emergency. . . . But we know from the same experience that, to be effective, such a system must employ strong compulsions. . . .

The proponents of the centralized approach tell us that their system need not involve compulsion. Certainly there is no need to see serfdom staring us in the face every time some government bureau issues a regulation. . . . But what of the effectiveness of such a system? We have every reason to be skeptical. In all probability we would have the worst of two worlds—the freewheeling consumption and relatively low savings of the free economy, and the loss of initiative and the frictions of the controlled system. Conservatives conclude that free enterprise is superior economically to democratic control, and a better way of life than an effective but dictatorial regime.

To call free enterprise a way of life is more than a pretty phrase.

. . . Successful conservatism must keep its policies in line with the changing pattern of American life. The United States, for the most part, is now a thoroughly urban and industrialized community—a century removed from the nation of independent farmers and small traders that it started out to be. It is very rich, and yearly is becoming even richer. From these familiar facts flow needs, opportunities, and obligations.

The social and economic problems of an industrialized urban society cannot be solved by laissez faire. Whatever the beauties of its abstract logic, as a practical proposition laissez faire long ago joined the dodo. There is no place for it in modern conservative philosophy. Ours is a mixed economy, in which the government plays a large role. To this fact we largely owe the good functioning of the economy since the war. Conservatism today must accept most of the changes of the last 25 years, and must go on from there to improve them and to initiate further constructive action of its own.

An industrial urban society needs broad social security coverage—unemployed workers can't go home to the farm, and the aged can't go to live with their children. It needs protection against illness—medicine is no longer in the stage of simple remedies bought for little money. It needs better housing—the social conditions of urban living create strains that are not solved readily by supply and demand. It needs more education. And fortunately, the prime mover of all these needs—our growing economy—also enables us to afford them.

Many of these expanding requirements can be filled by private enterprise, and as many as can should. Much, however, will have to be done by government—local if possible, federal if necessary. Is this a march into socialism? Those who take that view disregard the dynamics of a free economy. They overlook the fact that changing living conditions and greater wealth create new situations. It happens that some of the things for which need increases with rising income are of the kind that, in Lincoln's phrase, the people cannot do so well for themselves and which the government can do better. Should private enterprise be the dog in the manger and object to anything being done that it cannot do itself?

What counts is that these services which a rich economy can afford be provided in a way that preserves incentives. There is no greater difference in the world than that between a man who is trying hard and one who is not. To keep alive the play of rewards and penalties, we must not make unemployment more attractive than hard work. We must not make illness, imagined or real, more profitable than good health. But when the living standards of the great bulk of the population are rising further and further above what used to be called subsistence, there is plenty of room for decent social services without risk of softness. . . .

A further touchstone of conservative sincerity in calling free enterprise a way of life is its concern for equality of opportunity. We have equality today for the highly talented. A really bright boy can get an education and can get to the top in any walk of life, no matter where he starts. We do not have it for the moderately talented. A moderately talented son of an Ivy League alumnus will go to his father's college and spend his life in a reasonably good job. The moderately talented son of a working man stands a good chance of being overlooked by life. More education, and easier access to it, is the key. Progress in racial integration, as fast as is possible without social and political disintegration, is another step toward fuller equality of opportunity.

Still another requirement for free enterprise as a way of life is to be serious about free markets, competition, and decentralization of power. They are the simple but potent devices by which we call forth initiative, ensure fair treatment to all who participate in the economy, and ultimately safeguard our freedoms. We shall never achieve perfect competition nor perfect markets. But unless we work at them everlastingly, we shall in time have very little of either.

This calls for steadfast application of the anti-trust laws, not to combat bigness as such, but to ensure that bigness does not become monopoly. It means giving small business a chance—through the tax system, through government contracts, through monetary and credit policy. It means further progress toward a self-supporting agriculture, through flexible price-supports and the ending of our habitual crop surpluses. It means willingness of industry and labor to face competition not only at home, but also from abroad, through gradual tariff reduction. Lastly, it means preference for private or local action over federal wherever possible without great sacrifice of efficiency.

These are, it seems to me, the main elements of a conservative economic policy. If conservatism makes progress on these fronts, it . . . will accomplish that most constructive of all political performances: conservative evolution.

3.18 Liberal Versus Conservative Strands of Neo-Keynesianism

Robert Lekachman

The 1960s deserve their fame in the record of public action as the years in which Keynesian economics became the open as well as the implicit national premise upon which two Presidents based their fiscal recommendations. This is the decade which has converted an esoteric theory into the annual exercise of distributing a fiscal surplus between tax reduction and social welfare. Possibly more startling still was business' discovery that economic expansion was assisted by the termination of the traditional civil war between Democratic national administrations and the business community. Business' recognition that prudent Keynesian fiscal policies actually promote larger markets and higher profits has had an unexpected effect. Keynesian prescriptions, the monopoly of reformers and radicals during the 1930s and 1940s, have very nearly become the favorite medicines of the established, propertied interests in the community.

The major economic question which faces Americans in the Keynesian era is no longer a matter of whether modern fiscal policy should or should not be employed. For the reasonable, this is an issue finally resolved. It has been superseded by a much harder set of choices dependent on social valuations more complex than the simple preference of prosperity to depression, growth to stagnation, and progress to retrogression. These are the choices which were foreshadowed by the controversy in the Kennedy administration over the best way to stimulate the American economy.

* * *

The expansionists were themselves divided into two groups. The Galbraith group strongly urged a substantial expansion of public spending. As Galbraith analyzed the needs of the time, the public spending would not only stimulate the economy but would also feed the starved public services and do something to rectify the existing social imbalance between public and private spending. . . . Theoretically, however, it is just as possible to stimulate a sluggish economy by reducing taxes as by enlarging social welfare programs or, for that matter, military spending. Hence the second expansionist school, organized by the Council of Economic Advisers, committed themselves with growing urgency to the superiority of a tax reduction over a public spending policy, partly on technical administrative grounds and partly on arguments of political feasibility. As stimulating devices, tax cuts produce their effects much more rapidly than new spending programs, which take time to get started. On the political front, Congress was believed much more receptive to tax reduction

Excerpted from Robert Lekachman, *The Age of Keynes* (New York: Random House, 1966). Reprinted by permission of the publisher.

than to additional government spending, even when the budgetary impact was identical. . . .

When a President and a Congress acknowledge the need for fiscal stimulus, *how* should this stimulus be supplied? The practical choice, the major social valuation, and the continuing political argument focus upon the two routes to economic expansion which are open, the twentieth-century liberal route and the twentieth-century conservative alternative.

The modern economic conservative is no longer a budget balancer; he is perfectly willing to recognize deficiencies in aggregate demand as they present themselves. He may well accept the current diagnosis that the economic malaise of the 1950s and early 1960s was the consequence of insufficient private investment and a tax structure which withdrew the fruits of economic expansion too quickly and too copiously from the pockets of consumers and entrepreneurs. Defining the problem in this fashion, the conservative expansionist is prone to pin his hopes on a refashioning of the federal tax system and periodical infusions of fiscal stimulus in the shape of additional tax reductions. He is likely to be wary of large expenditures on social welfare and still suspicious of the enlargement of federal influence. Nevertheless, more and more he esteems the federal government as a partner in business prosperity.

* * *

The thrust of two Democratic Presidents' legislative programs and administrative actions has been at the least consistent with the expectations of modern economic conservatives. The familiar roster of liberalized depreciation, investment tax credit, reduced corporate income tax rates, moderated personal tax progression, and excise tax alteration all have amounted to direct or indirect attempts to stimulate business confidence, enlarge private investment, and emphasize the significance of private economic production. The Kennedy and Johnson appointments to the federal regulatory agencies and the Cabinet, and the decision to vest control of the communications satellite in private corporate hands, are additional acts of solicitude for business feelings and preferences. It is accurate rather than invidious to term the faith of modern businessmen commercial Keynesianism, and it is only sensible to welcome the perception by intelligent businessmen that private activity can be aided by a government sympathetic both to business and to high employment. Commercial Keynesianism is a giant step beyond older policies preferred by the business community.

Nevertheless, the opposing contemporary position also has its just claims. The liberal expansionist stance owes a debt to the Galbraith of *The Affluent Society,* the Harrington of *The Other America,* and the unemployment analyses of Charles Killingsworth. Liberal expansionists unite in denying that commercial Keynesianism is capable of meeting adequately the economic challenges of the next decade. By itself expansionary policy will not prepare the nation for a changing labor market.

Clearly the persistence of poverty, the presence of structural unemployment, and the looming menace of automation all demand specific programs of public intervention. So also does the fact, in the Galbraithian view, that Americans allocate far too many resources to private activity and far too few to public purposes. . . .

Liberal expansionists are convinced that the nation's schools, houses, hospitals, and social services will never be so high in quality as its automobiles, cosmetics, and detergents until large amounts of resources are shifted from low-priority private uses to high-priority public uses. The practical import of the judgment is that in a time of prosperity as in a time of recession, the role of the federal government should increase, not decrease.

Therefore, whether they emphasize poverty, structural unemployment, or the starvation of the public services, liberal expansionists favor public spending over tax reduction. It is exactly at this point in the practical politics of fiscal policy that they part company from conservative expansionists. Since each time taxes are reduced it is harder to achieve larger federal appropriations, liberal expansionists must in logic be the opponents of tax cuts and the friends of larger expenditures on urban redevelopment, regional rehabilitation, vocational education, manpower retraining, public recreation, aid to education, and low-cost, federally assisted housing. Liberal expansionists dislike tax reduction because they perceive it as the inevitable competitor of the superior policies which assist the unemployed young, the victims of segregated education, the technologically displaced, and the miserably housed.

3.19 The New Economics: Handmaiden of Inspired Truth

Richard B. Du Boff and Edward S. Herman

INTRODUCTION

Few who have followed the course of the marriage between the political Establishment and the brand names of the economics profession will be surprised by the way the leading liberal economists rallied to the support of President Nixon's August 15, 1971 "new economic policy" (NEP). Nor will they be puzzled by the ease with which Mr. Nixon has been able to invoke the prestige of the Keynesian-inspired "new economics" in launching a regressive, pro-business set of "reforms." As we shall see below, the New Economists,[1] de-

[1] "New economists" ordinarily refers to those using the analytical tools derived from Keynes and concerned with his problems and methods. In this article we focus attention on the leading practitioners of Keynesian economics in the United States, . . . who occupy the top rung of the economics profession in prestige, influence, and command over media attention, and who serve in high level councils and economic posts in Democratic administrations. For brevity we shall use New Economists (in caps) to refer to this core group. We recognize that there are some differences among them and that even greater variations are found in the profession outside of this group of relatively older and better established brand name economists. The New Economists, in sum, are not spokesmen for any independent, humanistic viewpoint. They have been handmaidens of an inspired, official, American truth.

Excerpted from Richard B. Du Boff and Edward S. Herman, "The New Economics: Handmaiden of Inspired Truth," *Review of Radical Political Economics* 4, no. 2 (Summer 1972). Reprinted by permission of the publisher and Richard B. Du Boff.

spite their vaunted liberalism, have formulated a "growth" dogma admirably suited to the needs of a government openly hostile to liberal reform itself. The emergence of this conservative doctrine is related to the fact that the New Economists share the ideology and values of the dominant power groups in American society. For this reason they have considerably more rapport with government and business executives than with, say, ghetto residents, union organizers, members of the Union for Radical Political Economics, or socially concerned Third World economists. . . .

Given their conservative and nationalist premises, it is understandable that the Economists have consistently looked upon the economic policies of Richard Nixon as reasonable, responsible, and "within the ball park"—in contrast to the "irresponsible" views of the New Left and other critics of American society. . . . Their disagreements with Nixon's pre-NEP game plan were technical, narrow, and partisan, never involving fundamental objectives.

GROWTH: THE NEW ECONOMISTS' ROAD TO MECCA

. . . The primary intellectual weapon that economists have furnished for regressive fiscal and monetary policies is the doctrine of "economic growth." The triumph of the "new economics" of growth took place during the "new frontier" of John F. Kennedy. . . .

Growth, for New Economists, is the overriding social priority for our country, the *sine qua non*. . . . Growth produces jobs, rising personal consumption (the chief goal of "economic man"), dynamic technology, national power, and, of course, the famous "growth dividend" that supposedly provides an ever-increasing quantity of resources to the public sector for dealing with the problems our society faces without any fundamental changes in political and social institutions. In this view, growth is the first requirement for solving our crises, since it is the *only* avenue open on the premise of "given" economic, social, and political arrangements (including the distribution of income and power).

To stimulate growth, and to do it quickly, a government will rarely, if ever, have the capacity, time, or energy to effect serious reforms at the same time, even if so inclined. For the measures taken to spur growth must actively enlist the assistance of the already entrenched spending sectors of the economy—especially private business investment, but also household consumption. In the context of the present-day United States—with strategic political influence and crucial decision-making power concentrated in large industrial, financial, and media enterprises—fiscal and monetary means employed to stimulate the economy as the first order of business will necessarily favor the big corporation, the military-industrial complex, and to a lesser degree the affluent middle class consumer. Any other scheme of priorities and benefits would touch off a contest with dominant power interests that might result in a total stalemate of policymaking. . . .

The establishment of "growth" as the supreme, number one priority is a formula for assuring that reforms, even mild ones, will be put off—often indefinitely. . . . Reforms, that is, must await the return of a healthy economy and the generation of the needed revenues; accordingly, Nixon recommended the postponement of revenue sharing and welfare "reform" in the interests of growth, with hardly a whimper from the New Economists.

These economists hold, or appear to believe, that however regressive the means for *initiating* growth, the resulting "dividend" will somehow become available to provide benefits later—so that out of reactionary choices *now* will come aid for the needy at home and abroad at some future date. This is a refined "trickle-down" theory. It rests on an extremely naive set of political beliefs as well. "Growth" is likely to consolidate the strength of the existing power structure and enhance its ability to capture any residual benefits. Thus, the idea that stimuli produced by tax advantages and other favors to big business and private consumption will eventually increase revenues available for broad social purposes is a product of wishful thinking. Logically, we should expect those able to command benefits for themselves in the first place to be able at the next stage to insist on further bounties for the private sector, rather than government spending for social needs. The most likely outcome would seem to be the appropriation of the "growth dividend" by the dominant power groups for their own purposes, not for those of liberal advisers.

The massive tax cut route to "growth" taken in 1962–64 led New Economists to look with anticipation to the expected flow of dividends that would soon permit the nation to turn its attention to pressing domestic problems. But those dividends were used to finance Vietnam. And the Vietnam "peace dividend" of 1969–71 (when war-related outlays were cut back from $29 to $13 billion) was devoured by the Pentagon for its "modernization" and "inflation" costs, as well as for military pay raises. . . .

The "growth" of the 1960's led to no reassessment of priorities on the part of America's ruling elites. And, . . . since August 1971 economists like Okun and Heller are still in the wings ready to rationalize growth without reform. For them, the diversions of the "growth dividend" over the past decade are merely unfortunate mishaps—random "errors"—or else they are attributable to a "failure of leadership." . . .

Finally, the New Economists have stood by their "growth" doctrine despite increasing public and scientific concern over the negative externalities associated with quantitative economic growth. They give short shrift to E. J. Mishan's thesis that "growth" in advanced capitalist countries, with modern technology and private profit systems, produces "disamenities" faster than amenities. In the world of the new economics, the phenomenon of multiplying negative externalities is a qualification, a correctible deviation on the primrose path to ever higher levels of GNP. . . .

In the interests of ecological balance and a more rational control of the human condition, social scientists of various political persuasions are experimenting with projections of zero growth rates, or a *smaller* national output, more equitably distributed, less lethal to mankind and its environment, and requiring fewer inputs of alienated labor. Such alternatives will become more urgent as the "economic growth" juggernauts of the Western nations (and their

Soviet Communist imitators) begin to run out of natural and environmental resources and as the other two-thirds of the world's people demands its share of a stabilized global output. The New Economists voice concern over these problems, but the radical solutions necessary to deal with them always turn out to be impractical in the short run; and at the onset of each crisis, the Economists retreat, as if by a conditioned reflex, to "growth" as the urgent, immediate answer to our problems. The result is that their doctrines have become not only pedestrian and conservative, but positively dangerous to rational social behavior. . . .

BONANZAS FOR BUSINESS UNDER KENNEDY, JOHNSON, AND THE PRAGMATIC LIBERALS

From the very first triumphs of the "new economics," starting in 1961, growth without reform was the order of the day. Whether the New Economists of the Kennedy administration accepted this strategy on the grounds of political expediency or principle, it is a fact that they surrendered unconditionally to the growth syndrome and, along with JFK, beat a total retreat from reform. Tax reform in particular was sold down the river; no real effort was ever made to close the gaping tax loopholes which were then becoming a matter of some national attention. Nixon's 1971 bonanzas for big business are, therefore, perfectly consistent with the economic policies of his two Democratic predecessors and follow logically from the *growth-über-alles* doctrine. . . .

The major Kennedy-Johnson tax policies were the investment credit of mid-1962 and the Revenue Act of 1964. . . . The first . . . allowed a 7 percent tax credit for business on purchases of machinery and equipment, as well as more favorable depreciation schedules. It is estimated to have reduced corporate taxes by $5 billion through 1966 and by $3 billion per year from 1967 through mid-1969 (when Nixon terminated it). The second—the "magnificent tax cut"—provided for regressive personal and corporate income tax cuts. These policies left virtually untouched all the notorious tax loopholes (capital gains, multiple trusts, charitable gifts, stock options, tax free municipal bond interest, and the oil and lumber depletion allowances). They returned over $12 billion to middle and upper income families, while the administration scrounged around to find $1 billion for a "war on poverty."

The ideological rationale for these regressive policies was effectively implanted in the councils of the federal government during Walter Heller's tenure as chairman of the CEA (January 1961-November 1964). . . . Heller viewed with pride the surging corporate profits arising from the investment credit and the other Kennedy business plums. . . . Tax reform, on the other hand, Heller regarded as hopelessly impractical: "Reforms come hard, the dream of a thorough tax reform is just that—a dream." On another occasion, in late 1963, Heller explained how "Traditionally, the Democratic Party has placed great stress on tax measures to benefit consumers. But the force of circumstance has raised investment in productive equipment to a higher and higher priority . . . Such measures would have been considered unnecessary, perhaps even 'un-

Democratic,' ten or fifteen years ago.'' A year earlier, just after the peak of the debate over ''tax cuts versus tax reform,'' Heller's fellow CEA member James Tobin had declared that

> *Redistribution of income and wealth by taxation and government transfer payments was in days gone by another rallying point for liberal political movements. The fire has gone out of this one too.* . . .

Whatever else this evidence may show, it indicates that Nixon's regressive modes of getting the economy moving again are in harmony with the growth dogma of the New Economists, in theory and in practice. . . .

THE NEW ECONOMISTS, PUBLIC INVESTMENT, AND THE FREE MARKET

An elementary economic truth provides the best insight into the malaise of conventional economics and its ''new'' practitioners. It is something every introductory economics student learns but that his teachers seem incapable of digesting: namely, that if private investment is one way to create jobs, public investment is another. Not a single liberal economist of national reputation has pushed vigorously for public investment in recent years, except for Galbraith, viewed by many of his colleagues as a sort of curious maverick. . . . The criticisms of Nixon's NEP by the New Economists, for instance, have focused almost entirely on its biases against consumers and, here their criticism becomes fainter, lower income groups. Walter Heller disagrees with NEP mainly on the grounds that it needs ''more balance between business and consumers'' and is ''biased against the consumer.'' Comparatively little is said about the unrelieved neglect of the nonmilitary and nonhighway public sector.

The New Economists . . . will go to nearly any lengths to avoid unequivocal advocacy of large-scale government spending for social projects.

The chronic unwillingness to come to grips with the public sector problem reveals once again where most New Economists stand—squarely in favor of the status quo, albeit with occasional discomfort. Their reformism is shriveled, limited by conservative premises and an unwillingness to depart from the politically feasible. As liberals and humane individuals, many of them desire an eradication of war, poverty, racism, urban decay, pollution, and social disintegration; but mainstream economists do not really care enough about these objectives to press for them in the light of their short-run ''impracticality'' and obnoxiousness to men of power. Furthermore, even insofar as these economists give any weight to reform or radical change, their own ''growth'' ideology leaves them being wagged by the dog's tail, constantly chasing after ''reforms'' that, somehow or another, seem to get put off and subordinated to the needs of one ''crisis'' or another.

The ''new frontier'' years, which gave the New Economists their first taste of power, brought out very clearly their attitude toward the public sector (as well as toward tax reform, military spending, and "growth"). In 1961 and 1962 Heller and Kermit Gordon of the CEA, along with Galbraith (then Ambassador to India) "favored" expansion of government expenditures on social welfare and public works projects then being proposed by Senator Joseph S. Clark, but they immediately capitulated on this issue (just as they did on tax reform). Only Galbraith held out for more nonmilitary public spending, and his persistence soon earned him a reputation as an obstructionist to those who wanted to get on with the job of spurring faster growth. . . .

No matter how brand name economists twist and turn, they cannot evade the stark fact that their values and politics are closely intertwined with those of the commanding heights of American capitalism. They bask in the sunlight of power, and they enthusiastically make themselves available and useful to that handful of men who control the major corporations, banks, research bureaus, and political organizations. They speak the language of the power elite and understand and sympathize with its "problems"; conversely, critiques such as this start off on value premises completely incomprehensible to the New Economists.

At this stage, New Economists do not even qualify as reformers, for they have abandoned all analytic as well as political efforts directed towards hemming in and eventually reducing the power of big corporations, shifting the distribution of income from property toward ordinary labor and from upper toward lower income recipients, rechanneling resources from private consumption and military spending toward the social public sector, and redirecting the energies of this society from free market exploitation toward a rational social and economic planning process.

The continuing emphasis of the New Economists is on increasing GNP, produced by "free enterprise." As Heller puts it, "decentralized decision making and freedom of choice are left untouched by the impersonal fiscal and monetary tools that government uses to carry out its responsibility for a high-level economy . . . [By contrast] microeconomic policy more often calls for unpleasant restraints like guideposts and antitrust laws than for welcome stimulants like tax credits for investments." . . .

In a system facing grave environmental problems inherited from unconstrained free market expansion of the past, with chronic deficiencies in housing and other capital-short areas neglected by private enterprise, with the military-industrial complex and Madison Avenue-fed consumerism still riding high and gobbling up the lion's share of our resources, the Growth + Free Enterprise philosophy is the New Economists' version of what C. Wright Mills so aptly labelled "crackpot realism."

CONCLUDING NOTE

The conservative and accommodationist politics of the New Economists should surprise no one. There was a brief period when Keynesian ideas were novel and were regarded as threatening by important segments of the business community. At the same time there was even a strand of Left Keynesianism, which used the new economics as a method of social analysis and emphasized its radical implications for income distribution and the role of the state. But there was always a larger group of Keynesians who stressed the "tool" aspects of the new doctrine, along with its "policy neutrality" and its serviceability to policymakers for carrying out whatever objectives they might choose to plug in.

The New Economists represent the triumph of that "pragmatic" school. In fact, the critical potential of Keynesian economics never was very great, and the extended prosperity following the Second World War led to its swift decline. The long economic boom, buttressed by massive government spending, was considered to be a vindication of applied macroeconomics. The practicality of this brand of Keynesianism, plus the opportunities it provided for technically oriented model-builders and statisticians, assured the growth and success of the pragmatic school. This was largely a case of a rising demand eliciting an appropriate supply response.

For economists who do effectively service the dominant forces of the system, the rewards are substantial—money, influence, power, and ready access to the media. By the same token, economists who seek such benefits can obtain them only through accommodation to the existing power structure, dealing with it on its own terms, and affiliating with its institutionalized elements (the Democratic Party, blue-ribbon panels, "think tanks," government committees, research and consulting firms). Once settled in this camp, economists become part of the economic and social elite itself—they develop natural ties to the dominant elements in society and similar personal interests in the status quo. They are subject to what Malthus called "the insensible bias of situation and interest," so that the inspired truth to which New Economists are dedicated is part of a class interest which they themselves share.

THE SHATTERED SYNTHESIS

In the final selection of this chapter, Fusfeld criticizes the post-Keynesian synthesis from the perspective of liberal-radical reform. It became increasingly evident in the late 1960s and early 1970s, Fusfeld contends, that cracks were emerging in the carefully forged Keynesian consensus. The closer the economy approached full employment, the greater the conflicts between full-employment and other policy goals (for example, price stability and balance of payments equilibrium) became. Furthermore, critics have increasingly dissented from the underlying values of the Keynesian consensus itself (for example, the imperative of economic growth), and have challenged the concentrations of economic power and the symbiosis between government and large corporations which have accompanied post-Keynesian "successes." Political economics in America has moved into a new phase of controversy and dissent, as will be illustrated more fully in succeeding chapters.

3.20 Post-Post-Keynes: The Shattered Synthesis

Daniel R. Fusfeld

Within the theoretical and political framework of the post-Keynesian synthesis, solutions seemed to be present for all of the great economic problems of the postwar world. Liberals and reformers flocked to embrace it. Yet, underneath the surface it was the economics of the status quo, of anti-communism and the Cold War, of reform around the edges of the social and economic order.

The post-Keynesian synthesis, in fact, reflected and provided justification for the concentration of power in American society in the years after World War II. The locus of governmental power had shifted to the federal government, and within the federal government to the Executive branch. With world power came a further concentration within the Executive branch itself, into the hands of the national security managers. This growing concentration of political power was paralleled by an increasing concentration of economic power in the business community. A recent Federal Trade Commission study showed that in 1968 the 100 largest manufacturing corporations held a larger share of manufacturing assets than the 200 largest in 1950 and that the 200 largest in 1968 controlled a share equal to that of the 1,000 largest in 1941.

Big business and big government have been coming together in an increasingly symbiotic relationship. Big government needs big business because the giant corporation has become the key to effective functioning of the economy—witness the Penn Central and Lockheed rescue operations—and because big business is the source of the weaponry on which national power rests. Government, in turn, provides the environment of economic growth within which the large corporation flourishes, educates the managers and technicians that big enterprises need, maintains the framework for settlement of labor disputes, and seeks to maintain a system of world order conducive to the growth of international corporations. Concentrated economic and political power are allies.

Sustained full employment and economic growth, emphasized by the post-Keynesian synthesis, became the twin keystones of an understanding between those who held and exercised power and those who did not. The levers of power remained in the hands of those who managed big business and big government. In exchange for allowing them a relatively free rein, the great middle-income majority obtained the material benefits that accrued from a quarter century of economic expansion.

How smoothly indeed the post-Keynesian synthesis seemed to be working, both in theory and in practice. Then, in the 1960s, at the height of its influence, the synthesis began to be faced with a group of problems that it could not handle effectively.

Inflation was the first to appear. The monetary and fiscal policies designed to achieve full employment and economic growth seemed to generate rising prices when full employment neared. Even during substantially slack economic periods, price levels showed an upward creep.

An incomes policy—government control of wages and prices—was never envisaged in the post-Keynesian synthesis, for one of its chief points is the idea that management of the economy need not extend into the microeconomic domain of wages, prices, profits, and incomes generally. But, of course, an incomes policy has come to us full force with the phases of the Nixon controls—an acknowledgment by a Republican administration that the private sector alone cannot be relied on to achieve stabilizing results in these areas.

Closely related to the problem of domestic inflation is a second problem: the continuing crisis in the international monetary system. The U.S. deficit in its balance of international payments, sustained since 1950 with the exception of the Suez crisis years, 1957–58, finally wrecked the system established at Bretton Woods in 1944. The immediate cause of the problem was U.S. private investment and military expenditures abroad on a scale too great to be financed by a favorable balance of trade. When our favorable trade balance fell victim to domestic inflation at the same time that military spending was vastly increased, the end quickly came. A historic devaluation of the dollar has resulted.

A deeper issue lurks beneath these events. A nation's domestic economic policies influence its balance of international payments, and its balance of payments limits the freedom it has in pursuing domestic economic goals. Moreover, the balance of payments of the United States, as the dominant nation in world trade and finance, affects the balance of payments of other nations, which affects their domestic economic policies and limits the alternatives among which they can choose. In this way, our domestic economic policies ultimately weigh on those of other nations. These are worldwide economic relationships that the post-Keynesian synthesis had hardly considered and for which it has almost no policy prescriptions.

A third problem to emerge in the 1960s concerned the underdeveloped countries. Growth of the advanced economies was supposed to generate capital resources that could be channeled into the less-developed economies, getting them started on the path to self-sustained growth. It didn't work out that way. Economic growth was spotty, and, as Gunnar Myrdal and others pointed out, in many areas there was a reverse drain of capital and skilled manpower out of the underdeveloped areas and into the advanced international economy. Meanwhile, the public health technology of the advanced countries was imported into the backward nations, causing declining death rates and rapid population growth that literally ate up the gains from economic growth. The gap between the rich and poor nations tended to widen rather than narrow, which is just the opposite of the results suggested by economic orthodoxy.

These three issues—inflation, the international financial system, and underdeveloped nations—were serious problems, but they did not involve the implicit values and goals of the post-Keynesian synthesis. In recent years, however, a series of issues which do just that has come to the fore: economic growth, the environment, the racial problem, and militarism. The discussions of these issues did not center on the theoretical basis of the post-Keynesian synthesis. Rather, its implicit policy goals were questioned, along with the social and economic institutions it sought to explain.

The once sacrosanct goal of economic growth was the first to be criticized, with the onslaught being led in this country by John Kenneth Galbraith and in England by E. J. Mishan. Galbraith pointed out that an economy dominated by private decisions about consumption and production tends to starve its public sector. This is especially true when motivations center on individual gains in income and wealth. Private spending on luxuries and entertainment expands while such foundations of the future as education and basic science are slighted. Furthermore, modern marketing and advertising techniques are used by business firms to mold consumer spending to their needs as producers, instead of adjusting production to match a pristine pattern of consumer wants. The system as a whole operates for the benefit of producers rather than consumers, if Galbraith's analysis is reasonably correct, and its goal is the aggrandizement of business wealth instead of the individual's welfare.

Mishan went even further, arguing that a materialistic society interested primarily in piling up more and more material goods was destructive of humane values and pursued goals antithetical to human happiness. The important point about Mishan's argument is not its novelty—his views are even older than the science of economics itself—but in its popularity. It struck a note that many were eager to hear.

The views expressed by Galbraith and Mishan were echoed by a new generation of youth disenchanted with the materialism of middle-income America, by workers dissatisfied with the monotony of their jobs and the limited horizons of their lives, and by blacks and Latins condemned to low wages, poverty, and welfare. Disenchantment, hostility, and alienation became facts of life for the economist as well as the psychiatrist to consider.

The growing militarism of American life raised further questions about economic goals. In the 1950s and 1960s, the greatest industrial nation in the world was using between 10 and 15 per cent of its huge and increasing output for military and related purposes. The obvious question arose: What is the advantage of economic growth if a large portion of the gain is used for wasteful or destructive purposes? But underlying that was an even more basic question: What is it about the economic system that drives it (or allows it to be driven) to such ends? Had military expenditures created such strong vested interests in the "military-industrial complex" that there was no going back to a humane economy? If these questions generated breezes of doubt before 1965, after the war in Southeast Asia escalated to high levels, they brought storms of dissent.

An equally fundamental issue arose as many people became aware of the potential environmental crisis the industrial nations seemed to be heading for. A growing economy produces increasing amounts of waste, and one in which high consumption levels are a major feature contributes even more. Modern industrial technology, furthermore, was not developed with compatibility with the natural environment in mind. Would continued economic growth destroy the ecological base not only of the economy but of human life as well? The economics of the post-Keynesian synthesis had no answer to that question, and the ameliorative measures suggested were only partial responses to a huge problem.

Finally, the persistence of poverty and the emergence of the urban-racial crisis in the United States in the late 1960s pointed up the fact that a large portion of the American people was not participating adequately in the affluence achieved by many. A devastating social and economic conflict emerged in the midst of what should have been a society with reduced conflict—because of growing affluence. It became clear that the benefits of affluence were *not* being so widely diffused as to strengthen the social fabric.

By now, even the orthodox post-Keynesian economist has good reason to doubt that the private-enterprise, market-oriented economy can resolve its problems effectively. A high-pressure economy has brought new strains on the social fabric and exposed intractable problems. Growth is now seen as potentially unbalanced, misdirected, or destructive. Inflation, a succession of international financial crises, problems of the Third World, cities torn by conflict, an endangered natural environment, militarism, the persistence of poverty, and growing alienation—instead of increased well-being, there is a crisis of confidence.

The tacit agreement between the haves and the have-nots has broken up. The war in Southeast Asia laid bare the shift in the locus of power to a relatively small group whose control over the decision-making process is supplemented by careful manipulation of public opinion and political process. The gains from economic growth stopped as the costs of the war escalated. Many young people saw, perhaps more clearly than their elders, the essential polity compromise that traded affluence for power and refused to accept it. Blacks and other minority groups, segregated in their urban ghettos and developing a racial and political consciousness, refused to accept their continued status as second-class citizens. The whole system of polity broke down. Along with it went the orthodox post-Keynesian synthesis of theory and policy. The paradigm of a smoothly adjusting system of largely competitive markets that produces what consumers want, provides rewards appropriate to effort, and is assured of stable economic growth through Keynesian macroeconomics policies lost its credibility. A growing radical movement sees the economic and political systems as essentially malign rather than benign, antagonistic to humane values rather than supportive of them. Contemporary economics is in crisis because the social order is in crisis, unable to go back to the old and unwilling to strike boldly toward the new.

The problems of the present indicate the path to the future. A reconstruction of economics—a new synthesis and a new paradigm—will have to move toward greater concern for humane values, toward a humane economy on a worldwide scale.

A humane economy requires more than prosperity and economic growth, more than efficient allocation of resources. It demands changes in the framework of economic institutions to achieve greater equality and freedom. It requires dispersal of the economic power and governmental authority that support the present disposition of income, wealth, and power. It requires a social environment that brings a sense of community and fellowship into human relationships. It demands compatibility among man, his technology, and the natural environment. And all of these things must be done on a worldwide scale. These are the goals of the future, to which economists and everyone else will have to devote their energies.

4 JOSEPH SCHUMPETER AND THE THEORY OF CAPITALIST TRANSFORMATION

The post-Keynesian synthesis never commanded unanimous allegiance. Joseph Schumpeter, a contemporary of Keynes and the author of a major alternative theory of capitalism, maintained until his death (in 1950) a scholarly detachment from Keynesian economics and an analytical critique of Keynesian-style macroeconomic policies. Iconoclasts like John Kenneth Galbraith have stood apart from the synthesis and criticized several of its main tenets. At the University of Chicago, the University of Virginia, and elsewhere a highly vocal group of ''neoliberal'' or ''individualist-conservative'' economists (for example, Friedrich Hayek, Milton Friedman, James Buchanan), have constructed a philosophy and program for radical reform of the American economy based on a reaffirmation of the primacy of individual freedom of choice and the role of the competitive market-price system as a social coordinative process. Meanwhile, the civil rights movement, student protest, and anti-(Vietnam) war ferment created a political environment in the 1960s and early 1970s conducive to a rekindled interest in radical critiques of capitalism. Writings of the Old Socialist–Marxist Left (for example, those of Paul Sweezy and Paul Baran) were restudied, and a New Left critique of American capitalism emerged. The New Left has focused on the perceived need for radical reform, but resembles radical individualist-conservatism in its rejection of centralized bureaucracy as a viable alternative to the market system.

Schumpeter's critique of Keynes and the Schumpeterian alternative vision of the prospects for capitalism are considered in this chapter. Chapter 5 examines the economic thought of Galbraith. The critiques and dissents of the neo-liberals–individualist conservatives are discussed in chapters 6, and the Old and New Left socialists in chapter 7.

SCHUMPETER'S ANSWER TO MARX AND KEYNES

Joseph Schumpeter remained outside the emerging Keynesian consensus in the 1930s and 1940s, and he provided the most comprehensive analysis since Marx of the development and future of capitalism. Schumpeter's analysis, considered in broad historical perspective, retains much of its timeliness today and takes its intellectual place among other major dissents from the post-Keynesian synthesis.

Schumpeter is sometimes called a conservative, antisocialist Marxist! There is certainly a strong Marxian influence upon his three major works: *The Theory of Capitalist Development* (1911), the brilliant intellectual vision of his youth that provided a framework for his subsequent studies; *Business Cycles* (1939), a comprehensive theoretical, historical, and statistical analysis of capitalism; and *Capitalism, Socialism, and Democracy* (1943, 1950), the broadest and most popular of his works. Recognition of the historical transience of economic systems, an economic interpretation of history, emphasis upon class conflicts, focus upon the dynamics of economic development and cyclical economic fluctuations, identification of the key role of the creation, distribution, and investment of an economic surplus by a capitalist entrepreneurial elite—all of these are similarities between the Schumpeterian and Marxian analyses of capitalism.

At the same time, Schumpeter's analysis provides a conservative and antisocialist answer to both Marx and Keynes. In perhaps overly simplified terms, we may characterize the relations among Marx, Keynes, and Schumpeter as follows: Marx (1) identified some major properties of capitalist behavior (for example, depressions, inequality in income distribution), (2) designated these properties as flaws or contradictions of the system, and (3) predicted the death of capitalism because of its economic failures. Keynes also (1) identified leading properties of capitalism (notably its proclivity toward unemployment because of the absence of a viable self-regulatory mechanism), and (2) designated them as failures of the system, *but* (3) proposed (limited) reforms of the system to eradicate or control them. Schumpeter agreed with both Marx and Keynes on (1), disagreed with both on (2), and agreed with Marx on (3), partly because of undesirable side effects of liberal-labor reforms of the Keynesian variety.

Schumpeter agreed that capitalism *is* characterized by economic instability and periodic depressions and unemployment. But, he argued, economic instability is not necessarily an indicator of failure in the capitalist system. Indeed, Schumpeter emphasized in *The Theory of Economic Development* and in *Business Cycles* that economic instability is the normal and necessary path by which the capitalist economy develops. Heroic and creative entrepreneurs, financed by bank credit, make investments in economic innovations (for example, new products, methods of production, markets, sources of supply) embodying new technologies, resource discoveries, and so on. *If* these innovative investments are successful, imitators follow, in the original industry and elsewhere (for example, successful innovations in the automobile industry encourage secondary innovation and investment in petroleum, rubber tires, glass, and so on) and the economy embarks upon a dramatic upward surge: prosperity. Eventually, innovations are completed and investment subsides, an avalanche of consumer goods pours onto the market with dampening effects on prices; rising costs and interest rates squeeze profit margins, and the economy contracts: recession. In effect, recession is a normal process of adaptation and adjustment following prosperity and is the normal means or route to economic development in a capitalist economy. Historically, recessions have not prevented economic growth, because expansions generally have been stronger and longer than contractions. Further, contractions serve the useful function of eliminating inefficient, noninnovating businesses, as new products, methods, and markets replace the old in a process of "creative destruction." Lastly, historical perspective shows us that some depressions are more severe than others because there are "long waves" in cyclical activity as well as shorter cycles, and that especially severe or long depressions, like those of the 1870s and 1930s, do not constitute breaks in capitalism's evolution or signal its impending demise.

Similarly, economic inequality is not a flaw or failure of capitalism. In a static and stationary world, without innovation and economic development, competition eventually would reduce profits to "normal" levels. But in a dynamic, developing economy, above-normal profits are often the reward for innovation. Because of the tremendous uncertainties surrounding innovations, that is, the possibility of failure and the likelihood of competitive encroachment in the event of success—the lure and occasional realization of extraordinary profits may well be the price society pays for the revolutionary contributions of its business leaders. Further, capitalism in practice reduces inequality in several ways: first, by increasing equality of opportunity relative to earlier, more class-bound societies; second, by the creation of mass-produced products that benefit working masses more than they do any other sector of the economy; third, by philanthropy and social legislation underwritten by the process of capitalist economic growth; and fourth, because although "relative poverty" or inequality is necessary for the sustainment of capitalism, "absolute poverty" falls as capitalist development proceeds.

Schumpeter's theory of the business cycle is summarized by Rendigs Fels in selection 4.1. The thesis that cyclical economic fluctuations and economic inequality do not constitute a failure of capitalism's basic engine for economic development—Schumpeter's answer to Marx and, in part, to Keynes—is described in selection 4.2.

4.1 Summary of Schumpeter's Theory of the Business Cycle

Rendigs Fels

THE ENTREPRENEUR

Innovation plays the central role in Schumpeter's theory. He defined it "as the setting up of a new production function. This covers the case of a new commodity, as well as those of a new form of organization such as a merger, of the opening up of new markets, and so on." Innovation is different from invention. The individuals who introduce new production functions are called entrepreneurs. Innovation is more difficult than the ordinary running of a business for it involves a choice not between the tried and the tried but between the tried and the untried. But once the way has been shown it becomes easier for others (1) to do the same thing, (2) to improve upon it, and (3) "to do similar things in similar lines"; the latter two categories represent what Schumpeter called "induced innovation," though the first presumably is not innovation at all. This provides the explanation for the observed facts that innovations are not evenly distributed over time but come in clusters and that they "are not at any time distributed over the whole economic system at random, but tend to concentrate in certain sectors and their surroundings."

Schumpeter assumed that innovations are carried out by new men and new firms. Innovation enables the new firm to make profits for a time, but eventually they are competed away, and the firm goes into decay. There are exceptions, cases of giant companies which are just shells for changing personnel carrying out a succession of innovations. This Schumpeter called trustified capitalism, to distinguish it from competitive capitalism. At the time Schumpeter wrote the exceptions were not yet great enough to invalidate the model.

Innovations usually require the building of new plant and equipment (or the rebuilding of old), involving time and expenditure. The money comes ultimately from credit creation.

EQUILIBRIUM

The concept of equilibrium plays an important part in the model. Schumpeter used equilibrium in the Walrasian sense of every firm, industry and household having no incentive to do anything but what they are already doing. The importance of the Walrasian system lies in the tendency, which can be observed in real life, for the economy to move towards it.

Real life of course does not fulfill the requirements of the Walrasian system, but this does not destroy its value. Some of the exceptions are important for business cycles. In particular, equilibrium is compatible with a considerable amount of unemployment (estimated for England at 3.3 per cent prior to 1914), which Professor Schumpeter called normal unemployment. . . . Thus, even at equilibrium, the economy can expand output, an elasticity which is increased by the possibility of overtime. There are other imperfections too so that it is more appropriate to think of the real economy as passing through neighborhoods rather than points of equilibrium. Equilibrium involves saving and real investment due to (population) growth and deepening of capital but no innovation.

FIRST APPROXIMATION

Schumpeter started the description of his model with many simplifications which he later dropped—perfect competition, perfect equilibrium, no saving, constant population. The first approximation, therefore, is a long way from historical fact. In this simplified economy, mere increase in knowledge plus the profit motive induce an entrepreneur to undertake something new and unfamiliar, borrowing money to build his plant and equipment. "Then other entrepreneurs follow, after them still others in increasing number, in the path of innovation, which becomes progressively smoothed for successors by accumulating experience and vanishing obstacles." Under the simplifying assumptions used at this stage of the argument, no increase in output is possible while the first entrepreneur is building his plant: indeed, output of consumers goods declines as entrepreneurs bid factors away from them with their newly created bank balances. (Later it will be seen that output in fact increases during the innovating period because employment rises above normal.) This upsets the partial equilibria of firms and industries throughout the economy, spelling losses for some and gains for others; but at this stage the non-innovating firms in the aggregate increase profits (which had been zero), because they pay out only part of the increase in incomes but in the second round, before the new products come to market, receive all of them.

When the products of the entrepreneurs at length come to market, total output of the economy is increased more than it formerly was reduced. Old firms now face a new source of disequilibrium, but whereas formerly the difficulties of adaptation were tempered, even for those firms which had to undergo losses, by the increase in expenditure, the new disequilibrium requires more difficult readjustments.

Entrepreneurial activity eventually slackens and stops. . . . First, because in any instance its possibilities are limited and eventually it results in the competing-away of profits, by which time the innovating impulse will have spent itself; and, second, because innovation upsets equilibrium, meaning "fluctuations and successive attempts at adaptation to changing temporary situations" and "the impossibility of calculating costs in a satisfactory way."

Cessation of entrepreneurial activity brings new borrowing to an end (still under simplified conditions), tending to depress the price level and bring discomfiture to many firms. But in addition "auto-deflation"—repayment of (bank) debts by entrepreneurs, destroying balances—accentuates the effects. The process which now takes place—"adaptation to the new things created, including the elimination of what is incapable of adaptation, resorption of the results of innovation into the system, reorganization of economic life so as to make it conform to the data as altered by enterprise, remodeling of the system of value, liquidation of indebtedness . . . under our assumptions and with but minor qualifications . . . leads up to a new neighborhood of equilibrium . . . " The stage is now set for innovation to begin again.

The above sequence of events corresponds to what are generally known as prosperity and recession. The model in its present form brings out some essential points: prosperity is a period of abstaining from consumption for the sake of investment; recession is a period of reaping the harvest.

SECOND APPROXIMATION—THE SECONDARY WAVE

In the prosperity phase, investment from innovating activity increases consumers spending almost as quickly as producers spending. ". . . old firms will react to this situation and . . . many of them will 'speculate' on this situation. . . . New borrowing will then no longer be confined to entrepreneurs, and 'deposits' will be created to finance general expansion, each loan tending to induce another loan, each rise in prices another rise.'' This is the well-known cumulative process Schumpeter called ''the secondary wave.'' It is quantitatively so important that it obscures the phenomena of the primary wave.

''The break in secondary prosperity is similarly induced by the turn of the underlying process.'' The reckless, fraudulent, speculative or otherwise unsuccessful enterprise of the secondary wave means much more liquidation than the primary wave implies. ''All this does not necessarily amount to panic or crisis . . . but it easily induces panics or crises.'' It leads to the ''vicious spiral'' which is defined by two effects: (1) ''any fall in values which enforces liquidation, induces quite mechanically another fall in values;'' and (2) pessimism may enter as a causal role as people realize how much there is to liquidate or even get hysterical about it. As a result the process is likely to overrun the neighborhood of equilibrium toward which it is moving and enter another phase—depression—which is characterized by ''Abnormal Liquidation, that is to say, by a downward revision of values and a shrinkage of operations that reduce them, often quite erratically, below their equilibrium amounts. While in recession a mechanism is at work to draw the system toward equilibrium, new disequilibrium develops now: the system again draws away from a neighborhood of equilibrium as it did during prosperity, but under the influence of a different impulse . . . But when depression has run its course . . . the system starts to feel its way back to a new neighborhood of equilibrium.'' This constitutes the fourth phase, called recovery or revival. ''. . . while recession and—if depression occurs—revival are necessary parts of the cyclical process of economic evolution, depression itself is not . . . Whether it occurs or not is a question of fact and depends on accidental circumstances, such as the mentality and temper of the business community and the public, the prevalence of get-rich-quick morals, the way . . . in which credit is handled in prosperity, the ability of the public to form an opinion about the merits of propositions, the degree to which it is given to belief in phrases about prosperity plateaus and the wonders of monetary management and so on.''

It is conceivable that the depression phase might go on indefinitely, but buffers in the economy tend to limit it. Closing down of a factory may force a grocery out of business, but the grocer's market does not entirely disappear; and while some of the factory's creditors may be forced into bankruptcy, others will be able to stand the strain. Moreover, ''total income fluctuates less than total output, the item wages plus salaries less than total income, expenditure on consumers' goods less than wages plus salaries'' partly because of the dilution of effects just described but partly because there are incomes little affected by depression. On the other hand, the spiral is often accentuated by external factors. The depression phase is longer than the spiral. Once depression stops, revival to a neighborhood of equilibrium follows as a matter of course. To assert the contrary is to claim that business men will deliberately incur losses or forego profits. Once equilibrium has been reached, conditions are sufficiently stable to induce another burst of innovating. Then the cycle repeats itself.

If depressive forces can gather momentum so that the economy outruns equilibrium into the depression phase, why cannot revival similarly gather momentum and outrun equilibrium into prosperity without benefit of innovation? This is less likely because there is nothing in revival analogous to the breakdown of the secondary wave during recession. But even if excess optimism lifted the economy above equilibrium, it would soon relapse in the absence of innovation (though perhaps with a damped fluctuation around equilibrium).

THIRD APPROXIMATION—MANY SIMULTANEOUS CYCLES

So far, the model has been discussed as if there were only one wave-like motion. Actually, there are three reasons for expecting the simultaneous operation of many different waves.

First, "The periods of gestation and of absorption of effects by the economic system will not, in general, be equal for all the innovations that are undertaken at any time. There will be innovations of relatively long span, and along with them others will be undertaken which run their course, on the back of the wave created by the former, in shorter periods."

Second, "Major innovations hardly ever emerge in their final form or cover in one throw the whole field that will ultimately be their own . . . One railroad or a few lines may be all, and more than all, that can be successfully built in a given environment at a given time . . . In such cases, innovation is carried out in steps each of which constitutes a cycle. But these cycles may display a family likeness, and a relation to one another which is easy to understand and which tends to weld them into a higher unit that will stand out as a historical individual. The case is entirely different from the previous one. There we had a multiplicity of cycles each of which was an independent entity. Here we have a sequence of cycles of one type only, and the cycle of higher order is but a product or composite of these and has no existence of its own."

Third, there may be a cumulation of effects from all the commercial and industrial processes of an epoch which take the form of a long cycle. "Railroadization may again serve as example. Expenditure on, and the opening of, a new line has some immediate effects on business in general, on competing means of transport, and on the relative position of centers of production. It requires more time to bring into use the opportunities of production newly created by the railroad and to annihilate others. And it takes still longer for population to shift, new cities to develop, other cities to decay, and, generally, the new face of the country to take shape that is adapted to the environment as altered by the railroadization."

Strictly speaking, we should expect an indefinite number of cycles. For analytic *convenience,* however, Schumpeter in his historical outline used a three-cycle schema: the forty-month or Kitchin cycle, the ten-year or Juglar cycle, and the 60-year or Kondratieff cycle. The first Kondratieff cycle was that of the industrial revolution, from the 1780's to 1842; the second that of steam and steel, from 1842 to 1897; the third that of electricity, chemistry, and motors, from 1898 on.

Since the three cycles interfere with each other, nothing is known a priori about the net result, other than the presumption that when all three are in the same phase, particularly if it is depression, the movement will be of unusual intensity. In history, Schumpeter found three Kitchins to each Juglar, and six Juglars to each Kondratieff, though there is nothing in his model which would lead him to expect such regularity.

4.2 Schumpeter's Answer to Marx and Keynes: Inequality and Instability

Joseph A. Schumpeter

* * *

Suppose that the capitalist engine keeps on producing at that [2%] rate of increase for another half century starting from 1928. To this assumption . . . it cannot be objected . . . on the ground that in the decade from 1929 to 1939 capitalism had already failed to live up to that standard. For the depression that ran its course from . . . 1929 to . . . 1932 does not prove that a secular break has occurred in the propelling mechanism of capitalist production because depressions of such severity have repeatedly occurred—roughly once in fifty-five years—and because the effects of one of them—the one from 1873 to 1877—are taken account of in the annual average of 2 per cent. The subnormal recovery to 1935, the subnormal prosperity to 1937 and the slump after that are easily accounted for by the difficulties incident to the adaptation to a new fiscal policy, new labor legislation and a general change in the attitude of government to private enterprise all of which can . . . be distinguished from the working of the productive apparatus as such.

* * *

Well, if from 1928 on available production under the conditions of the capitalist order continued to develop . . . at a long-run average rate of increase of 2 per cent per year, it would after fifty years, in 1978, reach an amount of roughly 2.7 times the 1928 figure. . . . Average income per head during those fifty years would increase to a little more than double its 1928 amount. . . .

Perhaps some readers feel that a proviso should be added about the distribution of the total monetary income. Until about forty years ago, many economists besides Marx believed that the capitalist process tended to change relative shares in the national total so that the obvious inference from our average might be invalidated by the rich growing richer and the poor growing poorer, at least relatively. But there is no such tendency. Whatever may be

Abridged from pp. 64-71, 125-26, 152-55 in *Capitalism, Socialism and Democracy,* 3rd ed., by Joseph A. Schumpeter.

thought of the statistical measures devised for the purpose, this much is certain: that the structure of the pyramid of incomes, expressed in terms of money, has not greatly changed during the period covered by our material—which for England includes the whole of the nineteenth century—and that the relative share of wages plus salaries has also been substantially constant over time. There is, so long as we are discussing what the capitalist engine might do if left to itself, no reason to believe that the distribution of incomes or the dispersion about our average would in 1978 be significantly different from what it was in 1928.

One way of expressing our result is that, if capitalism repeated its past performance for another half century starting with 1928, this would do away with anything that according to present standards could be called poverty, even in the lowest strata of the population, pathological cases alone excepted.

Nor is this all. Whatever else our index may do or may not do, it certainly does not overstate the actual rate of increase. It does not take account of the commodity, Voluntary Leisure. New commodities escape or are inadequately represented by an index which must rest largely on basic commodities and intermediate products. For the same reason improvements in quality almost completely fail to assert themselves although they constitute, in many lines, the core of the progress achieved. . . .

One more point: . . . I have stated . . . that . . . relative shares in national income have remained substantially constant over the last hundred years. This, however, is true only if we measure them in money. Measured in real terms, relative shares have substantially changed in favor of the lower income groups. This follows from the fact that the capitalist engine is first and last an engine of mass production which unavoidably means also production for the masses, whereas, climbing upward in the scale of individual incomes, we find that an increasing proportion is being spent on personal services and on handmade commodities, the prices of which are largely a function of wage rates.

Verification is easy. There are no doubt some things available to the modern workman that Louis XIV himself would have been delighted to have yet was unable to have—modern dentistry for instance. On the whole, however, a budget on that level had little that really mattered to gain from capitalist achievement. Even speed of traveling may be assumed to have been a minor consideration for so very dignified a gentleman. Electric lighting is no great boon to anyone who has money enough to buy a sufficient number of candles and to pay servants to attend to them. It is the cheap cloth, the cheap cotton and rayon fabric, boots, motorcars and so on that are the typical achievements of capitalist production, and not as a rule improvements that would mean much to the rich man. Queen Elizabeth owned silk stockings. The capitalist achievement does not typically consist in providing more silk stockings for queens but in bringing them within the reach of factory girls in return for steadily decreasing amounts of effort.

The same fact stands out still better if we glance at those long waves in economic activity, analysis of which reveals the nature and mechanism of the capitalist process better than anything else. Each of them consists of an "industrial revolution" and the absorption of its effects. For instance, we are able to observe statistically and historically—the phenomenon is so clear that even our scanty information suffices to establish it—the rise of such a long wave toward the end of the 1780's, its culmination around 1800, its downward sweep and then a sort of recovery ending at the beginning of the 1840's. This was the Industrial Revolution dear to the heart of textbook writers. Upon its heels, however, came another such revolution producing another long wave that rose in the forties, culminated just before 1857 and ebbed away to 1897, to be followed in turn by the one that reached its peak about 1911 and is now in the act of ebbing away.

These revolutions periodically reshape the existing structure of industry by introducing new methods of production—the mechanized factory, the electrified factory, chemical synthesis and the like; new commodities, such as railroad service, motorcars, electrical appliances; new forms of organization—the merger movement; new sources of supply—La Plata wool, American cotton, Katanga copper; new trade routes and markets to sell in and so on. This process of industrial change provides the ground swell that gives the general tone to business: while these things are being initiated we have brisk expenditure and predominating "prosperity"—interrupted, no doubt, by the negative phases of the shorter cycles that are superimposed on that ground swell—and while those things are being completed and their results pour forth we have elimination of antiquated elements of the industrial structure and predominating "depression." Thus there are prolonged periods of rising and of falling prices, interest rates, employment and so on, which phenomena constitute parts of the mechanism of this process of recurrent rejuvenation of the productive apparatus.

Now these results each time consist in an avalanche of consumers' goods that permanently deepens and widens the stream of real income although in the first instance they spell disturbance, losses and unemployment. And if we look at those avalanches of consumers' goods we again find that each of them consists in articles of mass consumption and increases the purchasing power of the wage dollar more than that of any other dollar—in other words, that the capitalist process, not by coincidence but by virtue of its mechanism, progressively raises the standard of life of the masses. It does so through a sequence of vicissitudes, the severity of which is proportional to the speed of the advance. But it does so effectively. One problem after another of the supply of commodities to the masses has been successfully solved by being brought within the reach of the methods of capitalist production. The most important one of those that remain, housing, is approaching solution by means of the prefabricated house.

And still this is not all. Appraisal of an economic order would be incomplete . . . if it stopped at the output which the corresponding economic conveyor hands to the various groups of society and left out of account all those things that the conveyor does not serve directly but for which it provides the means as well as the political volition, and all those cultural achievements that are induced by the mentality it generates. . . . Not only the modern mechanized plant and the volume of the output that pours forth from it, not only modern technology and economic organization, but all the features and achievements of modern civilization are, directly or indirectly, the products of the capitalist process. They must be included in any balance sheet of it and in any verdict about its deeds or misdeeds.

There is the growth of rational science and the long list of its applications. Airplanes, refrigerators, television and that sort of thing are immediately recognizable as results of the profit economy. But although the modern hospital is not as a rule operated for profit, it is nonetheless the product of capitalism not only, to repeat, because the capitalist process supplies the means and the will, but much more fundamentally because capitalist rationality supplied the habits of mind that evolved the methods used in these hospitals. And the victories, not yet completely won but in the offing, over cancer, syphilis and tuberculosis will be as much capitalist achievements as motorcars or pipe lines or Bessemer steel have been. In the case of medicine, there is a capitalist profession behind the methods, capitalist both because to a large extent it works in a business spirit and because it is an emulsion of the industrial and commercial bourgeoisie. But even if that were not so, modern medicine and hygiene would still be by-products of the capitalist process just as is modern education.

* * *

The technique and atmosphere of the struggle for social legislation obscures the otherwise obvious facts that, on the one hand, part of this legislation presupposes previous capitalist success (in other words, wealth which had previously to be created by capitalist enterprise) and that, on the other hand, much of what social legislation develops and generalizes had been previously initiated by the action of the capitalist stratum itself. Both facts must of course be added to the sum total of capitalist performance. Now if the system had another run such as it had in the sixty years preceding 1928, . . . it is easy to see that all the desiderata that have so far been espoused by any social reformers —practically without exception, including even the greater part of the cranks—either would be fulfilled automatically or could be fulfilled *without significant interference with the capitalist process*. Ample provision for the unemployed in particular would then be not only a tolerable but a light burden. Irresponsibility in creating unemployment and in financing the support of the unemployed might of course at any time create insoluble problems. But managed with ordinary prudence, an *average* annual expenditure of 16 billions on an *average* number of 16 million unemployed including dependents (10 per cent of the population) would not in itself be a serious matter. . . .

May I call the reader's attention to the reason why unemployment which everyone agrees must be one of the most important issues in any discussion of capitalism . . . will play a comparatively small role in my argument? I do not think that unemployment is among those evils which, like poverty, capitalist evolution could ever eliminate of itself. I also do not think that there is any tendency for the unemployment percentage to increase in the long run. The only series covering a respectable time interval—roughly the sixty years preceding the First World War—gives the English trade-union percentage of unemployed members. It is a typically cyclical series and displays no trend (or a horizontal one). Since this is theoretically understandable—there is no theoretical reason to call the evidence in question—those two propositions seem established for the prewar time to 1913 inclusive. In the postwar time and in most countries unemployment was mostly at an abnormally high level even before 1930. But this and still more the unemployment during the thirties can be accounted for on grounds that have nothing to do with a long-run tendency of unemployment percentages to increase *from causes inherent in the capitalist mechanism itself.* I have mentioned above those industrial revolutions which are so characteristic of the capitalist process. Supernormal unemployment is one of the features of the periods of adaptation that follow upon the "prosperity phase" of each of them. We observe it in the 1820's and 1870's, and the period after 1920 is simply another of those periods. So far the phenomenon is essentially temporary in the sense that nothing can be inferred about it for the future. But there were a number of other factors which tended to intensify it—war effects, dislocations of foreign trade, wage policies, certain institutional changes that swelled the statistical figure, in England and Germany fiscal policies (also important in the United States since 1935) and so on. Some of these are no doubt symptoms of an "atmosphere" in which capitalism will work with decreasing efficiency. That however is another matter. . . .

But whether lasting or temporary, getting worse or not, unemployment undoubtedly is and always has been a scourge. . . . Nevertheless, I hold that the real tragedy is not unemployment per se, but unemployment plus the impossibility of providing adequately for the unemployed *without impairing the conditions of further economic development:* for obviously the suffering and degradation—the destruction of human values—which we associate with unemployment, though not the waste of productive resources, would be largely eliminated and unemployment would lose practically all its terror if the private life of the unemployed were not seriously affected by their unemployment. The indictment stands that in the past—say, roughly, to the end of the nineteenth century—the capitalist order was not only unwilling but also quite incapable of guaranteeing this. But since it will be able to do so if it keeps up its past performance for another half century this indictment would in that case enter the limbo filled by the sorry specters of child labor and sixteen-hour working days and five persons living in one room which it is quite proper to emphasize when we are talking about the past social costs of capitalist achievement but which are not necessarily relevant to the balance of alternatives for the future. Our own time is somewhere between the disabilities of earlier stages in capitalist evolution and the abilities of the system in full maturity. In this country at least, the better part of the task could even now be accomplished without undue strain on the system. The difficulties do not seem to consist so much in the lack of a surplus sufficient to blot out the darkest hues in the picture: they consist, on the one hand, in the fact that the unemployment figure has been increased by anti-capitalist policies beyond what it need have been in the thirties and, on the other hand, in the fact that public opinion as soon as it becomes at all alive to the duty in question, immediately insists on economically irrational methods of financing relief and on lax and wasteful methods of administering it.

Much the same argument applies to the future—and to a great extent the present—possibilities held out by capitalist evolution for the care of the aged and sick, for education and hygiene and so on. Also, an increasing number of commodities might reasonably be expected, from the standpoint of the individual household, to pass out of the class of economic goods and to be available practically up to the satiety point. This could be brought about either by arrangements between public agencies and producing concerns or by nationalization or municipalization, gradual progress with which would of course be a feature of the future development even of an otherwise unfettered capitalism.

SCHUMPETER'S ANSWER TO KEYNES AND HANSEN

If we grant, with Schumpeter, that capitalism generates economic development (dynamic qualitative changes brought about by innovations) and growth (quantitative increases in output, income, leisure, and so on generated by economic development), that economic instability, unemployment, and inequality are not failures of the system but simply concomitants of capitalist development, and that economic growth reduces poverty and entails other benefits as well, then the question of capitalism's prospects resolves itself into whether the capitalist "engine" can be expected to continue to function in the future as it has in the past. The Keynes-Hansen theories of depression and secular stagnation say "no," as we observed in chapter 3, and it is this negative answer that essentially legitimizes the Keynesian critique of laissez-faire and the promotion of a governmentally guided or managed capitalism. Schumpeter explicitly dissented from the Keynesian analysis of depression, especially the theory of secular stagnation, and therefore also from the Keynesian prescriptions for public policy. Schumpeter's critique of Keynes and Hansen is presented in selection 4.3.

4.3 Schumpeter's Answer to Keynes and Hansen: Secular Stagnation

Joseph A. Schumpeter

The Vanishing of Investment Opportunity

. . . . The present generation of economists has witnessed not only a world-wide depression of unusual severity and duration but also a subsequent period of halting and unsatisfactory recovery. I have already submitted my own interpre-

Abridged from pp. 111–20 in *Capitalism, Socialism and Democracy*, 3rd ed., by Joseph A. Schumpeter.

tation of these phenomena and stated the reasons why I do not think that they necessarily indicate a break in the trend of capitalist evolution. But it is natural that many if not most of my fellow economists should take a different view. As a matter of fact they feel, exactly as some of their predecessors felt between 1873 and 1896—though then this opinion was mainly confined to Europe—that a fundamental change is upon the capitalist process. According to this view, we have been witnessing not merely a depression and a bad recovery, accentuated perhaps by anti-capitalist policies, but the symptoms of a permanent loss of vitality which must be expected to go on and to supply the dominating theme for the remaining movements of the capitalist symphony; hence no inference as to the future can be drawn from the functioning of the capitalist engine and of its performance in the past.

. . . . Even if the forces and mechanisms stressed by the theory of vanishing investment opportunity were in themselves adequate to establish the presence in the capitalist process of a long-run tendency toward ultimate deadlock, it does not necessarily follow that the vicissitudes of the past decade have been due to them and—which it is important to add for our purpose—that similar vicissitudes should therefore have to be expected to persist for the next forty years.

. . . . The factors that are held to justify a pessimistic forecast concerning the performance of capitalism in the near future and to negate the idea that past performance may be repeated [i.e., the] . . . main reasons for holding that opportunities for private enterprise and investment are vanishing are these: saturation, population, new lands, technological possibilities, and the circumstance that many existing investment opportunities belong to the sphere of public rather than of private investment.

1. For every given state of human wants and of technology (in the widest possible sense of the term) there is of course for every rate of real wages a definite amount of fixed and circulating capital that will spell saturation. If wants and methods of production had been frozen for good at their state in 1800, such a point would have been reached long ago. But is it not conceivable that wants may some day be so completely satisfied as to become frozen forever after? Some implications of this case will presently be developed, but so long as we deal with what may happen during the next forty years we evidently need not trouble ourselves about this possibility.

If ever it should materialize, then the current decline in birth rate, still more an actual fall in population, would indeed become an important factor in reducing opportunities for investment other than replacement. For if everyone's wants were satisfied or nearly satisfied, increase in the number of consumers would *ex hypothesi* be the only major source of additional demand. But independently of that possibility, decrease in the rate of increase in population does not per se endanger investment opportunity or the rate of increase in total output per head. Of this we can easily satisfy ourselves by a brief examination of the usual argument to the contrary.

. . . It is . . . held that a declining rate of increase in total population ipso facto spells a declining rate of increase in output and hence of investment because it restricts the expansion of demand. This does not follow. Want and effective demand are not the same thing. If they were, the poorest nations would be the ones to display the most vigorous demand. As it is, the income elements set free by the falling birth rate may be diverted to other channels and they are particularly apt to be so diverted in all those cases in which the desire to expand alternative demands is the very motive of childlessness. A modest argument can indeed be made out by stressing the fact that the lines of demand characteristic of an increasing population are particularly calculable and thus afford particularly reliable investment opportunities. But the desires that provide alternative opportunities are, in the given state of satisfaction of wants, not much less so. . . .

2. Next as to the opening up of new lands—that unique opportunity for investment which cannot ever recur. Even if, for the sake of argument, we grant that humanity's geographical frontier is closed for good—which is not in itself very obvious in view of the fact that at present there are deserts where once there were fields and populous cities—and even if we further grant that nothing will ever contribute to human *welfare* as much as did the foodstuffs and raw materials from those new lands—which is more plausible—it does not follow that total output per head must therefore decline, or increase at a smaller rate, during the next half-century. This would indeed have to be expected if the lands that in the nineteenth century entered the capitalist sphere had been exploited in the sense that diminishing returns would now be due to assert themselves. This however is not the case and, as was just pointed out, the decreasing rate of increase in population removes from the range of practical considerations the idea that nature's response to human effort either already is or must soon become less generous than it has been. Technological progress effectively turned the tables on any such tendency, and it is one of the safest predictions that in the calculable future we shall live in an *embarras de richesse* of both foodstuffs and raw materials, giving all the rein to expansion of total output that we shall know what to do with. . . .

There remains another possibility. Though the current output per head of foodstuffs and raw materials need not suffer and may even increase, the vast opportunities for enterprise and hence for investment that were afforded by the task of developing the new countries seem to have vanished with its completion and all sorts of difficulties are being predicted from the resulting reduction of outlets for savings. We will assume again for the sake of argument that those countries actually are developed for good and that savings, failing to adapt themselves to a reduction of outlets, might cause troubles and wastes unless other outlets open up instead. Both assumptions are indeed most unrealistic. But there is no necessity for us to question them because the conclusion as to the future development of output is contingent upon a third one that is completely gratuitous, viz., the absence of other outlets.

. . . . It is gratuitous to assume not only that the "closing of the frontier" will cause a vacuum but also that whatever steps into the vacant place must necessarily be less important in any of the senses we may choose to give to that word. The conquest of the air may well be more important than the conquest of India was—we must not confuse geographical frontiers with economic ones.

. . . . We can assert that the vanishing of the investment opportunities incident to the development of new countries—if they are already vanishing—*need* not cause a void that would necessarily affect the rate of increase in total output. We cannot assert that they actually will be replaced by at least equivalent ones. We may point to the fact that from that development further developments naturally arise in those same countries or in others; we may put some trust in the ability of the capitalist engine to find or create ever new opportunities since it is geared to this very purpose; but such considerations do not carry us beyond our negative result. . . .

3. An analogous argument applies to the widely accepted view that the great stride in technological advance has been made and that but minor achievements remain. So far as this view does not merely render the impressions conceived from the state of things during and after the world crisis —when an apparent absence of novel propositions of the first magnitude was part of the familiar pattern of any great depression—it exemplifies still better than did the "closing of humanity's frontier" that error in interpretation economists are so prone to commit. We are just now in the downgrade of a wave of enterprise that created the electrical power plant, the electrical industry, the electrified farm and home and the motorcar. We find all that very marvelous, and we cannot for our lives see where opportunities of comparable importance are to come from. As a matter of fact however, the promise held out by the chemical industry alone is much greater than what it was possible to anticipate in, say, 1880, not to mention the fact that the mere utilization of the achievement of the age of electricity and the production of modern homes for the masses would suffice to provide investment opportunities for quite a time to come.

Technological possibilities are an uncharted sea. . . . From the fact that some of them have been exploited before others, it cannot be inferred that the former were more productive than the latter. And those that are still in the lap of the gods may be more or less productive than any that have thus far come within our range of observation. Again this yields only a negative result which even the fact that technological "progress" tends, through systemization and rationalization of research and of management, to become more effective and sure-footed, is powerless to turn into a positive one. But for us the negative result suffices: there is no reason to expect slackening of the rate of output through exhaustion of technological possibilities.

4. [A] variant of this branch of the theory of vanishing investment opportunity remains to be noticed. . . . The great bursts of economic activity that used to spread the symptoms of prosperity all over the economic organism have of course always been associated with expansions of producers' expenditure that were in turn associated with the construction of additional plant and equipment. Now some economists have discovered, or think they have discovered, that at the present time new technological processes tend to require less fixed capital in this sense than they used to in the past, particularly in the epoch of railroad building. The inference is that spending for capital construction will henceforth decrease in relative importance. Since this will adversely affect

those intermittent bursts of economic activity that evidently have much to do with the observed rate of increase in total output, it further follows that this rate is bound to decline, especially if saving goes on at the old rate.

This tendency of new technological methods to become increasingly capital-saving has not so far been adequately established. Statistical evidence up to 1929—later data do not qualify for the purpose—point the other way. All that the sponsors of the theory in question have offered is a number of isolated instances to which it is possible to oppose others. But let us grant that such a tendency exists. We have then the same formal problem before us which exercised so many economists of the past in the case of labor-saving devices. These may affect the interests of labor favorably or adversely, but nobody doubts that on the whole they are favorable to an expansion of output. And this is—barring possible disturbances in the saving-investment process which it is the fashion to exaggerate—no different in the case of devices that economize outlay on capital goods *per unit of the final product*. In fact, it is not far from the truth to say that almost any new process that is economically workable economizes both labor and capital. Railroads were presumably capital-saving as compared with the outlay that transportation, by mailcoach or cart, of the same numbers of passengers and of the same quantities of goods that actually are being transported by railroads now would have involved. Similarly silk production by mulberry trees and silkworms may be more capital-consuming—I don't know—than the production of an equivalent amount of rayon fabric would be. That may be very sad for the owners of capital already sunk in the former. But it need not even mean decrease of investment opportunity. It certainly does not necessarily mean decrease in the expansion of output. Those who hope to see capitalism break down solely by virtue of the fact that the unit of capital goes further in productive effect than it used to, may have to wait long indeed.

5. Finally, since the subject is usually dealt with by economists who aim at impressing upon the public the necessity of governmental deficit spending, another point never fails to turn up, viz., that such opportunities for investment as remain are more suited for public than they are for private enterprise. This is true to some extent. First, with increasing wealth certain lines of expenditure are likely to gain ground which do not naturally enter into any cost-profit calculation, such as expenditure on the beautification of cities, on public health and so on. Second, an ever-widening sector of industrial activity tends to enter the sphere of public management, such as means of communication, docks, power production, insurance and so on, simply because these industries become increasingly amenable to the methods of public administration. National and municipal investment could thus be expected to expand, absolutely and relatively, even in a thoroughly capitalist society, just as other forms of public planning would.

But that is all. In order to recognize it we need not make any hypothesis about the course of things in the private sector of industrial activity. Moreover, for the purpose in hand it is immaterial whether in the future investment and the incident expansion of output will to a greater or a lesser extent be financed and managed by public rather than by private agencies. . . .

SCHUMPETER, CONSERVATISM, AND LIBERALISM

Schumpeter's creative reinterpretation of Marx and dissent from Keynes might seem to place him in juxtaposition if not union with such contemporary individualist-conservatives-neoliberals as Friedrich Hayek and Milton Friedman. Indeed, there are familial connections between Schumpeter's defense of modified laissez-faire and critique of many reforms of the Keynesian era and the neoclassicism of Friedman and other individualist-conservatives.

But there is one striking difference. The neo-liberalism of the contemporary individualist-conservatives, like the classical liberalism of Adam Smith and John Stuart Mill, rests squarely on the principle of atomistically competitive markets as social processes for economic coordination and control of business enterprise. By contrast, Schumpeter's analysis of the role of "big business" bears a striking resemblance to certain features of the laissez-faire conservatism and "social Darwinism" of the late nineteenth century. Schumpeter's hero is not the competitive market, but the creative, daring entrepreneur, the "captain of industry," who makes the innovations that introduce new products, embody resource discoveries and technological improvements, and open new markets, *and,* in the process, build new industrial empires.

On the one hand, the dynamic innovations of the entrepreneurial class —and Schumpeter assumed that their special qualities of vision, daring, and rugged empire building set them apart from ordinary capitalists or mere managers of existing enterprises—constitute a powerful competitive force in economic development. The "perennial gale of creative destruction," whereby new products and processes displace old ones, is vastly more important than price competition among existing firms and products. And because of the tendency for innovations to spread, by imitation and extension to allied fields, the monopoly position of the industrial pioneer is only temporary.

On the other hand, the possibility of retention, at least temporarily, of above-normal profits from innovations may well stimulate a higher rate of innovation and technological improvement. Short-run strategies and practices that protect the (temporary) monopoly position of the innovator thus may be the price society pays for technological progressivity and thereby a higher growth rate over the long run.

In any event, Schumpeter argued, to apply the "bloodless" concepts of pure or perfect competition to an interpretation of the actual historical experience of capitalist development implies the existence of an entirely imaginary "golden age" of atomistic competition and a "break" in the process of capitalist development with the advent of "big business" in the late nineteenth century. This view, Schumpeter contended, is doubly mistaken. In terms of dynamic performance (new products, processes, markets), big-business, oligopoly capitalism since the late nineteenth century has been more, not less, competitive than old-style proprietary, atomistically competitive capitalism. And the advent of big business has not been associated with a decrease in the growth rate of such capitalist economies as that of the United States.

Schumpeter's ideas about monopoly and innovations are presented in selection 4.4.

4.4 Creative Destruction and Monopoly

Joseph A. Schumpeter

The Process of Creative Destruction

The theories of monopolistic and oligopolistic competition and their popular variants may in two ways be made to serve the view that capitalist reality is unfavorable to maximum performance in production. One may hold that it always has been so and that all along output has been expanding in spite of the secular sabotage perpetrated by the managing bourgeoisie. Advocates of this proposition would have to produce evidence to the effect that the observed rate of increase can be accounted for by a sequence of favorable circumstances unconnected with the mechanism of private enterprise and strong enough to overcome the latter's resistance. . . . However, those who espouse this variant at least avoid the trouble about historical fact that the advocates of the alternative proposition have to face. This avers that capitalist reality once tended to favor maximum productive performance, or at all events productive performance so considerable as to constitute a major element in any serious appraisal of the system; but that the later spread of monopolist structures, killing competition, has by now reversed that tendency.

First, this involves the creation of an entirely imaginary golden age of perfect competition that at some time somehow metamorphosed itself into the monopolistic age, whereas it is quite clear that perfect competition has at no time been more of a reality than it is at present. Secondly, it is necessary to point out that the rate of increase in output did not decrease from the nineties from which, I suppose, the prevalence of the largest-size concerns, at least in manufacturing industry, would have to be dated; that there is nothing in the behavior of the time series of total output to suggest a "break in trend"; and, most important of all, that the modern standard of life of the masses evolved during the period of relatively unfettered "big business." If we list the items that enter the modern workman's budget and from 1899 on observe the course of their prices not in terms of money but in terms of the hours of labor that will buy them—i.e., each year's money prices divided by each year's hourly wage

Abridged from pp. 81–92, 106 in *Capitalism, Socialism and Democracy,* 3rd ed., by Joseph A. Schumpeter.

rates—we cannot fail to be struck by the rate of the advance which, considering the spectacular improvement in qualities, seems to have been greater and not smaller than it ever was before. If we economists were given less to wishful thinking and more to the observation of facts, doubts would immediately arise as to the realistic virtues of a theory that would have led us to expect a very different result. Nor is this all. As soon as we go into details and inquire into the individual items in which progress was most conspicuous, the trail leads not to the doors of those firms that work under conditions of comparatively free competition but precisely to the doors of the large concerns—which, as in the case of agricultural machinery, also account for much of the progress in the competitive sector—and a shocking suspicion dawns upon us that big business may have had more to do with creating that standard of life than with keeping it down.

* * *

The essential point to grasp is that in dealing with capitalism we are dealing with an evolutionary process. It may seem strange that anyone can fail to see so obvious a fact which moreover was long ago emphasized by Karl Marx. Yet that fragmentary analysis which yields the bulk of our propositions about the functioning of modern capitalism persistently neglects it. Let us restate the point and see how it bears upon our problem.

Capitalism, then, is by nature a form or method of economic change and not only never is but never can be stationary. And this evolutionary character of the capitalist process is not merely due to the fact that economic life goes on in a social and natural environment which changes and by its change alters the data of economic action; this fact is important and these changes (wars, revolutions and so on) often condition industrial change, but they are not its prime movers. Nor is this evolutionary character due to a quasi-automatic increase in population and capital or to the vagaries of monetary systems of which exactly the same thing holds true. The fundamental impulse that sets and keeps the capitalist engine in motion comes from the new consumers' goods, the new methods of production or transportation, the new markets, the new forms of industrial organization that capitalist enterprise creates.

. . . . The history of the productive apparatus of a typical farm, from the beginnings of the rationalization of crop rotation, plowing and fattening to the mechanized thing of today—linking up with elevators and railroads—is a history of revolutions. So is the history of the productive apparatus of the iron and steel industry from the charcoal furnace to our own type of furnace, or the history of the apparatus of power production from the overshot water wheel to the modern power plant, or the history of transportation from the mailcoach to the airplane. The opening up of new markets, foreign or domestic, and the organizational development from the craft shop and factory to such concerns as U.S. Steel illustrate the same process of industrial mutation—if I may use that biological term—that incessantly revolutionizes the economic structure *from within,* incessantly destroying the old one, incessantly creating a new one. This process of Creative Destruction is the essential fact about capitalism. It is what capitalism consists in and what every capitalist concern has got to live in. This fact bears upon our problem in two ways.

First, since we are dealing with a process whose every element takes considerable time in revealing its true features and ultimate effects, there is no point in appraising the performance of that process *ex visu* of a given point of time; we must judge its performance over time, as it unfolds through decades or centuries. A system—any system, economic or other—that at *every* given point of time fully utilizes its possibilities to the best advantage may yet in the long run be inferior to a system that does so at *no* given point of time, because the latter's failure to do so may be a condition for the level or speed of long-run performance.

Second, since we are dealing with an organic process, analysis of what happens in any particular part of it—say, in an individual concern or industry—may indeed clarify details of mechanism but is inconclusive beyond that. Every piece of business strategy acquires its true significance only against the background of that process and within the situation created by it. It must be seen in its role in the perennial gale of creative destruction. . . . In other words, the problem that is usually being visualized is how capitalism administers existing structures, whereas the relevant problem is how it creates and destroys them. . . .

Economists are at long last emerging from the stage in which price competition was all they saw. . . . In capitalist reality as distinguished from its textbook picture, it is not that kind of competition which counts but the competition from the new commodity, the new technology, the new source of supply, the new type of organization (the largest-scale unit of control for instance)—competition which commands a decisive cost or quality advantage and which strikes not at the margins of the profits and the outputs of the existing firms but at their foundations and their very lives. This kind of competition is as much more effective than the other as a bombardment is in comparison with forcing a door, and so much more important that it becomes a matter of comparative indifference whether competition in the ordinary sense functions more or less promptly; the powerful lever that in the long run expands output and brings down prices is in any case made of other stuff.

It is hardly necessary to point out that competition of the kind we now have in mind acts not only when in being but also when it is merely an ever-present threat. It disciplines before it attacks. . . . Now a theoretical construction which neglects this essential element of the case neglects all that is most typically capitalist about it; even if correct in logic as well as in fact, it is like *Hamlet* without the Danish prince.

Monopolistic Practices

* * *

We have just seen that, both as a fact and as a threat, the impact of new things—new technologies for instance—on the existing structure of an industry considerably reduces the long-run scope and importance of practices that aim, through restricting output, at conserving established positions and at maximizing the profits accruing from them. We must now recognize the further fact that restrictive practices of this kind, as far as they are effective, acquire a new significance in the perennial gale of creative destruction, a significance which they would not have in a stationary state or in a state of slow and balanced growth. In either of these cases restrictive strategy would produce no result other than an increase in profits at the expense of buyers except that, in the case of balanced advance, it might still prove to be the easiest and most effective way of collecting the means by which to finance additional investment. But in the process of creative destruction, restrictive practices may do much to steady the ship and to alleviate temporary difficulties. . . .

* * *

In analyzing . . . business stragety *ex visu* of a given point of time, the investigating economist or government agent sees price policies that seem to him predatory and restrictions of output that seem to him synonymous with loss of opportunities to produce. He does not see that restrictions of this type are, in the conditions of the perennial gale, incidents, often unavoidable incidents, of a long-run process of expansion which they protect rather than impede. . . .

This stands out most clearly in the case of those sectors of the economy which at any time happen to embody the impact of new things and methods on the existing industrial structure. The best way of getting a vivid and realistic idea of industrial strategy is indeed to visualize the behavior of new concerns or industries that introduce new commodities or processes (such as the aluminum industry) or else reorganize a part or the whole of an industry (such as, for instance, the old Standard Oil Company).

As we have seen, such concerns are aggressors by nature and wield the really effective weapon of competition. Their intrusion can only in the rarest of cases fail to improve total output in quantity or quality, both through the new method itself—even if at no time used to full advantage—and through the pressure it exerts on the preexisting firms. But these aggressors are so circumstanced as to require, for purposes of attack and defense, also pieces of armor other than price and quality of their product which, moreover, must be strategically manipulated all along so that at any point of time they seem to be doing nothing but restricting their output and keeping prices high.

On the one hand, largest-scale plans could in many cases not materialize at all if it were not known from the outset that competition will be discouraged by heavy capital requirements or lack of experience, or that means are available to discourage or checkmate it so as to gain the time and space for further developments. . . .

On the other hand, enterprise would in most cases be impossible if it were not known from the outset that exceptionally favorable situations are likely to arise which if exploited by price, quality and quantity manipulation will produce profits adequate to tide over exceptionally unfavorable situations provided these are similarly managed. . . .

Our argument however extends beyond the cases of new concerns, methods and industries. Old concerns and established industries, whether or not directly attacked, still live in the perennial gale. Situations emerge in the process of creative destruction in which many firms may have to perish that nevertheless would be able to live on vigorously and usefully if they could weather a particular storm. . . . Finally, there is certainly no point in trying to conserve obsolescent industries indefinitely; but there is point in trying to avoid their coming down with a crash and in attempting to turn a rout, which may become a center of cumulative depressive effects, into orderly retreat. . . .

. . . . "Restraints of trade" of the cartel type as well as those which merely consist in tacit understandings about price competition may be effective remedies under conditions of depression. As far as they are, they may in the end produce not only steadier but also greater expansion of total output than could be secured by an entirely uncontrolled onward rush that cannot fail to be studded with catastrophes. . . .

Even as now extended however, our argument does not cover all cases of restrictive or regulating strategy, many of which no doubt have that injurious effect on the long-run development of output which is uncritically attributed to all of them. And even in the cases our argument does cover, the net effect is a question of the circumstances and of the way in which and the degree to which industry regulates itself in each individual case. It is certainly as conceivable that an all-pervading cartel system might sabotage all progress as it is that it might realize, with smaller social and private costs, all that perfect competition is supposed to realize. This is why our argument does not amount to a case against state regulation. It does show that there is no general case for indiscriminate "trust-busting" or for the prosecution of everything that qualifies as a restraint of trade. Rational as distinguished from vindictive regulation by public authority turns out to be an extremely delicate problem which not every government agency, particularly when in full cry against big business, can be trusted to solve. But our argument, framed to refute a prevalent *theory* and the inferences drawn therefrom about the relation between modern capitalism and the development of total output, only yields another *theory*, i.e., another outlook on facts and another principle by which to interpret them. For our purpose that is enough.

* * *

Thus it is not sufficient to argue that because perfect competition is impossible under modern industrial conditions—or because it always has been impossible—the large-scale establishment or unit of control must be accepted as a necessary evil inseparable from the economic progress which it is prevented from sabotaging by the forces inherent in its productive apparatus. What we have got to accept is that it has come to be the most powerful engine of that progress and in particular of the long-run expansion of total output not only in spite of, but to a considerable extent through, this strategy which looks so restrictive when viewed in the individual case and from the individual point of time. In this respect, perfect competition is not only impossible but inferior, and has no title to being set up as a model of ideal efficiency. It is hence a mistake to base the theory of government regulation of industry on the principle that big business should be made to work as the respective industry would work in perfect competition. And socialists should rely for their criticisms on the virtues of a socialist economy rather than on those of the competitive model.

CAN CAPITALISM SURVIVE?

What, then, of the future? "Can capitalism survive?" Schumpeter asked pointedly. "No, I do not think it can," he answered. The paradox is this: Capitalism's demise is not in prospect (at least in the near term) because of economic failure. Schumpeter believed the capitalist engine to be sound and potentially capable of sustaining long-run economic growth and development. Instead, *because* of its very success, it will fail, in a process of "creative destruction." Economic development will bring institutional, political, and ideological changes inconsistent with the continued viability of capitalist institutions.

In part, these changes in the "superstructure" of society are illustrated by (misguided) Keynesian-type policies and other liberal-labor reforms characteristic of contemporary managed (Schumpeter called it "laborist") capitalism. These policies (especially when accompanied by government regulation of business and implemented by a political administration unsympathetic to business men and business interests) interfere with business decisions, increase the uncertainties of obtaining and retaining large-scale profits, and thereby frighten investors. As a consequence, investment may well be insufficient to sustain full employment, growth becomes sluggish, and the economy behaves *as if* it were characterized by Keynes-Hansen stagnation.

More broadly, Schumpeter saw a transformation and prospective demise of capitalism caused by a number of changes emanating from the very dynamism of the system: (1) the obsolescence of the entrepreneurial function—as innovation is "bureaucratized" in the large-scale corporation, itself a product of the capitalist developmental process; (2) destruction of the institutional framework of capitalism—via the transformation from atomistic competition to markets dominated by large-scale concentrations of economic power, and the separation of property ownership and management; (3) destruction of the "protecting strata" of precapitalist classes (for example, the feudal aristocracy), institutions, and values; and (4) growing hostility against the system (encouraged, for example, by Keynesian theory), and governmental policy emanating from that hostility. While praising the technological progressivity and dynamic performance of oligopoly and big business, Schumpeter contended that increases in the concentration of economic power, decreases in the relative role of small, proprietary businesses, and the greater bureaucratization and stability of large-scale corporations undercut political support for old-style laissez-faire capitalism and emasculate opposition, even within the business community, to liberal-labor reforms. In effect, capitalism's very economic success creates surrounding political, ideological, and psychological changes that prevent its viable functioning and thereby cause its demise.

Schumpeter describes these various changes and their implications for the future of capitalism in selection 4.5. A critical evaluation of Schumpeter's views is found in selection 4.6, by Allen Sievers.

4.5 Can Capitalism Survive?

Joseph A. Schumpeter

. . . . I am not going to argue that [capitalist] achievement and promise are in themselves sufficient to support an argument for allowing the capitalist process to work on and, as it might easily be put, to lift poverty from the shoulders of mankind.

There would be no sense in this. Even if mankind were as free to choose, . . . no determined value judgment necessarily follows from the facts and relations between facts that I have tried to convey. . . .

However, whether favorable or unfavorable, value judgments about capitalist performance are of little interest. For mankind is not free to choose. This is not only because the mass of people are not in a position to compare alternatives rationally and always accept what they are being told. There is a much deeper reason for it. Things economic and social move by their own momentum and the ensuing situations compel individuals and groups to behave in certain ways whatever they may wish to do—not indeed by destroying their freedom of choice but by shaping the choosing mentalities and by narrowing the list of possibilities from which to choose. If this is the quintessence of Marxism then we all of us have got to be Marxists. In consequence, capitalist performance is not even relevant for prognosis. Most civilizations have disappeared before they had time to fill to the full the measure of their promise. Hence I am not going to argue, on the strength of that performance, that the capitalist intermezzo is likely to be prolonged. In fact, I am now going to draw the exactly opposite inference.

* * *

Crumbling Walls

THE OBSOLESCENCE OF THE ENTREPRENEURIAL FUNCTION

. . . . Progress itself may be mechanized as well as the management of a stationary economy, and this mechanization of progress may affect entrepreneurship

Abridged from pp. 125–26, 129–35, 138–45 in *Capitalism, Socialism and Democracy*, 3rd ed., by Joseph A. Schumpeter.

and capitalist society nearly as much as the cessation of economic progress would. In order to see this it is only necessary to restate, first, what the entrepreneurial function consists in and, secondly, what it means for bourgeois society and the survival of the capitalist order.

We have seen that the function of entrepreneurs is to reform or revolutionize the pattern of production by exploiting an invention or, more generally, an untried technological possibility for producing a new commodity or producing an old one in a new way, by opening up a new source of supply of materials or a new outlet for products, by reorganizing an industry and so on. Railroad construction in its earlier stages, electrical power production before the First World War, steam and steel, the motorcar, colonial ventures afford spectacular instances of a large genus which comprises innumerable humbler ones—down to such things as making a success of a particular kind of sausage or toothbrush. This kind of activity is primarily responsible for the recurrent "prosperities" that revolutionize the economic organism and the recurrent "recessions" that are due to the disequilibrating impact of the new products or methods. To undertake such new things is difficult and constitutes a distinct economic function, first, because they lie outside of the routine tasks which everbody understands and, secondly, because the environment resists in many ways that vary, according to social conditions, from simple refusal either to finance or to buy a new thing, to physical attack on the man who tries to produce it. To act with confidence beyond the range of familiar beacons and to overcome that resistance requires aptitudes that are present in only a small fraction of the population and that define the entrepreneurial type as well as the entrepreneurial function. This function does not essentially consist in either inventing anything or otherwise creating the conditions which the enterprise exploits. It consists in getting things done.

This social function is already losing importance and is bound to lose it at an accelerating rate in the future even if the economic process itself of which entrepreneurship was the prime mover went on unabated. For, on the one hand, it is much easier now than it has been in the past to do things that lie outside familiar routine—innovation itself is being reduced to routine. Technological progress is increasingly becoming the business of teams of trained specialists who turn out what is required and make it work in predictable ways. The romance of earlier commercial adventure is rapidly wearing away, because so many more things can be strictly calculated that had of old to be visualized in a flash of genius.

On the other hand, personality and will power must count for less in environments which have become accustomed to economic change—best instanced by an incessant stream of new consumers' and producers' goods. . . .

Thus, economic progress tends to become depersonalized and automatized. Bureau and committee work tends to replace individual action.

* * *

But this affects the position of the entire bourgeois stratum. Although entrepreneurs are not necessarily or even typically elements of that stratum from the outset, they nevertheless enter it in case of success. Thus, though entrepreneurs do not per se form a social class, the bourgeois class absorbs them and their families and connections thereby recruiting and revitalizing itself currently while at the same time the families that sever their active relation to "business" drop out of it after a generation or two. Between, there is the bulk of what we refer to as industrialists, merchants, financiers and bankers; they are in the intermediate stage between entrepreneurial venture and mere current administration of an inherited domain. The returns on which the class lives are produced by, and the social position of the class rests on, the success of this more or less active sector—which of course may, as it does in this country, form over 90 per cent of the bourgeois stratum—and of the individuals who are in the act of rising into that class. Economically and sociologically, directly and indirectly, the bourgeoisie therefore depends on the entrepreneur and, as a class, lives and will die with him, though a more or less prolonged transitional stage—eventually a stage in which it may feel equally unable to die and to live—is quite likely to occur, as in fact it did occur in the case of the feudal civilization.

To sum up this part of our argument: if capitalist evolution—"progress"—either ceases or becomes completely automatic, the economic basis of the industrial bourgeoisie will be reduced eventually to wages such as are paid for current administrative work excepting remnants of quasi-rents and monopoloid gains that may be expected to linger on for some time. Since capitalist enterprise, by its very achievements, tends to automatize progress, we conclude that it tends to make itself superfluous—to break to pieces under the pressure of its own success. The perfectly bureaucratized giant industrial unit not only ousts the small or medium-sized firm and "expropriates" its owners, but in the end it also ousts the entrepreneur and expropriates the bourgeoisie as a class which in the process stands to lose not only its income but also what is infinitely more important, its function. The true pacemakers of socialism were not the intellectuals or agitators who preached it but the Vanderbilts, Carnegies and Rockefellers. This result may not in every respect be to the taste of Marxian socialists, still less to the taste of socialists of a more popular (Marx would have said, vulgar) description. But so far as prognosis goes, it does not differ from theirs.

THE DESTRUCTION OF THE PROTECTING STRATA

So far we have been considering the effects of the capitalist process upon the economic bases of the upper strata of capitalist society and upon their social position and prestige. But effects further extend to the institutional framework that protected them. In showing this we shall take the term in its widest acceptance so as to include not only legal institutions but also attitudes of the public mind and policies.

Capitalist evolution first of all destroyed, or went far toward destroying, the institutional arrangements of the feudal world—the manor, the village, the craft guild. . . .

Economically all this meant for the bourgeoisie the breaking of so many fetters and the removal of so many barriers. Politically it meant the replacement of an order in which the bourgeois was a humble subject by another that was more congenial to his rationalist mind and to his immediate interests. But, surveying that process from the standpoint of today, the observer might well wonder whether in the end such complete emancipation was good for the bourgeois and his world. For those fetters not only hampered, they also sheltered. . . .

* * *

Barring exceptional conditions, the bourgeois class is ill equipped to face the problems, both domestic and international, that have normally to be faced by a country of any importance. The bourgeois themselves feel this in spite of all the phraseology that seems to deny it, and so do the masses. Within a protecting framework not made of bourgeois material, the bourgeoisie may be successful, not only in the political defensive but also in the offensive, especially as an opposition. For a time it felt so safe as to be able to afford the luxury of attacking the protective frame itself; such bourgeois opposition as there was in imperial Germany illustrates this to perfection. But without protection by some non-bourgeois group, the bourgeoisie is politically helpless and unable not only to lead its nation but even to take care of its particular class interest. Which amounts to saying that it needs a master.

But the capitalist process, both by its economic mechanics and by its psycho-sociological effects, did away with this protecting master or, as in this country, never gave him, or a substitute for him, a chance to develop. . . .

In breaking down the pre-capitalist framework of society, capitalism thus broke not only barriers that impeded its progress but also flying buttresses that prevented its collapse. That process, impressive in its relentless necessity, was not merely a matter of removing institutional deadwood, but of removing partners of the capitalist stratum, symbiosis with whom was an essential element of the capitalist schema. . . .

THE DESTRUCTION OF THE INSTITUTIONAL FRAMEWORK OF CAPITALIST SOCIETY

* * *

It has been pointed out above that the very success of capitalist enterprise paradoxically tends to impair the prestige or social weight of the class primarily associated with it and that the giant unit of control tends to oust the bourgeoisie from the function to which it owed that social weight. The corresponding change in the meaning, and the incidental loss in vitality, of the institutions of the bourgeois world and of its typical attitudes are easy to trace.

On the one hand, the capitalist process unavoidably attacks the economic standing ground of the small producer and trader. What it did to the pre-capitalist strata it also does—and by the same competitive mechanism—to the lower strata of capitalist industry. . . .

Now it is important to realize precisely what these consequences consist in. . . . Even if the giant concerns were all managed so perfectly as to call forth applause from the angels in heaven, the political consequences of concentration would still be what they are. The political structure of a nation is profoundly affected by the elimination of a host of small and medium-sized firms the owner-managers of which, together with their dependents, henchmen and connections, count quantitatively at the polls and have a hold on what we may term the foreman class that no management of a large unit can ever have; the very foundation of private property and free contracting wears away in a nation in which its most vital, most concrete, most meaningful types disappear from the moral horizon of the people.

On the other hand, the capitalist process also attacks its own institutional framework . . . within the precincts of the big units. Excepting the cases that are still of considerable importance in which a corporation is practically owned by a single individual or family, the figure of the proprietor and with it the specifically proprietary interest have vanished from the picture. There are the salaried executives and all the salaried managers and submanagers, . . . the big stockholders, . . . the small stockholders. The first group tends to acquire the employee attitude and rarely if ever identifies itself with the stockholding interest. . . . The second group . . . is at one remove from both the functions and the attitudes of an owner. As to the third group, small stockholders often do not care much about what for most of them is but a minor source of income and, whether they care or not, they hardly ever bother. . . . No element of any of those three groups into which I schematized the typical situation unconditionally takes the attitude characteristic of that curious phenomenon, so full of meaning and so rapidly passing, that is covered by the term Property.

Freedom of contracting is in the same boat. In its full vitality it meant individual contracting regulated by individual choice between an indefinite number of possibilities. The stereotyped, unindividual, impersonal and bureaucratized contract of today—we may fasten upon the labor contract—which presents but restricted freedom of choice, . . . has none of the old features the most important of which become impossible with giant concerns dealing with other giant concerns or impersonal masses of workmen or consumers. . . .

Thus the capitalist process pushes into the background all those institutions, the institutions of property and free contracting in particular, that expressed the needs and ways of the truly "private" economy activity. Where it does not abolish them, as it already has abolished free contracting in the labor market, it attains the same end by shifting the relative importance of existing legal forms—the legal forms pertaining to corporate business for instance as against those pertaining to the partnership or individual firm—or by changing their contents or meanings. The capitalist process, by substituting a mere parcel of shares for the walls of and the machines in a factory, takes the life out of the idea of property. It loosens the grip that once was so strong—the grip in the sense of the legal right and the actual ability to do as one pleases with one's own; the grip also in the sense that the holder of the title loses the will to fight, economically, physically, politically, for "his" factory and his control over it, to die if necessary on its steps. And this evaporation of what we may term the material substance of property—its visible and touchable reality—affects not only the attitude of holders but also that of the workmen and of the public in general. Dematerialized, defunctionalized and absentee ownership does not impress and call forth moral allegiance as the vital form of property did. Eventually there will be *nobody* left who really cares to stand for it—nobody within and nobody without the precincts of the big concerns.

Growing Hostility

THE SOCIAL ATMOSPHERE OF CAPITALISM

* * *

The capitalist process, so we have seen, eventually decreases the importance of the function by which the capitalist class lives. We have also seen that it tends to wear away protective strata, to break down its own defenses, to disperse the garrisons of its entrenchments. And we have finally seen that capitalism creates a critical frame of mind which, after having destroyed the moral authority of so many other institutions, in the end turns against its own; the bourgeois finds to his amazement that the rationalist attitude does not stop at the credentials of kings and popes but goes on to attack private property and the whole scheme of bourgeois values.

The bourgeois fortress thus becomes politically defenseless. . . .

But, so it might well be asked . . . why should the capitalist order need any protection by extra-capitalist powers or extra-rational loyalties? . . . Cannot a perfectly good case be made out for it? . . . .

First, it is an error to believe that political attack arises primarily from grievance and that it can be turned by justification. Political criticism cannot be met effectively by rational argument. From the fact that the criticism of the capitalist order proceeds from a critical attitude of mind, i.e., from an attitude which spurns allegiance to extra-rational values, it does not follow that rational refutation will be accepted. Such refutation may tear the rational garb or attack but can never reach the extra-rational driving power that always lurks behind it. . . .

Second, the success of the indictment becomes quite understandable as soon as we realize what acceptance of the case for capitalism would imply. That case, were it even much stronger than it actually is, could never be made simple. People at large would have to be possessed of an insight and a power of analysis which are altogether beyond them. . . . But even if this is disregarded, rational recognition of the economic performance of capitalism and of the hopes it holds out for the future would require an almost impossible moral feat by the have-not. That performance stands out only if we take a long-run view; any pro-capitalist argument must rest on long-run considerations. In the short run, it is profits and inefficiencies that dominate the picture. In order to accept his lot, the leveler or the chartist of old would have had to comfort himself with hopes for his great-grandchildren. In order to identify himself with the capitalist system, the unemployed of today would have completely to forget his personal fate and the politician of today his personal ambition. The long-run interests of society are so entirely lodged with the upper strata of bourgeois society that it is perfectly natural for people to look upon them as the interests of that class only. For the masses, it is the short-run view that counts. . . .

THE SOCIOLOGY OF THE INTELLECTUAL

Nevertheless, neither the opportunity of attack nor real or fancied grievances are in themselves sufficient to produce, however strongly they may favor, the emergence of active hostility against a social order. For such an atmosphere to develop it is necessary that there be groups to whose interest it is to work up and organize resentment, to nurse it, to voice it and to lead it. The mass of people never develops definite opinions on its own initiative. Still less is it able to articulate them and to turn them into consistent attitudes and actions. All it can do is to follow or refuse to follow such group leadership as may offer itself. . . .

* * *

One of the most important features of the later stages of capitalist civilization is the vigorous expansion of the educational apparatus and particularly of the facilities for higher education. . . . There are several consequences that bear upon the size and attitude of the intellectual group.

First, inasmuch as higher education thus increases the supply of services in professional, quasi-professional and in the end all "white collar" lines beyond the point determined by cost-return considerations, it may create a particularly important case of sectional unemployment.

Second, along with or in place of such unemployment, it creates unsatisfactory conditions of employment—employment in substandard work or at wages below those of the better-paid manual workers.

Third, it may create unemployability of a particularly disconcerting type. The man who has gone through a college or university easily becomes psychically unemployable in manual occupations without necessarily acquiring employability in, say, professional work. . . .

All those who are unemployed or unsatisfactorily employed or unemployable drift into the vocations in which standards are least definite or in which aptitudes and acquirements of a different order count. They swell the host of intellectuals in the strict sense of the term whose numbers hence increase disproportionately. They enter it in a thoroughly discontented frame of mind. Discontent breeds resentment. And it often rationalizes itself into that social criticism which . . . is in any case the intellectual spectator's typical attitude toward men, classes and institutions especially in a rationalist and utilitarian civilization. Well, here we have numbers; a well-defined group situation of proletarian hue; and a group interest shaping a group attitude that will much more realistically account for hostility to the capitalist order than could the theory—itself a rationalization in the psychological sense—according to which the intellectual's righteous indignation about the wrongs of capitalism simply represents the logical inference from outrageous facts and which is no better than the theory of lovers that their feelings represent nothing but the logical inference from the virtues of the beloved. Moreover our theory also accounts for the fact that this hostility increases, instead of diminishing, with every achievement of capitalist evolution.

Of course, the hostility of the intellectual group—amounting to moral disapproval of the capitalist order—is one thing, and the general hostile atmosphere which surrounds the capitalist engine is another thing. The latter is the really significant phenomenon; and it is not simply the product of the former but flows partly from independent sources. . . . The role of the intellectual group consists primarily in stimulating, energizing, verbalizing and organizing. . . .

Capitalist evolution produces a labor movement which obviously is not the creation of the intellectual group. But it is not surprising that such an opportunity and the intellectual . . . should find each other. Labor never craved intellectual leadership but intellectuals invaded labor politics. They had an important contribution to make: they verbalized the movement, supplied theories and slogans for it . . . made it conscious of itself and in doing so changed its meaning. In solving this task from their own standpoint, they naturally radicalized it, eventually imparting a revolutionary bias to the most bourgeois trade-union practices. . . . Thus, though intellectuals have not created the labor movement, they have yet worked it up into something that differs substantially from what it would be without them.

The social atmosphere, for the theory of which we have been gathering stones and mortar, explains why public policy grows more and more hostile to capitalist interests, eventually so much so as to refuse on principle to take account of the requirements of the capitalist engine and to become a serious impediment to its functioning. The intellectual group's activities have however a relation to anti-capitalist policies that is more direct than what is implied in their share in verbalizing them. Intellectuals rarely enter professional politics and still more rarely conquer responsible office. But they staff political bureaus, write party pamphlets and speeches, act as secretaries and advisers, make the individual politician's newspaper reputation which, though it is not everything, few men can afford to neglect. . . . Moreover, in times of rapid expansion of the sphere of public administration, much of the additional personnel required has to be taken directly from the intellectual group—witness this country.

4.6 Joseph A. Schumpeter: A Critical Evaluation

Allen M. Sievers

SCHUMPETER'S CASE

Schumpeter insisted that he was a non-partisan scientist and that his personal wishes must not be confused with his analysis. That he did not welcome the socialist fate which his "science" detected in the future of the West, we can of course accept and can only wonder how any of his readers could possibly have misunderstood that point. On the other hand, it is equally clear that he did have commitments and antipathies. He was emotionally and spiritually dedicated to capitalism of a particularly "unfettered" variety, and he was equally opposed to socialism and its emissaries. His fundamental preoccupation was with freedom for the bearers and protectors of capitalist civilization, the bourgeois and aristocratic elite, and this orientation governs everything he has written. Schumpeter's "scientific" economic analysis must be construed as a rationale or apologia for capitalism, just as his great rival Marx erected a "science" to defend socialism. Indeed, the Schumpeterian system is a conservative capitalist's answer to the threat of the Marxian system. It is both an analytical and a polemical answer, though the polemics may be far too subtle to be effective. By capitalism here is meant Schumpeterian capitalism, which is laissez-faire and dynamic.

THE ANSWER TO MARX AND KEYNES

It should never be forgotten that Schumpeter was fascinated by Marx, and that Marx was both his forerunner and his opponent. It is not too much to say that Schumpeter's *Capitalism* is, first of all, an answer to Marx's *Capital*. Schumpeter borrowed extensively from his rival in the process of defending the merits of capitalism, though he always converted what he took to his own uses. Schumpeter agreed with Marx that society is an organic whole—that it must be understood in terms of process, dynamics, and growth. He also realized that the capitalist economy is somehow at the same time an analogue of a machine, which Schumpeter calls the economic engine. Moreover he concurred that the institutional fabric and the economic engine form an integrated whole.

On one basic issue Schumpeter agreed with Marx up to a point but disagreed with him in a crucial respect. Marx posited a dynamic at work which would inevitably lead to the collapse of capitalism and the emergence of socialism. Schumpeter also believed that there was such a thing as a capitalist dynamic and that it would *probably* eventually lead to socialism. The real dif-

---

Allen M. Sievers, *Revolutions, Evolution, and the Economic Order*, copyright © 1962, pp. 37, 42–43, 46, 50. Reprinted by permission of Prentice-Hall, Inc., Englewood Cliffs, N.J.

ference between them is that Schumpeter somehow conceived his theory as a vindication of capitalism. The eventual death of capitalism, according to Schumpeter, would not be the result of the failure of the capitalist engine —which is still functioning as effectively as it ever did and gives every indication of being able to continue to function at top efficiency. Capitalism would collapse, paradoxically, as a result of its own success. The fatal flaw is not in the economy itself (that is, the capitalist engine), but rather in the ideas and motivations and policies and institutions of the civilization which is a reflex of the economy. These anti-capitalist forces are by-products of the virtues of capitalism, not of its frailties. Like Marx, Schumpeter had a dialectical approach, but his dialectic was concerned with the conflict between benign economic dynamics and disintegrating forces in the supporting structure.

This is an ingenious solution to a difficult intellectual problem and a clever attack on prevailing public policy. Schumpeter was conceding to his socialist opposition that capitalism is doomed and that socialism is its natural heir (though to his allies he pointed out that this is merely a present tendency and that there is no such thing as absolute and irrevocable inevitability). He answered the revisionist Marxists with his own version of amended Marxism. As a moral proposition he defended the integrity of the capitalist process, and he interpreted the coming of socialism as more of an abdication by the capitalists than a victory of the socialists. In pragmatic terms, speaking in quasi-Marxist language, he told the socialists to wait, in their own interest, until the time was ripe. To all groups he gave warning against improper types of government intervention for the sake of smooth development up to the stage at which the socialists would naturally take over. Just as Marx had converted Hegel and the classical economists to his own ends, so Schumpeter attempted to convert Marx to his.

There is considerable aesthetic satisfaction to be derived from contemplating Schumpeter's system, and it is one of those inexplicable matters of the sociology of intellectual movements that Schumpeter's practical impact has been so nugatory. Perhaps his message was ill-timed. Perhaps he was too subtle for his audience. Or perhaps he simply was not convincing. Whatever the reasons, Schumpeter must be counted a failure in the political sense, as contrasted, for example, with his great rival, Lord Keynes.

If Marx was Schumpeter's ostensible and honorable opponent, Keynes was his deadly foe, though perhaps not openly avowed. As for Hansen, he was never referred to by name, although Schumpeter undoubtedly identified him with Keynes. It takes just a little reading between the lines for Schumpeter's hostility towards Keynes to emerge. First, it might be noted that Schumpeter had professional occasion to comment on Keynes the man in two works other than *Capitalism.* In 1946 he wrote an article on Keynes in the *American Economic Review,* which was posthumously published in 1951 in a collection called *Ten Great Economists.* The title was perhaps not of Schumpeter's own choosing. In the foreword his widow and editor saw fit to comment, with great understatement, that Schumpeter and Keynes were never "close." The text of the essay provides reason enough. Schumpeter calls Keynes the "rationalizer of anti-capitalist volition.'' Keynes pulled down the last pillar (admiration for thrift) which supported the capitalist edifice which socialists wanted to destroy. Most damning of all, Schumpeter called Keynes an intellectual ''a little *déraciné*.'' Although ostensibly punctiliously courteous, this essay, in these words, was as devastatingly insulting as Schumpeter could have been. That this judgment of Keynes was quite deliberate is clear from the fact that it was repeated in Schumpeter's monumental *History of Economic Analysis,* where he called Keynes an ''unattached intellectual.'' Remembering what Schumpeter had to say about intellectuals in *Capitalism,* this epithet labels Keynes as irresponsible and as virtually a public enemy. While never actually calling him a socialist, Schumpeter clearly considered him to be the kind of quasi-socialist whose writings have the net effect of abetting the socialist cause.

Schumpeter took issue with Keynes's theory of saving and his view of the consumption function, with his conviction that investment opportunities are vanishing, but above all with his over-all diagnosis of chronic stagnation. Schumpeter held that there is no problem of saving in the Keynesian sense because saving normally follows after a decision to invest. Schumpeter thought it ludicrous that anyone could really believe that there can be a deficiency of consumption.

The essay in the *Ten Great Economists* traces the fundamental stagnationist ''vision'' of Keynes back to Keynes's earlier *Economic Consequences of the Peace* and *A Revision of the Treaty*. What most disturbed Schumpeter was his realization that Keynes's stagnation thesis is two-pronged. It is based on doubts about the internal forces propelling the capitalist economy, as well as the external forces. Schumpeter recognized that Keynes's long-run theory is one of ''*secular* stagnation,'' because it posits an inherent tendency towards the ''stationary'' (stagnation) state. The economic engine itself, sacrosanct to Schumpeter, is to Keynes the cause of capitalist break-down. At the same time, Keynes (and Hansen) thought that the capitalist engine would run out of fuel, and that it no longer has nineteenth-century levels of investment opportunity upon which to feed. Schumpeter and Keynes agree that this deficiency of capitalism is an external factor, but it is one which is based upon objective reality. Schumpeter thought that neither the engine nor the objective milieu in which it operates is tending to weaken. To Schumpeter, the weakness lies in man-made circumstances and in the psychological responses to these conditions. This distinction is of the greatest importance to Schumpeter because of the difference in policy implications between his theory and that of the stagnationists.

These arguments reduce to a single thesis. Given Schumpeter's faith in the adequacy of demand and in the power of entrepreneurs to discover ever new opportunities for investment, it does not really matter whether Keynes and his disciples are right or not about investment outlets. If old opportunities for investment vanish, there will always be new ones. Scientific and technological invention alone, and the innovations which are based upon such invention, can be relied upon to fuel the capitalist engine indefinitely.

Schumpeter at one point criticizes Keynes for having an overly simple model, and perhaps Schumpeter's is pleasingly complex by contrast. There can be no doubt, however, that Schumpeter's complex model centers around a simple process—the entrepreneur making innovations and thus generating the dynamic of creative destruction. Granting the accuracy of this vision, it follows that the system will collapse, should the process ever fail. Since the process depends upon two things—the objective opportunity to innovate and the disposition of entrepreneurs to take advantage of the opportunity—it is enough for one of them to fail. The Keynesians thought that the opportunities for "innovation" have been failing in the twentieth century. Schumpeter thought rather that the motivation of the entrepreneur might be flagging, but not fatally thus far. This simple difference is of profound significance to Schumpeter.

Schumpeter was willing to admit that capitalism will, or at least may, one day stagnate. But it mattered greatly to him to understand truly exactly what does and what does not conduce to stagnation, for in this knowledge is appreciation of the greatness of capitalism and discovery of the road to redemption. To Schumpeter the prime consideration was that the tendency towards stagnation is at this moment in history the result of a failure of nerve, a failure of entrepreneurial motivation and energy. The capitalist engine remains intact and will continue to perform as well in the future as in the past. Schumpeter did quietly admit, however, that the very dynamic of capitalism is producing a change in the institutional sector which must in any case eventually spell stagnation for the engine. Progress or success will eventually produce stagnation, but if properly understood, the evil day can be long postponed. Even when stagnation finally occurs, it will be the fault not of the capitalist engine itself but of the institutional complex which will stultify the human driving power behind the engine. The difference between the Schumpeterian and the Keynesian concept of stagnation makes for diametrically opposite programs. Keynes's stagnation calls for government intervention. Schumpeter's views call for an abandonment of all government actions which might inhibit profits.

Schumpeter's case appears to be weak on two grounds. One is the inadequacy of his response to the stagnationists. If some historical outlets for investment are in fact closing down, it would seem to be a legitimate question whether the remaining outlets will be adequate to take up the slack. For example, there is real meaning in the question of whether capitalism could have ever gotten started if Europe had been the only habitable part of the globe. The discovery of America and commerce with the East certainly provided a stimulus for which it is difficult to conceive a substitute. The second half of this argument is that it is as much blind faith to assume that science and technology will be endlessly fruitful as it is wishful thinking to "hope" (in Schumpeter's language) that investment opportunities will fail. It is just as unscientific to project a continually rising curve of invention into the future as it is to project a falling curve. Schumpeter argued that because we have no reason to project the latter we may continue to project the former. In the absence of knowledge there is nothing left but ignorance.

As a matter of fact, the state of knowledge on this subject is somewhat better than Schumpeter indicated. It is possible to forecast upon the basis of present scientific developments what further developments may be expected along the same lines. For this reason there is some basis for optimism. On the other hand, it is much more difficult to predict discoveries in the field of pure science. The actual technological dividend from the scientific progress of the depression and war years has probably been less than might reasonably have been expected, except in fields which have no relation to consumer demand. Military technology, space technology, and even cost-saving technology in industry have made measurable progress. But there have been no really major break-throughs in the form of new industries based upon new inventions, comparable to those series of technological revolutions which began in the 1870's and continued up to the Great Depression. Television is perhaps the most conspicuous new industry but it was clearly "in the works" in the 1930's. It may be that we are in ignorance of a backlog of new industries which have been similarly in the works in recent decades, but there can be no doubt that promising scientific developments have not yielded their promise. Practical industrial uses of atomic energy is an example of a major disappointment thus far.

On a priori grounds it might further be argued—science fantasy aside—that there is a limit to the major ways in which technological novelty might improve human existence. Mechanics, electricity, electromagnetic waves, chemistry, and even biochemistry have all been put to economic use. Problems of rapid transportation, cheap food for an urban population, cheap textiles of high quality, artificial light, wife-saving appliances in the home, and devices for centralized production and mass distribution of the entertainment arts have all been reasonably solved. It would be foolish to say that improvements and preferable variations will not be forthcoming, but surely new directions seem less likely. It is always possible that some unknown force of nature remains to be exploited (telepathy by brain waves, for instance), but the known forces have been put to work for man in a way that might have been predicted ahead of time and now can no longer be predicted. After almost two centuries of this kind of progress, the advent of new industries, creating major shifts in living patterns or displacing major existing industries, can no longer be assumed to be inevitable. As the prophecy of technological progress was once a bold hypothesis justified by events, current evidence today justifies the equally bold hypothesis that future technology will be limited to less revolutionary changes.

Taking such a strong negative outlook is not necessary to question the logical grounds for Schumpeter's boundless faith in innovation. It is enough that there is no basis for a favorable prognosis. The second fundamental weakness in Schumpeter's position is the insistence that his kind of stagnation implies the robust health of the business process itself, whereas the Keynesian thesis challenges, as does Marxism, the innate power of the capitalist engine. The question is not whether Keynes and Hansen distrust the laissez-faire capitalist system—which they *do*—but whether the careful distinction Schumpeter tried to make can be logically upheld. Is it possible, consistent with Schumpeter's strong avowal of the organic approach, to make the kind of inner-outer distinction he posits?

The key to this distinction is the entrepreneur. The innovating activity of the entrepreneur, according to Schumpeter, is a part of the business process. His innovations constitute the very quintessence of capitalist dynamics. But at the same time the opportunity to innovate comes from outside, as does the motivation of the entrepreneur. It would seem clear that the definition of the capitalist process as the sum of all market behavior is not self-subsistent. If inventions should fail, the capitalist dynamic would come to a halt. Thus an external element is necessary to the process, and the process alone is not enough to guarantee progress. This is why Schumpeter had to insist that the force of invention, an inexhaustible fuel for the capitalist engine, is perennially given. It is not part of the engine, but since it is always there, the engine, *ceteris paribus,* is a perpetual motion machine. The metaphysical question of whether or not the fuel is logically part of the engine is not worth arguing about, perhaps, but it is certain that capitalism fails if the fuel fails. If the stagnationists should be right about the tendency to exhaust investment opportunities, this would be an indictment of laissez-faire capitalism itself. For it is the economic organization of the society which has failed. Presumably other forms of organization could function even if the opportunities for profitable investment do not exist.

Schumpeter's expectation of stagnation is based upon the weakening of the capitalist institutional framework or what Marx calls the superstructure. To Marx the superstructure merely acts out on its own level the dialectic drama of the capitalist mode of production; there is no independent causality. Schumpeter intended to divorce the productive from the institutional sectors. In an evolving capitalist society, the institutional framework must change, and this change in turn acts back upon the engine. Human discretion, however, has an independent role to play on the institutional level. Capitalists, for example, may or may not succumb to the propaganda which enervates their profit-making motivation and they may or may not acquiesce in the policy of the state which inhibits their profit-making potential. Other sections of society likewise may or may not support attitudes and policies which undermine the conditions for free operation of the capitalist engine. If capitalism fails, it will be because of the smothering of the engine and not because of its wearing out.

This position as an abstraction may or may not be logically tenable. But the assumption that New Deal policies were as a matter of historical fact adopted out of malevolence towards capitalism is highly questionable. The cogent argument of Karl Polanyi in *The Great Transformation* would seem to support the Keynesian position on this point rather than the Schumpeterian, while avoiding the trap of Marxist determinism. Polanyi's argument is simply that the process of laissez-faire capitalism must be understood in terms of the dynamic of an institutional complex, and that this particular dynamic inevitably led to collapse. The automaticity of the market evoked counter forces of self-protection throughout the society, which in time destroyed automaticity. This necessity was not a function of the deterministic nature of some Marxian demiurgos but simply the consequence of its own special logic. That is, a market system of the pre-1933 variety was inherently non-viable, and its fate was sealed from its inception. Not capitalism in itself but laissez-faire capitalism of necessity destroyed itself. Consequently the New Deal is to be understood as a spontaneous social response to the needs of society. It is not necessary in Polanyi's theory to distinguish the engine from the capitalist institutions, for they interact and the total action is what is significant. Laissez-faire capitalism was the system as a whole, and it is this whole system which had its own dynamic and which collapsed. Leaving Polanyi aside, there is little reason not to take Keynes and Hansen and Harrod and others at face value when they said that they sought to save capitalism by reforming it. Moreover, the American people in supporting the reforms of the New Deal were not coerced or seduced but pressured by economic reality. Though Schumpeter had faith that the Great Depression would cure itself, most people did not. Perhaps most significant of all, the subsequent political history of the United States has not revealed any great disposition or any genuine power to restore laissez faire. The country turned to a Republican administration in due time; but though this administration may be said, in contrast to the previous Democratic administrations, to have embraced the business community and to have been duly requited, the objective evidence would indicate that institutional changes towards any sort of counter-reform were minimal.

For all this, it is possible that Schumpeter was right. Economics is clearly not in a position to prove any one interpretation definitive. It is also clear that Schumpeter's apology for laissez-faire capitalism was urbane, rational, and humane. It was just not polemically effective. Since it is impossible to experiment with history, the Schumpeterian alternative must remain a theoretical model as against the reality of the non-laissez-faire world.

SCHUMPETER, CONTEMPORARY ECONOMIC THOUGHT, AND PUBLIC POLICY

Schumpeter's apparent determinism mitigated against drawing positive proposals for public policy. However, beneath the rhetoric and paradoxes, the implications for public policy are clear. First, the major dynamic benefits from capitalist development do not accrue from atomistic competition, but from large-scale oligopolistic corporations. Thus, corporations must not be dismantled just because they are large. This rationale for big business has become an essential ingredient in the economic philosophy of managerial capitalism, and it has helped provide a reformulation of the theory of antitrust policy focusing upon (oligopolistically) competitive economic performance rather than (atomistically) competitive economic structure.

Second, Schumpeter implied, don't kill the goose that lays the golden eggs. If it is believed to be necessary to extend government activity in economic life, do so in ways that sustain opportunities for at least occasional large-scale business profits, intervene as little as possible in entrepreneurial decisions, and minimize antagonism and maximize cooperation between business and government. It is not sufficient that government policy work through the market system; it is also necessary that the prerogatives and privileges of capitalist industrialists be disturbed as little as possible. This too has become a strategic ingredient in conservative Keynesianism, and thereby in the post-Keynesian synthesis itself. In some measure at least, the post-Keynesian consensus has attempted to avoid the trauma of the Schumpeterian predictions by incorporating some of the insights of his critique. Indeed, growing criticism of the post-Keynesian synthesis from the Left (chapter 7) has arisen in part from the very symbiosis of big business and big government, and from the perceived capture of the apparatus of government by large-scale corporations. In the view of liberal social reformers and socialist critics, the post-Keynesian synthesis has absorbed too much from the Schumpeterian lessons.

In closing, it should be noted that Schumpeter's analysis has linkages with other theories of dissent from the post-Keynesian synthesis. Schumpeter's spirited defense of an old-style, more-or-less laissez-faire economic individualism makes common bond with the individualist-conservatives (chapter 6). Schumpeter's heavy intellectual debt to Marx and his essentially Marxist methodology, outlook, and vision, have made him well-read and highly respected among the Marxist Left (chapter 7). And Schumpeter's defense of large corporations as the vehicles of economic development and technological progress is carried forth by John Kenneth Galbraith, to whose ideas we now turn.

5 JOHN KENNETH GALBRAITH: POWER, AFFLUENCE, AND THE NEW INDUSTRIAL STATE

The economic ideas of John Kenneth Galbraith—Harvard economics professor, author of numerous best-sellers, former ambassador to India, past president of the American Economic Association, former chairman of the Americans for Democratic Action, adviser to prominent political leaders—are not subject to neat classification in terms of the post-Keynesian synthesis. On numerous issues (for example, government expenditures versus tax cuts, the social imbalance between private and public sectors of the economy), Galbraith's positions lie clearly in the liberal wing. Some of his ideas (notably the concept of countervailing power and the defense of big business), are, by contrast, akin to the philosophy of managerial capitalism and readily adaptable as an integral ingredient in the synthesis' conservative strand. Largely, however, Galbraith has stood apart from the Keynesian consensus in economic thought and policy while providing a prominent critique of the organization and functioning of contemporary American capitalism—a sort of dissenting tradition from the Center. It should be noted that Galbraith's dissent from mainstream economics is as often methodological as it is substantive. He is critical of some of the underlying assumptions of mainstream economics (for example, the worth of competition), and wants to extend the boundaries of the discipline by asking questions about the changing structure and functioning of the capitalist system as a whole.

COUNTERVAILING POWER

Galbraith has written four main critical works directly germane to our discussion: *American Capitalism: The Concept of Countervailing Power* (1952); *The Affluent Society* (1958); *The New Industrial State* (1967); and *Economics and the Public Purpose* (1973). The central issue of *American Capitalism* is economic power. The classic case for decentralized private economic decision making, Galbraith suggests, rested on the theory of competition. Traditionally, competition was perceived as a (self-) regulatory mechanism within the capitalist economy; private economic power was to be restrained through the existence of (a large number of) competitors on the *same* side of the market. But the growth of oligopoly and the concentration of private economic power has eroded faith in the competitive market place as a regulatory and coordinative process. The result, in popular discussion and to some extent within the economics profession, has been a pronounced ambivalence. We extoll the dynamic efficiency and technological progressiveness of large oligopolistic corporations, but we view with alarm the presumed disappearance of effective restraints on corporate power.

In practice, Galbraith contends, a new regulatory process (with occasional government assistance) has emerged within the private sector of the economy. Despite, and in part because of, the prevalence of large-scale corporations and the concentration of economic power, "countervailing" power blocs have arisen. In brief, Galbraith's theory states that "original" power on one side of the market encourages the emergence of opposing or "countervailing" power on the opposite side—partly as a means of self-protection, partly from the lure of a share in monopoly-monopsony profits. Three prominent examples of groups that have acquired countervailing power (and the means they have used) are: labor unions (collective bargaining, pressures for favorable labor legislation), large retail chain stores (who have bargained for lower prices from manufacturers and, prodded by competition in retailing, have to some extent passed on these gains to consumers), and farm organizations (cooperatives for marketing farm products, political pressures to establish agricultural price supports).

According to Galbraith, countervailing power may decrease and on occasion has decreased the exploitation of consumers and workers by corporations. Insofar as this is true, countervailing power de facto approaches the results of competitive markets. But a second, and more persuasive, case for countervailing power lies in its contributions to improving the positions of repressed groups, for example, workers and farmers, and thereby alleviating social tensions.

Galbraith notes certain exceptions and limitations to the functioning of countervailing power. First, it has not arisen in certain important areas (for example, housing construction, where builders have not developed countervailing power against suppliers and unions). Second, it requires some minimum of opportunity and capacity for organization. Third, it tends to break down in periods of inflation, at least in certain respects; excess demand combined with market power enables large firms to increase prices (especially when under the pressure of rising wages negotiated through the countervailing power of unions), but protection for the general public ceases to exist. As already noted, Galbraith suggests that countervailing power is in many instances a self-generated force. Where it is not, and where its creation would yield important social benefits, government should make its promotion an objective of public policy. In formulating public policy, a distinction should be made between original and countervailing power. A good case can be made, Galbraith argues, for decreasing original power (for example, through antitrust action) if countervailing power does not arise to offset it. But because (1) past efforts at reducing market power have not been very successful, (2) oligopolistic corporations, though wielders of economic power, have often been characterized by efficient and progressive performance, and (3) there are positive advantages to countervailing power insofar as it alleviates social tensions, a good case can be made also for promoting countervailing power as a means of creating a balance.

In practice, notes Galbraith, government policy has done some of each. In instances where the number of sellers is small, and their absolute and relative size is large (for example, manufacturing industry), government policy has striven (though not always consistently or vigorously) to reduce market power. But in instances where the number of sellers is large, and their absolute and relative power is small (for example, labor, agriculture), government action, especially from the New Deal onward, has attempted to increase countervailing power.

Selection 5.1 provides an exposition of the basic model, excerpted from *American Capitalism*. Selection 5.2 is a critical evaluation by Walter Adams, prominent and uncompromising advocate of "effective competition."

5.1 Countervailing Power: Exposition

John K. Galbraith

. . . . With the widespread disappearance of competition in its classical form and its replacement by the small group of firms if not in overt, at least in conventional or tacit collusion, it was easy to suppose that since competition had disappeared, all effective restraint on private power had disappeared.

In fact, new restraints on private power did appear to replace competition. They were nurtured by the same process of concentration which impaired or destroyed competition. But they appeared not on the same side of the market but on the opposite side, not with competitors but with customers or suppliers. It will be convenient to have a name for this counterpart of competition and I shall call it *countervailing power*.

To begin with a broad and somewhat too dogmatically stated proposition, private economic power is held in check by the countervailing power of those who are subject to it. The first begets the second. The long trend toward concentration of industrial enterprise in the hands of a relatively few firms has brought into existence not only strong sellers, as economists have supposed, but also strong buyers as they have failed to see. The two develop together, not in precise step but in such manner that there can be no doubt that the one is in response to the other.

The fact that a seller enjoys a measure of monopoly power, and is reaping a measure of monopoly return as a result, means that there is an inducement to

Excerpted from John K. Galbraith, *American Capitalism*, pp. 111–12, 114–23, 137–38, 147–48.

those firms from whom he buys or those to whom he sells to develop the power with which they can defend themselves against exploitation. It means also that there is a reward to them, in the form of a share of the gains of their opponents' market power, if they are able to do so. In this way the existence of market power creates an incentive to the organization of another position of power that neutralizes it.

The contention I am here making is a formidable one. It comes to this: Competition which, at least since the time of Adam Smith, has been viewed as the autonomous regulator of economic activity and as the only available regulatory mechanism apart from the state, has, in fact, been superseded. Not entirely, to be sure. I should like to be explicit on this point. Competition still plays a role. There are still important markets where the power of the firm as (say) a seller is checked or circumscribed by those who provide a similar or a substitute product or service. . . . However, this is not the only or even the typical restraint on the exercise of economic power. In the typical modern market of few sellers, the active restraint is provided not by competitors but from the other side of the market by strong buyers. . . .

It was always one of the basic presuppositions of competition that market power exercised in its absence would invite the competitors who would eliminate such exercise of power. The profits of a monopoly position inspired competitors to try for a share. In other words competition was regarded as a *self-generating* regulatory force. The doubt whether this was in fact so after a market had been pre-empted by a few large sellers, after entry of new firms had become difficult and after existing firms had accepted a convention against price competition, was what destroyed the faith in competition as a regulatory mechanism. Countervailing power is also a self-generating force and this is a matter of great importance. Something, although not very much, could be claimed for the regulatory role of the strong buyer in relation to the market power of sellers, did it happen that, as an accident of economic development, such strong buyers were frequently juxtaposed to strong sellers. However the tendency of power to be organized in response to a given position of power is the vital characteristic of the phenomenon I am here identifying. As noted, power on one side of a market creates both the need for, and the prospect of reward to, the exercise of countervailing power from the other side. This means that, as a common rule, we can rely on countervailing power to appear as a curb on economic power. There are also, it should be added, circumstances in which it does not appear or is effectively prevented from appearing. . . . For some reason, critics of the theory have seized with particular avidity on these exceptions to deny the existence of the phenomenon itself. It is plain that by a similar line of argument one could deny the existence of competition by finding one monopoly.

* * *

ILLUSTRATIONS

The operation of countervailing power is to be seen with the greatest clarity in the labor market where it is also most fully developed. Because of his comparative immobility, the individual worker has long been highly vulnerable to private economic power. The customer of any particular steel mill, at the turn of the century, could always take himself elsewhere if he felt he was being overcharged. Or he could exercise his sovereign privilege of not buying steel at all. The worker had no comparable freedom if he felt he was being underpaid. Normally he could not move and he had to have work. Not often has the power of one man over another been used more callously than in the American labor market after the rise of the large corporation. As late as the early twenties, the steel industry worked a twelve-hour day and seventy-two-hour week with an incredible twenty-four-hour stint every fortnight when the shift changed.

No such power is exercised today and for the reason that its earlier exercise stimulated the counteraction that brought it to an end. In the ultimate sense it was the power of the steel industry, not the organizing abilities of John L. Lewis and Philip Murray, that brought the United Steel Workers into being. The economic power that the worker faced in the sale of his labor—the competition of many sellers dealing with few buyers—made it necessary that he organize for his own protection. There were rewards to the power of the steel companies in which, when he had successfully developed countervailing power, he could share. . . .

By contrast there is not a single union of any consequence in American agriculture, the country's closest approach to the competitive model. The reason lies not in the difficulties in organization; these are considerable, but greater difficulties in organization have been overcome. The reason is that the farmer has not possessed any power over his labor force, and at least until recent times has not had any rewards from market power which it was worth the while of a union to seek. As an interesting verification of the point, in the Great Valley of California, the large farmers of that area have had considerable power vis-á-vis their labor force. Almost uniquely in the United States, that region has been marked by persistent attempts at organization by farm workers.

Elsewhere in industries which approach the competition of the model one typically finds weaker or less comprehensive unions. The textile industry, boot and shoe manufacture, lumbering and other forest industries in most parts of the country, and smaller wholesale and retail enterprises, are all cases in point. I do not, of course, advance the theory of countervailing power as a monolithic explanation of trade-union organization. No such complex social phenomenon is likely to have any single, simple explanation. . . . Nevertheless, as an explanation of the incidence of trade-union strength in the American economy, the theory of countervailing power clearly fits the broad contours of experience. There is, I venture, no other so satisfactory explanation of the great dynamic of labor organization in modern capitalism. . . .

The labor market serves admirably to illustrate the incentives to the development of countervailing power and it is of great importance in this market. However, its development, in response to positions of market power, is pervasive in the economy. As a regulatory device one of its most important manifestations is in the relation of the large retailer to the firms from which it buys.

The way in which countervailing power operates in these markets is worth examining in some detail.

One of the seemingly harmless simplifications of formal economic theory has been the assumption that producers of consumers' goods sell their products directly to consumers. . . . In fact goods pass to consumers by way of retailers and other intermediaries and this is a circumstance of first importance. Retailers are required by their situation to develop countervailing power on the consumer's behalf.

. . . Retailing remains one of the industries to which entry is characteristically free. It takes small capital and no very rare talent to set up as a seller of goods. Through history there have always been an ample supply of men with both and with access to something to sell. The small man can provide convenience and intimacy of service and can give an attention to detail, all of which allow him to co-exist with larger competitors.

The advantage of the larger competitor ordinarily lies in its lower prices. It lives constantly under the threat of an erosion of its business by the more rapid growth of rivals and by the appearance of new firms. This loss of volume, in turn, destroys the chance for the lower costs and lower prices on which the firm depends. This means that the larger retailer is extraordinarily sensitive to higher prices by its suppliers. It means also that it is strongly rewarded if it can develop the market power which permits it to force lower prices.

* * *

Countervailing power in the retail business is identified with the large and powerful retail enterprises. Its practical manifestation, over the last half-century, has been the rise of the food chains, the variety chains, the mail-order houses (now graduated into chain stores), the department-store chains, and the co-operative buying organizations of the surviving independent department and food stores.

This development was the countervailing response to previously established positions of power. The gains from invading these positions have been considerable and in some instances even spectacular.

* * *

At the end of virtually every channel by which consumers' goods reach the public there is, in practice, a layer of powerful buyers. . . .

The buyers of all these firms deal directly with the manufacturer and there are few of the latter who, in setting prices, do not have to reckon with the attitude and reaction of their powerful customers. The retail buyers have a variety of weapons at their disposal to use against the market power of their suppliers. Their ultimate sanction is to develop their own source of supply as the food chains, Sears, Roebuck and Montgomery Ward have extensively done. They can also concentrate their entire patronage on a single supplier and, in return for a lower price, give him security in his volume and relieve him of selling and advertising costs. This policy has been widely followed and there have also been numerous complaints of the leverage it gives the retailer on his source.

* * *

When the comprehensive representation of large retailers in the various fields of consumers' goods distribution is considered, it is reasonable to conclude—the reader is warned that this is an important generalization—that most positions of market power in the production of consumers' goods are covered by positions of countervailing power. As noted, there are exceptions and, as between markets, countervailing power is exercised with varying strength and effectiveness. The existence of exceptions does not impair the significance of the regulatory phenomenon here described. To its devotees the virtues of competition were great but few if any ever held its reign to be universal.

Countervailing power also manifests itself, although less visibly, in producers' goods markets. . . . The more normal operation of countervailing power in producers' goods markets has, as its point of departure, the relatively small number of customers which firms in these industries typically have. Where the cigarette or soap manufacturer numbers his retail outlets by the hundreds of thousands and his final consumers by the millions, the machinery or equipment manufacturer counts his customers by the hundreds or thousands and, very often, his important ones by the dozen. But here, as elsewhere, the market pays a premium to those who develop power as buyers that is equivalent to the market power of those from whom they buy. The reverse is true where weak sellers do business with strong buyers.

* * *

GOVERNMENT POLICY

The role of countervailing power in the economy marks out two broad problems in policy for the government. In all but conditions of inflationary demand, countervailing power performs a valuable—indeed an indispensable—regulatory function in the modern economy. Accordingly it is incumbent upon government to give it freedom to develop and to determine how it may best do so. The government also faces the question of where and how it will affirmatively support the development of countervailing power. It will be convenient to look first at the negative role of the government in allowing the development of countervailing power and then to consider its affirmative role in promoting it.

At the outset a somewhat general distinction must be made between countervailing and original power. When, anywhere in the course of producing, processing or distributing a particular product, one or a few firms first succeed in establishing a strong market position they may be considered to be the possessors of original market power. They are able, as the result of their power over the prices they pay or charge, to obtain more than normal margins and profits. . . .

The rule to be followed by government is, in principle, a clear one. There can be a very good reason for attacking positions of original market power in the economy if these are not effectively offset by countervailing power. There is at least a theoretical justification for opposing all positions of market power. There is no justification for attacking positions of countervailing power which leaves positions of original market power untouched. On the contrary, damage both in equity and to the most efficient operation of the economy will be the normal consequence of doing so.

* * *

A number who have accepted as desirable the development of countervailing power by previously disadvantaged groups have been nonetheless careful to point out that it is decidedly a second-best solution. Given the power of the modern industrial corporation, it is doubtless well that those who do business with it have the capacity to protect themselves. But how much better to have avoided this struggle between the behemoths. There is something frightening and possibly dangerous about this bargaining between vast aggregations. How much better to have denied power to all. The world of countervailing power may be tolerable but it is highly imperfect.

This is an appealing argument although it is not likely to appeal to anyone who is interested in results. Past efforts to extirpate economic power have been notably unavailing. One cannot suppose that they will be more successful in the future. Economic power may indeed be inherent in successful capitalism. We had better be content with restraints we have than to search for a never-never land in which they would be rendered unnecessary.

Finally, there has been special concern over the role which government has played in the development of countervailing power. As noted, farmers, workers and numerous other groups have sought and received government assistance, either in the form of direct support to their market power or in support to organization which in turn made market power possible. In short, the government has subsidized with its own power the countervailing power of workers, farmers and others. . . . This assistance, clearly, explains some part of the self-confidence and well-being which these groups display today.

* * *

We can now see that a large part of the state's new activity—the farm legislation, labor legislation, minimum-wage legislation—is associated with the development of countervailing power. As such it is neither adventitious nor abnormal; the government action supports or supplements a normal economic process. Steps to strengthen countervailing power are not, in principle, different from steps to strengthen competition. Given the existence of private market power in the economy, the growth of countervailing power strengthens the capacity of the economy for autonomous self-regulation and thereby lessens the amount of over-all government control or planning that is required or sought.

5.2 Countervailing Power: Critique

Walter A. Adams

Professor J. K. Galbraith—in an attempt to explain not just the workability of specific industries but of the whole economy—theorized that the American economy can perform quite brilliantly in spite of the widespread prevalence of industrial oligopoly.

The following discussion will be concerned with an examination of the countervailing power thesis in terms of its practical as well as theoretical applicability. Without attempting to discredit the fundamental plausibility and attractiveness of the thesis, we shall point to some of its limitations: (1) countervailing power is often undermined by vertical integration and top-level financial control; (2) bilateral monopolies created through the process of countervailance are not a happy solution of the economic power problem; (3) the countervailing influence of technological and inter-industry competition is not a meaningful substitute for competition in the neoclassical sense; (4) countervailance through government action is often subverted by unduly intimate affiliation between regulator and regulatee; and (5) the whole thesis rests on the dubious assumption that giant sized firms are the inevitable result of twentieth century technology and economics. These are the points which will now be discussed.

TOP-LEVEL FINANCIAL CONTROL AND VERTICAL INTEGRATION

According to Galbraith, the existence of concentrated power on one side of the market will eventually give rise to countervailing power on the other side of the market. Powerful sellers will cause the growth of powerful buyers and vice versa. As a result, the concentration of the steel barons will be offset by similar concentration among their automobile manufacturing customers, thus precluding, or at least reducing, the likelihood of monopolistic exploitation.

This argument leaves out of account the possibility of undermining and subverting the effectiveness of countervailing power as a regulatory mechanism. This objective can be accomplished by the co-ordination and centralization of both the buyer's and the seller's business policy within a single decision-making unit. It can be achieved through the common techniques of top-level financial control and vertical integration. Countervailing power can be exercised only so long as the forces on opposite sides of the market engage in arm's length bargaining, only so long as they are controlled by separate and financially independent decision-making units. Once we admit, however, the

Excerpted from Walter A. Adams, "Competition, Monopoly, and Countervailing Power," *Quarterly Journal of Economics,* November 1953. Reprinted by permission of the publisher.

existence of economic interest groupings and giant vertical integrations, the opposing sides of the market are blended into one and any potential countervailance is automatically vitiated.

BILATERAL MONOPOLY AND COUNTERVAILING POWER

As was pointed out above, countervailing power operates primarily through the creation of bilateral monopoly and/or oligopoly situations. A monopoly on one side of the market finds its power neutralized by the appearance of a monopoly on the other side of the market. There thus develops a system of checks and balances, built on the foundation of bilateral power concentrations.

The labor market is cited as an area where this process can be observed with the greatest clarity, for it is in the labor market that giant unions bargain on a national, industry-wide scale against groups of employers acting jointly either through a trade association or an informal ad hoc bargaining committee.

Bilateral monopoly in the labor market is thus justified on the grounds that it prevents unilateral exploitation, while simultaneously allowing one monopolist to share in whatever exorbitant gains may accrue to the other.

The fly in this ointment is self-evident, viz., that unions and management—without necessarily conspiring—can jointly exploit the consumer. This is true especially in times of inflation when employers may grant wage increases with relative impunity, and then pass their higher costs on to the consumer in the form of higher prices. These higher prices thereupon become the basis for new wage demands, and the inflationary spiral is sent on another merry spin. The bilateral monopoly of union and management fuels the engine for accelerating and perpetuating inflation.

TECHNOLOGICAL AND INTER-INDUSTRY COMPETITION

The advocates of the countervailing power thesis maintain that competition in the neoclassical sense, i.e., competition among sellers and among buyers within a particular industry, is outmoded. Their argument runs somewhat as follows. Old-fashioned intra-industry competition tends to promote maximum output, minimum prices, and optimum utilization of capacity; in short, it stimulates efficiency. But this efficiency is static and unprogressive in character. It makes no allowance for the research, development, and innovation required for economic growth. While it prevents concentration, it stifles progress. To have progress, we need more, not less concentration. Only bigness can provide the sizable funds necessary for technological experimentation and innovation in the industrial milieu of the twentieth century. Only monopoly earnings can provide the bait that lures capital on to untried trails. While progress may thus require high power concentration in many industries, this need not be a source of concern to society at large. Technological development will serve as an offset against any short-run position of entrenchment which may be established. The monopoly of glass bottles will be countervailed by the introduction of the tin can; and the dominance of the latter will in turn be undermined by the introduction of the paper container. The consumer need not rely, therefore, on the static competition between large numbers of small firms as protection against exploitation. In the long run, he can find far greater safety—and better things for better living, to boot—in the technological competition of a small number of large firms, which through research and innovation eventually destroy any position of market control that may be established.

There are two basic flaws in this argument. The first is that history seems to contradict it.

It must always be remembered that the phenomenal performance of American capitalism over the last hundred years may have been achieved not primarily because of the behavior of well entrenched large-scale firms, but "because there was still enough virility left in the competitive process to permit innovations and the breaking into established fields to go on." Certainly we would be guilty of the *post hoc ergo propter hoc* fallacy were we to argue that since monopolization accompanied the long-run growth of output, it also was its cause. Certainly, the European experience with the restrictionism of monopoly capitalism should give us pause before society places exclusive reliance on the countervailing influence of technological competition as a protective device against exploitation, inefficiency, and monopolistic retrogression.

There is another flaw in the argument that inter-industry, product, or technological competition is an effective offset against entrenchment or market domination in any one industry. The facts are that when the paper container began to threaten the tin can duopoly, Continental Can entered the paper container industry; when magnesium threatened the aluminum monopoly, Alcoa started its participation in the magnesium cartel; when aluminum began to be used as a substitute for copper, Anaconda embarked on its venture in the aluminum industry.

It would seem too much to expect full, vigorous and unrestricted competition between different parts of the same company when the obvious result of such activity would rebound to the disadvantage and loss of the company's total operations. Truly, the Brandeis maxim that "one cannot be expected to compete against one's self" is as applicable today as it was forty years ago. Inter-industry competition and technological innovation become a farce when public policy permits them to be subverted by merger and combination. Yet that is exactly what has been happening recently to an increasing extent. That is exactly why the argument of the countervailing power advocates is unconvincing if not outright erroneous.

THE ROLE OF GOVERNMENT

According to its exponents, countervailing power does not always arise autonomously. Indeed, in some cases, its development may require positive promotion by government action. Galbraith looks upon this promotive activity as the main peacetime function of the federal government and applauds, for example, the enactment of New Deal measures designed to give a group market power it did not previously possess. As a rule of thumb, Galbraith simply suggests that the government "attack positions of original market power in the economy if these are not effectively offset by countervailing power." He regards such action as neither adventitious nor abnormal, since its purpose is merely to support a "natural" economic process. Given the existence of private market power, Galbraith considers governmental countervailance a desirable technique for strengthening the "capacity of the economy for autonomous self-regulation," and deems it an indirect method for lessening the "amount of over-all government control or planning that is (eventually) required or sought." So, at least, the countervailing power doctrine would have us believe.

This thesis rests on the doubtful assumption that there is a sharp dichotomy between the economy, on the one hand, and government, on the other. It assumes that government is an autonomous, monolithic, and self-contained organism. This view is, unfortunately, an intellectual amusement of the past. It ignores the fact that economic interest groups are today largely politicized units, making their claims upon and through the institutions of the state.

Legislation

In the legislative consideration of many economic measures, the absence of countervailing power is painfully apparent.

There is little doubt that particularistic, politically vocal, economic pressure groups can use the legislative process for their own advantage. They can demand, and often obtain, governmental aid in countervailing the power of entrenched interests. This does not mean, however, that the form of this countervailance will redound to the general welfare as it does to a narrowly-defined private welfare. Nor does it mean, that the basic problems underlying the demand for governmental countervailance will thereby be solved.

In short, the countervailing action expected of government tends more often than not merely to be an appeasement of special interest pressures. Legislation designed to countervail the power of "economic royalists" is not the product of an independent governmental unit functioning in a vacuum, but the result of a log-rolling process involving compromise with, adjustment to, and appeasement of a variety of special interest claims. Everybody who is somebody seems to get what he wants; only the sum total of these wants is not always equivalent to the needs and desires of the community as a whole.

Regulation

The independent regulatory commissions are a second example of how difficult it is to achieve countervailing power through governmental action. The Interstate Commerce Commission is a case in point. This Commission, created to protect the public from the abuses of a highly concentrated power group, today seems mainly to protect the railroads against effective regulation by the public.

While it defends the railroads from encroachment by rival means of transportation, the Commission also serves as an effective lobby on behalf of railroad interests.

SIZE, TECHNOLOGY AND EFFICIENCY

The final limitation of the countervailing power thesis is inherent in its basic assumption, viz., that the giant size of America's dominant enterprises is the inevitable result of twentieth century technology and economics.

This explanation of the concentration process is the cornerstone of the whole countervailing power theory. If it is valid, then antitrust litigation is obviously outmoded, and countervailing power becomes *one*—if not *the*—method of dealing with huge economic power aggregates. If the explanation is inadequate, however, other public policy alternatives may become more desirable.

We must examine, therefore, the crucial assumption of the Galbraith thesis, viz., that firms are big because they are efficient; that firms are big because consumers want them to be big; that bigness is little more than the natural result of modern technological and economic forces.

The data on the relation between size and efficiency are by no means conclusive; efficiency is not always the concomitant of giant size; in aluminum and steel, for example, the largest firms are neither great technical innovators nor paragons of efficient operation.

The record of antitrust prosecutions is replete with cases which demonstrate that industrial pre-eminence is often achieved as much by resort to coercive practices as by "natural" growth processes.

Many cases could be cited to show that competition often dies from other than natural causes, while those responsible for its euthanasia advertise themselves as victors in an unfettered Darwinian struggle. There is evidence that at times the survival of the fittest is promoted, not alone through a process of natural selection, but with the helping hand of a benevolent authority. Government supported research activity is a case in point.

An examination of the allocations and priority system, the accelerated amortization program, the disposal of war surplus establishments, the structure of business taxes reveals the same pattern of promoting concentration—at times through unconscious, at times through deliberate action by the most powerful economic unit in the world. The net effect is that established giants remain dominant while the competition of newcomers is effectively handicapped.

CONCLUSION

In conclusion, we can say that the countervailing power thesis is not without merit; that it rightly calls attention to the existence of potential checks and balances which, in our economy, supplement competition as a device for counteracting concentrated economic power. This does not mean, however, that countervailing power is a suitable substitute for competition; or that it can long survive in the absence of competition; or that it affords any clear and administratively feasible guidelines for public policy.

Some measure of countervailing power is obviously ubiquitous. It exists in a socialist state where the steel monopoly countervails the aluminum monopoly and where the trades union congress offsets the power of the central industry planning board. It is present, to some degree, in a fascist corporate state as well as in a sovietized society. This hardly affords any assurance, however, that the people will be protected against actual or potential abuse of concentrated economic power.

Before we discard competition as the cornerstone of national economic policy, we might well recall that even our socialist critics regard competition as the oldest and strongest defense of private capitalism and enterprise.

THE PROBLEMS OF AFFLUENCE

In *The Affluent Society,* Galbraith challenges the very core of the post-Keynesian synthesis by raising doubts concerning the importance of its underlying values: production and growth. In reality, Galbraith contends, American capitalism has become an "affluent society" in which the production of goods, especially private goods, has diminished in importance. But conventional (now including Keynesian) economic thought, which emerged under earlier, less affluent circumstances, has become increasingly obsolete and characterized by numerous illusions.

Illusion 1. Production is important for consumer welfare. But this is belied by diminished marginal utility of goods and by the "dependence effect," for example, by the creation of wants by and through the process of production itself, especially through sales promotion.

Illusion 2. Production is strategic for maintaining national defense and satisfying foreign commitments. But in a rich society, allocation to the defense sector, not necessarily the size of the GNP, is what is crucial; and expanded output is accompanied by expanded wants.

Illusion 3. Economic growth is necessary for the reduction of poverty. But residual poverty in an affluent society is largely of the "case" or "insular" variety; and neither is reduced directly by a rising GNP. ("Case" poverty includes that inflicted by society on particular groups, for example, racial minorities, the aged, the disabled, migrant agricultural workers. "Insular" poverty characterizes economically isolated sectors, such as Appalachia.) Furthermore, poverty in an affluent society is largely "relative," the result of inequalities in income distribution, and economic growth often simply widens the gap between rich and poor.

Illusion 4. Monetary and fiscal policy adapted to the promotion of full employment can be reversed to promote price stability when aggregate demand is excessive. Actually, Galbraith contends, there are important barriers to the efficacious application of monetary and fiscal measures as anti-inflationary devices (not the least barrier being their political unpopularity), and the successful application of the Keynesian orthodoxy to the promotion of full employment has reinforced tendencies toward inflation.

Adherence to earlier, obsolete ideas, Galbraith argues, prevents progress and change in social institutions, and creates tensions and imbalances that threaten the stability of the system, and thus its affluence. The major tensions of affluent capitalism are the treadmill, squirrel cage character of the economy, emanating from the "dependence effect," and the pressures for inflation —generated both by closer approximation to full employment (demand-pull) and by market power of sellers (supply-push). The main social imbalance, Galbraith avers, is a misallocation of resources between private sector goods (relatively overproduced) and public sector goods (relatively underproduced).

Recommendations for public policy in an affluent society follow easily from the identification of its illusions and imbalances. First, suggests Galbraith, production should be largely divorced from economic security (which continues to be of considerable importance) through the adoption of the principle of "cyclically guaranteed compensation," for example, a program of unemployment compensation benefits whose magnitude and length vary directly with the severity of unemployment. This plan would adjust compensatory payments to the severity of the business cycle, thereby functioning more effectively as an automatic stabilizer and helping prevent mild unemployment from leading to larger depressions. And it would eliminate financial discrimination against unemployment, making more tolerable the unemployment associated with a more forceful pursuit of price stability. Second, argues Galbraith, social imbalance could be partially rectified by increased use of sales taxes at state and local levels where the needed redress between public poverty and private opulence is greatest. Third, because case and insular poverty are largely impervious to economic growth, they must be attacked directly. Although redistributive welfare measures will continue to have a place, the great potential payoff is in breaking vicious circles of poverty, notably by educational investment in children.

Selections 5.3 and 5.4 provide exposition and critique of two important Galbraithian themes, the "dependence effect" and "social imbalance."

5.3 Problems of Affluence

John K. Galbraith

The Dependence Effect

If the individual's wants are to be urgent they must be original with himself. They cannot be urgent if they must be contrived for him. And above all they must not be contrived by the process of production by which they are satisfied. For this means that the whole case for the urgency of production, based on the urgency of wants, falls to the ground. One cannot defend production as satisfying wants if that production creates the wants.

Were it so that a man on arising each morning was assailed by demons which instilled in him a passion sometimes for silk shirts, sometimes for kitchenware, sometimes for chamber pots, and sometimes for orange squash, there would be every reason to applaud the effort to find the goods, however odd, that quenched this flame. But should it be that his passion was the result of his first having cultivated the demons, and should it also be that his effort to allay it stirred the demons to ever greater and greater effort, there would be question as to how rational was his solution. Unless restrained by conventional attitudes, he might wonder if the solution lay with more goods or fewer demons.

So it is that if production creates the wants it seeks to satisfy, or if the wants emerge *pari passu* with the production, then the urgency of the wants can no longer be used to defend the urgency of the production. Production only fills a void that it has itself created.

The point is so central that it must be pressed. Consumer wants can have bizarre, frivolous, or even immoral origins, and an admirable case can still be made for a society that seeks to satisfy them. But the case cannot stand if it is the process of satisfying wants that creates the wants. For then the individual who urges the importance of production to satisfy these wants is precisely in the position of the onlooker who applauds the efforts of the squirrel to keep abreast of the wheel that is propelled by his own efforts.

That wants are, in fact, the fruit of production will now be denied by few serious scholars. And a considerable number of economists, though not always in full knowledge of the implications, have conceded the point.

The even more direct link between production and wants is provided by the institutions of modern advertising and salesmanship. These cannot be reconciled with the notion of independently determined desires, for their central function is to create desires—to bring into being wants that previously did not exist. The path for an expansion of output must be paved by a suitable expansion in the advertising budget. Outlays for the manufacturing of a product are not more important in the strategy of modern business enterprise than outlays for the manufacturing of demand for the product. None of this is novel. All would be regarded as elementary by the most retarded student in the nation's most primitive school of business administration. The cost of this want formation is formidable. In 1956 total advertising expenditure—though, as noted, not all of it may be assigned to the synthesis of wants—amounted to about ten billion dollars. Obviously, such outlays must be integrated with the theory of consumer demand. They are too big to be ignored.

But such integration means recognizing that wants are dependent on production. It accords to the producer the function both of making the goods and of making the desires for them. It recognizes that production, not only passively through emulation, but actively through advertising and related activities, creates the wants it seeks to satisfy.

The businessman and the lay reader will be puzzled over the emphasis which I give to a seemingly obvious point. The point is indeed obvious. But it is one which, to a singular degree, economists have resisted. They have sensed, as the layman does not, the damage to established ideas which lurks in these relationships. As a result, incredibly, they have closed their eyes (and ears) to the most obtrusive of all economic phenomena, namely modern want creation.

And so the notion of independently determined wants still survives. In the face of all the forces of modern salesmanship it still rules, almost undefiled, in the textbooks. And it still remains the economist's mission—and on few matters is the pedagogy so firm—to seek unquestioningly the means for filling these wants. This being so, production remains of prime urgency. We have here, perhaps, the ultimate triumph of the conventional wisdom in its resistance to the evidence of the eyes. To equal it one must imagine a humanitarian who was long ago persuaded of the grievous shortage of hospital facilities in the town. He continues to importune the passers-by for money for more beds and refuses to notice that the town doctor is deftly knocking over pedestrians with his car to keep up the occupancy.

The fact that wants can be synthesized by advertising, catalyzed by salesmanship, and shaped by the discreet manipulations of the persuaders shows that they are not very urgent. A man who is hungry need never be told of his need for food. If he is inspired by his appetite, he is immune to the influence of Messrs. Batten, Barton, Durstine & Osborn. The latter are effective only with those who are so far removed from physical want that they do not already know what they want. In this state alone men are open to persuasion.

The general conclusion is of such importance for this essay that it had perhaps best be put with some formality. As a society becomes increasingly affluent, wants are increasingly created by the process by which they are satisfied. This may operate passively. Increases in consumption, the counterpart of increases in production, act by suggestion or emulation to create wants. Or producers may proceed actively to create wants through advertising and salesmanship. Wants thus come to depend on output. In technical terms it can no longer be assumed that welfare is greater at an all-round higher level of production than at a lower one. It may be the same. The higher level of production has, merely, a higher level of want creation necessitating a higher level of want satisfaction. There will be frequent occasion to refer to the way wants depend on the process by which they are satisfied. It will be convenient to call it the Dependence Effect.

Among the many models of the good society no one has urged the squirrel wheel. Moreover, as we shall see presently, the wheel is not one that revolves with perfect smoothness. Aside from its dubious cultural charm, there are serious structural weaknesses which may one day embarrass us. For the moment, however, it is sufficient to reflect on the difficult terrain which we are traversing. We are committed to production for reasons of economic security. Not the goods but the employment provided by their production was the thing by which we set ultimate store. Now we find our concern for goods further undermined. It does not arise in spontaneous consumer need. Rather, the dependence effect means that it grows out of the process of production itself. If production is to increase, the wants must be effectively contrived. In the absence of the contrivance the increase would not occur. This is not true of all goods, but that it is true of a substantial part is sufficient. It means that since the demand for this part would not exist, were it not contrived, its utility or urgency, ex contrivance, is zero. If we regard this production as marginal, we may say that the marginal utility of present aggregate output, ex advertising and salesmanship, is zero. Clearly the attitudes and values which make production the central achievement of our society have some exceptionally twisted roots.

The Theory of Social Balance

The final problem of the productive society is what it produces. This manifests itself in an implacable tendency to provide an opulent supply of some things and a niggardly yield of others. This disparity carries to the point where it is a cause of social discomfort and social unhealth. The line which divides our area of wealth from our area of poverty is roughly that which divides privately produced and marketed goods and services from publicly rendered services. Our wealth in the first is not only in startling contrast with the meagerness of the latter, but our wealth in privately produced goods is, to a marked degree, the cause of crisis in the supply of public services. For we have failed to see the importance, indeed the urgent need, of maintaining a balance between the two.

The family which takes its mauve and cerise, air-conditioned, power-steered, and power-braked automobile out for a tour passes through cities that are badly paved, made hideous by litter, blighted buildings, billboards, and posts for wires that should long since have been put underground. They pass on into a countryside that has been rendered largely invisible by commercial art. . . . They picnic on exquisitely packaged food from a portable icebox by a polluted stream and go on to spend the night at a park which is a menace to public health and morals. Just before dozing off on an air mattress, beneath a nylon tent, amid the stench of decaying refuse, they may reflect vaguely on the curious unevenness of their blessings. Is this, indeed, the American genius?

In the production of goods within the private economy it has long been recognized that a tolerably close relationship must be maintained between the production of various kinds of products. The output of steel and oil and machine tools is related to the production of automobiles. Investment in transportation must keep abreast of the output of goods to be transported. The supply of power must be abreast of the growth of industries requiring it. . . .

Just as there must be balance in what a community produces, so there must also be balance in what the community consumes. An increase in the use of one product creates, ineluctably, a requirement for others. If we are to consume more automobiles, we must have more gasoline. There must be more insurance as well as more space on which to operate them. Beyond a certain point more and better food appears to mean increased need for medical services. This is the certain result of the increased consumption of tobacco and alcohol. More vacations require more hotels and more fishing rods. And so forth. With rare exceptions—shortages of doctors are an exception which suggests the rule—this balance is also maintained quite effortlessly so far as goods for private sale and consumption are concerned. The price system plus a rounded condition of opulence is again the agency.

However, the relationships we are here discussing are not confined to the private economy. They operate comprehensively over the whole span of private and public services. It will be convenient to have a term which suggests a satisfactory relationship between the supply of privately produced goods and services and those of the state, and we may call it social balance.

The problem of social balance is ubiquitous, and frequently it is obtrusive. As noted, an increase in the consumption of automobiles requires a facilitating supply of streets, highways, traffic control, and parking space. The protective services of the police and the highway patrols must also be available, as must those of the hospitals. Although the need for balance here is extraordinarily clear, our use of privately produced vehicles has, on occasion, got far out of line with the supply of the related public services. The result has been hideous road congestion, an annual massacre of impressive proportions, and chronic colitis in the cities. As on the ground, so also in the air. Planes collide with disquieting consequences for those within when the public provision for air traffic control fails to keep pace with private use of the airways.

But the auto and the airplane, versus the space to use them, are merely an exceptionally visible example of a requirement that is pervasive. The more goods people procure, the more packages they discard and the more trash that must be carried away. If the appropriate sanitation services are not provided, the counterpart of increasing opulence will be deepening filth. The greater the wealth the thicker will be the dirt. This indubitably describes a tendency of our time. As more goods are produced and owned, the greater are the opportunities for fraud and the more property that must be protected. If the provision of public law enforcement services do not keep pace, the counterpart of increased well-being will, we may be certain, be increased crime.

The case for social balance has, so far, been put negatively. Failure to keep public services in minimal relation to private production and use of goods is a cause of social disorder or impairs economic performance. The matter may now be put affirmatively. By failing to exploit the opportunity to expand public production we are missing opportunities for enjoyment which otherwise we might have had. Presumably a community can be as well rewarded by buying better schools or better parks as by buying bigger automobiles. By concentrating on the latter rather than the former it is failing to maximize its satisfactions. As with schools in the community, so with public services over the country at large. It is scarcely sensible that we should satisfy our wants in private goods with reckless abundance, while in the case of public goods, on the evidence of the eye, we practice extreme self-denial. So, far from systematically exploiting the opportunities to derive use and pleasure from these services, we do not supply what would keep us out of trouble.

The conventional wisdom holds that the community, large or small, makes a decision as to how much it will devote to its public services. This decision is arrived at by democratic process. Subject to the imperfections and uncertainties of democracy, people decide how much of their private income and goods they will surrender in order to have public services of which they are in greater need. Thus there is a balance, however rough, in the enjoyments to be had from private goods and services and those rendered by public authority.

It will be obvious, however, that this view depends on the notion of independently determined consumer wants. In such a world one could with some reason defend the doctrine that the consumer, as a voter, makes an independent choice between public and private goods. But given the dependence effect —given that consumer wants are created by the process by which they are satisfied—the consumer makes no such choice. He is subject to the forces of advertising and emulation by which production creates its own demand.

The competition is especially unequal for new products and services. Every corner of the public psyche is canvassed by some of the nation's most talented citizens to see if the desire for some merchantable product can be cultivated. No similar process operates on behalf of the nonmerchantable services of the state. Indeed, while we take the cultivation of new private wants for granted we would be measurably shocked to see it applied to public services. The scientist or engineer or advertising man who devotes himself to developing a new carburetor, cleanser, or depilatory for which the public recognizes no need and will feel none until an advertising campaign arouses it, is one of the valued members of our society. A politician or a public servant who dreams up a new public service is a wastrel. Few public offenses are more reprehensible.

So much for the influences which operate on the decision between public and private production. The calm decision between public and private consumption pictured by the conventional wisdom is, in fact, a remarkable example of the error which arises from viewing social behavior out of context. The inherent tendency will always be for public services to fall behind private production. We have here the first of the causes of social imbalance.

5.4 Private Versus Public: Could Kenneth Galbraith Be Wrong?

Henry C. Wallich

Public needs are underfinanced while private tastes are overindulged—that is the proposition.

The two parts of the proposition seem neatly to complement each other—too much of one, therefore too little of the other. In fact they don't. It is one thing to be irritated by certain manifestations of our contemporary civilization—the gadgets, the chrome, the tailfins, and the activities that go with them. It is quite another—and something of a non sequitur—to conclude from this that the only alternative to foolish private spending is public spending. Better private spending is just as much a possibility. My contention here will be that to talk in terms of "public vs. private" is to confuse the issue. More than that, it is to confuse means and ends. The choice between public and private money is primarily a choice of means. The sensible approach for those who are dissatisfied with some of the ends to which private money is being spent, is to specify first what other ends are important and why. Having determined the ends, the next step is to look to the means. That is the order in which I propose to proceed here.

WHAT IS WRONG WITH PRIVATE SPENDING?

One may share the irritation of the new social critics as they look upon some of the fluff and the floss on our standard of living. The critics may want to bear in mind, however, that not all the money in this country is spent by people for whom life begins at $25,000. The median family income is $5600. Would these critics of the affluent society want to try living on much less than that? When Galbraith inveighs eloquently against switchblades, narcotics, and other phases of juvenile delinquency, he deserves the support of all right-thinking representatives of what he calls the "conventional wisdom." But are the sources of these aberrations more intimately tied to affluence or to poverty? The exponents of the new social criticism may also want to remember the outcome of that "noble experiment," Prohibition. It should have taught us that it is futile to become our brother's dietitian. I hope that it has also imbued us with wholesome doubt about the moral right of some members of the community to regulate the lives of the rest.

SIGNS OF QUALITY

Obviously, the quality of our culture could be greatly improved by public expenditures for education and support of the arts. The sales of good paperbacks and LPs are encouraging signs. But if contemporary materialism is to be leavened by such pursuits, it will be principally because large numbers of individuals make private decisions to that end. Social criticism is constructive if it helps precipitate these decisions. It obstructs a desirable evolution if it suggests that public creature comforts are the only alternative to private.

But while emphasis on nonmaterial ends seems sadly lacking in the new social criticism, the critics are right in pointing out that new material needs also have been carried to the fore by social and economic evolution, even though they mislabel them as public needs. In the good old days, when this was still a nation of farmers, most people had no serious retirement worries, there was no industrial unemployment problem, good jobs could be had without a college degree, most diseases were still incurable—in short, social security, education, and health care found primitive and natural solutions within the family and among the resources of the neighborhood. Today, these solutions are neither adequate nor usually even possible.

Meanwhile mounting wealth and advancing technology have brought within reach the means of meeting these needs. We can afford to live better in every way—more creature comforts, more leisure, more attention to matters of the mind and the spirit. At the same time we can take better care of retirement, of unemployment, of illness, of education, of the possibilities opened by research, than ever before.

There are indeed new needs. The citizen-taxpayer has his choice of meeting them, as well as all his other goods or services he wants privately, for cash or credit. Or he can buy them from the government, for taxes.

The nation as a whole pays taxes to buy public services as it pays grocery bills to buy groceries. The tax burden may be heavier for some individuals than for others. But the nation as a whole has no more reason to complain about the "burden" of taxes than about the "burden" of grocery bills—and no more reason to hope for relief.

Of the two stores, the private store today still is much the bigger. The public store is smaller, but it is growing faster.

Each store has some exclusive items. The private store sells most of the necessities and all of the luxuries of life, and in most of these has no competition from the government side. The public store has some specialities of its own: defense, public order and justice, and numerous local services that the private organization has not found profitable. But there is a wide range of items featured by both stores: provision for old age, health services, education, housing, development of natural resources.

THE NEW NEEDS

The bulk of the new needs are in this competitive area. The fashionable notion is to claim them all for the public store and to label them public needs. The statistics say otherwise. They say in fact two things. First, the supply of this group of goods and services has expanded very rapidly in recent years; and second, they are being offered, in varying degrees, both by the private and the public suppliers. Let us run down the list.

Provision for old age is predominantly private.

Health expenditures are still mainly private.

Education: the bulk of it is public; but a good part, particularly of higher education, is private.

So much for the allegation that the "new needs" are all public needs. What of the public store, which is said to have been neglected? Some of them could make an investor in private growth stocks envious.

Some parts of federal, state, and local budgets have expanded rapidly, others less rapidly. The massive build-up in defense expenditures from the late 'forties to the 'fifties has squeezed other programs. Unfortunately, some programs that both political parties have favored—including aid to education, to depressed areas, for urban renewal—have been delayed unduly by the vicissitudes of politics. But the figures as a whole lend little support to the thesis that politicians don't spend enough, and that the government store is not expanding fast enough.

THE CITIZEN IN THE STORES

The two stores—private and public—work very hard these days to capture the business of the citizen-taxpayer. Here is what he hears as he walks into the private store:

"The principal advantage of this store," the private businessman says, "is that you can shop around and buy exactly what you want. If I don't have it, I'll order it. You, the consumer, are the boss here. To be sure, I'm not in business for charity but for profit. But my profit comes from giving you what you want. And with competition as fierce as it is, you can be sure the profit won't be excessive."

If the proprietor has been to Harvard Business School, he will perhaps remember to add something about the invisible hand which in a free economy causes the self-seeking of competitors to work for the common good. He will also, even without benefit of business school, remember to drop a word about the danger of letting the public store across the street get too big. It might endanger freedom.

As the citizen turns this sales talk over in his mind, several points occur to him. Without denying the broad validity of the argument, he will note that quite often he has been induced to buy things he did not really need, and possibly to neglect other, more serious needs. Snob appeal and built-in obsolescence promoted by expensive advertising don't seem to him to fit in with the notion that the consumer is king. Looking at the brand names and patents and trademarks, he wonders whether most products are produced and priced competitively instead of under monopoly conditions. The invisible hand at times seems to be invisible mainly because it is so deep in his pocket.

Bothered by these doubts, the citizen walks across the street and enters the public store.

"Let me explain to you," says the politician who runs it—with the aid of a horde of hard-working bureaucrats doing the chores. "The principles on which this store is run are known as the political process, and if you happen to be familiar with private merchandising they may seem unusual, but I assure you they work. First of all, almost everything in this store is free. We simply assess our customers a lump sum in the form of taxes. These, however, are based largely on each customer's ability to pay, rather than on what he gets from the store. We have a show of hands from the customers once a year, and the majority decides what merchandise the store is to have in stock. The majority, incidentally, also decides how much everybody, including particularly the minority, is to be assessed for taxes.

"You will observe," the politician continues, "that this store is not run for profit. It is like a co-operative, run for the welfare of the members. I myself, to be sure, am not in politics for charity, but for re-election. But that means that I must be interested in your needs, or you would not vote for me. Moreover, there are some useful things that only I can do, with the help of the political process, and in which you and every citizen have an interest. For instance, everybody ought to go to school. I can make them go. Everybody ought to have old-age insurance. I can make that compulsory too. And because I don't charge the full cost of the service, I can help even up a little the inequalities of life.

"By the way," the politician concludes, "if there is any special little thing you want, I may be able to get it for you, and of course it won't cost you a nickel."

The citizen has some fault to find with the political process too. He notes that there is not even a theoretical claim to the benefits of an invisible hand. Majority rule may produce benefits for the majority, but how about the other 49 percent? Nor is there the discipline of competition, or the need for profits, to test economy of operation. There is no way, in the public store, of adjusting individual costs and benefits. And the promise to get him some small favor, while tempting, worries him, because he wonders what the politician may have promised to others. The political process, he is led to suspect, may be a little haphazard.

He asks himself how political decisions get to be made. Sometimes, obviously, it is not the majority that really makes a decision, but a small pressure group that is getting away with something. He will remember that—after payments for major national security and public debt interest—the largest single expenditure in the federal budget is for agriculture, and the next for veterans.

THE EXPANDING BELT

Next, the citizen might consider the paralyzing "balance-of-forces" effect that often blocks a desirable reshuffling of expenditures. The allocation of public funds reflects the bargaining power of their sponsors, inside or outside of the government.

What is the consequence of the balance-of-forces effect? If the proponents of one kind of expenditure want to get more money for their projects, they must concede an increase also to the advocates of others. More education means more highways, instead of less; more air power means more ground forces. To increase a budget in one direction only is as difficult as letting out one's belt only on one side. The expansion tends to go all around. What this comes down to is that politicians are not very good at setting priorities. Increases in good expenditures are burdened with a political surcharge of less good ones.

THE CITIZEN'S FAILURES

The citizen would be quite wrong, however, if he blamed the politician for the defects of the political process. The fault lies with the process, or better with the way in which the process, the politician, and the citizen interact. The citizen therefore would do well to examine some of his own reactions and attitudes.

First, when he thinks about taxes, he tends to think of them as a burden instead of as a price he pays for a service. As a body, the nation's taxpayers are like a group of neighbors who decide to establish a fire department. Because none is quite sure how much good it will do him, and because each hopes to benefit from the contribution of the rest, all are prudent in their contributions. In the end they are likely to wind up with a bucket brigade.

But when it comes to accepting benefits, the citizen-taxpayers act like a group of men who sit down at a restaurant table knowing that they will split the check evenly. In this situation everybody orders generously; it adds little to one's own share of the bill, and for the extravagance of his friends he will have to pay anyhow. What happens at the restaurant table explains—though it does not excuse—what happens at the public trough.

Finally, in his reaction to public or free services, the citizen takes a great deal for granted, and seldom thinks of the cost. Public beaches mistreated, unmetered parking space permanently occupied, veterans' adjustment benefits continued without need—as well as abuses of unemployment compensation and public assistance—are some examples. This applies also, of course, to privately offered benefits, under health insurance, for instance. The kindly nurse in the hospital—"Why don't you stay another day, dearie, it won't cost you anything, it's all paid for by Blue Cross"—makes the point.

THE POLITICAL DOLLAR AT A DISCOUNT

These various defects of the political process add up to an obvious conclusion: the dollar spent by even the most honest and scrupulous of politicians is not always a full-bodied dollar. It often is subject to a discount. It buys less than it should because of the attrition it suffers as it goes through the process, and so may be worth only 90 cents or 80 cents and sometimes perhaps less. The private dollar, in too many cases, may also be worth less than 100 percent. But here each man can form his own judgment, can pick and choose or refuse altogether. In the political process, all he can do is say Yes or No once a year in November.

The discount on the public dollar may be compensated by the other advantages of the government—its ability to compel, to subsidize, to do things on a big scale and at a low interest cost. Whether that is the case needs to be studied in each instance. Where these advantages do not apply, the private market will give better service than the political process. For many services, there is at least some leeway for choice between the private and public store—health and retirement, housing, research, higher education, natural-resource development. Defense, on the other hand, as well as public administration, public works of all kinds, and the great bulk of education—while perhaps made rather expensive by the political process—leave no realistic alternative to public action.

The argument I have offered is no plea to spend more or less on any particular function. It is a plea for doing whatever we do in the most effective way.

CORPORATE POWER, TECHNOLOGY, AND POLICY

The New Industrial State incorporates the concepts of power and affluence in its description of the changing structure and functioning of American capitalism, but it also extends Galbraith's analysis. As in *American Capitalism,* Galbraith focuses upon concentrated economic power in the large-scale corporation. And as in *The Affluent Society,* he perceives consumer "sovereignty" as rendered largely meaningless by the sales promotion activities of powerful and persuasive corporations. But this more recent work goes beyond any of his earlier books by emphasizing the strategic role of technology. First is the now-familiar theme that modern technologies have fostered the tremendous expansion of both the absolute and the relative size of big business, and of the economic power of large-scale corporations in the economy as a whole. Second, like Thorstein Veblen before him, Galbraith perceives technology as *the* strategic resource, and control over technology as the main basis for economic power. Accordingly, power has shifted from capitalists to a loosely defined group, the *technostructure,* which, through its specialized technical knowledge, is the real repository of power within the corporate hierarchy. Third, the tremendous economic power of large-scale corporations, coupled with the highly expensive and time-consuming character of modern production, has reduced the role of the market as a process for social control and increased the importance of the *planning* activities of corporations—thereby creating a transformation to a largely "planned" economy. (Presumably, corporations to some extent countervail one another, as postulated in *American Capitalism,* but this theme is not developed in *The New Industrial State.)*

Corporate power also profoundly affects government policy. In the new industrial state, government serves the corporate community by providing (1) education and technical training and thus a skilled labor force, (2) collective goods that complement and enhance consumption of private goods, for example, highways for the automobile industry, and (3) high levels of aggregate demand, to ensure that sales promotion endeavors are not nullified by recession and unemployment. Monetary and fiscal policy are also biased in favor of business, especially large corporate interests. To encourage expansion in the 1960s, for instance, the federal government applied a conservative Keynesian strategy of tax cuts (to facilitate business expansion) rather than a liberal Keynesian strategy of expanded public works and really generous antipoverty programs. In anti-inflationary policy, tight money hits small businesses (dependent upon borrowed funds) more heavily than it does giant corporations, with their lush undistributed profits.[1]

Throughout all his works, Galbraith focuses upon the big questions of the changing structure of the economic system and the inadequacy of traditional economic analysis to answer such questions. Like Marx and Veblen, Galbraith perceives the industrialization process in terms of compelling technological changes that, in turn, generate new institutions, for example, emergence of large-scale corporations in the late nineteenth century. Ideas lag behind technological and institutional change, serving the essentially conservative function of defending existing, and often socially harmful, institutions in terms of traditional, accepted beliefs. Most notably, the concepts of consumer (and citizen) sovereignty and competitive markets provide a ''conventional wisdom'' concealing the realities of corporate, military, and political power, and the social consequences thereof—pollution, social imbalance between private and public goods, excessive growth, economic and political inequality, and imperviousness of the highly organized industrial sector to social control. What are the prospects for reform? In contrast to Marx, Galbraith does not look to the working class to play a strategic role in social change. As did Veblen, he pauses on the brink of proposals for reform, having identified some of the major problems and trends and having chastised orthodox economic theory for failing to provide meaningful answers and explanations. Perhaps, he suggests, an ''educational and scientific estate'' can provide an independent base of persuasion and influence to temper if not countervail completely the power of giant corporations, big government, and the military.

The following selections provide exposition and critique of the ''new industrial state.'' Galbraith gives a synopsis of his main themes in selection 5.5. A critical view—by mainstream economist Scott Gordon—is presented in selection 5.6.[2]

5.5 The New Industrial State

John K. Galbraith

Change and the Industrial System

A curiosity of modern economic discussion is the role of change. It is imagined to be very great; to list its forms or emphasize its extent is to show a reassuring

[1] This paragraph, and the succeeding one, are taken and adapted from John E. Elliott, *Economics: A Student Resource Book* (Pacific Palisades: Goodyear, 1973), p. 253.

[2] As selection 5.8 shows, dissent from Galbraith's challenging views is by no means restricted to mainstream economists. See also Ralph Miliband, ''Professor Galbraith and American Capitalism,'' *Socialist Register,* 1968; and Robert Fitch, ''A Galbraith Reappraisal: The Idealogue as Gadfly,'' *Ramparts,* May 1968 for critical evaluation from democratic socialist and New Left perspectives.

grasp of the commonplace. Yet not much is supposed to change. The economic system of the United States is accepted by all but the malcontent as a largely perfect structure. It is not easy to perfect what has been perfected. There is massive change but, except as the output of goods increases, all remains as before.

As to the change there is no doubt. The innovations and alterations in economic life in this century, and more especially since the beginning of World War II, have, by any calculation, been great. The most visible has been the application of increasingly intricate and sophisticated technology to the production of things. Machines have replaced crude manpower. And increasingly, as they are used to instruct other machines, they replace the cruder forms of human intelligence.

Machines and sophisticated technology require, in turn, heavy investment of capital. They are designed and guided by technically sophisticated men. They involve, also, a greatly increased elapse of time between any decision to produce and the emergence of a salable product.

From these changes come both the need and the opportunity for the large business organization. It alone can deploy the requisite capital; it alone can mobilize the requisite skills. It can also do more. The large commitment of capital and organization well in advance of result requires that there be foresight and also that all feasible steps be taken to insure that what is foreseen will transpire. It can hardly be doubted that General Motors will be better able to influence the world around it—the prices and wages at which it buys and the prices at which it sells—than a man in suits and cloaks.

Nor is this all. The high production and income which are the fruits of advanced technology and expansive organization remove a very large part of the population from the compulsions and pressures of physical want. In consequence their economic behavior becomes in some measure malleable. No hungry man who is also sober can be persuaded to use his last dollar for anything but food. But a well-fed, well-clad, well-sheltered and otherwise well-tended person can be persuaded as between an electric razor and an electric toothbrush. Along with prices and costs, consumer demand becomes subject to management. This adds an important further element of control over environment.

When investment in technological development is very high, a wrong technical judgment or a failure in persuading consumers to buy the product can be extremely expensive. The cost and associated risk can be greatly reduced if the state pays for more exalted technical development or guarantees a market for the technically advanced product. Suitable justification—national defense, national prestige, deeply felt public need such as for supersonic travel—can readily be found. Modern technology thus defines a growing function of the modern state.

And technology and associated requirements in capital and time lead even more directly to the regulation of demand by the state. A corporation, contemplating an automobile of revised aspect, must be able to persuade people to buy it. It is equally important that people be able to do so. This is vital where heavy advance commitments of time and money must be made and where the product could as easily come to market in a time of depression as of prosperity. So there must be stabilization of overall demand.

I am concerned to show how, in this larger context of change, the forces inducing human effort have changed. This assaults the most majestic of all economic assumptions, namely that man in his economic activities is subject to the authority of the market. Instead, we have an economic system which, whatever its formal ideological billing, is in substantial part a planned economy. The initiative in deciding what is to be produced comes not from the sovereign consumer who, through the market, issues the instructions that bend the productive mechanism to his ultimate will. Rather it comes from the great producing organization which reaches forward to control the markets that it is presumed to serve and, beyond, to bend the customer to its needs.

The Imperatives of Technology

Technology means the systematic application of scientific or other organized knowledge to practical tasks. Its most important consequence, at least for purposes of economics, is in forcing the division and subdivision of any such task into its component parts. Thus, and only thus, can organized knowledge be brought to bear on performance.

Nearly all of the consequences of technology, and much of the shape of modern industry derive from this need to divide and subdivide tasks and from the further need to bring knowledge to bear on these functions and from the final need to combine the finished elements of the task into the finished product as a whole. Six consequences are of immediate importance.

First. An increasing span of time separates the beginning from the completion of any task. The more thoroughgoing the application of technology—in common or at least frequent language, the more sophisticated the production process—the farther back the application of knowledge will be carried. The longer, accordingly, will be the time between the initiation and completion of the task.

Second. There is an increase in the capital that is committed to production aside from that occasioned by increased output. The increased time, and therewith the increased investment in goods in process costs money. So does the knowledge which is applied to the various elements of the task. The application of knowledge to an element of a manufacturing problem will also typically involve the development of a machine for performing the function. (The word technology brings to mind machines; this is not surprising for machinery is one of its most visible manifestations.) This too involves investment as does equipment for integrating the various elements of the task into the final product.

Third. With increasing technology the commitment of time and money tends to be made ever more inflexibly to the performance of a particular task. That task must be precisely defined before it is divided and subdivided into its component parts. Knowledge and equipment are then brought to bear on these fractions and they are useful only for the task as it was initially defined. If that task is changed, new knowledge and new equipment will have to be brought to bear.

Fourth. Technology requires specialized manpower. However, technology does not make the only claim on manpower; planning, to be mentioned in a moment, also requires a comparatively high level of specialized talent. To foresee the future in all its dimensions and to design the appropriate action does not necessarily require high scientific qualification. It does require ability to organize and employ information, or capacity to react intuitively to relevant experience.

Fifth. The inevitable counterpart of specialization is organization. This is what brings the work of specialists to a coherent result. If there are many specialists, this coordination will be a major task. So complex, indeed, will be the job of organizing specialists that there will be specialists on organization. More even than machinery, massive and complex business organizations are the tangible manifestation of advanced technology.

Sixth. From the time and capital that must be committed, the inflexibility of this commitment, the needs of large organization and the problems of market performance under conditions of advanced technology, comes the necessity for planning. Tasks must be performed so that they are right not for the present but for that time in the future when, companion and related work having also been done, the whole job is completed. And the amount of capital that, meanwhile, will have been committed adds urgency to this need to be right. So conditions at the time of completion of the whole task must be foreseen as must developments along the way. And steps must be taken to prevent, offset or otherwise neutralize the effect of adverse developments, and to insure that what is ultimately foreseen eventuates in fact.

Market Coordination-Versus Planning

In the market economy the price that is offered is counted upon to produce the result that is sought. Nothing more need be done. The consumer, by his offer to pay, obtains the necessary responding action by the firm that supplies his needs. By offering to pay yet more he gets more. And the firm, in its turn, by similar offers gets the labor, materials and equipment that it requires for production.

Planning exists because this process has ceased to be reliable. Technology, with its companion commitment of time and capital, means that the needs of the consumer must be anticipated—by months or years. When the distant day arrives the consumer's willingness to buy may well be lacking. By the same token, while common labor and carbon steel will be forthcoming in response to a promise to pay, the specialized skills and arcane materials required by advanced technology cannot similarly be counted upon. The needed action in both instances is evident: in addition to deciding what the consumer will want and will pay, the firm must take every feasible step to see that what it decides to produce is wanted by the consumer at a remunerative price. And it must see that the labor, materials and equipment that it needs will be available at a cost consistent with the price it will receive. It must exercise control over what is sold. It must exercise control over what is supplied. It must replace the market with planning.

As viewed by the industrial firm, planning consists in foreseeing the actions required between the initiation of production and its completion and preparing for the accomplishment of these actions. And it consists also of foreseeing, and having a design for meeting, any unscheduled developments, favorable or otherwise, that may occur along the way. As planning is viewed by the economist, political scientist or pundit, it consists of replacing prices and the market as the mechanism for determining what will be produced, with an authoritative determination of what will be produced and consumed and at what price. It will be thought that the word planning is being used in two different senses.

In practice, however, the two kinds of planning, if such they may be called, are inextricably associated. A firm cannot usefully foresee and schedule future action or prepare for contingencies if it does not know what its prices will be, what its sales will be, what its costs including labor and capital costs will be and what will be available at these costs. If the market is unreliable, it will not know these things. Hence it cannot plan. If, with advancing technology and associated specialization, the market becomes increasingly unreliable, industrial planning will become increasingly impossible unless the market also gives way to planning. Much of what the firm regards as planning consists in minimizing or getting rid of market influences.

A variety of strategies are available for dealing with the increasing unreliability of markets. Not all, in fact, require their replacement.

But the more common strategies require that the market be replaced by an authoritative determination of price and the amounts to be sold or bought at these prices. There are three ways of doing this:

1. The market can be superseded.
2. It can be controlled by sellers or buyers.
3. It can be suspended for definite or indefinite periods by contract between the parties to sale and purchase.

All of these strategies are familiar features of the industrial system.

The Technostructure

The need to draw on, and appraise, the information of numerous individuals in modern industrial decision-making has three principal points of origin. It derives, first, from the technological requirements of modern industry. It is not that these are always inordinately sophisticated; a man of moderate genius could, quite conceivably, provide himself with the knowledge of the various branches of metallurgy and chemistry, and of engineering, procurement, production management, quality control, labor relations, styling and merchandising which are involved in the development of a modern motorcar. But even moderate genius is in unpredictable supply, and to keep abreast of all these branches of science, engineering and art would be time-consuming even for a genius. The elementary solution, which allows of the use of far more common talent and with far greater predictability of result, is to have men who are appropriately qualified or experienced in each limited area of specialized knowledge or art. Their information is then combined for carrying out the design and production of the vehicle. The real accomplishment of modern science and technology consists in taking ordinary men, informing them narrowly and deeply and then, through appropriate organization, arranging to have their knowledge combined with that of other specialized but equally ordinary men. This dispenses with the need for genius. The resulting performance, though less inspiring, is far more predictable.

The second factor requiring the combination of specialized talent derives from advanced technology, the associated use of capital and the resulting need for planning with its accompanying control of environment. The market is, in remarkable degree, an intellectually undemanding institution. Much of the appeal of the market, to economists at least, has been from the way it seems to simplify life. Better orderly error than complex truth.

For complexity enters with planning and is endemic thereto. The manufacturer of missiles, space vehicles or modern aircraft must foresee the requirements for specialized plant, specialized manpower, exotic materials and intricate components and take steps to insure their availability when they are needed. For procuring such things, we have seen, the market is either unreliable or unavailable. And there is no open market for the finished product. Everything here depends on the care and skill with which contracts are sought and nurtured in Washington or in Whitehall or Paris.

The same foresight and responding action are required, in lesser degree, from manufacturers of automobiles, processed foods and detergents. They too must foresee requirements and manage markets. Planning, in short, requires a great variety of information. It requires variously informed men and men who are suitably specialized in obtaining the requisite information. There must be men whose knowledge allows them to foresee need and to insure a supply of labor, materials and other production requirements; those who have knowledge to plan price strategies and see that customers are suitably persuaded to buy at these prices; those who, at higher levels of technology, are so informed that they can work effectively with the state to see that it is suitably guided; and those who can organize the flow of information that the above tasks and many others require. Thus, to the requirements of technology for specialized technical and scientific talent are added the very large further requirements of the planning that technology makes necessary.

Finally, following from the need for this variety of specialized talent, is the need for its coordination. Talent must be brought to bear on the common purpose. More specifically, on large and small matters, information must be extracted from the various specialists, tested for its reliability and relevance, and made to yield a decision.

In the past, leadership in business organization was identified with the entrepreneur—the individual who united ownership or control of capital with capacity for organizing the other factors of production and, in most contexts, with a further capacity for innovation. With the rise of the modern corporation, the emergence of the organization required by modern technology and planning and the divorce of the owner of the capital from control of the enterprise, the entrepreneur no longer exists as an individual person in the mature industrial enterprise. Everyday discourse, except in the economics textbooks, recognizes this change. It replaces the entrepreneur, as the directing force of the enterprise, with management. This is a collective and imperfectly defined entity; in the large corporation it embraces chairman, president, those vice presidents with important staff or departmental responsibility, occupants of other major staff positions and, perhaps, division or department heads not included above. It includes, however, only a small proportion of those who, as participants, contribute information to group decisions. This latter group is very large; it extends from the most senior officials of the corporation to where it meets, at the outer perimeter, the white- and blue-collar workers whose function is to conform more or less mechanically to instruction or routine. It embraces all who bring specialized knowledge, talent or experience to group decision-making. This, not the management, is the guiding intelligence—the brain—of the enterprise. There is no name for all who participate in group decision-making or the organization which they form. I propose to call this organization the Technostructure.

The Revised Sequence

In virtually all economic analysis and instruction, the initiative is assumed to lie with the consumer. In response to wants that originate within himself, or which are given to him by his environment, he buys goods and services in the market. The opportunities that result for making more or less money are the message of the market to producing firms. They respond to this message of the market and thus, ultimately, to the instruction of the consumer. The flow of instruction is in one direction—from the individual to the market to the producer. All this is affirmed, not inappropriately, by terminology that implies that all power lies with the consumer. This is called consumer sovereignty. There "is always a presumption of consumer sovereignty in the market economy." The unidirectional flow of instruction from consumer to market to producer may be denoted the Accepted Sequence.

We have seen that this sequence does not hold. And we have now isolated a formidable apparatus of method and motivation causing its reversal. The mature corporation has readily at hand the means for controlling the prices at which it sells as well as those at which it buys. Similarly, it has means for managing what the consumer buys at the prices which it controls. This control and management is required by its planning. The planning proceeds from use of technology and capital, the commitment of time that these require and the diminished effectiveness of the market for specialized technical products and skills.

Supporting this changed sequence is the motivation of the technostructure. Members seek to adapt the goals of the corporation more closely to their own; by extension the corporation seeks to adapt social attitudes and goals to those of the members of its technostructure. So social belief originates at least in part with the producer. Thus the accommodation of the market behavior of the individual, as well as of social attitudes in general, to the needs of producers and the goals of the technostructure is an inherent feature of the system. It becomes increasingly important with the growth of the industrial system.

It follows that the accepted sequence is no longer a description of the reality and is becoming ever less so. Instead the producing firm reaches forward to control its markets and on beyond to manage the market behavior and shape the social attitudes of those, ostensibly, that it serves. For this we also need a name and it may appropriately be called The Revised Sequence.

5.6 The Close of the Galbraithian System

Scott Gordon

THE NEW INDUSTRIAL STATE AS A PLANNED ECONOMY

The pivotal point of Galbraith's economic thought is the theme of *American Capitalism*—that the American economy is characterized by a high degree of concentration and that the analysis of economic processes by means of the traditional models of economic theory is therefore meaningless. In *The New Industrial State* he carries this argument further, not in the direction of the "theory of countervailing power," which was the constructive analysis of the earlier book, but toward the conclusion that the American economy is not only no longer a competitive economy but that it is not even a market economy. The independence of consumer preferences and factor offers, the profit incentives of the producing units, and the price mechanism which, in traditional theory, knits the system together, are all swept away, and the "heartland of the economy" (the industrial sector) is represented as "managed" by the giant corporations which dominate its various industries. "The firm controls the prices at which it buys materials, components and talent, and takes steps to insure the necessary supply at these prices. And it controls the prices at which it sells and takes steps to insure that the public, other producers or the state take the planned

---

Excerpted from Scott Gordon, "The Close of the Galbraithian System," *Journal of Political Economy* (1967). Reprinted by permission of the publisher and the author.

quantities at these prices. So far from being controlled by the market, the firm, to the best of its ability, has made the market subordinate to the goals of its planning'' (1967, p. 110). The qualification in the last sentence quoted would suggest an examination of the constraints which act as exogenous controls over the firm, but Galbraith does not proceed in this direction. The qualification disappears utterly, and the picture that emerges of the modern large corporation is that it has unlimited power to reach forward and control its product demands and to reach backward and control its factor supplies. The demand and supply functions of the Galbraithian world all have price elasticities that are either infinite or zero, and often they degenerate to single points. Under such assumptions, it is not surprising that traditional market theory is regarded as yielding little insight into the mechanism of economic organization. In *American Capitalism* the business firm was considered to be constrained by the other major institutions of the economy, labor unions, and government, but in *The New Industrial State* these are viewed not as competing repositories of power but as complementary organisms which have joined with the great corporation to assist it in its ''planning.''

These developments, in Galbraith's view, have not resulted from fortuitous circumstances; they are inherent in the logic of modern technology. The day of the ''entrepreneurial firm'' is over. The modern industrial firm is operated by a ''technostructure'' of talents which manages the various processes of the firm down through its hierarchical levels and whose goals are primarily to maintain the autonomy of the organization itself and to promote its growth. What makes the modern giant corporation effective in the pursuit of its aims is organization. If there is genius at work, it is not to be found in any human frame; the ''technostructure'' consists of quite ordinary men who are welded into a managerial team. The English language does not contain a voice that is passive enough to express the essential idea. The corporation is simply ''doing its thing,'' as the Hippies would say, and its managerial members are doing theirs, governed by the imperatives of modern technology. Moreover, Galbraith asserts, these imperatives are not confined to capitalistic economies. Technological determinism is a law of industry which transcends political ideologies and social systems. He sees, accordingly, a convergence of the economic systems of all mature industrial states not, as some have claimed, because the Soviet-type economies are introducing some markets and capitalistic economies are introducing some macromanagerial elements, but because in both cases the ''heartland'' of the economy consists, as it *must,* of planning systems.

The Galbraithian view of the modern economy has innumerable antecedents in the sense that the death of the market has often been announced and with it, usually, the impotence of traditional economic analysis. But one need not linger over this. In specific terms, Galbraith's picture most distinctly evokes memories of Thorstein Veblen, who foresaw a kind of revolution by the technocrats who would take over the operation of the economy. Galbraith tells us that this revolution is already complete. Veblen's ''Soviet of Engineers'' is essentially the same as Galbraith's ''technostructure.'' In both views, these developments are considered to evolve from the inherent nature of modern production technology. There are normative similarities too. Veblen looked forward to the replacement of the price system by "engineers" as an advance in logic, order, and efficiency; yet he could not keep from speaking of it with a tinge of irony and even bitterness. The same is true of Galbraith. When he writes on these matters, his adjectives and adverbs carry reproaches and misgivings, but the substance of the argument is that the new world that is managed by the technostructures of the large corporations is far more efficient, both in the static sense and in the promotion of innovation, than a world of market organization. In the last chapters of *The New Industrial State,* Galbraith pleads for intellectuals to bestir themselves over the problems of political and economic power that these developments have created and asks, rather vaguely, for the use of government as a controlling and directing force. His main difficulty is, however, the same as Veblen's in the end: there is no practical (and perhaps no philosophical) difference between asserting that something is inevitable and considering it to be desirable.

Galbraith's analysis of the American economy is constructed upon his conception of the legal and organizational nature of the modern industrial firm. The essentials of this conception derive from Berle and Means' classic of thirty years ago, *The Modern Corporation and Private Property.* The delineation of the modern firm offered in *The New Industrial State* is, in such terms, largely conventional, but it is expressed vividly and effectively. There are some people left, including some economists, who persist in regarding the corporation as a purely instrumental device, an association of individual venturers of capital, and there are some areas of economic policy where anachronistic conceptions of this sort have been seriously misleading. Because it is likely to be so widely read, *The New Industrial State* may render good service in bringing, once again, to the attention of a wide audience one of the most momentous facts of the modern age, the emergence of the corporation as a primary social institution.

Galbraith's concept of the "technostructure," however, overstresses the monolithic nature of the corporate managerial system, and it is more likely to become a cliché than a useful tool of analysis. The decentralization of modern managerial organization indicated by Peter Drucker's *The Concept of the Corporation* has no reflection in *The New Industrial State,* though this development is, one would think, of the utmost importance in appraising the corporation's role as an economic and social institution. Galbraith also has little to say about other important modern developments, such as the growth of the conglomerate-type corporation and the phenomenal rise of pension funds as actual and potential owners of corporate stocks. In short, *The New Industrial State* does not enter upon an examination of the important recent and current developments in corporate evolution, some of which would seem to this reviewer to be very germane to the central thesis there presented. That the picture of the corporation contained in the book is consequently somewhat old hat and commonplace should not, however, obscure the fact that it is essentially true, and very important. The modern large corporation *is* largely free of stockholder control; it *does* supply internally a large part of its capital requirements; it *is* run by its managers; and the managerial bureaucracy *is* a coherent social-psychological system with motives and preferences of its own.

When we turn from Galbraith's picture of the internal organization of the modern corporation to his view of the external environment in which the corporation operates, however, the picture becomes much less satisfactory. The corporation here appears as a very strange organism indeed. It controls completely all the important elements of its environment. It has no need to accommodate itself to any exogenous circumstances; it is able to mold these to suit itself. Such a corporation would be like no organism, biological or social, that ever was, for it would encounter no constraints upon what it wishes (or is impelled) to do, which is to grow. Theoretically, we should observe all major industrial firms growing infinitely large, each of them—moreover, instantaneously! This is a caricature, but it serves to focus attention on the important question, which is: What are the factors that prevent this from occurring and how do they operate? It is not sufficient simply to say that "of course" rabbits or ants or humans or General Motors cannot overrun the earth, eliminating all other organisms. One must discover the mechanism that prevents this from happening. Scientific explanation is an essay on the constrained maximum; no less so when we examine the growth of firms. But the Galbraithian firm knows no constraints. "The size of General Motors is in the service not of monopoly or the economies of scale but of planning. And for this planning—control of supply, control of demand, provision of capital, minimization of risk—there is no clear upper limit to the desirable size. It could be that the bigger the better" (1967, p. 76).

But it can't be the bigger the better (relative to the total economy) for General Motors, United States Steel, and General Dynamics all at once. The Galbraithian picture is only plausible at all if one considers one firm at a time. It may be plausible to say that there is no market, as economists understand it, for automobiles or for steel, but what happens in the case of automotive steel where two "technostructures" confront one another? It is hardly sufficient to say, as Galbraith does, that they make contracts with one another (1967, p. 30) without describing what governs the terms they arrive at. The "countervailing power" thesis of *American Capitalism* might be invoked here, but Galbraith does not employ it in the analysis of *The New Industrial State,* and nothing else is introduced that might play a similar explanatory role. We are left with a microeconomics without Walras—a particular equilibrium analysis in which the equilibrium is nonsensical.

This points to the main defect of Galbraith's conception. He deals with the organization of the individual firm, but he says nothing about the organization of the *economy*. How is the economy organized into a coherent system? By means of what mechanism or procedure are the activities of the "five or six hundred firms" that constitute "the heartland of the modern [U.S.] economy" (1967, p. 9) made to mesh? Galbraith rejects the market mechanism of traditional economics, but he offers no answer of his own to these fundamental questions. *The New Industrial State* fails to present a coherent picture of what it sets out to describe, the organization of the American economy. It seems to me that Galbraith slips from the proposition that the firm plans to the proposition that the economy is planned, without realizing that such statements possess only a verbal similarity. His view of the forces making for a convergence of Soviet-type and capitalistic economies is marked by similar elisions.

Nevertheless, this does not mean that the traditional conception of American capitalism is a satisfactory one. There is no central planning agency which commands the economy, but there has been an immense proliferation of governmental policies at federal, state, and local levels over the past fifty years, and it is conceivable that the United States today is, in this way, more of a planned economy than is, say, Yugoslavia. On another plane, we have to recognize that fundamental changes have taken place in the control of American industry and that the traditional concept of private property is now inapplicable to this sphere of American life. Perhaps "private enterprise" as a concept for the analysis of the American economy and "socialist enterprise" for the Soviet Union are of little use, and we should regard both economies as essentially bureaucratic systems. Perhaps the "iron law of oligarchy" is necessary to make the "imperatives of modern technology" into a fruitful analytical conception. Galbraith, however, does not explore any of these avenues of investigation, nor does he develop any others to amplify his analysis. The main lines he draws are correct (though not as novel as he consistently implies), but though he writes at length, he puts very little upon his canvas that does more than ink over ever more heavily the first broad intuitive strokes.

ECONOMICS AND THE PUBLIC PURPOSE

A common criticism of *The New Industrial State* is that the economy is not "General Motors writ large." Galbraith readily agrees. To support his point that this was a purposeful omission rather than an error of commission, he has presented in his most recent work, *Economics and the Public Purpose,* a descriptive model of American capitalism composed of two major and roughly coequal sectors. One, the "planning system," consists of about one thousand Brobdingnagian corporations producing more than half of the GNP. Analysis of their organization and behavior provided the core of *The New Industrial State*. The other, the "market system," consists of about twelve million smaller firms and farms, in trade, light manufacturing, and services; it constitutes roughly the "other half" of the national economy.

Both sectors endeavor to control their economic environment, but by different means. The giant corporations do so by sheer size relative to their markets; the smaller firms, farms, and labor groups can do so only through collective action or government assistance. Further, the market system is part of the environment that the planning system seeks to control: large corporations both sell to and buy from smaller firms, but at prices controlled by the giants. Consequently, inequalities in economic power generate inequalities in income between the two sectors. From this analysis, and the judgment that these inequalities in power and income are irrational and unfair, Galbraith derives his major policy conclusion: government should assist, protect, and promote the market system so as to more or less equalize its power and rewards relative to those of the planning system. (The main themes of *Economics and the Public Purpose* are summarized in selection 5.7.)

If this sounds familiar, it should, for it essentially returns full circle to Galbraith's policy recommendation in *American Capitalism*: the utilization of government as an agency of countervailing power to succor the small and weak relative to the large and powerful. This raises two questions for critical evaluation. First, should this happen? Second, will (or can) it happen? As we have noted and will see (recall selection 5.2 and see selection 6.10), traditional advocates of competition such as Walter Adams—and neoliberals or individualist-conservatives such as George Stigler—answer "No" to the first question, on the grounds that countervailing power may simply serve to supplement monopoly in the planning system with monopoly (or greater monopoly) in the market system and that a more direct and desirable answer is to reduce economic power in the planning system through the promotion of effective competition. (Galbraith, of course, regards such an approach as utopian.)

In selection 5.8, Paul Sweezy, prominent neo-Marxist (see selection 7.2), further observes that not all members of the market system are victims of the economic system. Many (for example, relatively small but rich Texas ranchers) are its beneficiaries. But Sweezy focuses the major thrust of his criticism (of this aspect of Galbraith's analysis) on the second question. Is it plausible, he asks, to expect government, itself controlled by the dominant interests in the economic system,[3] to emancipate society from the technostructure and become the instrument of the "public purpose"? Without allies (notably, the working class) to "unseat the class now in power," Galbraith's proposals, Sweezy avers, are so much "utopian reformism."

Whatever one's response to this critique, it is clear from his latest work that America's most well-known contemporary economist has not lost his facility for raising fundamental questions concerning the organization and development of the modern industrial system. It is also clear that Galbraith cannot be cast (as he has on occasion been cast) as a Panglossian apologist for big business, oligopoly capitalism. *Economics and the Public Purpose* reinforces Galbraith's image as dissenting gadfly and demonstrates a close link with philosophies of liberal social reform. He has thus increasingly come to dissent both from neo-Keynesian orthodoxy, especially its conservative strand (recall chapter 3), and from recent endeavors by Milton Friedman and others to restate and update classical liberal views in a contemporary setting (see chapter 6).

[3] As a neo-Marxist, Sweezy continues to emphasize the dominant role played by capitalist industrial and financial interests in the seats of power. But the question remains even if we accept Galbraith's views concerning the shift in power to the technostructure.

5.7 Economics and the Public Purpose

John K. Galbraith

The Planning System and the Market System

The combination of a powerful thrust to the expansion of the firm in some parts of the economy with effective restraints on growth in other parts produces a remarkably skewed pattern of economic development. In the United States one may think of one thousand manufacturing, merchandising, transportation, power and financial corporations producing approximately half of all the goods and services not provided by the state. In manufacturing the concentration is greater. In the first quarter of 1971, the 111 industrial corporations with assets of a billion dollars or more had more than half of all the assets employed in manufacturing and received substantially more than half of the earnings on more than half of the sales. The 333 industrial corporations with assets of more than $500 million had a full 70 percent of all assets employed in manufacturing. In transportation, communications, power utilities, banking and finance, although the concentration is somewhat less, the tendency is similar; in merchandising the concentration is also high.

Making up the remainder of the economy are around twelve million smaller firms, including about three million farmers whose total sales are less than those of the four largest industrial corporations; just under three million garages, service stations, repair firms, laundries, laundromats, restaurants and other service establishments; two million small retail establishments; around nine hundred thousand construction firms; several hundred thousand small manufacturers; and an unspecified number serving the multivariate interests of an advanced society in what is collectively called vice.

No agreed level of assets or sales divides the millions of small firms which are half the private economy from the handful of giant corporations which are the other half. But there is a sharp conceptual difference between the enterprise that is fully under the command of an individual and owes its success to this circumstance and the firm which, without entirely excluding the influence of individuals, could not exist without organization. This distinction, which may be thought of as separating the twelve million small firms from the one thousand giants, underlies the broad division of the economy here employed. It distinguishes what is henceforth called the market system from what is called the planning system.

That the planning system does not conform to the neoclassical model—that its firms are not passive in response to the market or the state—will not be difficult to establish. Mainly it is a matter of breaking with accustomed and stereotyped thought. To this part of the economy we will return. The market system, in its admixture of monopoly and competition, does conform in broad outline to the neoclassical model. The latter model is a rough description of half of the economy; it has lost touch with the other and, in many ways decisive, half. Precisely because of its capacity for radical change the nonmarket part has transformed itself into something very different. But the market system also departs from the neoclassical model in two respects: Intervention by the state in this part of the economy is more extensive and altogether more normal than the theory suggests. And the market system must exist alongside the planning system. As might be imagined, its development is powerfully affected by this latter fact.

While the firm in the market system is subject to the market constraints and disciplines of the neoclassical model, it does not accept them with any pleasure. We may lay it down as a firm rule that all participants in the economic system will wish to modify such constraints in their own favor. They will try to influence prices, costs, consumer decisions and the actions of the community and the state. And this will be as true of the market system as the planning system. The difference is not in intent but ability.

The difference between the planning and the market systems does not lie in the desire to escape from the constraints of the market and to effect control over the economic environment. It is in the instruments by which these are accomplished and the success with which they are attended. Participants in the market system who want stabilization of their prices or control of their supply must act collectively or get the assistance of the government. Such effort is highly visible and often ineffective, unsuccessful or inefficient. Voluntary collective efforts can be destroyed by a few deserters. Legislators do not always respond—even to farmers. If action is taken, it is often taken apologetically, for it is recognized that the established economics disapproves.

In the planning system, in contrast, the firm wins its control over prices automatically and with no public fanfare merely by being large. Similarly over output. And it can be large because its tasks lend themselves to organization. There are also things for which it needs the support of the state. But its approach is not to the legislature but to the bureaucracy. This is more reticent. And, the bureaucracy being more powerful, it is also likely to be more effective. The consequence, not surprisingly, is that firms in the market system get much attention for accomplishing very little by way of setting aside market constraints or otherwise modifying the economic environment to which they are subject. And the large firms in the planning system get no attention for accomplishing much.

The planning system seeks to exercise control over its economic environment, and it succeeds. The market system manifests the same desire, is much more visible in its effort and is much less successful. The one system dominates its environment; the other remains generally subordinate to it.

But the planning system is very much a part of the environment to which the market system is subordinate. It supplies power, fuel, machinery, equipment, materials, transportation, communications that the market system uses. It also supplies a large share of the consumers' goods and services that participants in the market system purchase. And it is an important purchaser of the products of the market system—most notably in the case of agriculture. A prime feature of this relationship will already be evident. The market system buys at prices which are extensively subject to the power of the planning system. And an important part of its products and services are sold at prices which it does not control but which may be subject to the market power of the planning system. Given this distribution of power, there is a prima facie case that things will work better for the planning system than for the market system. The terms of trade between the two systems will have an insouciant tendency to favor the system that controls its prices and costs and therewith the prices and costs of the other system as well. A further effect, unless there is unimpeded mobility between the two systems, will be inequality of return—a relatively secure and favorable income for participants in the planning system, a less secure and less favorable return for those in the market system.

The neoclassical system accepts that differences in ability, energy and diligence are differently rewarded. Income accrues to property, and the ownership of property is not imagined to be equally distributed over the population. In some parts of the economy there are monopolies with their special capacity for enriching the recipients of monopoly gains. But the neoclassical system assumes that resource movement will work generally toward lessening inequality. And it does not allow of enduring differences in income among workers in different parts of the economy.

The present system leads, in contrast, to the expectation of an enduring difference in income between workers in different parts of the economy—and more generally. Five factors, all intrinsic to the system, suggest this result.

(1) The planning system resolves its conflict with unions by extensively conceding wage claims, including a share in productivity gains. The market system lacks both the power and, with some exceptions, the productivity gains.

(2) The control by the planning system over its prices and costs includes control over prices charged and paid to the market system. This allows it a substantial measure of control over its terms of trade with the market system. Being able to regulate its terms of trade, it naturally turns these (prices charged the market system, prices paid the market system) to its own advantage.

(3) This advantage is enhanced by the fact that the small entrepreneur in the market system remains in business in part because of his ability to reduce his own wage and in part because, unions being less frequent and less encouraged, he can on occasion reduce the wages of his workers. This exploitation has the sanction of the state, and the entrepreneur's self-exploitation is esteemed by the convenient social virtue.

(4) Measures to arrest inflation, as employed in the past, curtail demand, prices and incomes in the market system. In the planning system prices are under

control, and wages are subject to the authority of strong unions. The effect of restriction in demand in this part of the economy is thus on output and employment. Incomes of employed workers, overtime pay apart, do not fall. And the unemployment sharply reduces what chance there may be for workers in the market system to move to the higher-paid employment of the planning system.

(5) The planning system, especially in the technostructure, requires personnel of relatively high educational qualification—engineers, other technicians, accountants, lawyers, statisticians, computer programmers and many others. Educational requirements for employment in the market system—most notably in agriculture—have traditionally been much lower. The quality of the educational system accommodates to this difference. In addition some parts of the market system, agriculture again being the notable case, have relied extensively in the past on black and Mexican workers. Poor education, racial discrimination and the need to migrate from traditionally agricultural regions to areas of industrial employment have increased the wage differential between the market and the planning systems.

Policy for the Market System

The unequal development of the economy is the consequence of the power deployed differentially within the planning system and as compared with the market system. And the inequality in income as between the two systems has a similar source. The planning system, in the most general case, has power over the prices at which it sells to the market system and over the prices at which it buys from the market system. The terms of trade have, in consequence, a reliable tendency to be in its favor.

It will be evident that any fundamental correction of the relationship between the planning and the market systems must begin with the equalization of power between the two parts of the economy. This is no academic matter. It involves intensely practical questions of how prices, wages and incomes are established in the two systems—matters where necessity has already led to action that is not only unblessed by the accepted economics but is in conflict with its lessons. Viewed as we come to see it here, this action—agricultural price-fixing, other support to small businessmen, support to collective bargaining, minimum wage legislation, the proposed provision of a guaranteed minimum income, international commodity arrangements, even some protective tariffs—is an intensely logical response to the bargaining weakness of the market system. We have not moved too rapidly and incautiously with such legislation, as the accepted economics strongly holds. It is not a response to special circumstances or special hardship or politics, which is the normal explanation or justification. Given the structure of the modern economy—given the two systems—such action is the logical response to need. We suffer because we have moved too slowly and too cautiously and with too great a sense of guilt with measures to equalize the power wielded by the two systems.

The foregoing defines the nature and scope of efforts needed to remedy the weakness of the market system. It means that not reluctant, not merely passive, but strongly affirmative support must be accorded to its efforts to develop market power. In a rational and fair economy neglected and weak groups would be sought out and assisted in developing such power. There would be a general presumption not against but in favor of collective action by those who are numerous, small and weak. In specific terms this means the following:

(1) *General exemption for small businessmen from all prohibitions in the antitrust laws against combination to stabilize prices and output.* Any resulting abuse should be cured by regulation—not by efforts to restore competition. Further, where prices and incomes are notably low or erratic, there should be affirmative public support to organization to stabilize prices and production and to regulate entry into the business. Agreements to this end should be fully enforceable. And there should be particular encouragement to collective action limiting self-exploitation—limiting hours and conditions of work of self-employed entrepreneurs, notably in service industries, retailing and small manufacture.

The goal should not be in doubt. Nor should there be any effort at semantic concealment. The goal is to stabilize income and strengthen the bargaining position of the market system by collective and publicly reinforced power over the main determinants of income. For the consequence of what is here proposed is only to give the small businessman (and his workers) something of the security in prices and income, and therewith in investment and planning, that the large firm (and its employees) enjoys as a matter of course. It gives the service station operator, auto dealer, shoe manufacturer a modest fraction of the market power that General Motors, Ford or Exxon take for granted.

(2) *Direct government regulation of prices and production in the market system.* As in agriculture, self-organization to support prices, and thus to improve bargaining power and to raise and stabilize return, is often impractical in the market system. Any individual producer can get the advantages of the improved prices resulting from the cooperative action without accepting the restraints on output that such action normally requires. When enough discover this possibility, the cooperative action breaks down. In these circumstances government regulation of prices and production must be regarded as a wholly normal policy.

(3) *Strong and effective encouragement to trade union organization in the market system.* Nothing in economic life is more certain than that the evolution of economic society places the employee of the small firm in peculiar need of the support of a union. It is this employee whose bargaining position is weakest; it is his employer who survives because of that weakness. Even the briefest glance at the position of the farm worker, casual laborer, employee of the small service establishment, domestic worker, as compared with the trade union member in the planning system, affirms the point. Yet in the United States the law specifically denies the support of the National Labor Relations Act to such workers. It is hard to imagine a more illogical, even barbarous form of discrimination.

(4) *An extension and major increase in the minimum wage.* The market system, as it now operates, is a design for allowing the small entrepreneur to

survive by lowering his income. The first remedial step is to ensure that this is not involuntary—to allow collective action by producers to protect themselves against this tendency. And the second remedial step is to encourage trade union organization so that these employers cannot, at will, reduce the wages of their workers. For good reason such employers have a tradition of resisting trade unions. And, being small and geographically dispersed, these industries are often inherently difficult to organize. So the next line of defense is the minimum wage.

The minimum wage must be much more aggressively used than in the past. The test of the appropriate level, a most important point, is not what allows the small firm in the market system to survive. That is because the market system survives in part because of its superior ability to depress wages. Accordingly a minimum wage that is consistent with survival in the market system is one that perpetuates inequality. The ultimate purpose of the minimum wage is to eliminate the wage differential as between the market and the planning systems. This means, in effect, forcing those who patronize the market system to pay the full price for the product—one that reflects an equality of wage return with the planning system—or to go without. They must no longer be the beneficiaries of the bargaining weakness of workers in the market system. It is integral to this reform that no firm should be so small, no industry so weak, that (subject always to suitable time allowance for change and adjustment) it should be exempt from the minimum wage.

(5) *A revised view of international commodity organization and a cautiously revised view of tariff protection in the market system.* The large corporation extends its operations across international frontiers. Thus it is effectively protected against the special hazards of international trade. In other countries it participates in the oligopolistic convention that excludes price competition; foreign firms entering its home market operate under similar constraints. If its cost disadvantage is too great, it can produce in the low-cost country under its own brand. Having such protection, it does not need the further assistance of the protective tariff. It can take a large-minded view of the social merit of free trade.

Not so the firm in the market system. Its only hope for enjoying the same protection for prices and income that is enjoyed as a matter of course by the transnational firm will be an international agreement stabilizing prices and production by official action or a tariff. International agreements have been negotiated and operated with varying success in the past for wheat, coffee, rubber and sugar. The case for them is very strong. Less formal arrangements to stabilize prices or place quotas on shipments as between the market systems of different countries can similarly be justified. They only do for producers in such industries what transnational corporations accomplish far more efficiently for the planning systems. The difference is, that being visible, they arouse indignation.

The case for the use of national tariffs to protect the bargaining position of a national market system is less strong. Often there is advantage in replacing domestic with foreign production. The tariff is peculiarly likely—as international agreement is not—to invite retaliatory action with adverse consequence.

Still where tariff action is required as part of an effort to enhance the bargaining position of a domestic industry—as will normally be the case—such action cannot be excluded on doctrinal grounds. To do so is again to deny to the market system a protection that the planning system builds and enjoys as part of its basic structure.

(6) *A strong presumption in favor of government support to the educational, capital and technological needs of the market system.* The planning system, we have seen, can be viewed as an adaptation to the needs of modern technology. It has the ability to supply itself with the requisite capital. And it has a singular capacity to have its public needs, including those for qualified manpower, become public policy. The market system lacks such power. Actions by the state to provide the small firm with research and technical support, capital and qualified talent reflect not preferential but compensatory treatment. They are also essential elements of any policy designed to reduce the inherently unequal development as between the two systems.

5.8 Utopian Reformism

Paul M. Sweezy

Galbraith's newest critique of neoclassical (or orthodox or received) economics contains little that is new. It has been repeated, with variations and changing emphases, in all his works. And for the most part it is entirely justified. Economics as the subject is taught in establishment educational institutions has little relevance to reality and is thoroughly apologetic, in effect if not in intent. I will not dwell on this. What I wish to focus attention on is the "model" (the term is almost *de rigueur* these days) which he puts in the place of his version of the neoclassical picture of a consumer-dominated and producer-powerless self-adjusting market system which fails to perform satisfactorily only when deluded intellectuals and ignorant politicians meddle with it.

Galbraith's present model differs from his earlier versions in that he now divides the economy into two parts which he calls the "planning system" and the "market system." The planning system, as he acknowledges, is merely a new name for what is traditionally called the "monopolistic or oligopolistic sector": it comprises a thousand or so giant corporations which produce three quarters or more of the country's industrial output. The market system is the rest of the private economy, with agriculture, services, and retailing as its principal subdivisions. Having identified these two "systems," Galbraith proceeds to analyze the functioning of the economy as a whole in terms of their interaction with each other and with the state or public sector.

According to this analysis, the dominant role is played by the planning system. It is here that the driving force of the economy (the savings-and-

Excerpted from Paul M. Sweezy, "Utopian Reformism." *Monthly Review,* November 1973, pp. 1–11. Reprinted by permission of Monthly Review Press.

investment process) is centered. Given its overwhelming monopoly power, the planning system is able to exploit the largely competitive market system, enforcing on it unfavorable terms of trade in the manner of a metropolis and its colonies. This disparity in power is also reflected in the relations of the two systems to the state: the planning system has easy access to all branches of government and establishes effective control over most of them, while the market system is for the most part left out in the cold. "The modern state," he tells us, "is not the executive committee of the bourgeoisie, but it *is* more nearly the executive committee of the technostructure." (The "technostructure" is Galbraith's term for the controllers of the large corporation: we shall return to this presently.) The result of this lopsided distribution of power is that the planning system gets what it wants, especially money, from the state, while the market system is starved. This sets up a process of growing inequality between the two systems.

Compared to neoclassical theory, this two-systems model is undoubtedly an improvement. It integrates monopoly and state power, the dominant forces in the U.S. economy today, into the analysis of the system as a whole (neoclassical theory is artfully designed to avoid doing precisely this), and it succeeds quite well in offering plausible diagnoses of some of the system's major problems. One of these is the already-mentioned allocation of resources to and within the public sector. Another is inflation, which Galbraith recognizes to be endemic to the system, impervious to control through fiscal and monetary policies, and compatible with persistent high levels of unemployment.

I believe, however, that in many respects the Galbraithian model is seriously flawed and ends up as a kind of new, streamlined apologetic for monopoly capitalism. Since to develop this theme satisfactorily would require much more than a brief review, I will confine what follows to highlighting what seem to me to be some of the gravest weaknesses of his analysis.

THE PLANNING SYSTEM

Every economic enterprise, from the smallest to the largest, of course has to do a certain amount of planning. But as a group the large corporations do not do any planning together, and do not constitute a system in the usual sense of a collection of entites strongly interrelated among themselves and more weakly related to their environment. Galbraith as much as admits all this in numerous passages, as for example when he speaks of the need for measures "to ensure the interindustry coordination of which the planning system is incapable," or treats the energy "crisis" as precisely a symptom of the planning system's inability to plan. Apart from in-firm planning, which is real enough but not peculiar to Galbraith's planning system, what he seems generally to mean by "planning" is the power of the big corporations to throw their weight around in their relations with consumers and government, something which of course is emphasized by all theories of monopoly capitalism without any need to invoke the language of planning.

Why, then, is Galbraith so wedded to the notion of the planning system?

The reason, I think, is that it gives him one of the tools he needs for conceptualizing the U.S. power structure in a manner convenient to his own predilections and reform program. To explain this, we need first to understand another of Galbraith's key concepts.

THE TECHNOSTRUCTURE

It is pretty generally accepted by now that the typical big corporation is not controlled by majority vote of its shareholders or even by its board of directors, but by what it is usual to call its management, i.e., its top officers who (except in time of financial trouble) are normally a self-perpetuating group which selects the board of directors rather than vice versa. It is important to recognize that this does not mean what it is often taken to mean, that ownership and control are separated in the large corporation. Quite apart from cases in which management is picked by and represents large stockholders (majority or minority), executives of large corporations are, with few exceptions, wealthy men, owners of substantial amounts of stock in their own and other corporations. Far from being separated from ownership, they are simply the most active echelon of what C. Wright Mills called the corporate rich, who own a large part of the country's wealth. This being the case, one would naturally expect them to run their corporations with an eye single to maximum profit and the most rapid feasible accumulation of capital.

For reasons which will become clear as we proceed, however, this conclusion does not suit Galbraith's purposes at all. He would like to abolish the capitalist altogether, but since this is impossible, the next best thing is to transform him into a functionless (and relatively powerless) rentier. But this, as we have already seen, is not accomplished by the theory of managerial control: the managers are in fact capitalists in the fullest sense of the term. So Galbraith is driven to invent a new theory, the theory of the technostructure. The gist of the argument is that corporate managements, in the sense defined above, are not really in control at all. They lack the necessary knowledge, and knowledge is the basis of power. This knowledge is possessed by a large group of specialists. This is the technostructure. Not any single individual but the technostructure becomes the commanding power." In this way management is buried in, and subordinated to, the much larger technostructure, which derives its power from specialized knowledge and is in no way beholden to ownership.

It is only necessary to add that the technostructure is in charge of the planning system to control prices, manipulate the consumer, and dominate the state. Since, as we already know, the planning system also dominates and exploits the market system, it appears that we have here a complete picture of the power structure of American society. The technostructure sits at the center and runs the whole show.

In Galbraith's view, however, this is a pretty shaky arrangement. The technostructure doesn't really represent anyone but itself, and its power derives largely from its ability to hoodwink or brainwash most other people into believing that its purposes are identical with the public purpose. If the public, or sufficiently large segments of it, could be disabused of this way of looking at things, it should be relatively easy to break the society's thralldom to the technostructure. The state could then be "emancipated" and transformed into a "public state," and a whole series of reforms adding up to a "new socialism," or maybe several new socialisms, could be enacted and carried through.

Galbraith would nationalize a few sectors of the private economy, most notably the armament industries, but he is not naive enough to imagine that this by itself would change very much. For the rest, the ownership and organization of economic activity would be left as they are, with one exception. Every group would be encouraged, assisted, and in some cases perhaps even forced to organize to pursue its own economic interest. Since we can't have universal competition, he seems to be saying, let us universalize monopoly. And if one were to object that, judging from past experience, this seems a somewhat dubious method of achieving the "public purpose," Galbraith would probably reply that we have never had a "public state" presiding over the whole economy and imposing its benevolent dictates on all the conflicting but (in the new dispensation) relatively powerless groups and interests that make up the economy. The public state presumably embodies the public purpose, and Galbraith is the prophet of both.

But why call this a utopia rather than what Galbraith doubtless believes it to be, i.e., a hard-headed, realistic, and realizable program of social reform? The reason quite simply is that his conceptualization of the power structure is light years away from the reality of monopoly capitalist society.

The technostructure does not dominate the planning system, or anything else for that matter. Galbraith's contrary opinion is based on a confusion between making decisions within a given framework and deciding what goals are imposed by this framework on those operating within it. I do not think he is correct in maintaining that the technostructure rather than the management makes all the operating decisions—whether to build a new factory, how next year's model will differ from this year's, etc., etc.—but even if he were correct it would have no bearing on the ultimate purpose of the enterprise. This is determined not by any individual or group but by the very nature of the business system. *Real power in the enterprise is held by those who have the power to hire and fire, and it is precisely this power which inheres in management.* In exercising it, management acts as capitalists and on behalf of capitalists.

Once we realize that the capitalists dominate the giant corporations of today as completely as they did the smaller enterprises of a hundred years ago, we can hardly help wondering if Galbraith's theory is any more reliable in other respects. And the answer, not surprisingly (to use one of his favorite expressions), is that it is not.

For one thing, the picture of a more or less homogeneous "market system" confronting a handful of giant corporations is fanciful in the extreme. Not that the small exploited and self-exploiting enterprise doesn't exist in such areas of the economy as agriculture, retail trade, and services: it does exist and it is victimized by the system, just as Galbraith says. But there are also plenty of winners who are by no stretch of the imagination in Galbraith's planning system. To name only a few of the more important categories is to reveal how extensive and significant the phenomenon is: small and medium-sized corporations in manufacturing and trade, locally based construction firms (nearly the whole construction industry), large farmers and ranchers, real estate owners and operators, owners of radio and TV stations, local bankers, professionals (especially doctors and lawyers). Not all of those included in these categories are winners, of course. But literally millions of them are in no sense victims of the system: on the contrary, many are among its chief beneficiaries. Many of the people in the categories listed (and others not listed) are wealthy in their own right, with incomes and capital assets well above the average of the technostructure, and they are intertwined in many ways (e.g., through stock ownership) with the corporate rich. Politically, they dominate the communities and the electoral districts, often right up to the state level, in which they live and operate. Socially, they belong to the same class as the corporate rich, sharing the same life-style, the same values, the same ideology. They thus constitute what is, in terms of numbers and geographical spread, by far the largest part of a relatively homogeneous class which derives its enormous wealth and privileges from the economic status quo.

But is this also a ruling class in the sense of dominating the state? According to Galbraith's theory, the answer would have to be no. He makes a rather sharp distinction between the bureaucratic and elective branches of the government. The bureaucracies are similar in composition and outlook to the technostructure, with which they have a strong tendency to develop what he calls a symbiotic relationship: this indeed is the source of the technostructure's power over the state. The elective branches, congress and the presidency, on the other hand, are not necessarily tied to any power group. To be sure, the Republican Party and up to now a large part of the Democratic Party have bought the technostructure's line that what is good for it is good for the country. But these alliances are not unbreakable. As we have already seen, Galbraith believes that beginning with the elective branches, the state can be emancipated from the technostructure and turned into the instrument of the "public purpose."

From the standpoint of class analysis, things look rather different. The higher reaches of the government bureaucracies (including the judiciary) are overwhelmingly staffed by members of the dominant economic class and/or people dependent on them; and the political party organizations are controlled at every level by the vested interests which stand to gain most from the protection and favors which the local, state, and federal governments are in a position to hand out. These are facts which have been confirmed by innumerable empirical studies of cities, towns, and political institutions, though it is true that not all of the authors of these studies draw the logical conclusion that government in the United States is owned lock, stock, and barrel by exactly the same interests that own most of the country's wealth and control its economic life. These interests, taken together, constitute a ruling class in the fullest sense of the term, the richest and most powerful ruling class in the history of the world.

The implications of this for Galbraith's strategy of reform are of course devastating. If the enemy is a rootless, upstart technostructure which maintains itself in power mainly by selling a phony ideological bill of goods, then it makes sense to rely on an ideological counterattack followed by an effort to win over the Democratic Party to Galbraith's new brand of populism. But if the enemy is in fact an enormously powerful bourgeoisie with two centuries of experience in ruling behind it and absolutely no scruples about using every and any available means to achieve its ends, then a rather different strategy seems called for. Above all, one had better look around for possible allies who could enter upon a struggle to unseat the class now in power with a reasonable prospect of success. And I challenge Galbraith, or anyone else, to say where such allies might conceivably be found except in the working class, using the term in a broad sense to include the great majority of those who must work for a living regardless of the color of their collars. Workers have potential power not because they are in the majority—when the chips are down no ruling class cares for the arithmetic of minorities and majorities—but because they are indispensable to the process of production and hence to the very life of society.

Like most liberals, Galbraith sees little hope in the workers. If he is right, things will continue to deteriorate, as Galbraith now recognizes they have been deteriorating for a long time. But it might be more constructive to work on the assumption that at some stage in this process American workers will experience a political awakening, similar to that of the 1930s, only next time on a scale appropriate to the seriousness of the developing crisis of world capitalism. I would like to pay Galbraith the compliment of believing that, should this happen, he will be flexible enough to write another book explaining how and why he expected it all along.

6 RADICAL REFORM FROM THE RIGHT: THE INDIVIDUALIST CONSERVATISM OF THE NEO-LIBERALS

A third major strand of dissent from the post-Keynesian synthesis, and one that proposes radical reform of the economic order, is found in the writings of what is called variously "individualist-conservatism" or "neo-liberalism." In chapter 1, the term *classical liberalism* was used to encompass the social and economic philosophy of such figures as Adam Smith and John Stuart Mill. This philosophy embodied three prominent dimensions: freedom of individual economic choice, social coordination through the competitive market, and a strategic but limited role for government in economic life. Economists such as Hayek, Friedman, Buchanan, and others are self-consciously "liberal" and anti-conservative. They view their ideas as extensions and reformulations of classical liberalism (hence, *neo*-liberalism), and they specifically criticize conservatism. As defined by Hayek, conservatism embodies "paternalistic, anti-intellectual, and often mystical propensities. . . ." Without a social program, and characterized essentially by a timid distrust and "fear of change," a conservative movement "is bound to be a defender of established privilege and to lean on the power of the government for the protection of privilege."[1] At least since the New Deal in the United States, however, "liberalism" has popularly connoted left-wing democratic social reform, and has been identified with the extension of collective (especially governmental) control over economic life.[2] The neo-liberals' disassociation from liberal-labor reform, their critique of collective-governmental control of economic affairs, and their focus on freedom of individual choice explain their popular designation as conservative-individualist. And because many liberal reforms have been accepted or implemented under the auspices of the post-Keynesian synthesis, neo-liberals are often in the unenviable position of appearing to be in alliance with (laissez-faire) conservatives and opposed to progressive institutional change in general. Actually, neo-liberals are somewhat removed from both the "liberal" and

[1]Friedrich A. Hayek, *The Road to Serfdom* (Chicago: University of Chicago Press, 1949), p. xi.

[2]It should be reemphasized, however, that the rationale of contemporary social reform liberalism for extending the role of collective, especially governmental, measures is only as a means to the end of enhancing effective liberty for society as a whole, including workers, lower income groups, and racial minorities.

"conservative" strands of the post-Keynesian synthesis. Full implementation of their individualizing, decentralizing, market-oriented proposals would constitute a *radical* reconstruction of the American economic system. In this respect, neo-liberalism resembles the anticentralization, antibureaucracy New Left criticisms of the post-Keynesian synthesis.

Although lacking a strong political following, neo-liberalism has been highly influential within the economics profession, and its major ideas have percolated into broader criticisms of the post-Keynesian orthodoxy at a number of strategic points (for example, on the questions of monetary versus fiscal policy and on the possibility of a guaranteed annual income). Donald Watson sketches the general contours of the neo-liberal–individualist-conservative economic philosophy in selection 6.1.

6.1 Neo-Liberalism

Donald S. Watson

Neo-liberalism in its most uncompromising form is probably best represented by Ludwig von Mises, one of many Viennese economists who have come to the United States. So extreme indeed is his position on any question of economic policy that it is perhaps difficult to say where Mises really differs from the classical liberals of the last century. Moreover, other neo-liberals disagree sharply with Mises on many points. He has written much in exposition of his views on economic policy; in attempting to gain a popular following he has been able to interest only a few small groups of businessmen. Mises holds to an extreme individualism; all of his value judgments turn on questions of the achievements of the goals of individuals, whose means of social cooperation he sees as the market. To him the only proper function of government is to assist the smooth functioning of the market economy. He therefore subscribes explicitly to the laissez faire policy because it means that each individual can "choose how he wants to cooperate in the social division of labor."

The Road to Serfdom by Friedrich A. Hayek, is a well-known tract on the neo-liberal economic philosophy. Its theses are that the accumulation of large-scale government intervention in the economy leads to socialism, that freedom and democracy cannot exist under socialism, and that therefore the movement toward more government controls should be stopped. Hayek however does not advocate a return to nineteenth-century laissez faire, a slogan which he in fact specifically repudiates. Hayek's positive case is for the strengthening of competition and for economic policies in the form of "rules of law." He gives support to such policies as minimum wages, social security, and building regulations, provided that these and other economic policies are laid down clearly by the legislature as definite rules, infrequently changed, and applicable to all.

Of the American neo-liberals, perhaps the most outspoken and vigorous was the late Henry C. Simons. His general views on economic policy are stated in an essay published in 1934 with the arresting title *A Positive Program for Laissez Faire: Some Proposals for a Liberal Economic Policy*. Simons did not advocate laissez faire in the generally understood sense of that term. On the contrary, he proposed that government undertake a series of measures, all of them drastic, to establish a system under which freedom and equality will flourish. His drastic measures are the elimination of private monopoly by radical reform of the business corporation, the breaking up of large units, and the enforcement of competition; the resort to government ownership where competition is impossible; the gradual adoption of free trade; and a drastic reduction of inequalities of income through overhaul of the tax system. Radical, too, was Simons' proposal for a thorough transformation of the banking system. Among other things, he wanted bank deposits to have full (100 per cent) reserves instead of partial reserves. In general, this view is still held by neo-liberal economists.

The universities of Vienna and of Chicago have been centers of neo-liberal economic thought. Neo-liberalism in the United States has even been called "the Chicago School of economic policy." A few well-known British and German economists are also neo-liberal in their economic philosophies.

THE GENERAL CHARACTERISTICS OF NEO-LIBERALISM

The market is considered by neo-liberals as an institution or rather a complex of closely related institutions that on the whole works well. In the value judgments of neo-liberalism the market is assigned tasks of high importance and is found to fulfill those tasks. The purely economic task of directing production at low or minimum cost to the maximum satisfaction of consumers' wants is amply described by economic theory, on which many of the neo-liberals are authorities. Holding firmly to the philosophy of the rights of the individual, neo-liberals also assign, so it can be said, an ethical task to the market, as they would like to see it operate—the task of protecting and fostering the freedom of the individual. The market likewise has political tasks: the minimization of private power and the protection of the rights of minorities. Neo-liberals are inclined to meet adverse criticism of the market by replying that bad government restrictions or faulty legal institutions prevent or hamper the market from yielding the good results of which it is capable.

An economy composed of small units is an ideal of neo-liberalism, one of course following from the strong emphasis on the market. The market must be competitive and must therefore be composed of units small enough so that no one can wield private power and dominate others. In his *The Social Crisis of our Time* the German-Swiss neo-liberal Wilhelm Röpke sees Western civilization as torn between the remains of an outworn laissez faire philosophy and in danger of succumbing to the deceitful lures of collectivism. The solution to the social crisis is "the third way," which is Röpke's manner of describing his own version of a neo-liberal economic and social philosophy. A society following the third way would contain a competitive economy of small units; there would be no gigantic corporations or unions or any other large nongovernmental organizations. The American neo-liberal Henry C. Simons was also explicit and forthright in proposing a dismantling of large private economic organizations as a necessary step in establishing a thoroughly competitive economy. Other neo-liberals have hesitated to make such bold and sweeping recommendations, and in general have tended to confine themselves to narrower issues, such as stricter enforcement of the antitrust laws.

A preference for freedom and progress over stability is also a part of the system of value judgments of neo-liberalism. Like everyone else, neo-liberals of course want economic stability, but they are not willing to place this objective ahead of others they regard as equally or more important. Economic freedoms and conditions of economic progress come first in the minds of neo-liberals. To a considerable extent however this part of the neo-liberal doctrine is negative, in the sense that it is a protest against the heavy emphasis during the last generation upon full employment. In the late 1950's, neo-liberal economists stressed the desirability of price stability over the stability of employment; reform-liberal economists tended to take the opposite position.

The proper task of government is to maintain a strong framework of economic rules. Such is the positive role assigned to government in neo-liberal doctrine. In Röpke's words, "It is a permanent task of economic policy to lay down and enforce the norms and standards of economic life." In this respect neo-liberalism clearly differs from classical liberalism. Where the latter assigned a minimum role to government, neo-liberalism prescribes a long list of important functions to government. The functions however are all of one kind—they are the establishment of "rules."

This feature of neo-liberalism will now be given closer attention. The distinction between rules and authorities (i.e., discretionary controls) was most certainly not explicit in classical liberalism. The distinction furthermore dismisses the issue of laissez faire. To the neo-liberals the issue is not *whether* there should be government economic controls, but rather *what kinds,* and *how* they should be executed. Still another reason for a close look at the distinction is the contrast with reform liberalism. And again, public debates on economic policies frequently turn on controversies over means rather than ends.

"RULES VERSUS AUTHORITIES"

The neo-liberal economists generally make much of the distinction between "rules" and "authorities." The concepts are not entirely clear, nor is it easy to draw a line between them. The issue is nonetheless fundamental because it lies at the heart of the neo-liberal economic philosophy.

In the neo-liberal economic philosophy, rules are ends-means structures establishing boundaries for the economic activity of individuals. There may be few of them or many. Wilhelm Röpke uses the terms "compatible" and "incompatible," that is, compatible or incompatible with the market. To Röpke, any form of government intervention that does not impair the functioning of the price mechanism is compatible with it. Such intervention, he contends, is absorbed by the market. An example is a tariff; being a rise in the cost of importing, it affects importers, consumers, and domestic producers, all of whom adjust their demands and supplies. The flows of production and consumption are altered, but they continue to be determined by the decisions of private individuals. To call a tariff compatible is not of course to give it a stamp of approval, but only to draw attention to its character. In contrast, foreign exchange control and import quotas are classed by Röpke as incompatible with the market and the price mechanism, because these methods of control mean that government itself determines directly the amounts and kinds of imports.

Characteristics of Rules

(1) Once established, a rule is not changed frequently, and thus becomes a firm basis for the long-range decisions of all those affected. Examples of comparatively infrequent change are the federal minimum wage, and formerly, the tariff duties on imports; in these examples the intervals between changes have been several years. On the other hand, some instruments of economic policy, such as member-bank reserve requirements and the margin requirements for trading on the stock exchanges, possess some of the attributes of rules, but have in fact been altered fairly frequently in some periods, although they have often remained unchanged for several years at a time. The infrequent change that is supposedly a characteristic of a rule is to be contrasted with the exercise of continuous supervision by an administrative body, as in the efforts to manipulate farm prices. Here the firms and individuals directly concerned are faced with the additional uncertainty of having to guess the actions of the regulating body. (2) Rules are general or universal in both intent and application. Neoliberals like further to stress their impersonal and nondiscriminatory nature. Where the effect of a rule is to alter a market price, the market mechanism continues to function, and individuals continue to make their own adjustments to it. (3) Rules are simple to enforce. The principle of their administration is simple, even where questions of fact may be complicated, because the task of enforcement is only to see whether or not the minimum wage is paid, the duty on imports is collected, the zoning laws are obeyed, or whatever it may be. For the enforcement of rules the administrative machinery is small and relatively uncomplicated, consisting in most instances of a few attorneys and inspectors, and their clerical staffs.

Characteristics of Authorities

(1) The market is replaced or supplanted, as in the example of an import quota; the amount of a commodity to be imported is directly decided, as a definite physical or dollar volume. In contrast, the effects of a higher tariff are nearly always uncertain, because importers make the decisions as to how much to import. Where the operations of the market are not superseded, they are modified, as in the control of farm prices—the federal government enters on the

demand side as a buyer or on the supply side to keep farm commodities off the market. (2) Control is continuous, being altered from time to time as facts, circumstances, and opinions change. If, for example, imports are regulated by means of a quota, the regulating body modifies the quota once a year at the least. The business firms and individuals directly affected have the tasks both of guessing what the regulating body's decisions will be, and if possible of influencing the decisions in their favor. (3) If the administrators have wide discretion and can settle individual cases according to merit, then the ends of the policy in question are decided or modified by the administrators. (4) Where the administrators of an economic policy have wide discretion and where their legal powers are sufficient to direct the uses of economic resources, they can select the persons or classes of persons (including of course corporations) to be benefited or punished. Such control can then be discriminatory in the sense in which a rule is not. (5) Control by administrative discretion with wide and flexible powers can mean precision and speed. These are virtues significant and necessary in times of grave emergency.

THE MEANING OF NEO-LIBERALISM FOR CONTEMPORARY ECONOMIC POLICY

To a large extent the attitude and positions taken by neo-liberals on questions of contemporary economic policy are negative. As adverse critics of many of the current economic policies, neo-liberals have much to contribute, even to those in fundamental disagreement, because as good economists, the neo-liberals can point to the otherwise unappreciated implications of economic policies. Lacking any mass support or popular following, the neo-liberal views have, however, slight impact upon the course of most actual economic policies. Nevertheless the neo-liberals do exert some influence in the sense that they furnish powerful intellectual support for the continuation and strengthening of monetary policy, of the antitrust policy, and of policies directed toward the lowering of barriers to international trade. There are certain areas of economic policy on which neo-liberals have had little to say. In some cases this is because they perhaps consider the policies, though hopelessly wrong, too firmly imbedded to be changed. In other instances neo-liberals have been relatively silent because it can be hazarded that the policies in question make them uncomfortable; possible examples are the regulation of public utilities and of labor relations.

THE ROAD TO SERFDOM

Basic to the neo-liberal critique is the view that the modern mixed economies, established in the United States and elsewhere in accord with principles of the post-Keynesian synthesis, are institutionally unstable, and that if not radically reconstructed in a decentralized, market-oriented direction, they will be transformed eventually into systems of central planning and comprehensive governmental control. "Fundamentally, there are only two ways of coordinating the economic activities of millions," contends Friedman. "One is central direction involving the use of coercion—the technique of the army and of the modern totalitarian state. The other is voluntary cooperation of individuals—the technique of the marketplace."[3] But to launch a democratic capitalist economy on large-scale programs of left-wing, centralist economic reform is to virtually guarantee its deterioration into (first) socialism and, thereby (second) totalitarianism. This is the grand theme of Hayek's *The Road to Serfdom* (1944). First, departure from and interference with the competitive market system leads to socialism.

1. Once private monopoly power is allowed to become entrenched, the only viable alternative is government control of monopoly, which, to be effective, must become ever more detailed.

2. Once government control, through taxation and collective expenditure, becomes a substantial part of the economy (say, 30 to 50 percent), it thereby dominates the whole.

3. Government controls, by intervening in the market, prevent it from functioning and thereby create pressures for greater controls.

4. To be effective, controls of one type (for example, price control) must be accompanied by others (for example, wage control).

5. As the scope of government control is extended, impersonal market forces (which people accept as beyond their control) play a smaller role and conscious political decisions (which people do not accept as beyond their control) play a larger role in determining income and employment; consequently, pressures to influence government on behalf of various groups increase.

Second, democratic socialism or collectivist democracy is an illusion, or at best a short-lived phenomenon. Socialism will lead to totalitarianism, and the loss of democracy and individual freedoms.

1. Socialism is characterized, by definition, by the loss or absence of individual economic freedoms (for example, loss of free enterprise, substitution of central political choice for consumer sovereignty).

2. Socialism is inconsistent with political democracy and individual political freedom. Because of the complexities of centralized economic planning, democratic legislatures cannot plan effectively and will increasingly delegate economic authority to the executive and its agencies, far removed from democratic control. Socialist planning then leads to dictatorship, because dictatorship "is the most effective instrument of coercion and the enforcement of ideals, and, as such, essential if central planning on a large scale is to be possible."[4] Then, since dictatorial planning would be more successful if government were free from criticism and dissent, totalitarian control over political life is a frightening likelihood.

These themes are developed in greater depth by Hayek in selection 6.2. In selection 6.3 they are critically evaluated by Henry Wallich, noted advocate of conservative, but "middle-of-the-road," positions on economic issues. (Recall selections 3.18 and 5.4.)

[3] Milton Friedman, *Capitalism and Freedom* (Chicago: University of Chicago Press, 1962), p. 13.

[4] Hayek, *The Road to Serfdom*, p. 70.

6.2 The Road to Serfdom: Exposition

Friedrich A. Hayek

INDIVIDUALISM AND COLLECTIVISM

Socialism may mean, and is often used to describe, merely the ideals of social justice, greater equality, and security, which are the ultimate aims of socialism. But it means also the particular method by which most socialists hope to attain these ends and which many competent people regard as the only methods by which they can be fully and quickly attained. In this sense socialism means the abolition of private enterprise, of private ownership of the means of production, and the creation of a system of "planned economy" in which the entrepreneur working for profit is replaced by a central planning body.

To nearly all those to whom socialism is not merely a hope but an object of practical politics, the characteristic methods of modern socialism are as essential as the ends themselves. Many people, on the other hand, who value the ultimate ends of socialism no less than the socialists refuse to support socialism because of the dangers to other values they see in the methods proposed by the socialists. The dispute about socialism has thus become largely a dispute about means and not about ends—although the question whether the different ends of socialism can be simultaneously achieved is also involved.

The situation is still more complicated by the fact that the same means, the "economic planning" which is the prime instrument of socialist reform, can be used for many other purposes. We must centrally direct economic activity if we want to make the distribution of income conform to current ideas of social justice.

But such planning is no less indispensable if the distribution of incomes is to be regulated in a way which to us appears to be the opposite of just.

It must always be remembered that socialism is a species of collectivism and that therefore everything which is true of collectivism as such must apply also to socialism. Nearly all the points which are disputed between socialists and liberals concern the methods common to all forms of collectivism and not the particular ends for which socialists want to use them; and all the consequences with which we shall be concerned follow from the methods of collectivism irrespective of the ends for which they are used.

The difficulties caused by the ambiguities of the common political terms are not yet over.

The idea of central economic planning owes its appeal largely to the very vagueness of its meaning; it is essential that we should agree on its precise sense before we discuss its consequences.

Excerpted from Friedrich A. Hayek, *The Road to Serfdom,* (Chicago: University of Chicago Press, 1944), pp. 32-35, 40-43, 56-62, 64-71, 88-95. Reprinted by permission of The University of Chicago Press, Routledge & Kegan Paul, Ltd., London, and the author.

"Planning" owes its popularity largely to the fact that everybody desires, of course, that we should handle our common problems as rationally as possible and that, in so doing, we should use as much foresight as we can command.

An economist, whose whole task is the study of how men actually do and how they might plan their affairs, is the last person who could object to planning in this general sense. But it is not in this sense that our enthusiasts for a planned society now employ this term.

According to the modern planners, it is not sufficient to design the most rational permanent framework within which the various activities would be conducted by different persons according to their individual plans. This liberal plan, according to them, is no plan—and it is, indeed, not a plan designed to satisfy particular views about who should have what. What our planners demand is a central direction of all economic activity according to a single plan, laying down how the resources of society should be "consciously directed" to serve particular ends in a definite way.

The dispute between the modern planners and their opponents is, therefore, *not* a dispute on whether we ought to choose intelligently between the various possible organizations of society; it is not a dispute on whether we ought to employ foresight and systematic thinking in planning our common affairs. It is a dispute about what is the best way of so doing. The question is whether for this purpose it is better that the holder of coercive power should confine himself in general to creating conditions under which the knowledge and initiative of individuals are given the best scope so that *they* can plan most successfully; or whether a rational utilization of our resources requires *central* direction and organization of all our activities according to some consciously constructed "blueprint."

What in effect unites the socialists of the Left and the Right is this common hostility to competition and their common desire to replace it by a directed economy.

Yet, though all the changes we are observing tend in the direction of a comprehensive central direction of economic activity, the universal struggle against competition promises to produce in the first instance something in many respects even worse, a state of affairs which can satisfy neither planners nor liberals: a sort of syndicalist or "corporative" organization of industry, in which competition is more or less suppressed but planning is left in the hands of the independent monopolies of the separate industries. This is the inevitable first result of a situation in which the people are united in their hostility to competition but agree on little else. By destroying competition in industry after industry, this policy puts the consumer at the mercy of the joint monopolist action of capitalists and workers in the best organized industries. Yet, it is not a state which is likely to persist or can be rationally justified. Such independent planning by industrial monopolies would, in fact, produce effects opposite to those at which the argument for planning aims. Once this stage is reached, the only alternative to a return to competition is the control of the monopolies by the state—a control which, if it is to be made effective, must become progressively more complete and more detailed.

Although competition can bear some admixture of regulation, it cannot be combined with planning to any extent we like without ceasing to operate as an effective guide to production. Nor is "planning" a medicine which, taken in small doses, can produce the effects for which one might hope from its thoroughgoing application. Both competition and central direction become poor and inefficient tools if they are incomplete; they are alternative principles used to solve the same problem, and a mixture of the two means that neither will really work and that the result will be worse than if either system had been consistently relied upon. Planning and competition can be combined by planning for competition but not by planning against competition.

THE "INEVITABILITY" OF PLANNING

It is a revealing fact that few planners are content to say that central planning is desirable. Most of them affirm that we can no longer choose but are compelled by circumstances beyond our control to substitute planning for competition. The myth is deliberately cultivated that we are embarking on the new course not out of free will but because competition is spontaneously eliminated by technological changes which we neither can reverse nor should wish to prevent. This argument is rarely developed at any length—it is one of the assertions taken over by one writer from another until, by mere iteration, it has come to be accepted as an established fact. It is, nevertheless, devoid of foundation. The tendency toward monopoly and planning is not the result of any "objective facts" beyond our control but the product of opinions fostered and propagated for half a century until they have come to dominate all our policy.

PLANNING AND DEMOCRACY

The various kinds of collectivism, communism, fascism, etc., differ among themselves in the nature of the goal toward which they want to direct the efforts of society. But they all differ from liberalism and individualism in wanting to organize the whole of society and all its resources for this unitary end and in refusing to recognize autonomous spheres in which the ends of the individuals are supreme. In short, they are totalitarian in the true sense of this word.

The "social goal," or "common purpose," for which society is to be organized is usually vaguely described as the "common good," the "general welfare," or the "general interest." It does not need much reflection to see that these terms have no sufficiently definite meaning to determine a particular course of action. The welfare and the happiness of millions cannot be adequately expressed as a single end, but only as a hierarchy of ends, a comprehensive scale of values in which every need of every person is given its place. To direct all our activities according to a single plan presupposes that every one of our needs is given its rank in an order of values which must be complete enough to make it possible to decide among all the different courses which the planner has to choose. It presupposes, in short, the existence of a complete ethical code in which all the different human values are allotted their due place.

The essential point for us is that no such complete ethical code exists. Not only do we not possess such an all-inclusive scale of values: it would be impossible for any mind to comprehend the infinite variety of different needs of different people which compete for the available resources and to attach a definite weight to each.

This is the fundamental fact on which the whole philosophy of individualism is based. It starts from the indisputable fact that the limits of our powers of imagination make it impossible to include in our scale of values more than a sector of the needs of the whole society.

From this the individualist concludes that individuals should be allowed, within defined limits, to follow their own values and preferences rather than somebody else's; that within these spheres the individual's system of ends should be supreme and not subject to any dictation by others.

When individuals combine in a joint effort to realize ends they have in common, the organizations, like the state, that they form for this purpose are given their own system of ends and their own means. But any organization thus formed remains one "person" among others, in the case of the state much more powerful than any of the others, it is true, yet still with its separate and limited sphere in which alone its ends are supreme. The limits of this sphere are determined by the extent to which the individuals agree on particular ends; and the probability that they will agree on a particular course of action necessarily decreases as the scope of such action extends. There are certain functions of the state on the exercise of which there will be practical unanimity among its citizens; there will be others on which there will be agreement of a substantial majority; and so on, until we come to fields where, although each individual might wish the state to act in some way, there will be almost as many views about what the government should do as there are different people.

We can rely on voluntary agreement to guide the action of the state only so long as it is confined to spheres where agreement exists. But not only when the state undertakes direct control in fields where there is no such agreement is it bound to suppress individual freedom. We can unfortunately not indefinitely extend the sphere of common action and still leave the individual free in his own sphere. Once the communal sector, in which the state controls all the means, exceeds a certain proportion of the whole the effects of its actions dominate the whole system. Although the state controls directly the use of only a large part of the available resources, the effects of its decisions on the remaining part of the economic system become so great that indirectly it controls almost everything. Where the central and local authorities directly control the use of more than half the national income, they control indirectly almost the whole economic life of the nation.

It is not difficult to see what must be the consequences when democracy embarks upon a course of planning which in its execution requires more agreement than in fact exists. Agreement will exist only on the mechanism to be used. But it is a mechanism which can be used only for a common end; and the question of the precise goal toward which all activity is to be directed will arise as soon as the executive power has to translate the demand for a single plan into a particular plan. Then it will appear that the agreement on the desirability of planning is not supported by agreement on the ends the plan is to serve.

It may be the unanimously expressed will of the people that its parliament should prepare a comprehensive economic plan, yet neither the people nor its representatives need therefore be able to agree on any particular plan. The inability of democratic assemblies to carry out what seems to be a clear mandate of the people will inevitably cause dissatisfaction with democratic institutions. Parliaments come to be regarded as ineffective "talking shops," unable or incompetent to carry out the tasks for which they have been chosen. The conviction grows that if efficient planning is to be done, the direction must be "taken out of politics" and placed in the hands of experts—permanent officials or independent autonomous bodies.

It is important clearly to see the causes of this admitted ineffectiveness of parliaments when it comes to a detailed administration of the economic affairs of a nation. The fault is neither with the individual representatives nor with parliamentary institutions as such but with the contradictions inherent in the task with which they are charged. They are not asked to act where they can agree, but to produce agreement on everything—the whole direction of the resources of the nation. For such a task the system of majority decision is, however, not suited. Majorities will be found where it is a choice between limited alternatives; but it is a superstition to believe that there must be a majority view on everything. There is no reason why there should be a majority in favor of any one of the different possible courses of positive action if their number is legion. Every member of the legislative assembly might prefer some particular plan for the direction of economic activity to no plan, yet no one plan may appear preferable to a majority to no plan at all.

Nor can a coherent plan be achieved by breaking it up into parts and voting on particular issues.

An economic plan, to deserve the name, must have a unitary conception. A complex whole in which all the parts must be most carefully adjusted to each other cannot be achieved through a compromise between conflicting views. To draw up an economic plan in this fashion is even less possible than, for example, successfully to plan a military campaign by democratic procedure. As in strategy it would become inevitable to delegate the task to the experts.

But the ends of an economic plan, or of any part of it, cannot be defined apart from the particular plan. It is the essence of the economic problem that the making of an economic plan involves the choice between conflicting or competing ends—different needs of different people. But which ends do so conflict, which will have to be sacrificed if we want to achieve certain others, in short, which are the alternatives between which we must choose, can only be known to those who know all the facts; and only they, the experts, are in a position to decide which of the different ends are to be given preference. It is inevitable that they should impose their scale of preferences on the community for which they plan.

This is not always clearly recognized, and delegation is usually justified by the technical character of the task. But this does not mean that only the technical detail is delegated, or even that the inability of parliaments to understand the technical detail is the root of the difficulty.

It is not the delegation of law-making power as such which is so objectionable. The objectionable feature is that delegation is so often resorted to because the matter in hand cannot be regulated by general rules but only by the exercise of discretion in the decision of particular cases. In these instances delegation means that some authority is given power to make with the force of law what to all intents and purposes are arbitrary decisions (usually described as "judging the case on its merits").

The expedient of delegation cannot really remove the causes which make all the advocates of comprehensive planning so impatient with the impotence of democracy. The delegation of particular powers to separate agencies creates a new obstacle to the achievement of a single co-ordinated plan. Even if, by this expedient, a democracy should succeed in planning every sector of economic activity, it would still have to face the problem of integrating these separate plans into a unitary whole. Many separate plans do not make a planned whole—in fact, as the planners ought to be the first to admit, they may be worse than no plan. But the democratic legislature will long hesitate to relinquish the decisions on really vital issues, and so long as it does so it makes it impossible for anyone else to provide the comprehensive plan. Yet agreement that planning is necessary, together with the inability of democratic assemblies to produce a plan, will evoke stronger and stronger demands that the government or some single individual should be given powers to act on their own responsibility. The belief is becoming more and more widespread that, if things are to get done, the responsible authorities must be freed from the fetters of democratic procedure.

The argument by which the planners usually try to reconcile us with this development is that, so long as democracy retains ultimate control, the essentials of democracy are not affected.

Parliamentary discussion may be retained as a useful safety valve and even more as a convenient medium through which the official answers to complaints are disseminated. It may even prevent some flagrant abuses and successfully insist on particular shortcomings being remedied. But it cannot direct. It will at best be reduced to choosing the persons who are to have practically absolute power. The whole system will tend toward that plebiscitarian dictatorship in which the head of the government is from time to time confirmed in his position by popular vote, but where he has all the powers at his command to make certain that the vote will go in the direction he desires.

It is the price of democracy that the possibilities of conscious control are restricted to the fields where true agreement exists and that in some fields things must be left to chance. But in a society which for its functioning depends on central planning this control cannot be made dependent on a majority's being able to agree; it will often be necessary that the will of a small minority be imposed upon the people, because this minority will be the largest group able to agree among themselves on the question at issue. Democratic government has worked successfully where, and so long as, the functions of government were, by a widely accepted creed, restricted to fields where agreement among a majority could be achieved by free discussion; and it is the great merit of the liberal creed that it reduced the range of subjects on which agreement was necessary to one on which it was likely to exist in a society of free men. It is now often said that democracy will not tolerate "capitalism." If "capitalism" means here a competitive system based on free disposal over private property, it is far more important to realize that only within this system is democracy possible. When it becomes dominated by a collectivist creed, democracy will inevitably destroy itself.

We have no intention, however, of making a fetish of democracy. It may well be true that our generation talks and thinks too much of democracy and too little of the values which it serves.

Democracy is essentially a means, a utilitarian device for safeguarding internal peace and individual freedom. As such it is by no means infallible or certain. Nor must we forget that there has often been much more cultural and spiritual freedom under an autocratic rule than under some democracies—and it is at least conceivable that under the government of a very homogeneous and doctrinaire majority democratic government might be as oppressive as the worst dictatorship. Our point, however, is not that dictatorship must inevitably extirpate freedom but rather that planning leads to dictatorship because dictatorship is the most effective instrument of coercion and the enforcement of ideals and, as such, essential if central planning on a large scale is to be possible. The clash between planning and democracy arises simply from the fact that the latter is an obstacle to the suppression of freedom which the direction of economic activity requires. But in so far as democracy ceases to be a guaranty of individual freedom, it may well persist in some form under a totalitarian regime. A true "dictatorship of the proletariat," even if democratic in form, if it undertook centrally to direct the economic system, would probably destroy personal freedom as completely as any autocracy has ever done.

The fashionable concentration on democracy as the main value threatened is not without danger. It is largely responsible for the misleading and unfounded belief that, so long as the ultimate source of power is the will of the majority, the power cannot be arbitrary.

Democratic control *may* prevent power from becoming arbitrary, but it does not do so by its mere existence. If democracy resolves on a task which necessarily involves the use of power which cannot be guided by fixed rules, it must become arbitrary power.

ECONOMIC CONTROL AND TOTALITARIANISM

Most planners who have seriously considered the practical aspects of their task have little doubt that a directed economy must be run on more or less dictatorial lines. That the complex system of interrelated activities, if it is to be consciously directed at all, must be directed by a single staff of experts, and that ultimate responsibility and power must rest in the hands of a commander-in-chief whose actions must not be fettered by democratic procedure, is too obvious a consequence of underlying ideas of central planning not to command fairly general assent. The consolation our planners offer us is that this authoritarian direction will apply "only" to economic matters.

Unfortunately, the assurance people derive from this belief that the power which is exercised over economic life is a power over matters of secondary importance only, and which makes them take lightly the threat to the freedom of our economic pursuits, is altogether unwarranted. It is largely a consequence of the erroneous belief that there are purely economic ends separate from the other ends of life. Yet, apart from the pathological case of the miser, there is no such thing. The ultimate ends of the activities of reasonable beings are never economic. What in ordinary language is misleadingly called the "economic motive" means merely the desire for general opportunity, the desire for power to achieve unspecified ends. Many people believe that anything which, like economic planning, affects only our economic interests cannot seriously interfere with the more basic values of life.

This, however, is an erroneous conclusion. Economic values are less important to us than many things precisely because in economic matters we are free to decide what to us is more, and what less, important.

The question raised by economic planning, is not merely whether we shall be able to satisfy what we regard as our more or less important needs in the way we prefer. It is whether it shall be we who decide what is more, and what is less, important for us, or whether this is to be decided by the planner.

The authority directing all economic activity would control not merely the part of our lives which is concerned with inferior things; it would control the allocation of the limited means for all our ends. And whoever controls all economic activity controls the means for all our ends and must therefore decide which are to be satisfied and which not. This is really the crux of the matter. Economic control is not merely control of a sector of human life which can be separated from the rest; it is the control of the means for all our ends. And whoever has sole control of the means must also determine which ends are to be served, which values are to be rated higher and which lower—in short, what men should believe and strive for. Central planning means that the economic problem is to be solved by the community instead of by the individual; but this involves that it must also be the community, or rather its representatives, who must decide the relative importance of the different needs.

The power of the planner over our private lives would be no less complete if he chose not to exercise it by direct control of our consumption. Although a planned society would probably to some extent employ rationing and similar devices, the power of the planner over our private lives does not depend on this and would be hardly less effective if the consumer were nominally free to spend his income as he pleased. The source of this power over all consumption which in a planned society the authority would possess would be its control over production.

Our freedom of choice in a competitive society rests on the fact that, if one person refuses to satisfy our wishes, we can turn to another. But if we face a monopolist we are at his mercy. And an authority directing the whole economic system would be the most powerful monopolist conceivable. While we need probably not be afraid that such an authority would exploit this power in the manner in which a private monopolist would do so, while its purpose would presumably not be the extortion of maximum financial gain, it would have complete power to decide what we are to be given and on what terms. It would not only decide what commodities and services were to be available and in what quantities; it would be able to direct their distribution between districts and groups and could, if it wished, discriminate between persons to any degree it liked.

The power conferred by the control of production and prices is almost unlimited. In a directed economy, where the authority watches over the ends pursued, it is certain that it would use its powers to assist some ends and to prevent the realization of others. And since the authority would have the power to thwart any efforts to elude its guidance, it would control what we consume almost as effectively as if it directly told us how to spend our income.

Not only in our capacity as consumers, however, and not even mainly in that capacity, would the will of the authority shape and "guide" our daily lives. It would do so even more in our position as producers. These two aspects of our lives cannot be separated; and as for most of us the time we spend at our work is a large part of our whole lives and as our job usually also determines the place where and the people among whom we live, some freedom in choosing our work is, probably, even more important for our happiness than freedom to spend our income during the hours of leisure.

Most planners, it is true, promise that in the new planned world free choice of occupation will be scrupulously preserved or even increased. But there they promise more than they can possibly fulfil. If they want to plan, they must control the entry into the different trades and occupations, or the terms of remuneration, or both. In almost all known instances of planning, the establishment of such controls and restrictions was among the first measures taken. If such control were universally practiced and exercised by a single planning authority, one needs little imagination to see what would become of the "free choice of occupation" promised. The "freedom of choice" would be purely fictitious, a mere promise to practice no discrimination where in the nature of the case discrimination must be practiced, and where all one could hope would be that the selection would be made on what the authority believed to be objective grounds.

There would be little difference if the planning authority confined itself to fixing the terms of employment and tried to regulate numbers by adjusting these terms. By prescribing the remuneration, it would no less effectively bar groups of people from entering many trades than by specifically excluding them.

WHO, WHOM?

The choice open to us is not between a system in which everybody will get what he deserves according to some absolute and universal standard of right, and one where the individual shares are determined partly by accident or good or ill chance, but between a system where it is the will of a few persons that decides who is to get what, and one where it depends at least partly on the ability and enterprise of the people concerned and partly on unforeseeable circumstances.

That the ideal of justice of most socialists would be satisfied if merely private income from property were abolished and the differences between the earned incomes of different people remained what they are now is true. What these people forget is that, in transferring all property in the means of production to the state, they put the state in a position whereby its action must in effect decide all other incomes.

What our generation has forgotten is that the system of private property is the most important guaranty of freedom, not only for those who own property, but scarcely less for those who do not. It is only because the control of the means of production is divided among many people acting independently that nobody has complete power over us, that we as individuals can decide what to do with ourselves. If all the means of production were vested in a single hand, whether it be nominally that of "society" as a whole or that of a dictator, whoever exercises this control has complete power over us.

We have already seen that the close interdependence of all economic phenomena makes it difficult to stop planning just where we wish and that, once the free working of the market is impeded beyond a certain degree, the planner will be forced to extend his controls until they become all-comprehensive. These economic considerations, which explain why it is impossible to stop deliberate control just where we should wish, are strongly reinforced by certain social or political tendencies whose strength makes itself increasingly felt as planning extends.

Once it becomes increasingly true, and is generally recognized, that the position of the individual is determined not by impersonal forces, not as a result of the competitive effort of many, but by the deliberate decision of authority, the attitude of the people toward their position in the social order necessarily changes. There will always exist inequalities which will appear unjust to those who suffer from them, disappointments which will appear unmerited, and strokes of misfortune which those hit have not deserved. But when these things occur in a society which is consciously directed, the way in which people will react will be very different from what it is when they are nobody's conscious choice.

Inequality is undoubtedly more readily borne, and affects the dignity of the person much less, if it is determined by impersonal forces than when it is due to design.

While people will submit to suffering which may hit anyone, they will not so easily submit to suffering which is the result of the decision of authority.

Once government has embarked upon planning for the sake of justice, it cannot refuse responsibility for anybody's fate or position. In a planned society we shall all know that we are better or worse off than others, not because of circumstances which nobody controls, and which it is impossible to foresee with certainty, but because some authority wills it. And all our efforts directed toward improving our position will have to aim, not at foreseeing and preparing as well as we can for the circumstances over which we have no control, but at influencing in our favor the authority which has all the power.

As soon as the state takes upon itself the task of planning the whole economic life, the problem of the due station of the different individuals and groups must indeed inevitably become the central political problem. As the coercive power of the state will alone decide who is to have what, the only power worth having will be a share in the exercise of this directing power. There will be no economic or social questions that would not be political questions in the sense that their solution will depend exclusively on who wields the coercive power, on whose are the views that will prevail on all occasions.

I believe it was Lenin himself who introduced to Russia the famous phrase "who, whom?"—during the early years of Soviet rule the byword in which the people summed up the universal problem of a socialist society. Who plans whom, who directs and dominates whom, who assigns to other people their station in life, and who is to have his due allotted by others? These become necessarily the central issues to be decided solely by the supreme power.

That a government which undertakes to direct economic activity will have to use its power to realize somebody's ideal of distributive justice is certain. But how can and how will it use that power? By what principles will it or ought it to be guided?

There is only one general principle, one simple rule which would indeed provide a definite answer to all these questions: equality, complete and absolute equality of all individuals in all those points which are subject to human control.

But nothing is further from the truth than that people in general regard mechanical equality of this kind as desirable. No socialist movement which aimed at complete equality has ever gained substantial support. What socialism promised was not an absolutely equal, but a more just and more equal, distribution. Not equality in the absolute sense but "greater equality" is the only goal which is seriously aimed at.

Though these two ideals sound very similar, they are as different as possible as far as our problem is concerned. While agreement on complete equality would answer all the problems of merit the planner must answer, the formula of the approach to greater equality answers practically none.

These difficulties need not lead to open clashes so long as socialism is merely the aspiration of a limited and fairly homogeneous group. They come to the surface only when a socialist policy is actually attempted with the support of the many different groups which together compose the majority of a people. Then it soon becomes the one burning question which of the different sets of ideals shall be imposed upon all by making the whole resources of the country serve it. It is because successful planning requires the creation of a common view on the essential values that the restriction of our freedom with regard to material things touches so directly on our spiritual freedom.

So long as the socialist movement in a country is closely bound up with the interests of a particular group, usually the more highly skilled industrial workers, the problem of creating a common view on the desirable status of the different members of society is comparatively simple. The movement is immediately concerned with the status of one particular group, and its aim is to raise that status relatively to other groups. The character of the problem changes, however, as in the course of the progressive advance toward socialism it becomes more and more evident to everyone that his income and general position are determined by the coercive apparatus of the state, that he can maintain or improve his position only as a member of an organized group capable of influencing or controlling the state machine in his interest.

6.3 The Road to Serfdom: Critique

Henry C. Wallich

"In social evolution," says Friedrich Hayek in his *Road to Serfdom,* "nothing is inevitable but thinking makes it so." This applies eminently, I believe, to Hayek's own social argument of the alleged totalitarian effects of centralization. They are not inevitable. True enough, planning is probably much harder without dictatorship. In consequence, it is likely to be much worse and less effective. But there is no compelling reason why a nation strongly imbued with a democratic tradition should not succeed in maintaining its freedom under planning. Among the three possible roads that democratic planning might take—the road to serfdom, the return to free markets, or simply the unchanging route of continued democratic planning—none seem to be prima facie ruled out.

Let us follow the supposed march into socialism step by step. How far could the dismantling of economic freedom go, before the man in the street would feel seriously incommoded? First to go would be the business man's freedom, and with it probably his ability to make and keep large amounts of money. The business man can be relied upon to be vocal in his own defense. But whether his protestations would find much of an echo among the lower income groups is debatable. Next in line, if the planning screws are tightened, is the consumer. He would find his range of choice narrowed, through import restrictions, rationing, standardization, and perhaps heavier taxation. Here popular resistance might be expected. If postwar experience in the United States is any guide, strong consumer restraints are not well received by the American public. In some European countries, on the other hand, people seem to have taken queing up without much protestation so long as the rations were adequate.

The next turn of the screw, if there is one, would probably squeeze labor. After production and consumption controls loom controls over manpower. Manpower controls are at the watershed between economic and political freedom. Here is where the British planners suffered their Waterloo. If manpower controls can be made to stick, any further tightening seems to lead into clear civil rights territory. Wide administrative discretion, severe penalties for noncompliance, efforts to whip up support and stifle opposition, may become necessary to back up the controls. What still separates us at this point from Soviet or Nazi style practices is the power of the people to change the government if this kind of planning does not suit them. How real a power is it?

Leftwingers argue that it is adequate, and that it is all that matters. Because they tend to identify freedom with security and welfare, they are undismayed by loss of choice and opportunity. Because not a few of them are technicians, they are impatient of imperfections and compromises. For many, this means impatience with the free market, with indirect fiscal and monetary controls, and with the political process.

Their embattled libertarian opponents dispute this case. They deny that an ultimate right to recall the government means much in the way of democracy or freedom. They argue that the mere formulation of detailed plans implies far-reaching delegation of power to the bureaucracy. Without this delegation, planning is likely to amount to no more than governmental rubber-stamping of whatever the market decides. The execution of the plans, if it is to be possible at all, will require that even more discretion be entrusted to the bureaucrats, and very able bureaucrats at that. To plan is human, to fulfill divine—or nearly so.

The powers of the legislature, therefore—so the libertarian argument goes on—are progressively watered down. Popular government becomes a figurehead. A change of government, under such conditions, will not bring a real turn of the tide, campaign oratory to the contrary not withstanding. The great powers of the administration, indeed, may make it increasingly difficult to mount an effective opposition. People know where their bread is buttered, however stingily, and dare not risk real opposition. The great weight of the decisions to be made, that reach deep into everybody's life, make issues tense and compromises problematical. Strong authority, the libertarians continue, beckons as a way out. Dictatorship, of course, does not solve problems, but it can liquidate them. Democracy, when it cannot solve them, must find a way to survive them. Life with major unresolved problems may become so uncomfortable that democracy breaks down.

Tension under planning, the libertarians say, may destroy democracy in yet another way. If the issues at stake threaten the very way of life of some group, that group may refuse to accept the verdict of the democratic process and resort to force. Rumblings along these lines have occasionally been heard from the left wing of European socialist parties. When we arrive at this margin of intolerance, dictatorship may prove the last refuge of a planner.

The old-fashioned liberal's case against the centralized economy is a persuasive one. It is marred, however, by the frequent use of the word "must" where "may" would be more appropriate. History, which can prove no rules but often does prove the exceptions, has already handed down rebuttals to the indictment, as in the cases of Britain, the Scandinavian countries, and Australia. In these and other countries much exposed to planning, democracy and freedom have survived without serious difficulty.

Hayek, in appraising the evident fact that the British did not travel down the road to serfdom, stresses what he calls the softening of the British character under the Labor Government. Thus he shifts his apprehensions to the long run. I would argue that a case that may be almost watertight in countries where democracy and freedom are weak does not necessarily apply to countries where both are strong. A vigorous people that knows its mind and how to speak it is not likely to let its planners run away with the economy. It will want them to submit to existing habits, tastes, and prejudices. It will expect them to be nice to the consumer. It will expect them to be particularly nice, in an expensive way, to special interest groups. It will expect the planners, in fact, to do the very things that snarl up an economy in special privileges, restrictions, and over-organization, and that hold up progress.

This gentle kind of planning seems entirely compatible with freedom. The people of the country so governed might find that though their life was not bad, it was curiously slow in getting better. They might come to believe that dilatory progress was the price of liberty, a penalty they would willingly go on paying to protect their freedom. Or they might decide to shift to a freer economy.

THE NEO-LIBERAL CASE FOR COMPETITIVE MARKETS

The neo-liberals' corollary to the critique of socialism and central planning is their case for an atomistically competitive market economy, a case that rests primarily on the market's alleged contributions to economic efficiency and (especially) to individual freedom. (Recall Keynes' observations on this point, which are quite similar.)

The efficiency argument is stated succinctly by Carl Christ in selection 6.4. Although neo-liberals do not suggest that the American economy would be "perfectly" competitive as a result of their proposed reforms, an atomistically competitive economy would approach the welfare norm of perfect competition much more closely than does an economy characterized by large dosages of monopoly and oligopoly. In addition, contends Hayek, a workably competitive market economy provides the most efficacious means of utilizing individuals' dispersed and decentralized knowledge of the "particular circumstances of time and place" in which they live and work.[5]

[5]Hayek, *Individualism and Economic Order* (Chicago: University of Chicago Press, 1948), pp. 77–89.

The freedom argument is presented by Milton Friedman in selection 6.5. In a market economy, Friedman avers, individuals are free to exchange, and will do so only if exchange is perceived as more beneficial to them than any other alternative. A system of private competitive enterprise also disperses power and, by separating private economic power from public political power, checks and balances the later. C.B. Macpherson provides a critique of Friedman's views on economic and political freedom in selection 6.6.

6.4 The Competitive Market and Optimal Allocative Efficiency

Carl F. Christ

My argument may be summarized in a somewhat oversimplified fashion, as follows:

(1) With certain important qualifications that I shall discuss, in a private-property, free-contract economy, public policy is not properly concerned with the relative prices at which particular goods and services are exchanged in the market. This is because relative prices have a job to do in allocating resources, and, with the qualifications alluded to, this job is done in what economists call an optimal way if the relative prices are determined by free contract.

(2) Again with certain important qualifications that I shall discuss, in a private-property, free-contract economy, public policy is not properly concerned with the quantities of particular goods and services produced by the economy as a whole, or consumed by particular individuals. This is because, with the qualifications alluded to, freedom of contract leads to what economists call an optimal allocation of resources.

(3) There is an important area within which public policy is properly concerned with particular relative or absolute prices, and/or with the quantities of particular goods and services consumed by particular individuals. This area provides the qualifications referred to under points (1) and (2). Most of these qualifications involve one or more of the following situations: An individual is not well informed about the alternatives facing him or about the consequences of his actions; an individual is not the best judge of his own interests; an individual cannot sell or mortgage himself as he can other wealth; an individual's deed brings about gains or losses to himself that are greater or less than the gains or losses to society, so that an individual who pursues his own private gain is not advancing the interests of society as much as he might. Familiar examples of the last are theft, fraud, extortion, tax evasion, monopolization, etc.; others will be discussed below.

Excerpted from *The Relationship of Prices to Economic Stability and Growth* 85th Congress, 2d Session (Washington, D.C.: U.S. Government Printing Office, 1958).

PRIVATE PROPERTY AND FREE CONTRACT

A society based on private property and freedom of contract takes the initial distribution of property as given, and lets the subsequent distribution arise from free contracting. There are rules for deciding who owns each piece of property. Each person has control over the use of his own property, except that we do not permit a person to sell or mortgage himself or his children. Property can change hands only by free contract agreed to by all parties to the contract (this usually involves exchange), or by free gift. A person's wealth increases rapidly if he receives large gifts, if he produces much, if others become willing to offer high prices for what he owns, and if he saves much. Because of freedom of contract, no person is forced to accept a material position that he thinks is inferior to the one that his original property will provide for him. If anyone can produce property that he regards as more valuable than the resources he consumes in the process, then he can gain from production. And if he can find other people who will give him in trade things that he regards as more valuable than the things he gives up in return, then he can gain from exchange.

Under certain conditions, this kind of an arrangement would lead to what economists call an optimal allocation of resources. The conditions, of course, are the source of the qualifications mentioned in connection with points (1) to (3) at the beginning of the paper. Let me now turn to the economists' definition of "optimal allocation of resources," then state the conditions, and then argue that if they are met, private property and freedom of contract do lead to the economists' optimal allocation of resources.

DEFINITION OF AN OPTIMAL ALLOCATION OF RESOURCES

An optimal allocation of resources, in the technical language of the economist, means a situation in which no individual can be made better off without making some other or others worse off. It may help to give examples of situations that are not optimal allocations. For example, if I own a house and I want to sell it provided I can get at least $25,000 for it, and if you want to buy it provided that you can get it for $30,000 or less, then (if we are both well informed about the matter, and if the interests of third parties are not affected) the existing allocation of resources is not optimal, and it can be improved by a contract for the sale of the house from me to you at some price in the range of $25,000 to $30,000.

Take another example that is more typical in that it involves production as well as exchange: Suppose that you are willing to buy a widget for $120 or less, and that I can cause a widget to be produced with resources that I can buy for $90 or more from their owners (including myself). Then, again if all parties are well informed and the interests of persons not party to the action are not affected, the existing allocation of resources is not optimal; it can be improved by a contract for the sale of a widget from me to you for a price somewhere in the range from $90 to $120, and another contract for the sale of the required resources from their owners to me at a combined price somewhere in the same range, but at or below the price of the widget. Gains from the improvement in allocation will accrue to you, me, and the owners of the resources that are used to produce the widget, in a manner depending upon the prices agreed on for the widget and the resources. An optimal allocation is a situation in which no more contracts agreeable to all parties remain to be made.

Notice that I said "an optimal allocation," not "the optimal allocation." This is not an accident; it is important. There is an infinite number of optimal allocations, according to this definition. When an economist says that an allocation of resources is an optimal one, he is taking the currently existing distribution of wealth as given, and is saying that the economy is satisfying efficiently the wants that are regarded as most important by those people who happen to have the wealth. No judgment is made at all on the question of whether the currently existing distribution of wealth is too unequal, too equal, fair, proper, justified, or anything of the sort.

CONDITIONS FOR AN OPTIMAL ALLOCATION OF RESOURCES UNDER PRIVATE PROPERTY AND FREE CONTRACT

Now it is time to state the conditions under which private property and free contract will lead to an optimal allocation of resources, thus defined:

(a) Motivation.—Each individual seeks intelligently to satisfy his wants as completely as he can with the means he has. In particular, he will always buy from the lowest priced seller he knows of, and will always sell to the highest priced buyer he knows of.

(b) Information.—Each individual knows what his present and future wants are and how important they are to him; he also knows what present and future actions are open to him and what the consequences of his actions will be. In particular, he knows everyone else's present and future bid and asked prices for all wealth, he knows what and how much he can produce now and in the future with any given combination of resources, and he knows to what extent his present and future wants will be satisfied by each kind of wealth.

(c) Mobility.—Resources are perfectly mobile, that is, it takes no time and costs nothing to convert from one kind of productive activity to another, or to exchange goods in the market.

(d) Competition.—Every individual is such a small buyer and seller of the things he deals in, relative to the total transactions of the market, that his decisions to bid or ask or buy or sell have no perceptible effect on the prices bid or asked by others.

(e) Third parties.—Every individual deed affects only the doer, and every contract affects only the parties to the contract. In particular, this excludes contracts by which third parties are injured and also contracts by which third parties are benefited.

(f) The institution of private property and free contract as we know it is modified to permit individuals to sell or mortgage their persons in return for present and/or future benefits.

These conditions have been deliberately designed so that if they were fulfilled, then each individual would seek and find others with whom he can make mutually advantageous contracts, and such contracts would be made, until no more remain to be made. When that state of affairs occurs, an optimal allocation of resources has been achieved.

THE ROLE OF RELATIVE PRICES IN RESOURCE ALLOCATION

It is now easy to explain the role of relative prices in the process of resource allocation. First, note that if everyone seeks the best price he can get, and no one can control prices, and everyone knows what prices are being quoted, then it will turn out that for each good or service there is a single market price: No one will pay more and no one will accept less. Market prices may change in response to changes in resource availability, technology, tastes, or wealth distribution, but they are not perceptibly influenced by any individual's action.

Market prices, and in particular relative prices, have several jobs to do in allocating resources; these jobs can conveniently be grouped into three related but more or less distinct main groups. The first is to decide how much of each product is to be made, and for whom. The second is to decide what combination of resouces is to be used in making each product. And the third is to decide how much of current output shall be consumed and how much shall be saved and invested for increasing future output.

Relative prices perform these jobs in several ways. They carry information throughout the economy concerning products that are being made in larger or smaller than optimal amounts, and concerning products that are not being produced with the optimal combination of resources. They provide the incentive for people to shift toward an optimum. And they distribute the product among resource owners, since each resource owner is paid the market price for his resources, thus receiving an income that he can use in the way most satisfying to him.

The price of a product, relative to the combined price of the resources used to produce it, tells whether the right amount of that product is being produced or not. If the relative price of a product is high, so that the rate of return to capital in that industry is higher than elsewhere in the economy, then too little of this product is being produced, because buyers can induce resource owners to shift resources from elsewhere to make more of it, at prices that will satisfy both the buyers of the extra product and the owners of the transferred resources. (Recall the example of the widgets.) And the fact that the rate of return in that industry is higher than elsewhere in the economy provides the incentive for more resources to come into it. Similarly, if the price of a product is low relative to its cost, that is a sign that too much of it is being produced, and provides the incentive for resources to leave that industry.

If the price of a resource is low, relative to the value of the output it can produce in a certain firm, that is a sign that too little of the resource is being used in that firm, and the firm will induce owners of the resource to shift some of it from elsewhere in the economy to that firm, at a price that will satisfy both the firm and the owners of the resource. Similarly, if the price of a resource is high relative to the value of the output it can produce in a firm, then the firm is using too much of the resource, and the firm is led to cut down on the use of it.

Thus, in the end, producers are induced to make for each buyer the things he values most highly. Resource owners are induced to apply their resources where they can produce things that are most highly valued by buyers. And each producer is induced to make his product with the combination of resources that costs least; i.e., that is the least useful to other producers.

Interest rates form the relative prices of future versus present goods and services (if the absolute price level is stable). Through interest rates, consumers decide how much to consume and how much to save, and entrepreneurs are induced to invest in activities whose products will be most highly valued relative to their cost; i.e., relative to the things that must be foregone to obtain them.

It is important to remember that relative prices established under free contract will not lead to these optimal results unless resource owners are permitted to receive the market price for each unit of resources they own, for otherwise the incentive to allocate optimally is affected. This means that large incomes will be received by those who own large amounts of valuable resources.

One of the most important advantages of free contract is that it provides automatic adjustments to changes in tastes and technology. Resources shift out of industries whose products have become less desirable or more expensive to produce and into industries whose products have become more desirable or cheaper to produce. Equally important, producers who feel that they have ideas for useful new products or better techniques are free to try them out, and if buyers find they are worthwhile, they will be adopted.

PUBLIC POLICY TO CORRECT RESOURCE MISALLOCATION UNDER FREE CONTRACT

In the real world the conditions under which free contract leads to optimum resource allocation do not always hold.

A familiar case is that of monopoly, which is distinguished by the seller's ability to affect the price of his product significantly by selling more or less of it. A monopolist, if he exploits his position, turns out less product than would a competitive industry in his place, and charges a higher price, in order to make more profit than would a competitive industry. In effect, he prevents some resources from being used to make his product, even though there are would-be buyers who are willing to pay more for the product than the resource owners could get for the necessary resources if they sold them elsewhere. Economic analysis can demonstrate that the gains that the resource owners and would-be buyers would get, if they were allowed to exchange, are great enough to pay the monopolist's profit and still leave something over. Hence the monopolist creates a misallocation of resources, because he creates a situation in which someone could be made better off without making anyone worse off. Public policy to prevent monopoly is accordingly proper.

A second example is that of protection against common disasters, e.g., activities such as national defense, fire and police protection, and sanitation. Here the distinguishing characteristic is that if one individual contracts for protection for himself, he thereby protects his neighbors at least to some extent, whether they agree to help pay for the protection or not: He cannot have the fire in his own house put out without reducing the risk that his neighbor's will catch fire, he cannot protect himself from attack without reducing the likelihood that his neighbor will be attacked, and he cannot practice sanitation without reducing the chance that his neighbors will become infected.

If everyone else is going to pay for protection, it may be in the private interest of a single individual not to do so, because he gets substantial protection anyway from the fact that others are providing it for themselves. This is not fair. More important, since many people pursue their interests in this way, the cost of protection for the remaining ones may be so great that they do not think it is worthwhile. For this reason, some private multiparty contracts that would benefit all parties never get made. Therefore, provided it can be shown that a community enterprise financed by appropriately apportioned taxes or assessments could convey to each person benefits that he values more highly than he values his share of the cost, public policy for this purpose improves the allocation of resources and is proper. Indeed, in such a case, the public policy is merely an effective substitute for the private contract that does not get made. However, the proviso is crucial: If it is not possible to apportion the costs of the enterprise in such a way that everyone will value his benefits more highly than his share of the costs, then the enterprise represents a misallocation of resources, and public policy to create it must be justified, if at all, on some other ground.

A third case is that of resources whose competitive exploitation would result in a waste of the resources. For example, when many people own land lying above an oil deposit, it is in the private interest of each person to drill and pump oil as fast as possible, before his neighbors have time to get a very big share. But when everyone does this, total costs will be greater and less of the oil in the deposit will be recovered than if just a few wells were drilled in the right places. Everyone could be better off under a unified drilling and pumping operation, and there is a clear case for community action requiring this. Fishing is another industry where this problem can arise.

There are many public policies whose justification rests on the premise that people are not well informed, either about their own true interests, or about the alternatives open to them, or about the consequences of their actions, or about all of these. Rules requiring the disclosure of information about the contents of food and drugs, and about the nature of corporations whose stock is offered for sale, are of this kind. So also are certain health, safety, and building regulations.

A more basic policy that is justified this way in part is the prohibition against a person's selling or mortgaging himself: Freedom is a paramount value, and whenever a person feels that he wants to sell himself for something else offered in return, he should be protected against his own poor judgment. I feel that there is another quite different justification for this policy, namely that human beings are simply not like other property, that they have a dignity that demands they not be treated so, even though it is true that human beings are an important form of wealth, constituting a large share of total wealth.

THE PROPER PROVINCE OF FREE CONTRACT

I now argue that there remains a significant field within which the allocation of resources under free contract is better than if public policy concerns itself with the prices of particular commodities or the quantities consumed by particular persons (these are the first two points stated at the beginning).

Clearly there is a significant field where individuals do know what they want better than the government does, and seek it fairly intelligently; where they are reasonably well informed about their opportunities; where resources are reasonably mobile between different uses; where substantial competition prevails; and where effects of private contracts on third parties are unimportant by comparison with what it would cost to administer compensating payments. This field includes a large part of the consumer goods area of the economy, and of the area where techniques and capital goods and other resources are marshaled for the production of desired goods and services. The mechanism by which relative prices established under free contract allocate resources is described briefly above; that section is an important part of the argument here.

6.5 Capitalism and Freedom

Milton Friedman

Economic arrangements play a dual role in the promotion of a free society. On the one hand, freedom in economic arrangements is itself a component of freedom broadly understood, so economic freedom is an end in itself. In the second place, economic freedom is also an indispensable means toward the achievement of political freedom.

The first of these roles of economic freedom needs special emphasis because intellectuals in particular have a strong bias against regarding this aspect of freedom as important. They tend to express contempt for what they regard as material aspects of life, and to regard their own pursuit of allegedly higher values as on a different plane of significance and as deserving of special attention. For most citizens of the country, however, if not for the intellectual, the

Excerpted from Milton Friedman, *Capitalism and Freedom* (Chicago: University of Chicago Press, 1962), pp. 8–21. Reprinted by permission of the publisher and the author.

direct importance of economic freedom is at least comparable in significance to the indirect importance of economic freedom as a means to political freedom.

The citizen of Great Britain, who after World War II was not permitted to spend his vacation in the United States because of exchange control, was being deprived of an essential freedom no less than the citizen of the United States, who was denied the opportunity to spend his vacation in Russia because of his political views. The one was ostensibly an economic limitation on freedom and the other a political limitation, yet there is no essential difference between the two.

The citizen of the United States who is compelled by law to devote something like 10 per cent of his income to the purchase of a particular kind of retirement contract, administered by the government, is being deprived of a corresponding part of his personal freedom. How strongly this deprivation may be felt and its closeness to the deprivation of religious freedom, which all would regard as "civil" or "political" rather than "economic," were dramatized by an episode involving a group of farmers of the Amish sect. On grounds of principle, this group regarded compulsory federal old age programs as an infringement of their personal individual freedom and refused to pay taxes or accept benefits. As a result, some of their livestock were sold by auction in order to satisfy claims for social security levies. True, the number of citizens who regard compulsory old age insurance as a deprivation of freedom may be few, but the believer in freedom has never counted noses.

A citizen of the United States who under the laws of various states is not free to follow the occupation of his own choosing unless he can get a license for it, is likewise being deprived of an essential part of his freedom. So is the man who would like to exchange some of his goods with, say, a Swiss for a watch but is prevented from doing so by a quota. So also is the Californian who was thrown into jail for selling Alka Seltzer at a price below that set by the manufacturer under so-called "fair trade" laws. So also is the farmer who cannot grow the amount of wheat he wants. And so on. Clearly, economic freedom, in and of itself, is an extremely important part of total freedom.

Viewed as a means to the end of political freedom, economic arrangements are important because of their effect on the concentration or dispersion of power. The kind of economic organization that provides economic freedom directly, namely, competitive capitalism, also promotes political freedom because it separates economic power from political power and in this way enables the one to offset the other.

Historical evidence speaks with a single voice on the relation between political freedom and a free market. I know of no example in time or place of a society that has been marked by a large measure of political freedom, and that has not also used something comparable to a free market to organize the bulk of economic activity.

Because we live in a largely free society, we tend to forget how limited is the span of time and the part of the globe for which there has ever been anything like political freedom: the typical state of mankind is tyranny, servitude, and misery. The nineteenth century and early twentieth century in the Western world stand out as striking exceptions to the general trend of historical development. Political freedom in this instance clearly came along with the free market and the development of capitalist institutions. So also did political freedom in the golden age of Greece and in the early days of the Roman era.

History suggests only that capitalism is a necessary condition for political freedom. Clearly it is not a sufficient condition. Fascist Italy and Fascist Spain, Germany at various times in the last seventy years, Japan before World Wars I and II, tzarist Russia in the decades before World War I—are all societies that cannot conceivably be described as politically free. Yet, in each, private enterprise was the dominant form of economic organization. It is therefore clearly possible to have economic arrangements that are fundamentally capitalist and political arrangements that are not free.

Even in those societies, the citizenry had a good deal more freedom than citizens of a modern totalitarian state like Russia or Nazi Germany, in which economic totalitarianism is combined with political totalitarianism. Even in Russia under the Tzars, it was possible for some citizens, under some circumstances, to change their jobs without getting permission from political authority because capitalism and the existence of private property provided some check to the centralized power of the state.

The relation between political and economic freedom is complex and by no means unilateral. In the early nineteenth century, Bentham and the Philosophical Radicals were inclined to regard political freedom as a means to economic freedom. . . . Recognizing the implicit threat to individualism, the intellectual descendants of the Philosophical Radicals—Dicey, Mises, Hayek, and Simons, to mention only a few—feared that a continued movement toward centralized control of economic activity would prove *The Road to Serfdom,* as Hayek entitled his penetrating analysis of the process. Their emphasis was on economic freedom as a means toward political freedom. . . .

Collectivist economic planning has indeed interfered with individual freedom. At least in some countries, however, the result has not been the suppression of freedom, but the reversal of economic policy. . . .

The proximate explanation of these shifts in policy is the limited success of central planning or its outright failure to achieve stated objectives. However, this failure is itself to be attributed, at least in some measure, to the political implications of central planning and to an unwillingness to follow out its logic when doing so requires trampling rough-shod on treasured private rights. . . .

Historical evidence by itself can never be convincing. Perhaps it was sheer coincidence that the expansion of freedom occurred at the same time as the development of capitalist and market institutions. Why should there be a connection? What are the logical links between economic and political freedom? In discussing these questions we shall consider first the market as a direct component of freedom, and then the indirect relation between market arrangements and political freedom. A by-product will be an outline of the ideal economic arrangements for a free society.

As liberals, we take freedom of the individual, or perhaps the family, as our ultimate goal in judging social arrangements. Freedom as a value in this sense has to do with the interrelations among people . . . .

The basic problem of social organization is how to co-ordinate the economic activities of large numbers of people. . . .

Fundamentally, there are only two ways of co-ordinating the economic activities of millions. One is central direction involving the use of coercion —the technique of the army and of the modern totalitarian state. The other is voluntary co-operation of individuals—the technique of the market place.

The possibility of co-ordination through voluntary co-operation rests on the elementary—yet frequently denied—proposition that both parties to an economic transaction benefit from it, *provided the transaction is bi-laterally voluntary and informed*.

Exchange can therefore bring about co-ordination without coercion. A working model of a society organized through voluntary exchange is a *free private enterprise exchange economy*—what we have been calling competitive capitalism. . . .

Specialization of function and division of labor would not go far if the ultimate productive unit were the household. In a modern society, we have gone much farther. We have introduced enterprises which are intermediaries between individuals in their capacities as suppliers of service and as purchasers of goods. And similarly, specialization of function and division of labor could not go very far if we had to continue to rely on the barter of product for product. In consequence, money has been introduced as a means of facilitating exchange, and of enabling the acts of purchase and of sale to be separated into two parts.

Despite the important role of enterprises and of money in our actual economy, and despite the numerous and complex problems they raise, the central characteristic of the market technique of achieving co-ordination is fully displayed in the simple exchange economy that contains neither enterprises nor money. As in that simple model, so in the complex enterprise and money-exchange economy, co-operation is strictly individual and voluntary *provided: (a)* that enterprises are private, so that the ultimate contracting parties are individuals and *(b)* that individuals are effectively free to enter or not to enter into any particular exchange, so that every transaction is strictly voluntary. . . .

So long as effective freedom of exchange is maintained, the central feature of the market organization of economic activity is that it prevents one person from interfering with another in respect of most of his activities. The consumer is protected from coercion by the seller because of the presence of other sellers with whom he can deal. The seller is protected from coercion by the consumer because of other consumers to whom he can sell. The employee is protected from coercion by the employer because of other employers for whom he can work, and so on. And the market does this impersonally and without centralized authority.

Indeed, a major source of objection to a free economy is precisely that it does this task so well. It gives people what they want instead of what a particular group thinks they ought to want. Underlying most arguments against the free market is a lack of belief in freedom itself.

The existence of a free market does not of course eliminate the need for government. On the contrary, government is essential both as a forum for determining the "rules of the game" and as an umpire to interpret and enforce the rules decided on. What the market does is to reduce greatly the range of issues that must be decided through political means, and thereby to minimize the extent to which government need participate directly in the game. The characteristic feature of action through political channels is that it tends to require or enforce substantial conformity. The great advantage of the market, on the other hand, is that it permits wide diversity. It is, in political terms, a system of proportional representation. Each man can vote, as it were, for the color of tie he wants and get it; he does not have to see what color the majority wants and then, if he is in the minority submit.

. . . Political freedom means the absence of coercion of a man by his fellow men. The fundamental threat to freedom is power to coerce, be it in the hands of a monarch, a dictator, an oligarchy, or a momentary majority. The preservation of freedom requires the elimination of such concentration of power to the fullest possible extent and the dispersal and distribution of whatever power cannot be eliminated—a system of checks and balances. By removing the organization of economic activity from the control of political authority, the market eliminates this source of coercive power. It enables economic strength to be a check to political power rather than a reinforcement.

Economic power can be widely dispersed. There is no law of conservation which forces the growth of new centers of economic strength to be at the expense of existing centers. Political power, on the other hand, is more difficult to decentralize. There can be numerous small independent governments. But it is far more difficult to maintain numerous equipotent small centers of political power in a single large government than it is to have numerous centers of economic strength in a single large economy. There can be many millionaires in one large economy. But can there be more than one really outstanding leader, one person on whom the energies and enthusiasms of his countrymen are centered? If the central government gains power, it is likely to be at the expense of local governments. There seems to be something like a fixed total of political power to be distributed. Consequently, if economic power is joined to political power, concentration seems almost inevitable. On the other hand, if economic power is kept in separate hands from political power, it can serve as a check and a counter to political power. . . .

6.6 A Note on Friedman's Freedom

C. B. Macpherson

This note deals with (1) an error which vitiates Friedman's demonstration that competitive capitalism coordinates men's economic activities without coercion;

From C. B. Macpherson, "Elegant Tombstones: A Note on Friedman's Freedom," *Canadian Journal of Political Science*, March 1968. Reprinted by permission of the publisher and the author.

(2) the inadequacy of his arguments that capitalism is a necessary condition of political freedom.

Professor Friedman's demonstration that the capitalist market economy can coordinate economic activities without coercion rests on an elementary conceptual error. His argument runs as follows. He shows first that in a simple market model, where each individual or household controls resources enabling it to produce goods and services either directly for itself or for exchange, there will be production for exchange because of the increased product made possible by specialization. But "since the household always has the alternative of producing directly for itself, it need not enter into any exchange unless it benefits from it. Hence no exchange will take place unless both parties do benefit from it. Cooperation is thereby achieved without coercion" (p. 13). So far, so good. It is indeed clear that in this simple exchange model, assuming rational maximizing behavior by all hands, every exchange will benefit both parties, and hence that no coercion is involved in the decision to produce for exchange or in any act of exchange.

Professor Friedman then moves on to our actual complex economy, or rather to his own curious model of it:

> *As in* [*the*] *simple model, so in the complex enterprise and money-exchange economy, cooperation is strictly individual and voluntary provided: (a) that enterprises are private, so that the ultimate contracting parties are individuals and (b) that individuals are effectively free to enter or not to enter into any particular exchange, so that every transaction is strictly voluntary (p. 14).*

One cannot take exception to proviso *(a)*: it is clearly required in the model to produce a cooperation that is "strictly individual." One might, of course, suggest that a model containing this stipulation is far from corresponding to our actual complex economy, since in the latter the ultimate contracting parties who have the most effect on the market are not individuals but corporations, and moreover, corporations which in one way or another manage to opt out of the fully competitive market. But to concentrate attention on proviso *(a)* is to miss the fault in proviso *(b)*, which is more fundamental, and of a different kind. It is not a question of the correspondence of the model to the actual: it is a matter of the inadequacy of the proviso to produce the model.

Proviso *(b)* is "that individuals are effectively free to enter or not to enter into any particular exchange," and it is held that with this proviso "every transaction is strictly voluntary." A moment's thought will show that this is not so. The proviso that is required to make every transaction strictly voluntary is not freedom not to enter into any *particular* exchange, but freedom not to enter into any exchange *at all*. This, and only this, was the proviso that proved the simple model to be voluntary and noncoercive; and nothing less than this would prove the complex model to be voluntary and noncoercive. But Professor Friedman is clearly claiming that freedom not to enter into any *particular* exchange is enough: "The consumer is protected from coercion by the seller because of the presence of other sellers with whom he can deal. . . . The employee is protected from coercion by the employer because of other employers for whom he can work . . ." (pp. 14–15).

It is easy to see what Professor Friedman has done, but it is less easy to excuse it. He has moved from the simple economy of exchange between independent producers, to the capitalist economy, without mentioning the most important thing that distinguishes them. He mentions money instead of barter, and "enterprises which are intermediaries between individuals in their capacities as suppliers of services and as purchasers of goods" (pp. 13–14), as if money and merchants were what distinguished a capitalist economy from an economy of independent producers. What distinguishes the capitalist economy from the simple exchange economy is the separation of labor and capital, that is, the existence of a labor force without its own sufficient capital and therefore without a choice as to whether to put its labor in the market or not. Professor Friedman would agree that where there is no choice there is coercion. His attempted demonstration that capitalism coordinates without coercion therefore fails.

Since all his specific arguments against the welfare and regulatory state depend on his case that the market economy is not coercive, the reader may spare himself the pains of attending to the careful and persuasive reasoning by which he seeks to establish the minimum to which coercion could be reduced by reducing or discarding each of the main regulatory and welfare activities of the state. None of this takes into account the coercion involved in the separation of capital from labor, or the possible mitigation of this coercion by the regulatory and welfare state. Yet it is because this coercion can in principle be reduced by the regulatory and welfare state, and thereby the amount of effective individual liberty be increased, that liberals have been justified in pressing, in the name of liberty, for infringements on the pure operation of competitive capitalism.

The argument that competitive capitalism is necessary to political freedom is itself conducted on two levels, neither of which shows a necessary relation.

(a) The first, on which Friedman properly does not place very much weight, is a historical correlation. No society that has had a large measure of political freedom "has not also used something comparable to a free market to organize the bulk of economic activity" (p. 9). Professor Friedman rightly emphasizes "how limited is the span of time and the part of the globe for which there has ever been anything like political freedom" (p. 9); he believes that the exceptions to the general rule of "tyranny, servitude and misery" are so few that the relation between them and certain economic arrangements can easily be spotted. "The 19th century and early 20th century in the Western world stand out as striking exceptions to the general trend of historical development. Political freedom in this instance clearly came along with the free market and the development of capitalist institutions" (pp. 9–10). Thus, for Professor Friedman, "history suggests . . . that capitalism is a necessary condition for political freedom" (p. 10).

The broad historical correlation is fairly clear, though in cutting off the period of substantial political freedom in the West at the "early 20th century"

Friedman seems to be slipping into thinking of economic freedom and begging the question of the relation of political freedom to economic freedom. But granting the correlation between the emergence of capitalism and the emergence of political freedom, what it may suggest to the student of history is the converse of what it suggests to Professor Friedman: i.e., it may suggest that political freedom was a necessary condition for the development of capitalism. Capitalist institutions could not be fully established until political freedom (ensured by a competitive party system with effective civil liberties) had been won by those who wanted capitalism to have a clear run: a liberal state (political freedom) was needed to permit and facilitate a capitalist market society.

At any rate, the historical correlation scarcely suggests that capitalism is a necessary condition for political freedom.

(b) Passing from historical correlation, which "by itself can never be convincing," Professor Friedman looks for "logical links between economic and political freedom" (pp. 11–12). The link he finds is that "the kind of economic organization that provides economic freedom directly, namely, competitive capitalism, also promotes political freedom because it separates economic power from political power and in this way enables the one to offset the other" (p. 9). The greater the concentration of coercive power in the same hands, the greater the threat to political freedom (defined as "the absence of coercion of a man by his fellow men"). The market removes the organization of economic activity from the control of the political authority. It thus reduces the concentration of power and "enables economic strength to be a check to political power rather than a reinforcement" (p. 15).

Granted the validity of these generalizations, they tell us only that the market *enables* economic power to offset rather than reinforce political power. They do not show any necessity or inherent probability that the market *leads* to the offsetting of political power by economic power. We may doubt that there is any such inherent probability. What can be shown is an inherent probability in the other direction, i.e., that the market leads to political power being used not to offset but to reinforce economic power. For the more completely the market takes over the organization of economic activity, that is, the more nearly the society approximates Friedman's ideal of a competitive capitalist market society, where the state establishes and enforces the individual right of appropriation and the rules of the market but does not interfere in the operation of the market, the more completely is political power being used to reinforce economic power.

Professor Friedman does not see this as any threat to political freedom because he does not see that the capitalist market necessarily gives coercive power to those who succeed in amassing capital. He knows that the coercion whose absence he equates with political freedom is not just the physical coercion of police and prisons, but extends to many forms of economic coercion, e.g., the power some men may have over others' terms of employment. He sees the coercion possible (he thinks probable) in a socialist society where the political authority can enforce certain terms of employment. He does not see the coercion in a capitalist society where the holders of capital can enforce certain terms of employment. He does not see this because of his error about freedom not to enter into any particular exchange being enough to prove the uncoercive nature of entering into exchange at all.

The placing of economic coercive power and political coercive power in the hands of different sets of people, as in the fully competitive capitalist economy does not lead to the first checking the second but to the second reinforcing the first. It is only in the welfare-state variety of capitalism, which Friedman would like to have dismantled, that there is a certain amount of checking of economic power by political power.

The logical link between competitive capitalism and political freedom has not been established.

Professor Friedman, in arguing that freedom would be increased if most of the regulatory and welfare activities of contemporary Western states were abandoned, did not take into account the coercion involved in the separation of capital from labor or the possible mitigation of this coercion by the regulatory and welfare state. But in Chapter 10, on the distribution of income, he does deal with a closely related problem. Here he sets out the ethical case for distribution according to product, as compared with "another [principle] that seems ethically appealing, namely, equality of treatment" (p. 162). Distribution according to product he describes, accurately enough, as the principle "To each according to what he and the instruments he owns produces" (pp. 161–162): to be strictly accurate this should read "resources" or "capital and land" instead of "instruments," but the sense is clear. This is offered as "the ethical principle that would directly justify the distribution of income in a free market society" (p. 161). We can agree that this is the only principle that can be offered to justify it. We may also observe that this principle is not only different from the principle "to each according to his work," but is also inconsistent with it (except on the fanciful assumption that ownership of resources is always directly proportional to work). Professor Friedman does not seem to see this. His case for the ethical principle of payment according to product is that it is unthinkingly accepted as a basic value-judgment by almost everybody in our society; and his demonstration of this is that the severest internal critics of capitalism, i.e. the Marxists, have implicitly accepted it.

Of course they have not. In the first place, [Marx's view was] at most, the principle "to each according to his work," not "to each according to what he and the instruments he owns produces" or "to each according to his product." In the second place, Marx accepted "to each according to his work" only as a transitionally valid principle, to be replaced by the ultimately desirable principle "to each according to his need."

Having so far misread Marx, Professor Friedman gives him a final fling.

> *Of course, the Marxist argument is invalid on other grounds as well . . .* [*most*] *striking, there is an unstated change in the meaning of "labor" in passing from the premise to the conclusion. Marx recognized the role of capital in producing the product but regarded capital as embodied labor. Hence, written out in full, the*

> *premises of the Marxist syllogism would run: "Present and past labor produce the whole of the product." The logical conclusion is presumably "Past labor is exploited," and the inference for action is that past labor should get more of the product, though it is by no means clear how, unless it be in elegant tombstones* [*pp. 167–168*].

This nonsense is unworthy of Professor Friedman's talents. The Marxist premises are: Present labor, and the accumulation of surplus value created by past labor and extracted from the past laborers, produce the whole value of the product. Present labor gets only a part of that part of the value which it creates, and gets no part of that part of the value which is transferred to the product from the accumulated surplus value created by past labor. The logical conclusion is presumably that present labor is exploited and past labor was exploited, and the inference for action is that a system which requires constant exploitation should be abandoned.

Ignorance of Marxism is no sin in an economist, though cleverness in scoring off a travesty of it may be thought a scholarly lapse. What is more disturbing is that Professor Friedman seems to be satisfied that this treatment of the ethical justification of different principles of distribution is sufficient. Given his own first postulate, perhaps it is. For in asserting at the beginning of the book that freedom of the individual, or perhaps of the family, is the liberal's "ultimate goal in judging social arrangements," he has said in effect that the liberal is not required seriously to weigh the ethical claims of equality (or any other principle of distribution), let alone the claims of any principle of individual human development such as was given first place by liberals like Mill and Green, against the claims of freedom (which to Friedman of course means market freedom). The humanist liberal in the tradition of Mill and Green will quite properly reject Friedman's postulate. The logical liberal will reject his fallacious proof that the freedom of the capitalist market is individual economic freedom, his undemonstrated case that political freedom requires capitalism, and his fallacious defense of the ethical adequacy of capitalism. The logical humanist liberal will regret that the postulate and the fallacies make *Capitalism and Freedom* not a defense but an elegant tombstone of liberalism.

MODIFIED LAISSEZ-FAIRE: THE ECONOMIC ROLE OF GOVERNMENT

Complementing the neo-liberals' vision of a resuscitated atomistically competitive market economy is their specification of the proper role and functions of government. Because the extension of economic power to government invites the use of coercion, the scope and agenda of government's activities should be restricted. As in classical liberalism, the criterion for limitation of proper government action is by *function* rather than size. Governments should be restricted to those functions in which their activity is completely consistent with individual freedom and/or those functions which cannot be provided (or provided as well) by the market. In general, these conditions are most likely to be met when government action is confined to impersonal "rules of the game" which are changed infrequently and are simple to enforce, thereby leaving individuals free to organize and coordinate their affairs through market exchange.

A neo-liberal discussion of appropriate and inappropriate governmental economic functions is provided by Hayek in selection 6.7. In *The Constitution of Liberty (1960),* Hayek describes the growing obsolescence of socialist visions centering around nationalization of industry and government planning, and the emergence of the contemporary welfare state. In that context, he makes consistency with individual freedom the key criterion for assessing the appropriateness and proper extent of government actions.[6]

The neo-liberal critique of government's role in economic life reflects also an evaluation of the likely efficiency and effectiveness of government action. Neo-liberals argue that simply because the market contains a particular flaw, it does not follow that government's role should be extended in an attempt to remedy it. A given problem may or may not be subject to remediation through government action. Inquiry into the behavior and functioning of government will show that government, too, has its limitations in making and implementing rational economic decisions. This theme is an integral part of Murray Rothbard's critique of the welfare state in selection 6.8.

6.7 The Economic Role of Government

Friedrich A. Hayek

It is the character rather than the volume of government activity that is important. A functioning market economy presupposes certain activities on the part of the state; there are some other such activities by which its functioning will be assisted; and it can tolerate many more, provided that they are of the kind which are compatible with a functioning market. But there are those which run counter to the very principle on which a free system rests and which must therefore be altogether excluded if such a system is to work. In consequence, a government that is comparatively inactive but does the wrong things may do much more to cripple the forces of a market economy than one that is more concerned with economic affairs but confines itself to actions which assist the spontaneous forces of the economy.

The rule of law provides the criterion which enables us to distinguish between those measures which are and those which are not compatible with a

[6] See also Milton Friedman, *Capitalism and Freedom,* pp. 23–36. What is perhaps most striking in Friedman's presentation is that even many activities that virtually "everyone" (within the post-Keynesian synthesis) would consider to be appropriate functions of government, Firedman singles out as being proper and feasible for private enterprises.

Excerpted from Friedrich A. Hayek, "*The Constitution of Liberty* (Chicago: University of Chicago Press, 1960), pp. 257–61. Reprinted by permission of the publisher and the author.

free system. Those that are may be examined further on the grounds of expediency. Many such measures will, of course, still be undesirable or even harmful. But those that are not must be rejected even if they provide an effective, or perhaps the only effective, means to a desirable end. We shall see that the observation of the rule of law is a necessary, but not yet a sufficient, condition for the satisfactory working of a free economy. But the important point is that all coercive action of government must be unambiguously determined by a permanent legal framework which enables the individual to plan with a degree of confidence and which reduces human uncertainty as much as possible.

Let us consider, first, the distinction between the coercive measures of government and those pure service activities where coercion does not enter or does so only because of the need of financing them by taxation. In so far as the government merely undertakes to supply services which otherwise would not be supplied at all (usually because it is not possible to confine the benefits to those prepared to pay for them), the only question which arises is whether the benefits are worth the cost. Of course, if the government claimed for itself the exclusive right to provide particular services, they would cease to be strictly non-coercive. In general, a free society demands not only that the government have the monopoly of coercion but that it have the monopoly only of coercion and that in all other respects it operate on the same terms as everybody else.

A great many of the activities which governments have universally undertaken in this field and which fall within the limits described are those which facilitate the acquisition of reliable knowledge about facts of general significance. The most important function of this kind is the provision of a reliable and efficient monetary system. Others scarcely less important are the setting of standards of weights and measures; the providing of information gathered from surveying, land registration, statistics, etc.; and the support, if not also the organization, of some kind of education.

All these activities of government are part of its effort to provide a favorable framework for individual decisions; they supply means which individuals can use for their own purposes. Many other services of a more material kind fall into the same category. Though government must not use its power of coercion to reserve for itself activities which have nothing to do with the enforcement of the general rules of law, there is no violation of principle in its engaging in all sorts of activities on the same terms as the citizens. If in the majority of fields there is no good reason why it should do so, there are fields in which the desirability of government action can hardly be questioned.

To this latter group belong all those services which are clearly desirable but which will not be provided by competitive enterprise because it would be either impossible or difficult to charge the individual beneficiary for them. Such are most sanitary and health services, often the construction and maintenance of roads, and many of the amenities provided by municipalities for the inhabitants of cities. Included also are the activities which Adam Smith described as "those public works, which, though they may be in the highest degree advantageous to a great society, are, however, of such a nature, that the profit could never repay the expense to any individual or small number of individuals." . . .

Furthermore, a free system does not exclude on principle all those general regulations of economic activity which can be laid down in the form of general rules specifying conditions which everybody who engages in a certain activity must satisfy. They include, in particular, all regulations governing the techniques of production. . . .

If, for instance, the production and sale of phosphorus matches is generally prohibited for reasons of health or permitted only if certain precautions are taken, or if night work is generally prohibited, the appropriateness of such measures must be judged by comparing the over-all costs with the gain; it cannot be conclusively determined by appeal to a general principle. This is true of most of the wide field of regulations known as "factory legislation." . . .

We must now turn to the kinds of governmental measures which the rule of law excludes in principle because they cannot be achieved by merely enforcing general rules but, of necessity, involve arbitrary discrimination between persons. The most important among them are decisions as to who is to be allowed to provide different services or commodities, at what prices or in what quantities—in other words, measures designed to control the access to different trades and occupations, the terms of sale, and the amounts to be produced or sold.

So far as the entry into different occupations is concerned, our principle does not necessarily exclude the possible advisability in some instances of permitting it only to those who possess certain ascertainable qualifications. The restriction of coercion to the enforcement of general rules requires, however, that any one possessing these qualifications have an enforcible claim to such permission and that the grant of the permission depend only on his satisfying the conditions laid down as a general rule and not on any particular circumstances (such as "local need") which would have to be determined by the discretion of the licensing authority. . . .

There are several reasons why all direct control of prices by government is irreconcilable with a functioning free system, whether the government actually fixes prices or merely lays down rules by which the permissible prices are to be determined. In the first place, it is impossible to fix prices according to long-term rules which will effectively guide production. Appropriate prices depend on circumstances which are constantly changing and must be continually adjusted to them. On the other hand, prices which are not fixed outright but determined by some rule (such as that they must be in a certain relation to cost) will not be the same for all sellers and, for this reason, will prevent the market from functioning. A still more important consideration is that, with prices different from those that would form on a free market, demand and supply will not be equal, and if the price control is to be effective, some method must be found for deciding who is to be allowed to buy or sell. This would necessarily be discretionary and must consist of *ad hoc* decisions that discriminate between persons on essentially arbitrary grounds. As experience has amply confirmed, price controls can be made effective only by quantitative controls, by decisions on the part of authority as to how much particular persons or firms are to be allowed to buy or sell. And the exercise of all controls of quantities must, of necessity, be discretionary, determined not by rule but by the judgment of authority concerning the relative importance of particular ends.

It is thus not because the economic interests with which such measures interfere are more important than others that price and quantity controls must be altogether excluded in a free system, but because this kind of controls cannot be exercised according to rule but must in their very nature be discretionary and arbitrary. To grant such powers to authority means in effect to give it power arbitrarily to determine what is to be produced, by whom, and for whom. . . .

The range and variety of government action that is, at least in principle, reconcilable with a free system is thus considerable. The old formulae of laissez faire or non-intervention do not provide us with an adequate criterion for distinguishing between what is and what is not admissible in a free system. There is ample scope for experimentation and improvement within that permanent legal framework which makes it possible for a free society to operate most efficiently. . . .

6.8 The Great Society: A Libertarian Critique

Murray N. Rothbard

The Great Society is the lineal descendant and the intensification of those other pretentiously named politics of twentieth-century America: the Square Deal, the New Freedom, the New Era, the New Deal, the Fair Deal, and the New Frontier. All of these assorted Deals constituted a basic and fundamental shift in American life—a shift from a relatively *laissez-faire* economy and minimal state to a society in which the state is unquestionably king. In the previous century, the government could safely have been ignored by almost everyone; now we have become a country in which the government is the great and unending source of power and privilege. . . .

The basic reason for this development is not difficult to fathom. It was best summed up by the great German sociologist Franz Oppenheimer; Oppenheimer wrote that there were fundamentally two, and only two, paths to the acquisition of wealth. One route is the production of a good or service and its voluntary exchange for the goods or services produced by others. This method—the method of the free market—Oppenheimer termed "the economic means" to wealth. The other path, which avoids the necessity for production and exchange, is for one or more persons to seize other people's products by the use of physical force. This method of robbing the fruits of another man's production was shrewdly named by Oppenheimer the "political means."

Excerpted from Murray N. Rothbard, "The Great Society: A Libertarian Critique," in *The Great Society Reader,* edited by Marvin E. Gettleman and David Mermelstein (New York: Random House, 1967). Reprinted by permission of the publisher and the authors.

Throughout history, men have been tempted to employ the "political means" of seizing wealth rather than expend effort in production and exchange. . . . To regularize and order a permanent system of predatory exploitation, men have created the state.

Every act of the state is necessarily an occasion for inflicting burdens and assigning subsidies and privileges. By seizing revenue by means of coercion and assigning rewards as it disburses the funds, the state *creates* ruling and ruled "classes" or "castes." . . .

Since the state, nakedly observed, is a mighty engine of organized predation, state rule, throughout its many millennia of recorded history, could be preserved only by persuading the bulk of the public that its rule has not really been exploitative: that, on the contrary, it has been necessary, beneficient, even in the Oriental despotisms, divine. Promoting this ideology among the masses has ever been a prime function of intellectuals, a function that has created the basis for co-opting a corps of intellectuals into a secure and permanent berth in the state apparatus. . . .

In the United States, a strong libertarian and antistatist tradition prevented the process of statization from taking hold at a very rapid pace. The major force in its propulsion has been that favorite theater of state expansionism, . . . war. For although in wartime various states find themselves in danger from one another, every state has found war a fertile field for spreading the myth among its subjects that *they* are the ones in deadly danger, from which their state is protecting them. In this way states have been able to dragoon their subjects into fighting and dying to save them under the pretext that the *subjects* were being saved from the dread Foreign Enemy. In the United States, the process of statization began in earnest under cover of the Civil War (conscription, military rule, income tax, excise taxes, high tariffs, national banking and credit expansion for favored businesses, paper money, land grants to railroads), and reached full flower as a result of World Wars I and II, to finally culminate in the Great Society.

The recently emerging group of "libertarian conservatives" in the United States have grasped a part of the recent picture of accelerated statism, but their analysis suffers from several fatal blind spots. One is their complete failure to realize that war, culminating in the present garrison state and military-industrial economy, has been the royal road to aggravated statism in America. On the contrary, the surge of reverent patriotism that war always brings to conservative hearts, coupled with their eagerness to don buckler and armor against the "international Communist conspiracy," has made the conservatives the most eager and enthusiastic partisans of the Cold War. Hence their inability to see the enormous distortions and interventions imposed upon the economy by the enormous system of war contracts.

Another conservative blind spot is their failure to identify *which groups* have been responsible for the burgeoning of statism in the United States. In the conservative demonology, the responsibility belongs only to liberal intellectuals, aided and abetted by trade unions and farmers. Big businessmen, on the other hand, are curiously exempt from blame (farmers are small enough businessmen, apparently, to be fair game for censure). . . . Almost never is *interest* pinpointed as an overriding reason for statism among businessmen. This failure is all the more curious in the light of the fact that the *laissez-faire* liberals of the eighteenth and nineteenth centuries (e.g., the Philosophical Radicals in England, the Jacksonians in the United States) were never bashful about identifying and attacking the web of special privileges granted to businessmen in the mercantilism of their day.

In fact, one of the main driving forces of the statist dynamic of twentieth century America has been big businessmen, and this long before the Great Society. Gabriel Kolko, in his path-breaking *Triumph of Conservatism,* has shown that the shift toward statism in the Progressive period was impelled by the very big business groups who were supposed, in the liberal mythology, to be defeated and regulated by the Progressive and New Freedom measures. Rather than a "people's movement" to check big business, the drive for regulatory measures, Kolko shows, stemmed from big businessmen whose attempts at monopoly had been defeated by the competitive market, and who then turned to the federal government as a device for compulsory cartellization. This drive for cartellization through government accelerated during the New Era of the 1920s and reached its apex in Franklin Roosevelt's NRA. . . .

The formal corporatism of the NRA is long gone, but the Great Society retains much of its essence. The locus of social power has been emphatically assumed by the state apparatus. Furthermore, that apparatus is permanently governed by a coalition of big business and big labor groupings, groups that use the state to operate and manage the national economy. The usual tripartite *rapprochement* of big business, big unions, and big government symbolizes the organization of society by blocs, syndics, and corporations, regulated and privileged by the federal, state, and local governments. What this all amounts to in essence is the "corporate state." . . .

The indispensable intellectual role of engineering popular consent for state rule is played, for the Great Society, by the liberal intelligentsia, who provide the rationale of "general welfare," "humanity," and the "common good" (just as the conservative intellectuals work the other side of the Great Society street by offering the rationale of "national security" and "national interest"). The liberals, in short, push the "welfare" part of our omnipresent welfare-warfare state, while the conservatives stress the warfare side of the pie. This analysis of the role of the liberal intellectuals puts into more sophisticated perspective the seeming "sellout" of these intellectuals as compared to their role during the 1930s. Thus, among numerous other examples, there is the seeming anomaly of A. A. Berle and David Lilienthal, cheered and damned as flaming progressives in the thirties, now writing tomes hailing the new reign of big business. Actually, their basic views have not changed in the least. In the thirties, these theoreticians of the New Deal were concerned with condemning as "reactionaries" those big businessmen who clung to older individualist ideals and failed to understand or adhere to the new monopoly system of the corporate state. But now, in the 1950s and 1960s, this battle has been won, big businessmen are all eager to be privileged monopolists in the new dispensation, and hence they can now be welcomed by such theorists as Berle and Lilienthal as "responsible" and "enlightened," their "selfish" individualism a relic of the past.

The cruellest myth fostered by the liberals is that the Great Society functions as a great boon and benefit to the poor; in reality, when we cut through the frothy appearances to the cold reality underneath, the poor are the major victims of the welfare state. The poor are the ones to be conscripted to fight and die at literally slave wages in the Great Society's imperial wars. The poor are the ones to lose their homes to the bulldozer of urban renewal, that bulldozer that operates for the benefit of real estate and construction interests to pulverize available low-cost housing. All this, of course, in the name of "clearing the slums" and helping the aesthetics of housing. The poor are the welfare clientele whose homes are unconstitutionally but regularly invaded by government agents to ferret out sin in the middle of the night. The poor (e.g., Negroes in the South) are the ones disemployed by rising minimum wage floors, put in for the benefit of employers and unions in higher-wage areas (e.g., the North) to prevent industry from moving to the low-wage areas. The poor are cruelly victimized by an income tax that left and right alike misconstrue as an egalitarian program to soak the rich; actually, various tricks and exemptions insure that it is the poor and the middle classes who are hit the hardest. The poor are victimized too by a welfare state of which the cardinal macroeconomic tenet is perpetual if controlled inflation. The inflation and the heavy government spending favor the businesses of the military-industrial complex, while the poor and the retired, those on fixed pensions or Social Security, are hit the hardest. . . . And the burgeoning of compulsory mass public education forces millions of unwilling youth off the labor market for many years, and into schools that serve more as houses of detention than as genuine centers of education. Farm programs that supposedly aid poor farmers actually serve the large wealthy farmers at the expense of sharecropper and consumer alike; and commissions that regulate industry serve to cartellize it. The mass of workers is forced by governmental measures into trade unions that tame and integrate the labor force into the toils of the accelerating corporate state, there to be subjected to arbitrary wage "guidelines" and ultimate compulsory arbitration.

The role of the liberal intellectual and of liberal rhetoric is even more stark in foreign economic policy. Ostensibly designed to "help the underdeveloped countries," foreign aid has served as a gigantic subsidy by the American taxpayer of American export firms, a similar subsidy to American foreign investment through guarantees and subsidized government loans, an engine of inflation for the recipient country, and a form of massive subsidy to the friends and clients of US imperialism in the recipient country.

* * *

In sum, the most important fact about the Great Society under which we live is the enormous disparity between rhetoric and content. In rhetoric, America is the land of the free and the generous, enjoying the fused blessings of a free market tempered by and joined to accelerating social welfare, bountifully distributing its unstinting largesse to the less fortunate in the world. In actual practice, the free economy is virtually gone, replaced by an imperial corporate state Leviathan that organizes, commands, exploits the rest of society and, indeed, the rest of the world, for its own power and pelf.

NEO-LIBERALISM AND MAJOR ECONOMIC ISSUES

MONETARY AND FISCAL POLICY

Neo-liberals are at their most incisive and provocative in their dual role as critics of discretionary government management and control of the economy and proponents of reform in the structure and organization of public policy. This is illustrated by neo-liberal views on monetary and fiscal policy, monopoly and big business, economic inequality, and economic growth.

The relationship between neo-liberalism and contemporary macroeconomic theory and policy is subtle and complex. On the one hand, neo-liberals dissent from specific elements of Keynesian theory, as well as from the Keynesian claim to have demonstrated the likelihood of macroeconomic equilibrium at less than full-employment utilization of resources. Gottfried Haberler has argued that *if* the price system is not permitted to do its work (that is, if prices and wages are rigid, and do not fall to accommodate excess supplies of goods or labor), then of course unemployment may well occur; but that if prices and wages are perfectly flexible in a downward direction, then deflation, by increasing the real value of wealth, will eventually result in upward shifts in the propensity to consume and, thereby, a return to "true" equilibrium at full employment.[7]

On the other hand, neo-liberals recognize the possibility of excessive or insufficient aggregate demand for goods (especially caused by expansions or contractions in the money supply) as important factors in generating inflation or depression, and they support the provision of what Henry Simons called a general "monetary framework" as an appropriate function of government policy. Indeed, Milton Friedman's best-known contributions to economics are in the fields of monetary theory and policy—notably his arguments for monetary rather than fiscal policy and his critique of discretionary (as opposed to automatic) monetary (and fiscal) policy. Friedman proposes, for example, to put monetary management on an automatic basis by means of a simple "rule" to increase the money supply by a specified percentage annually.

[7] Gottfried Haberler, "The General Theory," in Seymour Harris, editor, *The New Economics* (N.Y.: Knopf, 1952), pp. 166–76. In more technical terms, this process is sometimes called the "Pigou effect" in honor of British neo-classicist A. C. Pigou. See his "The Classical Stationary State," *Economic Journal,* December, 1943, pp. 343–51. Rechristened the "real balance effect" by Don Patinkin, this theme has been explored in greater depth in his *Money, Interest, and Prices* (New York, Harper & Row, 1965).

Although Friedman's contributions to the theory of macroeconomic policy are probably the best-known of contemporary neo-liberal efforts, his general penchant for automaticity and for identification of the perils of discretionary action is widely shared by individualist-conservative critics of neo-Keynesian orthodoxy. As observed in chapter 3, neo-liberals such as James Buchanan dissent vigorously from the concept of "functional finance" in fiscal policy (compare selections 3.4 and 3.15), commend the concept of budgetary balance at high-level employment, and even have some kind words to say for the annually balanced budget as an instrument for providing control over government expenditures. Selection 6.9 illustrates the neo-liberals' acceptance of the need for macroeconomic policy to promote stable prosperity together with their preference for automatic rules rather than discretionary action.[8]

[8] The contrast between Keynes (or such Keynesians as Abba Lerner) and such neo-liberals as Friedman and Buchanan should not be drawn too sharply, however. As already seen in chapter 3 (recall selection 3.5), on the basic logic of deficit versus surplus financing Buchanan's discussion is essentially similar to the Keynesian analysis. Similarly, the young Friedman's description of the combination of monetary and fiscal policy—financing deficits by monetary creation, accompanying surpluses by destruction of money—is very similar to the Keynesian idea of financing deficits by the sale of bonds to the central bank, for example, by the creation of money. See his "A Monetary and Fiscal Framework for Economic Stability," *American Economic Review,* June 1948, pp. 245–64, and selection 6.11. See also Dudley Dillard, *The Economics of John Maynard Keynes* (Englewood Cliffs: Prentice-Hall, 1946), pp. 113–15.

6.9 A Monetary and Fiscal Framework for Economic Stability

Milton Friedman

Proposed Long-Run Reform in Our Monteary and Fiscal Framework[1]

The monetary and fiscal framework that follows is designed to promote economic stability and, at the same time, to be entirely automatic and to involve no discretionary action by governmental authorities. It covers the fiscal, as well as the monetary, framework because of the intimate connection between the two.

[1] This statement is largely a summary of a proposal described and analyzed at greater length in my article entitled "A Monetary and Fiscal Framework for Economic Stability," published in American Economic Review, XXXVIII (June 1948), pp. 245–64, and reprinted in Readings in Monetary Theory (Blakiston Co., 1951), pp. 369–93.

Excerpted from Milton Friedman, *Monetary Policy and the Management of the Public Debt.* Joint Economic Committee, 82d Congress, 2d Session, 1952 and Testimony of October 30, 1959, *Hearings, Employment, Growth, and Price Levels.* Joint Economic Committee, 86th Congress, 1st Session, 1959.

The proposal involves four main elements: the first relates to the monetary system; the second, to Government expenditures on goods and services; the third, to Government transfer payments; and the fourth, to the tax structure. Throughout, it pertains entirely to the Federal Government and all references to "government" should be so interpreted.

1. A reform of the monetary and banking system to eliminate both the private creation or destruction of money and discretionary control of the quantity of money by central bank authority. The private creation of money can perhaps best be eliminated by adopting the 100-percent reserve proposal. The adoption of 100-percent reserves would also reduce the discretionary powers of the reserve system by eliminating rediscounting and existing powers over reserve requirements. To complete the elimination of the major weapons of discretionary authority, the existing powers to engage in open market operations and the existing direct controls over stock market, consumer, and real estate credit should be abolished.

Under the 100-percent reserve proposal, existing commercial banks would, in effect, be separated into two parts. One part would provide depositary facilities. This part would essentially be a "warehouse" of funds, since it would be required to hold reserves, in the form either of currency or of deposits in a central governmental depositary, equal to 100 percent of its deposits. Its income would come from service charges to depositors, unless as a matter of public policy, it were thought desirable to subsidize this activity.

The other part of the existing commercial banks would take over its lending and investing functions. It would be an "investment trust," and would operate entirely with its own capital, or with funds obtained by the issuance of securities.

These modifications would leave as the chief monetary functions of the banking system the provision of depositary facilities, the facilitation of check clearance, and the like; and as the chief function of the monetary authorities, the creation of money to meet Government deficits or the retirement of money when the Government has a surplus.[2]

2. A policy of determining the volume of Government expenditures on goods and services—defined to exclude transfer expenditures of all kinds—entirely on the basis of the community's desire, need, and willingness to pay for public services. Changes in the level of expenditure should be made solely in response to alterations in the relative value attached by the community to public services and private consumption. No attempt should be made to vary expenditures, either directly or inversely, in response to cyclical fluctuations in business activity. Since the community's basic objectives would presumably change only slowly—except in time of war or immediate threat of war—this

[2] The adoption of 100 percent reserves is essential if the proposed framework is to be entirely automatic. It should be noted, however, that the same results could, in principle, be achieved in a fractional reserve system through discretionary authority. In order to accomplish this, the monetary authorities would have to adopt the rule that the quantity of money should be increased only when the Government has a deficit, and then by the amount of the deficit, and should be decreased only when the Government has a surplus, and then by the amount of the surplus.

policy would, with the same exception, lead to a relatively stable volume of expenditures on goods and services.

3. A predetermined program of transfer expenditures, consisting of a statement of the conditions and terms under which relief and assistance and other transfer payments will be granted. Such a program is exemplified by the present system of social security under which rules exist for the payment of old-age and unemployment insurance. The program should be changed only in response to alterations in the kind and level of transfer payments the community feels it should and can afford to make. The program should not be changed in response to cyclical fluctuations in business activity. Absolute outlays, however, will vary automatically over the cycle. They will tend to be high when unemployment is high and low when unemployment is low.

4. A progressive tax system which places primary reliance on the personal income tax. Every effort should be made to collect as much of the tax bill as possible at source and to minimize the delay between the accrual of the tax liability and the actual collection of the tax. Rates, exemptions, etc., should be set in light of the expected yield at a level of income corresponding to reasonably full employment at a predetermined price level. The budget principle might be either that the hypothetical yield should balance Government expenditure, including transfer payments (at the same hypothetical level of income) or that it should lead to a deficit sufficient to provide some specified secular increase in the quantity of money. The tax structure should not be varied in response to cyclical fluctuations in business activity, though actual receipts will, of course, vary automatically. Changes in the tax structure should reflect changes in the level of public services or transfer payments the community chooses to have. A decision to undertake additional public expenditures should be accompanied by a revenue measure increasing taxes. Calculations of both the cost of additional public services or transfer payments and the yield of additional taxes should be made at the hypothetical level of income suggested above rather than at the actual level of income. The Government would thus keep two budgets: the stable budget, in which all figures refer to the hypothetical income, and the actual budget. The principle of balancing outlays and receipts at a hypothetical income level would be substituted for the principle of balancing actual outlays and receipts.

Under the proposal, Government expenditures would be financed entirely by either tax revenues or the creation of money, that is, the issue of non-interest-bearing securities. Government would not issue interest-bearing securities to the public; the Federal Reserve System would not operate in the open market. This restriction of the sources of Government funds seems reasonable for peacetime. However, in time of war or immediate threat of war, involving a substantial expansion of governmental expenditures expected to be temporary, it would probably be desirable to finance part of these expenditures by borrowing from the public through the issuance of interest-bearing securities. Provision should therefore be made for this exception under the stated conditions.

Under the proposal, deficits or surpluses in the Government budget would be reflected dollar for dollar in changes in the quantity of money; and, conversely, the quantity of money would change only as a consequence of deficits or surpluses. A deficit means an increase in the quantity of money; a surplus, a decrease.

Deficits or surpluses themselves become automatic consequences of changes in the level of business activity. When national money income is high, tax receipts will be large and transfer payments small; so a surplus will tend to be created, and the higher the level of income, the larger the surplus. This extraction of funds from the current income stream makes aggregate demand lower than it otherwise would be and reduces the volume of money, thereby tending to offset the factors making for a further increase in income. When national money income is low, tax receipts will be small and transfer payments large, so a deficit will tend to be created, and the lower the level of income, the larger the deficit. This addition of funds to the current income stream makes aggregate demand higher than it otherwise would be and increases the quantity of money, thereby tending to offset the factors making for a further decline in income.

The proposal therefore automatically produces monetary and fiscal effects promoting stability in aggregate income, output, and prices.

A Monetary and Fiscal Framework Revisited [1959]

Wars aside, the chief economic threats to the preservation of a free society have come from the sharp fluctuations that have occurred from time to time in economic activity and in prices and that have threatened to tear the social fabric asunder. In devising means to prevent such fluctuations, it is well to be clear about their source.

One view, which the great depression did more perhaps than any other single event to instill and reinforce, is that a private market economy is inherently unstable and has been the source of the major periods of economic instability in our history.

In this view, only a vigilant government offsetting continuously the vagaries of the private economy has prevented or can prevent such periods of instability. This view seems to me fundamentally mistaken.

As I read the historical record, including the record of the great depression, I reach almost the opposite conclusion. The major inflations and depressions in the United States have in almost every instance been produced, or at the very least, strongly reinforced, by the failure of government to discharge properly the tasks assigned to it, in particular the task of providing a stable monetary framework. Perhaps the most remarkable feature of the record is the adaptability and flexibility that the private economy has shown under such extreme provocation.

This conclusion is almost self-evident for the major inflations of our history. These have all been associated with war and were quite clearly produced by use of the printing press or its equivalent to finance governmental expenditures.

But it can also, I believe, be shown to be in accord with the major contractions in the history of our country, from the contraction of 1839 to 1843 which was greatly exacerbated by the aftermath of the bank war; to the contraction of 1873 to 1879, which was intensified by the deflation incidental to creating the monetary conditions for resumption of gold payments at pre-Civil War parity; to the unsettled conditions of the 1890's, which owed much to agitation for free silver and uncertainty whether the Government could maintain the gold standard; to the major price contraction after the post-World War I inflation, resulting from the inexperience of the Federal Reserve System in handling its new tools; to the great depression, in which a system established in large measure to prevent a banking panic permitted the most severe and widespread panic in our history to occur and by its actions helped to produce a decline of one-third in the stock of money, although it had ample power to prevent either development; to the severe contraction of 1937 to 1938, when a collapse in investment in reaction to unwise and erratic governmental policies was reinforced by deflationary action by the monetary authorities.

Our monetary performance has been far better in the postwar period. But even in that period it has probably on balance contributed to instability. And this is almost surely true of the Government's fiscal performance.

The most unstable major sector of the national income has in the postwar period been Government expenditures. Fluctuations in expenditures have arisen partly from the changing needs of defense. But they have also arisen from the response to recurrent recessions. Increases in governmental expenditures designed to offset the recessions have taken so much time that they have come into play in important measure only after the economic tide has turned and recovery has been resumed, thus reinforcing rather than offsetting cyclical fluctuations.

What is true about economic fluctuations is true also, I believe, about growth. While a stable legal framework and preservation of free markets are essential prerequisites for healthy economic growth, and while government has done much in these respects to promote and facilitate growth, it has taken other measures that have tended to inhibit growth. These include not only the promotion of instability just considered, but also such interferences with the effective operation of the free market as price fixing, subsidies to particular activities, tariffs and quotas affecting foreign trade, and taxes seriously distorting economic incentives.

If my reading of history is right, it means that the central task for government at the present time is not to construct a highly sensitive set of instruments that can continuously offset instability introduced by other factors or that can facilitate economic growth, but rather to mend its own ways, to cease from being itself a primary source of instability and a primary obstacle to the effective utilization of resources by individuals.

What we urgently "need is not a skilled driver of the economic vehicle continuously turning the steering wheel to adjust to the unexpected irregularities of the route but some means of keeping the passenger who is in the back seat as ballast from occasionally leaning over and giving the steering wheel a jerk that threatens to send the car off the road."

I have tried to make my suggestions specific and to keep my comments on them brief.

MONETARY POLICY

1. Replace the present vague guides to the monetary authorities by the instruction that they increase the stock of money in the hands of the public at a fixed rate specified in advance and that they not alter the rate in response to changes in business conditions. The rate of growth chosen should be designed to produce an approximately constant level of prices over the long run.

Evidence to date suggests that this would require a rate of increase somewhere between 3 and 5 percent per year, if the money stock is defined as including currency in the hands of the public and demand and time deposits in commercial banks. This rule would avoid the monetary uncertainties that have plagued us in the past, provide a stable monetary background for short-run adjustments, and assure long-run stability in the purchasing power of the dollar.

2. Streamline present Federal Reserve powers by eliminating obsolete and unnecessary powers that interfere with the ability of the System to control the stock of money and that introduce unnecessary instability. The major changes required are the elimination of rediscounting and of the power to vary reserve requirements. These are highly defective tools of monetary management. Their elimination would leave open market operations as the major tool of monetary management.

3. Reform our present banking arrangements. The most satisfactory reform would be to separate the depositary from the lending and investing activities of banks by requiring depositary institutions to have reserves of 100 percent in the form of Federal Reserve notes and deposits. If this were done, it would be desirable to pay interest on the reserves, to remove any limitations on the interest rates commercial banks may pay to depositors, to permit free entry into the depositary banking business, and to eliminate present government controls over lending and investing activities.

This reform would eliminate instability arising out of shifts in the fraction of its money the public wishes to hold in the form of currency and in the fraction of their assets banks want to hold in the form of cash or Federal Reserve deposits. It would establish a closer link between Federal Reserve action and the money supply.

A less far-reaching yet desirable reform would be to make member bank reserve requirements uniform for all classes of banks and all deposits, whether demand or time; to put into effect the recently enacted power to treat vault cash as satisfying reserve requirements; to pay interest on reserves held in the form of Federal Reserve deposits; to remove the present prohibition of the payment of interest on demand deposits, and to repeal the present power of monetary authorities to limit the interest payable on time deposits. The change in reserve requirements should be made in such a way that the net effect is neither expansionary nor contractionary.

FISCAL ARRANGEMENTS

1. To promote economic stability, it is desirable to avoid erratic and sudden changes in governmental expenditure programs so far as possible, and in particular, in response to changes in economic conditions.

With a stable program of expenditures and a stable tax structure, changes in economic conditions automatically produce shifts in the governmental budget toward a surplus in time of expansion and a deficit in time of contraction. This built-in flexibility is all to the good. Attempts to go still further have in practice had the effect of fostering rather than curing instability.

2. To promote economic productivity and growth, a thorough reform of our tax structure is required. The present structure distorts incentives and discourages effort, and thereby leads to much waste, and it does so in ways that produce glaring inequities. The major reforms that seem to me desirable are:

[*a*] The ultimate elimination of the corporation income tax. Instead, corporations should be required to attribute their undistributed income to stockholders and stockholders should be required to include their pro rata share of undistributed income in income subject to the individual income tax.

[*b*] Reform of the individual income tax to reduce drastically the nominal rates imposed in the high brackets and to widen greatly the tax base. These high nominal rates have been responsible for the proliferation of provisions reducing the amount of income subjected to them. This has mitigated the adverse effect of the rates on incentive but only at the cost of producing a misdirection of resources to take advantage of the provisions, and a largely arbitrary distribution of the tax burden, with persons in essentially the same economic position paying vastly different taxes, depending on their accidental capacity to take advantage of special provisions.

Taxes finally paid would be both more equitably levied and less disturbing to efficiency if rates were drastically lowered and the base expanded and changed. The most important changes required in the base are the elimination of percentage depletion on oil and other raw materials; the elimination of tax exemption of interest on State and local securities; the coordination of income, estate, and gift taxes; and provision for averaging income over a period, which would also permit a more satisfactory treatment of capital gains.

MONOPOLY AND BIG BUSINESS

Neo-liberalism contains both an assumption of competitive markets and a corollary indictment of monopoly power. But if, as such classical liberals as Adam Smith contended, market transactors have a natural propensity to monopolize (for example, through collusion, expansion of size, exclusion of competitors, and so on), facilitated and even encouraged by government action, free enterprise may well require government encouragement and protection. A departure from laissez-faire and a restriction of "freedom" (for example, freedom to monopolize, collude, restrict entry, etc.) is implied. This creates a dilemma for neo-liberals. Proposed solutions vary from vigorous trust-busting to more or less acceptance of the status quo.

Friedman, for example, criticizes the restrictive properties of private monopoly, but refrains from advocacy of wholesale dissolution of giant monopoly or oligopoly corporations, on four grounds. First, although private monopoly is bad, its major alternatives—public regulation and public ownership—are worse. Public regulation envelops private enterprise in a web of government bureaucracy that, if effective, stifles managerial initiative and, if ineffective, adds the costs of government bureaucracy to those of private monopoly power. Public ownership removes the efficiency-creating stimulus of the profit motive and the protection for the consumer of competition (even if only among monopolists). Second, although the degree of monopoly power may have increased in the latter decades of the nineteenth century, it has been remarkably stable since then.[9] Third, pure monopoly is extremely rare. Most "monopoly power" is really big business oligopoly, which includes a good deal of competition. Fourth, government itself (through, for example, government licensing, tariffs, agricultural price supports) is a major source of monopoly. If government were to cease and desist its support of monopoly, the remaining degree of monopoly would probably be tolerable, especially because, in a dynamic economy, much monopoly power is temporary and short-lived in any event.

By contrast, vigorous trust-busting is a very strong plank in at least one strand of neo-liberal thought (which thereby converges with or parallels the populist, social reform liberal views of the progressive era of the early twentieth century). The most uncompromising of the antimonopoly strand among neo-liberals was Henry Simons, University of Chicago economist of the 1930s and 1940s.[10] Sharply critical of Keynesian economists (Hansen for instance,) and the liberal-labor reforms of the New Deal, especially its support of labor unions, Simons at the same time vigorously presented a truly radical program for (classical) liberal reform. Where feasible, he argued, "drastic measures" should be taken to eliminate monopoly, including dissolution of giant corporations, prosecution of collusive behavior, repudiation of the "rule of reason" in antitrust cases, elimination of interlocking stock acquisitions and corporate officerships in the same line of business, abolition of tariffs, restrictions on sales promotion, and federal incorporation of corporations. Where competition is not feasible, transition should be made to government operation and ownership. The half-way house of public utility regulation, he felt, was ineffectual at best and unduly restrictive of private initiative at worst. In selection 6.10, George Stigler, prominent contemporary neo-liberal, carries on this dimension of Simons' program and illustrates the uncompromising position of at least some neo-liberals in arguing for dissolution as the appropriate remedy for monopoly power in business.

[9] See G. Warren Nutter, *The Extent of Enterprise Monopoly in the United States, 1899–1939* (Chicago: University of Chicago Press, 1951) and George J. Stigler, *Five Lectures on Economic Theory* (London: Longmans, Green and Co., 1949), pp. 46–65.

[10] See his *Economic Policy for a Free Society*. Chicago: University of Chicago Press, 1948.

6.10 Critique of Big Business

George Stigler

WHAT IS BIGNESS?

Bigness in business has two primary meanings. First, bigness may be defined in terms of the company's share of the industry in which it operates: a big company is one that has a big share of the market or industry. By this test Texas Gulf Sulphur is big because it produces more than half the sulfur in America, and Macy's (whose annual sales are much larger) is small because it sells only a very small fraction of the goods sold by New York City retail stores. By this definition, many companies that are small in absolute size are nevertheless big—the only brick company in a region, for example—and many companies that are big in absolute size (Inland Steel, for example) are small. Second, bigness may mean absolute size—the measure of size being assets, sales, or employment as a rule. Then General Motors and U.S. Steel are the prototypes of bigness.

These two meanings overlap because most companies that are big in absolute size are also big in relation to their industries. There are two types of cases, however, in which the two meanings conflict. On the one hand, many companies of small absolute size are dominant in small markets or industries. I shall not discuss them here for two reasons: they seldom have anywhere near so much power as the companies that are big relative to large markets and industries; and they raise few political problems of the type I shall discuss below. On the other hand, there are a few companies that are big in absolute size but small relative to their markets. These companies are not very important in the total picture, and I shall also put them aside in the following discussion.

For my purposes, then, big businesses will mean businesses that are absolutely large in size and large also relative to the industries in which they operate. They are an impressive list: U.S. Steel, Bethlehem, and Republic in steel; General Electric and Westinghouse in electrical equipment; General Motors, Ford, and Chrysler in automobiles; du Pont, Union Carbide, and Allied Chemical among others in chemicals; Reynolds, Liggett & Myers, and American Tobacco in cigarettes.

The fundamental objection to bigness stems from the fact that big companies have monopolistic power, and this fundamental objection is clearly applicable outside the realm of corporate business. In particular, big unions are open to all the criticisms (and possibly more) that can be levied against big business. I shall not discuss labor unions, but my silence should not be construed as a belief that we should have a less stringent code for unions than for business.

Excerpted from George Stigler, "Critique of Big Business," ***Fortune*** **Magazine, May 1952, pp. 123 ff. Reprinted with permission.**

INDICTMENT OF BIGNESS

There are two fundamental criticisms to be made of big business: they act monopolistically, and they encourage and justify bigness in labor and government.

First, as to monopoly. When a small number of firms control most or all of the output of an industry, they can individually and collectively profit more by cooperation that by competition.

From this conclusion many reasonable men will dissent. Does not each brand of cigarettes spend huge sums in advertising to lure us away from some other brand? Do not the big companies—oligopolists, the economists call them—employ salesmen? Do not the big companies introduce constant innovations in their products?

Competition of a Kind

The answer is that they do compete—but not enough, and not in all the socially desirable ways. Those tobacco companies did not act competitively, but with a view to extermination, against the 10-cent brands in the 1930's, nor have they engaged in price competition in decades (*American Tobacco* vs. *United States, 328 U.S. 781*). The steel companies, with all their salesmen, abandoned cartel pricing via basing-point prices only when this price system was judged a conspiracy in restraint of trade in cement (*Federal Trade Commission* vs. *Cement Institute, 333 U.S. 683*). The plain fact is that big businesses do not engage in continuous price competition.

Nor is price the only area of agreement. Patent licensing has frequently been used to deprive the licensees of any incentive to engage in research; General Electric used such agreements also to limit other companies' output and fix the prices of incandescent lamps (*U.S.* vs. *General Electric, 82 F. Supp. 753*).

Very well, big businesses often engage in monopolistic practices. It may still be objected that it has not been shown that all big businesses engage in monopolistic practices, or that they engage in such practices all, or even most of, the time. These things cannot be shown or even fully illustrated in a brief survey, and it is also not possible to summarize the many court decisions and the many academic studies of big business. But it is fair to say that these decisions and studies show that big businesses usually possess monopolistic power, and use it. And that is enough.

For economic policy must be contrived with a view to the typical rather than the exceptional, just as all other policies are contrived.

Second, as to bigness in labor and government. Big companies have a large—I would say an utterly disproportionate—effect on public thinking. The great expansion of our labor unions has been due largely to favoring legislation and administration by the federal government. This policy of favoring unions rests fundamentally upon the popular belief that workers individually competing for jobs will be exploited by big-business employers—that U.S. Steel can in separate negotiation (a pretty picture!) overwhelm each of its hundreds of thousands of employees. In good part this is an absurd fear: U.S. Steel must compete with many other industries, and not merely other steel companies, for good workers.

Yet the fear may not be wholly absurd: there may be times and places where big businesses have "beaten down" wages, although I believe such cases are relatively infrequent. But it cannot be denied that this public attitude underlies our national labor policy, the policy of local governments of condoning violence in labor disputes, etc.

Big business has also made substantial contributions to the growth of big government. The whole agricultural program has been justified as necessary to equalize agriculture's bargaining power with "industry," meaning big business.

Business Across the Board

Big business is thus a fundamental excuse for big unions and big government. But in light of the widespread monopolistic practices—our first criticism of bigness—it is impossible to tell the public that its fears of big business are groundless. We have no right to ask public opinion to veer away from big unions and big government—and toward big business.

EFFICIENCY AND BIG BUSINESS

Are we dependent upon big businesses for efficient methods of production and rapid advances in production methods? If we are, the policy of breaking up big businesses would lower our future standard of living and many people would cast about for other ways than dissolution to meet the problems of bigness.

A company may be efficient because it produces and sells a given amount of product with relatively small amounts of material, capital, and labor, or it may be efficient because it acquires the power to buy its supplies at unusually low prices and sells its products at unusually high prices. Economists refer to these as the social and the private costs of production respectively. Big businesses may be efficient in the social sense, and usually they also possess, because of their monopoly position, private advantages. But the ability of a company to employ its dominant position to coerce unusually low prices from suppliers is not of any social advantage.

It follows that even if big companies had larger profit rates or smaller costs per unit of output than other companies, this would not prove that they were more efficient in socially desirable ways. Actually, big businesses are generally no more and no less efficient than medium-sized businesses even when the gains wrung by monopoly power are included in efficiency. This is the one general finding in comparative cost studies and comparative profitability studies. Indeed, if one reflects upon the persistence of small and medium-sized companies in the industries dominated by big businesses, it is apparent that there can be no great advantages to size. If size were a great advantage, the smaller companies would soon lose the unequal race and disappear.

If big businesses are not more efficient as a rule, how did they get big? The answer is that most giant firms arose out of mergers of many competing firms, and were created to eliminate competition. Standard Oil, General Electric, Westinghouse, U.S. Steel, Bethlehem, the meat packers, Borden, National

Dairy, American Can, etc.—the full list of merger-created big businesses is most of the list of big businesses. A few big businesses owe their position to an industrial genius like Ford, and of course future geniuses would be hampered by an effective antitrust law—but less so than by entrenched monopolies or by public regulatory commissions.

We do not know what share of improvements in technology has been contributed to big businesses. Big businesses have made some signal contributions, and so also have small businesses, universities, and private individuals. It can be said that manufacturing industries dominated by big businesses have had no large increases in output per worker on average than other manufacturing industries. This fact is sufficient to undermine the easy identification of economic progress with the laboratories of big businesses, but it does not inform us of the net effect of monopolies on economic progress.

REMEDIES FOR BIG BUSINESS

A considerable section of the big-business community seems to have taken the following position. The proper way to deal with monopolistic practices is to replace the general prohibitions of the Sherman Act by a specific list of prohibited practices, so businessmen may know in advance and avoid committing monopolistic practices. Even when the request for a specific list of prohibitions is made in all sincerity, it cannot be granted: No one can write down a full list of all the forms that objectionable monopoly power has taken and may someday take.

We must look elsewhere for the solution of the problems raised by big business. Our present policy is not a satisfactory solution. The Sherman Act is admirable in dealing with formal conspiracies of many firms, but—at least with the Supreme Court's present conception of competition and of the proper remedies for demonstrated restraint of trade in oligopolistic industries—it cannot cope effectively with the problem posed by big business. In industries dominated by a few firms there is no need for formal conspiracies, with their trappings of quotas, a price-fixing committee, and the like. The big companies know they must "live with" one another. Any competitive action one big company takes will lead to retaliation by the others. An informal code of behavior gradually develops in the industry: Firm X announces the new price, and except in very unusual circumstances Y and Z can be relied upon to follow. So long as there are a few big businesses in an industry, we simply cannot expect more than the tokens of competitive behavior.

This conclusion, I must emphasize, is not merely that of "economic theorists," although most (academic) economists will subscribe to it. It is also the conclusion our generation is reaching, for our generation is not satisfied with the behavior of big business. More and more, big businesses are being asked to act in "the social interest," and more and more, government is interfering in their routine operation. The steel industry, for example, what with congressional review of prices and presidential coercion of wages, is drifting rapidly into a public-utility status. And the drift will not be stopped by slick advertising.

DISSOLUTION THE REMEDY

No such drastic and ominous remedy as the central direction of economic life is necessary to deal with the problems raised by big business. The obvious and economical solution, as I have already amply implied, is to break up the giant companies. This, I would emphasize, is the minimum program, and it is essentially a conservative program. Dissolution of big businesses is a one-for-all measure in each industry (if the recent anti-merger amendment to the Clayton Act is adequately enforced), and no continuing interference in the private operation of business is required or desired. Dissolution involves relatively few companies: one dissolves three or four big steel companies, and leaves the many smaller companies completely alone. Dissolution does not even need to be invoked in a large part of the economy: some of our biggest industries, such as textiles, shoes, and most food industries, will require no antitrust action.

A policy of "trust busting" requires no grant of arbitrary powers to any administrative agency; the policy can be administered by the Antitrust Division acting through the courts. It is sufficient, and it is desirable, that the policy be directed against companies whose possession of monopoly power is demonstrated, and that dissolution be the basic remedy for the concentration of control in an industry that prevents or limits competition. Indeed, the policy requires new legislation only to the extent of convincing the courts that an industry which does not have a competitive structure will not have competitive behavior.

The dissolution of big businesses is only a part of the program necessary to increase the support for a private, competitive enterprise economy, and reverse the drift toward government control. But it is an essential part of this program, and the place for courage and imagination. Those conservatives who cling to the status quo do not realize that the status quo is a state of change, and the changes are coming fast. If these changes were to include the dissolution of a few score of our giant companies, however, we shall have done much to preserve private enterprise and the liberal-individualistic society of which it is an integral part.

INEQUALITY AND THE DISTRIBUTION OF INCOME

Income distribution and economic inequality constitute a third set of issues that illustrate well the neo-liberal penchant for combining social reform with faith in the efficacy and automaticity of market processes.

On the one hand, many neo-liberals profess at least some support for the social desirability of reducing inequality in the distribution of income. As in the issue of monopoly, Henry Simons probably represents the most radical stance of the neo-liberals in his specification of reduction of income inequality as "per se immensely important" and his identification of progressive income taxation and expansion of the range of "socialized consumption" (for example, medical care) and social welfare programs as appropriate means for pursuing this objective.[11]

[11] Ibid., pp. 65–68.

Other neo-liberals, for example, Friedman, Hayek, and Stigler, are somewhat less enthusiastic in their endorsement of equality as a social goal, and emphasize the possible conflicts between policies to reduce inequality and individual freedom. Still, the neo-liberal view in general gives at least qualified support for this social concern prominent in reform liberalism, especially in regard to the elimination of poverty, reduction of inequalities based on monopoly power and special privileges, and promotion of greater equality of opportunity.

On the other hand, neo-liberals place great faith in the efficacy of competitive markets as processes for income distribution, and essentially accept the orthodox view that distribution of income in accordance with market-determined marginal productivities of resources, given the distribution of property in society, is ethically fair as well as consistent with efficient and consumer-directed allocation of resources. (Recall selection 6.4.) Additionally, neo-liberals stress the wisdom and simplicity of making policies to reduce inequality and poverty as "automatic" as possible, for example, as free as possible from discretionary and potentially arbitrary and capricious decisions of government authorities. For example, Milton Friedman proposes to substitute a "negative income tax"—whereby individuals with very low incomes would automatically receive a negative tax, that is, a subsidy, just as individuals today with sufficiently high taxable incomes pay a positive tax—"for the present rag bag of measures directed at the same end," such as welfare payments, old age insurance, social security programs, and public housing.

In selection 6.11, Henry Wallich, whose middle-of-the-road approach to economic philosophy and policy places him alternatively in the conservative strand of the post-Keynesian synthesis (recall selection 3.17) and in sympathy with some of the positions of the neo-liberals, assesses the major arguments concerning equality versus inequality in the distribution of income.

6.11 Inequality and Income Distribution

Henry C. Wallich

TRADITIONAL ARGUMENTS FOR INEQUALITY

Wherever the question [of economic inequality] arises, one observes two extremes between which the great majority find their places: Those who see nothing wrong with the existing distribution of incomes, or one even more unequal, and those who take for granted that the only fair shares are equal shares. Each side has its arguments to demonstrate that its position is "naturally just."

Those who approve of inequality usually point to the obvious facts of life. Human beings are biologically unequal. The equality that the Constitution speaks of is one of rights, not of condition—before God and the law, not in the market place. The basic truth of these propositions is undeniable, even though the readiness of their proponents to bear other people's poverty with fortitude is sometimes a little irritating. Yet perhaps not much is proved by truths such as these. If man is the master of his fate, why should he not correct the consequences of biological inequality if he finds them unattractive? We have gone some way in evening up what nature made uneven—why not go the whole way?

The supporters of inequality are fond also of saying that, after all, anybody can get rich if he tries hard enough; this is a free country and those who remain poor have only themselves to blame. That is true enough in any particular case—leaving aside the question of whether the "case" has the ability to work his way to the top. It is conspicuously fallacious for the people as a whole. Even if the population of the United States consisted exclusively of men with the ability and determination of Rockefeller, Ford and Carnegie, they could not all be presidents of corporations. Circumstances—luck, connections and whatever—must inevitably lead a few to the top and keep the vast majority in the lower echelons. We cannot all get ahead of one another.

Finally, one often hears it said in support of income inequality that, after all, a man has a right to the fruits of his labor.

This principle carried conviction in the days when craftsmen and farmers really "made" what they lived by. Today it does not speak to us quite so clearly. When a man "makes" a million in business today, what is it he really makes, and how much of it is his own contribution? How much is contributed by his collaborators, his predecessors, by society at large? How much of it depends on the state of competition, the state of business and a host of other factors not demonstrably under his control? Economists believe that, under favorable conditions, they can calculate the contribution that an individual makes to the flow of production with the help of the marginal productivity doctrine. But they rarely have the courage to extract a moral claim from such calculations.

If those who regard economic inequality as "natural" fail to make a convincing case, those who go for equality as "the only just solution" perform no better. Righteous indignation and vicarious anguish at the sight of poverty do not add up to a logical demonstration. Equality of income as a principle of justice runs straight into the fact that men are unequal not only as producers but also as consumers. Some of us want an expensive education, some want to travel, some want great variety in clothes, living habits and entertainment—others may find all of this tiresome. Temperaments, moreover, may vary as well as tastes—we were created equal, but not equally cheerful. To endow everybody with equal income will certainly make for very unequal enjoyment and satisfaction. Perhaps some sort of allowance could be made for this. But in practice it would scarcely be feasible to determine for purposes of compensation how many drinks above or below par each individual happened to be born.

The plea for equality also offends the elementary feeling that there should be some relation between performance and reward. We cannot say, to be sure, that a man has a right to whatever he makes, because today there are few things of which we can say who really "made" them. Yet to say positively that a man has no right to what he makes seems to imply that someone else has a better right, which makes little sense. The right of any member of society to an equal share, moreover, would presumably depend on his having put forth a normal amount of effort. To hand a full share to those who not only do not succeed, but do not even try, will strike most people as perverse. Justice seems to escape the egalitarians as it has evaded those who believe in "natural" differences.

WHAT SORT OF INEQUALITY?

Looked at cold-bloodedly, what sort of an ideal is this economic equality? What claims to a fair minded man's allegiance does it have, what sense does it make as a goal?

Equality of rights before the law is intuitively appealing as a social goal. . . . The sum total of rights and powers in a community remains fixed—it adds up to 100 per cent. Any extra rights given to some mean extra obligations placed upon the rest. In such a situation, equal sharing of rights and powers offers the obvious solution.

This obvious solution does not translate smoothly into economics. Here the obvious goal seems to be, not equal welfare, but maximum welfare. A man can have more than others and yet not take anything from them, if he creates his own surplus. Economic equality as such seems to bestow no particular blessings. A community where some were rich and the rest well provided for presumably would be considered better off than one in which all were equally poor. Economic equality, unlike its political counterpart, plainly is not an end in itself. It is only a means, designed to reduce poverty; perhaps it is not the most effective means.

That economic equality does not rank with political equality as a moral ideal is plain on several grounds. To demand that none have privileges I do not enjoy seems fair. To insist that none be richer is merely spiteful. People's behavior, moreover, makes clear that economic equality is rarely their true goal. What they strive for is betterment. Insofar as they compare themselves with others, it seems that emulation, the creation of invidious distinctions, as Veblen has so well observed, turns out to be a stronger motive than desire for equality.

It seems clear that the debate over justice in distribution largely misses its point. The real issue is not which division, equal or unequal, is the more just. The issue is which of the two leads to higher welfare for all.

INEQUALITY AND PROGRESS

The Welfare Case for Equality

The case for greater equality can be established very simply. A dollar means less to a richer man than to a poorer. Therefore, if we take a dollar from the rich man and give it to the poor man, we hurt the rich man less than we help the poor. The sum total of their happiness rises by virtue of the operation. Happiness can be further increased by additional transfers and will reach its peak when everybody's income is up or down to the average and complete economic equality is achieved.

Scientific economics sees a fly in the egalitarian ointment. All we really know is that the millionth dollar means less than the thousandth *to the same man*. We cannot be sure that the millionth dollar means less to one man than the thousandth means to another. True enough, one of these men is rich, the other is poor. But perhaps the pauper is completely satisfied with what he has, while the millionaire is pressed for cash. Or perhaps the pauper is an insensitive clod, incapable of finer feelings, while the millionaire is a delicate aesthete who can exist only in complete luxury. More realistically, the millionaire is probably accustomed to his standard of living and the pauper to his. Even if they are fairly similar individuals, it may hurt the one more to cut his standard than it will cheer the other to increase his.

Rigorous economic theory, therefore, will not subscribe unqualifiedly to the egalitarians' doctrine that redistribution from rich to poor must increase total satisfaction. Nevertheless, for practical purposes, the case is pretty strong, the objections not very convincing. Individuals differ, but people in the mass fall into fairly stable patterns. I would hate to have to argue that the members of the upper income brackets are on average more sensitive and capable of greater enjoyment than the rest. And the unquestionable hardships that would result from a reduction of the upper living standards could be softened by spreading the process over a generation or two.

Thus put, the case for equality is impressive, simply on functional grounds and aside from questions of justice. It can hardly fail to predispose us in favor of greater rather than lesser equality, whenever this does not interfere with growth, or boomerang in other respects. In fact, however, it is apt to defeat itself in these respects more often than not. That will be the next step of the argument.

Growth vs. Redistribution

Once growth comes to be seen as an alternative to redistribution, its potential superiority in providing welfare becomes quickly apparent. Even those who are at the low end of the income scale stand to gain more, in the not-very-long run, from speedier progress than from redistribution. Redistribution is a one-shot operation. What it can do for the lower income groups amounts to less, as we have seen, than its enthusiasts claim. Soaking the rich yields political dividends, but not much consumable revenue. And once it is done, the toll of a lower rate of progress is exacted continually thereafter. If the rate of income growth in an egalitarian economy is 2 per cent per year, and 4 per cent in one allowing itself a higher degree of inequality, it will not be many years before the middle class of the egalitarian economy is outdistanced by the "poor" of the other.

The proposition that rapid progress is worth more than redistribution even to the poor has been challenged occasionally. The critics argue that the standard of poverty rises with the standard of living. Accordingly, if we succeeded in doubling or quadrupling the average standard of living, those who fell below it would feel just as poor as they do today. To redistribute, to raise the poor closer to the average, would thus be a surer road to happiness.

[This] gloomy premise . . . says that apparently we can never get ahead of our needs; . . . in fact it seems to put an end to all meaningful economic endeavor. No matter how rich we get, the doctrine says, no matter how equally we split our wealth, as a community we shall never feel any better off.

But . . . if man is constitutionally unable, as these critics seem to think, to achieve happiness, he can at least do something to reduce . . . pain. . . . With all our high standard of living, we still have enough sources of pain—illness, unprotected old age and, above all, lack of real leisure. So long as these are with us, there is little point in even wondering whether or not we would be made happier by more and more progress.

Creative Inequality

Let us put aside now the question of whether economic inequality is inequitable. Instead, let us look more searchingly at its constructive role in the economy.

One important explanation of, and reason for, inequality follows from the need to get the right people into the right jobs. It is wasteful if engineers do work that mechanics can handle, or if executives perform chores that could be done by their secretaries. A market economy avoids this by compelling business to compete for talent and to pay each man what he is worth in the job he can do best. The process admittedly works far from perfectly. Many of our income differentials arise from monopoly power rather than from greater productivity.

But even in more perfect markets, large differentials would arise.

Unless we pay people what they are worth, they may see to it that they are worth no more than they are paid. Therefore, if the selection process results in large bonuses, efficiency demands that, in good part, they be left where they land.

Another instance of creative inequality presents itself when we turn to incentives. Here again, the logic of our system produces inequalities that cannot be removed without slowing down the system itself. If we want good performance, we must hold out rewards. To be effective, rewards must raise one man above the other. Not their absolute level, but their differentiation is what counts, as we discovered in the discussion of incentives. Inequality once more proves to be the price of progress and efficiency.

It might be possible, of course, to shift the needed inequalities from the economic sphere to that of status, prestige and power. In part—to the extent that economic differentials are taxed away—that shift is likely to come automatically, even though unofficially. . . . I see no reason to think that power and prestige differentials are any more "just" than economic ones. Certainly they could be a great deal more unpleasant.

If a thoroughgoing economic egalitarianism were to take hold, its chief victim probably would be the incentive to take risks. Successful risk-taking has built most of the big fortunes. It is here that the egalitarians would find their most inviting targets. It is here, also, that the conjunction between equality and stagnation might make itself felt most strongly.

The incentive to invest, to be sure, is not exclusively wedded to the profit motive. It is related to other motivations—competition, sheer expansionism, prestige—which were duly noted in the preceding chapter. But remove profit and enough of the motive force probably will be gone to slow down the rest.

The ability to save is another important consequence of high incomes that has often been stressed. The rich, as has been correctly observed, can afford to save a good part of their incomes. The poor, unfortunately, save little or nothing. Leveling of incomes, it has therefore been thought, would perforce reduce the rate of saving. This argument was especially popular during the Great Depression, when saving tended to outrun investment opportunities. A cut in saving and a corresponding rise in consumption would then have aided recovery. Redistribution of income would have killed two birds with one tax hike.

To the credit of those who developed this doctrine and derived from it a pleasure perhaps more than intellectual, it must be said that they were also the first to discover that the doctrine may not fit the statistical evidence. What they discovered from income distribution data and personal budget studies was rather surprising. A man with $10,000 a year net may save $1,000 and a man with $4,000 may save nothing. But out of any dollar added to their respective incomes, both may save sums that are not so very different. In other words, it is true that the upper brackets save more of their *total* income; it is somewhat doubtful that they save much more than the poor also out of an *increase* in income. A change in income—up or down—seems to lead to a fairly similar change in saving for upper and lower brackets alike.

If this is so, a redistribution of income from rich to poor would cause the poor to begin saving possibly as much as the rich would cease to save. Redistribution, on these premises, would not greatly change the volume of saving out of current income. It would not help to cure a depression brought on by oversaving. By the same token, it would not greatly cut into the savings needed by a fast growing, high employment economy. The statistical facts which deprived the liberals of a favorite argument for redistribution have robbed conservatives of an old war horse in the struggle against the egalitarians.

The statistical findings, however, are not entirely clear cut. In Jacob Viner's phrase, there may be life in the old dogma yet. And it can be further reinvigorated by stressing that it is not only the quantity but also the quality of savings that counts. Industry needs venture capital, and that is not usually supplied by insurance companies buying bonds nor even by pension funds buying blue chip stocks. Venture capital typically comes from wealthy individuals. To dry up their savings would still create an important gap in our financial structure, even though dollarwise they could be replaced from other sources. This much can fairly be argued by those who see a threat in equalization.

One further point deserves to be made. Economic inequality is not purely an economic affair. It touches also upon political stability and social cohesion. In an extreme case, inequality may lead to revolution. So may overzealous efforts to reduce it. A distribution of income that is widely resented may, even though it is economically efficient, do more political harm than economic good. A society that has got itself into this frame of mind will probably be wise to pay the economic price of its political idiosyncrasies. Slower progress would then have to be written off as the cost of political and social betterment.

Added to its probable price in terms of growth, action to alter the distribution of income determined by the market is likely to impose a non-economic cost. Typically, this cost takes the form of lengthening the reach of government. Something, somebody, has to be registered, regulated, controlled. A little freedom always goes by the board. Some economic resources, too, that could perhaps be more productively employed must be shifted to this function. If anyone thinks that this is altogether a negligible matter, let him note the lack of enthusiasm with which taxpayers vote the means for even the most pressing functions of government.

CRITIQUE OF ECONOMIC GROWTH

While neo-liberals, and such middle-of-the-road conservative allies as Henry Wallich, have generally given a high priority to economic growth as a social goal and to the efficacy of competitive markets in promoting growth, their endorsement has typically been given with reservations. For example, neo-liberals are quick to distinguish between *extensive* growth, created by increasing the labor force and capital accumulation, that is, by increasing the quantities of resources, and *intensive* growth, created by technological improvements and increases in efficiency, for example, by increasing the productivity of resources. A centrally planned economic system that saves and invests 30 percent of national income and thereby achieves a higher growth rate than does a more market-oriented economy whose households and businesses save and invest 15 percent, does not necessarily demonstrate a "better" economic performance. In general, the "supreme goal" (Stigler) for neo-liberals is sustenance of individual freedoms. The optimum growth rate, with exceptions centering around the concept of "externalities," is essentially that which emerges from the market coordination of individual choices of consumers and businesses.

In the 1960s, as we observed in chapter 3, the "post-Keynesian synthesis" became a new orthodoxy. Its central focus was economic growth, both in the short-run sense of expanding output and employment to full-employment levels, and in the long-run sense of increasing society's productive capacity. Interestingly, the possible adverse effects of economic growth, for example, pollution and environmental destruction, noise, traffic congestion, while recognized by neo-Keynesian economists, have been identified more pointedly by "radical" critics from both Left and Right. Selection 3.19 summarized some of the criticisms of the neo-orthodox emphasis upon the social desirability of growth and growth-promotion policies raised by "new radicals" from the Left. Selection 6.12, by E. J. Mishan, provides a critique of growth from the perspective of more traditional and conservative values, for example, loss of a "code of morality" and socially unifying religious beliefs.

6.12 Critique of Economic Growth

E. J. Mishan

THE DESIRABILITY OF SUSTAINED ECONOMIC GROWTH

Assuming that per capita growth could be maintained indefinitely at current rates, we must still ask whether such growth is desirable. Has economic growth promoted social welfare in the recent past, and is it likely to do so in the future? An odd assortment of arguments come up in this debate, a number of which are definitely "nonstarters." We can save time and heat by recognizing some of them before going any farther.

First, there is the frequent statement that technology—the main force behind current economic growth—is itself neutral. One cannot associate it with good or evil attributes and "it all depends on how man uses it." But the *potential* of science and technology is not the issue. Their *actual* effects are. Intelligent conjecture about the future presupposes some knowledge of the reach of modern science and also some idea of the probable scientific developments over the foreseeable future. From this we can speculate about some of the more likely consequences on our lives, bearing in mind the limitations of men and the driving forces of modern institutions, economic and political.

A related response, the invocation of a "challenge" to man to "face the future" or to "be worthy of his destiny," must also go off the board. Otherwise we shall find ourselves with a two-headed penny. For wherever science and technology can be seen to have created problems, the technocrats exclaim "challenge" and perceive an immediate need for more technology. We must be alert to the possibility that some of the problems inflicted upon us by the advance of technology can also be solved by using less of the existing technology.

Nor is it, for similar reasons, legitimate to argue that we should seek the "optimal," or just-right, rate of growth. One can imagine some distillation of

---

Excerpted from E. J. Mishan, "Growth and Antigrowth: What Are the Issues?" *Challenge*, May/June 1973. Reprinted by permission of the publisher.

economic growth, some essence purified of all harmful external effects, which cannot fail to result in ideal human progress. But such flights of inspiration offer no plausible picture of the future and no guide to action. Economists all know that a narrow range of adverse spillovers—such as air and water pollution, noise, congestion and tourist blight—can be reduced given some political effort. Yet in judging the quality of life over the last two decades, we obviously cannot abstract from the brute facts of expanding pollution. So, also, in debating the foreseeable future, it is not the potential ideal that is at issue, but the political likelihood of realizing significant reductions in each of the familiar forms of pollution.

The "need" to maintain the momentum of economic growth in order to enable us to do good deeds like helping the poor, promoting high culture, or expanding higher education is also not on the agenda. This argument might win ethical support even if it were agreed that economic growth actually entailed a decline in social welfare for the majority of people. But the fact is that such worthy objectives can all be realized *without* sustained economic growth. In the United States, so much is produced which is trivial, inane, if not inimical, that we already have more than enough to transfer resources for these more meritorious purposes.

It is convenient for the professional economist to interpret people's economic behavior as reflecting their mature judgment about what is most conducive to their happiness. But I hope that he is not such a fool as really to believe it. It is also convenient for the economist to champion the right of the citizen to spend his money as he wishes. For my part, I have no objection if he prefers to sleep on a mattress stuffed with breakfast cereal. For I am not questioning his right to choose; I am questioning the consequences of his choice. We can sharpen the debate by focusing not on motivation, but only on the consequences.

Having, hopefully, cleared away some of the verbal undergrowth that tends to impede the progress of this debate, we are better able to perceive the issues that can be decisive. The issues can be divided, arbitrarily perhaps, into two categories:

1. In the first are the conventional array of adverse spillovers—air pollution, water pollution, solid waste pollution, noise, uglification of town and country—all of which have increased alarmingly since the war. The question is whether they have more than offset the "normal" expectations of welfare gains from economic growth.

2. In the second category are the remaining consequences of economic growth. How much weight is to be given to those pervasive repercussions that are less tangible and more complex than the familiar external diseconomies? Unwittingly, through the process of continually and unquestioningly adapting our style and pace of life to technological and commercial possibilities, we may be losing irrevocably traditional sources of comfort and gratification.

It is difficult to draw a balance sheet summarizing the net welfare effects of the increased output of goods and the concomitant spillovers in the last few years. Even if we had all the physical data—from the hazards of chemical pesticides to rising levels of noise, from oil-fouled beaches the world over, to forest-cropping and earth-stripping—we should, in a closely interdependent economic system, be faced with the almost impossible task of evaluation. My inclination is to describe what has been happening on the advancing pollution front in impressionistic terms, taking it for granted that the balance of the argument will be restored by the unremitting efforts of commercial advertising, establishment politicians, company chairmen, and the spate of articles in our newspapers and magazines that speak loudly of the goodies we have and of goodies yet to come.

The incidence of a single spillover alone—be it foul air, endless traffic bedlam, noise, or fear of criminal violence—can be enough to counter all of the alleged gains of economic prosperity. Let a family have five television sets, four refrigerators, three cars, two yachts, a private plane, a swimming pool, and half a million dollars' worth of securities. What enjoyment is left if it fears to stroll out of an evening, if it must take elaborate precautions against burglary, if it lives in continuous anxiety lest one or another, parent or child, be kidnapped, mutilated or murdered? A fat bag of consumer goods, an impressive list of technical achievements, can hardly compensate for any one of such perils that have come to blight the lives of millions of Americans.

The old-fashioned notion of diminishing marginal utility of goods and the increasing marginal disutility of "bads" can also bear more emphasis. For one thing, choosing from an increasing variety of goods can be a tense and time-consuming process. For another, as Stefan Linder observes in his admirable and amusing *Harried Leisure Classes,* Americans cannot find time to make use of all the gadgets and sports gear they feel impelled to buy.

In addition, the "relative income hypothesis" (or, more facetiously, the "Jones effect") argues strongly against continued economic growth, if only because it is a predicament for which the economists can propose no remedy consistent with such growth. In an affluent society, people's satisfactions, as Thorstein Veblen observed, depend not only on the innate or perceived utility of the goods they buy but also on the status value of such goods. Thus to a person in a high consumption society, it is not only his absolute income that counts but also his *relative* income, his position in the structure of incomes. In its extreme form—and as affluence rises we draw closer to it—only relative income matters. A man would then prefer a 5 percent reduction in his own income accompanied by a 10 percent reduction in the incomes of others to a 25 percent increase in both his income and the incomes of others.

The more this attitude prevails—and the ethos of our society actively promotes it—the more futile is the objective of economic growth for society as a whole. For it is obvious that over time everybody cannot become relatively better off. The economist can, of course, continue to spin his optimal equations even in these conditions, but he has no means of measuring the loss in terms of utter futility. Since the extent of these wealth-dissipative effects are never measured, estimates over the last few years of increments of "real" income (or "measured economic welfare") must be rejected as wholly misleading.

Reflecting on the unmeasurable consequence of economic growth, Gilbert and Sullivan's dictum "Things are never what they seem" is a proper leitmotif.

Consider first the motive force behind economic growth. Bernard Shaw once remarked that "discontent is the mainspring of progress." The secret of how to keep people running is to widen the gap between their material condition and their material expectations. That gap is a fair measure of their discontent, and it was never wider than it is today. It is institutionalized by the agencies of Madison Avenue and hallowed by our system of higher education.

If continued discontent with what they have is required to keep people buying the increasing output of industry, and continued discontent with their status is necessary to keep them operating the machine, can we really believe that people are nonetheless happier as they absorb more goods? Does not the consequent struggle for status in an increasingly anonymous society become so obsessive as to cut a person off from enjoyment of the largeness of life? Does not this "virtue" of motivation act to shrivel a person's generous impulses, to make him use other people as a means to advancement, corrupting his character and his capacity for friendship?

Next, let us look at the "knowledge industry," whose products fuel the engine of economic growth. In a society that pays ritual homage to our great secular cathedrals of knowledge, the words "scientific research" are holy and scholarship is almost synonymous with saintliness. But the social consequences of the disinterested pursuit of knowledge are not all beyond dispute. The harrowing degree of specialization that results from the attempt to advance the expanding boundary of any discipline can crush the capacity of men for instinctual pleasure and can make communication between scientists, even those working in the same field, increasingly difficult.

The advance of scientific knowledge enhances the secular to the detriment of the sacred. One wonders if the loss of the great myths, the loss of belief in a benevolent deity, in reunion after death, has not contributed to a sense of desolation. One wonders also if a code of morality can be widely accepted in a society without belief in any god or in any hereafter.

As decisions are increasingly influenced by experts, democracy becomes more vulnerable. As historical knowledge grows, and hawk-eyed scholars find a vocation in debunking national heroes and popular legend, the pride of peoples in their common past is eroded and, along with it, their morale as well.

We might also want to ponder briefly some of the unexpected repercussions of a number of much-heralded inventions. Consumer innovations over the recent past and foreseeable future appear to be largely labor-saving—inventions that reduce dependence on others, or, rather, transfer dependence to a machine. Given that the machine is incomparably more efficient, can its efficiency in yielding services compensate for the inevitable loss of authentic human experience? Packaged and precooked foods save time for the busy housewife. Personal contacts necessarily decline with the spread of more efficient labor-saving devices. They have already declined with the spread of supermarkets, cafeterias, and vending machines. And they will continue to decline with the trend toward computerization in offices and factories, toward patient monitoring machines and computer-diagnoses in hospitals, toward closed-circuit television instruction, automated libraries and teaching machines.

Thus the compulsive search for efficiency, directed in the main toward innovations that save effort and time, must continue to produce for us yet more elegant instruments for our mutual estrangement. We might ask if the things commonly associated with the good life—a more settled way of natural beauty and architectural dignity, a rehabilitation of norms of propriety and taste—can ever be realized by affluent societies straining eternally to woo the consumer with ever more outlandish and expendable gadgetry and seeking eternally for faster economic growth.

If it is conceded that, once subsistence levels have been passed, the sources of man's most enduring satisfactions spring from mutual trust and affection, from sharing joy and sorrow, from giving and accepting love, from open-hearted companionship and laughter; if it is further conceded that in a civilized society the joy of living comes from the sense of wonder inspired by the unfolding of nature, from the perception of beauty inspired by great art, from the renewal of faith and hope inspired by the heroic and the good—if this much is conceded, then is it possible to believe that unremitting attempts to harness the greater part of man's energies and ingenuity to the task of amassing an ever greater assortment of material possessions can add much to people's happiness? Can it add more than it subtracts? Can it add anything?

Recognizing the darker side of economic growth, we must conclude that the game is not worth the candle. And the answer to the question of whether continued economic growth in the West brings us any closer to the good life cannot be other than a resounding No.

RADICAL CRITIQUE OF AMERICAN CAPITALISM: CONVERGENCE OF EXTREMES

In the final selection in this chapter, Mancur Olson and Christopher Clague raise the intriguing hypothesis of convergence of neo-liberals and the New Left in their thinking about economic policy. Olson and Clague incorporate thinking of the "Virginia School" (James Buchanan and Gordon Tullock) as well as that of Friedman and other "Chicago School" economists in their composite picture of neo-liberalism. (This selection may profitably be read in conjunction with "New Left" selections 7.5 through 7.8 and with Fusfeld's analysis of the "shattering" of the post-Keynesian synthesis in selection 3.20.)

6.13

Dissent in Economics: The Convergence of Extremes

Mancur Olson and Christopher K. Clague

DISSENT IN ECONOMICS

The most conspicuous dissenters in economics today are the "radical economists." They are an outgrowth of the "new left," or more precisely proponents of the new left who happen to be economists. Some of those who are casually categorized with the new left are simply orthodox Marxists, and some of those who are called radical economists are in reality classical economists of the Marxian persuasion. But the sense of growth and novelty, at least in the United States and probably also in some parts of continental Europe, comes from what is actually new in the new left and from what is truly radical in radical economics, and this new left or radical development is what interests us here. The other main group of discontented economists are those who object to the passing of *laissez faire,* to "Keynesian" and post-Keynesian fiscal policies, to the threat to individual liberties they see in the welfare state, and to the economic analyses and prescriptions that have encouraged a generation or more of "creeping socialism."

The prototypical economists of this sort are those who speak of themselves as the "Virginia School" and have been greatly influenced by the work of James Buchanan. Buchanan and many of his disciples point out that, when most economists today find externalities, monopoly, or other problems that can lead markets to fail to operate in an optimal way, they typically advocated government intervention. This, Buchanan and those of his persuasion emphasize, involves a non sequitur. It does not follow from the fact that a market fails to bring optimality that government intervention will improve matters.

The Virginia School descends from Frank Knight and other forebears of the Chicago School, which has the same enthusiasm for *laissez faire* libertarianism, the same susceptibility to politicians like Goldwater, and the same dislike of Keynesian economics and the welfare state. Though it seems odd to treat so eminent an economist as discontented, an examination of Milton Friedman's views on practical policy, particularly as they are expressed in his book on *Capitalism and Freedom,* shows that he is in a profound sense a dissenter. He treats all government actions, and particularly those of central governments, as above all an actual or potential threat to individual freedom. He would like to return the schools to private enterprise (with compulsory attendance and financial vouchers), cut out most public support for higher educa-

Excerpted from Mancur Olson and Christopher K. Clague, "Dissent in Economics: The Convergence of Extremes," *Social Research,* Winter 1971, pp. 751–76. Reprinted by permission of the publisher and the authors.

tion, eliminate compulsory saving through social security, replace most social and welfare services by a (very modest) negative income tax, see labor unions lose most of their power, rely on a nondiscretionary monetary policy, and repeal all laws prohibiting racial discrimination by individuals. Anyone with these views is apt to be profoundly disturbed (even, perhaps alienated) by the direction in which the United States and most other societies are moving.

THE CONTENT OF DISSENT

If it is accepted that the growth and vitality of dissent in American economics has come from the radical economists on the one side and the Chicago-Virginia Schools on the other, the next question is: What are the discontents? There are a great many, but four are particularly significant: First there is the complaint that mainstream economics is often a rationalization for the prevailing public policies, political leadership, and the social system; second, the complaint that orthodox economics fails to take political or social factors into account; third, that economics today is preoccupied with technical elegance and detail to the neglect of policy relevance; fourth, that traditional economics neglects the forces that form and change preferences.

Some of these discontents, and the policy recommendations that are related to them, bring us to the point that, far to the left as the radicals are, and far to the right as the Chicago-Virginia groups are, and harsh as their comments about one another can sometimes be, there is an underlying unity in the discontents, and to a degree even in the policy objectives, of these two sides.

This unity is evident in some of the discontents mentioned above. With respect to the first discontent, we have already pointed out that both sides often regard mainstream economics as the servant of the "liberal establishment." The radical economists could hardly be more explicit about this. The Chicago-Virginia group does not make the same complaint in such a striking way, but some of its members have said almost the same thing.

The second complaint is that mainstream economics neglects or is naive about government and politics. Though several mainstream economists have worked on models of public choice, it is certainly true that most mainstream economists have no explicit model of government and politics. The typical economist, while naturally mindful of the desirability of free markets when they are feasible and competitive, may also often implicitly assume that public officials will normally be reasonable and well intentioned. He often also has the faith that the government, despite acknowledged faults, can recognize problems and devise and implement solutions that will serve the public reasonably well. This faith underlies the claim that his research has relevance for policy.

The radical economists regularly deplore the fact that most economists abstract from (or deal implicitly and naively with) government and politics. They believe that an economic theory that abstracts from the relationship between the economy and political or social developments cannot be relevant to the great questions of our time. Like Marx, they believe that governments reign in the interests of the ruling class. As they see it, those policies that appear to favor the oppressed classes were in fact passed to preserve the existing system.

Interestingly enough, the effort to incorporate political and governmental behavior explicitly into economic theory is the principal distinguishing feature of the Virginia School. Buchanan and Tullock proclaim that the central shortcoming in most economics today is the failure to incorporate government and politics into the framework of economic theory.

Though the members of the Chicago branch have not usually developed abstract models of political behavior, some of them have emphasized the need for such models. And they almost surely share the assumption that political behavior is normally self-interested and the pessimistic predictions about how governments will work in practice.

The third complaint is that economics is preoccupied with technical intricacies that have little relevance to the urgent problems of our time. Economists on the far left are fond of saying that elaborate mathematical models are being developed to answer questions that are utterly trivial. Some of the radical economists who make this complaint are themselves adept at technical economics and, strangely, even continue to practice it part of the time. Again, this complaint comes from the right wing as well. Buchanan and Tullock argue that the Virginia School's analysis is more "relevant" than other varieties of economics. Though his substantial theoretical contributions make it clear that Buchanan has a considerable aptitude for technical reasoning, he argues that too many economists are concerned with esoteric technical questions that are about as practical as the medieval disputes about how many angels could dance on the head of a pin. The same point seems to hold true, though perhaps less clearly, for the Chicago School.

Yet there probably is a genuine causal connection between the degree and intensity of political commitments of economists and their success in treating the technical tools of economics as a means rather than an end. The economists with political passions as intense as those at the poles of the political spectrum want to tell us something about the real world as they see it and accordingly tend to use elaborate technical arguments only when they are needed to make the point.

The fourth complaint—against the neoclassical assumption that peoples' tastes are fixed, or at least determined exogenously (outside the system neoclassicists study)—shows that the argument offered in this paper can easily be pushed too far. The assumption that tastes can be taken as given lies at the core of the mainstream economics, for its abandonment calls into question not only the efficiency of the competitive market, but also many of the tools economists use to study efficiency. Radical economists often attack this assumption, not only because they are aware that this is the Achilles heel of neoclassical economics, but probably also because they are particularly interested in the factors that influence individual preferences or "consciousness." Many radicals dislike the preferences that most people in the modern world now have; they feel that capitalist society makes people competitive, selfish, materialistic, submissive, and insufficiently spontaneous. In the United States today (and most of them would say, probably in the Soviet Union as well) most work is boring and dehumanizing, but instead of changing the nature of work, which is perfectly possible, society trains children, particularly through the schools, to submit to an alienating environment. Some radicals believe that appropriate changes in socialization could bring about substantial changes in human nature, and perhaps even create a "new man," who would not have to be offered material incentives.

At the same time, we should not forget that radical economists and others in the counterculture implicitly or explicitly assume that individual wants, even given the indoctrination by the present system, have some stability and legitimacy, as when they emphasize that everyone should be allowed to do "his own thing" and encourage individual spontaneity.

On the other side, the Chicago-Virginia Schools have been particularly defiant in saying individual tastes are beyond their purview. In their view, neither the economist nor anyone else should presume to judge the propriety of other individuals' tastes. Nor are they very interested in why tastes are what they are. They have moreover been particularly skeptical about the possibility of changing human nature and vigorously opposed to any government efforts to try.

POLICY PREFERENCES

The similarity of new left and classical liberal economists shows up not only in complaints but in policy preferences as well. Fundamentally, both the new left and classical liberal economists want societies in which the individual has what the new left calls his right to do "his own thing," and what economists of the right call "individual liberty." The "liberation" that both sides believe in is mainly the almost unlimited right for each *individual* to *do* what he pleases, whatever the majority through democratically elected government or private social pressure might have ordained. It is the rights of the minority, even the minority of one, against the majority, that they cherish. The concern about what the classical liberals call "economic freedom" and "individual liberty" goes back, of course, to the nineteenth century liberals and utilitarians, among whom John Stuart Mill is perhaps prototypical; it is what has always distinguished them from Burkean or Hegelian conservatives. The concern about what the new left calls unresponsive bureaucracy and the right to choose a new life style is what mainly distinguishes it from the old left with its familiar fondness for nationalization, central planning, and the Soviet example.

The old right advocacy of *laissez faire* (or something close to it) obviously rests to a considerable degree on the argument that it protects the rights of individuals, especially those in minorities. In a market free of externalities or public goods each individual can use his resources in whatever way he prefers and consume any mix of goods he can afford. Thus the free market provides a range of freedom of action that will be especially important to those with unusual preferences, which a society without markets could not provide, however complete its adherence to the usual democratic procedures.

The new left directs most of its enmity at the "power structure" or "establishment" rather than at markets (except insofar as markets are thought to lead to a concentration of wealth and hence of political power). The main policy proposals that have come from the new left concern "decentralization" and "democratic participation," and these proposals could hardly be directed against the market. This suggests not only a gradual abandonment of the old left antipathy to markets, but also a skepticism about bureaucracy, government, and majority rule quite like that of the Chicago and Virginia Schools.

Though the main source of new left skepticism about government and organized authority is the feeling that hierarchies push people around, there is also the belief of radical economists and other new leftists that bureaucracies are inefficient. In emphasizing the ineptness of government and bureaucracy the radical economists again obviously have much in common with the classical liberals. Each argues that the government's manpower training programs, criminal rehabilitation efforts, and social welfare services have accomplished little for the poor and cannot be expected to accomplish much, at least given present institutions.

It is entirely possible that the radical demands for decentralization and democratic participation can usefully be interpreted as embryonic left-wing versions of the political economy of the Virginia School.

On this interpretation, the new left plea for decentralization is the belief that each neighborhood or minority should have some of the authority that now is exercised by higher levels of government. Similarly, the demand for democratic participation, when applied as it is to societies that already have democratically elected governments, can be interpreted as an argument that each minority should have the right to veto at least some legislative and administrative actions, even when these actions have been decided upon by constituted bodies or authorities in democracies operating by majority rule.

Even if, as may well be the case, this interpretation of the new left approach to decentralization and democratic participation goes too far, it is nonetheless indisputable that the radical economists are far more cautious about government, hierarchy, and centralized planning than any other group of dissenting economists, except the classical liberals.

There is an historical precedent for the curious unity of the new left and old right economists. Marx was developing his ideas at about the same time that *laissez faire* liberalism was coming into ascendancy. This was also the period when anarchism was developing. It is surely significant that all three of the great ideologies of the mid-nineteenth century had within them a profound distrust of government. As is well known, Marx believed that the government was always the instrument of the dominant class, so that in capitalist societies it was controlled by the hated bourgeoisie; he opposed all of the governments that existed in his day. And as for his ultimate ideal, it was a stateless as well as a classless society. Obviously the *laissez faire* ideology wanted as close to a stateless society as was feasible. Anarchism fits the generalization as well as any ideology conceivably could. The suspicion of government in all three of these diverse ideologies suggests that, while the new-left/classical-liberal approach is not in keeping with the intellectual trends since the depression of the 1930s, it nonetheless has deep historical roots.

THE VALUE OF DISSENT

Can the gripes and ideas of the dissenting economists have any value to those who are not on the political extremes? We believe that they can, not only because there is no necessary connection between the political affiliation of those who express a view and its truthfulness or usefulness, but also because the new left and old right economists have been concerned about problems that are probably becoming more important as time goes on.

It would seem that the new left conviction that those who already have the private and public power will run things in their own interest, and the Virginia School models of political behavior, deserve a wider examination.

Giving the ubiquity of large hierarchies and the apparently increasing resentment of their power structures, there is surely a case for more careful research into the substantial area of nonmarket economics and social and political interaction within the large bureaucracy.

There is surely also something to be said for the radical economists' complaint about the assumption that tastes are exogenous. Clearly the corporations and other large organizations of the private sector spend a good deal on advertising and community relations. Clearly governments spend a lot on schools and the comments of their leaders are a principal subject of the media of public communication. A lot of this expenditure of resources is designed to change individual tastes or values, and it would be surprising if it were all without effect.

To be sure, the complaint is sometimes exaggerated; it is certainly not true that consumers buy whatever corporate hierarchies dictate that they buy.

There is probably also a need to give serious attention to the dissenters' complaints about the preoccupation with technical intricacy at the expense of relevance in mainstream economics.

These areas of neglect and difficulties in mainstream economics might seem to justify the demands of some radical economists for a new paradigm.

We would conjecture that if there is a paradigm change in economics, as there could be at any time, it will add a great deal more than it throws away. Surely no complete or ideal theory could do without some of the concepts economists use today. Yet we must be uneasy about the many aspects of reality that interact with variables that the economist studies, but which he often leaves out of account. As the dissenting economists have reminded us, we economists (or someone else) must take better account of the government and the other hierarchies that increasingly influence our lives, and grapple with the forces that change tastes. Someone must, in short, take account of the politics in large organizations and the sociology behind changing values. Perhaps, if there is a paradigm change in economics, it will be in the form of a unified approach to social science.

7 RADICAL REFORM FROM THE LEFT: NEO-MARXISM, THE NEW LEFT, AND DEMOCRATIC SOCIALISM

The fourth major strand of dissent from the post-Keynesian synthesis, incorporating both radical criticism and proposals for comprehensive economic reform, comes from the left wing of the American political spectrum. We have already noted some of the similarities between the dissent of the (New) Left and that of the neo-liberals. We now turn specifically to left-wing critiques. Although lines of demarcation are fuzzy, it is convenient to distinguish among the neo-Marxist, New Left, and contemporary democratic socialist variants of radical left-wing economic philosophy.

NEO-MARXISM

The most prominent and influential of the neo-Marxists are Paul Sweezy and the late Paul Baran. Sweezy, a student of Joseph Schumpeter and currently an editor of and leading contributor to the prominent Marxist publication *Monthly Review,* is best known for a comprehensive and scholarly statement of classical Marxian economic theory *(The Theory of Capitalist Development,* 1942). Until his death in 1964, Paul Baran, professor of economics at Stanford University, was undoubtedly America's preeminent academic Marxist economist. Both Baran and Sweezy are well known for their contributions to the economic theory of (centralized) socialism. Centralized socialism is representative of the traditional Old Left emphasis on government ownership and central planning, both as the identifying properties of a socialist economy and as the major institutional factors in the rapid industrialization and economic development of Soviet Russia. Prospectively, the Russian model is seen as applicable in the less-developed economies of Asia, Africa, and Latin America.[1] But we are concerned here with Sweezy and Baran as joint authors of the seminal, now classic, work *Monopoly Capital* (1966). In this and other writings, Sweezy and

[1] See John E. Elliott, *Comparative Economic Systems* (Englewood Cliffs, N.J.: Prentice-Hall, 1973), Chapter 11. In recent years, Sweezy's view on the role of government ownership as necessary and sufficient for the establishment of a socialist economy has been modified somewhat. See his discussion with Bettelheim in *Monthly Review,* March 1969 and December 1970.

Baran develop a modernized reassessment of classical Marxian theory (hence: *neo-*Marxist) and provide a radical critique of the functioning of contemporary American capitalism. Although unrepresentative of the New Left in terms of their centralized-socialist alternative to contemporary capitalism, in their dissent from the post-Keynesian consensus, and in their critique of monopolistic and "irrational" elements in American economic life they have profoundly influenced radical and socialist economists generally.

In *Monopoly Capital,* Baran and Sweezy examine the problems of a capitalist economy characterized by powerful concentrations of capital, including oligopoly as well as monopoly in the strict sense. Although Marx had forecast increasing concentration and centralization of capital, he emphasized that "even" a competitive capitalist system contained within it self-destructive contradictions. Although monopoly seemed likely to aggravate capitalism's problems and become one of the means through which capitalism proceeded to its doom, it was not the fundamental cause of its demise, and its elimination would not enable capitalism to survive. Baran and Sweezy, however, observe that "monopoly capitalism" differs from competitive capitalism in important ways, and that while aggravating some of capitalism's problems, monopoly actually makes others more manageable.

Monopoly capitalism is analyzed through the concept of the "economic surplus," defined as the difference between society's total output and the portion of output going to consumption and depreciation. While advanced capitalist countries have acquired the potential to produce enormous economic surpluses, they have not developed the necessary mechanisms to ensure that potential surpluses are in fact realized and then utilized rationally. Thus, the stability of the capitalist system becomes increasingly fragile.

The tendency of the surplus to rise is even more pronounced in monopoly capitalism than in competitive capitalism. Monopoly-oligopoly control over prices and sales, together with powerful pressures and opportunities for cost reduction, cause an absolute and relative increase in the economic surplus. "The law of rising surplus," Baran and Sweezy contend, must be assigned the role in monopoly capitalism that Marx gave to "the law of the falling rate of profit" in his study of competitive capitalism. How to absorb the rising economic surplus is the basic problem of monopoly capitalism.

A rising surplus can be absorbed in various ways. Because dividend payments tend to lag behind rising profits in a growing economy, the consumption of capitalists, though increasing in absolute terms, tends to decline relatively as the surplus increases. Because profitable investment opportunities depend on consumption, which tends to decline relative to income, the amount of the surplus that can be invested profitably is also likely to increase, but not at the rate at which the potential surplus rises. This will remain true despite a gigantic sales effort that makes investment more profitable while itself using up large amounts of the surplus. The potential for government spending on useful civilian projects is enormous, but the political realities of a capitalist system place sharp limits on what is actually possible. Thus, a heavy burden of surplus absorption falls upon militarism and imperialism.

But military expenditures, though politically popular, impose heavy limitations and risks. Enormous amounts of surplus are channeled into unproductive projects. Further, it is doubtful whether massive military spending can continue indefinitely in times of peace, and the prospect of nuclear war is generally unacceptable to capitalists as both unprofitable and potentially fatal. Imperialism becomes riskier and less profitable as Third World nations assert political and economic independence. The conclusion is that capitalism is not likely to last. If the major capitalist powers avoid annihilating themselves and others in full-scale war, eventually capitalism's contradictions should bring to power a government determined and able to remedy the problem in the only possible way: by rejecting the system itself in favor of socialism.

Selection 7.1 provides a synopsis by Baran and Sweezy of the neo-Marxist theory of monopoly capitalism. Selection 7.2 is a critique of the theory by Robert Heilbroner. The classical Marxist analysis of capitalist transformation to socialism focused on two major aspects of the transition process: first, capitalist crises, depression, and unemployment and, second, class conflict between capitalists and workers and consequent emergence of the working class as the agency for revolutionary change. (Recall selection 2.4.) Baran and Sweezy have reevaluated the first issue within the context of "monopoly capitalism." In selection 7.3, prominent European neo-Marxist Ernest Mandel reassesses the revolutionary potential of the working class in contemporary "neo-capitalism." According to Mandel, despite the industrialization, affluence, and social reforms of contemporary capitalism, the "revolutionary mission" of the working class remains essentially intact, grounded in three fundamental properties of modern labor: "its key role in the productive process, its basic alienation, its economic exploitation." Rising living standards and Keynesian-style monetary and fiscal policy notwithstanding, faith in the prospect of rebellion against oppression and injustice is "fully justified."

In selection 7.4, Arthur MacEwan describes the expansionist and imperalist proclivities of contemporary capitalism and the role of the state in protecting the foreign economic interests of the advanced nations. MacEwan's essay illustrates the important impact of Marx and the neo-Marxists upon the writings of the younger radical Left and the difficulty of making a sharp division between neo-Marxism and the New Left.

7.1 Monopoly Capitalism

Paul A. Baran and Paul M. Sweezy

With regard to the cost discipline which it imposes on its members the monopoly capitalist economy is no less severe than its competitive predecessor; in addition it generates new and powerful impulses to innovation. There can

Excerpted from Paul A. Baran and Paul M. Sweezy, *Monopoly Capital: An Essay on the American Economic and Social Order* (New York and London: Monthly Review Press, 1966). Reprinted by permission of the publisher.

therefore be no doubt about the downward trend of production costs under monopoly capitalism.

On the face of it this would seem to be an argument for monopoly capitalism's being considered a rational and progressive system. And if its cost-reducing proclivities could somehow be disentangled from monopoly pricing and a way could be found to utilize the fruits of increasing productivity for the benefit of society as a whole, the argument would indeed be a powerful one. But of course this is just what cannot be done. The whole motivation of cost reduction is to increase profits, and the monopolistic structure of markets enables the corporations to appropriate the lion's share of the fruits of increasing productivity directly in the form of higher profits. This means that under monopoly capitalism, declining costs imply continuously widening profit margins. And continuously widening profit margins in turn imply aggregate profits which rise not only absolutely but as a share of national product. If we provisionally equate aggregate profits with society's economic surplus, we can formulate as a law of monopoly capitalism that the surplus tends to rise both absolutely and relatively as the system develops.

This law immediately invites comparison, as it should, with the classical-Marxian law of the falling tendency of the rate of profit. Without entering into an analysis of the different versions of the latter, we can say that they all presuppose a competitive system. By substituting the law of rising surplus for the law of falling profit, we are therefore not rejecting or revising a time-honored theorem of political economy: we are simply taking account of the undoubted fact that the structure of the capitalist economy has undergone a fundamental change since that theorem was formulated. What is most essential about the structural change from competitive to monopoly capitalism finds its theoretical expression in this substitution. . . .

THE ABSORPTION OF SURPLUS

We now come to the problem of the absorption or utilization of the surplus.

In general, surplus can be absorbed in the following ways: (1) it can be consumed, (2) it can be invested, and (3) it can be wasted. . . .

To the extent that surplus is consumed by capitalists, the amount available for investment is correspondingly reduced. . . . The question therefore [is]: does capitalists' consumption tend to rise as a share of surplus? If not, the investment-seeking part of surplus must rise relatively to total income [in order to absorb the surplus].

Let us assume that capitalists consume the entire amount of distributed profits. This is not true, of course, but if it can be shown that even in this case capitalists' consumption does not tend to rise as a share of surplus, then the conclusion which follows will hold *a fortiori* for cases in which capitalists save out of their distributed profits.

. . . Most large companies have a target dividend payout rate which remains remarkably constant over long periods of time (50 percent seems to be the most common figure). When profits rise, however, they do not immediately adjust dividends to maintain the target rate.

Under these circumstances, capitalists' consumption would increase absolutely, which of course is to be expected, but it would decline as a proportion of surplus and even more as a proportion to total income. Since these conclusions hold *a fortiori* to the extent that capitalists save out of their dividend incomes, it is clear that no solution of the problem of surplus absorption can be expected from this quarter.

Not only surplus, then, but also the investment-seeking part of surplus tends to rise as a proportion of total income. Whether this tendency will be realized, however, is another question. In attempting to answer it, we must first determine whether the system normally provides investment outlets large enough to absorb a rising share of a rising surplus.

The logic of the situation is as follows: if total income grows at an accelerating rate, then a larger and larger share has to be devoted to investment; and, conversely, if a larger and larger share is devoted to investment, total income must grow at an accelerating rate. What this implies, however, is nonsensical from an economic standpoint. It means that a larger and larger volume of producer goods would have to be turned out for the sole purpose of producing a still larger and larger volume of producer goods in the future. Consumption would be a diminishing proportion of output, and the growth of the capital stock would have no relation to the actual or potential expansion of consumption.

Quite apart from the fact that such an explosive growth process would sooner or later exceed the physical potentialities of any conceivable economy, there is simply no reason to assume that anything like it has ever occurred or is likely to occur in the real world.

If accelerating growth is ruled out as totally unrealistic, one is left with the inescapable conclusion that the actual investment of an amount of surplus which rises relatively to income must mean that the economy's capacity to produce grows more rapidly than its output. Such an investment pattern is certainly not impossible; indeed, it has frequently been observed in the history of capitalism. But what is impossible is that it should persist indefinitely. Sooner or later, excess capacity grows so large that it discourages further investment. When investment declines, so do income and employment and hence also surplus itself. In other words, this investment pattern is self-limiting and ends in an economic downturn—the beginning of a recession or depression. . . .

. . . On the other hand, if the economy moves up from a position of less-than-capacity production, both surplus and the investment-seeking segment of surplus swell absolutely and relatively. . . . Surplus swells when capacity is fully utilized and surplus rapidly shrinks when investment outlets fail and aggregate demand declines. As surplus shrinks, the investment-seeking part of it shrinks more than in proportion. On the downswing, in other words, the ratio of consumption to both surplus and total output rises, and this sooner or later puts a stop to the contraction. The lower turning point is reached when the amount of surplus seeking investment is exactly absorbed by available investment outlets. At this point, a temporary equilibrium is reached which is characterized by the existence of excess productive capacity and unemployed workers. The reverse side of the coin is that an upswing, however initiated, generates a similar rapid absolute and relative increase of surplus. As soon as the investment-seeking part of surplus exceeds available investment outlets, the expansion comes to an end. And it should be remembered that this upper turning point may be reached long before full utilization of capacity or full employment of labor is achieved. . . .

We have seen that . . . mechanisms tend to generate a steady rising supply of investment-seeking surplus, but that in the nature of the case they cannot generate a corresponding rise in the magnitude of investment outlets. . . .

. . . A large part of investment over the years has been embodied in improved or altogether new types of producer goods. Does this mean that technological progress automatically provides outlets for investment-seeking surplus and that any shortage of outlets could in principle be overcome by an appropriate increase in the rate of technological progress? . . .

. . . Under monopoly capitalism there is no necessary correlation, as there is in a competitive system, between the rate of technological progress and the volume of investment outlets. Technological progress tends to determine the *form* which investment takes at any given time rather than its amount.

This is not a rigid rule to which there are no exceptions. Particularly in the case of new products, as distinct from new versions of existing products, there may be a rush to get into the market first in order to enjoy for a time an unchallenged monopoly position.

The importance of this point should not be exaggerated; . . . there are also factors which work in the opposite direction, inhibiting bursts of investment associated with the introduction of new products:

> *Capital investment particularly tends to lag because the expenditures required to begin output of a* new product *are usually quite small. Often existing facilities, or a part of them, can be converted to turn out trial quantities of the new product. And the really heavy expenditures required to build a complete new plant are not made until a year or two later. Similarly, expenditures to introduce a* new process *are not usually made until there is a relatively large production volume to justify these outlays.*

To the extent that this argument applies, there is little reason to distinguish between new products and new processes: both tend to be introduced in a controlled fashion and to determine the form which investment takes rather than its magnitude. The new product takes the place of the old, just as the new process takes the place of the old; there is little of that "creative destruction" which Schumpeter saw as the chief dynamic force of the capitalist economy. . . .

. . . Where the amount of depreciation is very large, as in present-day monopoly capitalism, it is quite possible that business can finance from this source alone all the investment it considers profitable to make in innovations (both new products and new processes), leaving no "innovational" outlets to help absorb investment-seeking surplus. Technological progress may, in other words, do little more than shape the most profitable uses for funds made available to corporate managements through their own "generous" depreciation policies. To the extent that this is so, technological progress makes no contribution at all to solving the problem of outlets for the "visible" part of investment-seeking surplus: whatever investment may be required to embody available innovations may well be less than enough to absorb the rising tide of depreciation allowances. . . .

Our conclusion is that technological progress is not . . . likely . . . to make a significant contribution to solving the problem of surplus absorption. . . .

Twist and turn as one will, there is no way to avoid the conclusion that monopoly capitalism is a self-contradictory system. It tends to generate ever more surplus, yet it fails to provide the consumption and investment outlets required for the absorption of a rising surplus and hence for the smooth working of the system. Since surplus which cannot be absorbed will not be produced, it follows that the *normal* state of the monopoly capitalist economy is stagnation. With a given stock of capital and a given cost and price structure, the system's operating rate cannot rise above the point at which the amount of surplus produced can find the necessary outlets. And this means chronic underutilization of available human and material resources. . . .

Counteracting forces do exist. If they did not, the system would indeed long since have fallen of its own weight. It therefore becomes a matter of the greatest importance to understand the nature and implications of these counteracting forces. . . .

The self-contradictory character of monopoly capitalism—its chronic inability to absorb as much surplus as it is capable of producing—impresses itself on the ordinary citizen in a characteristic way. To him, the economic problem appears to be the very opposite of what the textbooks say it is: not how best to utilize scarce resources but how to dispose of the products of superabundant resources. And this holds regardless of his wealth or position in society. If he is a worker, the ubiquitous fact of unemployment teaches him that the supply of labor is always greater than the demand. If he is a farmer, he struggles to stay afloat in a sea of surpluses. If he is a businessman, his sales persistently fall short of what he could profitably produce. Always too much, never too little.

This condition of affairs is peculiar to monopoly capitalism. The very notion of "too much" would have been inconceivable to all pre-capitalist forms of society; and even in the competitive stage of capitalism, it described a temporary derangement, not a normal condition. In a rationally ordered socialist society, no matter how richly endowed it might be with natural resources and technology and human skills, "too much" could only be a welcome signal to shift attention to an area of "too little." Only under monopoly capitalism does "too much" appear as a pervasive problem affecting everyone at all times.

From this source stem a whole series of attitudes and interests of crucial importance for the character and functioning of monopoly capitalist society. On the one hand, there is a stubborn spirit of restrictionism which pervades the institutional structure. Union featherbedding and Henry Wallace's plowing under of little pigs are only the best publicized example of practices which are all but universal in business and government: the most primitive reaction to an excess of supply is simply to cut back.

But cutting back as a remedy for "too much," even if beneficial to particular groups or individuals, only aggravates the situation as a whole. A secondary and more sophisticated set of attitudes and policies therefore emerges. . . . Their rationale derives from the simple fact that the obverse of "too much" on the supply side is "too little" on the demand side; instead of cutting back supply they aim at stimulating demand.

The stimulation of demand—the creation and expansion of markets—thus becomes to an ever greater degree the leitmotif of business and government policies under monopoly capitalism. . . . There are many conceivable ways of stimulating demand. If a socialist society, for example, should find that through some planning error more consumer goods were being produced than could be sold, given the existing structure of prices and incomes, the simplest and most direct remedy would clearly be to cut prices.

Such a course of action is obviously not open to a monopoly capitalist society, in which the determination of prices is the jealously guarded prerogative of the giant corporations. The plain fact is that the pricing process is controlled by the most powerful vested interests in monopoly capitalist society. To imagine that it could possibly be regulated in the public interest would be to imagine away the very characteristics of that society which make it what it is.

If stimulation of demand through price reduction is impossible within the framework of monopoly capitalism, this cannot be said of other possible methods. Take, for example, advertising and related forms of salesmanship . . . Every giant corporation is driven by the logic of its situation to devote more and more attention and resources to the sales effort. And monopoly capitalist society as a whole has every interest in promoting rather than restricting and controlling this method of creating new markets and expanding old ones.

Just as with price cutting and salesmanship, other forms of stimulating demand either are or are not compatible with the pattern of interests, the structure of power, the web of ideology that constitute the essence of monopoly capitalist society. Those which are compatible will be fostered and promoted; those which are incompatible will be ignored or inhibited. The question for monopoly capitalism is not whether to stimulate demand. It must, on pain of death.

With the law of rising surplus replacing the law of the falling tendency of the rate of profit, and with normal modes of surplus utilization patently unable to absorb a rising surplus, the question of other modes of surplus utilization assumes crucial importance. That they should be there in large and growing volume becomes a life-and-death issue for the system. And as they grow relative to capitalists' consumption and accumulation, they increasingly dominate the composition of social output, the rate of economic growth, and the quality of society itself.

One of these alternative modes of utilization we call the sales effort. . . . In its impact on the economy, it is outranked only by militarism. In all other aspects of social existence, its all-pervasive influence is second to none.

The tremendous growth of the sales effort and the spectacular intensification of its sway stem from its having undergone a far-reaching qualitative change. Price competition has largely receded as a means of attracting the public's custom, and has yielded to new ways of sales promotion: advertising, variation of the products' appearance and packaging, "planned obsolescence," model changes, credit schemes, and the like.

In an economic system in which competition is fierce and relentless and in which the fewness of the rivals rules out price cutting, advertising becomes to an ever increasing extent the principal weapon of the competitive struggle. . . .

What indeed would happen to a market continually plagued by insufficient demand? And what would happen to an economic system suffering from chronic underconsumption, underinvestment, and underemployment? For the economic importance of advertising lies not primarily in its causing a reallocation of consumers' expenditures among different commodities but in its effect on the magnitude of aggregate effective demand and thus on the level of income and employment. This has been readily grasped by professors of marketing and advertising as well as by business journalists, but with few exceptions it has been ignored by economic theorists.

The function of advertising, perhaps its dominant function today, thus becomes that of waging, on behalf of the producers and sellers of consumer goods, a relentless war against saving and in favor of consumption. And the principal means of carrying out this task are to induce changes in fashion, create new wants, set new standards of status, enforce new norms of propriety. The unquestioned success of advertising in achieving these aims has greatly strengthened its role as a force counteracting monopoly capitalism's tendency to stagnation. . . .

Just as advertising, product differentiation, artificial obsolescence, model changing, and all the other devices of the sales effort do in fact promote and increase sales, and thus act as indispensable props to the level of income and employment, so the entire apparatus of "finance, insurance, and real estate" is essential to the normal functioning of the corporate system and another no less indispensable prop to the level of income and employment. The prodigious volume of resources absorbed in all these activities does in fact constitute necessary costs of capitalist production. What should be crystal clear is that an economic system in which *such* costs are socially necessary has long ceased to be a socially necessary economic system. . . .

Under monopoly capitalism, . . . the normal condition is less than capacity production. The system simply does not generate enough "effective demand" (to use the Keynesian term) to insure full utilization of either labor or productive facilities. If these idle resources can be put to work, they can produce not only necessary means of subsistence for the producers but also additional amounts of surplus. Hence if government creates more effective demand, it can increase its command over goods and services without encroaching on the incomes of its citizens. This creation of effective demand can take the form of direct government purchases of goods and services, or of "transfer payments" to groups which can somehow make good their claims for special treatment (subsidies to businessmen and farmers, doles to the unemployed, pensions to the aged, and so on). . . .

The structure of the monopoly capitalist economy is such that a continually mounting volume of surplus simply could not be absorbed through private channels; if no other outlets were available, it would not be produced at all. What government absorbs is in addition to, not subtracted from, private surplus. Even more: since a larger volume of government spending pushes the economy nearer to capacity operation, and since up to this point surplus grows more rapidly than effective demand as a whole, it follows that both the government and the private segments of surplus can and indeed typically do grow simultaneously. It is only when government absorption continues to expand even after full utilization has been reached, as during the later years of the Second World War, that private surplus is encroached upon. . . .

The American ruling class, at any rate its leading echelon of managers of giant corporations, has learned these lessons through the rich experience of three decades of depression, war, and Cold War. And its attitude toward taxation and government spending has undergone a fundamental change. The older hostility to any expansion of government activities has not of course disappeared. In the realm of ideology, deeply rooted attitudes never disappear quickly. Moreover, in some sections of the ruling class—especially rentiers and small businessmen—hatred of the tax collector dominates feelings about the role of government. But the modern Big Businessman, though he sometimes speaks the traditional language, no longer takes it so seriously as his ancestors. To him, government spending means more effective demand, and he senses that he can shift most of the associated taxes forward onto consumers or backward onto workers. In addition—and this point is of great importance in understanding the subjective attitudes of Big Businessmen—the intricacies of the tax system, specially tailored to fit the needs of all sorts of special interests, open up endless opportunities for speculative and windfall gains. . . .

Given the power structure of United States monopoly capitalism, the increase of civilian spending had about reached its outer limits by 1939. The forces opposing further expansion were too strong to be overcome.

We can postulate that for every item in the budget there is some minimum amount which has general approval and which evokes no appreciable opposition. As this amount is exceeded, approval for further increments gradually declines and opposition builds up until an equilibrium is reached and further expansion stops. . . .

In the case of almost every major item in the civilian budget, powerful vested interests are soon aroused to opposition as expansion proceeds beyond the necessary minimum. This occurs whenever a significant element of competition with private enterprise is involved, but it is also true of other items where competition with private enterprise is largely or even wholly absent.

There are many urgent social needs which government can satisfy only by entering into some form of competition with private interests. River valley development, for example, an area in which private enterprise could never hope to operate effectively, is essential for flood control, water conservation, rebuilding eroded soils, etc. But it also produces electric power which competes with private power and thus provides a yardstick by which the performance of the private power monopolies can be measured. For this reason, river valley development is bitterly opposed not only by the utilities themselves but also by the entire Big Business community. . . .

Public housing, potentially a vast field for welfare spending, is another activity which encroaches upon the realm of private enterprise. A really effective low-cost housing program would necessarily call for extensive building in open spaces, which abound in most cities in the United States. But this is precisely what the powerful urban real estate interests are against. On the rock of this opposition, all attempts to launch a serious attack on the twin problems of insufficient and inadequate housing have foundered. Instead we have had fine-sounding "slum clearance" or "urban renewal" programs, which, while liberally rewarding the owners of run-down property, typically throw more people on the streets than they house. . . .

It would be possible to run through the gamut of civilian spending objects and show how in case after case the private interests of the oligarchy stand in stark opposition to the satisfaction of social needs. Real competition with private enterprise cannot be tolerated, no matter how incompetent and inadequate its performance may be; undermining of class privileges or of the stability of the class structure must be resisted at any cost. And almost all types of civilian spending involve one or both of these threats. There is just one major exception to this generalization in the United States today, and it is very much the type of exception which proves the rule: government spending on highways.

The New Deal managed to push government spending up by more than 70 percent, but this was nowhere near enough to bring the economy to a level at which human and material resources were fully employed. Resistance of the oligarchy to further expansion in civilian spending hardened and held with unemployment still well above 15 percent of the labor force. By 1939 it was becoming increasingly clear that liberal reform had sadly failed to rescue United States monopoly capitalism from its own self-destructive tendencies. As Roosevelt's second term approached its end, a profound sense of frustration and uneasiness crept over the country.

Then came the war, and with it salvation. Government spending soared and unemployment plummeted. At the end of the war, to be sure, arms spending was cut back sharply; but owing to the backlog of civilian demand built up during the war (compounded of supply shortages and a massive accumulation of liquid savings), the downturn associated with this cutback was relatively mild and brief and soon gave way to an inflationary reconversion boom. And the boom was still going strong when the Cold War began in earnest. Military spending reached its postwar low in 1947, turned up in 1948, received a tremendous boost from the Korean War (1950-1953), declined moderately during the next two years, and then in 1956 began the slow climb which continued, with a slight interruption in 1960, into the 1960's.

During the interval 1929–1957, total government spending increased from roughly one tenth to one quarter of GNP, most of the difference representing absorption of surplus which would otherwise not have been produced. . . .

It is of course in the area of defense purchases that most of the expansion has taken place—from less than 1 percent of GNP to more than 10 percent, accounting for about two thirds of the total expansion of government spending relative to GNP since the 1920's. This massive absorption of surplus in military preparations has been the key fact of postwar American economic history.

. . . The need of the American oligarchy for a large and growing military machine is a logical corollary of its purpose to contain, compress, and eventually destroy the rival world socialist system. . . .

. . . What really interests the giant multinational corporations which dominate American policy. What they want is *monopolistic control* over foreign sources of supply and foreign markets, enabling them to buy and sell on specially privileged terms, to shift orders from one subsidiary to another, to favor this country or that depending on which has the most advantageous tax, labor, and other policies—in a word, they want to do business on their own terms and wherever they choose. And for this what they need is not trading partners but "allies" and clients willing to adjust their laws and policies to the requirements of American Big Business. . . .

It would be misleading to leave the impression that only the oligarchy has favored the steady increase in military spending during these years. If one assumes the permanence of monopoly capitalism . . . one must decide whether one prefers the mass unemployment . . . characteristic of the Great Depression or the relative job security and material well-being provided by huge military budgets. . . . Since most Americans, workers included, still do assume without question the permanence of the system, it is only natural that they should prefer prosperity. And in order to rationalize this preference, they have accepted the official ideology of anti-Communism which appears to justify an unlimited expansion of the military establishment as essential to national survival.

THE IRRATIONAL SYSTEM

It is of the essence of capitalism that both goods and labor power are typically bought and sold on the market. In such a society relations among individuals are dominated by the principle of the exchange of equivalents, of *quid pro quo,* not only in economic matters but in all other aspects of life as well.

Not that the principle of equivalent exchange is or ever has been universally practiced in capitalist society. As Marx showed so convincingly in the closing chapters of the first volume of *Capital,* the primary accumulation of capital was effected through violence and plunder, and the same methods continue in daily use throughout capitalism's dependent colonies and semi-colonies. Nevertheless the ideological sway of *quid pro quo* became all but absolute. In their relations with each other and in what they teach those over whom they rule, capitalists are fully committed to the principle of *quid pro quo,* both as a guide to action and as a standard of morality.

This commitment reflected an important step forward in the development of the forces of production and in the evolution of human consciousness. Only on the basis of equivalent exchange was it possible to realize the more rational utilization of human and material resources which has been the central achievement of capitalism. At the same time, it must never be forgotten that the rationality of *quid pro quo* is specifically capitalist rationality which at a certain stage of development becomes incompatible with the underlying forces and relations of production. To ignore this and to treat *quid pro quo* as a universal maxim of rational conduct is in itself an aspect of bourgeois ideology, just as the radical-sounding assertion that under socialism exchange of equivalents can be immediately dispensed with betrays a utopian view of the nature of the economic problems faced by a socialist society.*

But even during the life span of capitalism itself, *quid pro quo* breaks down as a rational principle of economic and social organization. The giant corporation withdraws from the sphere of the market large segments of economic activity and subjects them to scientifically designed administration. This change represents a continuous increase in the rationality of the parts of the system, but it is not accompanied by any rationalization of the whole. On the contrary, with commodities being priced not according to their costs of production but to yield the maximum possible profit, the principle of *quid pro quo* turns into the opposite of a promoter of rational economic organization and instead becomes a formula for maintaining scarcity in the midst of potential plenty. Human and material resources remain idle because there is in the market no *quid* to exchange against the *quo* of their potential output. And this is true even though the real cost of such output would be nil. In the most advanced capitalist country a large part of the population lives in abysmal poverty while in the underdeveloped countries hundreds of millions suffer from disease and starvation because there is no mechanism for effecting an exchange of what they could produce for what they so desperately need. Insistence on the inviolability of equivalent exchange when what is to be exchanged costs nothing, strict economizing of resources when a large proportion of them goes to waste—these are obviously the very denial of the rationality which the concept of value and the principle of *quid pro quo* originally expressed.

The obsolescence of such central categories of bourgeois thought is but one symptom of the profoundly contradictory nature of monopoly capitalism, of the ever sharpening conflict between the rapidly advancing rationalization of the actual processes of production and the undiminished *elementality* of the system as a whole. This conflict affects all aspects of society. While rationality

*Marx emphasized in his *Critique of the Gotha Program* that the principle of equivalent exchange must survive in a socialist society for a considerable period as a guide to the efficient allocation and utilization of human and material resources. By the same token, however, the evolution of socialism into communism requires an unremitting struggle *against* the principle, with a view to its ultimate replacement by the ideal "From each according to his ability, to each according to his need." In a fully developed communist society, in which social production would be organized as in one vast economic enterprise and in which scarcity would be largely overcome, equivalent exchange would no more serve as the organizing principle of economic activity than at the present time the removal of a chair from one's bedroom to one's sitting room requires charging the sitting room and crediting the bedroom with the value of the furniture. This is obviously not to imply that the communist society of the future can dispense with rational calculation; what it does indicate is that the nature of the rationality involved in economic calculation undergoes a profound change. And this change in turn is but one manifestation of a thoroughgoing transformation of human needs and of the relations among men in society.

has been conquering ever new areas of consciousness, the inability of bourgeois thought to comprehend the development of society as a whole has remained essentially unchanged, a faithful mirror of the continuing elementality and irrationality of the capitalist order itself.

Social reality is therefore conceived in outlived, topsy-turvy and fetishistic terms. Powerless to justify an irrational and inhuman social order and unable to answer the increasingly urgent questions which it poses, bourgeois ideology clings to concepts that are anachronistic and moribund. Its bankruptcy manifests itself not so much in the generation of new fetishes and half-truths as in the stubborn upholding of old fetishes and half-truths which now turn into blatant lies. And the more these old fetishes and half-truths lose whatever truth content they once possessed the more insistently they are hammered, like advertising slogans, into the popular consciousness.

The claim that the United States economy is a "free enterprise" system is a case in point. At no time was enterprise really free in the sense that anyone who wanted to could start a business of his own. Still the concept conveyed an important aspect of the truth by pointing up the difference between the relative freedom of competitive capitalism on the one hand and the restrictions imposed by the guild system and the mercantilist state on the other. Having long ago lost this limited claim to truthfulness and referring as it now does to the freedom of giant corporations to exercise undisturbed their vast monopoly powers, "free enterprise" has turned into a shibboleth devoid of all descriptive or explanatory validity.

Bourgeois ideology is no longer a world outlook, a *Weltanschauung,* which attempts to discern order in the existing chaos and to discover a meaning in life. It has turned into a sort of box of assorted tools and gimmicks for attaining the central goal of bourgeois policies. And this goal—which in its younger days the bourgeoisie defined in terms of material progress and individual freedom—is more and more explicitly limited to one thing only: preservation of the status quo, alias the "free world," with all its manifest evils, absurdities, and irrationalities.

It is of course impossible to advance a reasoned defense of this status quo, and indeed the effort is seldom made any more. Instead of taking the form of a demonstration of the rationality and desirability of monopoly capitalism, the defense increasingly focuses on the repudiation of socialism which is the only real alternative to monopoly capitalism, and on the denunciation of revolution which is the only possible means of achieving socialism. All striving for a better, more humane, more rational society is held to be unscientific, utopian, and subversive; by the same token the existing order of society is made to appear not only as the only possible one but as the only conceivable one.

The contradiction between the increasing rationality of society's methods of production and the organizations which embody them on the one hand and the undiminished elementality and irrationality in the functioning and perception of the whole creates that ideological wasteland which is the hallmark of monopoly capitalism. But we must insist that this is not, as some apologists of the status quo would have us believe, "the end of ideology"; it is the displacement of the ideology of rising capitalism by the ideology of the general crisis and decline of the world capitalist order. That its main pillar is anti-Communism is neither accidental nor due to a transient conjunction of political forces, any more than is the fact that the main content of the political and economic policies of modern capitalism is armaments and Cold War. These policies can only be *anti;* there is nothing left for them to be *pro*.

7.2 Critique of Monopoly Capital

Robert Heilbroner

[The] Baran-Sweezy analysis can be best considered, I think, in three ways: as a moral indictment, as an economic model, and as a theory of power. Of the three I find the first to be the most effective. This is not because the material is new—we are all familiar with the dreary statistics of poverty, misallocation of resources, aborted education, etc. What in most books, however, are only complaints, are in this book particulars of one central accusation: that the social order peculiar to capitalism is irrational. By this Baran and Sweezy mean that, at bottom, it is the institution of private property that inhibits, deflects, or simply defeats efforts to undo the social inequities we all learn to live with and not to think about.

This stress on the systemic roots of our failure to repair the slums, to relieve poverty, to improve our educational efforts, is something to be mulled over by those all-too-many social scientists who have ignored the most elementary social judgments in the name of "value-free" inquiry, or as theologians of pure competition. Unfortunately, I fear that Baran's and Sweezy's accusations will not be very effective with most of them. . . .

In part this failure of persuasion lies in the avowedly exaggerated argument of the book. Every bit of available evidence is brought to bear against the system, but not a word is said in its defense.

The argument backfires for another reason. Whereas capitalism is portrayed as a system of class relations which does nothing but foist irrationality upon social action, socialism is pictured as the very paradigm of sweet reason. Thus, "Militarism and conquest are completely foreign to Marxist theory, and a socialist society contains no group or class which, like the big capitalists of the imperalist countries, stands to gain from a policy of subjugating other nations and peoples." This after Hungary, and at a time when we face the threat of a major Russo-Chinese conflict!

But the main failure of the moral indictment lies elsewhere in the authors' refusal to allow for any causes of social evil outside the realm of economic relations. Behind every instance of human weakness, indifference, or cruelty they show us the underlying cause to be the defense of class interests. In the

Excerpted from Robert Heilbroner, *Between Capitalism and Socialism* (New York: Random House, 1970. Reprinted by permission of the publisher.

end, this insistence, valid enough when thoughtfully applied, becomes invalid because it is indiscriminately used. . . .

However much I share their concern for social morality, I suspect that the authors are more interested in their description of monopoly capitalism as a system. . . . What they have presented is nothing less than a neo-Marxian theory of capitalism—a theory in which those time-honored categories of Marxian analysis, surplus value and the falling rate of profit, have been excluded and in which a new central tendency takes their place.

This central tendency they call the Law of Rising Surplus. By this the authors mean two somewhat different things. The first is that in an industrially progressive society there will be a steadily increasing capacity to produce more than is needed simply to sustain the working population at minimally acceptable levels and to replace worn-out equipment. This concept in itself is not particularly different from our ordinary ideas of rising productivity, except that by focusing on the mass of available "surplus product," we are forced to examine qualitatively as well as quantitatively the ends to which society applies its wealth. . . . In an appendix to the Baran-Sweezy book, Joseph D. Phillips estimates the amount of surplus in the United States in 1963 as $327,725,000,000, or fifty-six percent of GNP.

But Baran and Sweezy are more interested in a second use of the term surplus. To give a somewhat inexact parallel, the word is used as a kind of expanded version of "savings-and-investment," referring to those particular flows of revenue and outlay as they exist in a capitalist economy. Surplus can then be looked at (as can savings) as the money accruing to various individuals or businesses in a capitalist economy, or (like investment) as those economic acts which constitute the "real" counterpart of these financial changes. Specifically, in the Baran-Sweezy model, surplus becomes on the one hand a series of gains, such as monopoly profits, excess depreciation, property income, etc., and on the other, a series of activities, namely, investment, luxury consumption, and capitalist waste into which those gains are absorbed.

Here the authors discover a deep-seated problem. For they maintain that the amount of financial surplus will tend to grow, in large part because of an alleged tendency of corporate profits to rise, whereas the modes of expenditure available to mop up this surplus—the investment, waste, and luxury consumption needed to offset the rising stream of property and privileged income—will, for various reasons, lag behind. Indeed, Baran and Sweezy believe that a condition of chronic stagnation must therefore be the norm for a highly developed monopoly capitalism—a condition from which it has been rescued only by the fortuitous advent of epochal inventions (the steam engine, the railroad, and the automobile) and by the stimulating effects of wars.

. . . . I am myself not entirely easy with many of Baran's and Sweezy's definitions of "surplus," in particular their treatment of taxes and their failure to include any wage or middle-class salary payments as part of surplus. In addition, I am not convinced of their argument that corporate profits tend to grow within the economy, since I believe they overlook the prevailing permissive corporate attitude toward wage raises, and ignore the possibility . . . that corporate output is a declining proportion of total national output.

Meanwhile, however, the Baran-Sweezy model brings us to the third, and in my view the weakest, aspect of the book. This is their theory of the structure and exercise of power within monopoly capitalism. For essentially their argument as to the inability of the system to absorb its surplus hinges on a political rather than an economic obstacle. This is the refusal of the ruling oligarchy to utilize the surplus for nonmilitary purposes.

This is not a willful or arbitrary refusal. According to Baran and Sweezy, the ruling oligarchy is *unable* to pour the surplus of society into housing or education or other such things because expenditures for these purposes would jeopardize its economic and social interests.

What is wrong with this assertion? To begin with, it treats the oligarchy as if it were a compact body of men who acted in concert with one will and one aim. Yet studies of the interests of the big corporations reveal profound divisions of interest among them.

Second, Baran and Sweezy credit the oligarchy with immense operative power: "In constitutional theory the people exercise sovereign power; in actual practice a relatively small moneyed oligarchy rules supreme." If this were true, one would ask why—until the debacle of Vietnam—no Republican had been elected to the Presidency since Herbert Hoover, the sole exception being the "national" candidate, Eisenhower.

Finally, the oligarchy that emerges from the Baran-Sweezy analysis strikes me as a deceptive stereotype. There have been, I know, ruling classes so set in their ways, so blind to reality, that they have been unable to make those accommodations needed to assure their own survival: the French aristocracy comes to mind. But there have been other ruling classes—the English—who have managed their affairs very adroitly.

This same objection must be brought to bear against Baran's and Sweezy's portrait of the capitalist class. Could not, after all, such a class learn to consume its surplus through public housing on the grand scale? Baran and Sweezy tell us flatly that it cannot: "Such planning and such action . . . will never be undertaken by a government run by and for the rich, as every capitalist government is and must be." How, then, are we to explain the slum clearance programs in Sweden or Norway; the family allowances in Germany; the medical programs in England? If these kinds of remedial action are possible in America, what we need to understand are the reasons why capitalists here are different from those abroad. It is the principal defect of Baran's and Sweezy's analysis that they provide no means of answering this critical question.

The reason for this seriously distorted argument lies, I think, in a fatal Marxian predilection for "closed systems" of thought that can then proceed with a delicious inexorability to their assigned destinations. In such systems, it is very hard to incorporate models of thought or action that partake of uncertainty, indeterminateness, or changeability. As a result, beliefs and attitudes that are perfectly correct as first approximations of social behavior—such as the predisposition of the American government and business class to defend its system of privileges—are frozen in ways that leave no room for compromise, retreat, adaptation, or learning. No wonder, then, that the historic drama has so often defied Marxist predictions—the "hopeless" English Tories of the 1930's becoming the most enlightened Conservative party in Europe, the "militant" unionists of the New Deal becoming the fat cats of the 1960's, the "reactionary" middle class leading the revolutions of the underdeveloped world.

These failures of prediction—based, I believe, in large measure on an overly abstract conception of power and class—lead me to discount much of the future Baran and Sweezy envisage. At home they see a static monopoly capitalism, suffering from increasing psychic malaise, while abroad the champions of liberty and freedom rally mankind under the banners of national liberation. What they do not see are possibilities for a long-run emergence of rationality in America, as the new elites of science and social science gradually emerge; or the chances that retrograde movement may follow from the revolutionary tendencies of the underdeveloped world. I would agree with them that capitalism as a system of function and privilege will be and should be eventually replaced by a more rational system, and that revolutions will be needed in the underdeveloped world before those miserable peoples can achieve the national will to make the enormous developmental effort required of them. But I am certain that the road to the future will not run as straight to heaven or hell as the one that Baran and Sweezy describe.

7.3 Workers Under Neo-Capitalism

Ernest Mandel

The proletarian condition is, in a nutshell, the lack of access to means of production or means of subsistence which, in a society of generalized commodity production, forces the proletarian to sell his labor-power. In exchange for this labor-power he receives a wage which then enables him to acquire the means of consumption necessary for satisfying his own needs and those of his family.

This is the structural definition of the wage earner, the proletarian. From it necessarily flows a certain relationship to his work, to the products of his work, and to his overall situation in society, which can be summarized by the catchword "alienation." But there does not follow from this structural definition any necessary conclusions as to the level of his consumption, the price he receives for his labor-power, the extent of his needs or the degree to which he can satisfy them. The only basic interrelationship between structural stability of status and conjunctural fluctuations of income and consumption is a very simple one: Does the wage, whether high or low, enable the proletarian to free himself from the social and economic obligation to sell his labor-power? Does it enable him to go into business on his own account?

Starting either with the great depression of 1929–32 or with the second world war, capitalism entered into a third stage in its development, which is as different from monopoly capitalism or imperialism described by Lenin, Hilferd-

---

Excerpted from Ernest Mandel, "Workers under Neo-Capitalism," *International Socialist Review*, November/December 1968. Reprinted by permission of the publisher.

ing and others as monopoly capitalism was different from classical 19th century laissez-faire capitalism. We have to give this child a name; all other names proposed seem even less acceptable than "neo-capitalism."

We shall define neo-capitalism as this latest stage in the development of monopoly capitalism in which a combination of factors—accelerated technological innovation, permanent war economy, expanding colonial revolution—have transferred the main source of monopoly surplus profits from the colonial countries to the imperialist countries themselves and made the giant corporations both more independent and more vulnerable.

More independent, because the enormous accumulation of monopoly surplus profits enables these corporations, through the mechanisms of price investment and self-financing, and with the help of a constant buildup of sales costs, distribution costs and research and development expenses, to free themselves from that strict control by banks and finance capital which characterized the trusts and monopolies of Hilferding's and Lenin's epoch. More vulnerable, because of shortening of the life cycle of fixed capital, the growing phenomenon of surplus capacity, the relative decline of customers in non-capitalist milieus and, last but not least, the growing challenge of the non-capitalist forces in the world (the so-called socialist countries, the colonial revolution and, potentially at least, the working class in the metropolis) has implanted even in minor fluctuations and crises the seeds of dangerous explosions and total collapse.

For these reasons, neo-capitalism is compelled to embark upon all those well-known techniques of economic programming, of deficit financing and pump-priming, of incomes policies and wage freezing, of state subsidizing of big business and state guaranteeing of monopoly surplus profit, which have become permanent features of most Western economies over the last 20 years. What has emerged is a society which appears both as more prosperous and more explosive than the situation of imperialist countries 30 years ago.

It is a society in which the basic contradictions of capitalism have not been overcome, in which some of them reach unheard-of dimensions, in which powerful long-term forces are at work to blow up the system. I will mention here in passing only some of these forces: The growing crisis of the international monetary system, the trend towards a generalized economic recession in the whole capitalist world, the trend to restrict or suppress the basic democratic freedoms of the working class, in the first place, free play of wage bargaining, the trend toward deep and growing dissatisfaction of producers and consumers with a system which forces them to lose more and more time producing and consuming more and more commodities which give less and less satisfaction and stifle more and more basic human needs, emotions and aspirations, the contradictions between the accumulation of wasteful "wealth" in the West and the hunger and misery of the colonial peoples, the contradictions between the immense creative and productive potentialities of science and automation and the destructive horror of nuclear war in the shadow of which we are forced to live permanently, epitomize the basic contradictions of today's capitalism.

The question has been posed: Hasn't the role of the working class been fundamentally changed in this changed environment? Hasn't the long-term high level of employment and the rising real wage undercut any revolutionary potential of the working class? Isn't it changing in composition, and more and more divorced from the productive process, as a result of growing automation? Doesn't its relations with other social layers, such as white-collar workers, technicians, intellectuals, students, undergo basic modifications?

Affirmative answers to these questions lead to political conclusions of far-reaching consequence. For some, the stability of the capitalist system in the West cannot be shaken any more.

For others, that stability could be shaken only from outside: Others, while not questioning the basic instability of neo-capitalism, see no positive outcome at all because they believe that the system is able to drug and paralyze its victims. Finally, there are those who believe that neo-capitalism raises its gravediggers from within its bosom but see these gravediggers coming from the groups of outcasts: national and racial minorities, superexploited sections of the population, revolutionary students, the new youth vanguard. All these conclusions share in common the elimination of the proletariat of metropolitan countries from the central role in the worldwide struggle against imperialism and capitalism.

It would be easy to limit oneself to stating an obvious fact: All these theories spring from a premature rationalization of a given situation, the fact that the Western proletariat has receded into the background of the world revolutionary struggle for the past 20 years, between 1948 and 1968.

Such an answer, valid though it may be, would remain insufficient and incomplete. For some of the theories we have just mentioned, while being obvious rationalizations of the *fait accompli,* have enough sophistication and candor not to limit themselves to description pure and simple. They try to draw conclusions about the declining revolutionary role of the proletariat in the West from changes introduced into the very fabric of neo-capitalist society by technological, economic, social and cultural transformations of historic proportions and importance. So we have to meet these arguments on their own ground, and critically reexamine the dynamics of working class struggles, consciousness and revolutionary potential against the background of the changes which neo-capitalism has effected in the classical *modus operandi* of the capitalist system.

Our starting point must be the same as that adopted not only by Karl Marx but also by the classical school of political economy: the study of the place human labor occupies in the economic life of contemporary monopoly capitalism. Three basic facts immediately demand our attention in that respect.

First, contemporary production and distribution of material wealth is more than ever based upon modern industry and the factory. Indeed, one could say that the third industrial revolution at one and the same time both reduces industrial labor in the factory as a result of growing automation and increases industrial labor on a vast scale in agriculture, distribution, the service industries and administration. For the automation revolution must be seen as a vast movement of *industrialization* of these different sectors of economic activity, both economically and socially. We shall have to draw important conclusions from this trend. But what stands out is the fact that industrial labor in the broadest sense of the word—men forced to sell their labor-power to the manufacturing, cotton-growing, data-processing or dream-producing factory!—more than ever occupies the central place in the economy's structure.

Second, whatever the increase in consumption of the working class may have been, neo-capitalism hasn't modified in any sense whatsoever the basic nature of work in a capitalist society as alienated labor. One could even say that in the same way as automation extends the industrialization process into every single corner of economic life, it likewise universalizes alienation.

In any case, labor under neo-capitalism is more than ever alienated labor, forced labor, labor under command of a hierarchy which dictates to the worker what he has to produce and how he has to produce it. And this same hierarchy imposes upon him what to consume and when to consume it, what to think and when to think it, what to dream and when to dream it, giving alienation new and dreadful dimensions. It tries to alienate the worker even from his consciousness of being alienated, of being exploited.

Third, living labor remains more than ever the sole source of surplus value, the only source of profit, which is what makes the system tick.

But all these contradictions and absurdities are real, living contridictions and absurdities of capitalism. These would attain their absolute limit in universal and total automation which, however, lies completely beyond its reach because living labor is indispensable for the further accumulation of capital. One has only to observe how the billion-dollar corporations haggle and shout like fishwives over a 50-cent wage increase here and two hours off the workweek there to see that, whatever ideologues and sociologists might argue, the hard facts of life confirm what Marx taught us: Capital's unlimited appetite for profit is an unlimited appetite for human surplus labor, for hours and minutes of unpaid labor. The shorter the workweek becomes, the higher the actual productivity of labor, the closer and more strictly do capitalists calculate surplus labor and haggle ever more furiously over seconds and fractions of seconds as in time and motion studies.

Now precisely these three characteristics of modern labor—its key role in the productive process, its basic alienation, its economic exploitation—are the objective roots of its potential role as the main force to overthrow capitalism, the objective roots of its indicated revolutionary mission. Any attempt to transfer that role to other social layers who are unable to paralyze production at a stroke, who do not play a key role in the productive process, who are not the main source of profit and capital accumulation, takes us a decisive step backwards from scientific to utopian socialism, from socialism which grows out of the inner contradictions of capitalism to that immature view of socialism which was to be born from the moral indignation of men regardless of their place in social production.

Here we have to meet an objection often voiced both by so-called dogmatic Marxists and by avowed revisionists or opponents of Marxist theory. Haven't we given too general a definition of the working class under neo-capitalism? Shouldn't we restrict this category to the same group which came under this definition in the classical period of the socialist labor movement, to wit the manual workers actually engaged in production? Isn't it true that this category tends to decline, first relatively and then even in absolute figures, in the most advanced industrial countries of the West? Are not the mass of wage and salary earners to which we have constantly referred too vague and heterogeneous a grouping to be considered a social class in the Marxist sense of the word? And isn't the fading of the revolutionary potential of the working class in the Western metropolitan countries causally linked to this diminution of the manual production workers in the gainfully employed population?

The productive process of today tends more and more to *integrate* manual and non-manual workers, conveyor-belt semi-skilled and data-processing semi-skilled, highly skilled repair and maintenance squads and highly-skilled electronics experts.

Just as the third industrial revolution, just as automation, tends to industrialize agriculture, distribution, the service industries and administration, just as it tends to universalize industry, so it tends to integrate a constantly growing part of the mass of wage and salary earners into an increasingly homogeneous proletariat.

This conclusion needs further elucidation. What are the indicators of the enhanced proletarian character of these "new" layers of workers which become progressively integrated into the working class?

We could cite offhand a series of striking facts: reduced wage differentials between white-collar and manual workers, which is a universal trend in the West; increased unionization and union militancy of these "new" layers, which is equally universal (in Brussels as in New York, schoolteachers, electricians, telephone and telegraph workers have been among the militant trade unionists in the last five years); rising similarities of consumption, of social status and environment of these layers; growing similarity of working conditions, i.e., growing similarity of monotonous, mechanized, uncreative, nerve-racking and stultifying work in factory, bank, bus, public administration, department stores and airplanes.

If we examine the long-term trend, there is no doubt that the basic process is one of growing homogeneity and not of growing heterogeneity of the proletariat. The difference in income consumption and status between an unskilled laborer and a bank clerk or high-school teacher is today incommensurably smaller than it was fifty or a hundred years ago.

But there is an additional and striking feature of this process of integration of new layers into the working class under neo-capitalism: That is the equalization of the conditions of reproduction of labor-power, especially of skilled and semi-skilled labor-power. In the days of 19th century capitalism, there was elementary education for the manual worker, lower-middle-school education for the white-collar worker, high-school education for the technician; the reproduction of agricultural labor-power often didn't need any education whatsoever. Universities were strictly institutions for the capitalist class.

The very technological transformation, of which neo-capitalism is both a result and a motive force, has completely modified the levels of education.

Today, outside of completely unskilled laborers for whom there are very few jobs any more in industry, strictly speaking, and for whom tomorrow there might be no jobs available in the whole economy, conditions of reproduction of skill for industrial workers, technicians, white-collar employees, service workers and clerks are completely identical in generalized high-school education. In fact, in several countries, radicals are fighting for compulsory education up to 18 years in a single type of school, with growing success.

Uniform conditions of reproduction of labor-power entail at one and the same time a growing homogeneity of wages and salaries (value and price of labor-power), and a growing homogeneity of labor itself. In other words, the third industrial revolution is repeating in the whole society what the first industrial revolution achieved inside the factory system: a growing indifference towards the particular skill of labor, the emergence of generalized human labor, transferable from one factory to another, as a concrete social category (corresponding historically to the abstract general human labor which classical political economy found as the only source of exchange-value).

Let us restate the first conclusion we have arrived at. Neo-capitalism in the long run strengthens the working class much as did laissez-faire capitalism or monopoly capitalism in its first stage. Historically, it makes the working class grow both numerically and in respect to its vital role in the economy. It thereby strengthens the latent power of the working class and underlines its potential capacity to overthrow capitalism and to reconstruct society on the basis of its own socialist ideal.

Immediately new questions arise. If this be so, will not the increased stability of the neo-capitalist system, its wide use of neo-Keynesian and macroeconomic techniques, its avoidance of catastrophic economic depressions of the 1929–33 type, its capacity to shape the workers' consciousness through manipulation and the use of mass media, permanently repress these revolutionary potentialities? These questions boil down to two basic arguments which we shall deal with successively. One is the system's capacity to reduce economic fluctuations and contradictions sufficiently to assure enough reforms to guarantee a gradual easing of social tensions between capital and labor. The other is the system's capacity of integrating and engulfing the industrial proletariat as consumers and ideologically conditioned members of the society.

Granted that the phases of rapid economic growth—more rapid in the last 20 years than in any comparable past period in the history of capitalism—create the material possibilities for increasing real wages and expanding mass consumption. But the attempts to base pessimistic predictions about the revolutionary potential of the working class on this trend of rising real wages overlooks the dual effect of the economic booms under capitalism on the working class.

On the one hand, a combination of near-full employment and a rapid rise of productive forces, especially under conditions of rapid technological change, likewise leads to an increase in the needs of the working class. That portion of the value of labor-power which Marx calls historically determined and is attributable to the given level of culture tends to increase most rapidly under such conditions, generally much more rapidly than wages. Paradoxically, it is precisely when wages rise that the gap between the value and the price of labor-power tends to grow, that the socially determined needs of the working class grow more rapidly than its purchasing power.

Furthermore, rising real wages are constantly threatened by erosion. They are threatened by inflation. They are threatened by structural unemployment generated through technological change and automation. They are threatened by wage restraint and wage-freeze policies. They are threatened by recessions. The more the workers are accustomed to relatively high wages, the more they react against even marginal reductions in their accustomed level of consumption, the more all the just-named threats are potential starting points of real social explosion.

Even more important than the basic instability and insecurity of the proletarian condition which neo-capitalism hasn't overcome and cannot overcome is the inherent trend under neo-capitalism to push the class struggle to a higher plane. As long as the workers were hungry and their most immediate needs were unattended to, wage increases inevitably stood in the center of working class aspirations. As long as they were threatened by mass unemployment, reductions in the work-week were essentially seen as means of reducing the dangers of redundancy. But when employment is relatively high and wages are constantly rising, attention becomes gradually transferred to more basic aspects of capitalist exploitation.

The "wage drift" notwithstanding, industry-wide wage bargaining and attempts of neo-capitalist governments to impose incomes policies tend to focus attention more on the division of national income, on the great aggregates of wages, profits and taxes, than on the division of the newly created value at the factory level. Permanent inflation, constant debates around government fiscal and economic policies, sudden disturbances of the labor market through technological innovation and relocation of whole industries, draw the workers' attention in the same direction.

Classical capitalism educated the worker to struggle for higher wages and shorter working hours in his factory. Neo-capitalism educates the worker to challenge the division of national income and orientation of investment at the superior level of the economy as a whole.

Growing dissatisfaction with labor organization in the plant stimulates this very tendency. The higher the level of skill and education of the working class—and the third industrial revolution leaves no room for an uneducated and unskilled working class!—the more do workers suffer under the hierarchical and despotic work organization at the factory. The stronger the contradiction between the potential wealth which productive forces can create today and the immeasurable waste and absurdity which capitalist production and consumption implies, the more do workers tend to question not only the way a capitalist factory is organized but also what a capitalist factory produces.

The logic of all these trends puts the problem of workers' control in the center of the class struggle. Capitalists, bourgeois politicians and idealogues, and reformist Social Democrats, understand this in their own way. That is why different schemes for "reform of the enterprises," for "co-management," "co-determination" and "participation" occupy the center of the stage in practically all Western European countries.

But parallel to these various schemes of mystification and deception is the growing awareness in working class circles that the problem of workers' control is the key "social question" under neo-capitalism. Questions of wages and shorter working hours are important; but what is much more important than problems of the distribution of income is to decide who should command the machines and who should determine investments, who should decide what to produce and how to produce it.

There remains the last objection. Have the monopolists and their agents unlimited powers of manipulating the ideology and consciousness of the working class, and can they not succeed in preventing revolt, especially successful revolt, notwithstanding growing socio-economic contradictions?

Marxists have recognized the possibility of "manipulation" for a long time. Marx wrote about the artificially induced needs and consumption of the workers a hundred and twenty-five years ago. Marxists have many times reiterated that the "ruling ideology of each society is the ideology of the ruling class."

But one should guard against losing a sense of proportion in respect to this problem. After all, the working class movement arose in the 19th century under conditions where the mass of workers were far more dominated by the ideas of the ruling class than they are today.

In the last analysis the question boils down to this: Which force will turn out to be stronger in determining the workers' attitude to the society he lives in, the mystifying ideas he receives, yesterday in the church and today through TV, or the social reality he confronts and assimilates day after day through practical experience? For historical materialists, to pose the question this way is to answer it, although the struggle itself will say the last word.

The problems of the revolutionary potential of the working class cannot be answered by references to what goes on every day or even every year; revolutions do not erupt every day. The revolutionary potential of the working class can be denied only if one argues that the sparks of revolt which have been kindled in the working class mass through the experience of social injustice and social irrationality are smothered forever; if one argues that the patient and obstinate propaganda and education by revolutionary vanguard organizations cannot have a massive effect among the workers anywhere, anytime, whatever may be the turn of objective events. After all, it is enough that the flame is there to ignite a combustible mass once every 15 or 20 years for the system ultimately to collapse. That's what happened in Russia. That's what the May revolution in France has shown can happen in Western Europe too.

What the socialist revolution is all about, in the last analysis, is faith in the unconquerable spirit of revolt against injustice and oppression and confidence in the ability of mankind to build a future for the human race. Coming from a continent which went through the nightmares of Hitler and Stalin, and emerged hardly a generation later holding high the banner of social revolution, of emancipation of labor, of workers' democracy, of proletarian internationalism, and witnessing in France more youth rallying around that banner than at any time since socialist ideas were born, I believe that faith is fully justified.

7.4 Capitalist Expansion, Ideology, and Imperialism

Arthur MacEwan

While United States imperialism operates in many spheres—political, economic, cultural—it is in its most fundamental sense an economic phenomenon. That is, this international extension of control has its basis in the economic organization of American society. Within a capitalist economic system—and the U.S. is the most advanced capitalist system in history—there are basic forces which push that system toward expansion. This expansion carries with it an extension of control; hence, a capitalist system necessarily develops into an imperialist system.

THE EXPANSION OF CAPITAL

The fundamental principle of operation for the capitalist firm is the search for profits. This principle has its origins in purely competitive conditions, where a failure to continually find new ways to expand the profit margin will lead to the failure of the firm. In the modern capitalist economy of the United States, where monopolistic market conditions dominate, it is certainly not the case that at every moment the survival of the large firm is in danger if it slackens its search for profits. Nonetheless, foreign firms, smaller domestic firms, and firms producing substitutable products present a challenge that cannot be ignored. Moreover, in order to protect their profits, large firms must be attuned to shifts in demand and changes in labor and resource supply conditions. These pressures translate into the general operating rule: continually pursue the search for profits.

The search for profits is a process which takes on many forms. One form is the introduction of new techniques of production and organization which allow cost reductions. The introduction of new techniques is often associated with a dependence upon expansion in the size of the enterprise's operation. For example, an extension of the division of labor—that hallmark of capitalist efficiency—is almost always dependent upon an expansion of sales. In this manner, technical change in the production process is often intricately bound up with another form of the search for profits, namely, the search for new markets. Whether or not cost-cutting innovations are introduced, the opening of

---

Abridged and reprinted by permission of the author from Arthur MacEwan, "Capitalist Expansion, Ideology, and Intervention." Copyright © 1972 by Arthur MacEwan. The article originally appeared in *The Capitalist System: A Radical Analysis of American Society,* R. C. Edwards, M. Reich, and T. E. Weisskopf, editors. Englewood Cliffs, N.J.: Prentice-Hall, Inc., 1972.

new markets allows an expansion of sales without a corresponding decline in price. In the absence of increasing costs, new markets thus provide a basis for expanding profits.

Particularly important for the purposes of this essay is that the search for markets will often involve an expansion of the geographic sphere of operations. Geographic expansion has many advantages. For a firm operating in a competitive industry, geographic expansion allows the exploitation of markets where the downward pressure on prices is not so severe. For firms selling a relatively new product, the size of the local market may not be sufficient to take advantage of economies of scale, and international sales are necessary if production is to be profitable. In each case profitability is, of course, the criterion of geographic expansion, but profitability is often limited by uncertainty, lack of information, and political or economic instability. These factors can be significant barriers to the geographic expansion of the small firm.

For the large monopolistic firm, such matters of information, uncertainty, and instability are of less importance. In confronting each of these problems, the large firm has a natural advantage. It has the facilities to gain knowledge and gauge the possibility for profits, and it can help insure its investments against instability. There are additional reasons why the monopolistic firm is apt to place particular importance upon international expansion of its markets. First, simply in order to maintain its monopolistic position, it must control markets outside its original sphere of operation. Otherwise new firms may develop in those areas and eventually threaten the original base of operation. The consequences of a failure to control new markets is clear from the development of the European and Japanese automobile industries and their subsequent inroads on U.S. markets. While U.S. firms did attempt to control through the purchase of some European firms (e.g., Opel) they were unable to halt the European competition.

Second, in the same manner that it will search for new products rather than expand its own product line, the monopolistic firm will seek to expand in new markets rather than expand and cut profits (through a lowering of the price) in its basic market.

In addition to the search for new markets, there are other forms of the international search for profits. The availability of raw materials has always drawn capitalist enterprises throughout the world. While a firm of any size may be attracted by the profitability of obtaining raw materials, it is the large monopolistic firm that is particularly active and successful. In the first place, the exploitation of raw materials often requires large capital resources. Second, the large firm which is vertically integrated (e.g., the bauxite-aluminum-aluminum products companies) and thus uses the raw materials and sells the final product often has a special advantage. Third, and perhaps most important, the monopolistic firm is concerned about control. Whatever the narrow profitability of obtaining particular raw materials, controlling their supply is often important to the large firm which must continue to insure that other firms do not make inroads on its realm. The petroleum industry is the most prominent example of an international exploiter of raw materials, and it exhibits each of these advantages of monopolistic operation. Aluminum, copper, and other mineral industries also provide good examples.

Another form which the internationalization of business takes is the extension to new areas of the production process itself. On the one hand, the establishment of production operations in new areas is a means to exploit the markets of those areas. Sometimes the nature of the product is such that it is necessary or desirable to undertake production, or at least the final stages of production, close to the market in which it is sold. The refining of oil, the processing or packaging of food products (Coca-Cola!), the provision of a service, and construction projects all provide examples. Sometimes legal restrictions of the host country—tariffs, for example—require that a product be produced in the area where it is to be sold. This is true of the automobile industry in Mexico and in several other Latin American countries. Insofar as the establishment of production operations in a new area is based on such motives, it often involves not a complete operation but only the final assembly of a product.

On the other hand, production activities are frequently established in a new area in order to exploit the relatively low-cost labor in that area. The assembly of electronic components in Taiwan, punching IBM cards in Hong Kong, making shoes in Italy, and hand typesetting in several countries have all been developed by U.S. industries to avoid the relatively high labor costs at home. As with other types of international expansion, we can expect the monopolistic enterprise to take the lead in the international exploitation of labor. In terms of its ability to control and to transfer technology, its ability to secure sufficient demand for the new production enterprise, and its political ability to cope with the local population as a work force, the large firm has marked advantages.

In summary, the basic method of operation of the capitalist firm leads to international expansion in several ways. While the overall motivation is always profit, the particular medium through which the profits are gained can be the extension of markets, the obtaining of raw materials, or the exploitation of new sources of labor. In general, monopolistic enterprises can be expected to take the leading role in the internationalization of capital.

The internationalization of capital is a process which does not take place in a political vacuum. Capital requires direct protection and the institutions through which it operates must be protected. Thus the expansion of the area of operation of capital is always associated with an expansion of the political influence of the state with which that capital is associated. In the following section I shall examine the historical operation of state and capital in the expansionary process.

STATE AND CAPITAL IN THE PROCESS OF EXPANSION

In the history of capitalist development, we may distinguish three broad stages of expansionary activity. These stages, while they do not conform in a precise way to historical eras, are useful analytical tools for examining the internationalization of capital. First is the stage of creating *national economies* in which the locus of economic activity moves from cities or small regions toward a national framework. Second is the stage of *colonialism and spheres of influence* in which the business interests of advanced nations extend their control beyond their own boundaries but with each nation operating in separate geographic areas. Third is the stage of *international capitalist integration,* or *modern imperialism,* in which barriers to economic activity among capitalist countries tend to be eliminated and domination of the international economy becomes centralized in one nation. In each of these stages the state can be seen providing the essential framework for expansion.

The First Stage: The Development of National Economies

The early development of capitalism required the expansion of the size of the capitalist economic unit. In this expansion the state played a crucial role.

The key aspect of capitalist production is that the worker must be separated from the control of any productive factors other than his or her own labor and that the production process must be controlled by the owner of capital. The process of separating workers from their means of production, and thus forcing them into the labor market and into capitalist production relationships, was facilitated by the power of the state. The state was instrumental in the development of capitalism in England, for example, through promotion of the enclosure movement in the eighteenth century and through legislation forcing the poor to enter the work force in the nineteenth century. It played a similar role in other parts of Western Europe and in Japan (after the Meiji Restoration in 1868), where the persistence of feudal institutions threatened to impede the growth of capitalism.

The profitable use of a developing labor force by the capitalist firm depends upon an expansion in the size of the unit of production. The division of labor which provides the basis for capitalist efficiency could not take place in a small craft shop of the precapitalist era. However, an enterprise could be profitably expanded only to the extent that there was a market for increased output. Thus it was necessary for capitalist development that local restrictions on trade be broken down, that means of transportation and communication be developed, that a uniform system of law and order be established over a wide area—in short, it was necessary that national economic units be developed and strengthened.

The Second Stage: Colonies and Spheres

The stage in capitalist development which followed the political and economic development of the nation was characterized by colonial expansion and the creation of spheres of influence. As in the preceding stage, the economic integration of a larger geographic area was the key to the expansion process. However, while the need for markets and labor played some role, the effort to develop sources of supply for important foodstuffs and raw materials became particularly important in the second stage. The role of the state remained as before: to break down local restrictions on economic activity: to create a labor force; to create means of transportation and communication; to insure stability through the imposition of law and order.

Britain, for example, united the regional economies of India and opened the whole subcontinent to penetration by British capital. Each colonial power established its own currency as the medium of exchange throughout its realm. The European colonial powers in Africa imposed monetary taxes on the local population, forcing them to leave the traditional economy and enter the capitalist labor force to earn cash incomes to pay the taxes. Throughout the colonial world, railways directed toward import-export activity were given priority. Britain, France, Germany, and all of the colonial powers backed up their economic decisions in the most direct manner—with armed force.

In organizing trade within its particular sphere, each nation reserved for its own capitalist class special economic priviliges—both with respect to the subordinate areas in its control, as well as with regard to other leading capitalist powers. Thus, for example, Portugal prohibited the development of manufacturing in Brazil, reserving the market for goods produced in the parent country, and England restricted the trade of its North American colonies with other European powers.

The Third Stage: United States Hegemony

It is not surprising that the United States was a latecomer in building spheres of influence and establishing colonies. First, the United States itself had been under the control of Britain and became a nation only when many European nations were well-established as international powers. Second, as long as the United States was able to expand westward within the North American continent, there was little pressure for the more typical overseas expansion.

As continental boundaries were reached, the United States began to enter seriously the competition among the big powers for new areas of exploitation. Around the turn of the last century, the U.S. and Britain were instrumental in ushering in a new era of capitalist international relations. The policies of the new era were typified by the U.S. demand for an "open door" in the Far East. With several European powers scrambling to establish control in China, the U.S. in 1899 demanded that all countries be allowed commercial access to this area—that the door be left open to all. This policy signified a movement away from national spheres of influence toward a single integrated international capitalist economy. Two world wars were to be fought, however, before this final stage would be firmly established.

Part of the reason that the U.S. government took a diplomatic lead in altering the relations of international capitalism was that U.S. business interests were latecomers to international activity. Thus, short of all-out war with other imperialist powers, the government had no way other than diplomatic initiative to gain access to many areas for U.S. business. More important, the government's demand for open access and equal terms was natural since the nation was rapidly becoming the world's greatest economic power. Under conditions of open access, the emerging political and economic strength of the U.S. would insure that its interests would prevail more often than not.

Coincidentally with the rising international power of U.S. business, the

U.S. government engaged in numerous military interventions around the beginning of the century.

Military interventions, however, should not necessarily be taken as typical of the operation of U.S. imperialism. More often than not control has been exercised through economic power or through nonmilitary political pressure.

IDEOLOGY AND INTERVENTION

Acceptance of the pursuit of profit as a guiding principle means that the behavior of capitalist firms will be expansionary. In order for capitalist expansion to be successful, it is necessary that basic capitalist institutions be created and maintained: the labor market and other basic factor and commodity markets; private property; legal sanction for economic contracts; control of the work process by the owners of capital.

Translated into the realm of foreign policy, the task of the capitalist state then becomes that of facilitating and protecting the international business activities of its nationals. On the level of particular interests, for example: the U.S. diplomatic mission in India sees to it that U.S. pharmaceutical companies are allowed to produce and sell under "reasonable" conditions; in Bolivia and Peru, when U.S. owned oil companies are nationalized, it is the business of the U.S. government; when Brazilian coffee producers begin to sell instant coffee below the price at which U.S. companies can produce, the U.S. government "encourages" the Brazilian government to impose an export duty. On a broader level, the government provides mechanisms for the general expansion of U.S. interests abroad: the U.S. government encourages foreign governments to lower tariffs for U.S. goods and to enter reciprocity arrangements with the U.S.; the U.S. government provides insurances against nationalization or other political "disasters" in unstable areas; the international sections of various government departments—e.g., commerce, labor—devote themselves to providing U.S. business with investment and trade information on countries throughout the world. Finally, on the broadest level, the role of the government in protecting the international business interests of its citizens is the protection of the system that allows those interests to operate, i.e., the protection of international capitalism.

The need to preserve the system of international capitalism has extremely broad implications. For example, to explain the government's actions, from aid-giving to military intervention, we need not point to any particular interests or set of interests that are being served. It need only be argued that the system is being threatened, that the rules of international capitalist operation are in jeopardy.

Imperialist Control

Economic power provides the basis for control in a modern imperialist system. Imperialism is simply the internationalization of capitalist economic relations, and this includes the internalization of capitalist power relations. In the first place, the rationale of commodity markets is that those who can sell products the cheapest will hold the dominant position. Thus, important sectors of the economies of secondary capitalist countries are dominated by the more advanced enterprises of the primary imperialist nations. While such domination has an impact at all levels of the international system, it takes on its most overt form in the poor countries. Their indigenous industrial development is severely limited, and they tend to remain dependent upon the export of agricultural products and raw materials to the rich countries and upon the import of manufactures and technology from the rich.

Second, international capitalism tends to develop or reinforce a class structure in poor countries that serves its interests. Classes in subservience to and alliance with international capital tend to control the political apparatus; their power derives directly from their association with international capital. Both directly through the market and indirectly through the class structure, the economic power of the capitalist elite in the advanced capitalist nations enables them to dominate the economies of the poor countries.

The rapid growth in recent years of multinational corporations has greatly enhanced this economic power. The multinational corporations have a great deal of bargaining power in setting the terms on which their capital will be deployed in host countries simply because they have numerous options. They control technology and can regulate its dissemination according to their own priorities. They have the power, through internal pricing and bookkeeping adjustments, to artificially adjust the international location of their revenues and outlays and thereby affect the finances and balance of payments of host countries. The international capitalist market is like any national capitalist market: those who dominate the control of the means of production dominate the economy.

Imperialist control operates through political as well as economic channels. First, day-to-day control operates through normal diplomatic channels. The role of U.S. diplomatic missions throughout the world is defined as looking after the interests of its nationals, and this means in practice looking after the interests of U.S. business. Second, long-run control operates through the determination of the institutions of the international capitalist economy. Good examples are the negotiation of trade agreements favorable to U.S. capital and the establishment of an international monetary system in which the dollar is key. Such operations serve to maintain the long-run international hegemony of U.S. capital.

Finally, the dominance of the world capitalist economy by the United States is backed up by tremendous military strength. Modern imperialist operations depend on the actual deployment of the military only when problems arise which economic power and quiet political dealings cannot handle. But today imperialism is being presented with serious challenges, and as these challenges become a threat to the entire system, military responses become increasingly necessary.

THE NEW LEFT AND THE NEW RADICALISM

The radical dissent from the post-Keynesian orthodoxy that emerged and developed in the 1960s and early 1970s, while indebted to the neo-Marxist analysis, extends beyond it, especially in critique of large-scale organization and centralized bureaucracy (whether public or private). Many proponents of radical economic change in the United States have become convinced that both traditional socialism and modern liberalism are now incapable of inspiring any meaningful or far-reaching changes in American life. Reform proposals of moderate socialism seem to them to have been absorbed into liberalism, which in turn has since degenerated into mere rhetoric. Liberals are seen as doggedly repeating the slogans of progressive democracy, while in fact working to perpetuate the status quo within the United States, and supporting almost any political leaders abroad as long as they are avowedly anti-communist. Equally abhorrent to the New Left is the rigid state socialism (or state capitalism) of Eastern Europe, seen to be a gross distortion of Marxism and a collaborator with "the West" in the suppression of Third World interests.

Selections 7.5 through 7.8 provide an exposition and critical evaluation of the contemporary radical analysis of the New Left. In selection 7.5, Franklin and Tabb summarize the New Radical indictment of American capitalism. This critique, while drawing inspiration from the Old Left analysis of capitalism, goes much beyond it. New Left radicals argue that *even if* capitalism were successful, through Keynesian-style macroeconomic policy, in curbing large-scale depressions and unemployment, these other damning indictments of capitalism would remain. What is at issue is not merely "failure" versus "success" in terms of traditional capitalist values, but a challenge to those values themselves. The "challenge of radical political economics" however, is greater than one would infer from a catalog of the "ills of the capitalist system." As described by Franklin and Tabb, the new radicalism forcefully expands the scope of economics discipline (hence the phrase "political economics") at the same time that it turns the tools of economic analysis (some borrowed from Marx, some from traditional economics) to such issues as "urban malaise" and "waste and the GNP mania."

Like Galbraith in *The Affluent Society,* Calvert and Neiman (selection 7.6) identify affluence as a central characteristic of the new capitalism. And like Herbert Marcuse, contemporary Marxist philosopher who has significantly affected New Left analysis,[2] they return to the "early (humanist) Marx" of *The Economic and Philosophical Manuscripts* (recall selection 2.3) for inspiration. According to Calvert and Neiman, the basic "contradictions" of neo-capitalism are those of the "post-scarcity" society. Industrialization has created the potential, through vastly expanded increases in productivity, for a society characterized by the creative use of leisure. But capitalism remains wedded to the anachronistic device of the "work-income connection," churning out an ever-increasing GNP while creating numerous social costs in the process.

[2] See, for example, his *One Dimensional Man* (Boston: Beacon Press, 1964).

In his critique of the New Left (selection 7.7), Assar Lindbeck focuses upon three major issues: market versus bureaucratic processes for resource allocation and economic coordination, centralization versus decentralization of economic decision making, and public versus private ownership of the means of production. His key theme is that the writings of the New Left are internally inconsistent. Like neo-liberalism, they are critical of centralized concentrations of economic power and bureaucracy. But they are also critical of market processes. Lindbeck argues that greater reliance on markets is the only viable alternative to centralized state bureaucracy in coordination of modern economic life; you can choose between the two, but you cannot eliminate both as processes for economic coordination. The concluding selection in this section responds to Lindbeck's critique directly. Stephen Hymer and Frank Roosevelt (selection 7.8) dissent from Lindbeck's "economics paradigm" by suggesting that a Marxian-type analysis provides a more relevant and instructive framework for understanding and reforming capitalism's defects.

7.5 The Challenge of Radical Political Economics

Raymond S. Franklin and William K. Tabb

Radical economists are challenging mainstream views about the subject matter of economics and how the U.S. economy works. Mainstream orthodoxy not only is experiencing erosion as a result of its own inabilities to explain many current economic realities, but also is losing ground as a result of the emergence of new professional groups. Among these are the new grouping of institutional economists and the Union of Radical Political Economics (URPE), whose more than 1,850 members are devoted to radical scholarship and activities.

Perhaps of even greater importance is the fact that the elementary economics course is no longer monopolized by mainstream economics textbooks. This is due in no small part to the reasonably large quantity of new radical material and articles which have been published recently. This new state of affairs represents a sharp contrast to the 1950s, when departments of economics tended to be monolithically Keynesian. That bland Keynesianism complemented the consensus politics and blind optimism of the period.

This article is an interim summary of the major tenets and general orienta-

Excerpted from Raymond S. Franklin and William K. Tabb, "The Challenge of Radical Political Economics," *Journal of Economic Issues* 8, no. 1 (March 1974): 127–50. Reprinted by permission of the publisher and the authors.

tion of radical political economy by two authors who are themselves radical economists.

THE SCOPE OF RADICAL ECONOMICS

Defining the *scope* of radical economics is complex, but five major elements should be noted. These involve the structural transformation of society, centralized planning, the relationship between political and private economic power, wealth and income distribution, and participation in decision making.

Transforming Society

Unlike their welfarist, liberal mainstream counterparts who accept the broad institutional constraints of the existing system, radical economists are interested in the structural transformation of society. They see themselves as working toward ending, not stabilizing, monopoly capitalism, as working for the establishment of a socialist society which involves participatory planning, public ownership, the elimination of production for profit, and a genuinely egalitarian redistribution of income and wealth. They view theorizing not as an end in itself nor as an aesthetic ritual involving rigorous elegance, however irrelevant; rather, they see it as being linked to their advocacy of fundamental change or to their analysis of the barriers which obstruct such change. Economic analysis must deal with problems concerning political and economic power; rarely are solutions only technical in nature, unrelated to the ends or goals established by the given institutional arrangements. Radical economists, therefore, are devoted to providing the theoretical base for a social transformation; their politics are concerned with producing a political and ideological climate that would stimulate institutional changes.

Centralized Planning

While mainstream economists tend to view planning, especially centralized planning, as authoritarian and antidemocratic, radicals believe such a view is a gross oversimplification. They argue that we already have a great deal of such planning and regimentation in the economy, but it is mainly corporate planning for private ends done by a corporate oligarchy that is hierarchical, self-perpetuating, and largely invisible. Public planning with public ownership would broaden participation and widen the arena of public control over the economy. With respect to socialist planning, most radicals favor decentralized forms; decisions should be made as much as possible at the local level, and citizen-consumer and worker-producer planning groups should decide what and how to produce. Many radicals fear centralized control, whether by large corporations, a powerful Council of Economic Advisors, a Wage-Price Control Board, or a GOSPLAN. Decentralization is a critical element because many radical political economists believe "production" should be concerned not only with the goods and services produced but also, and equally, with the work process itself.

Political and Private Economic Power

Radicals see an intimate relationship between the political apparatus that governs society and the economic concentration of private power. Except for periods of widespread mass agitation, the typical state of affairs is one in which the government does not direct but instead reflects or facilitates the interests of wealth and concentrated economic power. In general, the acquisition of political position and power is seen as something akin to the buying of commodities by the highest bidders.

Income and Wealth Distribution

Because the connection of economic with political power is regarded as so crucial, radical economists assert that any basic understanding of the U.S. social order requires a careful analysis of the distribution of wealth and income and of its generation and transmission over time and between generations. They point to gross inequities in the distribution of wealth. Radical economists argue that the unequal distribution of income associated with an unequal distribution of wealth begets an unequal distribution of political power. This imbalance influences the political values, objectives, and policies of the government in ways which curtail social and economic justice and obstruct the economic system's ability to recognize and solve its plaguing problems. In other words, the system is flawed intrinsically by the nature of its hierarchical structure, not simply by the absence of "good" people in Congress or the presence of a "bad" president who did "wrong" things. Because mainstream economists either ignore or casually treat the relationship between political power and economic concentration, they do not understand the nature of the system's policy failures. The conscious overlooking of such interconnections, radicals believe, is *poor* not *pure* social science.

Mass Participation

The normative goals that guide the thinking of most radical economists are mass participation in decision making and the equal sharing of society's income and wealth. In practical terms, this implies that economic differences are to be kept to a minimum within a framework which gives cognizance to the variability in aptitudes, tastes, and psychological temperaments among individuals. This vision of society involves the rejection of the idea of individual gain without respect to the general gain or loss experienced by the group; it stresses the importance of moral over economic incentives.

Radicals reject the mainstream's concept of *efficiency,* which is defined in purely economic and technical terms and which necessitates inequality as a work stimulant. In contemporary U.S. capitalism, the important motivating force that keeps the system functioning "efficiently" is the maintenance of inequities which generate a fear of falling behind Smith and a desire to get ahead of Jones. In a good society, radical economists assert, *efficiency* should have far more than an economic meaning. In its profoundest sense it must involve self-realization through the work process, the worker's control over his own workspace, and a belief that the consumer goods being produced are needed and are important to a good life.

In a market-dominated society, cars are produced with built-in obsolescence in order to keep the wheels of profit rolling; the environment is polluted without consideration of its value to those who yearn for clean air and relish the beauty of a natural terrain; the ''mere'' sentimental value attached to an old landmark building and the security associated with stable neighborhoods is destroyed for the construction of an ''efficient'' superhighway needed by industry. Furthermore, man's morality, sexuality, and sensibility are manipulated for the purpose of the sale of commodities. In sum and substance, U.S. capitalism destroys human relations in order to maintain purely economic ones involving gain, getting ahead, and the private accumulation of things. To allow the market so much importance in the determination of a person's life-style is to attempt to make of man a one-dimensional creature.

These five general propositions and values which relate to the scope of radical economics will be employed below in the analysis of specific areas and problems. For illustrative purposes, we have selected [four] topics: market stratification, urban malaise, waste and the GNP mania, and inflation.

MARKET STRUCTURE AND STRATIFICATION

Mainstream economists tend to argue that the individual's income and his position in society are directly related to his ability, that altering income and social position is simply a function of acquiring a better education or more skills through work experience. Radical economists believe this is a gross oversimplification—so gross as to be erroneous. Far more goes into the determination of income and social position in the economy than education and work experience. A worker sweeping the floors of an automobile plant in Detroit earns much more than an identical worker sweeping the floor in a New York bank. Contrary to typical mainstream thinking on this matter, this difference has nothing to do with variations in education, work experience, native endowment, or I.Q.; it has little to do with the human capital explanation of the mainstream economists. This difference is a function of industry, location, unionism, and industrial structure.

In addition to institutional considerations, a basic part of the radical argument revolves about the role played by a stratified labor market. Because of the need to put people in various kinds of jobs that are undesirable, the system wittingly or unwittingly generates rules (based on race, sex, ethnic and class origin, and so forth) for allocating people to jobs.

At the bottom of the labor market are those who do the dirty work of the society—the lettuce pickers, chambermaids, dishwashers, janitors, messengers, car washers. For the most part these jobs are low paying, dead-end, and alienating. Such secondary jobs have an extremely high turnover rate; people work for awhile, quit or are fired, and then look for other similar jobs. These workers are mostly blacks, Puerto Ricans, Chicanos, women, or teenagers.

On the next rung up are workers who do routine primary work—tedious manual labor such as assembly-line work, construction work, menial sales or clerical work. Some of these jobs offer a chance for promotion, union protection, and better pay; these are mostly held by white ethnics.

The line between primary and secondary jobs is not always distinct; thus a typist in a typing pool or a keypunch operator is generally in the secondary job market, whereas a personal secretary would be in the primary one.

Below the secondary work force is the welfare population. Above the routine primary jobs are the creative workers, for example, professionals, media people, managers and executives. At the very top are those who receive their income from ownership rather than from participation in the labor market.

While not immutable, such stratification has a strong propensity to maintain itself; it will not be altered without profound change in the rules of the game. If, for example, welfare payments rise to levels that people could live on, then the poorly paid low status job loses its stranglehold. Welfare payments (or any income maintenance of minimum income scheme) must not be too adequate, otherwise secondary workers will lose the incentive to work in those jobs. Nor is it clear that a family assistance or negative income tax plan would overcome this incentive problem. If adequate income or decent housing is offered the very poor, then the working poor—who perceive themselves as bearing the tax burden of paying these costs—become upset. Therefore, the basic line for a negative income tax could not be set at livable levels. Again, when the unionized primary workers see government programs aimed at training secondary workers to compete for their jobs, they often turn to demagogues such as George Wallace. A real educational reform which would enable the sons and daughters of the poor and the working class to gain access in proportion to their numbers into Harvard, Yale, and Berkeley would, radicals believe, bring cries of outrage from upper-middle and high income groups.

The perspective of radical economists in examining institutions such as the educational system is that our economy needs stratification; therefore, it needs inequitable rules to maintain the economic privileges and social equilibrium of the existing order. Segmentation in the economy leads to the "freezing" of social distinctions. Job career ladders are superficially contrived in order to nurtuer intra- and intervocational status preoccupations among workers who have neither job satisfaction nor control over work. Occupational divisions of the kind we have been discussing are structured for control. In the absence of more intrinsic work motivation, control is the route to efficiency and profit in a capitalist system.

Mainstream economists, who tend to analyze the economy on the assumption that the structure of preferences and the distribution of income and wealth are exogenously determined, generally bypass the needs of those on the bottom of the economic and social ladder. This is not to argue that the class system is immutable, that its socializing institutions conform perfectly to its structure. To the contrary, a real source of pressure for change derives from the contradictions and dichotomies between the noneconomic and the economic components of the system. Unfortunately, because they lack "tidiness" for the use of "pure" economic tools and methods of measurement, the dynamics of such processes frequently are ignored by mainstream economists. When they make policy recommendations for upward occupational mobility, suggestions are linked closely to the changing economic requirements of the *given* system. This is illustrated by the efforts made over the past few years by human capital economists to justify modest improvements in the educational opportunities for minority groups; such changes are not aimed at eliminating an underclass or menial work. Mainstream economists simply do not think in such terms.

URBAN MALAISE

Consider next the urban scene. Whatever might be said about the condition of U.S. cities today as compared with that of fifty or one hundred years ago, few would disagree with the statement that the gap between what "could be" and "what is" has widened. Why has this happened?

The radical answer starts with the generally recognized fact that those higher up on the stratified pyramid have moved to the suburbs, leaving the poor and their problems in the central cities. Rural and suburban controlled legislatures have aggravated matters by their unwillingness to offer effective help. The advice the urban economist has offered for remedying these circumstances often has been harmful to the powerless. Urban renewal frequently has meant tearing down the homes of the poor and building for those who add to the tax base of the city—the nonpoor. In fact, the most sophisticated computer models often offer as policy the destruction of poor neighborhoods, forcing residents to relocate elsewhere. Such a policy enables average per capita income in the city to rise.

The highway program, if it follows standard economic efficiency criteria, builds highways to and for upper income suburbanites, not for the benefit of low income city dwellers. This is because most of the benefit from highway construction is in the commuting time saved, and time saved for the rich is worth more than the same amount of time saved for the poor. This policy usually is followed because of technical calculations and, more important, because of the relative power of the two groups in influencing decision making.

The logic of economic efficiency is the same logic which perpetuates the inequality of the system. Cities need good mass transit systems, but the system likely to be built will be one that meets the requirements of a stratified society. To build a system which meets the needs of lower income families and individuals, or one which might dramatically upset the automobile industry, would require that social and political struggles be waged against the class biases inherent in the system and against those interests which perpetuate a need for the given distribution of activities.

Mainstream's answer to many of these problems is governmental subsidies. When the radical looks at the nature of these subsidies, he finds that they frequently aid the rich rather than the poor. Contrary to official rhetoric, subsidy payments reflect biases similar to those discussed in relation to mass transit systems. It is not surprising to radicals that the largest single "welfare recipient" in recent times has been Lockheed Aircraft, which received a prize of $250 million for not being an efficient business; or that most farm subsidies go to agribusiness, very few to small farmers, and none to those in most need—the agricultural workers; or that the current methods of financing higher education lead to redistribution of income from the bottom echelons to the middle and upper ones; or that obsolescence in owning oil is given special tax consideration, but not obsolescence in owning a particular skill. Nor is it surprising that the largest single federal housing program is the tax write-off to middle and upper income homeowners.

In the radical view this is the way the state *normally* facilitates capitalist development. Such matters are ignored by mainstream economists, or they are viewed as deviations exposed by liberal muckrakers striving to make capitalism more honest.

WASTE AND THE GNP MANIA

Mainstream economists, at least until very recently, have never doubted the assumption that producing more goods and services automatically was good. John F. Kennedy's 1960 campaign was built around this unquestioned growth fixation. Behind him, giving intellectual credibility to his growth rhetoric, were the country's most prominent welfare liberal economists. Radical economists go beyond mere modification of the growth preoccupation; they see further growth of the kind that presently characterizes U.S. society as detrimental to the well-being of the American people.

The automobile industry is an example. This industry often has been identified as a symbol of the U.S. capacity for great physical output, the energy of its economy, and the well-being of its people. To the radical it has become a symbol of the opposite, a symbol of society's sickness.

A careful study made by a prominent group of mainstream economists estimated the cost of resources which would have been saved had cars with 1949 model lengths, weights, horsepower, transmissions, and so forth, been produced in each year up to 1960. They found that in that period it cost the U.S. public about $40 billion to produce a car which wears down sooner, uses more gas, is less safe, and costs more to maintain. In other words, billions of dollars have been spent in order to make a product which is in many ways inferior to that which we already had.

The automobile industry dramatically illustrates a phenomenon which occurs on a lesser scale in the production of many other goods. It is for good reason, therefore, that most radical economists believe that any serious analysis of the U.S. economy and social order which does not put the large corporation at center stage is irrelevant. To talk about the quality of American life as derived from some kind of value system which is unrelated to a corporation dominated society, as mainstream economists often do, is intellectually obscene.

INFLATION

In the economic history of U.S. capitalism, inflation has been a problem only during periods of acute shortages of goods. These periods all have been associated with war. In the aftermath of World War II and with the assimilation of Keynesian wisdom consisting of monetary manipulation and budgetary deficits, the nature of and explanation for inflation has become a problem to mainstream economists. While government has managed to prevent drastic downward swings in the economy, it has not succeeded in bringing about a sustained high level of employment. Some mainstream economists have described the new situation as being one of "high level stagnation"; that is, an economy in which extreme unemployment such as that of the 1930s has been avoided, but one which does not achieve anything approaching the full utilization of the U.S. labor force. The definition of *full employment* opportunistically has been changed from 2 percent to 4 percent unemployment, and currently there is discussion among some mainstreamers in favor of using 5 percent as the definition.

In a situation of high-level stagnation, a new challenge to mainstream orthodoxy has arisen, a challenge which significantly has disillusioned many mainstream economists. Their numerous *ad hoc* inflation theories involving cost pushes, wage-price spirals, and changing price expectations have not explained the existing situation. Moreover, these numerous theories (despite the high-powered statistical techniques frequently employed to test them) have tended to move farther away from empirical validation and from the standard micro assumptions made by mainstream economists. It was not an accident that very few mainstream economists anticipated the period between 1965 and 1972. That is, very few economists at the time came to grips with the nature of the inflationary process. Only in retrospect, after Richard Nixon did an about-face, did they tend to describe (without analyzing) something closer to the truth.

In a nutshell, the challenge stemmed from the simultaneous development of both inflation and unemployment. The current example of this dual process, which had its origin in the 1965 upsurge in military spending, illustrates what sent mainstream economists into a dither. Wanting to fight an unpopular war, but unwilling to tell the public what it eventually would cost them, the government not only continuously lied (as the Pentagon Papers show), but also did not raise taxes to pay for the war directly. The government feared that an increase in taxes would call attention to the real costs of the war and might lead to a taxpayer's revolt and a strengthening of the antiwar movement.

As the inflationary process at home became more and more unruly, an international monetary crisis developed which reflected a growing competitive struggle among the capitalist nations of Europe and Japan. To cope with domestic inflation, Nixon initially pursued a right-wing Keynesian set of policies, tightening the money supply and trimming the federal budget by reducing needed nonmilitary programs. The Nixon effort at controlling inflation was, in fact, a governmentally induced recession to stabilize prices. Nixon essentially was saying that the cost of slowing down the economy must be borne by workers through unemployment and severely limited wage increases. What went wrong, of course, was that governmentally induced unemployment did not abate the inflation. With one eye on the 1972 elections and another on the international monetary crisis, the President and his conservative Keynesian advisors panicked. Within a short period of time, Nixon moved ideologically from the position of a free market, Milton Friedman type of monetarist to that of a liberal, deficit-oriented Keynesian and then to a Bismarckian, wage-price "socialist" controller. In retrospect it turns out that mainstream fiscal economists underestimated the inflationary dangers and that mainstream money managers underestimated the amount of money supply tightening and of unemployment which would be necessary to stabilize prices.

Mainstream economists have no general explanation for the culmination of this process. At best, their views are ad hoc and fragmented. In contrast, the radical economist would point to the historical and structural context that defines the relations between the monopolistic, competitive, and public sectors. The lead sector in this triad is the monopolistic one, with its ability to maintain or increase profits because of its market power even in the face of restricted demand. Wage patterns established in the more productive monopolistic sector to some extent spill over into less productive public and competitive sectors. The politics of the public sector have led to accelerated increases in cost without corresponding increases in output or improvement in services by the public sector. The rising costs experienced in the competitive sector tend to lower its profits since businessmen in this sector are unable to pass on cost increases in the form of higher prices. Workers in this sector find it difficult to make a decent living; many appropriately have been identified as "the working poor."

In the postwar period large amounts of government funds have been funneled into the defense and other concentrated sectors of the economy, but the main benefits of such public expenditure have been appropriated by those least in need. Even though the profits in the monopolistic sector have been large at various intervals, they have not stimulated the absorption of the unemployed or the movement of workers from low wage to high wage sectors. This condition has not led to a revolt against corporate privilege; rather, it has stimulated the middle layers of society to focus their anger downward against the lower class. For social class reasons, the middle class erroneously has come to believe that the bulk of its hard-earned taxable income is funneled into wasteful governmental programs to help "ungrateful" blacks. As a result, the government has found it increasingly difficult to justify its expenditures and tax collections and therefore has had to pursue excessive deficit spending in a context of high-level stagnation. The outcome, despite all the governmental hustling and bustling, has been unemployment and inflation.

The public's seemingly misallocated distrust of the public sector, at a time when more and more of our problems appear to require an increase in the public sector's direct involvement, may be perfectly reasonable. The government simply is not delivering the goods. What the public does not understand sufficiently is why this is the case and how the government's deficiencies are related to the needs, power, and policies of the giant corporations. On this question mainstream economists with their neoclassical focus have little to say.

Radicals believe that a simplified Marxian macro model which divides the economy into its class components (for example, workers and capitalists) in the context of a specified structure explains more than the Keynesian groupings of the economy into consumers, investors, and government. In the radical view the mainstream's glib dismissal of a class analysis represents a basic conceptual deficiency in their mode of analysis of both developed and underdeveloped societies. The radical response to mainstream's more "functional" categories is to ask: Should we treat both Jim Bass and David Rockefeller as consumers? Is the corner gas station owner an investor in the same sense as the committee that runs Texaco or General Motors?

SUMMARY

Radical economists see the U.S. economy as primarily dominated by the monopolistic sector, consisting of corporate giants. More generally, the government acts to support class privilege and re-create it intergenerationally through the workings of its major institutions, for example, education, health, police, and the judiciary. This class bias on the part of the government does not necessarily eliminate the possibility of achieving modest reforms through the political process. But, from the radical perspective, reforms conceived within the *modus vivendi* of existing institutions cannot be consequential.

Most liberals and conservatives argue within a common framework. Both tend to accept as a premise that the key goal is economic growth, although they sometimes argue about how the benefits of this growth are to be distributed. For both, the key is how to use resources more efficiently. Since the basic instruments of economic growth in a capitalist economy lie within private corporations, the key to growth is to aid these corporations.

Mainstream economists begin with the question of how, given the existing market structure, legal framework, and so forth, we can best stabilize capitalism (prevent economic crises, help it grow, and so forth). Radicals ask how society can be restructured to fulfill different goals and needs, those which relate to cultivating a different national style of life: a different work process, a different sense of community and neighborhood, different social relations, and a different mode of solving society's problems. To radical economists, such changes cannot occur until commerce, private property and its corresponding privileges, and profit cease to dominate the main aspects of U.S. society. Their politics revolve around class agitation and advocacy programs aimed at nurturing new centers of power among the less privileged members of society. Their intellectual labor is devoted to criticizing mainstream arguments, ideas, theories, and policy recommendations and to exposing the class biases of mainstream recommendations.

While part of what ails U.S. society may be related to industrialism per se, a significant part of the malaise is related to the characteristics of U.S. capitalism itself. It is the radical claim that many of these specific characteristics are not being seriously analyzed by mainstream economists. The persistence of grave economic and social problems capable of breeding social unrest is the basis for the belief that the growth of a new group of radical economists is permanent.

7.6 Neocapitalism and the New Left

Greg Calvert and Carol Neiman

Neocapitalism and the New Contradictions

The appearance of the New Left in the advanced capitalist countries is the direct result of the development of new objective conditions and new economic, social, and political contradictions. Its political activists are people (especially young people) who are expressing human needs which break radically with the dominant culture and point toward a qualitatively different life and civilization. . . . The failure of the old Marxist-Leninist orthodoxy to face this new reality is basic to the dogmatic misunderstanding which characterizes the attitude of the Old Left towards new leftists.

Most importantly, it seems clear that material scarcity did not provide the basic conditions for the development of the New Left's negation of capitalist society in the industrialized world. The New Left is a reaction to societies characterized by a high level of individual consumption for an important segment of the population, production for waste in previously unimaginable proportions, and the relegation of the "class struggle" in the form of the fight for higher wages to the arena of collective bargaining for an increasingly large slice of an increasingly large pie. This is not to deny that poverty is the determining fact of life for an important segment of the population. The rural and urban poor and unemployed account for perhaps as much as twenty percent of the population of the advanced industrial world, and poverty remains the fundamental economic condition of much of the neocolonial Third World. Nevertheless, it is in the midst of the consuming strata of the consumer society that the New Left has grown and rebelled. Furthermore, poverty in the advanced capitalist world will not provide the basis for a broadly based movement for radical social transformation.

The last generation has witnessed the internal transformation of capitalist society in dimensions which are sufficient to assume the form of a new stage of capitalist development. The nature of this new era determines the conditions for the revolt of the New Left. . . .

We are living in [a] stage of capitalist development, . . . which is called

---

Excerpted from Greg Calvert and Carol Neiman, *A Disrupted History: The New Left and the New Capitalism* (New York: Random House, 1971). Reprinted by permission of the publisher.

variously "neocapitalism" or "corporate capitalism." After the stages of laissez faire and of monopolization, capitalism has entered a new era of development. Just as the era of laissez faire was characterized by competition and the building of the infrastructure of capitalist industrialization, and the era of monopoly capitalism was characterized by the consolidation of control by finance capital and the conquest of foreign markets through imperialism, so the third stage of development, neocapitalism, is characterized by the control of the economy by the giant corporations and the intensive expansion and development of investment, production, and the market within the advanced capitalist nations. The result is that a large majority of the "super profits" of capitalism are being reaped from domestic capitalist investments rather than from investment abroad. . . .

In this new stage, capitalism has developed agriculture through the application of industrial technology (mechanization and agricultural science); it has raised the living standards of the masses within the capitalist countries (through the development of the internal consumer market); and it has even created additional, nonproductive outlets for investment in the development of waste production (military investment and a variety of planned obsolescences).

. . . These developments . . . lead toward . . . an understanding of the real possibility and necessity of a revolutionary socialist transformation of capitalist society. What is required, however, is a much deeper understanding of the meaning of socialism and its potential for human liberation *and* a new strategy and new approach embodying an understanding of the new contradictions in neocapitalism, plus the conscious redefinition of the meaning of those values which are inseparable from a truly socialist perspective—freedom, democracy, and human creativity. It is precisely in these directions that the New Left must move if it is to develop a *radical* challenge to capitalism.

Furthermore . . . the problem is much more profound than the analysis of super profits and the buying off of a labor aristocracy. A much more basic phenomenon involves the *integration* of trade union demands for higher wages and shorter hours. After the period of primitive capital accumulation and the building of the economic infrastructure of industrial production, the need for the maintenance of wages and hours at their Draconian, mid-nineteenth century levels was less and less pressing. It became possible for capitalists to raise both real wages *and* real profits with rising per capita productivity. In fact, with the introduction of the new production techniques of the 1920s (and finally the methods of automated and cybernated production of the '50s and '60s), rising consumption levels among all working strata of the population became necessary to the economic survival of capitalist production—necessary in order to absorb the increased product and to avoid the cyclical crises of overproduction.

Thus the determinist theses of the Old Left—increasing material impoverishment and inevitable economic breakdown—are rendered less central by the internal development of advanced capitalism. Increased consumption to provide a growing domestic market and government intervention in order to stabilize the business cycle have become major concerns of the "enlightened" wing of the corporate governing class. This drawing together of corporate economic power and the structures of the state apparatus has yielded a variety of bureaucratic state capitalism which brings all aspects of social and economic existence under greater and greater centralized control.

* * *

COMPULSIVE CONSUMPTION AND WASTE

When Establishment sources express the fear that a new generation of young Americans is rejecting consumption as a goal and definition of their lives, it expresses a very real concern on the part of the corporate establishment about its economic future and its historical *raison d'etre*. In place of isolation, powerlessness, meaningless work, and lives defined as the production, ownership, and consumption of commodities, they are demanding community, love, creativity, and power over their own lives. It is a revolt of being, of Eros, against the plastic, boring, dehumanizing world, with its values of domination and exploitation, which brutalizes two-thirds of the world's people in order to maintain power and profit abroad while creating an anesthetized and deeroticized plastic population in the midst of a garbage heap at home.

Neocapitalist society, with its emphasis on compulsive individual consumption, waste production, and mass culture, lays the basis for the "one-dimensional society" which Marcuse describes so eloquently. The need for the total organization of economic life leads also to the totalitarian organization of culture and ideology. At the level of cultural life, mass culture becomes both a product for sale and a mechanism of social control and pacification. Mass media not only fill the compulsive neurotic needs which maintain the domestic market, but also produce the canned news which maintains the dominant ideology. Because neocapitalism demands steadily increasing consumption, it requires a break with the ideologies of scarcity which previously justified class society and provided solace for a suffering humanity.

The development of Madison Avenue techniques for the stimulation of compulsive individual consumption together with the vast expansion of consumer credit facilities has created new artificial needs for a people whose choices are limited and directed in the absence of rational economic organization for real human need and social development. Instead of a transportation system which would get people safely, quickly, comfortably, and cheaply from one place to another we are provided with a concrete-and-asphalt landscape, cars which are designed to fall apart, and slick advertising which offers us sexual fantasies in place of sexual freedom and real Eros. . . .

NEOCAPITALISM AND SOCIAL PACIFICATION

The success of the neocapitalist social order depends on its ability to deliver the goods (the consumer goods) and on the willingness of the vast majority of the working population to accept individual consumption as the sole measure of its freedom and well-being. Neocapitalist reforms have never been a totally coherent program in the United States quite simply because not all American capitalists have been as enlightened about their long-range self-interest as men like FDR and RFK. Roosevelt's neocapitalist New Deal was obtained in the face of virulent opposition from those representatives of the governing class who refused to recognize that in the era of advanced capitalism the policies of laissez faire cannot cope with the real problems.

The failure of integration and social pacification to maintain a totally docile population can only increase as the irrationality of advanced capitalist production becomes more apparent. In particular the emergence of the new technology of automation and cybernation and the potential for post-scarcity inherent in the present period creates a new vision, and the possibility of a qualitatively different kind of civilization—the possibility of nonrepressive society and the elimination of alienated labor.

* * *

Much of the New Left has remained justifiably uncomfortable with "Marxism" as a framework for revolutionary thought. Certainly the official mysticism of "the science of Marxism-Leninism" or "dialectical-materialism" can be rejected. Most of the recent attempts of the New Left to integrate Marxian theory into political practice have emphasized the "early (humanist) Marx" of the 1840s or have concentrated their efforts on the writings which directly preceded *Capital* (the *Grundrisse* and the *Contribution to the Critique of Political Economy*). This latter emphasis returns to the intriguing historical question of the nineteenth century: Is there a fundamental contradiction in capitalism which is based in the economic dynamics of the system itself? The answer seems to be yes, but a very different yes than that which has been passed off as "Marxist" and "scientific."

Scarcity, Post-Scarcity, and the Fundamental Contradiction

Capitalist industrialization, especially in the age of emerging cybernated production, offers the possibility for producing in abundance those material goods necessary for human survival, reproduction, and well-being, but frustrates the realization of this potential because of the necessity of maintaining the mechanisms for the appropriation of profit (surplus value). Put simply, this means that our productive resources are such that people could live without working but that capitalism requires that people work in order to live. The common-sense question might be: why not just give things away? The answer is that giving things away provides no mechanism (market) for appropriating profit, therefore people must work and earn incomes so that they can buy on the market the goods which are produced.

In its simplest terms, the fundamental socio-economic contradiction in capitalism grows out of the "work-income" relation as mediated by the market—the market for labor as well as goods. In neocapitalist society you have to work in order to live despite the fact that living without working is the potential of capitalist economic and technological development. Instead of abolishing the market and fully automating production in order to eliminate scarcity and alienated work, capitalism produces more waste, more alienating jobs, and encourages antisocial and repressive patterns of consumption. For capitalism there is no way out of this dilemma: the market must be maintained and jobs must be created (however useless) and consumption must continue to rise (even if it requires built-in obsolescence) in order that profits continue to be made no matter what the human cost of the whole enterprise. For, human costs are not entered in the account books of large corporations, and capitalism is a system of production for profit rather than for use.

* * *

[The capitalist] system may have produced an increasingly dehumanized and alienated society with all kinds of brutality and inhumanity, but it seemed to make a good deal of sense as long as the capitalists were involved in building up the productive forces of the economy. But what happens when that period of building-up (the period of primitive capital accumulation) is finished? What happens when the productive forces which the capitalists have organized begin to exceed the primitive needs which the system is designed to satisfy? What happens when the development of advanced technology brings a higher and higher rate of per capita productivity?

What happens is quite simple—and exceedingly explosive. On the one hand, human labor (manpower) becomes increasingly peripheral to the productive power of machines. On the other hand, human labor becomes increasingly utilized for nonproductive ends. And, increasingly for the capitalists, the problem is no longer a problem of how to produce more, but of how to dispose of what is produced. This is where the "fundamental contradiction" begins to produce serious difficulties; this is the point at which the "social relations of production" become a serious barrier to the "material forces of production" which capitalism has created. . . .

The fundamental contradiction in capitalism can be expressed as follows: it is the contradiction between the productive capacity (the material forces of production) and the necessity to extract a profit from production (based on the social relations of production, private ownership of capital and wage labor). Capitalism creates a productive potential which is capable of transcending the problem of scarcity, but, in order to maintain the profit system (or, rather, the system of appropriation of surplus value) it maintains the economy of scarcity. Although it is capable of producing abundance for all, the necessity of realizing a profit prevents it from either utilizing its full productive capacity or from a rational distribution of what it does produce. Capitalism has thus entered a phase (neocapitalism) where it is increasingly faced with the necessity of the expansion of the market in order to survive, in order to distribute (profitably) its excess surplus. Yet, it cannot expand its market by producing for the unemployed poor—that would not yield a profit.

In its simplest terms, the contradiction of advanced capitalism is expressed as the *necessity for the maintenance of the work-income connection*. In order to extract a profit, capitalism must maintain both sides of the market mechanism—wages for labor and prices for goods. It is not simply a matter of having to work in order to consume. One must work for wages (less than the value of the product produced) in order to have money to buy goods at a price which yields profits. Without money and the market mechanism, there is no capitalist system of profit accumulation and the economy would operate for human need (use-value) rather than for profit (exchange-value). The absolute necessity for the conversion of use value into exchange value (and the conversion of all relationships into relationships based on money) remains the fundamental characteristic of capitalist production. Break the work-income connection, and you will have destroyed the capitalist system—but that will not happen without the revolutionary transformation of the social relations of production.

In an underdeveloped or developing capitalism, the full weight of this contradiction is by no means apparent.

Under advanced neocapitalism, the real nature of the contradiction exposes itself in full force. Once scarcity is no longer the central focus, and once primitive capital accumulation has produced self-generating technological development, the full implication of the work-income connection is revealed as the very heart of capitalist society.

A primitive example of this phenomenon can be supplied from the agricultural sector of the economy. It is clear that the mechanization of agriculture in the United States has created a productive potential which far exceeds the needs of the American people. Yet, millions of poor people go hungry in this country. In order to maintain the high profits in agriculture which are the result of its capitalist nature (and which do not accrue for the most part to people who work the land), high food prices are maintained through the enforced limitation of production; land is taken out of cultivation (soil bank program) and sometimes produce is destroyed. Why not give it away?—the naïve observer asks again. You cannot give commodities away, for that would undermine the whole system of private ownership and the market mechanism!—the capitalist apologist is forced to reply. Even common sense is struck by the absurdity of this proposition.

It is at least clear from this example that although capitalist agriculture is capable of producing all that we need to eat, capitalism is incapable of transcending the realm of scarcity regarding the question of human nourishment. Thus the potential for post-scarcity which capitalism creates remains permanently unrealized as long as capitalist relations are maintained. The irrationality of such a system was apparent to many millions of hungry Americans during the Great Depression of the 1930s. While many went without food because there were no jobs whereby they could earn the wages necessary to subsist, the government was exhorting the farmers to "kill and plow under" in order to prevent the production of a "surplus" which would keep agricultural prices down—a highly irrational and inhuman solution to the problem of abundance. The only real solution would have involved the destruction of those "social relations of production" which fettered the "material forces of production"—but that is precisely what the neocapitalist regime of Roosevelt was determined to prevent.

* * *

The problem is much broader than food. Children in the ghetto are also without necessary shoes and clothing in an economy which spends millions of dollars on advertising designed to promote fads which encourage people to throw away their entire wardrobe every six months. But, because of the work-income necessity, ghetto children remain unclothed while plant and machinery remain idle or produce garbage. What's more, the fathers of ghetto children cannot find jobs because the economy does not need their labor. The machines could produce the goods—but he who would consume without working does not promote the necessary capitalist accumulation of profit.

There is only one logical deduction which any sensible person can make: the system which is based on profit accumulation is obsolete and the class which accumulates the profits is obsolete. Both the class and their system no longer serve a useful historical function: in fact they promote increasing absurdity and inhumanity in our lives when freedom from both scarcity and from alienated labor are possible.

THE NEW DEMANDS

Too often in the past, the question of social revolution was presented in the guise of a vengeful expropriation of the rich by the exploited. The have-nots would seize the wealth of the haves. This . . . . is a notion which makes some sense in the context of early industrialization and the reactions of an artisanry which finds itself face to face with proletarianization. It is, however, a naïve and primitive model of revolution which ignores the fact that real wealth is social wealth. It is not the "riches" of the "wealthy" which constitute the real wealth of an advanced industrial society but the enormous productive capacity of the society as a whole. The capitalist governing class is a historically reactionary force, not because it lives better or consumes more commodities, but because its power over society through control of the means of production prevents the realization of the historical potential for liberation which exists. The capitalist class is opposed not because it is "better off" but because it enslaves us in a system of commodity production and commodity consumption and is willing to resort to force and violence in order to maintain its control over production, resources, and markets.

The revolutionary transformation of capitalist society is not a question of "soaking the rich." It is rather the question of the transformation of a social system and social structures, of depriving those who have power of their control over social wealth in order that we may create a free society and contribute to the creation of a free world. When the New Left talks of transforming the relationships of power, it does not conceive of re-establishing the system of domination with a new form of dominative power. That kind of power is of no human interest and of no human use. Rather, the drive is aimed at the transformation of a system in which "power" is equivalent to "domination" and the creation of a society in which power becomes the ability of all men to realize their creative and productive potential as human beings in a common and collective effort. To reiterate, the major objection to the capitalist class and the capitalist system is not the "things" possessed by a few, but the fact that capitalism is a power over our lives which forces us to do wasteful and meaningless things when we want to do something radically different and marvelously new.

A key factor in the understanding of every period of human social and economic development is the "size and mode of utilization of the economic surplus." The key relationship (the social relations of production) in every socioeconomic configuration is based on the system of appropriation of that economic surplus. Thus, these social relations of production are the *class relationships* of every society and the *ruling class* in a given society is quite simply that group which determines the use of the economic surplus through its control of the means of production and exchange.

The historically progressive character of the capitalist class as the new ruling class in modern history grew out of the specific capitalist mode of utilization of the economic surplus. By sweeping aside the medieval order and instituting the total reorganization of production on the basis of wage labor, the capitalist class was able not only to increase the economic surplus but also to revolutionize the means of production through the investment of accumulated capital in the creation of modern industry. The industrial revolution, the greatest achievement of capitalist organization, gave rise first to the steady and rapid increase in per capita productivity. Secondly, it created an advanced technology, cybernated production, under which production is decreasingly tied to human labor power and increasingly the outgrowth of the application of scientific problem-solving. In so doing, the capitalist class has fulfilled its historic role and set the stage for a new era in human history.

The real challenge which the New Left can present in the midst of mature capitalism is based on precisely these issues. Its long-range potential lies in a struggle against the repressive uses of productive power, and for a new social order in which the liberating potential of post-scarcity can be realized. The New Left is the historical embryo of a new society in which men would be free from alienated labor and the restraints of repressive civilization and able to create a new culture of freedom on the basis of new human relationships and values.

Capitalism cannot create those new values nor can it realize the potential of post-scarcity. It is trapped within its own dynamic and must maintain the "upward spiral" of increasing production and increasing individual consumption. It has created the conditions in which human labor becomes increasingly superfluous and yet it cannot free human energy from alienated work. It has created "surplus labor" but it cannot create a free society.

It is only at this advanced stage of development that the contradiction between the economic potential and the way in which it is used and perverted emerges with full force. The frustration of that potential by capitalist structures gives rise to the new forms of social revolt in advanced capitalism and provides the social basis for the emergence of the New Left.

The changing basis of revolt is only barely perceived but its further development is inevitable. In the period of primitive capital accumulation, the very fact of surplus appropriation was seen as the heart of the capitalist system. In the neocapitalist period, it is not the raw fact of exploitation but rather the mode of utilization of the surplus which comes increasingly under attack. The growing utilization of human and material resources for wasteful and antisocial ends—experienced as oppression both in ''work'' and ''leisure''—becomes the basis for a whole new set of revolutionary demands; post-scarcity, the elimination of alienated labor, a nonrepressive culture. None of these can be achieved without the elimination of production for profit and its corollary, the marketplace, nor without decentralization and grass-roots democracy. Both the economic dynamics and the social relationships of capital must be transformed.

7.7 The Political Economy of the New Left: An Outsider's View

Assar Lindbeck

MARKETS VERSUS FORMALIZED ADMINISTRATIVE PROCESSES ("BUREAUCRACY")

One characteristic feature of the New Left movement is that most of its adherents are strongly opposed to markets. In the literature of the New Left, a market system is denounced as primitive, inefficient, chaotic, antisocial, unfair, and basically immoral.

One problem with this position is that most of the New Left's writers in this field are also strongly opposed to bureaucracy, that is, to formalized hierarchical administrative procedures. . . . It may be possible to make a strong case against either markets or administrative systems, but if we are against *both* we are in trouble; there is hardly a third method for allocating resources and coordinating economic decisions, if we eliminate physical force. Both markets and administrative procedures may, of course, take many different forms: Markets may be more or less competitive and administrative procedures more or less centralized, with some decision-making by vote, and so on. *Thus, the more strongly we are against bureaucracy, the more we should be in favor of markets.*

. . . . However, I think it is fair to say that most followers of the New Left have never faced up to the fact that we must have *some* mechanism for (1) obtaining *information* about preferences; (2) *allocating* resources to different sectors in accordance with these preferences; (3) deciding which *production*

Abridged from pp. 32–33, 35–37, 48–63, and 65–67 in *The Political Economy of the New Left* by Assar Lindbeck. Copyright © 1971 by Assar Lindbeck. By permission of Harper & Row, Publishers, Inc.

techniques to use; (4) creating *incentives* to economize in the use of resources, to invest, and to develop new technologies; and finally, (5) *coordinating* the decisions of millions of individual firms and households to make them consistent, so that each industry produces just so much and in exactly those quantities that are desired not only by households but also by firms producing millions of other commodities.

The need to specify a mechanism to perform all of these functions is also neglected by the best-known authors who have inspired the New Left. Instead of facing the problem, they usually propose such formulations as this one by Paul Baran: "a society can be developed in which the individual would be formed, influenced, and educated . . . by a system of rationally planned production for use, by a universe of human relations determined by and oriented toward solidarity, cooperation, and freedom." Or, as Baran has also said, optimal uses of resources in a planned economy "represent a considered judgement of a socialist community guided by reason and science." Others have commented simply that production should be directed toward the "true" needs of the individual and not toward the *wants* expressed in the marketplace. Such formulations are typical of what we find in New Left literature about allocation problems. . . .

Among the "anarchistic" wing of the New Left, the idea is presumably that economic decisions should be undertaken in about the same way as they are made in a democratic family in a primitive subsistence economy. The ideal seems to be some kind of "council democracy," in which people are supposed to convince one another or in which decisions are taken by general vote. It is possible that such a model would function in an agrarian society consisting of a number of rather isolated Robinson-Crusoe economies. However, it is an industrial society we live in, and the complexities inherent in the process of production and exchange not only call for specialization within individual firms but also presuppose that information is obtained regarding the wishes of millions of individuals *outside* the separate decision-making institutions and finally requires that billions of decisions by millions of different units be coordinated and made consistent. In a system of this type, central administrative planning and markets—or rather, various combinations of these two methods—are the only appropriate alternatives we know of.

* * *

In general, the New Left neglects, or is unaware of, the development of the theory of socialist planning which was largely inspired by the Lange-Lerner model for decentralized market socialism developed during the thirties. Similarly, New Left critics have not incorporated into their thinking the analysis of the techniques of economic planning in socialist as well as in capitalist market systems.

It is easy to find a rather scornful attitude in New Left literature toward the idea of a capitalist Welfare State. Sometimes this attitude seems to reflect a critical feeling toward the state in general, presumably partly a heritage from the Marxist theory of the state as a tool for the repression of workers by the capitalists. For example, Marcuse has argued that the Welfare State is "a state of unfreedom." The idea that workers are repressed by the modern Welfare State, a notion quite consistent with the Marxist theory of the state, surely must sound somewhat paradoxical to labor parties in Western Europe, which, though often opposed by the richest part of the population, contributed to the establishment of the modern Welfare State. Sometimes it is striking how closely some New Left criticism of the Welfare State resembles the old Right's fears that increased powers to public authorities would bring the end of individual freedom. This partial convergence of the New Left with the old Right seems, however, to be more characteristic of the American than the European scene. The antipathy toward government is so strongly shared by the extreme (libertarian) Right and part of the New Left that the line heads back on itself and joins a circle, with the extremes meeting. . . .

To some extent, New Left criticism of the Welfare State may also be a heritage from the classical dilemma of revolutionary socialism, where there has always tended to be a conflict between short-run and the long-run perspectives. If a Welfare State is established within the capitalist society, and many of the injustices and insecurities are thereby removed, how can a climate be created suitable for the overthrow of the system in the long run?

CENTRALIZATION VERSUS DECENTRALIZATION

Related to the problem of the choice between markets and bureaucracy, though not quite the same issue, is the choice between decentralization and centralization. An obvious link between these two problems is, of course, the fact that a market system is consistent with relatively far-reaching decentralization, whereas in a nonmarket system decisions have to be coordinated by some central authority. In fact, a market economy may be considered mainly as a method of achieving decentralization in economic systems, while at the same time bringing about coordination of economic decisions. *Thus, the more we like decentralization, the more we should favor market systems.* . . .

When economists advocate a heavy reliance on decentralized market systems with competing firms, they usually mention the high costs of collecting and processing information in highly centralized systems, as compared to those in market systems (in which changes in prices and in the quantities demanded transmit the necessary information to producers and consumers). Economists have also sometimes suggested that in systems based on central administrative processes some types of undistorted information may be virtually unobtainable at *any* cost. As regards consumer preferences, this conclusion, of course, follows directly from the theory of the subjective nature of individual preferences. However, there are also enormous difficulties on the production side because of the heterogeneity of products and production processes, which make *specific* knowledge about "time and place" crucial for rational decisions and hence for economic efficiency.

A specific problem affecting centralized administrative processes, designed to direct in detail the allocation of resources, particularly in complex economies, is that these processes in reality imply several "layers" of administrative bodies between the firm and top decision-makers. When information is "filtered" through these layers, it may be a reasonable hypothesis that most of the information is lost and that part of what remains is distorted. . . .

Obviously, deficiencies in information and coordination are not confined to central administrative systems. Decentralized systems also suffer from inadequate information and coordination. For instance, in decentralized systems there is an obvious risk that macroinformation (information about the economy as a whole, sometimes available to high-level administrative bodies) is not known or considered at the level of the firm. Individual firms may thus plan according to unrealistic and inconsistent assumptions about the *general* level of economic activity and the growth rate for the economy as a whole, running the risk of temporary overcapacity and various types of macroeconomic instabilities. In market economics this means that coordination of investment decisions might thus be improved by a centralized collection of information. This is, of course, one of the main arguments for some kind of "indicative planning" of the kind used in France, Japan and, perhaps to a smaller extent, in the Scandinavian countries.

These considerations are very relevant to an evaluation of the ideas of the New Left; very strong sympathies for decentralization are usually expressed in New Left literature. In this respect, the New Left also deviates from the main tradition of the old Left, which in general was more centralist in its outlook, with more emphasis on central planning. One reason for this difference may be that the young generation today has experienced the problems connected both with tendencies toward centralization in capitalist societies, in large corporations as well as in the state, and the much more far-reaching centralization in most communist countries. However, some of the "older" inspirers of the New Left have also expressed a strong antipathy to centralization, unlike the more "traditional" Marxists such as Maurice Dobb, and to some extent also Baran and Sweezy. An example is Mandel: It is his position that in an economy which is characterized by "planned bureaucracy and centralized fashion . . . sacrifices are imposed without the victims being asked their views and without obtaining *their prior consent*. Such a system of management is contrary to the principles of socialism, and furthermore it leads to economic results which are inferior to those of a more democratic system of management."

One basic dilemma for the New Left . . . is that its strong sympathy for decentralization is difficult to reconcile with its rejection of the market system, which presumably is the only type of economic system that permits far-reaching decentralization in complex industrial societies. The dilemma is complicated further by the fact that some New Leftists—sometimes also just those who favor decentralization—often also advocate more central social and economic planning. In this respect the New Left is to some extent confronted by the same dilemma that faced the syndicalist movement, which also simultaneously emphasized decentralization and central planning.

The classical way of escaping, rather than solving, this type of dilemma is presumably to argue that centralization is necessary in the short run but that in the future society far-reaching decentralization will in fact be implemented—an idea related to the Marxist notion of the ''withering away'' of the state in the long run. . . .

Finding an optimal combination of centralization and decentralization —and of markets and administrative procedures—is, of course, a *general* problem rather than a problem for the New Left specifically. What makes the dilemma particularly striking for the New Left, however, is that few groups in society are at the same time both so strongly against markets and bureaucracy and so much in favor of decentralization (though sometimes, as indicated, also demanding more central planning).

* * *

A related characteristic of the New Left movement is its advocacy of decentralization *within* firms and other organizations, often formulated as a criticism of the ''hierarchical structure'' in decision-making procedures within prevailing organizations, and its related assertions about alienation of employees. Many writers demand more democratic decision-making procedures, sometimes calling for ''participatory,'' or ''direct'' democracy. Mandel and Gorz are among those who have emphasized ''workers' control.''

In general, it seems that the New Left has made the lack of democracy in present capitalist societies one of the main targets in its criticism of capitalism. Thus, the old demand for workers' control of factories, or possibly community control, now often supplemented by the demand for student control of universities, has been one of the most characteristic features of the New Left's position, often expressed as a demand for ''control of our own lives.''

It can hardly be denied that most firms and other organizations in current societies have a hierarchical decision-making structure. Nor is it self-evident that these structures always result in the most efficient way of running organizations. And even if it were the most efficient way, there would, of course, still be the question of whether the gains in efficiency were worth possible, largely unknown, losses of other kinds, such as in ''personal satisfaction on the job.'' From this point of view, there seem to be strong reasons for experimentation with new forms of decision-making structures within various kinds of organizations and also to follow with interest the experiments with more ''democratic'' decision-making procedures in some countries: for example, workers' councils in Yugoslavia and, on a smaller scale and with more limited tasks, in Norway, where in a few selected firms, there have been experiments with ''self-managed'' groups of workers, a result of cooperation between employer and employee organizations.

Actually, the issue of more democratic decision-making procedures and workers' participation is, of course, closely connected with the issue of property rights and hence the ownership of the means of production; one important component of property rights is the choice of decision-making procedures within firms, which may vary considerably even without any change in the *formal* ownership of the means of production. The meaning of "ownership" is quite relative and depends entirely on the laws and administrative practices of the respective countries. This brings us to the next issue—the structure of ownership of the means of production.

OWNERSHIP OF CAPITAL

The New Left has a very egalitarian approach to society, thus following a basic theme in the socialist tradition. As among socialists in general, this leads to strong criticism of the structure of ownership in present societies.

The classical (and possibly the strongest moral and emotional) argument against private capitalism and in favor of collective ownership may be expressed by the rhetorical quest for equality: Why should wealth—and thereby also income and economic power—be as unevenly distributed as it is in present capitalist societies? . . . It has to be admitted, however, that some problems of private capitalism certainly are not solved by collective ownership and that some new problems would certainly arise.

Let us first look at some of the problems of private capitalism that are not solved automatically by public ownership. In present societies, capital in the form of physical and financial assets obviously accounts for only part of the total stock of wealth in the economy. A large and growing part of the capital stock consists of capital in the form of acquired education and training—what in recent years has been baptized "human capital." . . . Thus, assuming that human capital cannot be nationalized (provided slavery is not acceptable!), the nationalization of physical and financial capital would remove only part, and probably a diminishing part, of the total capital stock from private to collective hands. Of course, the nationalization of physical and financial capital by itself would have important, not to say drastic, effects on the distribution of income, wealth, and power in society.

The most obvious substitute for nationalization of human capital is probably nationalization of (part of) the *return* on human capital, for instance by progressive taxation. A much more efficient method, in the long run, is probably an expansion of the educational system to increase the supply of highly educated people, thus influencing wage differentials. However, then we are in the world of conventional liberal-social democratic policies, in which various kinds of inequalities in the distribution of income have always, though not necessarily successfully, been fought in this way.

* * *

Another problem that is not automatically solved by collective ownership is, of course, the distribution of *power* in society, particularly under a relatively centralized form of collective ownership and management. In several capitalist countries, such as the United States . . . there is an obvious tendency for economic, political, and military power to be concentrated in the same hands. Certainly this is illustrated by the amazing political power of economically strong and well-organized pressure groups in the United States; with the well-known ability in many cases to bring about legislation in their own favor—tax loopholes, subsidies and protection of agriculture and industry, regulation of certain industries—at the same time that underprivileged minorities are unable to obtain good education, elementary health care, and, in some cases, even sufficient food.

It is quite possible that a society with collective ownership of capital can solve some of these problems by wiping out privileges and helping poor minority groups to attain a decent life, depending on the values, honesty, and altruism of the administrators. It is not very likely, however, that the problem of the distribution of economic and political power will be solved. In the case of a centralist solution of the problem of collective ownership—nationalization—we would expect the problem to be accentuated, for then the bulk of economic power over physical assets would be concentrated in the "one hand" which also happens to exert political and military power: that is, the hand of centrally placed politicians and administrators. For instance, though in some capitalist countries today we have a strong military-industrial complex, sometimes stimulating an aggressive foreign policy, it does not seem convincing to argue that nationalization would necessarily make a country less inclined to use a combination of economic, political, and military force to promote high military spending and an aggressive foreign policy. . . .

No doubt there is some awareness among the New Left of the risks inherent in a concentration of power in nationalized economies as expressed both in its sympathy for decentralization and in its criticism of the Soviet system. . . .

Personally, I feel that the correlation between the structure of ownership, on the one hand, and political and social conditions, on the other, is in reality rather vague. . . . Thus, both the allocation of resources and social conditions—such as the quality of public services and the treatment of minorities—vary considerably among countries with (mainly) nationalized physical capital. Similar variations are to be found in countries with mainly private ownership. Compare, for instance, phenomena such as the level of military spending on defense (and attack!), the existence of slums, social security, the quality of public services, the existence of discrimination, racism, the commitment to redistribution of income, and so on, in different countries with (approximately) the same ownership structure in the industrial sector (90 percent private ownership of the capital in industry, banking, and agriculture), such as the United States and the Scandinavian countries. These dissimilarities in social conditions are partly related to the fact that different countries with the same *formal* structure of ownership, by way of legislation and social and economic policies, have given the concept of ownership different contents.

This is of course no denial of the possibility that in the future there may be instances where extensive nationalization results in such a strong concentration of power in the hands of government that a changeover to dictatorship is facilitated or generated. . . . It is also quite possible that the introduction of a decentralized market system into a political dictatorship helps to pave the way for decentralization and democratization of the political system as well. . . .

Thus, it is absurd to argue that there are *no* relations between economic and political structures. My main point about the limited correlations between economic and political conditions is that the relationships are so complicated that simple generalizations—whether by Hayek or the Marxists—are not convincing. This statement is, of course, not an attempt to minimize the risk of a substantial concentration of power and of a limitation on personal freedom in a society based mainly on public ownership. I think, however, that the more universal risks are bureaucratization, a lack of decentralization of initiative, and a propensity to abstain from criticism of highly placed public officials (for career reasons), rather than dictatorship (in the fascist or communist sense).

Some problems associated with the concentration of power in nationalized economies might, at least in principle, be solved by decentralization of economic powers to the level of the firm. Such a decentralization may, as already indicated, be quite consistent with the New Left sympathies in this regard. It seems that the ideal economic structure in much of New Left writing is an economy of autonomous (possibly rather small), firms, owned and operated by the employees themselves—a kind of producers' cooperative, or "collective capitalism." Mandel talks about "self-management of free communes of producers and consumers, in which everybody will take it in turn to carry out administrative work, in which the difference between 'directors' and 'directed' will be abolished, and a federation which will eventually cover the whole world." A great many such firms were in fact started on the European continent during the second half of the nineteenth century and the early years of the present century. The traditional explanation of their inability to compete with capitalist firms is that they never succeeded in solving the management problems, and possibly also the problems of accumulating capital and finance in general.

However, to make decentralization possible in complex industrial systems, it is necessary, as was already pointed out, to rely rather heavily on markets. . . .

A dilemma involved in bringing about far-reaching decentralization in economies dominated by collective ownership is that it is just those who hold political power who can decide *if* they want to abstain from this power or not. Under private capitalism, a considerable distribution of power is more or less automatically achieved when the ownership of capital is not concentrated in the hands of one or a few individuals or firms. Thus, a serious conflict easily emerges between the wish to reach decentralization and the desire for public (particularly government) ownership.

7.8 Economics of the New Left

Stephen Hymer and Frank Roosevelt

INTRODUCTION

Radicals usually have trouble communicating with economists.[1] The reason is that the two are generally interested in different questions. At the moment, however, we are fortunate enough to have an economist who is interested in the same questions that activate radicals. For this reason, Assar Lindbeck's *The Political Economy of the New Left—An Outsider's View* is a useful book for presenting the radical critique of economics and setting the stage for further dialogue.

The questions being asked by the New Left are (1) what is the connection between corporate capitalism and the obvious evils in our society, and (2) how do we go beyond capitalism towards the achievement of a decent society? Lindbeck begins his book explicitly accepting the validity of these questions: "The salient features of New Left economics are . . . its critique of present-day capitalist societies, with the important role played by large corporations, and the vision of how the economy should be reorganized" (p. 6).

The fact that Lindbeck begins with the right questions enables us to avoid sterile arguments about the internal consistency of his presentation and to concentrate instead on the general usefulness of economics in dealing with the questions we agree on. Along the way, however, we shall have to examine whether the method favored by Lindbeck does not in fact lead him to change the questions themselves—or dodge them altogether.

But the New Left will not tolerate changing the questions. For they have arrived at their questions not, as Lindbeck suggests most economists choose theirs, "by considerations of available analytical techniques" (p. 22), but through their experience. This experience began, as a rule, in the comfortable homes of the middle class. Having been reared in conditions of relative affluence and security, a new generation naturally became sympathetic to the plight of others subject to poverty, prejudice, and colonialism.

At first the new generation tried to overcome social injustice with the tools of its class: reason, technical knowledge, legal maneuvering, and electoral reform politics. The newly aroused young people operated on the assumption that the various evils they fought were only imperfections in a basically sound system.

[1] In this discussion we follow Lindbeck's general practice of using the words "economic" and "economist" to refer to the *neoclassical* (or orthodox, traditional, conventional, bourgeois) type of economist-economic theory.

Excerpted from Stephen Hymer and Frank Roosevelt, "Symposium: Economics of the New Left," *Quarterly Journal of Economics* 86 (November 1972). Reprinted by permission of the publisher, Frank Roosevelt, and the estate of Stephen Hymer.

The results obtained by the young activists, however, did not measure up to their expectations. From this experience, they began to wonder if there is not something fundamentally at fault in the system itself.

To the people who were now coming to see themselves as the New Left, the socioeconomic system appeared more and more clearly to be rotten at its roots. It tended both to encourage and to depend upon greed; it almost always placed a higher priority on things than on people; and its very foundations seemed to rest upon relations of domination and subordination.

The experience of the New Left led them to Marx. Finding themselves unable to deal with the waste, injustice, alienation, and entrenched power in their society, these young people had arrived existentially at the point from which Marx began his critique of capitalism. They found that he offered an explanation of social problems that went deeper than any they had previously encountered. And they were attracted by his vision of socialism and communism.

In what follows, we will argue that it is essential to take into account the class struggle—i.e., the fact of antagonistic relationships between groups of people—if one wishes to understand what is going on in the world. With Marx, we see this struggle occurring in modern society mainly between workers and capitalists. And it is important to observe, again following Marx, that capitalists and workers confront each other in two separate but interconnected realms: (1) the sphere of circulation, and (2) the sphere of production. The sphere of circulation is the realm of the market where the various actors meet each other as owners of commodities intent on exchanging them. The sphere of production is the more important realm where we find not only the production of commodities going on but also the capital-labor relationship itself being reproduced.

Until recently it did not seem that economists cared much one way or the other about the New Left. But now Lindbeck has come over from Sweden to tell us that the New Left has something to say to economists and to claim that economists, in turn, have something to offer to the New Left: To evaluate this claim is one of the main purposes of the present essay. We will proceed first by reconstructing the economics paradigm from Lindbeck's discussion and then by comparing it to the Marxian paradigm. We will let the reader judge which paradigm comes closest to answering the questions of the New Left.

THE ECONOMICS PARADIGM

In his survey of the New Left's critique of economics, Lindbeck presents us with a balance sheet of the strengths and weaknesses of his way of looking at the world. First, he tells us what tools economics *has* for analyzing various social problems, and, a moment later, he is good enough to indicate what economics *lacks* (in several cases associating the name of Marx with the excluded concepts). We will find that the items on the negative side of Lindbeck's balance sheet add up precisely to the Marxian set of tools, and we will contend that these tools, when brought together, prove more useful in dealing with the problems Lindbeck is addressing. Let us now take the problems one by one, in the order established by Lindbeck, and set up the balance sheet.

1. *Distribution.* Lindbeck takes up the New Left's charge that "academic economists . . . have insufficiently studied problems of the *distribution of income, wealth, and economic power* in society" (p. 9). He concedes "that 'academic' economic theories of the distribution of income are still based on the marginal productivity analysis—and hence on demand-supply models . . ." (p. 10) but dismisses the alternative theory of distribution that has recently been developed in Cambridge, England. Nowhere does he make clear that one of the chief differences between these two theories is that the first takes the existing distribution of wealth and economic power for granted (claiming that it will give the same results no matter who owns or controls what), while the second holds that nothing can be said until the general wage-profit division is determined (giving a central role to the distribution of wealth and economic power).

In contrast to the "academic" economists' theory of income distribution, Lindbeck correctly observes "that the emphasis in New Left writings is more on institutional arrangements and on the role of notions of the 'distribution of power' and the 'class struggle' in explaining the distribution of income" (p. 11).

2. *Tastes—Resource Allocation.* Here Lindbeck cites the New Left criticism "that economists tend to utilize too partial an approach in their analysis of . . . the problems of the *allocation of resources* . . . taking household preferences mainly as given, thereby leaving investigation of the formation of such preferences to other disciplines. . . ."

While Lindbeck clearly recognizes that preferences *change,* he proceeds throughout the book to make policy recommendations—e.g., in favor of markets, reliance on material incentives—on the basis that they result in the optimal satisfaction of *given* consumer preferences. This procedure would be justifiable only if it would be assumed that the policies and institutions recommended have no effect on preferences. Since this is clearly not the case, Lindbeck's arguments—and indeed all normative conclusions drawn from the theory of "efficient" allocation of resources—are undermined. It simply will not do to jump from ignorance of change to assumption of stasis.

3. *The Quality of Life.* Under this heading, Lindbeck brings up the New Left criticism that the quantitative orientation of economists leads them to "concentrate on the satisfaction of preferences for consumer goods, and possibly for leisure time, thus partly neglecting such problems as working conditions, the ways in which decisions are made, and the problem of the quality of the environment . . ." (p. 13). What strikes the critical reader of this section is that Lindbeck brings up *three* distinct problems (which in the next paragraph he refers to as: "Deterioration of the environment, alienation in work, and neglect of collective services") but only discusses *one* of them—the environment. This is no accident, for the only tool economists have to deal with "the quality of life" is the theory of "external effects."

Looking at qualitative problems in terms of "externalities" is a necessary consequence of the economists' focus on the sphere of circulation. If something is going wrong—e.g., poor working conditions, lousy decision making, fouled-up environment—it *must* be because people's preferences or firms' costs are not adequately represented in market prices. Hence the solution offered by the economists also falls in the realm of exchange: one must simply find out what the "external effects" are and induce people to take them into consideration by having the government tax or subsidize those market transactions that are causing all the trouble. (Cf. Lindbeck, pp. 14–15.)

Now this approach seems plausible when it is applied to environmental problems. (Companies might pump less waste into the river if they were taxed accordingly.) So this is the problem Lindbeck discusses. But what about "the ways in which decisions are made" and "alienation in work"? It is hard to see how any programs of taxes or subsidies might deal with these problems—even if we assume that such programs can actually be adopted and implemented by governments in capitalist societies. In fact one must leave the sphere of exchange and enter that of production even to understand these problems.

4. *Large Versus Small Changes*. Here Lindbeck presents the New Left's charge that "economists are obsessed with *marginal changes* within a given economic system" and fail to "discuss large, *qualitative changes* in the economic system." There are really two issues here.

First, there is an issue that can be seen in terms of comparative statics. As Lindbeck puts it, "economists are criticized for confining their studies mainly to 'local optima,' in the neighborhood of the initial position, rather than asking whether there may be some superior 'total optimum' position in a society organized quite differently from those we know" (p. 16). This is the framework in which economists are relatively comfortable. While refraining from value judgments, they may speculate about "comparative economic systems." In this regard, Lindbeck applauds "the vast literature on market systems and the differences between centralization and decentralization" but admits that "the literature on comparative economic systems is not among the strongest in economics" (p. 16).

The more serious omission on the part of economists is their neglect of the dynamics of historical change of economic systems. Here again, Lindbeck hints at the necessary but excluded analytical tools when he notes that "the criticism is given a Marxian touch by the New Left when they emphasize the need for the study of great historic processes and transformations of systems when their inherent 'contradictions' become too strong" (p. 16). That he himself has no use for such analysis is evident in his supercilious references to "the 'grand visions,' found in much of the New Left literature, of the historical development of capitalist societies" (p. 1). What the economists are left with is a comparative blueprints approach that does not help them determine what policies are relevant to any particular historical situation.

It is our contention that the basic tool kit of economics are insufficient for dealing with the New Left's questions. They relate exclusively to the sphere of circulation and thus cover only an arbitrarily circumscribed area of economic phenomena. Within this framework the economist is constrained to move in one dimension back and forth along a continuum with free markets at one end and central planning at the other.

But the capitalist process of production taken as a whole represents a synthesis of production and circulation. If we wish to understand the roots of the evils in our society and assess the possibilities of going beyond capitalism, we must be able to move also in the second dimension of production relations. This involves an analysis of excluded items which, taken together, form the basis of the Marxian paradigm.

THE MARXIAN PARADIGM

The Marxian system begins with the process of production. In every mode of production, labor and means of production are united to produce output. But it is the specific manner in which this union is accomplished that distinguishes the different socioeconomic formations from one another. Under capitalism they are united through the wage-labor contract under which the laborer alienates his labor power and agrees to submit to the control of the capitalist or his representative during the process of production.

In the market the laborer was a "free agent" who owned his own labor power and dealt with the capitalist on equivalent footing in pursuit of his own private interest. The bargain completed, however, he finds himself no longer free or equal or a property owner or an individual but a subordinate in an authoritarian hierarchy working with and on materials he does not own in a collective process of production.

The dualism between freedom in the marketplace and authoritarianism in the workplace is the essential characteristic of capitalist society. If the marketplace furnishes the economist with the model to justify capitalism in terms of freedom, equality, possession, and individualism, the actual conditions of work furnish the New Left with the critique of capitalism (with its nonfreedom and nonequality) as well as the clues to a future society (with a nonpossessive and nonindividualistic organization of work).

When the worker sells his labor, he in effect surrenders his freedom; but this does not mean that he passively accepts capitalist production. The laborer's daily work is involuntary, and so each day involves a struggle between capital and laborer. The capitalist tries to get the worker to do something he or she does not want to do; the worker tries to resist doing it. In Volume I of *Capital,* Marx analyzes the capitalist system of production in terms of this constant struggle, showing the forms of resistance put up by the workers and the types of pressure (e.g., organization, introduction of machinery, social legislation) devised by the capitalist to maintain control over the workers' labor time. These problems, which lie outside the market sphere, are hardly touched on at all in the modern economics curriculum.

How does the market fit into this? In the market numerous buyers and sellers confront each other under more or less competitive conditions and exchange commodities according to the laws of supply and demand. This aspect has been extensively analyzed by economists. But they have neglected a second aspect: the constraints placed on the market outcomes by the need to maintain the capitalist nature of production. Volume II of *Capital* attempts to deal with this problem by showing how the circular flow of goods and money reproduces the capital-labor relation—i.e., results in a distribution of income and wealth such that the capitalists end up again owning the means of production and the laborers end up again having to sell their labor in order to live. The wage must be sufficiently high to maintain the laborer but not high enough to allow him to become a capitalist. For example, if wages rise and eat into profits, investment dries up, growth slows down and unemployment results. This exerts a downward pressure on wage demands, restores the rate of profit, and allows the capitalist system to go on.

Since capitalism requires unequal relations of dominance and subordination in production, the game of the market must be a loaded game. The players begin with unequal endowments of wealth and education and at the end of play find themselves in much the same relative position as before. Of course a certain degree of mobility exists: a small number of people change ranks; but in cycle after cycle over the last two hundred years, the pyramid has remained a pyramid. In each round the top 10 percent of the population gets from 30 to 40 percent of the take, the bottom two thirds get only one third. The players are then ready to play again in production—the poor to work, the middle to manage, the rich to accumulate.

Much force was needed to bring this system into being. Economists have generally overlooked its brutal origins during the period of primitive accumulation in the sixteenth and seventeenth centuries.

Once free markets are established, force takes on more respectable forms. One of these respectable forms is the education system where people are trained to accept competition, discipline, authoritarianism, rigid schedules in preparation for life in capitalist production. This form of coercive socialization has been of particular interest to the New Left and is being extensively investigated by radical economists using the tools of class analysis rather than the market methodology of human capital.

Another respectable form of coercion is the propagation of ideologies that disguise the nature of human relations in our society. In our view, economics is one of the most important of these ideologies. By concentrating on market relations that mask the real nature of the transaction between capital and labor, economists have mystified the economic processes in our society and hindered the development of analytical tools for going beyond them.

CONCLUSION

In closing, let us return to consider the relevance of the two paradigms to the questions posed by the New Left. We remember that Lindbeck originally accepted the questions of the New Left and promised to show how economics can be applied to "its critique of present-day capitalist societies . . . and the vision of how the economy should be *reorganized*" (p. 6, italics added). By the end of the book, however, he has indicated his acceptance of the "mixed economy"—i.e., the capitalist Welfare State—and argued that the only trouble with the United States is that it is underdeveloped! Thus, Lindbeck has changed the questions.

The Marxian paradigm offers an alternative perspective and produces a different set of answers. It shows that capitalism, because it is based on private property and promotes an individualist point of view, places strict limits on how much government interference it will tolerate. It argues that as the system advances, the contradiction between its social nature and its private organization becomes increasingly intense. And it recommends that we supersede the mode of production based on wage labor by striving consciously to control our own everyday life in production as well as in consumption.

We hope that Lindbeck's book stimulates a fruitful dialogue between radical and traditional economists on how to go beyond our present limitations in thought and action.

DEMOCRATIC SOCIALISM AND ECONOMIC REFORM

American socialist thought has by no means been confined to the Marxian variety in the past, nor is it at present. A third subgroup of left-wing dissent, distinguishable both from neo-Marxism and from the New Left, is contemporary democratic socialism—exemplified here by Michael Harrington, a prominent member of the American Socialist party and president of the League for Industrial Democracy.

Like neo-Marxists and representatives of the New Left, democratic socialists diagnose deep ills within American capitalism. In *The Other America* (1962), for example, Harrington spotlighted the human plight and tragedy of individuals caught in the web of poverty in an otherwise affluent society, left largely beyond the redemption of the stability-growth-corporate expansion processes of the post-Keynesian synthesis. And, in *The Accidental Century* (1965), he demonstrated that the domination of technology by a corporate elite, subject to effective social control neither by the market nor by government, leaves technological progress and processes unplanned by society as a whole. But while democratic socialists have their visions and programs of comprehensive and radical change, they retain a deep sense of what is "politically feasible." Their variety of socialism blended with populist and progressive reform movements in earlier decades; now it has much in common with the liberal strand of the post-Keynesian synthesis, just as the neo-liberals overlap, at points, with the conservative strand. As Harrington stressed in his *Toward a Democratic Left* (1968), by framing their objectives modestly and employing a piecemeal approach, socialists attempt to attract wide political support and to use democracy as a process for economic reform, social control of the market, and reduction of poverty and inequality. The more open political environment of the 1960s and 1970s, in contrast to the 1950s, has extended the potential for economic reform as perceived by Harrington and other democratic socialists.

The influence of non-Marxian American socialists, now as in the past, is felt far more in terms of pressure for practical reforms than in proposals for a fundamental restructuring of society along socialist lines. Harrington's *The*

Other America, for example, is often credited for prodding the Liberal Establishment toward the creation of a War on Poverty, if not the pursuit of ultimate victory. This carries on an important historical tradition inherited from earlier democratic socialists, such as Eugene Debs and Norman Thomas. Many modifications in public policy and economic practice that the major political parties came to justify on pragmatic grounds were originally proposed or jointly sponsored by socialists. This has diluted the purity of socialist proposals, and makes it difficult to assess separately the exact contribution of socialism to economic reform. But at the same time it has been the willingness of democratic socialists to propose changes within the existing economic system, to focus (with social reform liberals) on democratic-collectivist reform, and to emphasize gradual, evolutionary institutional change that has made their proposals politically acceptable.

The various distinguishing characteristics of democratic socialism are illustrated in the following selection. Selection 7.9 contains Harrington's indictment of "reactionary Keynesianism" and the welfare state, and his case for democratic socialism. The modern welfare state, he argues, while expanding government's role in economic life, has skewed priorities and has built inequality into the system of public policy. Substantial further reform is needed to transform the inegalitarian welfare state into a true democratic socialist community.

In selection 7.10, C. A. R. Crosland, noted British economist, restates the fundamental concerns of the democratic socialist movement in terms of ends and criteria for a "certain kind of society," characterized by aspirations for cooperation, welfare, and (especially) equality. In selection 7.11, E. F. Schumacher, ecologist, self-designated Buddhist economist, student of British democratic socialist R. H. Tawney (recall selection 2.7), and critic of large-scale organization, evaluates industrialized capitalism *and* socialism in terms of irrational and dehumanizing properties common to both.

In selection 7.12, Gunnar Myrdal illustrates a point of convergence between democratic socialism and liberal democratic reform in his discussion of the potential for transition to a more decentralized and democratized "welfare community."

7.9 Why Socialism in America

Michael Harrington

Beyond the Welfare State

There are three basic reasons why the reform of the welfare state will not solve our most urgent problems: the class structure of capitalist society vitiates, or

Excerpted from Michael Harrington, *Socialism* (New York: E. P. Dutton, 1971), pp. 270–91. Reprinted by permission of the publisher.

subverts, almost every such effort toward social justice; private corporate power cannot tolerate the comprehensive and democratic planning we desperately need; and even if these first two obstacles to providing every citizen with a decent house, income and job were overcome, the system still has an inherent tendency to make affluence self-destructive.

Class Biases in Public Policies

In this context, the following analysis of the severe limits capitalism imposes on the welfare state is not designed to prove that liberals of the mass Left are foolish and deluded, but rather that their liberal values can only really be completely achieved on the basis of a socialist program.

First of all, the welfare state, for all the value of its institutions, tends to provide benefits in inverse relationship to human needs. And not—the point is crucial—because of a conspiracy by the affluent, but as a "natural" consequence of a society divided into unequal social classes.

It is possible to offset this inherent tendency within capitalist society to distribute public benefits according to the inequalities of private wealth, but only if there are vigorous radical reforms.

These are incremental in character, yet they have a revolutionary import since they involve actual shifts in the make-up and institutions of power itself. Thus, I will propose to vastly increase the proportion of resources allocated by democratic decision-making and to redistribute income so as to change the relationship between, and reality of, social classes.

The class divisions of welfare capitalism, which are the root cause of this problem within neo-capitalism, are not, it must be stressed at the outset, simply unfair in some abstract sense. Were that the case, a sophisticated conservative argument might be persuasive: since to some extent the growth of the economy benefits everyone, even those who are worst off, there is no point in endangering these gains on behalf of some ultimate egalitarianism. What really concerns the poor, this theory continues, is not the rise or fall of their *relative* share of affluence but the steady increase in their absolute standard of living. Actually, inequality does not merely mean that there are sharply unequal proportions of goods distributed among the various social sectors of the population. It signifies a socio-economic process, at once dynamic and destructive, which determines that public and private resources shall be spent in an increasingly anti-social way and thereby threatens the well-being of the entire society.

Housing is an excellent case in point. The Government, even under liberal administrations, has been much more solicitous about the comfort of the rich than the shelter of the poor. This policy is not only morally outrageous, it has had disastrous social consequences as well. Yet it must be emphasized that in thereby investing billions in the creation of public problems, Washington did not act maliciously but only followed—unconsciously, automatically, "naturally"—the priorities that are structured into America's class divisions. Thus: in 1962 the value of a single tax deduction to the 20 percent of Americans with the highest incomes was worth twice as much as all the monies spent on public housing for the one fifth who were poorest; and this figure does not even take into account Government support of below-market rates of interest to build suburbia; and, as the National Commission on Civil Disorders of 1968 computed the figures, the Government has helped to construct over ten million housing units for home builders, i.e., for the middle class and the rich, but provided only 650,000 units of low-cost housing for the poor.

But it would be a mistake to think that Washington discriminates only against the poor. For, as a White House Conference told President Johnson in 1966, *the entire lower half of the American population is excluded from the market for new housing,* a market that could not exist without massive Federal support. This point needs special emphasis, if only because many people, with the best of intentions, concluded from the rediscovery of poverty in America in the sixties that the bulk of the nation was affluent while only a minority were poor. But the statistics, far from describing a simple division between the rich and the poverty-stricken, show that we have in this country a *majority,* composed of the poor, the near-poor, more than half the workers and the lower middle class, which does not even have a "moderate standard of living" as defined by the Government itself.

So when Washington used its powers to improve conditions for a wealthy elite, the poor suffered most because they had the most urgent claim on the funds thus squandered on the upper class, but a majority of the people, including tens of millions who were not poor, were also deprived of benefits that should have rightfully been theirs. Worse, in carrying out these discriminatory policies, the Federal programs did positive harm to those most in need. As an American Presidential Commission recently reported, ". . . over the last decades, Government action, through urban renewal, highway programs, demolitions on public housing sites, code enforcement, and other programs, has destroyed more housing for the poor than government at all levels has built for them."

In the America of the seventies these fantastically skewed priorities have momentous social consequences. For Washington has, in effect, been aggravating the very social problems to which it would then point with alarm. By financing the flight of the middle class from the metropolis and helping industry locate in the suburbs, the central city was allowed to rot—with Federal encouragement. As a result, such related evils as violence, bitter old age, intensified racism and the decay of the traditional centers of culture all grew worse.

So the Government's discriminatory social policies have done much more than exacerbate inequality; they have helped to promote a fantastic anti-design for living. How, then, can we explain why sincere and dedicated men—as those who presided over these disastrous programs usually were—would lavish public funds to thus aggravate social problems? The answer is to be found in the class character of American society and the commercial logic which both derives from it and pervades governmental decisions.

The 1969 report of the Council of Economic Advisors provides candid documentation of this pattern. "Investing in new housing for low income families—particularly in big cities—," the Council said, "is usually a losing proposition. Indeed the *most profitable investment* is often one that demolishes homes of low-income families to make room for business and higher income families.'' (Emphasis added.) Now, it is obvious that the criterion of profitability to which the Council refers is private, since, as the gloomy projections of the Violence Commission demonstrate, the social cost of the present system is bankrupting the society. Yet this private calculus is precisely the one the Government follows.

For in a society based on class inequality and suffused with commercial values, it just doesn't ''make sense'' to waste resources on social uses or beauty or anything that cannot be quantified in dollars and cents. Our legislators, drawn almost exclusively from the middle and upper classes, cannot bring themselves to forget those principles, which are sacred to the private economy. To them it seems logical to invest the Federal dollar in those undertakings that run the lowest risk and will show the highest and most immediate return.

Housing is only one example of how the welfare state observes the priorities of maldistributed wealth even when it attempts to serve the common good. Other cases in point can be found in literally every department of government. The American welfare system in the sixties reached only a third of the poor and provided them, on a national average, with one half of what they needed. Meanwhile, in 1969 the richest one sixth among the farmers (individuals and corporations) received two thirds of the agricultural subsidies, or about $2.5 billion. Given the relation of social classes in the fields, America's commitment to promote ''agriculture'' is also a commitment to help the rich at the expense of the poor. And if one considers the various deductions in the tax codes as an indirect form of government expense—by not collecting money from an individual, Washington increases his income as surely as if it sent him a check—they total up to $50 billion, with the bulk of that sum going to oil men, home builders, stock-market speculators and others at the top of the economic pyramid.

But it is in education that the effect of systematic inequality is most damaging. America is becoming a ''knowledge economy'' in which higher and higher educational credentials are required (sometimes unnecessarily) in order to get a good job. The 1969 Manpower Report of the President said that the unprecedented recent boom had clearly revealed that ''economic expansion alone was insufficient to employ many people who had been bypassed in the general advance because of inexperience, lack of skills and cultural deprivation.'' Now, it is bad enough that such a group should exist, but what is truly intolerable is the extent to which social class structure denies it effective access to tax-supported education and works to make deprivation both self-perpetuating and hereditary.

So in education, housing, agriculture, welfare and every other area of social life it is necessary to attack the systematic concentration of economic power in order to achieve serious reform. The fulfillment of liberal values, in short, requires structural changes in our class relationships, changes that transcend the capitalist limits of today's welfare state.

The Need For Democratic Planning

Second, there must also be national economic and social planning on a scale that our present institutional arrangements will not tolerate.

There is no question but that the seventies will see planning in the United States. The really crucial questions are: What kind of planning? Planning for whom? The problems of welfare capitalist society are becoming so obvious and overwhelming that conservatives and even reactionaries have understood the need for state intervention—if only to maintain as much of the old order as possible.

Conservatives are sophisticated enough to understand that the "chaotic" growth of modern society is no longer tolerable and that, in order to hold back the future, a modicum of planning and discipline must be imposed on the corporations. What we must now confront is an entire historical period in which it is of the capitalist essence to plan. In the absence of a vigorous mass movement capable of democratizing this trend toward collectivism—in the absence, in other words, of a socialist alternative—planning will be conservative, manipulative and in the service of social and economic privilege. That is why it is so important to define the limits of neo-capitalist planning and to contrast it sharply with the socialist proposals in the same area.

The first distinction between capitalist and socialist planning has to do with money. Meeting social problems. In mid-1970, George Romney, the Secretary of Housing and Urban Development, estimated that 80 percent of U.S. families could not afford the average cost of a new house. To deal with a crisis of this magnitude will clearly require a shift of massive resources from the private to the public sector, since the market is not even reaching a majority of the people. But Mr. Nixon and his conservative colleagues are not about to propose basic revision in the uses of the national wealth. They sincerely believe that the common good is maximized by keeping the allocation of resources as private as possible. Given this basic, and capitalist, limit to their thinking, any planning measures they urge are going to be inadequately funded.

A second basic distinction between capitalist and socialist planning has to do with comprehensiveness.

When President Eisenhower proposed in May, 1968, that there be new, integrated communities with jobs, schools and parks and high-speed transportation links to the old cities, he was unwittingly committing himself to radical innovation. Assembling an integrated population and providing its members with decent work, education and transportation is not something to be accomplished by Adam Smith's "invisible hand." It requires long-range projections and a conscious coordination of Government policies. It could not be done, to take but one crucial example, if land were left to private speculation. For in order to assemble the huge areas needed for such extensive projects at a remotely reasonable cost, the public authority would have to use its power of eminent domain and establish land banks. So conservatives may be forced to recognize the magnitude of the urban crisis but they cannot solve it within their own economic calculus.

And yet, if it is easy enough to demonstrate that planning within a capitalist context is, at best, utterly and necessarily inadequate, this does not mean that socialist planning is without problems. These problems have to be faced candidly.

Socialist planning is not a total panacea; neither, for that matter, is democracy. The people are quite capable of making the wrong decision after having been given all the facts. But the only possibility of making a humane choice is if the institutions of democratic planning relentlessly encroach on the private sector in such areas of decisive importance as housing, transportation and education. Neo-capitalist planning with its commercial priorities is inherently limited and unable to solve the crises it recognizes. With socialist planning that is massive, comprehensive and democratic, there is at least the possibility that man will be able to master the environment he himself has created.

Capitalist Affluence is Self Destructive

The third major reason why capitalist society must be basically transformed is this: Let us assume that the system proves to be much more ingenious than the preceding analysis suggests. Suppose it constructs a welfare state that really does respond to the needs of the poor and that, without fundamental changes in structure, it manages to accommodate itself to democratic planning. Even then—and I admit this possibility for the purpose of argument only—even then, it would be necessary to go beyond capitalism to socialism. For if this society somehow found a way to deal with poverty, racism, inequality and unmet social needs, it would still be incapable of dealing with its own prosperity.

In traditional Marxist theory economic crisis was the result of overproduction within a society of systematically limited consumption. Many contemporary economists now argue that the cyclical breakdown of capitalism, which turned relative abundance into immediate want, has been mastered. That, as will be seen shortly, is much too optimistic an analysis, since the contradictions of capitalism bedevil Keynesians as well as anti-Keynesian conservatives. But even if we do assume for a moment that the cyclical crisis of capitalism is under control, it has been succeeded by an even more bizarre problem: that affluence itself is becoming increasingly counterproductive.

So—to cite one striking example—as the seventies began, the President of the United States told the nation in his Message on the Environment, "Based on present trends it is quite possible that by 1980 the increase in the sheer number of cars in densely populated areas will begin outrunning the technological limits of our capacity to reduce pollution from the internal combustion engine." One would think that such an apocalyptic presentiment would have been the prelude to decisive action. Yet only one week before he thus warned that the society was destroying the very air it breathes, Nixon proposed a budget in which mass transportation (which would cut down "the sheer number of cars" as well as serve a number of other social purposes) received 6 percent of the money assigned to building highways, i.e., to making sure that the sheer number of cars would indeed increase.

But the automobile is only one case in point. As Jerome C. Pickard of the Urban Land Institute has commented, "the concentrated character of future urban regional development will place a great strain on regional resources: on water supply, air and the land itself. The pollutants generated in such large scale urban and industrial concentration may threaten a large segment of the environment inhabited by a majority of the United States population."

It is precisely because capitalism has moderated the tendency toward periodic crises that it throws up a new form of the Marxian contradiction. For private decision-making is no longer capable of regulating a technology whose social consequences become more and more destructive.

In the example of the automobile is the essence of the problem: it is foolish to think that giant industries will voluntarily desist from the profitable spoilation of the environment; and it is impossible for a government committed to maximizing the autonomy of those corporations to take the drastic action that is required.

Finally, if neo-capitalism has ameliorated the more traditional forms of economic crisis, it has far from solved them. And here again, the private priorities of the corporation invade governmental policy.

When John F. Kennedy was elected President in 1960, the debate among his economic advisors had as much to do with the class struggle as it did with academic theory. The economists from the AFL-CIO and individuals like John Kenneth Galbraith and Leon Keyserling wanted Kennedy to adopt a social variant of Keynesianism and to eliminate the unemployment he inherited from Eisenhower by expanding consumption and making investments in public projects. Other advisors wanted a much more cautions—and business-oriented—policy. In 1962 there was a 7 percent tax credit for business investment and accelerated depreciation allowances for plant and equipment. These amounted to a multibillion-dollar increase in the cash flow of the giant corporations. These measures were then followed by a tax cut which, since it sought to increase private consumption spending and was based on the inequities of the tax code, assigned the largest benefits to the richest people.

This tactic, as I demonstrated in *Toward a Democratic Left,* promotes the values of Adam Smith with the techniques of John Maynard Keynes. It is the "natural" way for a capitalist society to fight crisis. For Kennedy could only have followed his more socially-oriented advisors if he had had a massive majority in the Congress to offset the political-economic power of the corporations. Under normal conditions, it was, and will be, the wisdom of capitalist reform to favor business in order to win its support. Thus, the full power of the Federal Government will be used to exacerbate the disparities of income in the society.

But then, such a policy also reproduces and intensifies the contradictions of the capitalist structure itself.

The tax credit and accelerated depreciation allowance had the effect of setting off a capital-goods boom. And that, of course, was the point of Richard Nixon's similar policy measures in 1971. However, by stimulating the economy in such a way, Washington is using its considerable power to maximize productivity but not the power to consume. In the short run, the capital-goods boom will generate employment and buying power, as the experience of the sixties shows. But in the absence of vigorous measures to raise the effective demand of the millions, these policies also lay the basis for a crisis of "overproduction" in which productivity outstrips consumption. By concentrating so many resources in the capital-goods sector, they also have an inflationary impact. Hence the simultaneous inflation-recession of the late sixties and early seventies was at least partly caused by Federal action.

And finally on this count, that state of equilibrium so dear to the classical economists still evades the Keynesians. When employment is high enough to approach a socially desirable level, unit labor costs for industry go up, profits go down and there are tendencies toward recession. And when unemployment is high enough to lower labor costs, there is an intolerable waste of human beings. But under a policy of structural reform, where working men and women would be shifted into extremely valuable social pursuits that would increase their productivity even as they provided needed goods and services in education, health care, environmental protection and the like, it would be possible to have full employment and price stability. That, however, would mean going beyond the basic principles of the capitalist use of human beings, for it would assign more and more workers to the ''nonprofit'' sector. Nonprofitable, that is, from the point of view of business, but enormously profitable for society.

So contemporary capitalism is not only heir to many of the traditional evils of the system, even if sometimes in ameliorated ways, it also cannot deal adequately, no matter how sophisticated it has become with either poverty or affluence. Left to itself, the system creates a welfare state that provides some benefits for all, yet favors the rich and discriminates against the desperate; it generates problems, like those of the urban environment, that demand comprehensive planning; and even when it functions to produce the highest standard of living the world has known, the social consequences of that achievement are so appalling as to vitiate much of it.

[In short] the fundamental solution of these problems requires measures that go beyond the limits of the capitalist economy.

7.10 Equality and Social Justice

C. A. R. Crosland

THE CONFUSION BETWEEN ENDS AND MEANS

If we are to reformulate socialist doctrine, the first task is clearly to decide what precise meaning is to be attached to the word 'socialism'.

This is not an easy question to answer. The word does not describe any present or past society, which can be empirically observed, and so furnish unimpeachable evidence for what is or is not 'socialism'. Thus statements about socialism can never be definitely verified; and we cannot treat it as being an *exact* descriptive word at all. There is therefore no point in searching the encyclopaedias for a definitive meaning; it has none, and never could.

But the worst source of confusion is the tendency to use the word to describe, not a certain kind of society, or certain values which might be attributes of a society, but particular policies which are, or are thought to be, means to attaining this kind of society, or realising these attributes. To rescue the word from these confusions, one must begin by asking what, if anything, is common to the beliefs of all, or almost all, of those who have called themselves socialists. The only constant element, common to all the bewildering variety of different doctrines, consists of certain moral values and aspirations; and people have called themselves socialists because they shared these aspirations, which form the one connecting link between otherwise hopelessly divergent schools of thought.

Thus the word first came on the modern scene with the early nineteenth-century Owenites, whom Marx contemptuously termed 'Utopian' socialists. They based their 'socialism' explicitly on an ethical view of society, a belief in a certain way of life and certain moral values. The means by which they thought this 'good society' could be attained are irrelevant to-day; and in fact they were quickly challenged by other socialist schools of thought, since when a continuous debate has proceeded, with no agreement, about what constituted the most suitable means. This debate would have no particular interest to-day, but for the fact that all the protagonists tried to appropriate the word 'socialism' to describe the particular means which they themselves favoured.

Thus Marx appropriated it for the collective ownership of the means of production on the false assumption that the pattern of ownership determined the character of the whole society, and that collective ownership was a sufficient condition of fulfilling the basic aspirations. And generally the word came to be applied to policies for the economic or institutional transformation of society, instead of to the ultimate social purposes which that transformation was intended to achieve; so one often hears socialism equated not only with the nationalisation of industry, but with government planning, or redistribution, or state collectivism. This of course is quite unhelpful, for although people may agree on ends, they may legitimately disagree about means. Moreover, the means most suitable in one generation may be wholly irrelevant in the next, and in any case (still more significant) a given means may lead to more than one possible end, as indeed has happened with each of the policies just mentioned.

Thus if, for example, socialism is defined as the nationalisation of the means of production, distribution and exchange, we produce conclusions which are impossible to reconcile with what the early socialists had in mind when they used the word: such as, that Soviet Russia is a completely socialist country (much more so, for instance, than Sweden)—even though it denies almost all the values which Western socialists have normally read into the word. Similarly, if socialism is defined as economic collectivism or State control of economic life, then Nazi Germany would correctly have been called a socialist country. But in neither case would the end-result be described as socialism by most socialists; the means of nationalisation and planning have proved adaptable to more than one purpose, which shows how unwise it is to identify the means with the end.

Not only is it unwise, but it is also semantically and historically incorrect. The various schools of thought which have called themselves, and been called by others, 'socialist'—Owenites and Marxists, Fabians and Christian Socialists, Syndicalists and Guild Socialists—have differed profoundly over the right means; and no one means has a better title to the label 'socialist' than any other. The one single element common to all the schools of thought has been the basic aspirations, the underlying moral values. It follows that these embody the only logically and historically permissible meaning of the word socialism; and to this meaning we must now revert.

THE BASIC SOCIALIST ASPIRATIONS

These ethical and emotional ideals have been partly negaitve—a protest against the visible results of capitalism—and partly positive, and related to definite views about the nature of the good society; though of course negative and positive strands are often inter-twined.

Perhaps one can list them roughly as follows. First, a protest against the material poverty and physical squalor which capitalism produced. Secondly, a wider concern for 'social welfare'—for the interests of those in need, or oppressed, or unfortunate, from whatever cause. Thirdly, a belief in equality and the 'classless society', and especially a desire to give the worker his 'just' rights and a responsible status at work. Fourthly, a rejection of competitive antagonism, and an ideal of fraternity and cooperation. Fifthly, a protest against the inefficiencies of capitalism as an economic system, and notably its tendency to mass unemployment. The first three formed the basis of socialism as 'a broad, human movement on behalf of the bottom dog'. The first and last were censures on the material results of capitalism; while the other three stemmed from an idealistic desire for a just, co-operative and classless society.

(I have listed only the social and economic aspirations. But of course underlying them, and taken for granted, was a passionate belief in liberty and democracy. It would never have occurred to most early socialists that socialism had any meaning except within a political framework of freedom for the individual. But since this political sssumption is shared by British Conservatives as well as socialists, no further reference is made to it.)

As thus formulated, even these basic aspirations are not all equally relevant to present-day society. Some are expressed in language adapted to conditions that no longer exist, and in particular are too negative in character. This is natural, for they were, in large part, a reaction against the actual results of pre-war capitalism; and with two million unemployed, widespread poverty and malnutrition, and appalling slums set against a background of flamboyant wealth amongst the richer classes, it was natural that the negative desire to abolish evils should outweigh more positive and detailed aspirations.

But to the extent that evils are remedied and injustices removed, negative statements become less and less appropriate. And they are seen to be inappropriate by the electorate, a growing section of which has no recollection of unemployment, or poverty.

Thus even when we go back to the basic aspirations, we still find the same, welcome, difficulty that the pace of change has overtaken the doctrine, and a re-formulation is needed.

How should we re-formulate these aspirations to-day in such a way as to preserve their basic emotional and ethical content, yet discarding what is clearly not germane to present-day conditions? Of the original five, the first and last are rapidly losing their relevance. Such primary poverty as remains will disappear within a decade, given our present rate of economic growth; and the contemporary mixed economy is characterised by high levels both of employment and productivity and by a reasonable degree of stability. In other words, the aspirations relating to the economic consequences of capitalism are fast losing their relevance as capitalism itself becomes transformed.

But the remaining three more positive ideals, described above as stemming either from a concern with the 'bottom dog', or from a vision of a just, co-operative and classless society, have clearly not been fully realised. No doubt we should phrase them differently to-day, but their basic content is still perfectly relevant. We have plenty of less fortunate citizens still requiring aid; and we certainly have not got an equal or classless society, nor one characterised by 'co-operative' social relations.

THE CO-OPERATIVE ASPIRATION

I propose to discuss the co-operative aspiration first, simply because I find it impossible to reach a definite conclusion about its relevance in contemporary conditions.

Matters look a good deal less clear-cut than when the co-operative ideal was first formulated over a century ago. On the one hand, the excesses of competitive individualism have been significantly moderated; on the other hand, competition is seen to have certain compensating advantages, not previously much discussed. However, let us consider the implications of endeavouring to realise the ideal more fully.

The [major] sphere in which the co-operative ideal is relevant is that of relations at work. The early socialists wanted people to work, not as separate individuals, but communally and co-operatively, organised in groups (co-operative guilds or communes) inspired with an altruistic collective purpose. To-day, since self-governing guilds are now impracticable, we should no doubt interpret this in terms of joint consultation or joint participation, that is, of groups within a large industrial unit (whether public or private) identified with, and working co-operatively for, the purposes of that unit.

But we now see that the difficulty is often not, as the early socialists thought it would be, to resolve a clash between individual and collective instincts, or to persuade people to form groups and adopt group standards. The human instinct towards gregariousness is so strong that groups form automatically, in industry as elsewhere, and quickly establish their own informal leaders and standards of behavior.

The difficulty is that these natural, self-created groups may be far from expressing the co-operative ideal. It is not merely that groups may develop extremely disagreeable characteristics—intolerance of dissent, excessive conformity, arbitrary cruelty in the exercise of their ultimate power to ostracise; but even if they do not, their purpose and function may be in no way communal or altruistic so far as objectives and institutions *outside* the group are concerned. On the contrary, their function and behaviour may be wholly selfish, and the element of identification or cooperation with the firm or industry entirely lacking. Thus they may, as industrial research has demonstrated, serve to restrict output, not to expand it; to worsen relations with management, not to improve them; to foster resentment and discontent, instead of harmony and a sense of common purpose.

The problem is to harness the group instinct in such a way as to create the desired social and co-operative atmosphere—to cause the natural groups to identify themselves with the larger unit in which they work. Unfortunately we scarcely know in detail how this is to be done. It does not follow automatically either from nationalisation, as the mines and the railways show, or from setting up joint consultation, which may simply impose a formal and rootless group on top of, and at cross-purposes with, the real groups below.

All we can say is that institutional change by itself is not enough; and that whether joint participation does or does not create a co-operative atmosphere depends on social forces on the exact nature of which industrial psychologists are not agreed—at any rate not to the extent that any clear national policy emerges.

This does not mean, of course, that there is no case for altering relations within industry, or for giving the worker more power. There is such a case. But it rests not on propositions about fraternity or social contentment, which our present knowledge does not justify, but on statements about social justice, the rights of workers, and equality. It is therefore subsumed, and so discussed under the aspiration towards social equality.

To sum up, the co-operative aspiration has at least been partially fulfilled, in that society is much less aggressively individualistic and competitive than a century ago; and indeed the trend toward 'sociability' is now so strong that we are more likely to be deprived of solitude than company. On the other hand we do not yet live in a co-operative Utopia. Most people still work mainly for personal gain, and not for the social good; and the ideal of communal, co-operative participation has scarcely begun to be realised in industry.

While, therefore, I realise that as a matter of verbal precision the co-operative ideal is certainly embraced by the word 'socialism', and while I accept that it would clearly be in some sense 'better' if there were a more general awareness of a common social purpose, I do not feel able, in what is intended to be a reasonably definite and practical statement of socialist aims, to include this as part of the goal.

THE WELFARE AND EQUALITY ASPIRATIONS

The two remaining aspirations—the concern with social welfare, and the desire for an equal and classless society—still have a perfectly clear relevance. The first implies an acceptance of collective responsibility and an extremely high priority for the relief of social distress or misfortune, in contrast to the much lower priority which it would receive in a 'free' economy guided mainly by an individualistic philosophy. This is the contemporary version of the traditional welfare and social-service philosophy, and of the instinct to side automatically with the less fortunate and those in need.

There is plenty of residual social distress. It is now caused less by primary poverty, though this can still be found, than by secondary poverty, natural misfortune, physical or mental illness, the decline in the size of the family, sudden fluctuations in income, and deficiencies in social capital. These last, for all the high level of average personal spending, are still appalling—ugly towns, mean streets, slum houses, overcrowded schools, inadequate hospitals, understaffed mental institutions, too few homes for the aged, indeed a general, and often squalid, lack of social amenities.

The relief of this distress and the elimination of this squalor is the main object of social expenditure; and a socialist is identified as one who wishes to give this an exceptional priority over other claims on resources. This is not a matter of the overall vertical equality of incomes; the arguments are humanitarian and compassionate, not egalitarian. It is a matter of priorities in the distribution of the national output, and a belief that the first priority should always be given to the poor, the unfortunate, the 'have-nots', and generally to those in need; from which follows a certain view about collective social responsibility, and thence about the role of the state and the level of taxation. This represents the first major difference between a socialist and a conservative.

The second distinctive socialist ideal is social equality and the 'classless society'. The socialist seeks a distribution of rewards, status, and privileges egalitarian enough to minimise social resentment, to secure justice between individuals, and to equalise opportunities; and he seeks to weaken the existing deep-seated class stratification, with its concomitant feelings of envy and inferiority, and its barriers to uninhibited mingling between the classes. This belief in social equality, which has been the strongest ethical inspiration of virtually every socialist doctrine, still remains the most characteristic feature of socialist thought to-day.

It is significant that these aspirations are not now primarily economic in character. The worst economic abuses and inefficiencies of modern society have been corrected; and this is no longer the sphere, as it has been for the greater part of the life of modern socialism, in which reforms are most urgently required.

IS SOCIALISM STILL RELEVANT

The ideals have so far merely been stated. They have not been justified in detail, nor any evidence adduced to show that their further fulfilment would definitely improve our society. All that has been argued is that they constitute 'socialism' in the only legitimate sense of the word, and that they are not embodied in our present society to such an extent that most people would describe it as socialist.

A few people would, it is true, so describe it—not explicitly, but by implication. That is, they take the view that we are at, or anyway in sight of, the final objective. This of course is a plausible view only if we select those more modest aspirations which have largely been fulfilled, and define these, and these alone, as socialism.

Now it is true that the planned full-employment welfare state is a society of exceptional merit and quality by historical standards, and by comparison with pre-war capitalism. It would have seemed a paradise to many early socialist pioneers. Poverty and insecurity are in process of disappearing. Living standards are rising rapidly; the fear of unemployment is steadily weakening; and the ordinary young worker has hopes for the future which would never have entered his father's head. There is much less social injustice; the economy works efficiently; and the electorate is in no mood for large-scale change, and certainly not for the complete overthrow of the present system. Many liberal-minded people, who were instinctively 'socialist' in the 1930s as a humanitarian protest against poverty and unemployment, have now concluded that 'Keynes-plus-modified-capitalism-plus-Welfare-State' works perfectly well.

Yet this is not socialism. True, it is not pure capitalism either; and it does fulfil some part of the traditional socialist aspirations, and to this extent has socialist features. Yet it could clearly be a great deal more socialist than it is—not, as people sometimes think, because it now has only 25% public ownership and is not fully planned down to the minutest detail, any more than Soviet society *is* more socialist because it has 100% public ownership and complete state planning: but simply because the traditional socialist ideals could be more fully realised than they are. To put the matter simply, we have won many important advances; but since we could still have more social equality, a more classless society, and less avoidable social distress, we cannot be described as a socialist country.

7.11 Small Is Beautiful: Critique of Industrialized Capitalism and Socialism

E. F. Schumacher

Buddhist Economics

'Right Livelihood' is one of the requirements of the Buddha's Noble Eightfold Path. It is clear, therefore, that there must be such a thing as Buddhist economics.

* * *

From E. F. Schumacher, *Small Is Beautiful: Economics As If People Mattered* (London: Blond & Briggs, New York: Harper & Row, 1973), pp. 50–53.

Let us take some fundamentals and see what they look like when viewed by a modern economist and a Buddhist economist.

There is universal agreement that a fundamental source of wealth is human labour. Now, the modern economist has been brought up to consider 'labour' or work as little more than a necessary evil. From the point of view of the employer, it is in any case simply an item of cost, to be reduced to a minimum if it cannot be eliminated altogether, say, by automation. From the point of view of the workman, it is a 'disutility'; to work is to make a sacrifice of one's leisure and comfort, and wages are a kind of compensation for the sacrifice. Hence the ideal from the point of view of the employer is to have output without employees, and the ideal from the point of view of the employee is to have income without employment.

The consequences of these attitudes both in theory and in practice are, of course, extremely far-reaching. If the ideal with regard to work is to get rid of it, every method that 'reduces the work load' is a good thing. The most potent method, short of automation, is the so-called 'division of labour' and the classical example is the pin factory eulogised in Adam Smith's *Wealth of Nations*. Here it is not a matter of ordinary specialisation, which mankind has practised from time immemorial, but of dividing up every complete process of production into minute parts, so that the final product can be produced at great speed without anyone having had to contribute more than a totally insignificant and, in most cases, unskilled movement of his limbs.

The Buddhist point of view takes the function of work to be at least threefold: to give a man a chance to utilise and develop his faculties; to enable him to overcome his ego-centredness by joining with other people in a common task; and to bring forth the goods and services needed for a becoming existence. Again, the consequences that flow from this view are endless. To organise work in such a manner that it becomes meaningless, boring, stultifying, or nerve-racking for the worker would be little short of criminal; it would indicate a greater concern with goods than with people, an evil lack of compassion and a soul-destroying degree of attachment to the most primitive side of this worldly existence. Equally, to strive for leisure as an alternative to work would be considered a complete misunderstanding of one of the basic truths of human existence, namely that work and leisure are complementary parts of the same living process and cannot be separated without destroying the joy of work and the bliss of leisure.

From the Buddhist point of view, there are therefore two types of mechanisation which must be clearly distinguished: one that enhances a man's skill and power and one that turns the work of man over to a mechanical slave, leaving man in a position of having to serve the slave. . . . It is clear, therefore, that Buddhist economics must be very different from the economics of modern materialism, since the Buddhist sees the essence of civilisation not in a multiplication of wants but in the purification of human character. Character, at the same time, is formed primarily by a man's work. And work, properly conducted in conditions of human dignity and freedom, blesses those who do it and equally their products. . . .

If a man has no chance of obtaining work he is in a desperate position, not simply because he lacks an income but because he lacks this nourishing and enlivening factor of disciplined work which nothing can replace. A modern economist may engage in highly sophisticated calculations on whether full employment 'pays' or whether it might be more 'economic' to run an economy at less than full employment so as to ensure a greater mobility of labour, a better stability of wages, and so forth. His fundamental criterion of success is simply the total quantity of goods produced during a given period of time. . . .

From a Buddhist point of view, this is standing the truth on its head by considering goods as more important than people and consumption as more important than creative activity. It means shifting the emphasis from the worker to the product of work, that is, from the human to the subhuman, a surrender to the forces of evil. The very start of Buddhist economic planning would be a planning for full employment, and the primary purpose of this would in fact be employment for everyone who needs an 'outside' job: it would not be the maximisation of employment nor the maximisation of production. Women, on the whole, do not need an 'outside' job, and the large-scale employment of women in offices or factories would be considered a sign of serious economic failure. In particular, to let mothers of young children work in factories while the children run wild would be as uneconomic in the eyes of a Buddhist economist as the employment of a skilled worker as a soldier in the eyes of a modern economist.

While the materialist is mainly interested in goods, the Buddhist is mainly interested in liberation. But Buddhism is 'The Middle Way' and therefore in no way antagonistic to physical well-being. It is not wealth that stands in the way of liberation but the attachment to wealth; not the enjoyment of pleasurable things but the craving for them. The keynote of Buddhist economics, therefore, is simplicity and non-violence. From an economist's point of view, the marvel of the Buddhist way of life is the utter rationality of its pattern—amazingly small means leading to extraordinarily satisfactory results.

For the modern economist this is very difficult to understand. He is used to measuring the 'standard of living' by the amount of annual consumption, assuming all the time that a man who consumes more is 'better off' than a man who consumes less. A Buddhist economist would consider this approach excessively irrational: since consumption is merely a means to human well-being, the aim should be to obtain the maximum of well-being with the minimum of consumption. Thus, if the purpose of clothing is a certain amount of temperature comfort and an attractive appearance, the task is to attain this purpose with the smallest possible effort, that is, with the smallest annual destruction of cloth and with the help of designs that involve the smallest possible input of toil. The less toil there is, the more time and strength is left for artistic creativity. It would be highly uneconomic, for instance, to go in for complicated tailoring, like the modern west, when a much more beautiful effect can be achieved by the skillful draping of uncut material. It would be the height of folly to make material so that it should wear out quickly and the height of barbarity to make anything ugly, shabby or mean. What has just been said about clothing applies equally to all other human requirements. The ownership and the consumption of goods is a means to an end, and Buddhist economics is the systematic study of how to attain given ends with the minimum means.

Modern economics, on the other hand, considers consumption to be the sole end and purpose of all economic activity, taking the factors of production—land, labour, and capital—as the means. The former, in short, tries to maximise human satisfactions by the optimal pattern of consumption, while the latter tries to maximise consumption by the optimal pattern of productive effort. It is easy to see that the effort needed to sustain a way of life which seeks to attain the optimal pattern of consumption is likely to be much smaller than the effort needed to sustain a drive for maximum consumption. We need not be surprised, therefore, that the pressure and strain of living is very much less in, say, Burma than it is in the United States, in spite of the fact that the amount of labour-saving machinery used in the former country is only a minute fraction of the amount used in the latter.

Simplicity and non-violence are obviously closely related. The optimal pattern of consumption, producing a high degree of human satisfaction by means of a relatively low rate of consumption, allows people to live without great pressure and strain and to fulfil the primary injunction of Buddhist teaching: 'Cease to do evil; try to do good.' As physical resources are everywhere limited, people satisfying their needs by means of a modest use of resources are obviously less likely to be at each other's throats than people depending upon a high rate of use. Equally, people who live in highly self-sufficient local communities are less likely to get involved in large-scale violence than people whose existence depends on world-wide systems of trade.

From the point of view of Buddhist economics, therefore, production from local resources for local needs is the most rational way of economic life, while dependence on imports from afar and the consequent need to produce for export to unknown and distant peoples is highly uneconomic and justifiable only in exceptional cases and on a small scale. Just as the modern economist would admit that a high rate of consumption of transport services between a man's home and his place of work signifies a misfortune and not a high standard of life, so the Buddhist economist would hold that to satisfy human wants from faraway sources rather than from sources nearby signifies failure rather than success. The former tends to take statistics showing an increase in the number of ton/miles per head of the population carried by a country's transport system as proof of economic progress, while to the latter—the Buddhist economist—the same statistics would indicate a highly undesirable deterioration in the *pattern* of consumption.

Another striking difference between modern economics and Buddhist economics arises over the use of natural resources. . . .

The teaching of the Buddha, on the other hand, enjoins a reverent and non-violent attitude not only to all sentient beings but also, with great emphasis, to trees. Every follower of the Buddha ought to plant a tree every few years and look after it until it is safely established, and the Buddhist economist can demonstrate without difficulty that the universal observation of this rule would result in a high rate of genuine economic development independent of any foreign aid. Much of the economic decay of south-east Asia (as of many other parts of the world) is undoubtedly due to a heedless and shameful neglect of trees.

Modern economics does not distinguish between renewable and non-renewable materials, as its very method is to equalise and quantify everything by means of a money price. Thus, taking various alternative fuels, like coal, oil, wood, or water-power: the only difference between them recognised by modern economics is relative cost per equivalent unit. The cheapest is automatically the one to be preferred, as to do otherwise would be irrational and 'uneconomic'. From a Buddhist point of view, of course, this will not do; the essential difference between non-renewable fuels like coal and oil on the one hand and renewable fuels like wood and water-power on the other cannot be simply overlooked. Non-renewable goods must be used only if they are indispensable, and then only with the greatest care and the most meticulous concern for conservation. To use them heedlessly or extravagantly is an act of violence, and while complete non-violence may not be attainable on this earth, there is nonetheless an ineluctable duty on man to aim at the ideal of non-violence in all he does.

Just as a modern European economist would not consider it a great economic achievement if all European art treasures were sold to America at attractive prices, so the Buddhist economist would insist that a population basing its economic life on non-renewable fuels is living parasitically, on capital instead of income. Such a way of life could have no permanence and could therefore be justified only as a purely temporary expedient. As the world's resources of non-renewable fuels—coal, oil and natural gas—are exceedingly unevenly distributed over the globe and undoubtedly limited in quantity, it is clear that their exploitation at an ever-increasing rate is an act of violence against nature which must almost inevitably lead to violence between men.

This fact alone might give food for thought even to those people in Buddhist countries who care nothing for the religious and spiritual values of their heritage and ardently desire to embrace the materialism of modern economics at the fastest possible speed. Before they dismiss Buddhist economics as nothing better than a nostalgic dream, they might wish to consider whether the path of economic development outlined by modern economics is likely to lead them to places where they really want to be. . . .

There is [a] question of whether 'modernisation', as currently practised without regard to religious and spiritual values, is actually producing agreeable results. As far as the masses are concerned, the results appear to be disastrous—a collapse of the rural economy, a rising tide of unemployment in town and country, and the growth of a city proletariat without nourishment for either body or soul.

It is in the light of both immediate experience and long-term prospects that the study of Buddhist economics could be recommended even to those who believe that economic growth is more important than any spiritual or religious values. For it is not a question of choosing between 'modern growth' and 'traditional stagnation'. It is a question of finding the right path of development, the Middle Way between materialist heedlessness and traditionalist immobility, in short, of finding 'Right Livelihood'.

Socialism

* * *

The strength of the idea of private enterprise lies in its terrifying simplicity. It suggests that the totality of life can be reduced to one aspect—profits. The businessman, as a private individual, may still be interested in other aspects of life—perhaps even in goodness, truth and beauty—but *as a businessman* he concerns himself only with profits. In this respect, the idea of private enterprise fits exactly into the idea of The Market, which, in an earlier chapter, I called 'the institutionalisation of individualism and non-responsibility'. Equally, it fits perfectly into the modern trend towards total quantification at the expense of the appreciation of qualitative differences; for private enterprise is not concerned with what it produces but only with what it gains from production.

* * *

But just as the powerful concentration of nineteenth-century science on the mechanical aspects of reality had to be abandoned because there was too much of reality that simply did not fit, so the powerful concentration of business life on the aspect of 'profits' has had to be modified because it failed to do justice to the real needs of man. It was the historical achievement of socialists to push this development, with the result that the favourite phrase of the enlightened capitalist today is: 'We are all socialists now.'

That is to say, the capitalist today wishes to deny that the one final aim of all his activities is profit. He says: 'Oh no, we do a lot for our employees which we do not really have to do; we try to preserve the beauty of the countryside; we engage in research that may not pay off,' etc., etc. All these claims are very familiar; sometimes they are justified, sometimes not.

What concerns us here is this: private enterprise 'old style', let us say, goes simply for profits; it thereby achieves a most powerful simplification of objectives and gains a perfect measuring rod of success or failure. Private enterprise 'new style', on the other hand (let us assume), pursues a great variety of objectives; it tries to consider the whole fullness of life and not merely the money-making aspect; it therefore achieves no powerful simplification of objectives and possesses no reliable measuring rod of success or failure. If this is so, private enterprise 'new style', as organised in large joint stock companies, differs from public enterprise only in one respect; namely that it provides an unearned income to its shareholders.

Clearly, the protagonists of capitalism cannot have it both ways. They cannot say 'We are all socialists now' and maintain at the same time that socialism cannot possibly work. If they themselves pursue objectives other than that of profit-making, then they cannot very well argue that it becomes impossible to administer the nation's means of production efficiently as soon as considerations other than those of profit-making are allowed to enter. If *they* can manage without the crude yardstick of money-making, so can nationalised industry.

On the other hand, if all this is rather a sham and private enterprise works for profit and (practically) nothing else; if its pursuit of other objectives is in fact solely dependent on profit-making and constitutes merely its own choice of what to do with some of the profits, then the sooner this is made clear the better. In that case, private enterprise could still claim to possess the power of simplicity. Its case against public enterprise would be that the latter is bound to be inefficient precisely because it attempts to pursue several objectives at the same time, and the case of socialists against the former would be the traditional case, which is not primarily an economic one, namely, that it degrades life by its very simplicity, by basing all economic activity solely on the motive of private greed.

A total rejection of public ownership means a total affirmation of private ownership. This is just as great a piece of dogmatism as the opposite one of the most fanatical communist. But while all fanaticism shows intellectual weakness, a fanaticism *about the means* to be employed for reaching quite uncertain objectives is sheer feeble-mindedness.

The whole crux of economic life—and indeed of life in general—is that it constantly requires the living reconciliation of opposites which, in strict logic, are irreconcilable. In macro-economics (the management of whole societies) it is necessary always to have both planning *and* freedom—not by way of a weak and lifeless compromise, but by a free recognition of the legitimacy of and need for both. Equally in micro-economics (the management of individual enterprises): on the one hand it is essential that there should be full managerial responsibility and authority; yet it is equally essential that there should be a democratic and free participation of the workers in management decisions. Again, it is not a question of mitigating the opposition of these two needs by some half-hearted compromise that satisfies neither of them, but to recognise them both. The exclusive concentration on one of the opposites—say, on planning, produces Stalinism; while the exclusive concentration on the other produces chaos. The normal answer to either is a swing of the pendulum to the other extreme. Yet the normal answer is not the only possible answer. A generous and magnanimous intellectual effort—the opposite of nagging, malevolent criticism—can enable a society, at least for a period, to find a middle way that reconciles the opposites without degrading them both.

The same applies to the choice of objectives in business life. One of the opposites—represented by private enterprise 'old style'—is the need for simplicity and measurability, which is best fulfilled by a strict limitation of outlook to 'profitability' and nothing else. The other opposite—represented by the original 'idealistic' conception of public enterprise—is the need for a comprehensive and broad humanity in the conduct of economic affairs. The former, if exclusively adhered to, leads to the total destruction of the dignity of man; the latter, to a chaotic kind of inefficiency.

There are no 'final solutions' to this kind of problem. There is only a *living* solution achieved day by day on a basis of a clear recognition *that both opposites are valid.*

Ownership, whether public or private, is merely an element of framework. It does not by itself settle the kind of objectives to be pursued within the framework. From this point of view it is correct to say that ownership is not the decisive question. But it is also necessary to recognise that private ownership of the means of production is severely limited in its freedom of choice of objectives, because it is compelled to be profit-seeking, and *tends* to take a narrow and selfish view of things. Public ownership gives *complete* freedom in the choice of objectives and can therefore be used for any purpose that may be chosen. While private ownership is an instrument that by itself largely determines the ends for which it can be employed, public ownership is an instrument the ends of which are undetermined and need to be consciously chosen.

There is therefore really no strong case for public ownership if the objectives to be pursued by nationalised industry are to be just as narrow, just as limited as those of capitalist production: profitability and nothing else. Herein lies the real danger to nationalisation . . . at the present time, not in any imagined inefficiency.

* * *

What is at stake is not economics but culture; not the standard of living but the equality of life. Economics and the standard of living can just as well be looked after by a capitalist system, moderated by a bit of planning and redistributive taxation. But culture and, generally, the quality of life, can now only be debased by such a system.

Socialists should insist on using the nationalised industries not simply to out-capitalise the capitalists—an attempt in which they may or may not succeed—but to evolve a more democratic and dignified system of industrial administration, a more humane employment of machinery, and a more intelligent utilisation of the fruits of human ingenuity and effort. If they can do that, they have the future in their hands. If they cannot, they have nothing to offer that is worthy of the sweat of free-born men.

Ownership

* * *

Systems are never more nor less than incarnations of man's most basic attitudes. Some incarnations, indeed, are more perfect than others. General evidence of material progress would suggest that the *modern* private enterprise system is—or has been—the most perfect instrument for the pursuit of personal enrichment. The *modern* private enterprise system ingeniously employs the human urges of greed and envy as its motive power, but manages to overcome the most blatant deficiencies of *laissez-faire* by means of Keynesian economic management, a bit of redistributive taxation, and the 'countervailing power' of the trade unions.

Can such a system conceivably deal with the problems we are now having to face? The answer is self-evident: greed and envy demand continuous and limitless economic growth of a material kind, without proper regard for conservation, and this type of growth cannot possibly fit into a finite environment. We must therefore study the essential nature of the private enterprise system and the possibilities of evolving an alternative system which might fit the new situation.

The essence of private enterprise is the private ownership of the means of production, distribution, and exchange. Not surprisingly, therefore, the critics of private enterprise have advocated and in many cases successfully enforced the conversion of private ownership into so-called public or collective ownership. Let us look, first of all, at the meaning of 'ownership' or 'property'.

As regards private property, the first and most basic distinction is between (a) property that is an aid to creative work and (b) property that is an alternative to it. There is something natural and healthy about the former—the private property of the working proprietor; and there is something unnatural and unhealthy about the latter—the private property of the passive owner who lives parasitically on the work of others. This basic distinction was clearly seen by Tawney who followed that "it is idle, therefore, to present a case for or against private property without specifying the particular forms of property to which reference is made".

> *For it is not private ownership, but private ownership divorced from work, which is corrupting to the principle of industry; and the idea of some socialists that private property in land or capital is necessarily mischievous is a piece of scholastic pedantry as absurd as that of those conservatives who would invest all property with some kind of mysterious sanctity.*

Private enterprise carried on with property of the first category is automatically small-scale, personal, and local. It carries no wider social responsibilities. Its responsibilities to the consumer can be safeguarded by the consumer himself. Social legislation and trade union vigilance can protect the employee. No great private fortunes can be gained from small-scale enterprises, yet its social utility is enormous.

It is immediately apparent that in this matter of private ownership the question of scale is decisive. When we move from small-scale to medium-scale, the connection between ownership and work already becomes attenuated; private enterprise tends to become impersonal and also a significant social factor in the locality; it may even assume more than local significance. The very idea of *private property* becomes increasingly misleading.

1. The owner, employing salaried managers, does not need to be a proprietor to be able to do his work. His ownership, therefore, ceases to be functionally necessary. It becomes exploitative if he appropriates profit in excess of a fair salary to himself and a return on his capital no higher than current rates for capital borrowed from outside sources.

2. High profits are either fortuitous or they are the achievement not of the owner but of the whole organisation. It is therefore unjust and socially disruptive if they are appropriated by the owner alone. They should be shared with all members of the organisation. If they are 'ploughed back' they should be 'free capital' collectively owned, instead of accruing automatically to the wealth of the original owner.
3. Medium size, leading to impersonal relationships, poses new questions as to the exercise of control. Even autocratic control is no serious problem in small-scale enterprise which, led by a working proprietor, has almost a family character. It is incompatible with human dignity and genuine efficiency when the enterprise exceeds a certain—very modest—size. There is need, then, for the conscious and systematic development of communications and consultation to allow all members of the organisation some degree of genuine participation in management.
4. The social significance and weight of the firm in its locality and its wider ramifications call for some degree of 'socialisation of ownership' beyond the members of the firm itself. This 'socialisation' may be effected by regularly devoting a part of the firm's profits to public or charitable purposes and bringing in trustees from outside. . . .

When we come to large-scale enterprises, the idea of private ownership becomes an absurdity. The property is not and cannot be private in any real sense. Again, R. H. Tawney saw this with complete clarity:

> *Such property may be called passive property, or property for acquisition, for exploitation, or for power, to distinguish it from the property which is actively used by its owner for the conduct of his profession or the upkeep of his household. . . .*

The so-called private ownership of large-scale enterprises is in no way analogous to the simple property of the small landowner, craftsman, or entrepreneur. It is, as Tawney says, analogous to "the feudal dues which robbed the French peasant of part of his produce till the revolution abolished them". . . .

To sum up:

a. In small-scale enterprise, private ownership is natural, fruitful, and just.
b. In medium-scale enterprise, private ownership is already to a large extent functionally unnecessary. The idea of 'property' becomes strained, unfruitful, and unjust. If there is only one owner or a small group of owners, there can be, and should be, a voluntary surrender of privilege to the wider group of actual workers. . . . Such an act of generosity may be unlikely when there is a large number of anonymous shareholders, but legislation could pave the way even then.
c. In large-scale enterprise, private ownership is a fiction for the purpose of enabling functionless owners to live parasitically on the labour of others. It is not only unjust but also an irrational element which distorts all relationships within the enterprise. . . .

There are many methods of doing away with so-called private ownership in large-scale enterprise; the most prominent one is generally referred to as 'nationalisation.'

* * *

Ownership is not a single right, but a bundle of rights. 'Nationalisation' is not a matter of simply transferring this bundle of rights from A to B, that is to say, from private persons to 'the State', whatever that may mean: it is a matter of making precise choices as to where the various rights of the bundle are to be placed, all of which, before nationalisation, were deemed to belong to the so-called private owner. Tawney, therefore, says succinctly: "Nationalisation (is) a problem of Constitution-making." Once the legal device of private property has been removed, there is freedom to arrange everything anew—to amalgamate or to dissolve, to centralise or to decentralise, to concentrate power or to diffuse it, to create large units or small units, a unified system, a federal system, or no system at all. As Tawney put it:

> *The objection to public ownership, in so far as it is intelligent, is in reality largely an objection to over-centralisation. But the remedy for over-centralisation is not the maintenance of functionless property in private hands, but the decentralised ownership of public property.*

* * *

7.12 The Democratic Welfare Community

Gunnar Myrdal

The State and the Individual

A REGULATED SOCIETY

Ours is a rather closely regulated society, leaving a certain amount of free enterprise to move within a frame set by a fine-spun system of controls, which are all ultimately under the authority of the democratic state.

PEOPLE LIKE IT

One of the explanations why people in general are rather well satisfied by living and working in these regulated national communities of the Western

Excerpted from Gunnar Myrdal, *Beyond the Welfare State* (New Haven: Yale University Press, 1960). Reprinted by permission of the publisher.

world is undoubtedly that they do not notice the controls so much, or do not react so violently, as they are becoming accustomed to them.

But partly, and I believe more significantly, the explanation of people's satisfaction with what has happened is that regulations in the democratic Welfare State are not pressed upon them from above, by a state dictatorship. They are felt to be the outcome of a social process, in the steering of which people are themselves participating. Also, these regulations, under this popular influence, are very broadly framed so as to give new rights to the masses of people: to increase their opportunities, open roads that were closed before by their poverty or ignorance, and to secure them against risks that in earlier times were disastrous for the individual and his family.

Most people have good reason to feel freer, not less free in the Welfare State. As the material and social limitations upon the individual's freedom to act and move are broken down, and replaced by rules laid down by legislation and collective agreements, they pass under democratic control, and can be changed by a process where nobody is without a voice.

And everybody also is aware, of course, of the fact that in spite of wars and other adverse events, production, incomes, and particularly the levels of living of the broader strata of our national communities have been rising more rapidly than ever, and that the prospects of the young are brighter than were those of their parents or grandparents when they started life. Economically as well as socially, the Welfare State has been a conspicuous success.

The fact that so many public policies are actually taking shape within the authorities for provincial and local self-government, and by agreements after collective bargaining amongst the numerous organizations within the infrastructure of organized society, contributes to the feeling of freedom amongst people, and the feeling that they are participating themselves in making the regulations they have to obey. In an advanced Welfare State, an increasingly large portion of the adult population is participating in government through membership on various municipal boards and councils responsible for the implementation of the laws and the disposal of funds—sometimes, as in Sweden, the payment of social security benefits and assessment of taxes—and, as they are elected, they have the officials as their subordinates. Other citizens are responsible for public policy as members of the boards of trade unions, cooperative associations of various types, and other interest organizations. In the advanced Welfare State with its high level of civic education and civic responsibility, these numerous office-holders are all "of the people," and not hired professionals. Everbody meets them in the workshops, in the streets, and in daily life. Many of the popular checks on their activity are informal and continuous, and thus not restricted to meetings and elections. The regulations which flow out of this ramifying organizational life appear to the whole community more as voluntary choices, more like the individual contracts and deals people would have to enter upon in the freest economy, as, of course, they do now. By also participating, directly or indirectly in the collective settlements, they feel that they have improved the conditions under which they make their individual moves. The increasing prevalence in the Western countries of this less formal type of public policy also means that its execution becomes smoother and more effective than it would be if it were all done by the state and its proper authorities.

This latter reason for satisfaction with the regulative activity of the Welfare State becomes stronger, of course, the more intense the democratic participation is on the different levels of collective decision making. When participation is on a low level, we should expect people to be more apt to feel that the regulations are imposed upon them from above and that they are being pushed around by "them"—the bosses, the bureaucrats, and the oligarchies in the organizations, and by the strange and distant forces in Wall Street and Washington. This might breed feelings of resentment, and will anyhow frustrate people's feelings of solidarity and identification with the purposes of the regulations.

As usual, the social mechanism works in circular cumulations of causes and effects. For such attitudes will, in their turn, inhibit the intensification of participation, the lack of which was among their causes. Viewed the other way, feelings of solidarity and identification will lead to participation, while it is only participation that can inspire such feelings. If people can come to realize a higher degree of participation, the conditions are also created for the organizations beneath the state level to gain in effectiveness and importance, which has the consequence that state regulations in many fields become less called for. The regulations can then be moved nearer to people's grasp and control.

REPLACING STATE INTERVENTIONS

Generally, as levels of living and education rise, and as people's participation in the affairs of the national community through the regular political processes and through all the organizations within the institutional infrastructure increases, we may approach a situation where many important public policies can be put into effect without much direct state intervention in the ordinary sense, and particularly without necessitating more than a minimum of state administration, simply by activating, as a means of communal control, the pressure of enlightened public opinion, and the bargaining strength of the organizations.

It is my judgment that in an advanced Welfare State, with democratically balanced interest organizations and a vigilant citizenry, the mere decision by parliament to make the restrictive practices in business part of general knowledge is quite an effective device for public control, and that often in such a country the need for legislation, prohibiting specific practices, and administrative controls enforcing the legislation can be kept to a minimum and reserved for strategic fields.

I am confident, too, to take another example, that there will come a time in America, perhaps not as very far off as many believe, when there will be no practical need to retain legislation, courts, and administration to defend Negroes against discrimination in the labor market and elsewhere.

But in the immediate future I am convinced there are many fields where we should prepare ourselves for a radical diminution of state regulations. Decisions as to the hours when shops are kept open could, in good communities, be left to be settled by agreements between the interested parties, if they were well organized, including the general public of buyers and consumers. Much legislation and inspection of food and many other things could also be simplified if the general public were better educated as consumers, and if their interests were effectively protected by strong and efficient consumers' organizations. The efforts and costs necessary to reach such a situation would be small, compared, for instance, with the huge expenditure on competitive advertising.

In many cases it is undoubtedly practical, not only to lay down certain general rules by legislation, but also to sanction their enforcement not only by courts but by administration. It is my conviction, however, that it should be possible to leave much more detailed regulations to be settled by the people themselves, in their local communities and through bargaining between their organizations. This will promote the coming into being of a more cooperative national community, with more identification, solidarity, and participation on the part of the individual citizen, who then will come to feel freer—and he actually will be more free. As I see it, this is the inherent ideal, which the developing democratic Welfare State is reaching towards. It implies the coming into existence of a "Welfare Culture" within the structure of the Welfare State.

THE NEXT PHASE

Let us assume that, in the next phase of growth and perfection of the Welfare State, we could achieve such a gradual diminution of direct state intervention by activating the people to take care of their own interests within the general rules laid down by the democratic state. The development would then, in a sense, have completed a full circle.

It started out from the quasi-liberal state of mass poverty, much social rigidity, and gross inequality of opportunity.

It went through a period when the old automatism went out of the system. Through a sequence of increasing public and private intervention and, flowing from this, intermittent attempts at their coordination by planning, we reached the present situation, where direct state intervention is still continually increasing in volume, though it is now only partially responsible for the social controls within the bounds of which we live.

In this transitional phase of the development towards the more perfect democratic Welfare State, while coordination and planning are becoming gradually more thorough, under the pressure of the continually growing volume of intervention, both by the state and by collective authorities and power groups beneath the state level, it often happens that people confuse planning with direct and detailed state regulations. The opposite, however, is true; there is still such a large volume of intervention because the measures are not ideally coordinated and planned. Planning should normally imply simplification and rationalization. We assume further that as planning proceeds, it will be seen to be in line with the ideals of the Welfare State to delegate, wherever it is safe and practicable, responsibility for detailed public regulations to local and sectional collective authorities instead of having them carried out by means of direct state intervention.

The third phase could thus mean an actual decrease of state intervention. The assumption is a continued strengthening of provincial and municipal self-government and a balanced growth of the infra-structure of effective interest organizations. This would, in its turn, presume an intensified citizens' participation and control, exerted in both these fields.

I do maintain that, in those of the Western countries that have advanced farthest in the accomplishment of the democratic Welfare State, we have already seen sporadic, and sometimes more than sporadic, auguries of this third phase. If we take these omens as representing the beginning of a development that we would like to see continued, and if we extrapolate that development, implying their generalization over the whole society, we would see a quite new situation emerging. The state as such could on the whole restrict itself to doing two main things, leaving the rest for local self-government and for cooperation and bargaining between the organizations in the infrastructure.

First, the state would have to maintain and strengthen a number of established, fundamental and—in the literal sense of the word—radical policy structures of a general character in such fields as international commerce and exchange, taxation, labor legislation, social security, education, health, and, of course, defense. In addition, the state will in most countries undoubtedly continue to run the railroads and to have the exclusive responsibility for the post, the telegraph, and the telephone. In cooperation with the municipalities it will own the public utilities, or at least control them closely. The state may or may not take over the businesses of banking and insurance and perhaps even increase the number of industries it is managing under its own regime; but for reasons already given in the last chapter it does not make much difference whether it does or not. By these policies the state would be organizing the national community in accordance with the public will as determined by the people's mandate, and also changing the conditions under which local self-government operates and the bargaining amongst the organizations goes on.

Second, the state would have to establish and continually adjust rules, and provide an umpire service, for life in the local and sectional compartments of the national community, as it evolves through provincial and municipal self-government and in the interest organizations operating in the several markets, and as it is conditioned by the first type of policy as well as by the rules themselves. One important part of these rules and this general supervision will concern the public desire that the organizations within the infrastructure be democratically governed, open and under satisfactory publicity controls, like other organs for public policy.

Within the general framework provided by these two types of state policies, the public will is then realized by an enlightened and active people, without calling for much direct state intervention *in casu*. The people will do this both directly through general community pressure, establishing and sanctioning what in reality is a system of social morals, and more indirectly through their participation in local self-government and in their interest organizations.

On the whole the state, as such, can keep out, after it has laid down the general rules for this dispersed activity and also after it has, by its major policy schemes of the type first mentioned, induced such fundamental changes of the conditions under which cooperation and bargaining go on that the arrangements reached are just and equitable, in line with the public will as ascertained by the political process in a democracy. All the main state policies of both types would, of course, have to be carefully planned and coordinated, so that the intended result is a development of the national economy as a whole, and all social relations within it in the desired direction.

The Welfare State of tomorrow would then realize a type of society which in many fundamentals would have deeply satisfied John Stuart Mill and all the earlier liberal philosophers more than a hundred years ago, if they had had the power of imagination to envisage the final implications of a development they barely saw the beginnings of. Even that angry old philosopher-historian, Karl Marx, who gave such an uncompromising expression of the old liberal vision, held since John Locke, of a society freed from class monopolies, and who enjoyed such a sadistic dream about the painful way it was determined to be reached by a natural development, would find much of his "realm of liberty." And Thomas Jefferson would most definitely see in the accomplished Welfare State a realization of "grass-root democracy," though in a very different, much more complicated, world than was within his vision. We would finally be reaching a state worthy of *consensus sapientium*.

THE UTOPIA AND THE REALITY

I have intentionally meant to depict a utopia. The reality in all our Western countries is far from realizing it. I would nevertheless insist on the relevance of the utopian, decentralized, and democratic state where, within the bounds of ever more effective overall policies laid down for the whole national community, the citizens themselves carry more and more of the responsibility for organizing their work and life by means of local and sectional cooperation and bargaining with only the necessary minimum of direct state interference. This utopia is, in my belief, a real goal. It is inherent in those ideals of liberty, equality, and brotherhood that are the ultimate driving forces behind the development of the modern democratic Welfare State. If we made the ideology of the Welfare State more explicit, i.e. if we clarified our direction and aims, this utopia would stand out as our practical goal.

Bureaucracy, petty administrative regulations, and generally a meddlesome state should not be the signum of our vision of a more accomplished democratic Welfare State. To fight against regimentation from above was always a rallying cause for the progressive elements in the Western countries. Now, when the state has been brought more effectively under the democratic control of the people, we have every reason to use state legislation and administration for fundamental economic and social policies of the two types mentioned in the last section. But we should not make peace with bureaucracy. I view as short-sighted those would-be reformers, both in the United States and in other Western countries, who, in their urge to improve society, place an almost exclusive trust in continual extension of state regulations, thereby presenting their fellow-citizens with a sort of "etatistic liberalism."

The obsolete or unnecessary state regulations are partly remnants from earlier phases of the development towards the Welfare State, when the gradual steps towards central coordination of the mass of unplanned and dispersed intervention were seldom radical enough, but left a sediment of needs for direct acts of state intervention, which now remains with us as rigid and often arbitrary bureaucracy. Some of them are a legacy from still earlier history and stem from a time when our countries were less democratic, more autocratic and more rigidly stratified into classes. And, now as always, bureaucracy has its own will to survive.

But more fundamentally the "etatism" of our Welfare States in their present development phase is a reflection of the fact that no country has, as yet, brought that simplifying coordination of the mesh of proliferating intervention of all sorts, which represents the Western type of planning, to anything like perfection. And meanwhile the volume of direct state intervention is still increasing everywhere, even if the central administration's relative share of community controls is decreasing. The process by which local self-government and a balanced and effective infrastructure of open and democratically controlled organizations are coming into their own is in none of the Western countries carried to completion; in some countries it sometimes seems as if this process of decentralization of government is reversed, at least temporarily and in some fields.

It is important, however, not least in the United States, to keep in mind as a long-range goal the values in decentralizing the community controls. As I see it, the strivings towards that goal are not hopeless. Even in America the conditions are gradually being created for more efficient collective authorities on the local and sectional levels.

To debureaucratize the state and liberate the people from petty interferences, exerted by authorities above their heads and outside their immediate control, is a progressive cause—today as in Jefferson's time. It can be accomplished only by perfecting and strengthening the Welfare State. The essence of the argument in this book is, that though planning is continually being necessitated by the rising volume of intervention, the purpose and accomplishment of planning in the Welfare State is, in fact, constantly to simplify, and largely to liquidate, old and new intervention: to substitute a few, mostly overall state policies for a growing mesh of detailed and direct ones, and, in particular, to recondition the national community in such a way that for the most part it can be left to the cooperation and collective bargaining of the people themselves, in all sorts of communities and organizations beneath the formal state level, to settle the norms for their living together.